DISCARDED

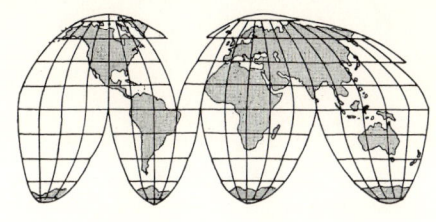

SECOND EDITION

INTERNATIONAL TRADE *and* FINANCE
THEORY • POLICY • PRACTICE

FRANKLIN R. ROOT, Ph.D.
Associate Professor of International Business

ROLAND L. KRAMER, Ph.D.
Professor of Commerce and Transportation

MAURICE Y. d'Arlin, M.B.A.
Lecturer on International Business,
Formerly Importer and International Factor

all of the
Wharton School of Finance and Commerce
University of Pennsylvania

South-Western  Publishing Company
Burlingame, Calif.   New Rochelle, N. Y.
S76 Cincinnati   Chicago   Dallas

Copyright ©, 1966

Philippine Copyright, 1966

by

SOUTH-WESTERN PUBLISHING COMPANY

Cincinnati, Ohio 45227

All Rights Reserved

The text of this publication, or any part thereof, may not be reproduced in any manner whatsoever without the permission in writing from the publisher.

Library of Congress Catalog Card Number: 66-15276

H368

Printed in the United States of America

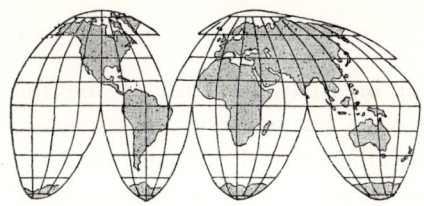

PREFACE

International Trade and Finance constitutes a major revision of the 1959 edition. Part 1 has been strengthened by two new chapters on the theory of trade and international payments adjustment; Part 2 has been expanded by three new chapters on the European Economic Community, the developing nations, and international monetary reform; and Part 3 has been completely rewritten. All of the other chapters have been revised—often substantially—to take account of new developments in both theory and policy.

This new edition preserves the integral treatment of theory, policy, and practice that distinguished its predecessor. By *theory* we mean the body of knowledge that explains the causal relationships that underlie international economic transactions. By *policy* we refer to the role of government in international trade and finance. By *practice* we mean the conduct of international business.

A grasp of theory enables us to analyze events occurring in the international economy and to evaluate the wisdom of national and business policies. A study of national policies helps to bring to us an understanding of the world in which all of us must live. The dominance of government policies in international trade and finance makes it especially important for persons engaged in international business to become acquainted with those policies and to perceive their influence on business operations. Finally, a study of the practice of international trade and finance brings us face to face with the individual business firms that are responsible for the vast majority of international economic transactions in the free world. In the last analysis, it is the activity of these firms that theory seeks to explain and that government policy seeks to influence. A knowledge of international trade and finance is vital for all those who may wish to enter an international business career or work for governments and organizations in the field of international economic relations.

Most textbooks in international trade and finance fall into one of two categories: (1) those dealing with theory and international economic policies with only an occasional reference to international

v

business, or (2) those dealing with international business and the foreign economic policies that bear on it, but omitting any systematic presentation of theory. Notwithstanding this dichotomy, we have found in our own teaching that theory, policy, and practice are alike indispensable to an understanding of contemporary international trade and finance. The Introduction, comprising two chapters, acquaints the reader with international trade through a discussion of its distinctive characteristics and empirical dimensions. The theory of international trade and finance is presented in Part 1, which covers Chapters 3 through 11. The theory of comparative costs, the transfer of international payments, the balance of international payments, foreign exchange rates, and the theory of adjustment are the principal topics of this part. Chapters 12 through 22 make up Part 2, which is concerned with policy. The means and ends of international economic policy; trade and payments restrictions; arguments for protection; cartels, state trading, and commodity agreements; international arrangements to liberalize trade and payments; the commercial policy of the United States; the European Economic Community; the developing nations and world trade; United States foreign investment; and the United States balance of payments and international monetary reform are taken up in order. Part 3 comprises Chapters 23 through 29 and examines the practice of international business. All of the principal aspects of international business are described and analyzed: the nature and scope of international business operations, researching foreign markets, international trading channels, foreign operations, financing international trade, supporting agencies, and international competition.

We have cooperated intimately in the preparation of this volume and it is offered as a joint product of our endeavors. The contents of every chapter have been improved through a process of mutual criticism and the "talking out" of ideas. We should like to acknowledge a deep sense of gratitude to our students and to many readers of the first edition; their reactions to our work have been most helpful in this revision.

This book is dedicated to Grover Gerhard Huebner, late Professor Emeritus, who introduced foreign trade courses in the Wharton School immediately following World War I. As teacher and counselor, he guided each of us in the prosecution of graduate study. As a colleague, he was always helpful and proved to be a true friend.

FRANKLIN R. ROOT
ROLAND L. KRAMER
MAURICE Y. D'ARLIN

CONTENTS

INTRODUCTION

Chapter 1 • page 1 • International Trade and the National Economy

	page		page
The National Interest in International Trade	2	Distinctive Features of International Trade	11
International Specialization and Trade	5	Summary	15

Chapter 2 • page 17 • The Dimensions of World Trade

Value and Volume of World Trade	17	Value and Volume of United States Trade	33
Composition of World Trade	26	Composition of United States Trade	36
Multilateral Structure of International Trade	27	Direction of United States Trade	39
The Role of the United States in World Trade	32	Dependence of the United States on International Trade	40
		Summary	44

PART I THEORY

Chapter 3 • page 47 • Comparative Costs and Gains from Trade

Why Nations Trade—The Theory of Comparative Costs	47	The Gains from International Trade	62
The International Mobility of Factors	58	Many Countries and Many Goods	67
		Summary	69

Chapter 4 • page 73 • Comparative Costs in the World Economy

Increasing Costs	73	Transportation and Other Transfer Costs	84
Decreasing Costs	77	Summary	92
Imperfect Competition	78		

Chapter 5 • page 95 • Comparative Costs in the World Economy (Concluded)

Change and Heterogeneity in Factor Endowments	95	International Trade in Services	110
Technological Innovation and Dissimilar Production Functions	102	Capital Movements	111
Unemployment and Comparative Costs	107	A Recapitulation of the Theory of Comparative Costs	112
		Summary	116

vii

Chapter 6 • page 119 • The Transfer of International Payments

	page		page
Transfer through Private Compensation	119	The Monetary Effects of International Payments	127
The Foreign Exchange Market	120	International Financial Centers	130
The Role of Commercial Banks	124	Summary	133

Chapter 7 • page 135 • The Balance of International Payments

The Compilation of the Balance of Payments	136	Why the Balance of Payments Always Balances	148
International Capital Movements	139	Summary	149
The Balance of Payments of the United States	141		

Chapter 8 • page 151 • Foreign Exchange Rates and Their Determination

The Rate of Exchange	151	Exchange Arbitrage	166
Freely Fluctuating Exchange Rates	153	Exchange Speculation and Capital Flight	168
Stable Exchange Rates	158	The Forward Rate of Exchange	170
Controlled Exchange Rates	164	Summary	173

Chapter 9 • page 175 • International Payments Disequilibrium and Adjustment

Balance of Payments Disequilibrium	176	The Need for Adjustment	185
Major Sources of Disequilibrium	181	Summary	187

Chapter 10 • page 189 • International Adjustment in a Stable-Rate System

Short-Run Adjustment	189	Payments Adjustment via the Foreign Trade Multiplier	201
The Classical Theory of Adjustment	192	The Role of Price Adjustment	207
National Income and Foreign Trade	194	Summary	211

Chapter 11 • page 213 • International Adjustment in a Variable-Rate System

Adjustment through Variable Rates	213	The Argument for Flexible Exchange Rates	228
The Effects of Exchange Depreciation	218	Summary	231

PART II POLICY

Chapter 12 • page 233 • The Means and Ends of International Economic Policy

The Definition and Scope of International Economic Policy	234	The Ends of International Economic Policy	238
The Means of International Economic Policy	235	The Diversity and Conflict of Ends	241
		Summary	244

Contents

Chapter 13 • page 247 • International Trade and Payments Restrictions

	page		page
Tariffs and Tariff Systems	247	Special Measures of Restriction	267
Quantitative Trade Restrictions	255	Summary	270

Chapter 14 • page 274 • Economic Effects of Trade and Payments Restrictions

Tariff Making and Tariff Functions	274	The Economic Effects of Exchange Control	289
Economic Effects of Tariffs	278		
Economic Effects of Quotas	285	Summary	294

Chapter 15 • page 298 • Arguments for Protection

The Case for Free Trade	298	Fallacious Arguments	308
The Case for Protection	299	Persistence of Protection	314
Arguments with Qualified Validity	301	Summary	315
Questionable Arguments	305		

Chapter 16 • page 317 • Cartels, State Trading, and Commodity Agreements

International Cartels	317	Intergovernmental Commodity Agreements	333
State Trading	328		
		Summary	338

Chapter 17 • page 341 • International Arrangements to Liberalize Trade and Payments

General Agreement on Tariffs and Trade	342	Regional Trade and Payments Arrangements	359
International Monetary Fund	351	Summary	370

Chapter 18 • page 373 • The Commercial Policy of the United States

Evolution of the United States Tariff Policy before 1934	374	The Trade Expansion Act of 1962	391
The Reciprocal Trade Agreements Program, 1934-62	378	Appraisal of United States Commercial Policy	394
		Summary	396

Chapter 19 • page 399 • The European Economic Community and World Trade

The Development of the European Economic Community	400	The United States and the Community	414
Place of the Community in World Trade	410	Summary	419

Chapter 20 • page 423 • The Developing Nations and World Trade

The Developing Nations and Their Potential Trade Gap	423	External Assistance to the Developing Nations: Private Investment and Government Aid Programs	446
Export Problems of the Developing Nations	436	Summary	451

Chapter 21 • page 455 • Foreign Investment of the United States

The Nature of Foreign Investment	455	The Foreign Investment Policy of the United States	470
The Investment Experience of the United States	461	Summary	477

Chapter 22 • page 480 • The United States Balance of Payments and International Monetary Reform

	page		page
The United States Payments Deficit	481	International Monetary Reform	500
Remedial Measures Taken by the United States Government	491	Summary	505

PART III PRACTICE

Chapter 23 • page 509 • The Nature and Scope of International Business

Relation of Sovereignty to International Business	509	Decision Making	511
What Is an International Business Enterprise?	510	The Structure of International Business	516
		Summary	517

Chapter 24 • page 520 • Researching Foreign Markets

Nature of Foreign Market Research	521	Foreign Market Survey Report	527
Characteristics of Sources of Foreign Market Information	521	Sources of Information for Foreign Market Surveys	529
Topics Covered in Foreign Market Surveys	523	Summary	536

Chapter 25 • page 539 • International Trading Channels

Organization of the Company	540	International Trading Agencies in the Foreign Market	545
International Trading Agencies in the Home Market	542	Summary	550

Chapter 26 • page 552 • Foreign Operations of United States Business

The Branch Office	553	Incentives to Foreign Operations	564
Foreign Branch Warehouse	553	Foreign Primary Production	566
Foreign Assembly	553	Licensing for Foreign Operations	568
Foreign Manufacturing	554	Control over Foreign Operations	570
Home Manufacturing	555	Joint Ventures	571
Obstacles to Foreign Operations	557	Summary	573

Chapter 27 • page 575 • Financing International Trade

Meaning of Finance	575	Terms of Payment	580
Nature of Finance	575	A Financing Package	584
Need for Credit Extension in International Trade	576	The Bank's Role	586
International Price Quotations	577	Government and International Banks	587
Sources of Foreign Credit Information	579	Summary	588

Chapter 28 • page 590 • Supporting Agencies in International Trade

Promotion	590	Risk Bearing	599
Merchandising	592	Communications	600
Legal	593	Education	601
Financial	595	Summary	602
Transportation	596		

Chapter 29 • page 605 • Meeting International Competition

Changing Factors in International Competition	605	Conclusion	622
Meeting International Competition	609	Summary	623

Index • page 625

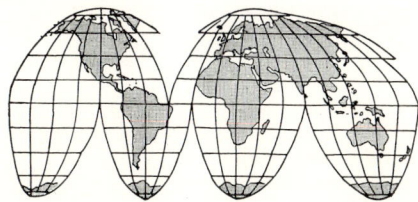

INTRODUCTION

What is the national interest in international trade? How is international trade related to international specialization? What are the distinctive features of international trade? What are the empirical dimensions of world trade? What is the nature of the foreign trade of the United States? These are the principal questions taken up in the next two chapters. Their consideration will prepare us for a more intensive study of the theory, policy, and practice of international trade and finance in the remainder of the text.

CHAPTER 1

INTERNATIONAL TRADE AND THE NATIONAL ECONOMY

No nation inhabits an economic vacuum. Its industries, its commerce, its technology, its standard of living, and all the other facets of its economy are related to the economies of foreign nations by a complex network of trade and finance. Each nation must take cognizance of this interdependence, and each can enlarge its bounty and lessen its risks through wise policies. The effective performance of international business is also of great importance. By furthering the advantages of international specialization and creating the conditions of economic advance, international business can provide a dynamic thrust toward higher levels of well-being for all peoples.

This conception of the vital significance of international trade animates and guides the present study. The first two chapters offer a general description of international trade and direct our thinking toward the remainder of the text. Then we shall turn to the explanation, or theory, of international economic relationships, and with this background we shall move on to the description and evaluation of national policies in the field of international trade and finance. These relationships and policies form the environment in which the business enterprise must function in the actual conduct of international trade. It is this conduct, or practice, of international trade that will occupy our attention in the closing part of the text.

THE NATIONAL INTEREST IN INTERNATIONAL TRADE

What is the national interest in international trade? This question has colored many debates down through the ages, and it will undoubtedly continue to do so in the future. In this section we shall discuss the interests of international business, of import-competing industries, and of consumers. We conclude by identifying the national interest in international trade with consumer welfare.

The Interest of International Business

The value of international trade to the producers, merchants, transportation agencies, financial institutions, and other business enterprises that engage in the export and import of merchandise, services, and capital, is easily understood. Simply stated, international trade is a source of income and profits.

Domestic producers gain from international trade in many ways. They depend upon imports to meet their industrial needs of raw materials and productive equipment at a lower cost than the same items can be acquired from domestic sources of supply. Exports afford domestic producers a profit on sales and they often make possible a larger scale of production with lower unit costs. Imports and exports, moreover, tend to moderate fluctuations in the supply, demand, and prices of individual goods. Sudden shifts in the availability of domestic raw materials may be offset by opposing shifts in raw material imports, and producers with substantial sales abroad are less sensitive to purely domestic economic conditions compared to producers in the same industries who dispose of their entire output at home.

A domestic concern may further find in export markets a means of additional growth that enables it to compete more effectively in the home market. Often the knowledge and experience gained from selling in foreign markets can be used to improve the efficiency and success of domestic marketing operations. In short, international trade allows domestic producers to escape the confines of the domestic market through imports that lower costs of production or improve the quality of the product and through exports that enhance sales and profits.

International trade cannot be carried on by producers alone. Many specialized middlemen and agencies are needed to conduct and facilitate its operations. This is particularly true of merchandise trade: the merchandise must be bought and sold; transportation services must be provided by railroads, ships, trucks, airplanes, and other agencies; international shipments must be insured, financed, and paid for; customs and other government requirements must be met; exports must be stimulated through advertising and other promotion devices; and so on. Specialized middlemen and agencies are also needed in the field of international investment, in the tourist trade, and in other nonmerchandise transactions of an international character. All of the many business concerns involved in carrying out these functions have a direct stake in international trade. When international trade is booming, they experience expansion and profits. Conversely, when international trade enters a slump, these concerns are the first to suffer losses.

The Interest of Import-Competing Industries

The contribution of international trade to the many business enterprises involved cannot be identified with the national interest since other groups are also part of the national economy. Domestic producers who face close competition from imports may be injured by an expansion of international trade. Moreover, the labor used by such producers may suffer from unemployment or lower wages as a consequence of import competition. The adverse effects of import competition are particularly noticeable when import-competing industries are concentrated in specific localities. In measuring the national gain from international trade, therefore, the losses experienced by these groups must be set against the benefits received by other groups.

It must not be supposed, however, that the losses experienced by domestic producers and others hurt by import competition are permanent or even undesirable. In an expanding economy labor, capital, and management are able to shift out of stagnant lines of production into more productive lines. Indeed, one of the virtues of a competitive economy lies in its flexibility in adjusting production to meet new technologies, new demands, and new competition—domestic or foreign.

The Interest of Consumers

As consumers all of us have an interest in international trade, although we are usually unaware of the influence of international trade on the prices and availability of goods. Goods are imported only because they are cheaper than domestic substitutes or have no close domestic substitutes. United States imports of textiles from Japan are an example of the first type of imports, while imports of bananas from Guatemala or dresses from Paris are examples of the second type. Without such imports the American consumer would pay a higher price for textiles and would not have the opportunity to enjoy bananas or Paris "creations."

Imports of raw materials and other industrial goods likewise benefit the consumer by lowering domestic costs of production and in some instances enabling the production of goods that depend exclusively on foreign sources of supply. The consumer also has an interest in domestic exports since they provide the means to pay for imports. Hence, as consumers we all benefit from the greater abundance and variety of goods and the lower prices that international trade makes possible.

Consumer Welfare and the National Interest

The contribution of international trade to the welfare of domestic consumers is the most basic of all. The end of economic activity is consumption; production is only a means to that end. A policy of production for the sake of production or of employment for the sake of employment ignores the fundamental reason for economic activity. For this reason, economists have usually identified the national economic interest with the economic well-being of a nation's people. It follows that a policy or economic activity that adds to the supply of goods and services that people wish to consume is a policy or activity in the national interest. Contrariwise, a policy or economic activity that brings about a level of national consumption that is below the level attainable by an alternative policy or activity is not in the national interest. This criterion of national interest may be modified to take account of illegal production, consumption harmful to health, the need to refrain from current domestic consumption in order to promote economic growth, and the like, but it differs from other criteria of national interest in its emphasis on consumer welfare. Of course, when a nation is at war, the aim of national survival takes precedence over consumer welfare or any other objective.

When we employ the criterion of consumer welfare to decide whether international trade is in the national interest, we find that it benefits the nation by increasing the supply of goods and services available for domestic consumption. Moreover, all trading nations gain from international trade. This gain rests squarely on the specialization that arises from the opportunity to buy and sell in foreign markets. If we are to understand the national interest in international trade, therefore, we must understand how international specialization leads to more productive employment of a nation's natural resources, capital, and labor.

INTERNATIONAL SPECIALIZATION AND TRADE

In this section we shall see first how international trade benefits the national economy by enabling a country to specialize in producing those goods and services whose production is best suited to its national endowments of natural resources, labor, and capital. Interregional trade, like international trade, also enables a country to specialize domestically and to secure gains. Finally we shall review some of the arguments that have been voiced against international specialization and trade.

The Gains from International Trade [1]

Although conceivably a nation might have a sufficient variety of productive factors to produce every kind of good and service, it would not be able to produce each good and service with equal facility. The United States *could* produce hand-woven rugs but only at a high cost since the production of such rugs requires great quantities of labor, which is expensive in this country. The production of hand-woven rugs, however, would afford a reasonable employment for the large supply of cheap labor in a country like India. It would be advantageous for the United States, therefore, to specialize in a commodity such as trucks whose production makes use of the abundant supply of capital in this country and to export trucks in exchange for hand-woven rugs from India.

This example illustrates in a very simple way the gains that result from international specialization—each nation is able to utilize its productive factors in their most productive combinations. By raising the productivity of national economies, international specialization increases the output of goods and services. This is its economic justification and the justification of the international trade that makes possible such specialization.

The contribution of international trade is so immense that few countries could become self-sufficient even with the greatest effort. Contemporary economies have been shaped by the international trade and specialization of the past, and their continued viability is closely

---

[1] The discussion of the basis and gains of international trade in this and the following subsections is introductory to the detailed analysis of Chapters 3, 4, and 5.

dependent on the world economy. For example, it is physically impossible for the United Kingdom and Japan to feed, clothe, and house their present populations without imports from other countries. Economic self-sufficiency for these two nations would mean mass starvation and poverty standards of living unless emigration proved possible on a stupendous scale. The survival of these countries depends essentially on the export of manufactures that require little space to produce in exchange for foodstuffs and raw materials which require great space to produce or are found in only certain areas of the earth.

The United Kingdom and Japan are examples of high dependence on international trade. But even countries that are able to supply their own peoples with the basic necessities of life out of domestic production would be faced with an unbearable decline in living standards if they were cut off from international trade.[2] New Zealand produces far more foodstuffs than are needed to nourish its sparse population, and it is able to trade this surplus for manufactures with industrial countries like the United Kingdom and Japan. Hence, for New Zealand economic self-sufficiency would not mean starvation but rather the deprivation of manufactured goods that are necessary to sustain its current standard of living. Of course, New Zealand could produce some manufactures to take the place of imports, but its efforts in that direction would be limited by its scarce supplies of labor, capital, and industrial raw materials. The New Zealand economy is itself the product of international specialization and trade, and a far different and poorer economy would have evolved in the absence of world markets.

The United States with its continental sweep and immense resources could afford economic self-sufficiency with the least cost of any nation, with the possible exception of the Soviet Union. Perhaps this explains why, far more than other peoples, Americans are inclined to underestimate the importance of international trade.

But even for this country, the cost of self-sufficiency would be formidable. American consumers would experience an immediate pinch in their standards of living. An entire range of foodstuffs would no longer be available or would be available only at exorbitant prices. That American institution—the cup of coffee—would become a luxury to all but a few, and most of us would be forced to do

---

[2] Much of the decline in living standards during a war is due to the cessation of international trade as illustrated by the experience of neutral countries such as Sweden and Switzerland in the last war.

without our daily stimulant or to use inferior substitutes. Even then, the sugar for our beverage would be an expensive item.

As regards basic foodstuffs, we should, of course, have a plentiful supply. In fact, we would become embarrassed by growing stockpiles of agricultural products as farmers lost export outlets for one fourth of their wheat crop, one third of their cotton crop, and large fractions of many other crops. Eventually many farmers would be ruined, and the agricultural sector of our economy would become less important.

Manufacturing industries would also face many difficulties. Without imports, many raw materials would no longer be available and inferior substitutes would replace them. Domestic supplies of other raw materials would no longer be supplemented by imports and their prices would rise to increase costs of production all along the line. The loss of export markets would also cause severe dislocations in many manufacturing industries.

Thus the outcome of economic self-sufficiency for the United States would be a noticeable decline in the American standard of living. Only those producers in direct competition with imports would benefit from self-sufficiency, but the improvement in their fortunes would be purchased at the cost of a general deterioration in the economic well-being of most Americans.

Actually, the United States is less self-sufficient than it used to be. Studies of our resource position, notably the report of the President's Materials Policies Commission in 1952, stress the growing dependence of this country on world markets for a wide variety of raw materials. In 1900 our production of materials (other than food and gold) was 15 percent greater than our consumption, but in 1950 this surplus had changed to a 9 percent deficit; and, on the basis of trends that are already visible, there will be a 20 percent production deficit in 1975.[3] It is clear that the national interest of the United States in foreign trade will grow in the future: more than at any time in the past our economic prosperity in the years ahead must rest upon an expanding world economy.

Domestic Specialization and Interregional Trade

The gains from specialization that are possible through international trade are fundamentally of the same nature as the gains

---

[3] President's Materials Policies Commission, *Resources for Freedom*, Vol. 1 (Washington, D. C.: Government Printing Office, 1952), p. 2.

from specialization achieved by interregional trade *within* a country. In a later section when we discuss the distinctive features of international trade, we shall discover that most of them originate in the political fact of national autonomy—not in economic conditions. Basically, trade within a country is identical with trade between countries. Both derive from the fact that individual regions and countries can gain through trade by specializing in the production of those goods and services that utilize the most productive combinations of their natural resources, labor, and capital.

At the present time over half of the foreign trade of Western European countries is with each other. If these countries should one day federate and become one nation, this trade would become interregional rather than international, but its virtues would be neither greater nor less by reason of that change alone.[4] International trade and interregional trade are substitutes for each other. Thus the explanation of the *relatively* small foreign trade of the United States is found in the vast interregional trade within its borders.

We readily comprehend the great advantages of regional specialization within the domestic economy. Nationalism may blind us to the gains from international trade, but it does not stand in the way of our appreciation of domestic trade. It is true that local producers and merchants may seek to turn consumers away from products "imported" from other domestic regions, but these efforts are largely wasted since localities and regions do not have the authority to impose restrictions on interregional trade.[5] Moreover, almost all of us consider the national economy to be a single economy rather than an agglomeration of regional economies, and we oppose any interference with trade in the domestic market.

To illustrate, we should view as absurd a petition by New England textile producers requesting the federal government to impose restrictions on the sale of textiles produced in the South. We might sympathize with the plight of several New England communities as their chief industry shut its doors and headed south, but we should

---

[4] Undoubtedly trade between European countries would expand greatly if these nations merged into one political unit, since the restraints now imposed on this trade by individual governments would disappear. But this would not make interregional trade any "better" than international trade. See Chapter 19.

[5] Interstate trade barriers are forbidden by the United States Constitution. Despite this fact, individual states do restrain interstate trade in certain products (mostly agricultural) through a variety of devices ostensibly employed for other purposes, such as pest control and public safety. Arrangements between domestic producers to restrain interstate trade are forbidden by the antitrust laws.

feel that such a situation is bound to occur now and then in a competitive economy and that in the long run everyone benefits by having goods and services produced in those places where costs are at a minimum. When, however, those same producers demand protection against imports of textiles from Japan, their appeal sounds reasonable to many of us despite the fact that the economic issue is the same, namely, whether domestic consumers are to have the right to purchase lower-cost textiles made in the South or in Japan.

To conclude, recognition of the basic similarity of interregional and international trade is essential to a proper understanding of the latter. That recognition will keep us from reaching the erroneous conclusion that, because of the many characteristics which distinguish international trade, it is a unique sort of trade and must be treated differently from domestic trade. Widespread awareness that the gains from international trade rest upon the same economic conditions as do the gains from domestic trade would eradicate much of the confusion and downright falsity that envelop public discussions of matters pertaining to our trade with other nations.

Some Arguments against International Trade

Some of the arguments that have been voiced against international trade include those stated below.

1. A nation dependent on foreign sources of supply is in a particularly vulnerable position during a war.

2. International trade is a source of instability and interferes with economic planning.

3. International trade creates losses for those domestic industries whose products are displaced by imports.

International specialization brings to a nation a higher standard of living, but it also implies dependence on foreign markets as sources of supply and as outlets for domestic production. Some persons contemplate this dependence with marked distaste and argue that the national interest demands that it be lessened or entirely eradicated. The aversion toward international specialization is rationalized in many ways, and it often camouflages the interests of private groups that stand to gain from the removal of import competition. The most important ally of attacks against international specialization and trade is nationalism—the ideology that holds the nation state to be the *only* source of political and economic security.

National Defense. It is argued that a nation dependent on foreign sources of supply is in a particularly vulnerable position during a war. The harrowing experience of the United Kingdom in both World Wars is cited as proof of this assertion—twice the German submarine blockade almost brought that country to her knees by cutting off imports of food and raw materials. This is, of course, a political or military argument rather than an economic one, but it has many economic implications. Its proper evaluation requires not only a careful forecast of the probable nature of a future war but a searching study of the relationships between economic strength and military capacity as well. For example, if another world war promises destruction of everyone's productive facilities within a few hours, then it is military strength in being that counts and the military argument for economic self-sufficiency falls by the wayside.

In conclusion, there is no assurance that greater economic self-sufficiency will enhance a nation's military power, and by the same token there is no justification to deny out of hand the compatibility of international specialization and a nation's ability to defend itself against armed aggression.

Instability and Economic Planning. International trade is also condemned as a source of economic instability. This attitude gained prominence in the 1930's when depression spread from one country to another by disrupting the international flow of goods, services, and capital. In particular, foreign observers were wont to protest the folly of close dependence on such a volatile economy as that of the United States. In our own day this argument against international trade has been reinforced by government policies directed toward full employment and economic development. To many economic planners, foreign trade is a nuisance unless carefully controlled to fit the master economic plan. This is not the place to evaluate the bearing of international trade and finance on domestic stability, employment, and economic development, but it may be pointed out that most nations are unable to achieve the objectives of full employment and the like except as members of a world trading system.

Protectionism. Traditionally, the attacks against foreign trade have been leveled against imports. Several arguments in addition to those already mentioned have been used to justify the protection of domestic industry against foreign competition. These arguments are described and analyzed in Chapter 15, and we shall say nothing about them here except to indicate that insofar as protectionism lowers a nation's imports, it also eventually lowers a nation's exports (unless the protectionist country loans or gives away its exports) since other nations must finance their imports through their exports.

The roll call of arguments against international specialization and trade is indeed a formidable one—national security, economic stability, full employment, economic development, economic planning, protectionism, and others of lesser note. All of these arguments pack a powerful emotional appeal to the man on the street. Nevertheless, international trade exhibits a vitality and growth that is difficult to reconcile with its alleged disadvantages. It would appear that the supreme economic advantages of international specialization and trade, when weighed against the supreme economic costs of national self-sufficiency, cannot be gainsaid by nationalistic fervor or the special pleading of private vested interests.

DISTINCTIVE FEATURES OF INTERNATIONAL TRADE

There are several distinctive features of international trade that are very closely related to the concept of national sovereignty—immobility of factors of production, national monetary systems, government regulation of international trade, and national economic policies. In addition to discussing each of these features, this section also briefly points out how different languages and customs influence the conduct of international business.

National Sovereignty

The nation recognizes no higher authority than its own in all matters that relate to its domestic affairs and its dealings with other nations. This is the essence of national sovereignty. Although international treaties and other agreements may pledge a nation to act in a certain way or not to act in a certain way, there is no question but that the nation retains its full sovereignty and, in the last analysis, may act as it chooses. The absence of supranational authority and the consequent right of nations to act unilaterally generate most of the differences that distinguish international from domestic trade. It is not surprising that international trade most closely approached domestic trade during the period before World War I when the nations of the world followed the economic and political leadership of Great Britain.

The Immobility of Factors of Production

In the nineteenth century, classical economists distinguished international trade from domestic trade by the criterion of factor mobility. It was assumed that the factors of production—natural resources, capital, management, and labor—moved freely within a country but did not move between countries. For this reason international trade obeyed laws of economic behavior that differed from those of domestic trade.

As the century progressed, these twin assumptions of perfect factor mobility within a country and perfect factor immobility between countries came more and more into conflict with the facts of economic life. On the one hand, it was noted that factors of production often do not move freely from one place to another inside the same country; and, on the other hand, it was observed that the substantial international migration of capital and people then going on illustrated an important degree of international factor mobility. Hence, contemporary economic theory posits no sharp distinction between international trade and domestic interregional trade; it considers both kinds of trade to be based on factor immobilities, that is, trade is a substitute for factor movements.

In the absence of political restrictions on the international movement of capital and persons, it is likely that factor mobility between countries would still be somewhat less than factor mobility within countries. International differences in customs and languages, distance, and the like would work in this direction. But under these circumstances no one would argue that factor movements between countries were essentially different from factor movements within countries. In actuality, as we all know, they *are* different, for nations throughout the world restrict immigration (and sometimes emigration) as well as the export and import of capital. Thus the exercise of national sovereignty has greatly lowered the international mobility of productive factors, and in so doing it has altered the scope and character of international trade. We may take, then, as one distinctive feature of international trade the high degree of factor immobility upon which it is based. People and capital do not move freely from one country to another and the movement of merchandise and services must act as substitutes.

National Monetary Systems

Unlike domestic trade, international trade takes place between economies that have different monetary systems. This gives rise to the need to exchange one currency for another at an agreed ratio. The purchase and sale of foreign currency is conducted in the foreign exchange market, and the exchange ratio between currencies is known as the *exchange rate*. Dealings in foreign exchange often appear mysterious to the layman, and perhaps more than anything else, except nationalism, they have convinced him that international trade is entirely distinct from the familiar domestic trade. Even some domestic producers have been daunted by the prospect of dealings in foreign exchange until relieved from their anxiety by the calm advice and aid of bankers.

Actually the presence of different monetary systems need not alter the character of international trade from its domestic counterpart. When exchange rates are stable and currencies are freely convertible into each other, international payments are just as easily made as are domestic payments. In these circumstances the national monetary systems comprise one international monetary system, and for all practical purposes they are one and the same. Before World War I such an international monetary system did in fact exist. National currencies were linked to gold and were freely transferable into each other; an international payment was no different from a domestic payment except that the former involved residents of different countries.

Today the situation is far different, and international trade is sharply set off from domestic trade by the restrictions imposed by many governments on transactions in foreign exchange and by variations in foreign exchange rates. Although the currencies of the industrial countries (mainly North America, Western Europe, and Japan) are for the most part freely convertible at stable rates, the currencies of most nonindustrial countries and of all Communist countries are inconvertible in one way or another and the exchange rates of the former are also frequently unstable. Currency inconvertibility can have profound effects on the conduct of international trade. An importer may not be able to buy merchandise from the country of his choice because he cannot buy the necessary foreign exchange from his government. He may be compelled, therefore, to import inferior or higher-priced goods from a country to which he is permitted to make payments. When currencies are freely convertible but unstable, foreign traders may suffer exchange losses unless they can hedge against them. We should remember, however, that it is more the **exercise of** national sovereignty to restrict international payments or vary exchange rates than the mere presence of different monetary systems that is a distinctive feature of international trade.

Government Regulation of International Trade

Nations have interfered with international trade ever since the beginning of the nation-state system some five hundred years ago. Even during the last half of the nineteenth century, when the majority of governments followed a policy of laissez faire with respect to domestic economic activities, the use of tariff protection was commonplace. Great Britain and the Netherlands were the only important trading nations that rid themselves of protective tariffs and adopted free trade in that period of liberal economic policies. Since World War I all nations without exception have regulated their foreign trade and have done so with many new control devices in addition to the traditional tariff.

We have already noted that many contemporary governments restrict the convertibility of their currencies. This is known as *exchange control* and allows a comprehensive regulation of the international movement not only of merchandise but of services and capital as well. Commodity trade is also regulated through quotas, licenses, tariffs, bilateral trading arrangements, commodity agreements, and other techniques. Restrictions are generally applied against imports, while exports may be stimulated by subsidies, exchange depreciation, bilateral agreements, as well as other methods. Mention should also be made of the fact that government regulation of international trade involves a great deal of red tape and bureaucratic delay that are often a potent deterrent to trade.

National Economic Policies

National economic policies may be compatible with the free flow of merchandise, services, and capital between nations or they may be responsible for the regulation and suppression of that flow. As we shall discover, national economic policies that are apparently wholly domestic in nature may have profound effects on international trade. To maintain an equilibrium in its international payments without resort to controls, a nation must keep its economy adjusted to the world economy. This means, for example, that it must pursue fiscal and monetary policies which keep its prices and costs competitive with those of other nations. It also means that there is sometimes a conflict between the aims of domestic policy and international adjustment. Because of political pressures this conflict is often resolved in favor of the former, while international maladjustment is frozen by the imposition of controls over foreign trade and payments.

When certain nations adopt domestic policies that are detrimental to their external stability, all trading nations suffer the consequences. For the international economy to function in an atmosphere of freedom there must be agreement among nations as to the criteria of sound domestic and international economic policies. It too often happens, however, that nations follow policies that are conceived in purely domestic terms, and the resulting welter of policies causes international maladjustments that are met by a rash of restrictive measures. Unlike interregional trade, therefore, international trade is subject to the influence of many separate national economic policies that are often in disharmony with each other.

Different Languages and Customs

Most nations have a distinctive linguistic and cultural identity in addition to a basic political identity. This is not always true; we can all call to mind nations that have more than one official language and more than one cultural group in their populations. Moreover, several nations may share a common language and a common cultural heritage. Nevertheless, it is true that people tend to be like each other in more ways when they belong to the same nation than when they belong to different nations. Hence, international trade—much more so than interregional trade—is apt to be trade between peoples whose languages, customs, attitudes, and other cultural traits are different. Such differences do not affect the basic economic similarity between interregional and international trade, but they do introduce many new elements into the conduct of international business.

SUMMARY

1. It is easy to understand the value of international trade to the business enterprises that are engaged in the export and import of merchandise, services, and capital. They are interested in international trade as a source of income and profits.
2. On the other hand, the interest of management, labor, and capital employed in domestic industries in close competition with imports from abroad may be injured by an expansion of international trade. It must be noted, however, that such injury is one of the costs of a competitive economic system.

3. The interest of domestic consumers is benefited by international trade because it lowers the prices of goods and makes available goods that cannot be produced at home.
4. If we agree that the proper end of economic activity is consumption, then we should agree that the interest of consumers in international trade is identical with the national interest. National welfare is enhanced by international trade because the latter permits international specialization that leads to a more productive use of the natural resources, capital, and labor of nations.
5. The contribution of international trade is so immense that few countries could become self-sufficient even with the greatest effort. Even the United States would find the costs of self-sufficiency formidable.
6. The gains from international specialization are fundamentally of the same nature as the gains from domestic interregional specialization. Thus, international trade and interregional trade are basically the same, and the distinctive features of international trade are largely owing to the political fact of national sovereignty.
7. There are several arguments against international specialization and trade —national security, economic stability, full employment, economic development, protection of domestic industries, etc. Nevertheless, the advantages of international trade are so great that it exhibits vitality and growth.
8. Most of the distinctive features of international trade—the low international mobility of factors of production, national monetary systems, government regulation, conflicting national policies—stem directly from the exercise of national sovereignty, the right of nations to do as they choose in all matters. We also take note that languages and customs tend to differ more between than within nations.

QUESTIONS AND APPLICATIONS

1. What is the nature of the national interest in international trade?
2. Why does not the United States forsake international trade and produce at home everything it consumes?
3. Domestic interregional trade is basically the same as international trade. Discuss.
4. There are several arguments against international trade. Which one do you consider the most formidable?
5. Discuss the implications of national sovereignty for international trade.

SELECTED READINGS

Ellsworth, P. T. *The International Economy*, 3d ed. New York: The Macmillan Company, 1964. Chapter 1.

Kindleberger, Charles P. *International Economics*, 3d ed. Homewood, Ill.: Richard D. Irwin, Inc., 1963. Chapter 1.

Towle, Lawrence W. *International Trade and Commercial Policy*, 2d ed. New York: Harper & Brothers, 1956. Chapter 1.

CHAPTER 2

THE DIMENSIONS OF WORLD TRADE

In its broadest sense international trade covers not only trade in merchandise but in services as well. International investment and other financial transactions between residents of different countries also contribute to international trade. The bulk of international economic transactions, however, involves merchandise exports and imports, and we shall restrict our attention to this category of international trade in this chapter. We shall become acquainted with the full range of international transactions in Chapter 7 when we describe the balance of international payments.

The approach in Chapter 2 is mainly statistical. We shall offer quantitative measures of different aspects of world trade with particular emphasis on the position of the United States. In so doing, our intent is to disclose important economic relationships that have a far greater significance than individual economic aggregates considered in isolation. These relationships are often the consequence of developments working slowly over decades, and they exhibit a degree of stability that contrasts with the ever-changing levels of international trade and its parts.

VALUE AND VOLUME OF WORLD TRADE

World trade is enormous even by American standards. In 1964 world merchandise exports (excluding the exports of Communist countries) were $151 billion—an amount equal to three tenths of the national income of the United States and to more than twice the national income of the United Kingdom. Another indication of the vast size of international trade is revealed by its comparison with the personal consumption of durable and nondurable goods in the United States, which was $234 billion in 1964.

Table 2-1 shows the dollar values of world exports for selected years since 1913.[1] These dollar values, however, cannot be used to measure the growth of world trade, particularly over a long period of years, because of changes in price levels. Between 1913 and 1964 the general price level of merchandise entering international trade more than doubled—mainly the consequence of inflation bred by two world wars only partially offset by the deflation of the 1930's. To trace changes in the *volume* of world trade since 1913, therefore, we must remove the effects of changes in the price level. This is done by calculating an index of quantum (volume) of world exports. The export quantum index in Table 2-1, based on 1953, indicates that the volume of world exports (and thus imports) has risen from 58

Table 2-1

WORLD TRADE: EXPORTS, QUANTUM EXPORTS, AND WORLD INDUSTRIAL PRODUCTION

Year	Exports (Billions of Dollars)	Index of Quantum of Exports (1953 = 100)	Index of World Industrial Production (1953 = 100)
1913	19.8 *	58	38
1928	32.7 *	74	55 †
1938	20.6	69	51
1948	52.7	70	73
1953	73.4	100	100
1958	94.4	128	116
1964	151.3	198	171

* Old gold dollars.
† 1929.

GENERAL NOTE: Data from 1948 on do not include Mainland China, U.S.S.R., East Germany, Bulgaria, Rumania, Albania, Czechoslovakia, Hungary, North Korea, and Poland.

SOURCES: W. S. Woytinsky and E. S. Woytinsky, *World Commerce and Governments* (New York: Twentieth Century Fund, 1955). United Nations, *Monthly Bulletin of Statistics* (various issues).

[1] The value of world exports is somewhat less than the value of world imports due to the fact that most nations value exports f.o.b. (free on board) at the point of exportation and imports c.i.f. (cost, insurance, freight) at the point of importation. Thus the value of world imports exceeds the value of world exports by the amount of transportation and other costs incurred in the physical movement of merchandise between countries. The United States, Canada, and a few other countries value imports as well as exports at their f.o.b. values. Free world imports were $159.2 billion in 1964.

in 1913 to 198 in 1964. This contrasts with the more than sevenfold increase in dollar values from $19.8 billion to $151.3 billion over the same period.

The growth in world trade since 1913 has not been steady. Both the value and volume of trade fell greatly in the early 1930's—the volume of world exports in 1932 was one fifth below the volume of 1928. Even in 1938 the volume of world trade was less than in 1928 and was not notably higher than in 1913. Since World War II, however, there has occurred a remarkable upsurge of world trade, and in 1964 the volume of exports was over 187 percent above the level of 1938.

International Trade and Industrial Production

Table 2-1 also suggests a relationship between the volume of world trade and world industrial production. Between 1913 and 1964 the volume of industrial production rose almost 350 percent while the volume of trade rose 241 percent. The higher growth rate for industrial production is mostly traceable to the years during and preceding World War II. Since 1948 world trade has outpaced industrial production—183 percent compared to 134 percent.

The relationship between industrial production and international trade is not fortuitous. As we shall observe later in the chapter, most of the world's trade is generated by the industrial countries. When the economies of these countries experience a rapid growth, international trade is stimulated and also expanded; conversely, depression in the industrial countries depresses world trade as well as domestic economic activity. Although industrial production is the dominant partner in this relationship, changes in world trade also cause changes in industrial production. This is particularly true of countries highly dependent on international trade, and in many instances domestic economic growth is limited by the growth of a country's exports.

In viewing the relationship between industrial production and international trade, we must also remember that nations have promoted industrialization and at the same time have restricted foreign trade. There is no way of knowing how greatly tariffs, quotas, exchange controls, and other restrictions have dampened the growth of world trade since 1913, but there is little question that its volume would be higher in their absence.

Principal Trading Countries

The United States, the United Kingdom, and West Germany are dominant in world trade. In 1963 these three countries alone accounted for 36.3 percent of the free world's exports and 30.3 percent of its imports. The ten leading countries in world trade in 1963 are shown in Table 2-2.

Table 2-2

PRINCIPAL TRADING COUNTRIES OF THE FREE WORLD IN 1963

(Billions of Dollars)

Exports		Imports	
United States	23.0	United States	17.1
West Germany	14.6	United Kingdom	13.1
United Kingdom	11.4	West Germany	13.0
France	8.1	France	8.7
Canada	6.5	Italy	7.5
Japan	5.5	Japan	6.7
Italy	5.0	Canada	6.1
Netherlands	5.0	Netherlands	6.0
Belgium-Luxembourg	4.8	Belgium-Luxembourg	5.1
Sweden	3.2	Sweden	3.4
Total	87.1	Total	86.7
Free World Exports	135.0	Free World Imports	142.5

GENERAL NOTE: All exports are f.o.b.; all imports are c.i.f., except the United States and Canada.

SOURCE: United Nations, *Monthly Bulletin of Statistics*, June, 1965.

Several points may be drawn from an examination of these data.

1. Seven of the major exporting nations and seven of the major importing nations are located in Europe. This underlines the tremendous significance of that area in the world economy.

2. The order of countries is not the same for both exports and imports. West Germany ranks second in exports but third in imports, just behind the United Kingdom. Canada ranks fifth in exports but only seventh in imports. These shifts result from the fact that some nations have net import balances, others have net export balances; and net balances, whether import or export, vary greatly in size. Although the precise ordering may change from one year to the next, the ten principal trading countries were the same in 1957 with only one exception—Venezuela (a major petroleum exporter) ranked tenth in exports, edging out Sweden, but did not place among the first ten importing countries.

3. The United States ranks first both in exports and imports, but its exports are far higher than its imports.

4. The ten principal trading countries were responsible for 60 percent of the free world's exports and 61 percent of its imports.

Table 2-3 exhibits the changes that have occurred in the relative *export* positions of the major international trading areas since 1913. The most striking development has been the rise of the United States to the position of first exporter among the countries of the world. In 1913 this position was occupied by the United Kingdom, but in the 1920's that country lost its export leadership to the United States although it retained its import leadership until 1950. In 1964 United States exports were 17.3 percent of free world exports.

Western Europe is by far the most important single trading *region* in world trade. Although slightly less important than in 1913, Western Europe accounted for 38.7 percent of world trade in 1964. Since World War II this region's international trade has been more dynamic than that of any other region, and today its share of world exports is substantially higher than in 1938.

Table 2-3

EXPORTS: UNITED STATES, UNITED KINGDOM, WESTERN EUROPE, JAPAN, AND REST OF WORLD

(Billions of Dollars)

Year	United States	United Kingdom	Western Europe *	Japan	Rest of World	Total World
1913 †	2.5	3.1	7.9	0.3	6.0	19.8
1928 †	5.1	3.5	9.9	0.9	13.3	32.7
1938	3.1	2.7	6.3	1.1	7.4	20.6
1948	12.7	6.4	11.0	0.3	22.3	52.7
1953	15.8	7.2	20.2	1.3	28.9	73.4
1958	17.9	9.0	31.5	2.9	33.1	94.4
1964	26.2	11.9	58.6	6.7	47.9	151.3

* Includes Austria, Belgium-Luxembourg, Denmark, Finland, France, West Germany, Greece, Italy, Netherlands, Norway, Portugal, Spain, Sweden, Switzerland, and Yugoslavia.

† Old gold dollars.

GENERAL NOTE: Data from 1948 on do not include Mainland China, U.S.S.R., East Germany, Bulgaria, Rumania, Albania, Czechoslovakia, Hungary, North Korea, and Poland.

SOURCES: United States Department of Commerce. League of Nations, *Industrialization and Foreign Trade* (1949). W. S. Woytinsky and E. S. Woytinsky, *World Commerce and Governments* (New York: Twentieth Century Fund, 1955). United Nations, *Monthly Bulletin of Statistics* (various issues).

The principal trading country located outside North America and Europe (including the United Kingdom) is Japan. This country has gained much ground since the early 1950's (when its share of world exports was less than 2 percent), but in 1964 its relative participation in world exports was still somewhat less than in 1938.

The relative importance of the rest of the world in total world exports is lower today than before World War II and substantially less than in 1928. This group of countries—mostly nonindustrial—suffered a steady decline in its share of world exports during the 1950's, mainly because of the more rapid growth in the trade of the industrial countries.

The Trade of Industrial and Nonindustrial Areas

It is a common misconception that most international trade consists in the exchange of foodstuffs and raw materials for manufactures between nonindustrial and industrial countries. The error of this view becomes apparent when we analyze the data in Table 2-4 on trade between industrial and nonindustrial areas.

The dominance of the industrial areas in international trade is clearly evident. In 1963 the countries of these areas originated 73.1 percent and absorbed 73.5 percent of free world trade. Trade *between* these same countries accounted for 53.2 percent of free world trade. In other words, over seven tenths of the exports of the *industrial* countries are with each other.

The countries of the nonindustrial areas originated 26.9 percent and absorbed 26.5 percent of free world trade in 1963. However, only 6.5 percent of free world trade arose out of trade *between* these same countries, that is, only about one quarter of the exports of the *nonindustrial* countries went to the *nonindustrial* areas. This fact underlines the dependence of the nonindustrial countries on the industrial countries.

In 1963, exports of the industrial areas to the nonindustrial areas were 19.9 percent of free world trade. Exports of the nonindustrial areas to the industrial areas were 20.3 percent of free world trade. This indicates that the nonindustrial areas have a small export balance in their trade with the industrial areas.

To sum up, in 1963, 53.2 percent of free world trade was between countries of the industrial areas, 6.5 percent between countries of the nonindustrial areas, and the remainder, 40.2 percent, was between the industrial and nonindustrial **areas**.

Table 2-4

TRADE WITHIN AND BETWEEN INDUSTRIAL AND NON-INDUSTRIAL AREAS AS A PERCENTAGE OF FREE WORLD TRADE

(Based on f.o.b. Values)

Exports From \ Exports To	Industrial Areas (%)	Nonindustrial Areas (%)	Total World (%)
Industrial Areas *			
1938	38.6	28.2	66.8
1950	35.2	24.6	59.8
1957	41.4	26.9	68.3
1963	53.2	19.9	73.1
Nonindustrial Areas †			
1938	25.0	8.2	33.2
1950	28.0	12.2	40.2
1957	21.7	10.0	31.6
1963	20.3	6.5	26.9
Total World ‡			
1938	63.6	36.4	100.0
1950	63.2	36.8	100.0
1957	63.1	36.9	100.0
1963	73.5	26.5	100.0

* Industrial areas comprise North America (United States and Canada), Western Europe, and Japan.

† Nonindustrial areas comprise Latin America, Southeast Asia, the Middle East, Oceania, and Africa.

‡ Data exclude Eastern Europe, U.S.S.R., and Communist Asia.

GENERAL NOTE: Data may not add precisely because of rounding.

SOURCE: General Agreement on Tariffs and Trade, *Trends in International Trade* (Geneva: October, 1958), Appendix, Table A. General Agreement on Tariffs and Trade, *International Trade 1963* (Geneva: 1964), Appendix, Table D.

The exchange of merchandise between industrial and nonindustrial countries has become a smaller share of world trade since 1938, 53.2 percent in that year compared to 40.2 percent in 1963. Moreover, this share has been dropping in recent years. At the same time trade between the industrial countries had risen from 38.6 percent of world trade in 1938 to 53.2 percent in 1963. Trade between the nonindustrial areas has also shown a downward drift since 1950.

Experts associated with the General Agreement on Tariffs and Trade ascribe the failure of the nonindustrial areas to retain their share of international trade, particularly exports to the industrial areas, to the industrial development that has occurred in many nonindustrial countries. Because of industrialization their production of the principal food and raw material exports has not been sufficient to meet domestic needs and at the same time maintain an adequate volume of exports to the industrial areas.[2] Hence industrial countries have had to turn to each other and to domestic production for food and raw materials to a growing extent in the postwar years. Undoubtedly, other factors have been at work, such as declining prices of primary products in the 1950's and, of course, the very rapid expansion of the exports of industrial areas.

The half of free world trade that occurs between industrial and nonindustrial countries is largely the traditional exchange of manufactured goods for foodstuffs and raw materials. In 1962, 81.5 percent of the exports of industrial areas to nonindustrial areas was classified as manufactures, and 87 percent of the exports of nonindustrial areas to industrial areas was classified as foodstuffs and raw materials. It may surprise us to learn that in 1962 foodstuffs and raw materials made up 32.1 percent of trade between the industrial areas while manufactures constituted the remainder. In that same year manufactures were 22.3 percent of trade between the nonindustrial areas.

East-West Trade

Up to this point we have looked at free world trade only. What of the international trade of the Eastern Trading Area—Eastern Europe, the Soviet Union, and Communist Asia? Together the countries in this area generated $18.7 billion of exports in 1963; the bulk of these exports ($12.5 billion) was to other Communist countries. Thus exports of the East in 1963 were about one eighth of aggregate world exports, and its exports to the West (including Cuba) made up only 3.7 percent of aggregate world exports.

Despite the relative smallness of East-West trade (about equal to the trade of the Netherlands in 1963), it has been growing rapidly and it has assumed a sizable volume for certain countries. Table 2-5 compares East-West trade for 1953 and 1963. The year 1953 marked the end of the Stalin era of dogmatic self-sufficiency and discouragement of Soviet trade relations with the West. Under Khrushchev, the Soviet leadership began to promote trade with the West, publicizing attractive opportunities for Western industrialists and pushing an aid-trade program with nonindustrial countries. At the same time, the West—notably Western Europe—eased its restrictions on trade with Communist countries and increasingly sought to expand exports

---

[2] General Agreement on Tariffs and Trade, *International Trade 1956* (Geneva: June, 1957), pp. 16-17.

Ch. 2 / The Dimensions of World Trade

to them. As a result of this bilateral shift in policy, trade between East and West more than trebled in the decade 1953-63.

Table 2-5 indicates that about two fifths of East-West trade involves the nonindustrial West. The other three fifths is accounted for by the industrial West, mostly Western Europe. The United States remains a very small trader with the East for a number of reasons. First, this country maintains very strict controls over exports to the Soviet bloc and prohibits *any* trade with Communist Asia. Second, the United States refuses to extend most-favored-nation (MFN) treatment to Communist countries so that imports from the East must pay the very high 1930 tariff rates. The United States also has other import restrictions that discriminate against imports from

Table 2-5
EAST-WEST TRADE, 1953 and 1963
(Millions of Dollars)

Country	Exports to East * 1953	Exports to East * 1963	Imports from East * 1953	Imports from East * 1963
Western Europe	764.0	2,287.6	852.8	2,790.5
W. Germany	78.7	454.0	99.7	494.1
United Kingdom	114.6	423.9	226.6	533.1
Italy	62.6	290.6	53.8	445.4
France	63.4	284.5	56.9	272.0
United States	1.8	166.4	43.2	80.8
Canada	0.5	276.7	6.2	23.7
Japan	4.5	241.7	31.9	255.0
Nonindustrial West †	576.9	1,948.8	605.8	2,020.5
All West †	1,347.7	4,921.2	1,539.9	5,170.5

* East includes Eastern Europe, U.S.S.R., and Mainland China. Yugoslavia, North Korea, and North Viet Nam are not included in table.
† Excluding Cuba.
SOURCE: Organization for Economic Cooperation and Development, Statistical Bulletins, Foreign Trade, Series A, *Overall Trade by Countries*.

the East, such as an embargo on certain furs. Third, the United States forbids private residents to grant credit to any Communist country beyond short-term commercial credit (normally six months). This stultifies trade because the Communist countries want to buy much more from the United States than this country wants to buy from them. Since the East does not generate significant earnings of convertible currencies in trade with Western Europe, it would be forced to deplete its gold reserves to finance any large expansion of trade with the United States.

In 1964 the United States shipped big quantities of wheat to the Soviet Union. This event started a controversy in this country regarding the wisdom of United States policy towards East-West trade. This is not the place to explore the many issues in this controversy. Suffice it to say that even a significant liberalization of United States export and import restrictions would probably induce not much more than a doubling of United States trade with the East unless long-term credit were also granted to the bloc countries. On the other hand, we can reasonably expect a continued expansion in overall East-West trade during the 1960's. Even so, East-West trade will remain a small percentage of the aggregate trade of free world countries.

COMPOSITION OF WORLD TRADE

Table 2-6 indicates the importance of manufactures, food, and raw materials in international trade for the years 1929, 1937, 1953, and 1963. In 1963 trade in manufactures comprised more than half (56.2 percent) the value of world trade; food, about one sixth (17.7 percent); and raw materials, about one quarter (24.6 percent).

The most significant change in the composition of international trade since 1929 is the enhanced importance of manufactures and the concomitant decline in the importance of raw materials and foodstuffs. We have already offered one explanation of this shift—the inability in the postwar period of the nonindustrial areas to sustain the level of their primary exports and the consequent turning toward domestic sources of supply by the industrial countries.

Other developments, however, have also contributed to this change. During the 1930's many countries, especially in Europe,

Table 2-6
PERCENTAGE COMPOSITION OF WORLD TRADE

	1929	1937	1953	1963
Manufactures	40.8	39.5	45.5	56.2
Food	24.2	22.4	22.1	17.7
Raw Materials	35.0	38.1	30.0	24.6
Residual	—	—	2.4	1.5
Total World Trade	100.0	100.0	100.0	100.0

SOURCE: W. S. Woytinsky and E. S. Woytinsky, *World Commerce and Governments* (New York: Twentieth Century Fund, 1955). General Agreement on Tariffs and Trade. United Nations, *Monthly Bulletin of Statistics*, March, 1965.

adopted government measures to increase self-sufficiency in foodstuffs by subsidizing domestic agriculture and restricting agricultural imports. Most countries have strengthened such programs since that time. Again certain technological advances have created substitutes for raw materials or have lowered the input of raw materials per unit of output. Artificial fibers and synthetic rubber are among the most outstanding examples of this technological displacement. These developments have tended to lower international trade in raw materials because many of the new products may be turned out by the use of domestic raw materials such as coal.

The most important explanation of the shift in the composition of international trade is probably the rapid growth of industrial output compared to primary production throughout the world. The world's physical production has become progressively dominated by manufactures, and this evolution has been reflected in the changing character of international trade. Contrary influences have also been operative. For example, the dependence of the United States on raw material imports is increasing rapidly as domestic sources become exhausted. When all the influences acting on the composition of world trade are taken into account, however, it appears that the share of manufactures will continue to rise in the future.

MULTILATERAL STRUCTURE OF INTERNATIONAL TRADE

We have already discussed the direction of world trade in terms of industrial and nonindustrial areas. Table 2-7 carries the analysis a step further by indicating the direction of trade among the major trading areas in 1963. In that year these areas conducted more than four fifths of world trade, including trade of the Communist countries.

A close scrutiny of Table 2-7 reveals the pattern of international trade in 1963. For example, the biggest export market of North America by far was Western Europe, followed by Latin America. Two thirds of Western Europe's exports went to Western Europe itself (intratrade); Western Europe's principal *external* market for exports was North America. Another point to be noted is that each area had export balances with some areas and import balances with others, with the exception of Western Europe which had import balances with all outside areas and Latin America which had export balances. In other words, the pattern of trade is *multilateral*. The same is true of the individual countries within the trading areas.

Table 2-7

THE DIRECTION OF FREE WORLD TRADE IN 1963

(Millions of Dollars f.o.b.)

Exports from \ Exports to	North America	Western Europe	Japan	Latin America	Other Non-industrial Areas	All Areas
North America * ...	7,670	8,420	1,975	3,360	5,370	26,795
Western Europe	5,540	40,380	610	2,430	11,210	60,170
Japan	1,645	715	—	320	2,380	5,060
Latin America	3,720	3,320	395	730	1,710	9,875
Other Nonindustrial Areas	3,795	12,080	2,300	380	6,585	25,140
All Areas	22,370	64,915	5,280	7,220	27,255	127,040

* Excludes United States "special category" exports which are not reported for security reasons.

SOURCE: General Agreement on Tariffs and Trade, *International Trade 1963* (Geneva: 1964), Appendix, Table D.

The Basis of Multilateral Trade

International trade develops a multilateral structure because of basic economic conditions. There is no reason why the exports of one nation or region to another nation or region should equal its imports from the latter. Indeed, there are several reasons why such an equality is not at all likely. For one thing, the basis of international trade is specialization and thus the exports of a particular commodity usually come from a relatively small number of nations. The following list indicates the major country sources of some representative exports:

Coffee	Brazil, Colombia, West Africa, Mexico, Salvador
Wheat	United States, Canada, Argentina, Australia, France
Sugar	Cuba, British West Indies, Philippines, Australia, Taiwan
Cotton	United States, Brazil, Egypt, Mexico, Pakistan
Rubber	Indonesia, Malaya, Thailand, Ceylon
Iron Ore	Sweden, Canada, Venezuela, France, United States
Coal	United States, West Germany, United Kingdom, Belgium
Automobiles ..	United States, Canada, United Kingdom, France, West Germany, Italy

The explanation of international specialization is taken up in

Chapters 3, 4, and 5; but it is clear that natural resources, to say nothing of people and capital, are not spread evenly over the earth.

At the same time that nations specialize in their exports, they tend to generalize in their imports; that is, they desire a wide variety of goods that can usually be obtained only from a great number of countries. There is no conflict between export specialization on the one hand and import generalization on the other when nations can buy and sell in world markets without the necessity of bilaterally balancing their trade with every other nation. Traditionally, the United Kingdom has had a large import balance with North America, but this caused no trouble before the war because that country had large export balances (counting services) in its trade with Latin America and other areas which, in turn, had export balances in their trade with North America. Thus the United Kingdom was able to finance its import balance with North America through multilateral settlement.[3] When we consider the international movement of services and capital, the basis for multilateral trade becomes even stronger.

Multilateral Structure of Contemporary International Trade

The multilateral structure of contemporary international trade is shown more clearly in Table 2-8 which indicates the net merchandise balances of the major trading areas in 1963. In that year North America had the biggest overall export balance and Western Europe the biggest overall import balance. These net balance positions have been persistent features of contemporary international trade. In 1957, for example, the export balance of North America was $3.9 billion and the import balance of Western Europe, $2.6 billion. The positions of Latin America and the Other Nonindustrial Areas, however, have varied considerably in the postwar period. In 1957 Latin America had an overall *import* balance of $105 million and the Other Nonindustrial Areas had an overall import balance of $2.0 billion. But in 1963 Latin America developed a large *export* balance

---

[3] Perhaps the most famous historical example of multilateral settlement is the triangular trade developed by New England merchants in the colonial period. New England had a large import balance with Great Britain because the mother country wanted few things other than ships from that region. This difficulty was overcome by New England's exporting to areas that had a positive balance in their trade with Great Britain. One triangular trade route involved the export of rum (made from molasses imported from the West Indies) to Africa in exchange for slaves which were then exchanged for molasses and pounds sterling in the West Indies. The pounds sterling were used to finance New England's import balance with Great Britain.

Table 2-8

NET BALANCES IN INTERNATIONAL TRADE IN 1963

(Millions of Dollars)

	North America	Western Europe	Japan	Latin America	Other Non-industrial Areas	All Areas
North America	—	+2,880	+330	−360	+1,575	+4,425
Western Europe	−2,880	—	−105	−890	−870	−4,745
Japan	−330	+105	—	−75	+80	−220
Latin America	+360	+890	+75	—	+1,330	+2,655
Other Nonindustrial Areas	−1,575	+870	−80	−1,330	—	−2,115

GENERAL NOTE: Net balances were calculated from the f.o.b. export values in Table 2-7. Thus they differ from net balances calculated by using c.i.f. import values. Table 2-8 reads from left to right. A plus sign indicates a *net* export balance; a minus sign, a *net* import balance.

SOURCE: Table 2-7.

while the Other Nonindustrial Areas experienced an import balance of about the same size as in 1957. For the most part these two areas are exporters of industrial raw materials and foodstuffs that are subject to wide swings in prices. When prices are high, these areas tend to develop export balances; when prices are low they tend to develop import balances. Other factors are also at work, such as conditions of export supply and the volume of foreign aid and investment received by these two areas.

The essence of multilateral *settlement* is the use of a net export balance in one direction to offset a net import balance in another direction. Multilateral settlement involves a "closed circuit" of net balances between the respective trading areas. To take a hypothetical example, multilateral settlement is possible between areas A, B, and C when, let us say, A has a net export balance with B; B has a net export balance with C; and C has a net export balance with A. Settlement will be complete, however, only when the net export balances of the three areas are equal.

Keeping this observation in mind, let us look again at Table 2-8. Can we find any closed circuits? The answer is no. The fly in the ointment is that both Western Europe and Latin America cannot participate in any multilateral circuits because their net balances with all other areas are in the same direction—negative for Western Europe and positive for Latin America. Nor is a closed circuit possible among North America, Japan, and the Other Nonindustrial Areas because North America has export balances with the other two. It is evident that the structure of contemporary *merchandise* trade is not well adapted to multilateral settlement on a global level. How, then, is settlement achieved? First, we must recognize that trade in services (particularly transportation and income on foreign investments) may open up the possibility of multilateral circuits. For example, it is possible that Western Europe has a surplus on merchandise *and* service trade with Latin America because of its sale of transportation and other services to the latter and its earnings on investments there. This could allow a limited multilateral clearance among Western Europe, Latin America, and Japan. It is probable, however, that the inclusion of service trade would not establish multilateral circuits on a *global* basis. The answer to our question, then, must be found in capital flows. By and large, the settlement of net balances in the contemporary international trading system is financed by a net outflow of capital from the United States (North America)—a substantial flow of private capital to Western Europe and Japan, and United States government foreign assistance to Latin America and the Other Nonindustrial Areas.

To conclude, the contemporary structure of international trade is very dependent on a sustained flow of private capital and government assistance from the United States to other trading areas. A sudden cessation of this flow would disrupt the pattern of world trade and force painful adjustments on all nations.

Prewar System of Multilateral Trade

The contemporary structure of world trade differs considerably from the system that existed before World War I. The latter system evolved in the last quarter of the nineteenth century as the improvement of transportation and communication coupled with the rapid expansion of industry in Europe led to an international specialization and trade that embraced the entire world. The structure of this system of trade was very complex, but its main outlines have been made clear by a study of the League of Nations.[4] It was centered on the United Kingdom, the leading international trader and financier of the period. The United Kingdom developed net merchandise import balances with all other regions except the "tropics"—Central Africa, India,

---

[4] League of Nations, *The Network of World Trade* (Geneva: League of Nations, 1942).

Burma, Ceylon, Southeast Asia, and Latin America excluding Argentina, Paraguay, and Uruguay. The net import balances with North America, Western Europe, and other regions were used to transfer the sizable British income from shipping, financial services, and overseas investments. The net export balance with the tropics was employed to transfer new investment capital from the United Kingdom to countries of that area. Under this system all currencies were freely convertible, and a region or a nation was able to buy and sell in the world market without regard to its balance of trade.

The prewar system of multilateral trade rested on the economic strength of the United Kingdom and the continuing export of capital from that country. In the twentieth century the relative decline of British power and the disruptive effects of two wars and a world depression have brought about its disintegration. As we have observed, we now have a different system of world trade that is based to a high degree on a foundation of United States private capital and foreign aid. The United States has replaced the United Kingdom as the key trading country, but, unlike the latter, it has a large export balance rather than an import balance. This places pressure on some foreign countries because they tend to buy more from this country than they sell to it.

In later chapters we shall trace the steps that have been taken to reconstruct a multilateral world trading system in which the individual trader is free to buy and sell in international markets in accordance with his own business judgment. In more significant terms, international trade can bring the highest gains to its participants only when it is allowed to develop a multilateral structure that fully reflects the comparative costs of national economies.

THE ROLE OF THE UNITED STATES IN WORLD TRADE

The United States is a giant in the world economy. This assertion may be documented in many ways, and we shall offer only a few salient observations.

>   1. With slightly over 6 percent of the world's population and less than 7 percent of its land area, the United States produces and consumes about one third of the world's goods and services. The production of this country is twice the combined production of the United Kingdom, France, West Germany, and Italy.
>
>   2. The United States generates over one half of the world's flow of saving—the source of investment and economic growth.

3. The average output per manhour in the United States is twice that of any other country except Canada.

4. As we have already observed, exports of the United States make up about 17 percent of the free world's exports and about 12 percent of its imports. Moreover, the United States is the principal international investor, and the foreign aid of its government is one of the main supports of the free world's trade.

In view of its tremendous strength, it is understandable that the economic fortunes of other free nations should depend, directly or indirectly, upon events within the United States economy. This country dominates the markets of the Western Hemisphere both as a buyer and supplier. Canada and many Latin American countries depend on the United States for more than half their exports and imports. Japan gets about one third of its imports from, and sends about one fourth of its exports to, the United States market. Most European countries depend on this country for about 10 percent of their imports and a smaller percent of their exports. But many of Europe's export markets are highly dependent on the United States market, and this relationship intensifies indirectly Europe's dependence. As we observed, the network of international trade is centered on the United States.

A serious depression in the United States would be a catastrophe not only for the American people but for other free peoples as well. Although the statement "when the American economy sneezes, the rest of the world catches a cold" has been invalidated by the resurgence of Western Europe, there is small doubt that a bad case of economic pneumonia in this country would soon spread to other nations. The sensitivity of foreign governments to American policy in the field of tariffs, agricultural quotas, export subsidies, private investment, and similar matters often surprises Americans; but it is based on an acute awareness of the deep impact of that policy on foreign economies. Undoubtedly the single most important feature of international trade is the key role of the United States. The future actions of this country will determine in large measure the evolution of international trade in the free world.

VALUE AND VOLUME OF UNITED STATES TRADE

Table 2-9 shows the value of United States merchandise exports and imports from 1871 to 1964. As was true of world trade, **values are misleading when they are used to measure changes in the volume** of exports and imports. Accordingly, this table also includes the quantity indexes of exports and imports for 1913 and for 1921 up to the present. Quantity indexes are not available for the years preceding 1913.

Table 2-9

UNITED STATES EXPORTS, IMPORTS, BALANCE OF TRADE, AND QUANTITY INDEXES OF EXPORTS AND IMPORTS, 1871–1964

(Millions of Dollars)

Yearly Average or Year *	Exports	Imports	Excess of Exports over Imports	Quantity Index of Exports (1957–59 = 100)	Quantity Index of Imports (1957–59 = 100)
1871–1900 ...	793	663	130		
1901–1915 ...	1,868	1,337	531	30 †	29 †
1916–1920 ...	6,521	3,358	3,163		
1921–1930 ...	4,587	3,741	846	39	46
1931–1940 ...	2,622	2,097	525	33	46
1941–1945 ...	10,051	3,514	6,537	82	52
1946–1955 ...	13,581	8,745	4,836	81	68
1956–1960 ...	19,292	14,025	5,237	103	99
1961	21,775	14,815	6,960	108	108
1962	22,024	16,612	5,464	112	123
1963	23,453	17,266	6,187	120	127
1964	26,086	18,685	7,401	142	135

* Fiscal years 1871-1915; calendar years thereafter.
† 1913.

SOURCE: United States Department of Commerce, *Statistical Abstract of the United States*, various editions.

Since 1913 neither export nor import volume has experienced a steady upward movement. During the 1930's the volume of exports sank below that of the 1920's and the volume of imports stayed the same. The explanation of this movement is, of course, the global depression of the 1930's. During those years the value of exports and imports fell more than their volumes because of falling price levels, but even by 1939 the volume of exports and imports had not regained the levels of 1929. This stagnation was ended by World War II. With the opening of war in the fall of 1939, American exports began the rapid climb that has brought them to the record levels of the 1960's.

In the 1950's United States imports grew more rapidly than exports, but in the 1960's exports have taken a lead in growth rate.

In recent years United States exports have been particularly stimulated by the dynamic economy of Western Europe.

The United States Export Balance

Until 1876 United States merchandise imports were usually in excess of merchandise exports. Since that year, however, this country has had a negative balance of trade only in 1888, 1889, and 1893, and then for only small amounts. The explanation of this shift from a chronic import balance to a chronic export balance lies in the evolution of the United States from a net international debtor to a net international creditor.

The excess of merchandise imports over exports before 1876 was used to transfer the capital that came to the young American economy from Europe, especially from Great Britain. As our country developed, the *net* inflow of investment capital slackened and in the last half of the 1870's an export balance arose to transfer the earnings from the earlier European investment. Later, at the turn of the century, the United States began to invest abroad and this investment further sustained the export balance. In the twentieth century America became the principal international lender and a net merchandise export balance continued to transfer capital to foreign countries. During the two world wars massive government loans and grants to Europe and elsewhere pushed the export balance to extraordinarily high levels, levels that have been substantially maintained up to the present by postwar foreign aid and private foreign investment. This behavior of the United States export balance since 1871-80 may be seen in Table 2-9.

Fallacies of Maintaining an Export Balance

Some people believe that a merchandise export balance is eminently desirable. The reasons behind this belief are discussed in later chapters, and at this time we shall make only a few observations that point to its fallacies.

First, a historical note—Great Britain maintained a chronic merchandise import balance all during the period of her economic supremacy in the nineteenth and early twentieth centuries. Second, when a nation has an export balance, it is sending more goods abroad than it is receiving from abroad. Temporarily, at least, it is lowering its standard of living. When we consider that the fundamental end of economic activity is the consumption of goods and services, then exports make sense only as a means of obtaining imports either immediately or at some time in the future. Third, when a country insists upon maintaining a chronic merchandise export balance, it raises obstacles to the eventual repayment of its international loans unless an import balance on services more than offsets the merchandise balance. A merchandise export balance may be desirable at some stage in a country's development, but it is never desirable *per se*. Finally, a merchandise export balance cannot be evaluated without reference to all the other items that comprise a nation's balance of international payments.[5]

COMPOSITION OF UNITED STATES TRADE

Tables 2-10 and 2-11 indicate the percentage composition of United States exports and imports respectively by major economic classes since 1871.

The most significant shift that has occurred in the composition of American exports since the nineteenth century has been a secular growth in the relative importance of semimanufactures and finished manufactures, and a secular decline in the relative importance of crude materials, crude foodstuffs, and manufactured foodstuffs. In 1964, the first two categories comprised 72.5 percent of all exports by value compared to 19.7 percent in the decade 1871-80. This shift in composition is the natural outcome of the transformation of

Table 2-10

COMPOSITION OF UNITED STATES EXPORTS, 1871–1964

(Percent)

Yearly Average or Year	Crude Materials	Crude Foodstuffs	Manufactured Foodstuffs	Semimanufactures	Finished Manufactures
1871–1880	38.6	19.7	22.0	4.6	15.1
1921–25	27.5	9.7	13.9	12.5	36.3
1936–40	19.0	3.8	5.5	19.3	52.4
1951–55	13.0	7.1	5.6	11.6	62.7
1956–60	12.9	7.4	6.0	15.0	58.7
1964	11.2	9.8	6.5	15.4	57.1

SOURCE: United States Department of Commerce, *Statistical Abstract of the United States*, various editions.

[5] The items that comprise a nation's balance of international payments are enumerated and described in Chapter 7.

Table 2-11
COMPOSITION OF UNITED STATES IMPORTS, 1871–1964
(Percent)

Yearly Average or Year	Crude Materials	Crude Foodstuffs	Manufactured Foodstuffs	Semimanufactures	Finished Manufactures
1871–1880	17.2	16.0	20.7	13.0	33.0
1921–25	37.4	11.1	13.0	17.7	20.9
1936–40	33.1	13.1	14.2	20.9	18.7
1951–55	26.3	19.5	10.1	23.7	20.4
1956–60	22.3	14.1	10.5	22.0	31.1
1964	18.5	10.9	9.7	21.5	39.4

SOURCE: United States Department of Commerce, *Statistical Abstract of the United States*, various editions.

the United States from a primary-producing country into the world's leading manufacturer.

Table 2-11 indicates that the share of finished manufactures in United States imports fell until the 1950's when it started to grow. In 1964, the share of finished manufactures was higher than in 1871-80. This is not too surprising when we recall that manufactures have become a much larger fraction of *world* trade since World War II. More specifically, the rising share of finished manufactures reflects both a growing dependence on foreign natural resources (notably refined petroleum products and newsprint) and higher standards of living that afford an expanding market for foreign "luxury goods" (such as passenger cars and bottled liquors).

Semimanufactures and crude materials also hold higher shares of United States imports today than in the period 1871-80. This comes from a higher dependence of United States industry on foreign sources of supply for material inputs in production. Imports of semimanufactures and crude materials should be considered together because crude materials are often transformed into semimanufactures by foreign processing industries. Note that the import share of crude materials has declined steadily since the 1930's, while the share of semimanufactures has stayed about the same.

Imports of crude foodstuffs such as coffee (almost 11 percent of United States imports in 1957 but only 7 percent in 1961) experienced a sharp fall in relative importance during the 1950's. Since World War II imports of manufactured foodstuffs (meat products, dairy products, beverages, etc.) have maintained their share of imports fairly well, but they are relatively less important than before the war.

Commodity Concentration of Imports

United States imports exhibit a substantial concentration in a relatively few commodities. There are approximately 5,000 United States import commodity classifications, but in 1961 ten commodities drawn from only sixteen classifications accounted for over one third of all United States imports. Ranked in order of importance as a percentage of total imports, they were as follows:

1. Coffee	7.0
2. Crude petroleum	6.5
3. Newsprint	4.8
4. Fuel oil and residual fuel	3.8
5. Raw cane sugar	3.3
6. Sawmill products	2.2
7. New passenger cars	2.1
8. Iron ores and concentrate	1.7
9. Crude rubber and allied gums	1.5
10. Bottle liquors, except brandy	1.4
All Ten	34.3

The high number of raw materials and semimanufactures in this list (Items 2, 3, 4, 6, 8, and 9) makes United States imports sensitive to changes in industrial activity within the American economy. It should also be noted that the ranking of leading imports changes over time in response to cyclical and secular movements in import demand. In 1952, raw wool, cocoa, and burlaps were among the first ten imports, but in 1957 their places were taken by automobiles, iron ore and concentrates, nickel, and manufactures. Compared to 1957, the 1961 list has dropped copper, wood pulp, and nickel, and has added fuel oil and residual fuel, sawmill products, and bottle liquors.

Commodity Concentration of Exports

Although the single commodity concentration of United States exports is less than that of imports, it is nonetheless significant. Out of approximately 2,500 export classifications, ten commodities and commodity types drawn from twelve classifications were responsible for over one fifth of all United States exports in 1961. Ranked in order of importance as a percentage of total exports, they were as follows:

1. Wheat	5.4
2. Raw cotton	4.2
3. Track-laying tractors and parts	1.6
4. Flue-cured leaf tobacco	1.5

5. Bituminous coal and lignite 1.5
6. Plastics materials 1.5
7. New trucks 1.4
8. Computing and related machines 1.3
9. Medicinal chemicals and pharmaceuticals 1.3
10. Refined copper and alloys 1.2
    All Ten 20.9

As is true of imports, the ranking of exports does not remain the same over time. Technological innovation is one factor in this change: plastics materials and computing and related machines did not appear among the first ten export commodities in 1957. Note that except for bituminous coal and lignite all of the leading exports are either temperate agricultural products (Items 1, 2, and 4) or manufactures (Items 3, 6, 7, 8, 9, and 10).

DIRECTION OF UNITED STATES TRADE

The origins of United States imports and the destinations of United States exports by geographical area since 1871 are indicated in Tables 2-12 and 2-13 respectively.

United States Imports

In the nineteenth century over half of all United States imports came from Europe, but that area was less important as a source of supply than as an export market. Since that time the growing population and industrialization of this country have placed heavy demands on imports of foodstuffs and raw materials from the other areas. Europe now ranks far below the Western Hemisphere (Canada and Latin America) as a source of United States imports.

Europe is still the *single* most important source of United States imports, however. It regained its traditional (prewar) leadership in 1959, and in the 1960's it has steadily gained at the expense of Latin America. Asia has also surged ahead in the 1960's as a source of imports, but has not achieved its relative importance of before World War II.

United States Exports

In the nineteenth century American exports were directed overwhelmingly to Europe. In the decade 1871-80, 81.8 percent of total exports by value went to that continent. In the twentieth century, however, Europe lost this imposing position, although it still

Table 2-12

UNITED STATES IMPORTS: PERCENTAGE DISTRIBUTION BY GEOGRAPHICAL AREAS

(Percent)

Yearly Average or Year	Canada	Latin America	Europe	Asia *	Africa
1871–1880	5.7	29.4	53.1	11.2	0.6
1921–25	11.5	27.1	30.4	28.9	2.1
1936–40	14.8	23.5	25.3	33.1	3.3
1946–50	21.5	36.5	15.2	21.2	5.6
1951–55	22.4	33.3	20.2	18.9	5.5
1956–60	21.2	29.7	26.6	18.4	4.1
1964	22.7	22.2	28.4	21.8	4.9

* Includes Australia and Oceania.

SOURCE: United States Department of Commerce, *Statistical Abstract of the United States*, various editions.

takes a greater share of exports than any other single area. At the same time other continents became more important as export markets. The greater significance of markets within the Western Hemisphere is particularly noticeable—Canada and Latin America took 36.5 percent of United States exports in 1964.

In the 1960's, however, the most dynamic markets for United States exports have been Western Europe and Japan—the two important industrial areas in the free world outside North America. This is shown in the sharp jump in the percentage shares of these two areas (Japan is the big market in Asia) since 1956-60. We have already observed that trade among the industrial areas is growing more rapidly than trade between the industrial and nonindustrial areas, and now we see that the United States is part of that trend.

DEPENDENCE OF THE UNITED STATES ON INTERNATIONAL TRADE

In a previous section we discussed the vital importance of the United States economy to the economy of the free world. We now take a brief look at the importance of the world economy to this country.

More than most peoples Americans are likely to underestimate the significance of exports and imports to the functioning of the domestic economy. This attitude toward international trade comes partly from our isolationist past, but it is also based on an awareness of the small size of our trade when measured against our total eco-

Table 2-13

UNITED STATES EXPORTS: * PERCENTAGE DISTRIBUTION BY GEOGRAPHICAL AREAS

(Percent)

Yearly Average or Year	Canada	Latin America	Europe	Asia †	Africa
1871–1880 ...	5.6	9.8	81.8	2.4	0.5
1921–25	14.3	16.9	52.7	14.5	1.6
1936–40	16.2	18.9	41.4	19.3	4.2
1946–50	16.2	24.2	35.2	17.2	5.2
1951–55	22.6	26.9	28.0	18.2	4.4
1956–60	21.9	24.0	30.9	19.3	4.0
1964	19.4	17.1	34.0	24.5	5.0

* Excludes "special category" commodities after January, 1950; these are not reported by geographical areas for security reasons.

† Includes Australia and Oceania.

SOURCE: United States Department of Commerce, *Statistical Abstract of the United States*, various editions.

nomic activity. The self-sufficiency of the American economy relative to foreign economies is easily demonstrated. One method is to compare the ratio of United States international trade (merchandise exports *plus* imports) to United States gross national product against similar ratios of other countries. The following enumeration showing the percentage that international trade held to gross national product for twelve countries in 1962 is representative: [6]

The Netherlands	76.4
Venezuela	65.2
Denmark	51.4
Canada	31.5
United Kingdom	29.9
West Germany	29.0
Australia	27.6
France	20.8
Japan	20.0
Brazil	19.1
India	9.8
United States	6.9

It would seem, therefore, that the United States could dispense with its international trade with only minor consequences to its econ-

---

[6] United Nations, *Yearbook of National Account Statistics*, 1963; and United Nations, *Yearbook of International Trade Statistics*, 1963.

Table 2-14

UNITED STATES IMPORTS ACCOUNTING FOR OVER 10 PERCENT OF NEW SUPPLY AND AMOUNTING TO MORE THAN $50 MILLION IN 1961

Product	Percent of New Supply
Coffee, cocoa, tea	100
Crude rubber, etc.	100
Diamonds for gemstones	100
Bananas and plantains	100
Carpet wools	100
Manganese ores and concentrates	94
Asbestos	93
Bauxite	87
Textile goods, mainly jute bagging	78
Raw cane sugar	69
Lapidary work, mainly cut diamonds	65
Scouring and combing mill products	50
Shellfish	44
Nonferrous smelter and refining products, n.e.c.*	41
Fin fish	34
Pulp mill products	32
Iron ores	28
Vegetable oil mill products, except cottonseed and soybeans	24
Wine and brandy	21
Distilled liquors, except brandy	21
Rubber footwear	19
Refined lead	18
Paper mill products, mainly newsprint	18
Watches and clocks	13
Crude petroleum	11
Sawmill products, hardwood dimension, and flooring	10

* Not elsewhere classified.

GENERAL NOTE: *New supply* is defined as United States production *plus* imports. Thus the percentage measures the ratio: imports/domestic production plus imports. Import values are values in the foreign country and do not include United States import duties, transportation costs, etc. Total import values, therefore, are understated relative to domestic output values.

SOURCE: United States Department of Commerce, *United States Commodity Exports and Imports as Related to Output, 1961 and 1960*, 1963, Chart 4, p. 5.

omy. Aggregate relationships, however, are often deceiving and especially so in this instance.

When we investigate the dependence of the American economy on specific imports as sources of supply and specific exports as outlets for domestic production, we come to closer grips with the question of the essentiality of international trade. The picture that we find does not agree with the image of United States self-sufficiency that is suggested by the comparison of international trade with gross national product.

Table 2-15
UNITED STATES EXPORTS ACCOUNTING FOR OVER 10 PERCENT OF DOMESTIC OUTPUT AND AMOUNTING TO MORE THAN $100 MILLION IN 1961

Product	Percent of Domestic Production
Grease and inedible tallow	53
Milled rice and byproducts	38
Construction and mining machinery, including wheel tractor parts	34
Cotton farm products	33
Leaf tobacco	30
Oil field machinery	29
Textile machinery	28
Metal-cutting machine tools	27
Metal-forming machine tools	25
Synthetic rubber	23
Cash grains	21
Computing and related machines	18
Railroad, streetcar, locomotives, and parts	18
Bituminous coal and lignite	17
Aircraft parts, propellers, engine parts, etc.	16
Internal combustion engines, excluding automotive and aircraft	16
Aircraft and engines	15
Pumps and compressors	12
Farm machinery, except tractor parts	11
Flour and meal	10
Photographic equipment	10

SOURCE: United States Department of Commerce, *United States Commodity Export and Imports as Related to Output, 1961 and 1960,* 1963, Table 4A, p. 56.

Dependence on Imports

Today there are only two metals—magnesium and molydenum—for which American industry is not partially or wholly dependent on foreign supplies. One hundred percent of our consumption of natural rubber, tin, and industrial diamonds; 90 percent or more of our consumption of nickel, cobalt, chromite, asbestos, and manganese; over 50 percent of our consumption of tungsten; and 35 percent or more of our consumption of lead, copper, and zinc must be met through imports. We are similarly dependent on imports of certain foodstuffs such as coffee, cocoa, and tea, which come entirely from foreign sources of supply. All studies point to an even greater dependence on imports of industrial raw materials in the future. Further examples of import dependence are offered in Table 2-14.

Dependence on Exports

Table 2-15 shows how important foreign export markets are to American farmers and many American manufacturers.

It is clear from a perusal of Table 2-15 that exports of many products represent a substantial portion of United States production. Farmers, in particular, are dependent on foreign markets for their livelihood. This country exports the equivalent of the output of more than 60 million acres—one harvested acre in five. In 1963 over half the United States production of wheat, rice, dry edible beans, and hops; two fifths of the soybeans, nonfat dry milk, and tallow; one fourth of the tobacco, prunes, raisins, cotton, and feed grains; and one fifth of dry edible beans, lard, and cottonseed were shipped to foreign countries. Not all of these exports were cash sales: the bulk of United States farm exports to nonindustrial countries is financed under United States foreign assistance programs.

Clearly the prosperity of American agriculture hinges on exports. The agricultural slump in the 1920's and the difficulties of farmers in the middle 1950's are traceable to the loss of foreign markets. Whatever protectionist groups may tell them, farmers have everything to gain from liberal govenment policies that foster an expanding world trade.

Foreign markets also represent the difference between profit and loss for many American manufacturers. Actually the importance of foreign markets is minimized when measured as a percentage of domestic production. The break-even point of many producers is so high that 5 or 10 percent of sales may be responsible for a disproportionate share of profits.

In conclusion, our dependence on both imports and exports is much greater than is suggested by the relationship between international trade and national income. Inability to obtain many imports would mean higher costs of production and in many instances the use of inferior substitutes. Exports are a necessity for farmers, and a large number of manufacturers would be forced into bankruptcy or seriously injured by the loss of foreign markets. Finally, millions of workers gain their livelihoods directly or indirectly from international trade.

SUMMARY

1. For the most part, Chapter 2 consists of statistical presentations of different aspects of world trade and the foreign trade of the United States. We are more interested in the relationships that are disclosed by the statistical data than in the data themselves.
2. Changes in the volume of world trade must be measured by a quantum index that removes the effects of changing price levels over time. The export quantum index indicates a rapid growth in the volume of world trade since World War II.

3. World trade and world industrial production are closely related since a large part of world trade is generated by the industrial countries. Trade has risen faster than industrial production in recent years.
4. The United States, the United Kingdom, and West Germany are dominant in world trade. Of the ten leading exporting and importing countries, seven are located in Europe. The United States has replaced the United Kingdom as the world's principal exporting and importing nation.
5. In 1963 two fifths of the world's trade was between industrial and nonindustrial areas while most of the remainder was between industrial areas. The trade of the nonindustrial areas has been falling as a share of world trade.
6. Trade between the free world and Communist countries (East-West trade) has increased rapidly since 1953, but it was still less than 4 percent of aggregate world exports in 1963.
7. The share of manufactures in world trade has grown at the expense of the share of foodstuffs and raw materials. In 1963, manufactures constituted over half of the world's trade.
8. The structure of international trade is multilateral. Today's system of trade differs from the prewar system, and it is highly dependent on United States private capital outflow and government foreign assistance.
9. The United States holds a dominant position in the world economy, and the economic fortunes of other free nations are dependent on its policies and actions. The volume of United States trade, both exports and imports, is far greater today than in the 1930's.
10. Since 1876 the United States has had a merchandise export balance except for the years 1888, 1889, and 1893. Such a balance may or may not be desirable, depending upon other items in the balance of payments.
11. Since the nineteenth century, American exports have shifted toward an emphasis on exports of semimanufactures and finished manufactures. Imports show a greater emphasis on industrial raw materials and semimanufactures. Both exports and imports exhibit a concentration in a relatively few commodities and commodity types.
12. Compared to the nineteenth century, Europe has become less imporant as an export market and as a source of supply. United States trade has become directed toward trade with the rest of the Western Hemisphere in particular. However, today Europe is once again the leading trading partner of this country for both exports and imports.
13. The United States is far more dependent on its international trade than is suggested by overall measures such as the relationship between international trade and gross national product. This is brought out by an examination of individual imports and exports.

QUESTIONS AND APPLICATIONS

1. Since 1913 the *value* of world trade has grown over sevenfold whereas the *volume* of world trade has almost quadrupled. How do you explain this apparent discrepancy?

2. "The connection between industrial production and world trade is not fortuitous." Explain.
3. (a) What are the principal trading countries?
   (b) How do you explain the rise of the United States to the position of first exporter and first importer?
4. "It is a common misconception that most international trade comprises the exchange of foodstuffs and raw materials for manufactures between nonindustrial and industrial countries." Discuss.
5. What have been the principal changes in the composition of world trade since 1929?
6. (a) What is multilateral trade?
   (b) What is the basis of multilateral trade?
7. What are the main differences between the multilateral structures of contemporary and prewar international trade?
8. Discuss the position of the United States in the world economy. What are the implications of that position?
9. What factors explain the merchandise export balance of the United States since 1876?
10. "A merchandise export balance is favorable to a nation and hence always desirable." Discuss.
11. What have been the main shifts in the composition of United States exports and imports since the last quarter of the nineteenth century?
12. "The United States could easily dispense with international trade because it is only a small fraction of United States national income." Discuss the validity of this statement.

SELECTED READINGS

(The following publications are the principal sources of statistics on international trade.)

General Agreement on Tariffs and Trade (GATT). *International Trade.* Geneva: Annual.

Organization for Economic Cooperation and Development (OECD). *General Statistics*, monthly; *Overall Trade by Countries*, monthly.

United Nations:
   Commodity Trade Statistics, quarterly.
   Direction of International Trade.
   Monthly Bulletin of Statistics.
   Yearbook of International Trade Statistics.

United States Department of Commerce:
   Historical Statistics of the United States.
   Statistical Abstract, annual.
   Survey of Current Business, monthly.

Woytinsky, W. S. and E. S. Woytinsky. *World Commerce and Governments.* New York: Twentieth Century Fund, 1955. Chapters 2, 3, and 4.

PART I

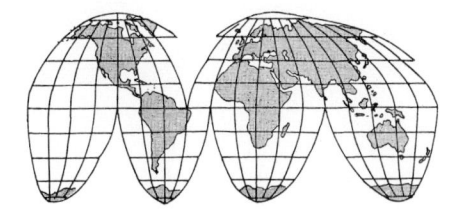

THEORY

To grasp the significance of everyday events occurring in the vast field of activity that we call international trade and finance, we must first gain an understanding of fundamental causal relationships, basic institutions, and unifying concepts. The nine chapters of Part I deal with these foundation stones of international trade and finance, which are the indispensable prerequisites of our later study of international economic policies and the practice of international business.

CHAPTER 3

COMPARATIVE COSTS AND
THE GAINS FROM TRADE

In this chapter we investigate the basis of international trade. Two broad questions guide our analysis: (1) Why does international trade take place? (2) What are the gains from international trade?

WHY NATIONS TRADE—THE THEORY OF COMPARATIVE COSTS

The basis of international trade is explained by the theory of comparative costs.[1] Because this theory is complex and easily misunderstood, we shall develop it in a series of steps. We begin with the proximate cause of international trade—absolute international differences in prices.

Absolute International Differences in Prices

Absolute differences between the prices of foreign goods and the prices of similar goods produced at home are the immediate basis of international trade. When these differences are greater than the costs of transferring goods from one country to another, it becomes profitable to import goods from the lower-price country to the higher-price country. An extreme case arises when a country *must* obtain a good from abroad (or else go without it) because of the physical impossibility of producing it at home. Thus, a country totally lacking

---
[1] We refer to the modern version of this theory based on the mutual interdependence theory of prices rather than the older classical version based on the labor theory of value.

coking coal has no choice but to import that commodity if it wishes to produce steel. In many instances, however, a country is physically able to produce the goods that it imports, but—and this is the important point—only at prices higher than it pays for imports. The United States *could* produce coffee and bananas but only at prices so high that few consumers could afford them.

Absolute international differences in prices come to light when there is an exchange rate that equates domestic and foreign currencies. For example, without an exchange rate between the dollar and the pound sterling it would not be possible to compare the prices of goods in the United States with the prices of similar goods in the United Kingdom. But when we know, say, that £1 equals $2, then direct price comparisons are possible and we can ascertain any absolute differences in the prices of specific goods.

Although absolute price differences are the immediate basis of international trade, they do not provide a final explanation. We want to know *why* such differences exist and whether they are fortuitous or systematic.

Absolute International Differences in Costs

Our first step is to note that absolute international differences in prices imply absolute international differences in costs. Prices are lower in one country than in another because costs are lower. When markets are purely competitive, prices and costs are identical.[2] Prices also equal costs of production when markets are monopolistically competitive, that is, when producers are able to differentiate their products but are unable to make long-run monopoly profits because of competition. Under oligopoly (few sellers) and monopoly (one seller), however, prices may be higher than costs of production due to the opportunity for long-run monopoly profits. In all instances prices must cover costs of production in the long run if a firm is to stay in business. With the exception of oligopoly and monopoly prices, then, prices equal costs of production in the long run although they may be greater or less than costs in periods of short-run adjustment to changes in demand.

---

[2] Pure or perfect competition exists for a product when (a) the number of buyers and sellers is so large that no one buyer or seller can influence its price, and (b) the product is homogeneous—it cannot be differentiated by sellers or buyers. Under pure competition, equilibrium costs of production include normal profits but not monopoly profits.

Dissimilar Cost Ratios

We have found that absolute international differences in prices are based on absolute international differences in costs. But what causes such cost differences? The answer to this question is most unexpected: absolute international differences in costs arise when cost ratios *within* each country are dissimilar. This assertion is the core of the theory of comparative costs and may be demonstrated by a simple arithmetical example.

Suppose there are only two countries (the United States and the United Kingdom); and, in isolation, each country produces two commodities (wheat and textiles). Assume further that the cost ratios between wheat and textiles *differ* between the two countries:

	UNITED STATES (Dollars)	UNITED KINGDOM (Pounds Sterling)
Unit cost (price) of wheat	1.00	3.00
Unit cost (price) of textiles ..	2.00	1.00

In the United States the cost ratio of wheat to textiles is 1:2 whereas in the United Kingdom the same ratio is 3:1. These ratios indicate that the United States has a *comparative cost advantage* in the production of wheat and a *comparative cost disadvantage* in the production of textiles. The converse situation exists in the United Kingdom. Gainful trade occurs when the United States exports wheat and imports textiles while the United Kingdom exports textiles and imports wheat.

We know this last statement to be true even though we have assumed no exchange rate that permits a direct comparison of absolute costs (prices) between the two countries. With the same cost the United States can produce either one unit of wheat or one-half unit of textiles. Since costs are determined by the inputs and prices of the productive factors (land, labor, management, and capital) required to carry on production, this means that the same quantity of factors can produce one unit of wheat or one-half unit of textiles in the United States. Factors devoted to wheat production cannot at the same time be used to produce textiles; consequently, the *real* cost of one unit of wheat in the United States is one-half unit of textiles. This is the *opportunity cost* of producing wheat in the United States.

In the United Kingdom, on the other hand, the opportunity cost of producing one unit of wheat is three units of textiles. Clearly, the United States has a lower opportunity cost of producing wheat, that is, it has a comparative advantage in that commodity; and, in the event of trade, it will be exported. Similarly, the opportunity cost of producing a unit of textiles in the United States is two units of wheat—resources used to produce one unit of textiles could have produced two units of wheat. In the United Kingdom, however, the opportunity cost of producing one unit of textiles is only one-third unit of wheat. Thus the United Kingdom will export textiles and the United States will import them. The United States has a comparative *dis*advantage in the production of textiles.[3]

To make this clearer, suppose that the exchange rate is £1 equals $1. Then the dollar price of wheat in the United Kingdom is $3 compared to $1 in the United States, and the dollar price of textiles is $1 in the United Kingdom compared to $2 in the United States. Trade is distinctly profitable with the United States exporting wheat and the United Kingdom exporting textiles.

Actually when cost ratios are dissimilar, there is a *range* of exchange rates that will permit the United States to export wheat and the United Kingdom to export textiles. One limit of this range is that exchange rate which makes the price of wheat the same in both countries. In our example this rate is £1 equals one third of a dollar ($1 equals £3) whereby the price of wheat becomes equivalent to $1 in both countries. The other limit is that exchange rate which makes the price of textiles the same in both countries. This rate is £1 equals $2 ($1 equals one half of a pound). The pound price of textiles in the United Kingdom then has a dollar equivalent of $2, the price of textiles in the United States. Trade is possible at either limit or at any exchange rate lying between them.

If trade occurs at an exchange rate marking one of the limits, then one country will neither gain nor lose from trade because the ratio of exchange between its exports and imports will equal its domestic ratio of exchange (the opportunity cost ratio) between the same products. To illustrate, when the exchange rate is £1 equals one third of a dollar, the United Kingdom must export three units of textiles (equivalent to $1) to obtain one unit of wheat from the United States.

---

[3] The role of dissimilar cost ratios may be expressed in general terms as follows: Let a_1 be the unit cost of product a in country 1 and b_1 the unit cost of product b in country 1. Let a_2 be the unit cost of product a and b_2 the unit cost of product b in country 2. Then trade is gainful when $a_1/b_1 \neq a_2/b_2$. If $a_1/b_1 > a_2/b_2$, then country 1 will import a and export b, while country 2 will export a and import b. If $a_1/b_1 < a_2/b_2$ (as in our example above) then country 1 will export a and import b, and conversely for country 2.

Ch. 3 / Comparative Costs and the Gains from Trade

But the United Kingdom could do just as well by producing wheat at home where its opportunity cost is also three units of textiles. At this rate of exchange, trade is possible although it makes no difference to the United Kingdom whether it trades or not since the entire gain goes to the United States.

If, however, the pound were to equal anything less than one third of a dollar, the United Kingdom would be able to obtain its wheat more cheaply from domestic production and would refuse to trade. Hence the opportunity cost ratio in the United Kingdom determines one limit of the range of exchange rates that permit trade between the two countries. The other limit is set by the opportunity cost ratio in the United States. When the dollar equals anything less than one half of a pound (the pound equals anything *more* than two dollars) the United States will not trade because it can obtain its textiles more cheaply from domestic production. At any exchange rate lying between the two limits both countries will gain from trade with each other.

To sum up, when cost ratios are dissimilar in two countries, there is a range of exchange rates between their respective currencies that will permit gainful trade between them. One limit of this range is determined by the opportunity cost ratio in one country; the other limit, by the opportunity cost ratio in the second country.

Identical Cost Ratios

The role of dissimilar cost ratios in providing the basis for international trade is further clarified by considering the effect of *identical* cost ratios. The following example differs from our first example only in the assumption of identical cost ratios:

	UNITED STATES (Dollars)	UNITED KINGDOM (Pounds Sterling)
Unit cost (price) of wheat	1.00	2.00
Unit cost (price) of textiles ..	2.00	4.00

In the United States the ratio of the dollar cost of a unit of wheat to the dollar cost of a unit of textiles is 1:2. In the United Kingdom the same ratio (expressed in pounds sterling) is identical—2:4 or 1:2. *Under these conditions no gainful trade is possible.* Any rate of exchange between the dollar and the pound will make the dollar (or sterling) prices of wheat and textiles either (1) the same in both countries, (2) higher in the United States, or (3) lower in the United States. The first possibility—the identity of dollar prices in both countries—clearly rules out international trade. If the second or third possibility exists, the United States will either import *both* commodities or export *both* commodities. But this is impossible since exports must equal imports in the absence of all loans or gifts—exports must pay for imports.

To illustrate, suppose that the exchange rate is £1 equals $1. At this rate the dollar price of wheat in the United Kingdom is $2 and the dollar price of textiles is $4—both higher than their respective prices in the United States. Since prices are lower at home, Americans will not buy either commodity from the United Kingdom; and the British, unable to export, will be unable to import. In short, no trade is possible. Again, suppose that the exchange rate is £1 equals 40 cents. Then the dollar price of wheat in the United Kingdom is 80 cents and the dollar price of textiles, $1.60. Prices of both commodities are now lower in the United Kingdom and again no trade is possible. Finally, suppose that the exchange rate is £1 equals 50 cents. At this rate the dollar prices of wheat and textiles are the same—there are no absolute price differences of any kind and trade is obviously out of the question.

In conclusion, trade between two countries is not possible when cost (price) ratios within each country are identical. In such circumstances neither country can gain from trading with the other.

Dissimilar Factor Price Ratios

In our search for the basis of international trade we have traced absolute international *price* differences to absolute international *cost* differences, and absolute international cost differences to dissimilar *cost ratios* within the trading countries. Once again, however, we are faced with a question: why do countries have dissimilar cost ratios?

The immediate explanation is that the marginal cost of production (which is equal to price under pure competition) is determined by the prices paid to the marginal inputs of the factors of production—land, labor, capital, and management; and the ratio of factor prices within each country may be dissimilar. Different commodities are made with different combinations of factor inputs. Consequently, the commodity cost ratio in each country reflects its factor price ratios—the ratios between rent, wages and salaries, interest, and normal profits. In one country wages may be low relative to rent, while in another country wages may be high relative to rent. Thus the first country will be able to produce goods that require a great deal of labor and

Ch. 3 / Comparative Costs and the Gains from Trade

not much land more cheaply than goods that require a great deal of land but not much labor. In the second country the opposite will be true.

To summarize, it is because factors of production are not perfect substitutes for each other and must be used in different combinations to produce different goods that dissimilar factor price ratios in two countries give rise to dissimilar cost ratios in the same countries.

The role of factor price ratios in the determination of cost ratios may be clarified by a simple illustration. We assume that in the United States the price of a unit of land is $1 and the price of a unit of labor is $2, and that in the United Kingdom, the price of a unit of land is £4 and the price of a unit of labor is £1. Thus land is relatively cheap in the United States and relatively expensive in the United Kingdom, while the converse is true of labor. We assume further that to produce a unit of wheat in either country requires five units of land and one unit of labor, and to produce a unit of textiles in either country requires one unit of land and ten units of labor. These inputs of land and labor per unit of output are the *technical coefficients of production*.[4] The following table results from these assumptions:

	UNITED STATES (Dollars)	UNITED KINGDOM (Pounds Sterling)
Unit price of land	1.00	4.00
Unit price of labor	2.00	1.00
Unit cost of wheat	7.00	21.00
Unit cost of textiles	21.00	14.00

The United States has a comparative advantage in the production of wheat (3:1), while the United Kingdom has a comparative advantage in the production of textiles (3:2). This follows from the

---

[4] We are assuming that the coefficients do not vary between countries and do not change with the level of output. At a given level of technology there is usually a fairly narrow range of possible factor combinations that may be used to produce a specific commodity, known as the *production function*. Which combination will be used within this range will depend on relative factor prices, that is, each producer will attempt to produce with the lowest-cost combination of factors. To make our example more realistic we might have assumed that somewhat higher land inputs and somewhat lower labor inputs are used in the production of wheat and textiles in the United States compared to production in the United Kingdom. The added realism, however, would not change our conclusions since the range of permissible variation is normally small; factors of production are only *partial* substitutes for each other. The bearing of the level of output on coefficients of production is discussed in Chapter 4. The possible existence of dissimilar production functions among nations is treated in Chapter 5.

fact that wheat production is *land-intensive* and the United States is able to use its relatively cheap factor (land) to greatest advantage in that production. On the other hand, the United States has a comparative *dis*advantage in textile production, which is *labor-intensive*, requiring comparatively large amounts of its relatively expensive factor (labor). The converse situation holds in the United Kingdom.

We conclude that when the ratios of factor prices in two countries are dissimilar, each country will have a comparative advantage in those goods whose production requires comparatively large amounts of its relatively cheap factor(s) and comparatively small amounts of its relatively expensive factor(s). It will have a comparable *dis*advantage in those goods whose production depends on comparatively large amounts of its relatively expensive factor(s) and comparatively small amounts of its relatively cheap factor(s).

The price of each factor is determined by its supply and the demand for its use in production. The demand for a factor is derived from the demand for the products that the factor helps to produce. Thus if the demand for automobiles goes up, the demand for workers, raw materials, capital, etc., that are required to increase the production of automobiles will also rise.[5] Since factor prices are determined by supply and demand, the existence of dissimilar factor price ratios in two countries implies dissimilar factor supply and/or factor demand ratios in the same countries.

Dissimilar Factor Supply Ratios

Countries differ greatly in their relative supplies of factors of production. A country like Canada has an abundant supply of natural resources relative to its supply of labor and capital. The Netherlands, on the other hand, has a relatively scarce supply of natural resources but a relatively abundant supply of labor and capital. Such differences multiply when we take into account the fact that the four factors of production are not homogeneous. Actually there are several kinds of land and many varieties of labor, management, and capital.[6] Thus one country has a temperate climate, another has a tropical climate; one country has coal but lacks iron ore, another has iron ore but lacks coal; one country has large supplies of educated skilled workers, another

---

[5] Raw materials are not an original factor of production, but the demand for raw materials stimulates a demand for the labor, land, etc., that produce them.

[6] Management is often considered a subtype of labor. We have distinguished it from labor, however, because of its key role in the organization and direction of production.

has a predominantly illiterate, unskilled labor force; one country has steel plants, another has none; and so on. The number of specific factors of production is so large that any one country is certain to have factor supply ratios that diverge in some respect from the ratios of other countries.

Disregarding factor demand for the time being, a factor in relatively abundant supply commands a price that is comparatively lower than the price of a factor in relatively scarce supply. We should expect, for example, that land rent relative to wages is low in Australia compared to land rent relative to wages in Belgium, since the former country has a density of population that is only a fraction of its density in the latter country. Again, the long-term interest rate relative to wages is lower in the United States than in Brazil because there is much more capital per worker in the former country than in the latter.

Common observation reveals that there are numerous dissimilarities in the factor supply ratios of different countries. Unless offset by relative factor demand, the prices of factors in relatively abundant supply are low compared to the prices of factors in relatively scarce supply. From this it follows that a country will have a comparative advantage in the production of those goods that require comparatively large amounts of its factors of production in relatively abundant supply, and a comparative *dis*advantage in the production of goods that use comparatively large amounts of factors in relatively scarce supply. Indirectly, therefore, a country exports the services of abundant factors of production and imports the services of scarce factors of production.

Dissimilar Factor Demand Ratios

Even if the relative supplies of land, labor, management, and capital were identical in two countries (a most unlikely condition), dissimilar demands for the use of these factors in production would create dissimilar factor price ratios and thereby provide a basis for international trade. This influence of demand on factor price *ratios* is likely to be weak, however, and it will seldom offset the influence of factor supplies. Per capita demand for wheat will not necessarily be high in a country that has relatively abundant land resources, and people must have food in order to live even though the land resources of its country are relatively scarce.

It is true that patterns of *consumption* differ considerably between countries that have dissimilar standards of living. But the differences are due more to income than to consumer tastes; and, as poor countries develop their economies, they tend to match the consumption patterns of the more-developed countries. Moreover, what appears as a difference in consumer tastes may often be traced to a difference in relative factor supplies. For example, the demand for shelter and clothing is usually less in a tropical climate than in a temperate climate. Although the ratio of factor demands may be a causative agent in the determination of relative factor prices, it is much less important than the ratio of factor supplies. In any event, the former is not likely to counteract the influence of the latter.

The Basis of International Trade

In our investigation of the basis of international trade we have moved from absolute international price differences to absolute international cost differences, from absolute international cost differences to dissimilar cost ratios within each country, from dissimilar cost ratios to dissimilar factor price ratios, and from dissimilar factor price ratios to dissimilar factor supply and factor demand ratios. Dissimilar factor supply ratios are the most fundamental links in this chain of causation. There is, however, no single *ultimate* basis of international trade—all of the market conditions that combine to determine prices in each country together constitute the basis of trade. These market conditions are mutually interdependent; each is both a cause and an effect. This interdependence is illustrated in Figure 3-1 which depicts the principal relationships that determine prices in a "closed economy" with no international trade.

Figure 3-1

PRICE DETERMINATION IN A CLOSED ECONOMY

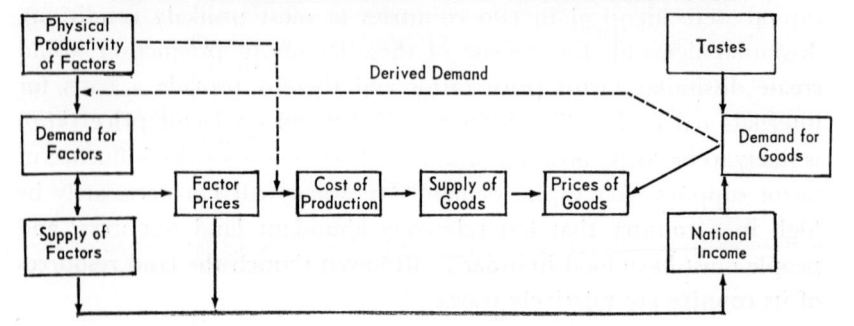

Ch. 3 / Comparative Costs and the Gains from Trade 57

Since consumption is the ultimate end of economic activity we start our analysis of Figure 3-1 with the demand for goods. The demand for goods is dependent on consumer tastes and the level and distribution of national income.[7] National income, in turn, derives from the prices and amounts of productive factors used to produce the national product, that is, the sum total of wages and salaries, interest, rent, and profits.[8] The demand for goods interacts with the supply of goods to determine prices. The supply of goods is itself determined by the cost of production and, as we have noted, when markets are purely competitive the price of a good equals its marginal cost of production. Because the production of goods requires the use of factors of production, the demand for goods creates a derived demand for factors of production. The demand for factors is also influenced by their physical productivity or physical input-output relationship (production function). If, for example, there is a demand for ten units of good A and each labor input contributes two units to the output of good A in accordance with the production function for good A, then there will be a demand for five inputs or units of labor. Other factors of production experience similar derived demands. Factor productivity depends on physical laws and the level of technology. Factor demand interacts with factor supply to determine factor prices, and factor prices multiplied by the factor quantities needed to produce a unit of output of each good make up its unit cost of production. Looked at the other way, the payments to factors for their productive services constitute the national income. And so, our analysis has come full circle as we have traced the major links in the mutual interdependence theory of prices.[9]

When a closed economy is opened up to international trade, its system of prices interacts with foreign price systems. The immediate impact of international trade is felt in the demand for goods—goods

---

[7] The *pattern* of consumption is dependent not only on the average per capita level of national income, but on its distribution as well, which is determined by the conditions of factor ownership. Two countries with the same per capita income and the same tastes may have contrasting patterns of consumption if in one country there are a very few rich consumers and a large number of poor consumers while in the other country most people are in the middle class with few very rich or very poor consumers.

[8] See Chapter 10 for a discussion of national income and product.

[9] Figure 3-1 greatly simplifies the mutual interdependence theory of prices. More correctly, it is the marginal supply and demand of factors and goods that determine prices, not the total supply and demand. However, consideration of marginalities would not change the basic relationships.

with a comparative cost advantage experience a new foreign demand, while goods with a comparative cost *dis*advantage lose their domestic markets to imports. These changes in demand then feed back to affect eventually the prices of productive factors. Over the long run, international trade may even bring about changes in factor supplies as they respond to shifts in factor prices. Given time, international trade may so transform the economy that it bears little resemblance to the sort of economy that would be feasible in the absence of trade.

The theory of comparative costs provides us with an understanding of the basis of international trade. Loosely speaking, we may say that dissimilar factor supply ratios in different countries are the basis of international trade. We must not forget, however, that the influence of factor endowments may be tempered by factor demands. Dissimilar factor endowments (relative to demand) give rise to dissimilar cost ratios that are transformed into absolute international cost differences upon the establishment of an exchange rate. These absolute differences in costs (and prices) are the immediate stimuli of international trade, but failure to understand their dependence on the cost ratios within each trading country leads to mistaken conceptions of trade and unwise government policies.

THE INTERNATIONAL MOBILITY OF FACTORS

The perpetuation of dissimilar factor supply ratios in different countries stems from the low international mobility of factors of production. If factors moved freely from one country to another, they would move until the supply of each factor was everywhere fully adapted to demand and the price of each factor was the same in every country and in every use. In that event the cost of producing each good would also be the same in every country, and there would be no basis for international trade. Thus perfect international mobility of factors of production is incompatible with the existence of international trade.[10] Even within a country, however, factors of production are only partially mobile, and this serves as the basis of interregional trade. Between countries the mobility of factors is especially low because of physical, social, and political obstacles.

---

[10] That international factor *immobility* is responsible for international trade was fully recognized by David Ricardo in 1817 in his *Principles of Political Economy and Taxation*. Ricardo and later classical economists assumed perfect factor *mobility* within each country and perfect *immobility* between countries.

The Mobility of Land Factors

Natural resources are completely immobile. It is not physically possible to move land area, climate, soil, forests, mines, landforms, and other "gifts of nature" from one place to another. Since the international distribution of natural resources is most haphazard, their immobility assures a permanent dissimilarity in the supplies of national land factors.

The Mobility of Labor and Management

The human agents of production, labor and management, are another story—they are physically able to move from one country to another. In practice, however, this potential mobility is sharply restricted by both motivations and opportunities.

People will not emigrate to a foreign country unless they are attracted by favorable prospects abroad or pressed by unhappy circumstances at home. Social inertia tends to keep people in their native countries. This inertia is the sum total of attachments to one's place of birth, one's family, and one's friends; of adaptation to the language, customs, and way of life of the native country; and of many similar conditions. Reluctance to move is fortified by the strange and unknown risks of emigration. Generally, the emigrant must face a new language, new customs, new laws, and an ignorance of specific economic opportunities. Despite these obstacles, however, large masses of people have moved from one country to another, particularly during periods of widespread unrest brought on by natural disasters, revolution, or war at home.[11]

In our own day the absence of motivations to emigrate has been much less important than limited opportunities to emigrate in explaining the low international mobility of labor. All contemporary governments restrict immigration and some, such as the Soviet government, also restrict emigration. With few exceptions, the international migrant must pass through a careful screening before admittance to a foreign country.[12] Actually, the international mobility

---

[11] Many waves of migration to the United States have been associated with unrest in Europe. The latest example is the influx of Hungarians.

[12] One exception deserves mention. Labor shortages in some western European countries have encouraged a substantial migration of workers in recent years, especially from southern Europe. In 1965 West Germany had more than one million foreign workers, and in Switzerland about one third of the labor force was foreign. Higher labor mobility is an important objective of the European Economic Community (see Chapter 19). This increase in international labor mobility *within* Western Europe has not been matched elsewhere in the world.

of labor is so low that international differences in relative labor supplies are probably growing wider due to disparate rates of population growth and of capital accumulation.

The Mobility of Capital

The international mobility of capital goods (construction, capital equipment, and inventories) varies with the nature of the good. Construction is largely tied to specific sites and is highly immobile while the mobility of capital equipment and inventories is limited only by transfer costs and government trade controls like any other commodities. It is important to realize, however, that a nation does not necessarily transfer capital to another nation by exporting capital goods to the latter. Instead, capital is transferred by international loans and investments (and occasionally by gifts) that provide the purchasing power needed to finance either the construction of capital goods in the borrowing country or the import of capital goods from abroad. Therefore, the criterion of the international mobility of capital is the ease of lending between nations.[13]

Viewed in this way, the international mobility of capital may be very high, and it is usually far higher than that of labor, to say nothing of land factors. Today this mobility has been lowered by political and economic instability, exchange control and depreciation, government expropriation, as well as other factors, that are commonly found in the newly developing nations. The international movement of capital that is now occurring does little to narrow international differences in relative capital supplies. Its greatest social contribution is the help it provides poor countries in their efforts to develop their economies—a contribution that adds to, rather than subtracts from, the opportunity for international trade. This contribution is strengthened by the movement of management factors that often accompanies foreign investment. Thus the mobility of management factors is heightened by a higher international mobility of capital.

International Trade as a Substitute for Factor Movements

The gist of these observations on factor mobility is that any existing dissimilarities in the relative supplies of national factors are not likely to be wiped out by international factor movements. Dissimilar factor ratios, therefore, provide a permanent basis of international trade. It follows that the movement of goods is a *substitute*

---

[13] The international transfer of capital is dealt with in Chapter 21.

Ch. 3 / Comparative Costs and the Gains from Trade   61

for the movement of factors of production. International trade allows a nation to reap the same economic gains that would accrue to it if factors of production moved freely between countries. By exporting goods in which it has a comparative advantage, the nation is able to export the services of its relatively abundant factors that must themselves remain at home. By importing goods in which it has a comparative *dis*advantage, the nation is able to import the services of relatively scarce factors that remain abroad. If it were possible to have a completely free international movement of factors, then there would be no need to export or import goods because all goods could be produced just as cheaply at home as elsewhere.

The Equalization of Factor Prices

That international trade is a substitute for factor movements is also shown by its effects on the factor prices of trading nations. Upon the opening of trade between two countries, the prices of international goods (exports and imports) become identical in both countries.[14] International trade merges both national markets into a single market, and in one competitive market there can be only one price for each good. But international trade goes beyond the equalization of the prices of goods; it also brings factor prices in the trading countries closer together. To trace this effect of international trade we must drop our assumption of constant unit costs for the more realistic assumption of increasing unit costs.[15] Then factor prices will be affected by the changes in supply and demand set in motion by the opening of trade.

Let us now return to our earlier example in which the United States has a comparative advantage in wheat production and a comparative *dis*advantage in textile production while the converse holds in the United Kingdom. The production of wheat is land-intensive and the United States has a relatively abundant supply of land that commands a relatively low rent. The production of textiles is labor-intensive and the United States has a relatively scarce supply of labor that commands a relatively high wage. The opposite is true in the United Kingdom.

When trade begins, the demand facing United States wheat rises as foreign demand is added to domestic demand. With increasing

---

[14] We are still assuming pure competition and the absence of transfer costs. The effects of imperfect competition and transfer costs upon international prices are treated in the next chapter.

[15] The source of increasing unit costs is explained in the following chapter.

unit costs, this higher demand leads to higher wheat prices and feeds back to create a higher demand and higher prices for the factors of production—especially land—used to produce wheat. At the same time, imports of textiles from the United Kingdom are displacing United States production of textiles. The falling demand for the latter initiates a falling demand and falling prices for the factors of production—especially labor—used to produce textiles. As a consequence, land rent rises relative to wages in the United States. Simultaneously, wages rise relative to land rent in the United Kingdom. Thus, the abundant factors (land in the United States, labor in the United Kingdom) become relatively more expensive while the scarce factors (labor in the United States, land in the United Kingdom) become relatively less expensive. It follows that the gap between the factor prices of the two countries becomes narrower. The same narrowing would occur if land moved from the United States to the United Kingdom (clearly impossible) while labor moved from the latter to the former country.

Will international trade ever achieve a full equalization of factor prices between the trading countries? Only under certain limiting assumptions: national factor endowments are not too unequal, there are no transfer costs, technology is the same in all countries, and there is only partial specialization—each country continues to produce some import-type goods. Only the last assumption may hold in the real world. We conclude, therefore, that international trade will bring national factor prices closer together but that it will not achieve a complete equalization.

THE GAINS FROM INTERNATIONAL TRADE

Through international trade a nation is able to obtain more goods with which to satisfy the needs and desires of its people (the ultimate end of economic activity) than if it were to produce all goods at home. This is the true gain from international trade; it is the fruit of international specialization in accordance with comparative cost advantages. International trade is indirect production. It enables each country to combine its factors of production more effectively by specializing in the production of those goods which are best produced by using large amounts of its relatively abundant factors and small amounts of its relatively scarce factors. In this way a country may produce for export those goods in which it has a comparative advantage and import those goods in which it has a comparative disadvantage.

The Division of Gains

Both countries will gain from international specialization and trade, but the exact division of gains between them will depend upon the rate of exchange between their two currencies. The rate of exchange itself is determined by the demand of each country for the other's goods.[16]

To illustrate the determination of the rate of exchange and the role that it plays in the distribution of the gains from trade we return to our earlier example of dissimilar cost ratios:

	UNITED STATES (Dollars)	UNITED KINGDOM (Pounds Sterling)
Unit cost (price) of wheat	1.00	3.00
Unit cost (price) of textiles .	2.00	1.00

With these cost ratios the range of exchange rates that allow gainful trade runs from £1 equals $2 to £1 equals one-third dollar. Over this range (including the two extremes) the exchange rate will be determined by the *reciprocal demand* of two countries. The exchange rate must be such that the exports and imports of each country are equal; this is the *equilibrium* rate of exchange.[17]

To show how reciprocal demand determines the equilibrium rate of exchange, let us assume an initial equilibrium rate of £1 equals $1, and that at this rate the United States imports 1,000 units of textiles while the United Kingdom imports 1,000 units of wheat. Then the *dollar* prices of wheat and textiles in both countries are as follows:

	UNITED STATES (Dollars)	UNITED KINGDOM (Dollars)
Unit cost (price) of wheat	1.00	3.00
Unit cost (price) of textiles ..	2.00	1.00

At this exchange rate the United States is able to import one unit of textiles (worth $1) from the United Kingdom for the export of each unit of wheat (worth $1). *Without* international trade the United States could acquire only one-half unit of textiles for each unit of wheat—the domestic opportunity cost ratio. Its gain from trade, therefore, is one-half unit of textiles for each unit of wheat.

---

[16] The determination of exchange rates is analyzed at length in Chapter 8.
[17] We are continuing to assume the absence of any international lending that would finance a gap between exports and imports.

Similarly, for the export of each unit of textiles (worth $1) the United Kingdom is able to import one unit of wheat (worth $1). *Without* trade the United Kingdom could obtain only one-third unit of wheat for each unit of textiles—the domestic opportunity cost ratio. Thus the United Kingdom gains two-thirds unit of wheat from the export of each unit of textiles. The *total* gain from trade for the United States is 500 units of textiles (1,000 times 0.5 units of textiles), which at the domestic cost equal $1,000. The *total* gain for the United Kingdom is 666.6 units of wheat, which at the domestic cost equal $2,000. Although the gain of the United Kingdom is twice that of the United States, both countries gain from trade and both would be worse off without trade.

Now suppose that the demand for textiles in the United States rises to 1,200 units at the current exchange rate while the demand for wheat remains the same in the United Kingdom. At the exchange rate of £1 equals $1, United States imports would be $1,200 and its exports $1,000. But this is not possible since exports must pay for imports. Therefore, the dollar price of pounds will now rise (the pound price of dollars will fall) until a new equilibrium rate of exchange is attained that brings about an equality between the exports and imports of both countries. The new equilibrium rate might be £1 equals $1.50 with the amount of textiles demanded by the United States, say 1,100 units, and the amount of wheat demanded by the United Kingdom, 1,650 units. The effect of the new exchange rate upon the *dollar* prices of wheat and textiles in the United Kingdom (the dollar prices in the United States and the pound prices in the United Kingdom remaining unchanged) is as follows:

	UNITED STATES (Dollars)	UNITED KINGDOM (Dollars)
Unit cost (price) of wheat	1.00	4.50
Unit cost (price) of textiles ..	2.00	1.50

At this new rate of exchange the total value of imports equals the total value of exports in both countries—$1,650. But it is obvious without detailed calculations that the United States gain from trade is now less (and the United Kingdom gain greater) than in the previous example when the exchange rate was £1 equals $1. The *commodity terms of trade* have worsened for the United States: it must now pay more for its imports (textiles) while the price of its exports

Ch. 3 / Comparative Costs and the Gains from Trade 65

(wheat) has remained constant.[18] Conversely, the terms of trade have bettered for the United Kingdom since the dollar price of its exports has risen while the dollar price of its imports has remained the same. Both countries, however, continue to gain from trade.

The lesson we draw from these two examples is that the country with the more intense demand for the other country's goods will gain less from trade than the country with the less intense demand.[19] In the extreme case the exchange rate is identical with the cost ratio in one country and that country neither gains nor loses from trade while the second country reaps all of the gain. This possibility, however, is exceedingly remote in the real world where international trade involves many commodities rather than only two. To conclude, the *division* of gains from international trade is determined by the relative intensities (and elasticities) of the demands of each country for the other's goods—reciprocal demand.

A Broader Interpretation of Gains

The preceding analysis provides us with a precise explanation of the gains from international trade and their division among the trading countries. This analysis, however, does not consider the enormous changes that international trade may bring to the economy of a country.

The contemporary economies of most countries would be radically different if they had not developed during a period of widespread trade. For example, the British economy produces only a small fraction of its food and raw material requirements—the cessa-

---

[18] The *commodity terms of trade* refer to the exchange ratio between exports and imports, that is, between wheat and textiles in our illustration. Arithmetically, the commodity terms of trade are expressed by a ratio of the *change* in the export price level over the *change* in the import price level, both changes being measured from a base year. An increase in the value of the ratio indicates an improvement in the commodity terms of trade (more imports per unit of exports). We should remember that a nation's gains from international trade are determined not only by its commodity terms of trade but also by the comparative cost ratios of the trading countries and the volume of trade. In our illustration on page 64, the terms of trade were altered by a movement of the exchange rate (a depreciation of the dollar vis-à-vis the pound) that was caused by a rise in the United States demand for textiles. If exchange rates were fixed, as under the gold standard, then adjustment to that shift in demand would involve an alteration in the terms of trade through changes in the domestic prices of the United States and the United Kingdom—a fall in the prices of the former country and a rise in the prices of the latter. See Chapters 10 and 11 for a fuller analysis of adjustments to restore equilibrium.

[19] The sensitivity (elasticity) of the amount demanded to changes in the exchange rate will also decide the equilibrium rate of exchange and therefore the division of gains from trade. See Chapter 8.

tion of all foreign trade would mean starvation for millions and a drastic reduction in the living standards of those fortunate enough to survive. To a lesser extent the same is true of Western Europe. In short, the basic structure of most national economies would be far different if nations were unable to specialize and trade with each other. Today's economies are largely a product of past international trade. Thus the gains from trade are commensurate with the whole economy, and they are evidenced by its long-run development in the direction of greater international specialization.

Absolute Differences in Productivity and Wages

In our discussion of the gains from trade we have taken no notice of different absolute levels of productivity and wages in the trading countries. Nor should we mention them now if it were not for certain misconceptions surrounding these topics.

It is sometimes argued that a country cannot gain from trade with a less productive country because it can produce everything with fewer man-hours at home. If this were true, the trade of the United States would be largely unprofitable since, in most production, this country enjoys a higher productivity than other nations. Of course, the answer to this assertion is that even though a country were able to produce everything with fewer man-hours than other countries, it would still gain from trade if its *ratio* of costs differed from foreign ratios, for then that country would have comparative advantages and disadvantages in production. The true significance of high productivity lies in the high incomes and standard of living that it affords a nation's people—not in the gains from trade. Fortunately, international trade is open to rich and poor nations alike.

Again, it is asserted that a country can only *lose* from trade with a low-wage country, since that country can undersell it. This argument has several weaknesses. First, it may be queried as to how any trade is possible if the domestic country is undersold in *all* products for, in that case, it could not export anything nor, therefore, import anything. If only *some* products are in question, then the argument is absurd since trade obviously requires that one country undersell the other country in some goods, and conversely. Second, it must be pointed out that wages may be low and unit costs high when productivity is low. Thus there is no necessary connection between low wages and low costs. Third, the low-wage argument **must** bow to the logic of the theory of comparative costs. As long as

Ch. 3 / Comparative Costs and the Gains from Trade

cost ratios are dissimilar, trade is profitable between countries regardless of absolute wage levels.

MANY COUNTRIES AND MANY GOODS

For simplicity we have assumed only two countries and two goods. How do the many countries and many goods of the actual world affect the theory of comparative costs?

The role of reciprocal demand in determining exports and imports is enhanced by the existence of several countries and several goods. We can show this most simply by first looking at an example of three countries and two commodities, and then looking at an example of two countries and several commodities.

Three Countries and Two Commodities

Let us suppose that the following prices for the same two commodities rule in the United States, the United Kingdom, and France:

	UNITED STATES (Dollars)	UNITED KINGDOM (Pounds Sterling)	FRANCE (Francs)
Unit (price) of wheat	1.00	2.00	1.00
Unit (price) of textiles	3.00	2.00	2.00

Before the opening of trade the prices of wheat and textiles in each country are such that one unit of wheat exchanges for one-third unit of textiles in the United States, one unit of wheat exchanges for one unit of textiles in the United Kingdom, and one unit of wheat exchanges for one-half unit of textiles in France. It is clear that the United States has a comparative advantage in the production of wheat, since the opportunity cost of its wheat is the lowest (one-third unit of textiles) among the three countries. Similarly, the United Kingdom has a comparative advantage in the production of textiles since the opportunity cost of its textiles is the lowest (one unit of wheat) among the three countries. But what of France? Its comparative advantage will be determined by the terms of exchange between wheat and textiles once international trade begins, and the terms of trade will be determined by reciprocal demand—the demand of each country for the exports of the other two countries.

Since the opportunity cost of a unit of wheat is one-half unit of textiles in France, it is apparent that France will export wheat whenever it can get for each unit of wheat more than (or at least as much as) one-half unit of textiles in exchange. If, for example, one unit of wheat exchanges for two-thirds unit of textiles, both the United States and France will export wheat to the United Kingdom in exchange for textiles. On the other hand, France will export textiles whenever it can get for each unit of textiles more than (or at least as much as) two units of wheat. Thus if one unit of textiles exchanges for two and one-half units of wheat, both the United Kingdom and France will export textiles to the United States in exchange for wheat. There is a third possibility that France will not trade in either commodity. This will happen if the terms of trade between wheat and textiles are identical with the ratio of exchange within France in the absence of trade, that is, one unit of wheat for one-half unit of textiles. In that event, the United States will export wheat to the United Kingdom in exchange for textiles.

The peculiar position of France is due to the fact that its domestic price ratio between wheat and textiles (1:2) lies between the price ratio in the United States (1:3) and in the United Kingdom (1:1). As we learned earlier in this chapter, trade is profitable between the United States and the United Kingdom over the range of exchange ratios marked off by their respective domestic price ratios, that is from $\frac{1}{3}$ to 1. We also learned that upon the opening of trade the exact exchange ratio is determined by reciprocal demand through its influence on the exchange rate. We now see in our present example that reciprocal demand determines whether France will trade or not and, if she does, the commodity that she will export and the commodity that she will import.[20] This substantiates our previous statement that the existence of many countries enhances the role of reciprocal demand.

Two Countries and Several Commodities

Let us suppose we have the domestic prices, shown in the table at the top of the next page, for a number of commodities in the United States and the United Kingdom.

It is obvious that the United States will export commodity A and the United Kingdom will export commodity G if there is trade between the two countries. Beyond that we can say nothing definite until a rate of exchange is established between the dollar and the pound, and the precise rate of exchange will depend upon reciprocal

---

[20] The possibility that a country will cease entirely to trade because of a shift in reciprocal demand is remote when we drop our assumption of two commodities.

Ch. 3 / Comparative Costs and the Gains from Trade 69

Commodity	United States (Dollars)	United Kingdom (Pounds Sterling)
A	1.00	15.00
B	2.00	13.00
C	4.00	11.00
D	7.00	11.00
E	9.00	12.00
F	10.00	6.00
G	12.00	1.00

demand. Any shift in demand that increases the number of pounds exchanged for a dollar (a slackening in demand for imports in the United States or a rise in demand for imports in the United Kingdom) will extend the number of commodities exported by the United Kingdom and lessen the number of commodities exported by the United States. Conversely, any shift in demand that decreases the number of pounds exchanged for one dollar will cause the United States to export a greater number of commodities and the United Kingdom to export a smaller number.

To conclude, reciprocal demand is of much greater importance in determining the nature of a country's trade than is suggested by our simple two-country, two-commodity model.

SUMMARY

1. The basis of international trade is explained by the theory of comparative costs. The immediate basis of trade lies in absolute differences between the prices of foreign goods and the prices of similar goods produced at home. Under perfect and monopolistic competition these price differences reduce to cost differences.

2. Absolute international differences in costs (prices) arise upon the establishment of an exchange rate when the cost ratios within each country are dissimilar, for then the opportunity costs of producing similar goods will differ between countries and each country will have a comparative cost advantage in producing some goods and a comparative cost *dis*advantage in producing other goods. When cost ratios are identical between countries, opportunity costs are also identical and there is no basis for gainful international trade.

3. When cost ratios are dissimilar, there is a range of exchange rates that permits gainful international trade. The two extremes of this range are determined by the cost ratios within each country. At exchange rates beyond these extremes, trade is unprofitable for one or the other countries and, therefore, will not take place.

4. Dissimilar cost ratios derive from dissimilar factor price ratios. This is because the factors of production (land, labor, capital, and management) are not perfect substitutes for each other and must be used in different combinations to produce different goods. Factor price ratios, in turn, are determined by the relative supply and demand of the factors of production.

5. Countries differ greatly in their relative supplies of factors of production. Since a factor in relatively abundant supply has a comparatively low price while a factor in relatively scarce supply has a comparatively high price, dissimilar national factor supplies give rise to dissimilar national factor prices. Dissimilar national factor demands may also cause dissimilar national factor prices. Although there is no single basis of international trade, we may say in a loose sense that the fundamental basis of international trade lies in dissimilar national factor endowments.

6. The gains from trade are great because international factor mobility is low. International trade is a substitute for the international movement of factors of production.

7. The gains from international trade stem from the greater production that is possible when nations specialize in accordance with their comparative advantages. The division of these gains between the trading nations will depend upon reciprocal demand. The gains from trade are not affected by absolute international differences in productivity or wages.

8. The presence of many countries and many goods enhances the role of reciprocal demand in determining the character of a country's foreign trade.

QUESTIONS AND APPLICATIONS

1. Why are absolute international differences in prices not the *final* explanation of international trade?
2. Assume that two countries (United States and France) each produce the same two commodities (wine and electric toasters) with the following costs:

	UNITED STATES (Dollars)	FRANCE (Francs)
Unit cost of wine	2.00	3.00
Unit cost of electric toasters	4.00	12.00

(a) What are the opportunity costs of producing wine and electric toasters in both countries?
(b) Is gainful trade possible between the two countries? If so, what will be its nature?
(c) Is there a range of exchange rates between the dollar and the franc that will permit gainful trade? If so, what is it?

Ch. 3 / Comparative Costs and the Gains from Trade

3. Why do identical cost ratios in two countries rule out any gainful trade between them?

4. "Loosely speaking, we may say that dissimilar factor supply ratios in different countries are the basis of international trade." Explain.

5. Why is international trade a substitute for international factor movements?

6. Referring to Question 2 above, what are the gains per unit of exports for each country when the exchange rate is one franc equals 0.5 dollars? Assuming that United States exports total 30 units at that rate of exchange, what is the number of units of United States imports? Why?

7. Explain how reciprocal demand determines the equilibrium rate of exchange and thus the division of gains from trade.

8. "The gains from trade depend on absolute differences in productivity and wages." What is the validity of this statement?

9. How does the existence of many countries and many goods affect the theory of comparative cost?

SELECTED READINGS

See the list of readings given at the end of Chapter 5.

CHAPTER 4

COMPARATIVE COSTS IN THE WORLD ECONOMY

To simplify the presentation of the theory of comparative costs in Chapter 3, we made a number of tacit assumptions: (1) constant unit costs of production, (2) perfect competition, (3) no transfer costs, (4) fixed supplies of the factors of production, (5) the sameness of production functions in different countries, (6) an unchanging level of technology, (7) full employment of all factors of production, and (8) no capital movements—the absence of international loans or gifts.

In the actual world economy, none of these assumptions holds at all times; and certain assumptions, such as no transfer costs, never hold. It is necessary, therefore, to modify or withdraw these assumptions if the theory of comparative cost is to explain the actual course of international trade. It will become apparent that in making the theory more relevant to the real world, we unavoidably add to its complexity.

INCREASING COSTS

In Chapter 3 we assumed that unit costs were independent of the level of production. Actually, the unit cost of producing any good will start to rise at *some* level of output although that level may be high or low, depending on the specific production process. Until the point of increasing unit costs is reached, unit costs may decrease slowly or rapidly, that is to say, the U-shaped cost curve may be shallow or deep.

The Principle of Diminishing Marginal Productivity

The basic cause of increasing unit costs is found in the *principle* of *diminishing marginal productivity*. This principle states that when inputs of one factor (or factors) are added one at a time to a fixed input of another factor (or factors), production at first will increase at an increasing rate, then level off, and eventually decrease. Accordingly, unit costs of production will first decrease, then level off, and finally increase.[1]

An example drawn from agriculture will clarify this principle. Suppose a farmer has twenty acres of land and he decides to produce wheat by combining labor with his land. (To simplify matters we assume the necessary seed and tools are provided without cost.) The production of wheat might respond to additional inputs of labor as follows:

Inputs of Labor (man-days)	Output of Wheat (bushels)	Change in Output of Wheat (bushels)
0	0	0
1	100	100
2	250	150
3	450	200
4	550	100
5	600	50
6	600	0
7	550	−50

With no labor inputs, the production of wheat is zero. When one labor input is combined with the twenty acres of land, production rises to 100 bushels. This change in production brought about by the last input of labor (the input first hired in this instance) is the *marginal product* of labor. As more inputs of labor are added to the fixed supply of land, the marginal product rises until the fourth labor input is hired. At this point the marginal product falls. The sixth input contributes nothing to production, and the seventh input actually lowers production because its marginal product is negative.

The principle of diminishing marginal productivity is applicable to all kinds of production because there are always certain factors of production that are relatively fixed in supply.[2] Together with transportation costs, the principle explains why all the world's wheat is not produced on one acre of land or all the world's textiles

---

[1] Unit costs will not vary precisely with the addition of factor inputs because of the cost of the fixed factor inputs.

[2] It follows that *constant costs* imply that factors are either perfect substitutes of each other and can be treated as a single factor or, what amounts to the same thing, factors are required in the same fixed proportions at all levels of production. Both of these conditions are absent in the real world.

Ch. 4 / Comparative Costs in the World Economy   75

Figure 4-1

PARTIAL SPECIALIZATION UNDER INCREASING COSTS: TWO COUNTRIES

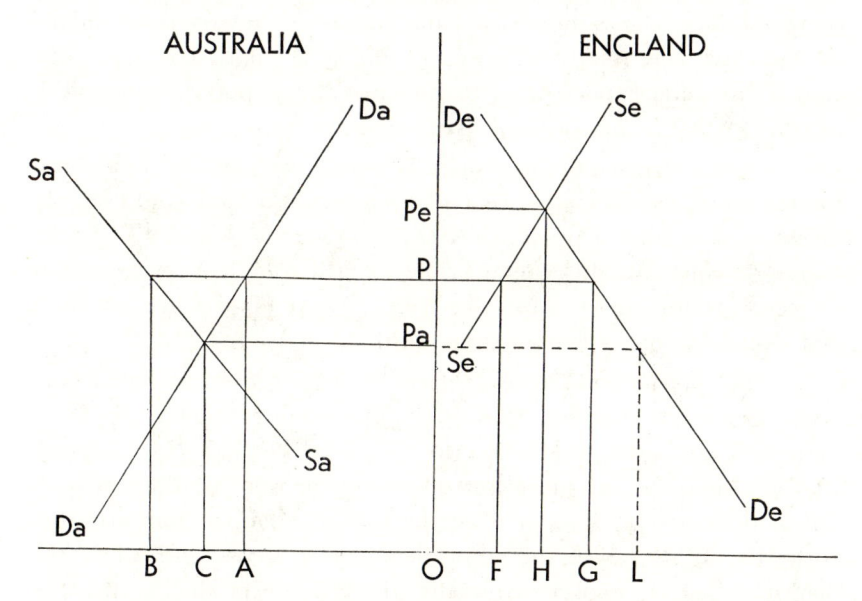

```
       AUSTRALIA              |          ENGLAND
                  Da          |De          Se
   Sa                         |
                              Pe
                              P
                              Pa    Se
                  Sa
                                                    De
   Da
   B  C  A          O    F   H   G       L
```

are not turned out by one factory. In manufacturing, the fixed factors are usually buildings, capital equipment, and technical and managerial personnel.

When a large firm or industry expands production, it may be able to obtain additional labor or other factors only at progressively higher prices. Higher factor prices, then, may be a second source of increasing unit costs.

The Effects of Increasing Costs on International Trade

The effects of increasing costs on international trade are two: (1) increasing costs generally rule out complete specialization of production between countries; and, (2) increasing costs as compared to constant costs narrow the opportunity for gainful trade. These effects are succinctly shown in Figure 4-1. The left half of Figure 4-1 shows the supply and demand schedules for wool in Australia: *Sa* and *Da*, respectively. With no international trade these schedules intersect to determine price, *O-Pa*; and at this price, *O-C* of wool is both supplied and demanded. Similarly, the supply and demand schedules for wool in England are indicated in the right half of Figure 4-1 as *Se* and *De*.

In isolation, the price of wool in England is $O\text{-}Pe$ and the amount demanded and supplied at this price, $O\text{-}H$. The price of wool is much lower in Australia because the production of wool requires comparatively large supplies of land, which are relatively abundant in Australia and relatively scarce in England. Both countries will gain if Australia exports wool to England and imports a commodity in which it has a comparative disadvantage.

If costs were constant, Australia would be able to supply unlimited units of wool at price $O\text{-}Pa$, whereas England could supply no units of wool at a price below $O\text{-}Pe$. Upon the opening of trade, therefore, constant costs would bring about a complete specialization of wool production in Australia—England would produce no wool and would import $O\text{-}L$ wool from Australia at price $O\text{-}Pa$.

Wool production, however, faces increasing costs in both countries. When trade begins, Australia will encounter higher unit costs as it expands wool production to meet the new English demand. At the same time, the unit cost of producing wool in England will fall as domestic production is cut back in the face of imports from Australia. This process of adjustment comes to an end when the marginal cost of wool in Australia—the cost of producing the last unit—has risen to $O\text{-}P$, and the marginal cost of wool in England has fallen to $O\text{-}P$. At this marginal cost, which is equal to price under pure competition, Australia will consume $O\text{-}A$ wool, produce $O\text{-}B$ wool, and export $A\text{-}B$ wool. England will consume $O\text{-}G$ wool, producing $O\text{-}F$ wool at home and importing $F\text{-}G$ wool. The price of wool is now the same in both countries ($O\text{-}P$), and exports ($A\text{-}B$) are equal to imports ($F\text{-}G$). Because of increasing costs, England continues to produce $O\text{-}F$ wool, and the volume of trade ($F\text{-}G$) is clearly smaller than it would be if costs were constant ($O\text{-}L$).

Despite the existence of increasing costs, there are many examples of complete international specialization in the world economy. At times a nation is physically unable to produce a specific commodity or cannot produce even a small amount except at a cost higher than foreign cost.[3] A large fraction of the international trade in minerals and food products falls into this category. Full international specialization also occurs when production is able to meet existing demand over a range of *decreasing* unit costs.

---

[3] In terms of Figure 4-1 this means that the domestic supply schedule of the importing country, despite an upward slope from left to right, lies entirely above the price of imports.

DECREASING COSTS

Although all production will experience increasing unit costs sooner or later, certain commodities may be produced at *decreasing* unit costs over a broad range of output.

Economies of Scale

Decreasing unit costs are mostly found in those manufacturing industries that use great quantities of capital to implement the techniques of mass production, such as the chemical, petroleum refining, steel, and automobile industries. The source of *internal* economies of scale lies in the indivisibility of specific factors of production. Giant machines, the assembly-line organization of production, managerial specialization, industrial research, etc., are economical only with mass production—they cannot be subdivided into the smaller units suitable for small-scale production. As production expands, these indivisible factors of production can be more fully utilized and thus a decrease in unit costs occurs.

Another source of decreasing unit costs may be found in *external* economies of scale that arise outside the firm or industry. The individual firm or industry functions within a broad economic environment and its costs of production are dependent upon the efficiency of the economy as a whole. As an economy develops, transportation and communication facilities, raw materials, capital equipment, supplies and parts, skilled labor, financing, etc., may become progressively more available and cheaper to the firm. The firm may also benefit from an expansion of its own industry. External economies—unlike internal economies—operate over the long run. Improvements in technology may also bring decreasing unit costs in the long run.

The Effects of Decreasing Costs on International Trade

Unlike increasing costs, decreasing costs enlarge the opportunity for international trade. Decreasing costs lead inevitably to complete international specialization unless their effects are blocked by tariffs or other restrictions. Thus the factor indivisibilities responsible for decreasing unit costs provide a basis for international trade along with differences in national factor endowments.

Assume, for example, that two countries (A and B) have the same factor proportions and the same level of technology. In terms of the simple model used in Chapter 3, no gainful trade is possible under these conditions because cost ratios are identical. But now let us suppose that country A has a big domestic market that allows it to achieve economies of scale in producing a manufactured good (say, automobiles) while country B has only a small domestic market that limits it to a high-cost, small-scale production of automobiles. Because of the economies of scale, country A now has a comparative advantage in automobiles and will export them to country B. In return, country A will import a good from country B in which it now has a comparative disadvantage because of the shift in opportunity cost ratios in country A that are induced by economies of scale. Thus economies of scale afford a basis for gainful trade even when factor ratios are identical among countries.

The United States has a comparative advantage in many mass-produced goods for two reasons: (1) the relatively abundant supply of capital in the United States, and (2) the economies of scale that are achieved by American producers in meeting the needs of domestic mass consumption. Many American producers are able to compete effectively in the world market because their unit costs of production have been lowered in satisfying the vast domestic demand. On the other hand, countries with relatively abundant supplies of capital but only small domestic markets are seldom able to secure the economies of scale and therefore have a comparative disadvantage in goods that lend themselves to mass production.[4] Since advances in technology are usually biased in favor of mass production, comparative advantages based on factor indivisibilities and domestic mass consumption are likely to grow with the passage of time.

IMPERFECT COMPETITION

Although a great deal of international trade in basic foodstuffs and raw materials is conducted in markets that are substantially purely competitive, most international trade in manufactured goods occurs in markets that depart in one way or another from the conditions of pure competition.[5] That is to say, manufactured goods are often differentiated rather than homogeneous among producers, and the number of producers may be small enough so that the individual producer's supply will influence the market price.

---

[4] If international trade is free of official restrictions, then a small country may obtain the advantages of large-scale production by producing for the world market. But this is difficult and risky in the real world where external markets may be suddenly closed off by foreign government action. One of the purposes of the European Economic Community is to overcome this obstacle to large-scale production by creating free trade among its members. See Chapter 19.

[5] Manufactures make up more than half of world trade. See Chapter 2.

The effects of this imperfect competition on international trade may be restrictive, neutral, or expansive, depending on the particular variety of imperfect competition in question and the policies of individual firms. In this section we shall briefly sketch the principal types of imperfect competition and their most likely influence on the course of international trade. In particular, we wish to know whether international trade differs significantly from what it would be if all markets were purely competitive.[6]

Types of Imperfect Competition

Imperfect competition in international trade may arise from monopoly, oligopoly, monopolistic competition, cartels, international commodity agreements, and state trading.

Briefly, monopoly refers to a single seller; oligopoly to a small number of sellers who produce the same or a somewhat differentiated product; and monopolistic competition to a large number of sellers, each of whom produces a differentiated product with close substitutes.

Cartels and commodity agreements involve restrictive arrangements among producers in various countries or among national governments. State trading occurs when part or all of the foreign trade of a country is in the hands of its government. Today the Communist countries exhibit the most extreme form of state trading; Communist government agencies are the sole buyers of all imports (monopsony) and the sole sellers of all exports (monopoly).[7]

Monopoly and oligopoly may affect international trade by the distortions they introduce into the price system due to the existence of *monopoly profits*. Monopolistic competition (and some oligopoly) may alter international trade through the *nonprice competition* which is its principal characteristic.

Monopoly Profits

Traditionally, economists have extolled perfect competition and, at the same time, have deplored imperfect competition. This attitude is based on the theoretical finding that the allocation of factors of production under imperfect competition does not maximize production and consumer satisfactions as under perfect competition. Under perfect competition the price of a good tends to equal its lowest unit

---

[6] See Footnote 2 on page 48 for a short definition of pure or perfect competition.

[7] Cartels, state trading, and commodity agreements are treated in Chapter 16.

cost of production, and cost of production includes only the profits necessary to attract and keep the management factor plus the other factor payments. Furthermore payments to an individual factor in any employment are equal to its marginal product in all employments. Thus it is *not* possible to increase national output by reallocating factor supplies among different lines of production. As observed in the preceding chapter, this means that national price and cost ratios are the same, and cost ratios reflect relative factor supplies and demands. Under the equilibrium conditions of perfect competition, therefore, comparative cost advantages and disadvantages are fully expressed in absolute international price differences.

Under monopoly and oligopoly, however, excess profits—profits not required to retain the management factor in production—may occur, although not necessarily. The existence of excess or *monopoly profits* makes the price of a good (or service) higher than its marginal cost of production, and for the nation as a whole the price ratios between goods differ from their cost ratios. In this way, the international allocation of production (international specialization) is not fully adjusted to opportunity costs; in other words, the gains from trade are less.

Monopoly and Oligopoly Prices

Although the presence of excess profits distorts the price system and tends to restrict the volume of international trade, it does not follow that monopoly and oligopoly prices are necessarily higher than perfectly competitive prices or that the volume of trade is necessarily less under monopoly and oligopoly than under perfect competition. A monopolistic or oligopolistic industry may be able to achieve economies of scale and a rate of technological discovery and capital investment that would not be possible if the same industry were perfectly competitive. Perfect competition may require that an industry be made up of small firms unable to achieve economies of scale or engage in research on new products and processes.[8] When there are significant economies of scale, therefore, monopoly or oligopoly prices

---

[8] Until recently, this sort of situation has characterized the United States cotton textile industry. Now bigger companies are being formed through mergers and acquisitions, and these companies are benefiting from economies of scale and more research. Many industries have started with a large number of small firms, but subsequently economies of scale have transformed them into oligopolies. The history of the United States automobile and steel industries offers instructive examples.

may be less than perfectly competitive prices, even though the former include excess profits and the latter do not. When this happens the volume of international trade is greater under monopoly or oligopoly than under pure competition. Of course, trade would be even greater if there were no excess profits.

The *net* effect of monopoly and oligopoly on international trade, therefore, may be detrimental or beneficial. Monopoly profits are always detrimental, but they may be more than offset by the economies of scale and rapid technological advance. The net effect of *pure* monopoly on trade is probably detrimental in most cases. Lacking the spur of competition, a monopoly firm may become stagnant or actually retard technological improvements in order to sustain high profits. Nor is a monopoly firm necessarily a large-scale producer enjoying decreasing unit costs. For these reasons a monopoly, particularly an old monopoly, is apt to restrict the opportunity for international specialization and trade by holding prices far above costs and charging "what the traffic will bear." Fortunately pure monopoly is exceedingly rare in international trade. Its effects on trade, however, are closely matched by cartels and state trading.

Oligopolies are very common in the mass-production industries where a few firms can supply the entire market. Oligopoly differs from monopoly in that there may be effective competition among oligopolists unless they organize a cartel or reach a less formal agreement not to compete, both forbidden by American law but often permitted in foreign countries.[9] The possibility that the relatively small number of producers will "gang up" on buyers by agreeing to hold up prices, allocate markets, freeze technology, and the like is the greatest danger of oligopoly. When competition does exist in an oligopolistic industry, it will usually be *nonprice* competition in quality, style, or services rather than in prices. The heavy burden of fixed costs in the mass-production industries creates such a great risk of price wars that the firms within those industries tend to raise and lower prices together. We are all familiar with this sort of price behavior in cigarettes, automobiles, and gasoline—all products of oligopolistic industries.

When there is effective competition between oligopolistic firms, international trade will generally benefit from economies of scale, rapid improvements in technology, etc. After all, the most dynamic

---

[9] The Webb-Pomerene Act, however, does allow American producers to organize an export cartel. See Chapter 16.

industries are likely to be the mass-production industries in which oligopoly is the usual market arrangement.[10] The aggressive competition of oligopolies in this country and their willingness and ability to exploit foreign sources of supply and foreign market opportunities are responsible in considerable measure for the expansion of United States trade.

Nonprice Competition

Most of the manufactured goods that enter international trade are sold in either oligopolistically or monopolistically competitive markets. In the latter variety of market each good is produced by a large number of producers, but each producer has succeeded in differentiating his product from competitive products in some way. This differentiation is achieved by the technique of nonprice competition, which is the hallmark of monopolistic competition. Although price competition is close and competitors' prices can never be disregarded, it is nonprice competition in quality, style, and services that makes up the aggressive front of monopolistic competition.

American consumers encounter nonprice competition at every turn. Television, radio, and other advertising media daily assault our eyes and ears with clever appeals to buy this or that product. Price appeals are relatively rare, and they are usually drowned out by the host of selling points centered on nonprice factors. We are warned, cajoled, sweet-talked, entertained, and implored—all with the intent to make us rush out to buy brand X. American advertising has a pervasiveness and vigor that are not matched in other countries, but the use of advertising is rising sharply in all countries of the free world, much of it sponsored by American companies that market abroad.[11]

Nonprice competition often employs appeals based on style factors. Not only is the style cycle of traditional style goods speeded up by this competition, but style is also created in goods that were formerly standardized. The evolution of the American automobile from the Model T to the contemporary stylized product is a case in point. Style introduces a rapid obsolescence of merchandise as the

---

[10] In 1963 the twenty largest industrial corporations in the United States were all members of oligopolistic industries—automotive, petroleum, steel, electrical, meat packing, chemical, business machines, agricultural machinery, and aircraft. See *The Fortune Directory*, August, 1964, p. 2.

[11] The place of advertising in the performance of international trade is treated in Chapter 28.

Ch. 4 / Comparative Costs in the World Economy   83

style has its day and then passes on; this raises problems of inventory, timing, and market information that are largely absent in the marketing of standardized merchandise. There is, however, another side of the coin—style obsolescence periodically renews demand by making buyers dissatisfied with their earlier acquisitions.

A great variety of services is also used to distinguish a product from its competitors—quick delivery, return guarantees, warranties, right of inspection before acceptance of merchandise, the availability of repair parts, servicing of the product and instruction in its use, etc. One reason behind the establishment of overseas branches and subsidiaries by domestic concerns is to facilitate service competition.[12]

The Effect of Nonprice Competition on International Trade

The effect of nonprice competition on international trade is expansive. Nonprice competition stimulates demand by acquainting buyers with goods, by transforming latent demand into active demand, by introducing new products and new uses for old products, by heightening the availability of products, and in other ways. The dynamism of nonprice competition in creating new demand contrasts with the passivity of price competition—accepting demand but doing nothing to change it.

It is sometimes argued that nonprice competition restricts international trade because selling costs make prices higher than they would be under pure competition. This accusation fails to note, however, that many goods do not sell themselves and that nonprice competition enlarges the sales of such goods beyond the levels attainable through pure competition.[13] Economies of scale may be possible only when production is bolstered through mass consumption induced by nonprice competition. The charge that nonprice competition is wasteful and costly is valid only when it does not enhance the demand for a product. This criticism is often leveled against cigarette advertising, which, it is alleged, does not raise the consumption of cigarettes but simply redistributes the existing demand among the individual producers.[14]

---

[12] See Chapters 25 and 26 for a discussion of the marketing channels and other foreign operations developed by American companies abroad.

[13] It is said that one of the most potent factors in the export of American consumer goods is the publicity given to the American standard of living throughout the world by Hollywood movies.

[14] Criticism of nonprice competition ultimately derives from welfare propositions, namely, that some things are better for society than others. The case for or

In the long run (the time needed to change productive capacity) monopolistic competition forces an identity between costs and prices. This absence of monopoly profits means that cost and price ratios are the same, and hence international trade moves in accordance with the principle of comparative advantage. We may conclude, therefore, that nonprice competition brings a dynamic, expansive element to international trade without the distortion of chronic monopoly profits. This is not to deny the importance of price competition; nonprice competition does not supplant price competition but rather supplements it. It means, however, that the theory of comparative cost must take account of nonprice competition as well as price competition if it is to explain the full scope of international trade.

TRANSPORTATION AND OTHER TRANSFER COSTS

The movement of merchandise from one country to another involves a number of transfer costs. They may be classified as (1) costs of physical transfer and (2) transfer costs associated with the government regulation of international trade. Costs of physical transfer include the costs incurred in packing, transporting, and handling merchandise. Such costs are omnipresent, and they affect the movement of goods both within and between nations. Transfer costs also arise out of the government regulation of foreign trade such as import duties, quotas, and exchange restrictions.[15] These transfer costs differ from physical transfer costs in that they pertain only to international trade. Their nature and individual effects on trade are described in later chapters; for the present we shall restrict our discussion to the significance of physical transfer costs.

Physical transfer costs influence international trade in two ways. First, transfer costs increase the prices of imports and thereby restrict the opportunity for gainful trade. Second, transfer costs affect international trade by their bearing on the location of industry and the geographical pattern of production.

---

against cigarette advertising is now complicated by the health issue. As for international advertising, a further point needs mention. International markets may differ greatly in their consumption levels and saturation percentages for the same product. Thus the promotional elasticity of the same advertising may, and often does, vary widely among national markets. Finally, much criticism of nonprice competition either ignores product innovations or denies their usefulness.

[15] Trade restrictions that prohibit trade either entirely or beyond specified amounts, such as import quotas, have the same economic effects as infinite transfer costs.

The Effects of Transportation Costs on International Trade

Transportation is the main source of physical transfer costs; handling and packing facilitate transportation and are subsidiary to it. To simplify matters, we shall confine our analysis to the effects of transportation costs on international trade. The effects of handling and packing costs are the same, but usually of lesser importance.

The restrictive effects of transportation costs on the volume of international trade may be seen by comparing Figures 4-1 and 4-2 which are drawn to the same scale. Figure 4-1 shows that Australia's wool exports (A-B) to England are equal to England's wool imports (F-G) from Australia at price O-P. Now let us introduce transportation costs. Instead of a single price ruling in both countries (O-P in Figure 4-1), there will be two prices that differ by the cost of transporting a unit of wool from Australia to England. We indicate this effect in Figure 4-2 by raising Australia's supply and demand schedules a distance O-O' higher than England's schedules. By so doing we recognize that the cost of Australian wool to English importers is the Australian price *plus* unit transportation costs represented by O-O'. The two equilibrium prices in Figure 4-2 are O'-P in Australia and O-P in England. At these prices Australia will export A-B wool and

Figure 4-2

EFFECTS OF TRANSPORTATION COSTS ON INTERNATIONAL TRADE

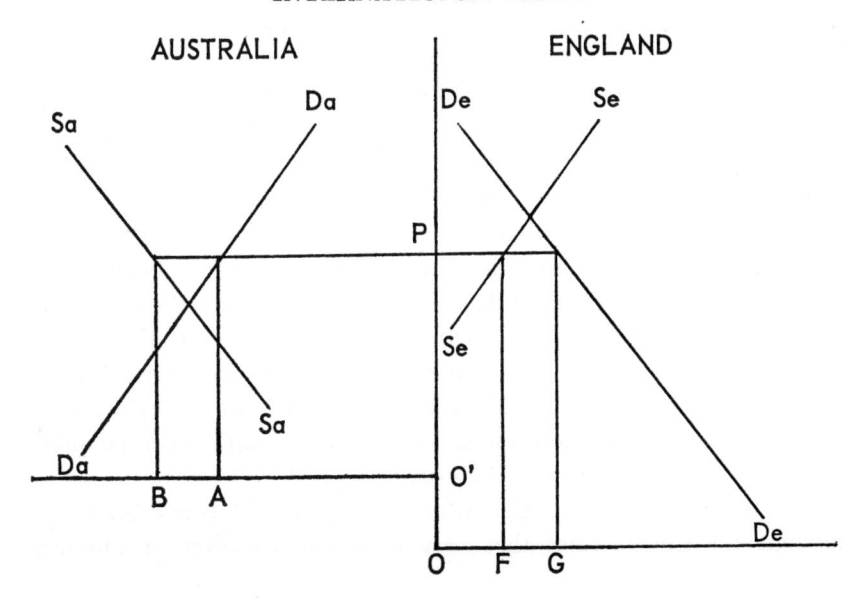

England will import *F-G* wool. Observe that the volume of trade in Figure 4-2 is less than the volume in Figure 4-1. Because of transportation costs the English now produce somewhat more wool at home (compare *O-F* in the two figures). Observe also that the English now pay a higher price for wool (*O-P* in Figure 4-2 is greater than *O-P* in Figure 4-1) but that the increase is somewhat less than transportation costs (*O-O'*) because the price in Australia has fallen in response to a smaller export demand (*O'-P* in Figure 4-2 is less than *O-P* in Figure 4-1). In this illustration Australia continues to export wool in spite of transportation costs. If transportation costs rose to equal *Pa-Pe* in Figure 4-1, however, Australia would cease to export any wool because transportation costs would entirely offset its pretrade price advantage.

Actually, commodities vary greatly in their capacity to absorb transportation costs. Commodities that are heavy, bulky, and hard to handle cannot absorb their transportation costs unless they command a high unit price. Bricks and sand are examples of this sort of commodity—to move them more than a short distance involves such high transportation costs that they cease to be competitive in price. On the other hand, commodities that take up little space or are easily handled may be economically transported over great distances even when their unit prices are low. The traditional staples of international trade, such as grains, wheat, cotton, and wool, fit the latter category of easy handling.

Transportation costs are not simply dependent on distance and the physical character of commodities. Transportation agencies, especially ocean shipping and railroad, have a very heavy investment in fixed capital and correspondingly high fixed costs. For this reason steamship and railroad companies have a strong incentive to utilize the full capacity of their ships and freight cars at all times. To do so, they tend to "charge what the traffic will bear." This means that freight rates vary among commodities far more than can be justified by differences in weight, bulk, ease of handling, or other physical factors. Commodities that can easily absorb freight costs because of high unit values, such as electronic equipment, are charged high rates. By the same token, bulky commodities of low unit value, such as wheat, are charged low rates. Generally speaking, manufactured goods pay much higher rates than primary goods.

This tendency to charge what the traffic will bear also helps account for freight rates that vary with the *direction* of physical movement. Frequently, the volume of trade between two ports, or geographical regions, is less in one direction than the other. To get full cargoes at ports where the volume of outgoing freight is low, steamship companies will charge shippers only low "backhaul" rates. In the nineteenth century, ships left Great Britain loaded down with coal and carried cargoes back to Britain at very low backhaul rates. These favorable rates undoubtedly stimulated British imports and the development of London as a reexport center for primary products.

The role of direction as a discriminatory factor in transportation rates is revealed in an investigation of ocean freight rates in United States trade by the Joint Economic Committee.[16] The Committee found that the international ocean freight rate structure was "weighted against" United States exports. In trade between the United States Pacific Coast and the Far East, freight rates on American exports exceeded rates on corresponding imports on 80 percent of the sampled items. Rate discrimination against American exports also occurred on 70 percent of the products traded between United States Atlantic and Gulf ports and the Far East, and on 60 percent of the goods shipped from the Atlantic Coast to Western Europe. For example, it cost $61.25 to ship radios from New York to Japan but only $40 to ship them from Japan to New York. The Committee also uncovered third country discrimination. A sample of rates on 40 export commodities showed that the average rate from the United States to ports in South America, South Africa, and India was $9.85 per 1,000 miles, whereas the average rate from Japan and from London to these same ports was $4.14 and $5.30, respectively. An American paid $39 to ship an automobile to Rio de Janeiro, Brazil, while an Englishman paid only $15.05, although New York is 500 miles closer to Rio de Janeiro than Liverpool.

In answer to the Committee's findings, ocean shipping spokesmen pointed out that United States liner exports were 1½ times greater in weight tons than imports, and rather than send vessels to the United States in ballast, shipowners charged only out-of-pocket, or variable, costs on shipments to the United States. The Committee rejected this explanation, asserting that even when the quantity and value of United States imports were roughly equal to United States

---

[16] Joint Economic Committee, Congress of the United States, *Discriminatory Ocean Freight Rates and the Balance of Payments* (Washington, D. C.: U.S. Government Printing Office, 1965). The data in this and the next paragraph are taken from this document.

exports it found discrimination. Furthermore, this argument did not apply to third country discrimination. The Committee felt that the monopolistic determination of ocean freight rates was more to the point. Most ocean freight rates are set by associations, or conferences, of steamship companies, and United States flag lines are outnumbered in all but seven of the more than 100 active steamship conferences involved in United States trade. The Committee obtained some evidence that foreign lines, regardless of flag, voted as a bloc against United States lines. The question of ocean freight rate discrimination in United States trade is a very complex subject, and we have merely touched on it here. Its importance, however, should not be underestimated. In 1962 ocean freight rates represented 12 percent of the value of United States exports and 10 percent of the value of United States imports.

We may generalize this discussion of transportation costs in international trade by stating that the existence of transportation costs separates goods into two classes—*domestic* goods and *international* goods. Domestic goods do not enter international trade because transportation costs make it impossible to sell them at competitive prices in foreign markets.[17] International goods, however, are able to absorb transportation costs and still meet foreign competition.

The existence of transportation costs, like increasing costs of production, means that international specialization will not be complete. When transportation costs are taken into account, there will be a number of goods that can be acquired more cheaply from domestic industries despite the fact that foreign industries can produce the same goods at a lower cost. Low-cost housing construction in one country will not benefit home buyers in another country. There is, however, no sharp dividing line between domestic and international goods. A higher foreign demand may make it economically feasible to export a good that has not entered foreign trade in the past. An improvement in transportation that greatly lowers cost will convert many domestic goods into international goods.

This last observation suggests the tremendous effects upon international trade of the "transportation revolution" that occurred in the nineteenth century, particularly in its last quarter. Before this

---

[17] Perishable goods are likely to be domestic goods unless techniques of preservation or very rapid means of transportation permit their sale at competitive prices in foreign markets. This is also true of interregional trade as is testified by the local character of milk and bread production.

revolution, the vast hinterlands of North and South America and the productive resources of such countries as Australia and New Zealand were unable to supply the world market, centered in Europe, because of prohibitive costs of transportation. Argentine beef was left to rot in the sun because only skins and horns could be exported to Europe. Australia was able to export wool but not mutton. North American wheat could not compete in European markets. Hence, the railroad, the steamship, refrigeration, and many other improvements in transportation that came thick and fast after 1870 completely altered the character of world trade. A worldwide system of multilateral trade evolved to bring an ever-widening exchange of goods, illustrating in reverse the restrictive effects of transportation costs.

The Effects of Transportation Costs on the Location of Industry

Transportation costs also influence international trade by affecting the *location* of production. In seeking to minimize costs of production, business firms must take full account of the transportation costs incurred in acquiring raw materials and in marketing final products. The best location for a firm is that location which minimizes total costs of production, including all transportation costs. This location may be near raw materials (*resource-oriented*), near the market or markets of the final product (*market-oriented*), or somewhere in between (*footloose*), depending upon the character of production processes.

When the cost of transporting raw materials used by an industry is substantially higher than the cost of shipping its finished products to markets, then the industry will usually locate closer to its raw material sources than to its markets. This situation exists when the industrial processes characterizing an industry use large quantities of bulky, low-value raw materials and fuels which do not enter into the final product. Such processes are described as "weight-losing" because the final product is so much less bulky or weighty than the materials and fuels necessary for its production. Steel, basic chemicals, aluminum, and lumber are among the products that utilize weight-losing industrial processes for their manufacture.

Steel production is an outstanding example of a resource-oriented industry. Loss of weight in production is very high: all of the coking coal and a big share of the iron ore are consumed in the smelting process. Thus a steel industry usually locates between deposits of coking coal and deposits of iron ore with a tendency to locate somewhat closer to coal deposits because of the greater weight loss. In the United States the bulk of the steel industry stretches from Buffalo and Pittsburgh westwards to Detroit and Chicago, getting its coal from Pennsylvania and West Virginia and its iron ore from the Lake Superior region of Minnesota. This locational pattern of steel mills had a profound influence on the creation of the American industrial heartland because so many industries are dependent on steel as a basic industrial commodity. Today the traditional locational forces are changing in the steel industry as the Mesabi ores become depleted and the United States becomes increasingly dependent on iron ore imports from Canada and South America.[18] Both the Bethlehem mill at Sparrow's Point near Baltimore and the Fairless Works at Morrisville near Philadelphia obtain iron ore by ship and are also favorably placed with respect to domestic coal, as well as **markets.**

Frequently, transportation costs are minimized for weight-losing industries at river or ocean ports where advantage can be taken of low freight rates for the water transportation of bulky products (sometimes made even more attractive by backhaul rate discrimination) and the avoidance of transshipping raw materials from one mode of transportation to another, such as from ship to railroad car. This explains, at least in part, why weight-losing industries are often found at ocean or river ports in the United States and Europe, why Sparrow's Point and the Fairless Works are favorably located even though their iron ore comes from mines thousands of miles away.

When the cost of transporting finished products is substantially higher than the cost of transporting the raw materials and fuels that are used in their manufacture, industries locate close to their markets. This relationship develops when industrial processes add bulk or weight in production, that is, they are *weight-gaining*. Then industries try to postpone manufacture of the final product until it is physically close to its market. Although United States automobile companies have concentrated basic manufacture in the Detroit area, they have established regional assembly centers within the United States and assembly centers in many foreign countries because it is much cheaper to ship unassembled auto parts than the whole vehicle.[19] Many other manufactured goods are shipped as parts to

---

[18] Technological changes such as beneficiation of iron ore at the mine, the oxygen converter process, and others are also affecting location economics in the United States steel industry.

[19] Many countries also impose high duties on whole vehicles and low or zero duties on vehicle parts in order to encourage assembly operations in their own territory.

assembly plants located near markets for the same reason. A prominent example of weight-gaining occurs in the construction of buildings where the final product is so much bulkier than its components. Thus building construction is mainly an assembly job at the construction site. Beverage manufacture offers another example of how weight-gaining processes push final manufacture towards the market. Coca Cola and Pepsi Cola ship syrup concentrate to plants all over the world which, in turn, add water to the concentrate and bottle the mixture. Recently, Scotch whiskey has started coming to the United States in concentrated form. Finally, mention should be made of the extreme market orientation shown by service industries such as wholesaling and retailing firms and transportation agencies.

When transportation costs are not an important factor on either the resource or market side or when they tend to neutralize each other, and when location close to the market is not particularly advantageous, then industries are highly mobile or footloose, locating where the availability and cost of labor and other factors of production give them the lowest manufacturing cost. Companies producing electronic components, shoes, garments, containers, and small housewares offer examples of high locational mobility.

The economics of location is extremely complex.[20] The fact that a firm may use several raw materials (including water, fuel, and power) drawn from different geographical areas and sell many products in several geographical markets can make it very difficult to determine the optimal location that minimizes transportation costs.[21] This difficulty is compounded by the need to consider also the availability and cost of factors of production (land, labor, and capital) at different locations.[22] The availability of unskilled and semiskilled labor is often decisive in location decisions, especially in market-oriented and footloose industries. In the simple two-country model we used in Chapter 3, the costs and availability (supply) of factors of production provided the basis (along with reciprocal demand) for international specialization. Now we see that the influence of trans-

---

[20] Readers interested in location theory should look into Edgar M. Hoover, *The Location of Economic Activity* (New York: McGraw-Hill Book Company, Inc., 1948); and Walter Isard, *Location and Space-Economy* (New York: The Technology Press and John Wiley and Sons, Inc., 1956).

[21] Linear programming can sometimes be used to solve this problem.

[22] Local taxes are also a factor in location. Many governments seek to attract industry to less-developed regions within their countries by offering preferential tax treatment to domestic and foreign investors. As part of its Mezzogiorno program, for example, Italy gives a 10-year tax holiday to manufacturing plants that locate in regions south of Rome.

portation costs on the location of industry adds another variable to the theory of comparative costs.

In effect, transportation inputs must be viewed, along with the traditional factors of production, as a determinant of a nation's opportunity cost and comparative advantage.[23] International specialization is dependent not only on the relative endowments of land, labor, and capital among the trading nations, but also on the cost of overcoming geographical distance, which for a given product may vary from one place to another both within and among nations, because of the location of raw materials or markets. In resource-oriented industries, transportation inputs may be a stronger influence on location and international specialization than relative supplies of productive factors. They will also be significant in determining international specialization in many market-oriented industries. Only in the case of footloose industries can we safely ignore the independent effects of transportation costs on location and international specialization. In broader terms, the influence of transportation costs on location suggests that countries which are distant from world markets for finished goods and have no substantial domestic markets will tend to have a comparative disadvantage in market-oriented industries, while countries close to world markets or with large domestic markets will attract market-oriented industries. Thus the location of a country may give it an advantage in export markets, even though its factor costs of producing some export goods are no lower (or are even higher) than the factor costs of producing similar goods in a country distant from those markets.

SUMMARY

1. In Chapter 3 several assumptions were made in order to simplify our presentation of the theory of comparative costs. In this and the next chapter we modify or withdraw these assumptions to make the theory more relevant to the actual course of international trade. In so doing, we unavoidably add to its complexity.

---

[23] In Chapter 9 of his book, *Location and Space-Economy*, Isard constructs an international trade model that utilizes "transport inputs." He states: "From the standpoint of trade theory we have introduced explicitly the distance factor (in the concept of transport inputs) and shown how the opportunity cost formulation can be easily extended to embrace industries which are typically transport-oriented intranationally." (page 215) However, Isard's model is highly simplified, and the integration of international trade and location theory to form a single theoretical system has not been accomplished as yet.

Ch. 4 / Comparative Costs in the World Economy

2. In the real world constant unit costs rarely hold in production. Because of the principle of diminishing marginal productivity, the unit cost of producing any good will start to rise at some level of output. Increasing unit costs of production generally rule out complete international specialization, and thereby narrow the opportunity for gainful international trade.
3. Although all production will experience rising unit costs if output is increased greatly, certain commodities may be produced at decreasing unit costs over a broad range of output because of internal and external economies of scale. Decreasing unit costs enlarge the opportunity for international trade and lead to complete international specialization. They provide a basis for international trade along with differences in national factor endowments.
4. Most of the international trade in manufactured goods is conducted in markets that depart in one way or another from the conditions of pure competition. The monopoly profits of monopolies and oligopolies lower the gains from international trade by introducing a discrepancy between national cost ratios and national price ratios. Monopoly and oligopoly prices, however, may be lower than purely competitive prices because of economies of scale and a rapid rate of technological advance. Nonprice competition brings a dynamic, expansive element to international trade; and, in the case of monopolistic competition, it does so without the distortion of monopoly profits.
5. Transfer costs may be divided into costs of physical transfer and the transfer costs associated with government regulation of foreign trade. Costs of physical transfer are mainly attributable to transportation. Transportation costs separate goods into two classes—domestic goods and international goods. Domestic goods do not enter international trade because transportation costs make it impossible to sell them at competitive prices in foreign markets. Hence the existence of transportation costs narrows the opportunity for international trade.
6. Transportation costs also influence the location of industry and, thereby, the international specialization of production. Location may be near raw materials (resource-oriented), near the market or markets of the final product (market-oriented), or somewhere in between (footloose), depending upon the character of production processes. In effect, transportation inputs must be viewed, along with the traditional factors of production, as a determinant of a nation's opportunity cost and comparative advantage.

QUESTIONS AND APPLICATIONS

1. (a) What is meant by "increasing costs"?
   (b) What are the effects of increasing costs on international trade? Why?
2. (a) What are the sources of economies of scale?
   (b) Why do decreasing costs lead inevitably to complete international specialization unless their effects are blocked by restrictions on trade?

3. What are the types of imperfect competition?
4. Why may the *net* effect of monopoly and oligopoly on international trade be detrimental or beneficial?
5. (a) What is nonprice competition?
   (b) Why is its effect on international trade likely to be expansive?
6. How do transportation costs directly affect the volume of international trade?
7. "Transportation costs are not simply dependent on distance and the physical character of commodities." Explain.
8. What is meant by "weight-losing" and "weight-gaining" industrial processes? How do these processes influence location?
9. Why is the "economics of location" so complex?

SELECTED READINGS

See the list of readings given at the end of Chapter 5.

CHAPTER 5

COMPARATIVE COSTS IN THE
WORLD ECONOMY (Concluded)

The task of modifying or withdrawing the assumptions underlying the simple model described in Chapter 3 in order to develop further the theory of comparative costs as an explanation of the actual patterns of world trade is continued in this chapter. In Chapter 4 the implications of increasing and decreasing costs, imperfect competition, and transportation costs were evaluated. We now look at change and heterogeneity in factor endowments, technological innovation and dissimilar production functions, unemployment, trade in services, and capital movements.

CHANGE AND HETEROGENEITY IN FACTOR ENDOWMENTS

In Chapter 3 we spoke of factors of production in terms of land, labor, and capital, and we tacitly assumed that a nation's factor endowments did not change. Actually, there are many varieties of land, labor, and capital that change both quantitatively and qualitatively over time. Technological innovations, in particular, are responsible for many shifts in factor quality and supply. In this section we consider the variability and heterogeneity of national factor endowments and their effects on international trade.

Land Factors

Land factors, or natural resources, comprise the many elements of the natural environment which contribute to the production of goods and services useful to man. Whether a natural element can and does contribute to production at any given time depends upon man's capacity and willingness to utilize it.

Contrary to popular understanding, natural resources are dynamic rather than fixed in supply. Elements of the natural environment *become* natural resources as mankind develops the need and ability to use them in production. Over the centuries man has transformed more and more of his natural environment into natural resources. Early man made only modest use of his natural environment as does the Australian bushman even today. The availability of coal had no effect on the economy of the American Indian because he had no productive use for coal and, consequently, it was not a natural resource to him. A generation ago much the same could be said of uranium for our own contemporary economy. One authority believes that the basic raw materials for industries of the future will be seawater, air, ordinary rock, sedimentary deposits of limestone and phosphate rock, and sunlight.[1] It is most likely that the oceans will become a much more important natural resource than they are at present. Fundamentally, therefore, what we call land factors, or natural resources, are dependent upon our technical knowledge and how we choose to use that knowledge. Man must be aware of the existence of natural elements, must recognize their usefulness to him, and must want and know how to exploit them before they can become natural resources possessing an economic significance.

Natural resources are conventionally classified as agricultural land, forests, fisheries, and mineral deposits. Viewed broadly, natural resources also include topographical land features, solar radiation, water, winds, and any other natural elements that contribute directly or indirectly to economic activities. Each of these natural resource types has many variations. Agricultural lands differ in natural fertility, insolation, rainfall, latitude, height, and in many other ways. Mineral deposits are even more diverse. Not only are there hundreds of different minerals, but deposits of one mineral will vary in size, accessibility, and quality. The many kinds of natural resources and the wide variations in their quality and other attributes preclude any precise measurement of the *totality* of national resource endowments or their comparison. Even international comparisons of one resource type, such as agricultural land, can be approximate only. Because of this complexity, sweeping statements about a country's resource endowment can be misleading. For example, although Switzerland is often described as "resource-poor," its topographical features (espe-

---

[1] Harrison Brown, *The Challenge of Man's Future* (New York: The Viking Press, 1956), p. 218.

Ch. 5 / Comparative Costs in the World Economy

cially the Alps) are a prime tourist attraction and also provide an abundant supply of waterpower for electricity generation.

Even though broad international comparisons of natural resources are only approximate, it is most evident that *specific* natural resources are distributed unevenly over the earth. Zimmerman classifies the frequency of resource occurrence as follows: (1) *ubiquities*, which occur everywhere, such as oxygen in the air; (2) *commonalities*, which occur in many places, such as tillable soil; (3) *rarities*, which occur in only a few places, such as tin; and (4) *uniquities*, which occur in one place, such as commercial cryolite.[2] He also points out that production processes generally involve a *combination* of materials so that usable combinations of (say) coal and iron may be quite rarely found in the same place even though both occur frequently alone. As we observed in Chapter 3, the uneven distribution of natural resources is an important cause of different factor proportions among nations.

So intimate is the relation between man and natural resources, the latter are sometimes indistinguishable from other factors of production, especially capital. We all know that much of Holland's land (about two fifths) has been reclaimed from the sea and is therefore as much capital as a natural resource. Less well known is how extensively the centuries of man's habitation in Western Europe have changed its physical nature:

> Sweat has flowed freely to bring European landscapes to their present shape. The climate and topography of the continent did not determine its present aspect. Once dense forests covered areas in France, Germany and Russia that are now almost treeless and completely under the plow. Where brush once predominated, pine woods grow. Where played the waves of the sea, rich harvests of wheat sway in the wind. Where desert marshes stretched, now great cities stand.[3]

The settlement of North America has likewise altered the landscape, soil conditions, and other aspects of the original natural environment. In more general terms, natural resources must first be discovered and then exploited, and this requires the complementary use of labor and capital.

It should be evident by now that national resource endowments are dynamic. Technological innovations develop new natural

---

[2] *Erich W. Zimmermann's Introduction to World Resources*, ed. Henry L. Hunker (New York: Harper and Row Publishers, 1964), p. 120.

[3] Jean Gottmann, *A Geography of Europe* (New York: Holt, Rinehart and Winston, 1962), p. 52.

resources from materials that had no previous economic use, and they also improve the accessibility of existing resources. New discoveries (also aided by technological advances) add to the known supply of resources. Offsetting this expansion is the exhaustion of natural resources through use and misuse. Oil wells run dry, iron mines peter out, forests sometimes disappear, fertile grasslands can become dustbowls, water tables sink, and so on. Because of this exhaustion process (as well as higher usage), the United States must now import many minerals, such as iron ore and copper, that were formerly supplied entirely from domestic sources or even exported in large quantities.

Human Factors

International variations in human factor endowments are both quantitative and qualitative. Aside from variations in overall size which derive mainly, although not exclusively, from variations in population, the *composition* of labor and management often differs markedly among nations. In poor, underdeveloped economies the bulk of the labor force is unskilled, occupied in traditional forms of agriculture, while only a small fraction is skilled in industrial pursuits, and an even smaller fraction has technical and management training. In contrast, the labor force in highly developed economies, such as the United States or Western Europe, is mainly composed of semiskilled and skilled workers in industry, white collar workers engaged in service occupations, and a significant proportion of technical and management people.

International differences in the quality of human factors are difficult to measure, but nonetheless important. Again they are most striking between poorly developed and highly developed economies. Qualitative variations arise because humans are shaped by an economic, political, social, and cultural milieu that is not everywhere the same nor ever likely to be. Thus there is a diversity among peoples in ways that influence economic performance, such as physical vigor, motivations and attitudes towards work, technical skills, organizational and management capacities, and many other attributes. In addition to disparities among individuals living in different cultures, there are also dissimilarities in social conditions which bear directly on economic performance. Some societies are rigid, offering little opportunity for lower-class individuals; other societies are open, allowing individuals to move upwards to higher social levels (or fall to lower levels). In a rigid society movement from one labor group to another is a slow, painful process which limits the capacity of the economy to make positive adaptations to change.[4]

Qualitative disparities among the human factors of different countries are so pervasive that skilled workers (or any other subtype of labor) in one country are never quite the same as in another country and may, in fact, be very dissimilar. Such qualitative disparities influence comparative costs in the same way as quantitative disparities. If workers in one country are generally twice as productive as workers in a second country because of quality differences (as distinguished from differences arising from the use of complementary factors, especially capital), then the effect on comparative costs is equivalent to doubling the size of the first country's labor force.

The gist of this discussion is that *at any point of time* the human factor endowment of a nation will be heterogeneous and will differ both in composition and quality from the human factor endowments of other nations. This, as we know, is a basis for profitable international trade. But this is not all. Each nation's human factor endowment changes *through time*, injecting a dynamic element into its comparative cost structure.

First, the overall supply of labor is strongly affected by the rate of growth and the age distribution of population. Second, the many subtypes of labor—unskilled, semiskilled, technical, etc.—are subject to different rates of change. The radical expansion in the number of whitecollar workers and the simultaneous decline in the number of unskilled workers in the United States since the turn of the century are illustrative. Third, the quality of labor alters with changes in education, technology, and economic opportunity. An upgrading of labor has been particularly pronounced in this country—jobs once staffed by high school graduates are now staffed by college graduates. Conversely, the quality of certain subtypes of labor may worsen. It is said that the productivity of coal miners in Europe is now less than before the war after full account is taken of relevant circumstances. Again, certain subtypes of labor may disappear along with their jobs due to technological displacement. These transformations

---

[4] Even in the mobile societies of advanced economies, the subtypes of labor tend to form "noncompeting" groups with little movement of people among them over the short run. The persistence of unemployment in the United States is a case in point. Many of the American unemployed are workers whose services are no longer in demand because of technological innovations which require more education and new skills. See pages 109-110 for further remarks on **structural unemployment.**

in the level, composition, and quality of the labor force introduce continuing changes in the relative factor endowments of a nation and hence in its foreign trade.

What we have said concerning labor is substantially true of the other human agent of production—management. Changes in the size and the quality of management are largely determined by the freedom of economic opportunity, the rate of growth of the economy, and the rate of technological advance. When economic opportunity is stultified by a social caste system or by monopoly organization of the economy, when the economy is stagnant, and when the techniques of production are static, the management factor will initiate few changes in its supply relative to the supplies of other factors of production.

In an economy like the United States, however, management is a most dynamic factor of production. In this country, management, adapted to the operation of large-scale business, has grown at a faster pace than other types of management; and the rapid rise of business schools suggests the qualitative changes that have occurred, and are occurring, in this factor.

Capital

Capital is the most dynamic factor of production, and it exhibits most strongly the influence of changing technology. An economy becomes more productive by increasing the supply of its capital relative to other factor supplies and by improving the quality of its capital. Today, the American factory worker produces more in less time than did his grandfather, primarily because he has more (and better) machines and more horsepower to help him.

Growth in the quantity and quality of capital is spurred by technological improvements. An advancing economy produces not only more factories, utilities, machines, and other varieties of capital, but also more productive factories, utilites, etc., to take the place of the old. The growth of capital may markedly alter the relative factor endowment of a country within a few generations. The outstanding contemporary example is the Soviet Union, which has been transformed from a predominantly agricultural economy into the world's second industrial power within a period of approximately thirty years.

Drastic changes in a nation's capital supply usually cause substantial shifts in the nature of its foreign trade. In Chapter 2 we observed that the United States was once primarily an exporter of agricultural products and raw materials, and an importer of manufactures. Now, with an abundant supply of capital, this country is a major exporter of manufactures and a heavy importer of raw materials.

Nations differ widely both in their stocks of capital goods and in their capacity to add to capital stocks through investment. Capital stocks constitute *real* capital which includes many varieties of equipment, buildings, and other instruments of production, as well as "social capital" such as transportation, communications, and educational facilities. Basically, however, real capital must be financed out of savings representing the surplus of current production over current consumption. Unlike real capital, investment funds (*financial* capital) may be viewed as a homogeneous factor of production commanding a single price which is the long-term interest rate adjusted for variations in risk.

Consumption exhausts most of the production of poor economies unless heroic austerity measures are undertaken by government authorities. Hence their rates of investment tend to be low, perpetuating international differences in capital endowments. Because the supply of investment funds is low, long-term interest rates are high. Unless stultified by government restrictions, political unrest, or other disturbances, investment funds will flow from advanced economies with high rates of saving to underdeveloped economies in order to earn higher returns. But even under the best of circumstances, international investment can do no more than supplement domestic investment which must carry the main burden of financing additions to a country's capital stock.[5] As a result of persisting disparities in existing capital stocks and the rate of new capital investment among nations, capital endowments will continue to be a key determinant of international differences in comparative costs.

Factor Change and Heterogeneity: Effects on Trade

This short appraisal of factor endowments has shown that each of the factors of production is subjected to many influences which alter its supply within a nation over time. Despite the generally low international factor mobility, factor changes are a continuing phenomenon within nations, causing shifts in factor proportions and in comparative cost structures. Hence a nation's trade is not stereotyped or static, but frequently changing in magnitude, composition, and

---

[5] Chapters 20 and 21 examine these and other aspects of underdeveloped economies and the international flow of investment capital.

direction at a rate which varies from time to time and from country to country. It follows that nations must adjust continuously to shifts in comparative advantage because they cannot reasonably expect their future trade to be a mere repetition of their present trade. In this dynamic world, nations that quickly adapt their trade and economies to change (regardless of its origin) have an obvious advantage over nations with sluggish responses.

This review has also pointed out that land, labor, and capital are heterogeneous, comprising many subfactors. This raises the possibility that a given subfactor may be *unique* to a nation with no counterparts in other nations. We can visualize this possibility most easily in the case of a mineral exploitable in only one country, but it could also happen with a labor or capital subfactor, at least in the short run. The possibility of subfactor uniqueness is heightened for labor and management when we take into account the many qualitative differences arising out of dissimilar socio-cultural environments.

The existence of a unique factor in a country's endowment may constitute a basis for trade independent of dissimilar proportions of the *same* factors, which is the basis for trade in the simple model. However, this exception is probably not too important: few subfactors are perfectly unique (without any substitutes), and even so, they are not likely to remain unique indefinitely in a world of rapid technological change. In this regard we can call to mind how Chile lost its sodium nitrate monopoly during World War I when chemists discovered an economical process for making nitrates out of nitrogen drawn from the air.

More important, the existence of numerous subfactors indicates that national comparative cost structures are highly complex, and that a broad similarity in the cost structures of two countries in terms of the three traditional factors most probably masks a rich diversity in their relative supplies of subfactors. For this reason the possibility of identical comparative costs among nations is a theoretical contingency only. Nations can always find a basis to trade profitably with each other.

TECHNOLOGICAL INNOVATION AND DISSIMILAR PRODUCTION FUNCTIONS

The role that technology plays in shaping economic activities must be included in a modern theory of trade. In the preceding section we spoke of technological innovation as an agent of change in factor endowments. In this section we take a closer look at the implications of technological innovation for the theory of comparative costs.

Technology is the accumulated knowledge, skills, and techniques that are applied to the production of goods and services. Inventions and discoveries are the source of technology, but they must be utilized in production to become technology. In our own age inventions and discoveries come mainly out of systematic research programs oriented towards technical innovations. The immense resources now devoted to research, coupled with the drive by management to apply its results to business enterprise, have created an environment of explosive technological change, especially in the advanced industrial economies. Technological innovations affect not only production and domestic and international trade, but also the living styles of countless millions of peoples around the globe. One innovation alone—the automobile— has already transformed American society and is starting to do the same in Europe and elsewhere.

Technological innovations assume two basic forms: (1) new and more economical ways of producing existing products (new production functions), whether by innovations specific to the production of certain products (such as a new way of making a chemical) or by general innovations that affect a broad range of production (such as automation); and (2) the production of wholly new products, industrial and consumer, such as electronic computers, television, plastics, jet airplanes, synthetic fibers (to name only a few of the more prominent products introduced since the end of World War II), and improvements in existing products. These two forms of technological innovation are closely interrelated; many new products, for example, are capital goods which make possible new production functions.

The simple comparative cost model in Chapter 3 made two implicit assumptions about technology: (1) the existence of a given state of technology, and (2) the same access to technology everywhere, that is, all countries use the same production functions. These assumptions do not hold in the real world. When we drop them, what happens to the factor proportions theory of trade?

International Differences in Production Functions

Technical discoveries do not occur in all countries at the same pace; nor are discoveries spread instantaneously from one country to another; nor are they applied to production at the same rate in different countries. Advanced industrial countries generate most of the new technology which then spreads to other countries after varying time lags. The most prominent example of this diffusion process is the Industrial Revolution (a combination of technical innovations, involving the steam engine, new kinds of machinery, the factory system of organization, and other developments adding up to a transformation of the entire economy) which started in England in the eighteenth century, then spread to Western Europe and North America during the following century, to Japan and Russia early in this century, and is still spreading to many parts of South America, Africa, and Asia. Because the diffusion process is not instantaneous, we can distinguish between nations that are technological leaders and nations that are technological followers.

At any given time, therefore, countries may be using different technologies to produce the same products, that is to say, dissimilar production functions.[6] Since the bulk of technological innovations takes the form of capital, a technological leader usually employs a capital-intensive method to produce a good which is traditionally labor or land-intensive. Dissimilar production functions are most strikingly evident in agriculture. In the United States a technical revolution has transformed agriculture over the past generation, encompassing a high level of mechanization, improved soil care, pest control, new varieties of seed, etc., and a large-scale organization of production which resembles a factory more than traditional farming. Agriculture in this country has become capital-intensive (there are only four million farmers and half of them produce almost all the commercial agricultural output) while in many parts of the world it has remained labor-intensive. The employment of capital-intensive production functions (made possible by new technology) explains how the United States has retained, and probably increased, its comparative advantage in agriculture despite rising wage and land costs.

The significance of this discussion is that *a good cannot be uniquely defined as capital-intensive or labor-(land) intensive because it may be produced in both ways in countries using different production functions.* Hence the link between factor endowments and the *specific* kinds of products a country will export and import is now broken.[7] We can still say a nation will export those goods that use

---

[6] A production function is the relationship between the output of a good and the necessary factor inputs. It may be most simply expressed as follows: $P = f(a, b, c \ldots)$ where P is output and $a, b, c \ldots$ are factor inputs.

[7] This may also be true even when countries use the *same* production function for a specific good if there is a high degree of factor substitutability (that is, the technical coefficients of production can assume a broad range of values) such that

relatively large inputs of its abundant factors and import those goods that use relatively large inputs of its scarce factors, but we cannot say what those goods will be without knowing the production functions in question. In brief, by creating dissimilar production functions among nations, technological innovation can serve as a basis of international trade, along with dissimilar factor endowments, economies of scale, and location.

We can show this by means of a simple two-country (A and B), two-product (wheat and textiles), two-factor (labor and capital) model in which both countries have the same factor proportions (providing no basis for trade) but use different production functions to produce wheat. Specifically, both countries produce textiles with the same production function which requires 3 units of labor and 2 units of capital to produce one unit of textiles. However, in producing one unit of wheat, country A uses one unit of labor and 4 units of capital (a capital-intensive process) while country B uses 5 units of labor and one unit of capital to produce wheat in the traditional labor-intensive way. Under these conditions, the two countries have different comparative costs: country A has a comparative advantage in wheat and country B, a comparative advantage in textiles, and both will gain from trade.

	Country A (dollars)	Country B (pesos)
Unit price of labor	2	4
Unit price of capital	1	2
Unit cost of textiles	8	16
Unit cost of wheat	6	22

Changing Technology and International Trade

Changing technology not only creates dissimilar production functions among countries at any given point of time, but also trans-

---

at one set of factor prices a product is (say) capital-intensive while at another set of factor prices it becomes labor-intensive. (See Footnote 4 on page 53 for an early comment on coefficients of production.) Technically, this situation is called *factor reversal;* its frequency is a matter of dispute among economists. Part of the problem lies in the difficulty of distinguishing the use of the *same* production function with different coefficients of production, on the one hand, from the use of *different* production functions, on the other, in concrete situations where both differences may be operative.

forms the trade of nations over time. We have already observed that technology determines what natural elements become land factors, making these factors dynamic rather than passive. Technology also vitally affects the training and education of labor, giving rise to qualitative differences among nations. Capital is directly influenced by technology because so much technology takes the form of capital equipment and, more basically, because technology contributes importantly to a nation's investment capacity by raising per capita productivity and real income.

The bearing of technology on international trade is not limited to the changes it provokes in the size and quality of factor endowments. Technology also furnishes a basis for economies of scale, and it has profoundly affected the scope of international trade through innovations in transportation and communication. By fostering new products, technology has a direct impact on the composition and growth of international trade. The competitive strength of United States exports owes much to product innovations in capital and consumer goods—as older products, such as automobiles, are displaced by foreign competition, they are replaced by new products, such as commercial jet aircraft, that for a time have no foreign counterparts. For this reason alone, a rapid rate of technological progress is a vital competitive weapon in world markets.

New products do not always expand the volume of world trade; they may simply displace older *export* products or actually contract the volume of trade as substitutes for *import* products. Nylon has largely eliminated the raw silk trade, synthetic rubber casts a pall over the long-run future of natural rubber, plastics have cut into the international trade of some traditional products, and coal, displaced by petroleum, has a relatively minor role in world commerce compared to the past. There is abundant evidence, however, that technological innovations in all their many forms have been, and continue to be, a positive force in world trade.

Technical knowledge is diffused among nations today more quickly than ever before. Diffusion occurs in several ways. Technical and other news media transmit knowledge of new discoveries from one country to another, as does trade in new products. Companies in advanced countries like the United States license technical know-how and assistance to foreign companies in return for royalty payments and fees, or set up their own operations abroad using new technology.[8] Diffusion is especially swift among the industrial countries because they have the capacity to use immediately the new technical knowledge. An outstanding example of this rapidity is the transistor. Developed by the United States, it was Japan that first used the transistor to make small radios which then found a big market in the United States. Technological leadership is constantly threatened, therefore, by innovations elsewhere. Technologically speaking, nations must run hard to avoid falling behind. In the nineteenth century, comparative advantages changed slowly over a generation or more; in our own times, a country may enjoy a comparative advantage in a product for only a few years before technical diffusion and imitation or new technical discoveries wipe it out.

UNEMPLOYMENT AND COMPARATIVE COSTS

In Chapter 3 we assumed that a nation's factors of production were fully employed at all times. Hence the production of one good could only be increased by decreasing the production of one or more other goods; that is, the opportunity cost of every good was positive. When, however, a nation's factors of production are not fully employed, it is possible to increase the production of one or more goods without lowering production elsewhere by using idle supplies of land, labor, management, and capital. In this event, the new production is a net addition to the national income, and its opportunity cost is zero.

Does the existence of unemployed factors of production invalidate the theory of comparative costs? Let us look first at the case of *cyclical* unemployment that results from a deflationary gap in effective demand and cuts across all sectors of the economy.

Cyclical Unemployment

It is sometimes argued that cyclical unemployment justifies any sort of production regardless of comparative costs since it will make a net addition to a country's national income. Thus a country will benefit by restricting imports and using idle factors to produce similar goods at home—the opportunity cost of imports is the exports that must be exchanged for them, whereas the opportunity cost of new domestic production is zero. Hence international specialization and trade must give way to self-sufficiency when unemployment arises in the domestic economy.

---
[8] See Chapter 26.

This argument was especially persuasive during the depression of the thirties, but it rests upon several questionable assumptions: (1) full employment is the overriding national economic objective; (2) international trade must be sacrificed to attain full employment; and (3) the international consequences of a domestic full-employment policy can be safely ignored. We now turn to a brief evaluation of these assumptions.

First, employment for the sake of employment cannot be a sound national objective. Full employment is most productive when the factors of production are allocated in accordance with comparative costs. In that way each factor is engaged in production in which its productivity is highest. Full employment is a means to the higher objective of national welfare, and this is maximized only when productivity cannot be raised by shifting factors of production from one economic activity to another. When imports are curtailed to afford opportunities for domestic employment, the losses occasioned by a lesser degree of international specialization must be set against any gains in national production.

Second, even though the gains in national production are greater than the losses brought about by the decline in international specialization, the policy of sacrificing international trade to increase domestic employment is not in the national interest, for there are other ways of stimulating employment that do not require the restriction of trade. An anticyclical employment policy should place main reliance on government fiscal and monetary policies that feed the inadequate stream of purchasing power in the economy. Not only will such policies alleviate unemployment in the domestic economy, but by sustaining or increasing imports they will also benefit foreign countries.

Third, the policy of curtailing imports to stimulate domestic employment is never in the interest of the community of nations. Actually that policy amounts to exporting unemployment to other nations since the decline in imports will depress foreign economies. Moreover, foreign countries can retaliate by restricting their own imports. As a consequence, international relations become embittered, international trade spirals downwards, and few countries are better off in terms of employment while many are much worse off in terms of economic welfare. This sequence took place to an unfortunate extent in the early thirties.

While condemning the policy of exporting one's unemployment, we must also recognize the fact that few nations are capable of overcoming any but a small amount of cyclical unemployment by the use of fiscal and monetary policies alone unless international economic cooperation is forthcoming. Such policies tend to increase imports while, at the same time, exports may be falling because of depression abroad, and few nations have the reserves to finance the resulting gap between their exports and imports until recovery sets in abroad. When, however, nations—particularly the major trading nations—cooperate with each other by extending credit and by harmonizing their domestic recovery measures, it may be possible for them to restore employment without seriously curtailing trade.

In treating cyclical unemployment in the preceding sections we have merely scratched the surface of this complex subject. For one thing, there is a wide difference between unemployment that affects only a minor trading country and unemployment that engulfs the entire community of nations. There is little doubt that large-scale unemployment, particularly in the United States, would have depressing effects upon international trade, although quick use of enlightened policy would keep us from making the mistakes of the thirties. We can conclude, however, that the presence of cyclical unemployment does not vitiate the gains from international specialization and trade even though it does place them in jeopardy. International trade can only thrive in a world economy whose productive resources are not idled by global depression.

Structural Unemployment

Unemployment can also occur when the composition of a nation's output and/or the quality and supply of its factors of production fail to adapt to new patterns of demand and competition. That is to say, the *structure* of the economy is no longer suited to changing markets. Declining industries and regions make their appearance, and workers gradually lose their jobs while the rest of the economy is growing. The basic disturbance causing structural unemployment may originate at home, abroad as specific export markets dry up or foreign competitors enter domestic markets (import competition), or both at home and abroad.[9]

---

[9] Structural unemployment in the United States today mainly results from changes in the domestic economy: the automation of industry is cutting the demand for unskilled and semiskilled workers and mechanization of agriculture is forcing the family farm out of existence. The Appalachian region, in particular, has been badly hurt by both changes.

When import competition appears to be causing structural unemployment, workers and management in the affected industry are quick to demand that government curtail imports by higher tariffs, quotas, or other means.[10] This protectionist solution attempts to preserve the status quo at the cost of losing the benefits of international specialization. If no other solution to the problem of structural unemployment were possible, protection would be justifiable as a way of utilizing labor and capital that would otherwise stand idle. But this is not the case. Basically, what is needed is a reallocation of productive factors, shifting them out of declining industries into expanding ones.

The capacity of an economy to adapt to change and thereby avoid or minimize structural imbalances is dependent primarily on the mobility of its factors of production and its overall rate of growth. When labor and capital move quickly out of declining industries into growing industries, then structural unemployment is transitional rather than prolonged. Mobility will be enhanced if the economy as a whole is growing, generating new opportunities for employment and capital investment. When, on the other hand, labor does not shift easily from one job to another or from one place to another, then structural unemployment may endure for a generation or more. Immobility is further intensified by a slowly growing economy.

All economies suffer from factor immobility, but it is most pervasive in underdeveloped countries where economic, social, and cultural conditions favor stability over change. For such countries import protection may be necessary to give them time to transform their economies, but the ultimate solution is to develop a capaciy to grow and adjust to change.[11] For developed countries, however, protection is not a reasonable alternative to measures that are aimed directly at increasing labor and capital mobility. In the last analysis, the cause of structural unemployment lies in a failure to adapt to technological and other changes. As we have stressed earlier, the world economy is dynamic, and nations can obtain the full advantages of international specialization only by responding quickly to new market opportunities and competitive challenges.

---

[10] See Chapter 15.
[11] See Chapter 20 for a further discussion of this point.

INTERNATIONAL TRADE IN SERVICES

Up to this point we have been talking explicitly only about the merchandise trade of nations. Actually, nations also exchange a great variety of services. The most important single service in international trade is transportation, amounting in value to about 10 percent of merchandise trade. Other important international services include personal travel, the use of foreign-owned capital, communications, and insurance.

Does the theory of comparative costs explain international trade in services? The answer is yes. Many services, notably transportation, are directly dependent on the movement of merchandise. Furthermore, the merchant marine of a country can be evaluated in terms of comparative costs just as any other industry. It is clear, for example, that the United States has a comparative disadvantage in merchant shipping vis a vis Western Europe and Japan. At present, only about one tenth of United States exports and imports are carried in United States bottoms despite government subsidies and cargo preference laws. Similarly, nations may have a comparative advantage (or disadvantage) in tourism, insurance, or in other international service industries.

To conclude, the theory of comparative costs can be applied to the analysis of service as well as to merchandise trade among nations. Service trade extends the range of industries that contribute to a country's exports and imports, adding to the complexity of international trade. By the same token, service trade enhances the gains from international specialization.

CAPITAL MOVEMENTS

When we drop the assumption of no international capital movements, a country's exports of goods and services need not equal its imports since international loans and/or gifts may be available to finance the gap between them. The function of short-term capital movements in helping to bring about equilibrium in a nation's balance of payments is explored in Chapter 9.

Apart from their equilibrating function, capital movements (especially long-term) can alter a nation's factor proportions by changing the supply and quality of its capital endowment. International capital movements may also act as carriers of technological innovations, and make possible economies of scale in borrowing countries. Finally, capital movements may accelerate the economic growth of recipient countries with manifold effects on the composition and volume of their imports and exports.

A RECAPITULATION OF THE THEORY OF COMPARATIVE COSTS

After all the modifications we have made in the assumptions underlying the simple trade model presented in Chapter 3, what can we say about the theory of comparative costs? Does the theory explain *actual* trade patterns?

The simple model attributes a country's comparative cost structure to its relative factor endowments. Although this theory recognizes the influence of demand on factor prices, it relegates factor demand to a minor role in the determination of comparative costs by assuming a similarity in national patterns of demand. Since countries differ in their relative factor endowments, they develop dissimilar comparative cost structures that serve as a basis for gainful trade. Specifically, a country will export those goods whose production requires large inputs of its relatively abundant (cheap) factors and import those goods whose production requires large inputs of its relatively scarce (expensive) factors.

This model is simple because it uses several restrictive assumptions. Some of these assumptions may be modified to make them more "realistic" without endangering the theory's fundamental proposition, namely, the dependence of comparative costs on factor endowments. Thus increasing costs, imperfect competition, changes in factor endowments, unemployment, service trade, and capital movements may be absorbed into the theory without difficulty although they undoubtedly complicate the explanation of trade. When we modify certain other assumptions, however, we call into question the essence of the theory or, at the very least, introduce additional explanations of trade.

We have encountered three conditions that would generate gainful trade among nations *even if there were no differences in factor endowments*. One is the presence of economies of scale that make possible decreasing unit costs over a broad range of output. In general terms, economies of scale create a comparative advantage for many industries located in developed countries with big domestic markets because such countries are most likely to initiate mass production and large-scale business organization. In the economic history of Western Europe and North America there are many examples of industries that developed comparative advantages, partly if not wholly, from economies of scale first experienced in supplying the home market.

Because of their bearing on industrial location, transportation inputs must also be considered, along with the traditional factors of production, as a determinant of a nation's opportunity cost and comparative advantage.

Technological innovations in production functions and products generate a third condition for gainful international trade, apart from any differences in factor endowments. Because technological innovations first appear in individual countries and spread to other countries only after varying time lags, the way of producing the same good (the production function) may differ from one country to another. In the United States agriculture is capital-intensive while in many other countries it is labor-intensive. Hence a good cannot be defined *uniquely* as capital-intensive or labor- (land-) intensive as was done in the simple trade model which assumed all countries have the same access to technology. In short, the link between factor endowments and the *specific* products a country will export and import is now broken.[12] Furthermore, the high degree of *factor heterogeneity* makes it very difficult, if not impossible, to validate empirically the relationship between factor endowments and comparative cost structures. In the words of Haberler:

> In general, we may say that with many factors of production, some of which are qualitatively incommensurable as between different countries, and with dissimilar production functions in different

---

[12] The "Leontieff paradox" is pertinent to this statement. Using input-output tables and 1947 foreign trade figures, Wassily Leontieff found that United States exports were less capital-intensive and more labor-intensive than United States imports. This finding provoked a fierce controversy in the economic literature (which we cannot discuss here) because it seemed to contradict the factor proportions theory of trade. According to that theory, United States exports should be more, not less, capital-intensive than United States imports. Leontieff himself tried to explain the paradox by suggesting that United States labor is three times as productive as labor elsewhere. A more satisfactory explanation, however, would appear to be the existence of dissimilar production functions among nations. It may be, for example, that import-competing industries in the United States are comparatively capital-intensive because United States capital is a better substitute than United States labor for foreign natural resources and labor. See W. W. Leontieff, "Factor Proportions and the Structure of American Foreign Trade: Further Theoretical and Empirical Analysis," *Review of Economics and Statistics*, November, 1956; and his original article "Domestic Production and Foreign Trade: The Amercan Capital Position Re-examined" which has been reprinted in *Economia Internazionale*, February, 1954. Gottfried Haberler gives a succinct treatment of the Leontieff paradox in *A Survey of International Trade Theory*, Special Papers in International Economics, Princeton University, No. 1, July, 1961, pp. 21-22.

countries, no sweeping *a priori* generalizations concerning the composition of trade are possible.[13]

We are led, then, to the following restatement of the theory of comparative costs. The presence of dissimilar cost ratios (opportunity costs) offers an opportunity for gainful trade among nations. These dissimilar cost ratios derive from dissimilar factor endowments, economies of scale, locational advantages (or disadvantages), and technological innovations. Which basis of trade is most important in a given instance will depend, among other things, on the country and product in question. It is reasonable to suppose that economies of scale and technological innovations are important determinants of the comparative costs of advanced industrial countries, whereas the comparative costs of nonindustrial countries are more related to factor endowments (especially natural resources.) If we believe, like Ellsworth, that most products are most efficiently produced by a process that uses intensively some particular factor or subfactor, then factor endowments provide the *main* explanation of trade for both industrial and nonindustrial countries.[14]

Some New Approaches to a Theory of Trade

Dissatisfaction with the factor-proportions version of comparative costs, especially in regard to trade in manufactured goods, has stimulated economists in recent years to develop new approaches to a theory of trade. Here are a few examples:

Linder argues that differences in factor proportions explain trade in natural resource-intensive products, but not in manufactures. A country, he says, cannot achieve a comparative advantage in a manufactured good that is not demanded in the home market. Only after the home market has grown enough to give an industry economies of scale can that industry successfully enter foreign markets. It follows that trade in manufactures will be most intensive among countries with similar markets, demand structures, and per capita incomes. Countries export manufactured goods that reflect their own consumption patterns and standards of living.[15] In effect, Linder makes economies of scale the *main* explanation of trade in manufactured goods.

---

[13] G. Haberler, *op. cit.*, p. 23.

[14] P. T. Ellsworth, *The International Economy*, (3d ed.; New York: The Macmillan Company, 1964), p. 157.

[15] Staffan B. Linder, *An Essay on Trade and Transformation* (New York: John Wiley and Sons, 1961), Chapter 3.

Kravis suggests that "availability" is the major determinant of trade. Trade tends to be limited to products that are *not* available at home either because they are not produced at all or because production can be increased only at much higher costs, that is to say, home supply is inelastic. Kravis attributes unavailability primarily to a lack of natural resources, but it can also result from technological innovation and product differentiation.[16] In brief, Kravis considers natural resources as the principal, although not exclusive, basis of trade in contrast to the factor proportions theory that explains trade in terms of *all* factors of production.

Posner stresses the role of technical changes that occur in some industries and in some countries, but not in others. Trade occurs during the lag before other countries catch up with the innovating country.[17]

Interest in economic growth has also stimulated the construction of models that trace the effects of many kinds of growth—capital accumulation, population increase, and technical innovation—on trade over time.[18] Economists are also devoting more attention to the impact of foreign trade on economic growth.[19] These are all efforts to *dynamize* international trade theory and thereby provide an explanation of the process (or processes) by which trade patterns change through time.

The theory of comparative costs, then, is a living theory that is being modified to explain the greater complexity of contemporary world trade. Although by no means fully satisfactory, the theory of comparative costs is a powerful instrument for the analysis and evaluation of trade patterns and international commercial policies.

Do Comparative Costs Explain Actual Trade Patterns?

Attempts have been made to test the empirical validity of the theory of comparative costs by measuring the extent to which differences in relative labor productivity and production costs in selected

---

[16] I. B. Kravis, "'Availability' and Other Influences on the Commodity Composition of Trade," *Journal of Political Economy*, April, 1956.

[17] M. V. Posner, "International Trade and Technical Change," *Oxford Economic Papers*, October, 1961.

[18] A concise description of these models is presented in W. M. Corden, *Recent Developments in the Theory of International Trade*, "Special Papers in International Economics, Princeton University, No. 7, March, 1965, Chapter III.

[19] A good example is Charles P. Kindleberger, *Foreign Trade and the National Economy* (New Haven: Yale University Press, 1962), Chapters 12, 13, and 14.

manufacturing industries are reflected in differences in the relative export performance of the United States and Great Britain.

MacDougall has investigated 24 industries participating in British-American trade before the Second World War when United States wages were double British wages. He found that United States exports to Britain were greater than British exports to the United States for seven of the twelve industries where United States ouput per worker was *more* than double British output. In contrast, British exports to the United States were greater than United States exports to Britain for all twelve of the industries where United States output per worker was *less* than double British output.[20]

Stern has carried MacDougall's study forward, using data for 1950. In that year American wages were 3.4 times as high as British wages. Sampling 39 industries, Stern found that for 15 industries where United States output per worker was *more* than 3.4 times British output, United States exports exceeded British imports in United States-British trade in eleven cases. However, for the 24 industries where United States output was *less* than 3.4 times British output, British exports were bigger than United States exports in 21 cases.[21]

The MacDougall and Stern studies are incomplete tests of the theory of comparative costs. For one thing, they consider only labor productivity which depends on all the factors of production, economies of scale, technology, etc. Thus these studies do not tell us why comparative costs are what they are. For another, their samples are drawn from the industrial sector only. Furthermore, they are limited to two countries. All things considered, however, these studies demonstrate that even a simplified version of comparative costs has empirical validity and can go a long way towards explaining actual patterns of trade.

SUMMARY

1. There are many varieties of land, labor, and capital that change both quantitatively and qualitatively over time. Technological innovations, in particular, are responsible for many shifts in factor quality and supply.

---

[20] G. D. A. MacDougall, "British and American Exports: A Study Suggested by the Theory of Comparative Costs," *Economic Journal,* Part I, December, 1951, and Part II, September, 1952.

[21] Robert M. Stern, "British and American Productivity and Comparative Costs in International Trade," *Oxford Economic Papers,* October, 1962.

2. National resource endowments are dynamic. Technological innovations develop new natural resources from materials that had no previous economic use, and they also improve the accessibility of existing resources.

3. Each nation's human factor endowment changes through time, and at any point of time it differs both in composition and quality from the human factor endowments of other nations.

4. As a result of persisting disparities in existing capital stocks and the rate of new capital investment among nations, capital endowments will continue to be a key determinant of international differences in comparative costs.

5. Nations must adjust continuously to shifts in comparative advantage. The existence of numerous subfactors indicates that national comparative cost structures are highly complex.

6. At any given time countries may be using different technologies to produce the same products, that is to say, dissimilar production functions. Hence there is no fixed relationship between factor endowments and the *specific* kinds of products a country will export and import.

7. Changing technology not only creates dissimilar production functions among countries at any given point of time, but also transforms the trade of nations over time.

8. The presence of *cyclical* unemployment does not vitiate the gains from international specialization and trade even though it does place them in jeopardy. In the last analysis, the cause of *structural* unemployment lies in a failure to adapt to technological and other changes.

9. The theory of comparative costs can be applied to the analysis of services as well as merchandise trade among nations.

10. When we drop the assumption of no international capital movements, a country's exports of goods and services need not equal its imports since international loans and/or gifts are available to finance the gap between them.

11. We have encountered three conditions that would generate gainful trade among nations *even if there were no differences in factor endowments:* economies of scale, locational advantages (or disadvantages), and technological innovations. We are led to say, then, that dissimilar cost ratios (opportunity costs) which offer an opportunity for gainful trade among nations may derive from any of these three conditions as well as from factor endowments.

12. Dissatisfaction with the factor-proportions version of comparative costs, especially in regard to trade in manufactured goods, has stimulated economists in recent years to develop new approaches to a theory of trade.

13. Statistical studies demonstrate that even a simplified version of comparative costs has empirical validity.

QUESTIONS AND APPLICATIONS

1. What are the effects on trade of factor change and heterogeneity?
2. What is technology? How does technological innovation give rise to dissimilar production functions among nations?
3. Illustrate with an arithmetical example how dissimilar production functions between two countries can create dissimilar cost ratios even when both countries have the same factor proportions.
4. Does the existence of cyclical unemployment invalidate the theory of comparative costs? the existence of structural unemployment? Explain.
5. What is the "Leontieff paradox"? Is it really a paradox?

SELECTED READINGS

Corden, W. M. *Recent Developments in the Theory of International Trade,* Special Papers in International Economics No. 7. Princeton: Princeton University Press, 1965. Chapters II and III.

Ellsworth, P. T. *The International Economy,* 3d ed. New York: The Macmillan Company, 1964. Part II.

Haberler, G. *A Survey of International Trade Theory,* Special Papers in International Economics No. 1. Princeton: Princeton University Press, 1961. Chapters II, III, and IV.

Harrod, Roy F. *International Economics,* Cambridge Economic Handbooks. Chicago: The University of Chicago Press, 1958. Chapters II, III, and IV.

Hoover, E. M. *The Location of Economic Activity.* New York: McGraw-Hill Book Company, Inc., 1948.

Kenen, P. B. *International Economics,* Foundations of Modern Economics Series. Englewood Cliffs, New Jersey: Prentice-Hall, Inc., 1964. Chapter 2.

Kindleberger, C. P. *Foreign Trade and the National Economy.* New Haven: Yale University Press, 1962.

Ohlin, B. G. *Interregional and International Trade.* Cambridge: Harvard University Press, 1935. Part II.

Ricardo, D. *Principles of Political Economy and Taxation,* Everyman's Library. New York: E. P. Dutton and Co., Inc., 1912. Chapter 7.

CHAPTER 6

THE TRANSFER OF INTERNATIONAL PAYMENTS

If one has money, making domestic payments presents no problem—dollars are acceptable throughout the United States, pounds sterling serve equally well in the United Kingdom, and the French need only francs in their dealings with each other. But suppose an American resident must make payment to a British resident, or a British resident must make payment to a French resident. What then? The American has only dollars, the Britisher desires payment in pounds sterling, and the French creditor asks for payment in francs. This problem of making payments internationally is solved by the mechanism of the foreign exchange market. The purpose of this chapter is to elucidate the fundamental principles that underlie the functioning of this market, to explain the role of commercial banks and international financial centers, and to trace the effects of international payments upon the money supply of the nation. The techniques and procedures that are followed in the actual financing of international trade are taken up in Chapter 27.

TRANSFER THROUGH PRIVATE COMPENSATION

One way to make international payments is the method of private compensation. Say an American resident *owes* a British resident 20 pounds sterling, which at the current rate of exchange is equivalent to $60. Suppose further that a second American resident is *owed* $60 by a second British resident. Then the following steps may be taken to solve the payments problem for all four parties. (1) The first American resident, a debtor, hands over $60 to the second American resident, a creditor. In this way the former is able to liquidate his debt in dollars while the latter receives in dollars what is owed him by the second British resident. (2) Simultaneously, the second British resident, a debtor, gives 20 pounds sterling to the first British resident, a creditor. Again, the debtor is able to pay in domestic currency and the creditor is paid in domestic currency. Thus by two simultaneous transactions, both of which are purely domestic, all four parties obtain satisfaction.

Private compensation demands considerable patience and a streak of luck on the part of the participants. Not only must the American debtor find an American creditor (or vice versa) and the corresponding British parties be brought together, but the amounts owing and owed must also be equal if there is to be a full cancellation of all obligations. This cumbersomeness rules out private compensation as a mode of international payments unless, for one reason or another, payments are not possible through the foreign exchange market. The real importance of private compensation lies in the fact that it illustrates in a clear-cut fashion the basic principle of all methods of international payment—*the clearance or offsetting of one international debt against another.* In our example the debt owed by the first American resident was offset against the debt owed by the second British resident, and since both debts were equal the clearance was perfect.

THE FOREIGN EXCHANGE MARKET

The overwhelming majority of international payments is made through the medium of foreign exchange traded in foreign exchange markets. We shall first examine the nature of foreign exchange and then the functions of the foreign exchange market.

Foreign Exchange

Foreign exchange is a financial asset involving a cash claim held by a resident of one country against a resident of another country. Foreign exchange is represented by a wide variety of credit instruments. Thus an American resident may hold foreign exchange in the form of foreign currencies, bank balances in foreign countries, bills of exchange drawn on foreign residents, or other highly liquid claims on foreigners. Despite this proliferation of forms, however, most foreign exchange used to effect international payments consists of bills of exchange of some sort. A clear conception of the essential nature of the bill of exchange, therefore, is necessary to an understanding of the transfer of international payments.

Ch. 6 / The Transfer of International Payments 121

The Bill of Exchange.[1] The bill of exchange is an extremely adaptable instrument, and many varieties have been developed to suit the particular needs of international finance. Basically, the bill of exchange is an unconditional order in writing, addressed by one person to another and signed by the former, that requires the person to whom it is addressed to pay on demand or at a fixed and determinable time in the future a specified sum of money to order.

There are three parties to a bill of exchange: (1) the *drawer* who orders payment and initiates the bill of exchange, (2) the *drawee* who is ordered to pay, and (3) the *payee* to whom payment is to be made. The bill of exchange is a negotiable instrument that may be transferred from one holder to another by endorsement. An example of a bill of exchange used in making international payments is illustrated below.

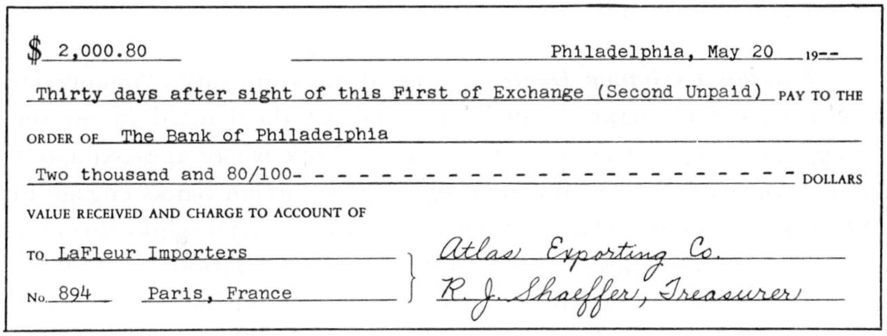

```
$ 2,000.80                                      Philadelphia, May 20    19--
Thirty days after sight of this First of Exchange (Second Unpaid)  PAY TO THE
ORDER OF  The Bank of Philadelphia
Two thousand and 80/100- - - - - - - - - - - - - - - - - - - - - - - DOLLARS
VALUE RECEIVED AND CHARGE TO ACCOUNT OF
TO LaFleur Importers                    }  Atlas Exporting Co.
No. 894    Paris, France                }  R. J. Shaeffer, Treasurer
```

Figure 6-1. A BILL OF EXCHANGE

Bills of exchange are distinguished in many ways. The nature of the drawee is of great significance. A *trade bill* is drawn against a commercial debtor who is usually an importer, whereas a *bank bill* is drawn against a bank.[2] Trade bills are usually drawn by exporters and other commercial creditors, while bank bills may be drawn by commercial creditors or by banks (banker's bill).

Both trade and bank bills may be payable immediately at sight or at some time in the future as expressed by a certain number of days after sight or a certain number of days after the date on which the bill was drawn. Thus we have sight bills, 30-day sight bills, 60-day sight bills, 30-day date bills, etc. Few bills of exchange used in international finance run beyond 90 days.

---

[1] This section offers only a brief explanation of the bill of exchange. A discussion of its use in international trade is reserved for Chapter 27.

[2] Actually most *domestic* payments are made with bank bills—"bills of exchange" drawn against domestic banks, which we call checks.

Another distinction arises out of the presence or absence of title documents. A bill of exchange that is accompanied by documents, such as a bill of lading, invoice, etc., is called a *documentary bill*, while one that is not accompanied by documents is known as a *clean bill*. These distinctions are not mutually exclusive—a bank or trade bill may be payable on sight and clean, payable 30 days after sight and documentary, and so on.

A bill of exchange becomes foreign exchange when it represents a highly liquid claim held by a domestic resident against a foreign resident, that is, when the payee is a domestic resident and the drawee is a foreign resident. Thus a trade bill drawn by an American exporter against an Italian importer, a banker's bill drawn by an American bank against a foreign bank, or a bill of exchange drawn by a foreign resident on another foreign resident but payable to a domestic resident are all examples of foreign exchange.

Foreign Exchange Dealers. Most dealers are large commercial banks located in major financial centers. In the United States the foreign exchange market is mainly in New York where approximately twelve American banks and some agencies of foreign banks engage in the bulk of foreign exchange transactions. Commercial banks throughout the United States maintain correspondent relations with these New York banks so that it is possible to buy or sell foreign exchange almost anywhere in the country. Foreign countries possess similar arrangements.

Dealers make up the foreign exchange market by standing ready at all times to buy and sell bills of exchange against domestic money. Dealers gain their livelihood by selling bills at a higher rate than they purchase them. Bills of exchange are bought from domestic exporters and others who have demand claims against foreign residents. Bills of exchange drawn by dealers on their bank balances abroad are sold to domestic importers and others who must make payment to foreign residents. Exchange brokers, acting as intermediaries between the exchange dealers, serve to unify the foreign exchange market and keep it competitive.

Functions of the Market

Foreign exchange markets perform three major functions: (1) the transfer of international payments, (2) the provision of credit, and (3) payment at a distance.

Transfer of International Payments. Foreign exchange markets relieve the individual and business concern from the problem of making or receiving foreign payments by using the same principle of debt clearance that was exemplified in private compensation. But the wholesale volume of clearance, the developed skills and facilities of the foreign exchange dealers, and the competitive nature of the market (barring exchange control by government) make for a far greater degree of efficiency and convenience.

Provision of Credit. Although the primary function of the foreign exchange market is the transfer of international payments, the market also acts as a source of credit. Most importers are neither willing nor prepared to pay cash for their purchases; they much prefer to delay payment until funds have been received from the resale of the merchandise. On the other hand, many exporters have little capacity or desire to extend credit to foreign buyers and thereby tie up their working capital. The fact that foreign buyers are residents of another country, conduct business in a different legal and political environment, and are usually quite distant as well, also makes exporters wary of affording them direct commercial credit.[3] The absence of a source of external credit, therefore, would sharply curtail the volume of international trade. By providing such credit, the foreign exchange dealer helps his own business by helping the business of the foreign trader.

Payment at a Distance. The ease with which the foreign exchange market carries out the transfer and credit functions is due, in large measure, to the means of instant communication that link exchange dealers in one country with dealers throughout the world. The cable, telegraph, and telephone enable payments to be made between distant points literally at the speed of light. Postal services offer a less expensive but relatively slower means of communication. The intimate contact of one foreign exchange dealer with another regardless of physical distance is exploited to the fullest degree through reciprocal and cooperative arrangements. Since all of the services that result from these facilities are available to any who deal in the foreign exchange market, we may consider them as representing a third function of the market.[4]

---

[3] The problems involved in granting foreign credits are discussed in Chapter 27.

[4] By permitting hedging against exchange risks, the forward **exchange market** performs a fourth function. See Chapter 8.

THE ROLE OF COMMERCIAL BANKS

Commercial banks located in the principal financial centers are the dominant dealers in foreign exchange, and the actual transfer of payments from one country to another is usually made through bills of exchange drawn by one bank against another. Commercial banks also provide most of the credit in foreign trade by purchasing time bills of exchange from exporters. As a consequence, international payments consist of interbank transfers, that is, of changes in the ownership of demand deposits which domestic and foreign banks maintain with each other.

The Banker's Bill

Commercial banks that deal in foreign exchange maintain demand deposits in foreign correspondent banks or in their own foreign branches. To transfer funds to a foreign resident, the bank needs simply to write a draft against its deposit in the resident's country and send it to him. This draft is a *banker's bill of exchange* drawn by a domestic bank against a foreign bank. If individuals or business firms were in the habit of maintaining balances in foreign banks, they could make international payments by personal drafts sent to foreign creditors. Actually large corporations with overseas branches sometimes follow this practice, and thereby circumvent the banker's bill of exchange. The considerable risks associated with variations in the exchange rate, however, and the imposition of exchange controls by governments, as well as inconvenience, are sufficient to limit this practice. Most individuals and business concerns prefer to rely on the banker's bill of exchange to effect foreign payments.

The Clearance of Interbank Debt

This chapter opened with a discussion of private compensation, pointing out that international payments are made through the offsetting or clearance of debt. We then asserted that private compensation is unnecessary when foreign exchange markets are in operation, but that clearance of debt remains the basic principle of international payments. We now inquire further into the nature of the debt clearance performed by the foreign exchange market.

We have remarked that the foreign exchange market effects international payments through the clearance of bank debt rather than private debt as was true in private compensation. To illustrate,

Ch. 6 / The Transfer of International Payments   125

let us return to our earlier example of private compensation. There, an American resident owed 20 pounds sterling (equivalent to $60) to a British resident while a second American resident was owed $60 by a second British resident. We saw how payment was made through the clearance of one private debt against the other, but we now suppose that this clearance occurs in the foreign exchange market. We further assume that the American creditor is an exporter and the American debtor, an importer; and that initiative for payment is taken by the Americans.

First, the American exporter draws, say, a bill of exchange payable in pounds sterling at sight against the British importer, and discounts this bill at his bank for dollars at the bank's buying rate for sterling.[5] The American bank now sends the bill to its correspondent bank in the United Kingdom, which, in turn, presents it to the British importer for immediate payment.[6] The British importer pays by drawing a sterling check for 20 pounds against his bank in favor of the American bank. In this way the latter acquires a sterling demand deposit of 20 pounds, which is held in its correspondent bank in the United Kingdom. At this stage the American bank has exchanged dollars, paid to the American exporter, for a sterling balance that makes it a creditor of its correspondent bank. Thus the original debt between the American exporter and the British importer has been transformed into an interbank debt.

The American bank is now able to draw a banker's bill of exchange against its foreign balance and thereby sell sterling exchange. The opportunity to do this occurs when an American importer comes to the American bank to buy 20 pounds sterling in order to pay a British exporter. The bank now draws a draft against its sterling deposit and sells it to the American importer at the bank's selling rate for sterling.[7] The importer then remits the draft to the British exporter who cashes it at his own bank. In selling this banker's bill for

---

[5] The exporter will not receive the full face value of his bill of exchange because it will take a few days before the bill can be presented to the British importer for payment. The longer the maturity of the bill, the greater the discount. The exporter has used the bank's buying rate for sterling in calculating the price of his export shipment.

[6] If the bill of exchange were a time bill, then the importer would "accept" the bill but would not pay it until the bill matured. See Chapter 27.

[7] Since the bank's selling rate is higher than its buying rate, a draft for 20 pounds sterling will cost something more than $60. This was taken into account by the importer in making his decision to buy from the British exporter.

20 pounds sterling, the American bank fully utilized the sterling deposit that arose from its previous purchase of a sterling bill of exchange from the American exporter—both payments offset each other and the clearance was perfect. The debt owed by the British importer to the American exporter was converted into a debt (demand deposit) owed by the British correspondent bank to the American bank. This interbank debt was then canceled when the American bank assumed the sterling debt of the American importer.

But suppose the American bank had no sterling to sell. In that event the American importer would not have been able to pay his sterling debt. The foreign exchange dealer must be able to buy and sell an equal amount of foreign exchange if he is to effect international payments; otherwise there is no basis, or only a partial basis, for clearance. Of course, this example is highly simplified. A single dealer need not clear his exchange transactions as long as the dealers making up the foreign exchange market are able to do so as a group. Moreover, dealers in one country may extend credit to dealers in another in order to permit the full clearance of foreign exchange transactions. Further, the supply of bills of exchange originates not only in the export of merchandise but also in all the credit items comprising the balance of payments. Similarly, the demand for bills of exchange arises out of all debit items in the balance of payments.[8] Nevertheless, there are times when the available supply of foreign exchange falls short of demand.

When the amount of foreign exchange in demand is equal to the amount of foreign exchange in supply, then foreign exchange dealers, taken as a group, are able to bring about a perfect clearance of international payments and the foreign exchange market is said to be in *equilibrium*. When, however, the amounts of foreign exchange demanded and supplied do not coincide, the market is in *disequilibrium*. In that event some sort of adjustment to achieve a balance is required whose nature will depend upon the institutional structure of the foreign exchange market and the character of the disequilibrium: gold and short-term capital movements may replenish a deficient supply of exchange, the rate of exchange may vary and remove the deficiency, or the government may ration the available supply of exchange by a regime of exchange control. These matters are more fully discussed in Chapters 9, 10, and 11.

---

[8] The balance of international payments is treated in Chapter 7.

The Exchange Risk

Today American banks that deal in foreign exchange maintain only minimum working balances in many foreign countries. This practice results from the prevalence of exchange control and the risk of variations in exchange rates. Exchange control often limits the availability and use of foreign balances owned by domestic banks while alterations in the exchange rate bring shifts in the value of foreign balances in terms of domestic money. Before World War I and for a short period in the 1920's most countries were on the international gold standard, and there was no risk of blocked funds or of wide swings in the exchange rate. Accordingly, exchange dealers were often willing to maintain substantial foreign deposits although, even then, they did not permit them to rise beyond a certain level. The foreign exchange dealer is able to get along with only a small inventory of foreign exchange by matching his sales and purchases of foreign exchange during each trading day. In this way he minimizes the risks of exchange rate variations and of exchange control.

THE MONETARY EFFECTS OF INTERNATIONAL PAYMENTS

It should now be clear that international payments are made through the clearance of debt between domestic and foreign banks. But this clearance of interbank debt also involves the increase or decrease of privately held demand deposits when bank debt is substituted for private debt; and because demand deposits are part of the national money supply, the result is a rise or fall in the supply of money.[9] Such changes in the supply of money constitute the *monetary effects* of international payments.

International Payments as Bank Debits and Credits

Since international payments cause changes in the assets and/or deposit liabilities of the respective national banking systems, we can trace the monetary effects of international payments by entering payments transactions in a simple T account drawn up for each banking system. The T account has two sides, one showing changes in assets,

---

[9] Banking systems are able to increase or decrease the money supply because they need maintain only fractional reserves behind their demand deposits. When a banking system acquires assets, they are paid for by the creation of demand deposits; and when assets are sold, demand deposits are liquidated. The reader who is unfamiliar with the monetary role of the banking system is referred to any modern text in basic economics.

the other showing changes in liabilities. Using T accounts, we now evaluate the monetary effects of a purchase and sale of sterling exchange by the American banking system. To simplify our presentation, we shall assume that the American banking system comprises only one bank and that the same is true of the British banking system.

Purchase of Sterling Exchange by an American Bank

When an American exporter sells a sterling bill of exchange to his bank, he gets paid in the form of a demand deposit at the bank. This transaction appears as follows in the T account of the American bank:

Assets	Liabilities
+ Sterling bill	+ Demand deposit (exporter)

The exporter can spend his demand deposit as he sees fit; the money supply of the United States (the creditor country) has *increased*.

Next, the American bank sends the sterling bill to its British correspondent bank which, after payment by the British importer, adds the proceeds to the demand deposit maintained with it by the American bank. The effect of this transaction upon the American bank is to convert one asset (sterling bill) into another asset (sterling deposit):

Assets	Liabilities
— Sterling bill + Sterling deposit	

At the same time the T account of the British correspondent bank is as follows:

Assets	Liabilities
	— Demand deposit (importer) + Demand deposit (American bank)

The purchase of a sterling bill by the American bank thus causes an *increase* in the money supply of the United States (the creditor country) and a *decrease* in the supply of money owned by domestic residents in the United Kingdom (the debtor country). In the latter country a demand deposit has been transferred from the ownership of the British importer to the ownership of the American bank.

Sale of Sterling Exchange by an American Bank

When the American bank sells a sterling bill to a domestic importer, the following changes occur in its assets and liabilities:

Assets	Liabilities
— Sterling bill	— Demand deposit (importer)

That is to say, the supply of money in the United States *decreases* as the demand deposit of the American importer is extinguished when he purchases the sterling bill from the bank.

At the same time the payment of the sterling bill by the British correspondent bank against which it was drawn involves a shift in the ownership of a sterling demand deposit from a foreign resident (the American bank) to a domestic resident (the British exporter who received the sterling bill from the American importer). This change appears as follows in the T account of the British bank:

Assets	Liabilities
	— Demand deposit (American bank)
	+ Demand deposit (British exporter)

Net Monetary Effects

In the previous sections we examined the monetary effects of a purchase and sale of sterling exchange by the American banking system. We might have chosen other examples of international payments, such as transactions in bills of exchange payable in dollars or in bills of a third currency rather than in sterling, but in every instance we should have found that the supply of money owned by domestic residents of the creditor or exporting country increased while the supply of money owned by domestic residents of the debtor country decreased. Over a period, therefore, the *net* effects of international payments upon the money supply of the nation will depend upon the net discrepancy between receipts and payments of foreign exchange.[10] If receipts exceed payments, the country will experience a rise in the money supply held by domestic residents; if receipts are less than payments, the opposite change in the money supply will occur. When receipts and payments are equal, there is no net change in money supply and, consequently, no net monetary effects; this is true when the foreign exchange market is in equilibrium.

The presence of net monetary effects is, therefore, a sign of disequilibrium in the foreign exchange market and in the balance of payments. Adjustment toward a balance between the receipts and the payments of foreign exchange is in order, and this adjustment will be facilitated by the influence exerted by the net monetary effects on the economic activity of the domestic and other countries unless this influence is counteracted by government measures. The role of net monetary effects in the removal of disequilibrium in the balance of payments is treated in Chapter 9.

INTERNATIONAL FINANCIAL CENTERS

Domestic and foreign banks are able to act as dealers in foreign exchange because they are willing to hold balances in other countries. The mechanism of international payments, therefore, is based upon a pattern of interbank debt that covers the entire world. This pattern may be decentralized, centralized, or somewhere between these two extremes.

Decentralized and Centralized Systems of International Payment

When the banking system in one country is linked to the banking systems in all other countries by a series of bilateral debt arrangements, the number of arrangements equal to the number of other countries, and when all international payments are cleared bilaterally, the system of international payment is fully decentralized. Figure 6-2 shows a fully decentralized payments system for a world of six countries.

When, on the other hand, banks in one country are linked to banks in other countries through balances maintained at *one* financial center, and when all international payments are cleared through this center, then the system of international payments is fully centralized. Figure 6-3 illustrates this system for a world of six countries.

---

[10] More precisely, the net effects of international payments will depend on the net discrepancy between receipts and payments of foreign exchange arising out of *autonomous* transactions in the balance of payments. See Chapter 9.

Figure 6-2
PERFECTLY DECENTRALIZED SYSTEM OF INTERNATIONAL PAYMENTS: SIX COUNTRIES

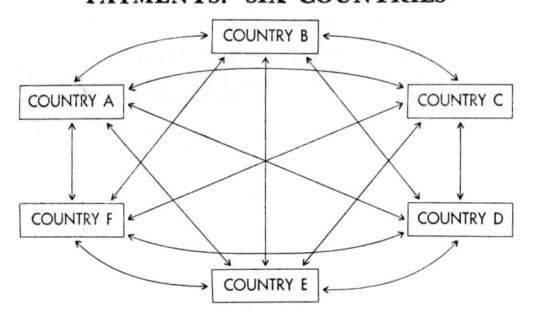

Arrows indicate reciprocal bank balances of foreign exchange dealers

Figure 6-3
PERFECTLY CENTRALIZED SYSTEM OF INTERNATIONAL PAYMENTS: SIX COUNTRIES

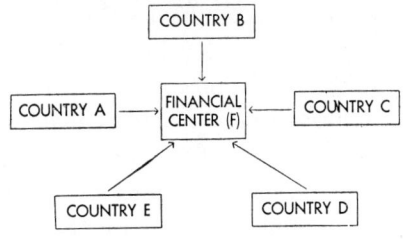

Direction of arrows indicates the location of foreign bank balances maintained by foreign exchange dealers

The London Financial Center

During the half century that preceded World War I, the system of international payments was highly centralized. The focus of this system was London: banks throughout the world maintained sterling balances in London and transferred funds from one country to another by drawing sterling bills. A Brazilian exporting coffee to the United States would draw a sterling bill on the American importer, who, when the time came to buy, would remit a sterling draft. In this way international payments occurred through shifts in the ownership of sterling balances located in London. Although most countries were on the gold standard at this time, it was the pound sterling that made up most of the world's payments.

The prominence of London was due to many factors. First, the United Kingdom was the world's greatest importer, and its policy of free trade permitted foreign suppliers an easy access to its domestic market. Second, the London money market was unparalleled in its efficiency and resources—banks, acceptance houses, discount houses, dealers, etc., made up a market in which sterling funds could be invested or borrowed on short term in any amount and at any time. Third, London was by far the paramount source of long-term investment capital; its highly evolved securities markets dealt in the securities of the entire world. First trader, first financier, and first investor of the world during a period when trade and finance were unrestricted by government policies, it was inevitable that most international payments should flow to, from, and through the London financial center.

The Rise of New York

During the 1920's New York and, to a lesser extent, Paris rose to challenge the financial supremacy of London. The blows that the United Kingdom had suffered during the war and the simultaneous emergence of the United States as the leading international creditor were the main factors responsible for this development.

The resulting decentralization of the international payments system brought to the fore certain problems that had not existed in the earlier payments system centered on London. For one thing, there was less economy in the use of the world's supply of monetary gold. When there is only one dominant international financial center, there is little need for gold on the part of the peripheral countries, aside from domestic reserves, since foreign exchange may be easily borrowed from the center. When there are several financial centers, however, each center must maintain gold reserves behind its international obligations, and the peripheral countries may also increase their gold holdings. In the twenties the shortage of gold was also heightened by the large acquisitions of the United States during the war.[11]

Another problem that arose in the twenties was the movement of speculative capital between London and New York, stemming from the general uncertainty regarding the future course of exchange rates and from lack of faith in the ability of certain countries to maintain their newly restored gold standard. The movement of this capital was made easier by the decentralization of the international payments

---

[11] United States Gold reserves rose from $1.7 billion in December, 1914, to $2.7 billion in December, 1918. Reserves continued to rise until December, 1924, when they reached $4.1 billion. Board of Governors of the Federal Reserve System, *Banking and Monetary Statistics* (1943), p. 544.

system; when there is only one financial center, there is less likelihood of a sudden flight of capital since it can move only to a peripheral country. In the twenties the volatility of short-term capital movements also heightened the gold shortage since each financial center was compelled to maintain greater reserves behind its foreign obligations. Despite these drawbacks the decentralized system of the twenties, based on the London-New York axis, would probably have developed into a more workable arrangement in time. It was destroyed, however, by the onset of world depression in the early thirties.

The Contemporary Payments System

Today the international monetary system rests on two financial centers—New York and London. Foreign governments (central banks) maintain balances at these centers which, together with gold, constitute their official international reserves. Private foreign banks rely mainly on dollar and sterling balances to finance their foreign exchange transactions. Probably two thirds of all international payments are made in dollars or in sterling. New York is the dominant center while London is important to Sterling Area countries in the Commonwealth. In recent years the balance of payments deficits experienced by the United States and the United Kingdom and the continuing growth in Western Europe's financial strength have stimulated demands for a reform of the international monetary system. The contemporary system, the difficulties that beset it, and proposed remedies are examined in Chapter 22.

SUMMARY

1. International payments involve the exchange of one country's money for the money of another country. This transfer function, along with the functions of credit and payment at a distance, is performed by the foreign exchange market. Dealers in foreign exchange are mainly commercial banks located in major financial centers, such as New York and London. The basic principle of the system of international payments is the clearance of debt whether private debt as in private compensation, or bank debt as in the foreign exchange market.
2. Foreign exchange is a money claim held by a resident of one country against a resident of another. Foreign exchange appears in tangible form as a wide variety of credit instruments all of which, however, are either money itself or other highly liquid claims. Despite the great number of forms of foreign exchange, most foreign exchange that is used to effect international payments consists of bills of exchange of some sort. Bills of exchange vary according to the nature of the drawer and the drawee, the maturity, and the existence of accompanying documents.

3. Dealers in foreign exchange transform private debt into interbank debt, and it is the clearance of this debt through banker's bills of exchange that provides the basis of the system of international payments. Since foreign exchange dealers are exposed to the risks of variations in the exchange rate and of exchange control, they seek to carry only a minimum inventory of foreign exchange by balancing sales against purchases during each trading day.

4. International payments cause a decrease in the domestic money supply of the debtor or importing country, and an increase in the domestic money supply of the creditor or exporting country. When payments and receipts do not coincide, there is a net monetary effect; the foreign exchange market and the balance of payments are also in disequilibrium. Adjustment to bring about a balance between payments and receipts of foreign exchange is then in order.

5. The system of international payments may be decentralized, centralized, or somewhere between these two extremes. Before World War I the London financial center was supreme, and the system of payments was highly centralized. During the twenties, however, New York rose to challenge London and the payments system became decentralized with certain resulting difficulties. Today New York is the dominant international financial center, but there are widespread demands for a reform of the world's monetary system.

QUESTIONS AND APPLICATIONS

1. How is international payment achieved through private compensation?
2. (a) What is foreign exchange?
   (b) What form of foreign exchange is usually used to effect international payments?
3. What are the functions of the foreign exchange market?
4. Explain how the foreign exchange market effects international payments through the clearance of interbank debt.
5. What is the exchange risk?
6. Using T accounts, trace the monetary effects of an international payment resulting from a sight draft drawn by an American exporter against a French importer.
7. What is the meaning of decentralized and centralized systems of international payment?

SELECTED READINGS

Crump, Norman. *The ABC of the Foreign Exchanges*. London: Macmillan Co., Ltd., 1951. Chapters 1-7.

Holmes, Alan R. and Francis H. Schott. *The New York Foreign Exchange Market*. New York: Federal Reserve Bank of New York, 1965.

Southard, Frank A. *Foreign Exchange Practice and Policy*. New York: McGraw-Hill Book Company, Inc., 1940.

CHAPTER 7

THE BALANCE OF
INTERNATIONAL PAYMENTS

During the course of a year the residents of one country engage in a vast number and variety of transactions with residents of other countries—exports and imports of merchandise and services, cash payments and receipts, gold flows, gifts, loans and investments, and other transactions. These transactions are interrelated in many ways, and together they comprise the international trade and payments of the national economy. Before we can analyze and evaluate a nation's international transactions, however, they must be classified and aggregated to make a balance of payments.

As a statistical classification and summary of all economic transactions between domestic and foreign residents over a stipulated period (ordinarily one year), the *balance of payments* of a nation affords an overall view of its international economic position. For this reason, the balance of payments is particularly helpful to government authorities—treasuries, central banks, stabilization agencies, etc.—who are directly charged with the responsibility of maintainng external economic stability. Moreover, international trade is so important to many countries that the balance of payments must be carefully considered in the formulation of domestic economic policies, such as employment, wages, and investment.

The balance of payments of a country may also influence the decisions of business. The experienced international trader or investor does not overlook the intimate bearing of the balance of payments upon the foreign exchange market and the course of government policy. A domestic exporter may hesitate to deal with an importer if he suspects that the authorities of the importer's country will shortly impose or tighten exchange controls in the face of an adverse balance

135

of payments. Dealers in foreign exchange also pay close attention to the balance of payments of countries whose currencies they handle in daily transactions. Failure to realize the close dependence of international business upon the balance of payments of the domestic and foreign countries has often led to losses or even outright business failures.

THE COMPILATION OF THE BALANCE OF PAYMENTS

Certain principles underlying the compilation of the balance of payments of a nation are worth emphasis. First, only economic transactions between domestic and foreign *residents* are entered in the balance of payments. Second, a distinction is made between *debit* and *credit* transactions. Third, a distinction is made between *current* and *capital* transactions. International transactions are entered in appropriate categories, such as merchandise, travel, and long-term capital movements, in accordance with these principles.

The Concept of Residence

The balance of payments summarizes all economic transactions between domestic and foreign residents. Residence should not be confused with the legal notions of citizenship or nationality.

Individuals who represent their government in foreign countries, including members of the armed forces, are always considered residents of their own country. Thus when an American serviceman buys a glass of wine in France, an international transaction occurs that enters the balance of payments of both the United States and France.

Individuals who do not represent a government are considered to be residents of that country in which they have a permanent residence and/or in which they find their "center of interest." In some instances an individual's center of interest may be in doubt; but ordinarily such criteria as customary place of work, residence of employer, or principal source of income are sufficient to determine it. In the event of conflict, the permanent place of habitation takes precedence over center of interest. For example, an individual working at the United Nations in New York who does not represent a foreign government, but who resides here permanently, is treated as a resident of the United States despite his foreign center of interest.

In preparing a balance of payments, the question of individual residence is much less important than the question of business residence. A corporation is a resident of the country in which it is incorporated, but its foreign branches and subsidiaries are viewed as foreign residents. Hence, shipments between an American concern and its overseas branch are international transactions and, as such, are entered in the United States balance of payments. At times the residence of a business may be difficult to decide. For example, a company may be incorporated in the domestic country, owned by residents of a second country, and conduct all of its business in a third country. In most instances, however, the residence of a business enterprise is readily apparent.

Government residence is the clearest of all: all government agencies are residents of their own country regardless of location.

International Transactions as Debits and Credits

Transactions between domestic and foreign residents are entered in the balance of payments either as debits or credits. *Debit transactions* are all transactions that involve payments by domestic residents to foreign residents. *Credit transactions* are all transactions that involve receipts by domestic residents from foreign residents.

This distinction is most clearly seen when we examine transactions between American and foreign residents and assume that all payments and receipts are made in dollars.[1] Then debit transactions involve dollar payments by Americans to foreigners, and credit transactions involve dollar receipts by Americans from foreigners.

What transactions involve dollar payments to foreign residents? They may be listed as follows:

1. Imports of merchandise.
2. Transportation services bought from foreign residents.
3. Purchases of American residents traveling abroad.
4. Services provided by foreign-owned capital in American production.
5. Miscellaneous services bought from foreign residents.
6. Gifts to foreign residents.
7. Investment abroad by American residents.
8. Imports of monetary gold.

Each of these transactions implies dollar payments by American residents to foreign residents. This is most apparent in the case of imports of merchandise and services. Americans must pay for the

---

[1] The balance of payments is usually drawn up in the currency of the domestic country. Regardless of the currency in which they are made, international payments and receipts may be expressed in the domestic currency by the use of appropriate exchange rates for conversion from foreign to domestic currencies.

merchandise, transportation, travel accommodations, and miscellaneous services that they buy from foreign residents. Americans must also pay interest and dividends for the use of foreign-owned capital in the United States. Similarly, American residents make dollar payments when they give to foreign residents or invest in foreign countries. Finally, Americans must pay for the gold that they import from abroad.

Conversely, the following transactions involve dollar receipts from foreign residents and are entered in the balance of payments as credits:

1. Exports of merchandise.
2. Transportation services sold to foreign residents.
3. Purchases of foreign residents traveling in the United States.
4. Services provided by American-owned capital in foreign production.
5. Miscellaneous services sold to foreign residents.
6. Gifts received from foreign residents.
7. Investments in the United States by foreign residents.
8. Exports of monetary gold.

Exports of merchandise and services are financed by dollar payments of foreign residents, which are, of course, dollar receipts for American residents. The services of American-owned capital abroad provide American investors with receipts of interest and dividends from foreign residents. Americans also receive dollars from the gifts of foreign residents and from investments made by foreign residents in the United States. Exports of gold, like merchandise exports, must be paid for by foreign residents and thereby create dollar receipts for Americans.

Current and Capital Transactions

Besides classifying international transactions as debits and credits, the balance of payments also distinguishes between *current transactions,* which involve merchandise and services, and *capital transactions,* which involve investments and monetary gold. All merchandise and service transactions are entered in the current account, while all investment and monetary gold transactions are entered in the capital account. Gift transactions and any other unilateral transfers may be entered in the current account or in a separate third account.

Ch. 7 / The Balance of International Payments   **139**

This distinction between current and capital transactions in the balance of payments facilitates the analysis of a country's international economic position. The current account tells us how much the nation is earning through the export of merchandise and services to other countries and how much the nation is spending through the import of merchandise and services. When the nation is earning more than it is spending internationally, then the net balance on the current account is a credit. When current payments exceed current receipts, the net balance on the current account is a debit.

The capital account shows whether domestic residents are investing abroad more or less than foreign residents are investing in the domestic country. It also indicates whether there is a net export or import of monetary gold.

The gift account reveals whether gifts to foreign residents are greater or less than gifts from foreign residents.

The relationships between the current, the capital, and the gift accounts of the balance of payments and their significance will become evident when we examine an actual balance of payments of the United States.

INTERNATIONAL CAPITAL MOVEMENTS

When American residents invest abroad, the United States is said to experience a *capital outflow*. Conversely, when foreign residents invest in the United States, this country experiences a *capital inflow*.[2]

A capital outflow gives rise to dollar payments to foreign residents and is, therefore, a debit entry in the balance of payments. In return for these dollar payments, American investors receive financial claims (bonds, stocks, deeds to property, etc.) against foreign residents that will be realized as dollar receipts at some future date when the investment is liquidated.[3]

A capital inflow is a credit in the balance of payments because it involves dollar receipts for Americans. In return, foreign investors receive financial claims against American residents.

When American investments abroad are liquidated, the dollars received by the investors constitute a capital inflow for the United

---

[2] International investment involves both loan and equity capital. See Chapter 21.

[3] Interest, dividends, and other income received by investors during the life of investments are entered as credits in the current account of the investing country's balance of payments.

States. Conversely, the liquidation of foreign-owned investments in the United States represents a capital outflow for this country.

We can look at international capital movements in a somewhat different way. A capital outflow occurs when either (1) domestically held financial claims against foreign residents are increased or (2) foreign-held financial claims against domestic residents (domestic liabilities) are decreased. That is to say, a country experiencing a capital outflow becomes more of an international creditor or less of an international debtor.

On the other hand, a capital inflow occurs when either (1) domestically held financial claims against foreign residents are decreased or (2) foreign-held financial claims against domestic residents (domestic liabilities) are increased. A capital inflow makes a country less of an international creditor or more of an international debtor.

Over the year the *net* international claims of a country will be increased, or its *net* international liabilities decreased, if its capital outflow exceeds its capital inflow, and conversely. The net capital movement over the year may be ascertained by an analysis of the capital account of the balance of payments.

There are many kinds of international claims and liabilities. Consequently, capital flows may occur in a number of ways. Securities representing creditor or ownership claims against private business firms and governments, and bank balances representing claims against banks, are the most common kinds of claims (or from the point of view of the other party, liabilities) involved in international capital movements.

A capital outflow is often referred to as a *capital export,* and a capital inflow, as a *capital import.* Although this terminology is apt, it often leads to confusion because the beginning student may be led to treat a capital export or import in the same way that he treats a merchandise export or import. This confusion can be avoided by keeping in mind that a capital outflow or export represents a dollar payment to foreign residents and hence is a debit item in the balance of payments. Conversely, a capital inflow or import involves dollar receipts by domestic residents and, accordingly, is a credit item in the balance of payments. In contrast, merchandise and service exports give rise to dollar receipts (credits), while merchandise and service imports give rise to dollar payments (debits).

THE BALANCE OF PAYMENTS OF THE UNITED STATES

We are now prepared to evaluate an actual balance of payments. For this purpose we shall use the balance of payments of the United States in 1958 as shown in Table 7-1.[4]

Table 7-1

BALANCE OF PAYMENTS OF THE UNITED STATES IN 1958
(Millions of Dollars)

	Debits (—)	Credits (+)
Current Account		
(1) Net military transfers under grants		$ 2,510
(2) Merchandise, excluding military	$12,944	16,207
(3) Transportation	1,477	1,644
(4) Travel	1,454	794
(5) Miscellaneous services	847	1,275
(6) Military transactions	3,365	279
(7) Income on investments	604	2,876
Total merchandise and services	20,691	25,585
(8) *Net balance on current account*		4,894
Unilateral Transfers		
(9) Private remittances (net)	517	
(10) Government (net):		
(a) Military	2,510	
(b) Other	1,790	
(11) *Total (net)*	4,817	
Capital Account		
(12) Long-term capital movements (net)	3,165	
(a) Net change in U. S. investment abroad	3,188	
(b) Net change in foreign investment in U. S.		23
(13) Short-term capital movements (net)		432
(a) Net change in U. S. investment abroad	699	
(b) Net change in foreign investment in U. S.		1,131*
(14) Monetary gold (net)		2,275
(15) Errors and omissions (net)		381

* Includes all transactions in United States government securities.

SOURCE: United States Department of Commerce, *Survey of Current Business* (March, 1959).

---

[4] United States balance of payments policy in the 1960's is treated in Chapter 22. There we shall learn that 1958 marked the beginning of big deficits in the United States balance of payments. We shall also learn that the balance of payments may be presented in different ways, but the distinction between debits and credits is always the same.

(1) Net Military Transfers under Grants

This entry records the net value of merchandise and service exports financed by military grants of the United States government. These exports have been classified separately because of their noncommercial nature.

(2) Merchandise, Excluding Military

The merchandise account includes all movable, tangible goods that are sold, given away, or otherwise transferred from domestic to foreign ownership (credits) and all movable, tangible goods that are bought, received gratis, or otherwise transferred from foreign to domestic ownership (debits). Aside from military transfers under grants, which are classified separately, there are two noteworthy exceptions to the rule that all tangible goods entering international trade be placed in the merchandise account—monetary gold and merchandise purchased by tourists. Monetary gold is classified in the capital account because of its financial character, and all merchandise (as well as services) purchased by tourists is entered in the travel account.

In 1958 United States merchandise exports exceeded merchandise imports by $3,263 million. This situation is sometimes referred to as a "favorable balance of trade" in that it requires net payments by foreign residents. This terminology derives from the mercantilists of the seventeenth and eighteenth centuries who considered the acquisition of gold a fundamental objective of foreign trade. Actually, the significance of the net merchandise balance cannot be determined without reference to the rest of the balance of payments. For this reason it is preferable to use the terms "export balance of trade," "positive balance of trade," or "credit balance of trade" to refer to a net excess of merchandise exports. The counterparts of these terms may be used to describe a net excess of merchandise imports.

(3) Transportation

The debit entry of this account includes all the services of transportation performed by residents of the rest of the world for American residents. Conversely, such services performed by American residents for foreign residents comprise the credit entry.

In 1958 this country had a positive balance of $167 million on transportation account, but during most of the years between the Civil War and World War II, it experienced a negative balance because of

Ch. 7 / The Balance of International Payments   143

the high construction and operating costs of the American merchant marine. After 1958 this balance resumed its traditional negative form.

(4) Travel

This account covers all the merchandise and services purchased by domestic residents while traveling abroad (debits) and all the merchandise and services purchased by foreign residents while traveling in the United States (credits). The travel account has consistently shown a net debit balance in the United States balance of payments because of the separate influences of the high incomes, the foreign extraction, and the general urge to travel of many American residents. In 1958 the net debit balance amounted to $660 million.

(5) Miscellaneous Services

This is a catchall account; it includes all current transactions not treated elsewhere. Typical items arising out of private transactions are exports and imports of services relating to communications, insurance, home office charges, rentals, royalties, and marketing costs. The export and import of services relating to diplomatic establishments and international agencies are also placed in this account. The United States had a credit balance of $428 million in these transactions in 1958.

(6) Military Transactions

The purchases by United States military agencies and personnel in foreign countries comprise the debit entry of this account. Purchases by foreign military agencies and personnel in this country make up the credit entry. The large-scale military establishments of the United States in Europe and elsewhere are responsible for the very heavy net debit balance of $3,086 million.

(7) Income on Investments

The debit entry of this account is the value of the services rendered by capital located in the United States but owned by foreign residents. The credit entry is the value of services rendered by capital located abroad but owned by American residents.

Capital is here conceived in real terms, namely, as a factor of production that contributes to the production of goods and services. The value of these capital services is measured by international receipts (credits) and payments (debits) of interest, dividends, rents, and branch profits.

In 1958 the United States had a net credit balance of $2,272 million on investment income account. A credit balance has existed since World War I, reflecting the development of this country as the leading international investor.

(8) Net Balance on Current Account

The net credit balance of $4,894 million in 1958 indicates that American residents transferred to foreign ownership that much more in merchandise and services than foreign residents transferred to domestic ownership. The net balance was financed in one way or another; otherwise it could not have come into existence. The remainder of the balance of payments tells us how the financing was accomplished.

(9) Private Remittances (Net)

This account includes the private (personal and institutional) gifts of American residents to foreign residents and conversely. The net debit entry of $517 million indicates the net private gifts of American residents. In terms of the balance of payments, this amount was available to foreign residents to help finance their excess purchases of merchandise and services from the United States.

(10) Government (Net)

The foreign aid of the United States government has increased enormously since the onset of World War II, and during the early 1950's it provided foreign residents with most of the dollars required to finance the excess exports of merchandise and services of this country. In 1958 net military aid amounted to $2,510 million, financing the net exports of military goods and services [Item (1)]. Other net unilateral transfers of the United States government (mostly economic aid but also including pensions, etc.) supplied foreign residents with $1,790 million.

(11) Total Unilateral Transfers (Net)

In 1958 net unilateral transfers, both private and government, aggregated a debit of $4,817 million. This amount was used by foreign residents to finance the net balance on current account of $4,894 million, leaving only $77 million to be financed in the capital account.

(12) Long-Term Capital Movements (Net)

The distinction between long- and short-term capital is one of maturity. Financial claims with an *original* maturity of more than one year, such as bonds, and financial claims that serve as instruments of long-term finance but lack a specific maturity, such as equity stocks, are entered in the long-term capital account when their ownership is transferred between domestic and foreign residents.

International transactions in financial claims with an original maturity of one year or less and in all financial claims that act as short-term credit instruments but which do not have a specific maturity (including demand deposits and currency) are placed in the short-term capital account.

As noted earlier, international capital movements may occur either through changes in domestically held financial claims against foreign residents or though changes in foreign-held financial claims against domestic residents (domestic liabilities). In 1958 both changes took place in the long-term capital account: United States long-term investment abroad (long-term financial claims against foreign residents) increased by $3,188 million, while long-term foreign investment in the United States increased by $23 million. The increase in United States investment abroad supplied dollars to foreign residents, and hence it was recorded as a debit, that is, a long-term capital outflow. On the other hand, the increase in foreign investment in the United States supplied dollars to American residents, and, accordingly, it was entered as a credit or long-term capital inflow. The net result of these two changes was a long-term capital outflow of $3,165 million. This amount received by foreign residents was far greater than the amount needed to finance the net current account balance after allowance for unilateral transfers ($77 million). What did foreign residents do with the extra $3,088 million? The answer lies in the remaining accounts of the balance of payments.

(13) Short-Term Capital Movements (Net)

Short-term capital movements provide the means of international payment for merchandise, services, unilateral transfers, and long-term financial claims; and in this sense they are "induced" by the latter. At times, however, short-term capital may move "autonomously" in response to speculation, fears of war, and the like.[5] Short-term financial claims take many forms: currency, demand deposits, time deposits.

---

[5] See Chapter 9.

bills of exchange, acceptances, treasury bills, commercial credits, etc. The outstanding characteristics of these claims are their extreme liquidity and the ease with which they move from one country to another unless prevented from doing so by government restrictions.

In 1958 there was a net inflow of short-term capital amounting to $432 million. This resulted from an increase in United States short-term investment abroad of $699 million (capital outflow) that was more than offset by an increase in foreign short-term investment in the United States of $1,131 million (capital inflow).[6]

The net inflow of short-term capital supplied American residents with $432 million and thus lowered the excess receipts of foreign residents derived from the previous accounts of the balance of payments from $3,088 million to $2,656 million.

(14) Monetary Gold (Net)

The special treatment of gold in the balance of payments stems from the unique role of gold in international payments. Gold, unlike other commodities, is freely accepted by all nations at a fixed price, and it is, therefore, a means of international payment. Like short-term capital movements, gold movements occur both in response to movements in merchandise, services, unilateral transfers, and long-term capital; and in response to speculation and fears of safety. In contrast to short-term capital movements, however, international gold movements are easily controlled by government agencies.

Not all gold movements are monetary in nature. For example, South Africa exports gold in the same way that other nations export merchandise. In compiling the balance of payments an attempt is sometimes made to distinguish between monetary and nonmonetary movements of gold. To avoid the expenses of physical movement, gold is often exported or imported by "earmarking." Thus the United States exports gold when gold is transferred from domestic ownership to foreign ownership but remains in the vaults of the Federal Reserve Bank of New York. The United States balance of payments indicates that in 1958 the United States "exported" $2,275 million of gold on a net basis. This net export of gold was paid for by foreign residents with the same amount of dollars and thereby decreased the extra receipts (receipts not needed to finance the preceding items of the balance of payments) from $2,656 million to $381 million. What

---

[6] Much of the foreign short-term investment in the United States is held by foreign governments, constituting their dollar reserves.

Ch. 7 / The Balance of International Payments   **147**

happened to this $381 million? We do not know precisely, but we do know that these extra receipts must appear somewhere in the balance of payments. Accordingly, we place them in an errors and omissions account.

(15) Errors and Omissions

In the actual compilation of the balance of payments, the statistical coverage is incomplete and a residual entry is necessary to bring about an accounting balance. There are several possible errors and omissions, but the most important are associated with short-term capital movements. The normal difficulties of tracing the movement of intangible short-term financial assets are compounded by attempts to conceal their movement when it is forbidden by foreign governments. The credit entry of $381 million suggests that a sizable inflow of short-term capital into the United States was not recorded. This would occur if, for example, private foreign residents secretly acquired dollar currency.

Summary of the Balance of Payments

This section summarizes what we have learned from examining the United States balance of payments for 1958.

United States exports of merchandise and services (including military transfers) totaled $4,894 million more than similar imports.

Net unilateral transfers from domestic to foreign residents financed $4,817 million of the net balance on current account, leaving only $77 million to be financed in the capital account.

Foreign residents received $3,165 million from the net long-term capital outflow of the United States. This amount was greater by $3,088 million than that needed by foreign residents to finance the net balance on current account after allowance for unilateral transfers.

American residents received $432 million from a net short-term capital inflow, but this still left foreign residents with extra receipts of $2,656 million.

These extra receipts were cut to $381 million when American residents (United States Treasury) made net exports of gold of $2,275 million.

We do not know the precise disposition of the net outstanding receipts accruing to foreign residents (net outstanding payments of American residents) because of the errors and omissions that are inevitable in the compilation of the balance of payments. The credit entry of $381 million suggests, however, that most of the outstanding receipts probably financed a short-term capital inflow.

WHY THE BALANCE OF PAYMENTS ALWAYS BALANCES

The balance of payments records total receipts from foreign residents and the disposition of those receipts (total payments to foreign residents) over the year. Hence, total debits are equal to total credits, and the balance of payments is always in accounting balance.[7] We have observed that, in the actual compilation of the balance of payments, the accounting balance is achieved by an errors and omissions entry.

We may gain a clearer understanding of why the balance of payments of a nation always balances by considering briefly the balance of payments of the individual family. The annual dollar receipts of the family may come from income, gifts, or borrowing (including any use of the family's own savings). In turn, these receipts are fully accounted for by spending on goods and services, gifts, and lending (including any addition to the family's own savings). Thus over the year family receipts and payments are equal.

This is also true of the nation in its dealings with the rest of the world. This is easily seen in Table 7-2, which presents a simplified version of the United States balance of payments in 1958. In that year total receipts were $28,673 million: $25,585 million came from exports of merchandise and services (income), $432 million came from a net inflow of short-term capital (short-term borrowing), and

Table 7-2
BALANCE OF PAYMENTS OF THE UNITED STATES IN 1958
(MILLIONS OF DOLLARS)

Dollar Receipts from Foreign Residents:	
Exports of merchandise and services	$25,585
Net inflow of short-term capital	432
Net gold exports	2,275
Net errors and omissions	381
Total Receipts	$28,673
Dollar Payments to Foreign Residents:	
Imports of merchandise and services	$20,691
Net unilateral transfers to foreigners	4,817
Net outflow of long-term capital	3,165
Total Payments	$28,673

SOURCE: Based on data in United States Department of Commerce, *Survey of Current Business* (March, 1959), p. 6.

---

[7] Conceptually, the balance of payments is a double-entry accounting statement.

Ch. 7 / The Balance of International Payments   **149**

$2,275 million from net gold exports (use of liquid assets), and $381 million was not precisely accounted for, but most likely consisted of an inflow of short-term capital. The payments side of the balance of payments shows how the total receipts were utilized to make up total payments: $20,961 million was spent on imports of merchandise and services, $4,817 million was used to make net gifts to foreign residents, and $3,165 million financed a net outflow of long-term capital (long-term lending).

The necessary equality of credits and debits in the balance of payments has no economic significance. The important question is *how* the accounting balance is achieved, that is, whether the balance of payments is in *equilibrium* or *disequilibrium*. This question is explored in Chapter 9.

SUMMARY

1. The balance of payments is a statistical classification and summary of all economic transactions between residents of one country and residents of other countries over a stipulated period of time, ordinarily one year.

2. Residence is primarily determined by permanent location, and secondarily by "center of interest."

3. The balance of payments classifies international transactions as debits or credits. Debit transactions involve payments by domestic residents to foreign residents; credit transactions involve receipts of domestic residents from foreign residents.

4. All merchandise and service transactions are placed in the current account of the balance of payments, while all investment and monetary gold transactions are placed in the capital account. Unilateral transfers may be entered in the current account or in a separate third account.

5. When Americans invest abroad, whether on a long- or short-term basis, the United States is said to experience a capital outflow or export. A capital outflow is a debit in the balance of payments because it involves payments to foreign residents. Conversely, when foreign residents invest in the United States, this country experiences a capital inflow or import, which is a credit in the balance of payments because it involves receipts from foreign residents.

6. An examination of the United States balance of payments for 1958 reveals how these principles and concepts are followed in practice, and it tells us much about the international economic position of this country in that year.

7. The balance of payments is always in accounting balance, that is, total debits equal total credits. The balance of payments records the total international receipts of the nation and their complete disposition as international payments.

QUESTIONS AND APPLICATIONS

1. What is the balance of international payments?
2. What three principles underlie the compilation of the balance of payments?
3. What determines whether a transaction is entered as a debit or a credit in the balance of payments?
4. What is the distinction between current transactions, unilateral transfers, and capital transactions?
5. Draw up a balance of payments for the United States and enter the following transactions as debits or credits in the appropriate accounts:
   (a) Export of merchandise.
   (b) Services sold to foreign travelers in the United States.
   (c) Gifts to foreign residents.
   (d) Import of gold.
   (e) Investments by foreign residents in the United States.
6. (a) Distinguish between a capital outflow and a capital inflow.
   (b) Why is a capital export and a merchandise export handled differently in the balance of payments?
7. "The net balance on the current account is financed in one way or another; otherwise it cannot come into existence." Explain.
8. Why is the balance of payments always in an accounting balance?

SELECTED READINGS

Badger, Donald G. "The Balance of Payments: A Tool of Economic Analysis," *International Monetary Fund Staff Papers,* Vol. II, No. 1 (September, 1951), pp. 86-197.

International Monetary Fund. *Balance of Payments Yearbook.* Washington, D. C.: annual.

Lary, Hal B. *Problems of the United States as World Trader and Banker.* New York: National Bureau of Economic Research, 1963.

Salant, Walter S., et al. *The United States Balance of Payments in 1968.* Washington, D. C.: The Brookings Institution, 1963.

CHAPTER 8

FOREIGN EXCHANGE RATES
AND THEIR DETERMINATION

Foreign exchange rates are of key significance in directing the flow of merchandise, services, and capital between nations. This chapter explores the different kinds of exchange-rate behavior and the relationship between exchange rates in the many financial centers.

THE RATE OF EXCHANGE

Foreign exchange is bought and sold in the foreign exchange market at a price that is called the *rate of exchange*. More specifically, the exchange rate is the *domestic* money price of foreign money, establishing an equivalence between dollars and British pounds sterling, dollars and French francs, dollars and Argentine pesos, and so on. The daily quotations of foreign exchange are based on the domestic money price of banker's bills of exchange transmitted by cable, the quickest means of international payment. Table 8-1 indicates the selling rates for cable transfers in New York on June 9, 1965.

The Pattern of Exchange Rates

The domestic price of cable transfers is the *base* rate of exchange; and other means of international payment—banker's sight and time bills and trade sight and time bills—usually sell at a discount from this base rate. These discounts reflect varying delays or risks of payment compared to the cable transfer. Even payment by a banker's sight draft sent airmail requires two or three days between New York and London, and during that time the foreign exchange dealer has the use of both the domestic money paid for the draft and the foreign balance against which the draft is drawn. Time drafts postpone payment for a much longer period. The discount on a given

Table 8-1

SELLING RATES FOR CABLE TRANSFERS IN NEW YORK ON WEDNESDAY, JUNE 9, 1965

EUROPE

	Wednesday	Tuesday	Week Ago	Year Ago
STERLING—$2.80 a pound. ($2.78–$2.82)				
Spot *	2.7932	2.7937	2.7935	2.7950
90 days'	2.7816	2.7829	2.7745	2.7906
BELGIUM—2.00 cents a franc. (1.9851–2.0151)				
Spot	2.0150	2.0150	2.0152	2.0073
DENMARK—14.477 cents a krone. (14.3678–14.5772)				
Spot	14.43¾	14.44½	14.43¾	14.47¾
FRANCE—20.255 cents a franc. (20.1045–20.4081)				
Spot	20.41	20.41	20.41	20.41
GERMANY (Fed. Rep.)—25.00 cents a mark. (24.8138–25.1899)				
Spot	25.01½	25.02½	25.03¾	25.16⅞
90 days'	25.05	25.06	25.08¼	25.22¾
ITALY—0.16 cent a lira. (.158856–.161160)				
Spot	0.16005	0.16006	0.16006	0.16005
NETHERLAND—27.62 cents a guilder. (27.-416–27.8357)				
Spot	27.72¾	27.73	27.74⅝	27.61½
NORWAY—14.00 cents a krone. (13.8888–14.1043)				
Spot	13.98¼	13.99	13.97¾	13.99½
PORTUGAL—3.4783 cents an escudo. (3.4458–3.5112)				
Spot	3.49	3.49	3.50	3.50
SPAIN—1.66667 cents a peseta. (1.6542–1.6792)				
Spot	1.68	1.68	1.68	1.68
SWEDEN—19.33 cents a krona. (19.1846–19.4741)				
Spot	19.39	19.39¼	19.42½	19.47½
SWITZERLAND—22.8675 cents a franc. (22.-4719–23.2828)				
Spot	23.08¾	23.08⅛	23.09	23.17⅝
90 days'	23.10⅝	23.10½	23.09½	23.19¾

OTHER COUNTRIES

	Wednesday	Tuesday	Week Ago	Year Ago
AUSTRALIA—$2.24 a pound. ($2.2176–$2.2624)				
Spot	2.2345	2.2349	2.2348	2.2360
CANADA—92.5 cents a Canadian dollar. (91.575–93.425)				
Spot	92.406	92.454	92.437	92.531
90 days'	92.50	92.531	92.516	92.577
NEW ZEALAND—$2.7809 a pound. (2.7530–2.8087)				
Spot	2.7842	2.7847	2.7845	2.7860
SOUTH AFRICA—$1.40 a rand. (1.3860–1.4140)				
Spot	1.3983	1.3986	1.3985	1.3993

FAR EAST

HONG KONG—17.5 cents a Hong Kong dollar. (17.325–17.675)				
Spot	17.50	17.50	17.50	17.55
INDIA—21.00 cents a rupee. (20.79–21.21)				
Spot	20.96	20.96	20.96	20.98
JAPAN—.2777 cents a yen (.279876–.275709)				
Spot	0.2763¾	0.2762	0.2760	0.2759
PAKISTAN—21.00 cents a rupee. (20.79–21.21)				
Spot	20.98	20.98	20.98	21.01

LATIN AMERICA

ARGENTINA—peso.				
Spot (fr)	0.59	0.59	0.59	0.73
BRAZIL—cruzeiro.				
Spot (fr)	0.0565	0.0565	0.0565	0.09
CHILE—Escudo.				
Spot (fr)	27.50	27.50	28.25	32.00
COLOMBIA—peso.				
Spot (fr)	5.65	5.65	5.75	10.06
MEXICO—8.00 cents per peso. (7.9936–8.0064)				
Spot	8.02	8.02	8.02	8.02
PERU—sol.				
Spot (fr)	3.75	3.75	3.75	3.75
URUGUAY—13.5135 cents per peso.				
Spot (fr)	2.10	2.10	2.20	5.40
VENEZUELA—29.8507 cents per bolivar.				
Spot	22.29	22.29	22.29	22.30

* Rate of exchange assuming immediate delivery.

GENERAL NOTE: In the quotations above, the sterling currencies are in dollars and decimals of a dollar; others represent cents and decimals of a cent. High and low support levels, in parentheses, follow official parities.

SOURCE: *New York Times*, June 10, 1965.

---

kind of foreign exchange, say a 30-day banker's bill, will depend upon the current rate of interest since, in effect, the buyer of the bill is lending money to the seller of the bill until its maturity date. Discounts from the base rate of exchange stem also from differences in the risk of payment. For that reason trade bills are quoted below bank bills of similar maturity.

The rates of different kinds of foreign exchange are, then, linked to the base rate of exchange by discounts that take account of liquidity and risk factors. Although these discounts will vary with the two aforementioned factors, the resulting pattern of exchange rates will rise and fall with the base rate. In our analysis of the determination of foreign exchange rates, therefore, we shall consider the pattern of rates as one rate, namely, the base rate of exchange for cable transfers.

The Behavior of Exchange Rates

The behavior of exchange rates will depend upon the nature of the foreign exchange market. When there are no restrictions on private trading in the market and official agencies do not stand ready to stabilize the rate of exchange, the exchange rate will fluctuate from day to day in response to changes in the supply and demand of foreign exchange. When, however, government authorities follow a policy of stabilization but do not interfere with private market transactions in foreign exchange, the exchange rate will move only within narrow limits, although these limits may be substantially altered from time to time by official action. Finally, the government may restrict private transactions by becoming the sole buyer and seller of foreign exchange; the rate of exchange is then no longer determined by supply and demand but is the end product of bureaucratic decisions. We now examine more closely the determination of these three sorts of exchange-rate behavior—freely fluctuating rates, stable rates, and controlled rates.

FREELY FLUCTUATING EXCHANGE RATES

When the rate of exchange is not stabilized or controlled by government authorities, the foreign exchange market approaches very closely the theoretical model of pure competition. Except for the liquidity and risk differentials that are allowed for by discounts, the foreign exchange of any given country is one homogeneous product. Moreover, the number of buyers and sellers of foreign exchange is so large that no one buyer or seller can measurably influence the rate of exchange but must accept it as given. In a free, unstabilized market, therefore, the rate of exchange is determined by the many individual acts of buying and selling, none of which singly is able to affect it but all of which interact to set its level.

The Demand for Foreign Exchange

In a free market the rate of exchange, like any other price, is determined by the interplay of supply and demand. The foreign exchange that is demanded at any time will depend upon the volume of international transactions that requires payments to foreign residents. That is to say, the demand for foreign exchange originates in the debit items of the balance of payments.

As is true of most goods, the amount of foreign exchange in demand varies inversely with its price—the amount demanded at a high rate is less than the amount demanded at a low rate provided that other conditions remain the same. A high exchange rate makes imports expensive to domestic buyers because they must offer more domestic money to obtain a unit of foreign money. As a result, a high rate of exchange reduces the volume of imports and thus lessens the amount of foreign exchange demanded by domestic residents. Conversely, a low rate of exchange, by stimulating imports, increases the amount of foreign exchange demanded.

This explanation points to the dependence of the demand for foreign exchange on debit transactions in merchandise, services, and capital items; but it also suggests the influence that the exchange rate itself exerts over the volume of those same transactions. The demand relationship of foreign exchange is indicated in Figure 8-1 by the familiar downward-sloping demand schedule D-D. In this instance the schedule shows the quantity of sterling exchange demanded at each rate of exchange in the New York market; thus it is an aggregate of all the individual demand schedules of domestic residents who wish to transfer funds abroad.

Figure 8-1

DEMAND FOR STERLING EXCHANGE IN NEW YORK

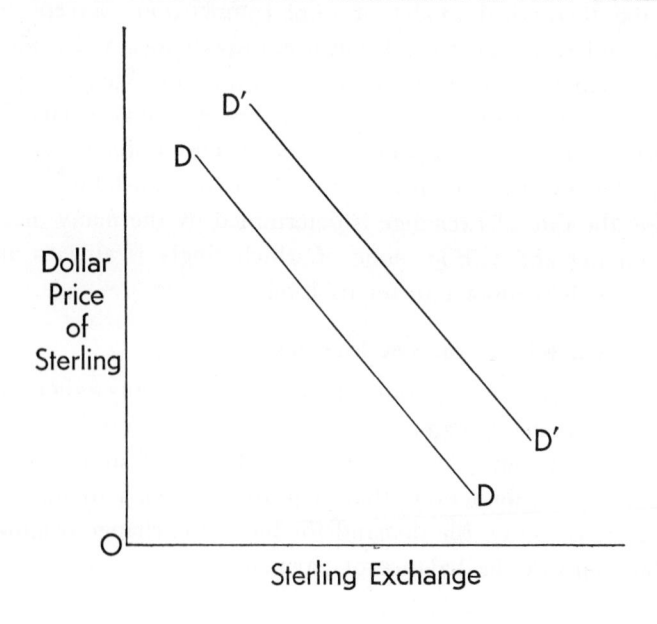

Dollar Price of Sterling

Sterling Exchange

In analyzing the determination of the exchange rate, it is important to distinguish between a movement along a given demand schedule (change in the amount demanded) and a shift in the entire schedule (change in demand). We have noted that a movement along the demand schedule is downward from left to right because the exchange rate determines the domestic price of imports and thereby affects their volume and the amount of foreign exchange demanded to pay for them. Changes in income, costs, prices, tastes, and other factors may, however, cause shifts in the debit items of the balance of payments independently of the exchange rate. When this happens, the entire demand schedule shifts either left or right, depending on whether there has been a decrease or an increase in the volume of debit transactions. For example, a rise in the national income of the United States will cause a rise in imports, and this will shift the demand schedule for foreign exchange to the right as more foreign exchange is demanded at each rate of exchange. Such a development is shown in Figure 8-1 by D'-D'.

The Supply of Foreign Exchange

The supply of foreign exchange in the foreign exchange market derives from international transactions that require money receipts from foreign residents, that is, from credit items in the balance of payments. Unlike the amount demanded, the amount of foreign exchange that is supplied the market varies *directly* with the rate of exchange. When the rate of exchange is high, domestic prices appear low to foreigners since they are able to acquire a unit of domestic money with a small expenditure of their own money. This cheapness stimulates domestic exports and thereby brings a larger supply of foreign exchange into the market. Conversely, a low exchange rate restricts exports and lowers the amount of foreign exchange offered to the market.

Figure 8-2 shows the supply relationship of foreign exchange by a schedule that slopes upward from left to right. A shift of the entire supply schedule either to the left or right occurs with a change in the credit items of the balance of payments brought about by factors other than the exchange rate. For example, a shift to the left would occur if deflation abroad caused a decrease in American exports. This would decrease the amount of foreign exchange supplied the market at each exchange rate. A decrease in the supply of sterling exchange in the New York market is shown in Figure 8-2 by S'-S'.

Figure 8-2

SUPPLY OF STERLING EXCHANGE IN NEW YORK

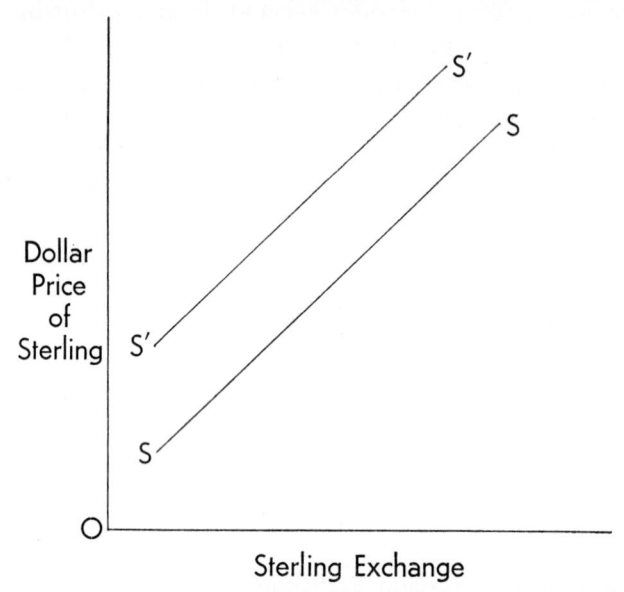

Dollar Price of Sterling

Sterling Exchange

Determination of the Rate of Exchange

The rate of exchange is determined by the intersection of the demand and the supply schedules. At this rate of exchange, and at no other rate, the market is cleared; the rate will remain stable until a shift occurs in either one or both schedules. It is unlikely that this equilibrium rate of exchange will last very long or even be attained in a free, unstabilized foreign exchange market, since continuing shifts in demand and supply will force continuing adjustments toward new equilibrium positions. Thus the exchange rate will fluctuate continuously just as the prices of securities traded in the security market. To simplify our analysis, however, we shall assume that there is time for the exchange rate to adjust fully to a change in demand or supply.

In Figure 8-3 the equilibrium rate of exchange is O-R; at this rate the amount supplied is equal to the amount demanded, and both suppliers and buyers of foreign exchange are satisfied. Suppose now that the demand for sterling increases from D-D to D'-D' as in Figure 8-4. In response to this increase, the equilibrium rate rises from O-R to O-R' where once again the amounts of sterling exchange supplied and demanded are equal. This higher rate calls forth an increase in the amount supplied of E-E', since it stimulates more American exports. Similarly, a shift of the demand schedule to the left (fall in

Ch. 8 / Foreign Exchange Rates and Their Determination 157

Figure 8-3

DETERMINATION OF EQUILIBRIUM STERLING EXCHANGE RATE IN NEW YORK

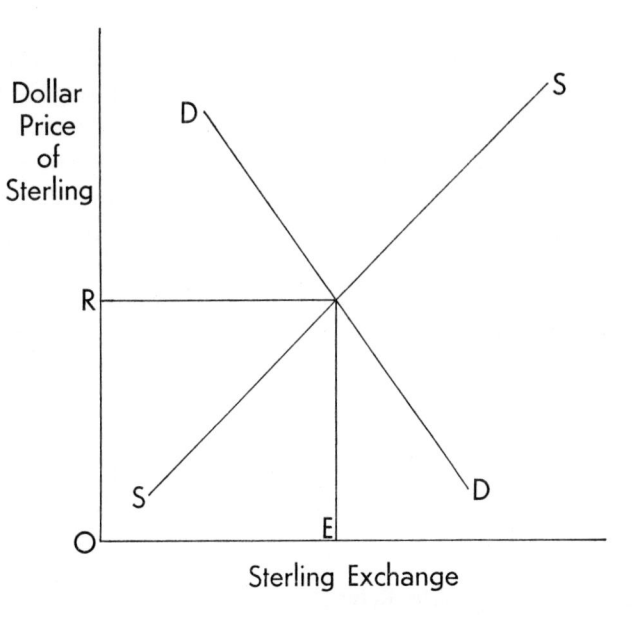

Figure 8-4

DETERMINATION OF A NEW EQUILIBRIUM STERLING EXCHANGE RATE IN NEW YORK

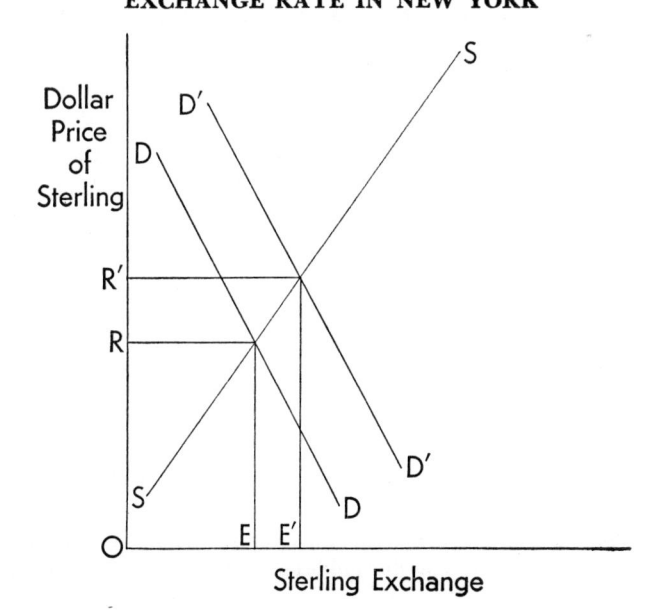

demand) will bring about a decline in the rate of exchange. On the other hand, a shift in the supply schedule to the left (fall in supply) will raise the exchange rate while a shift to the right (rise in supply) will lower it.

In summary, the exchange rate in a free, unstabilized market is determined by the supply of and the demand for foreign exchange, which derive from the credit and debit items of the balance of payments respectively. The exchange rate itself also influences the balance of payments and this influence is shown by the shape of the demand and the supply schedules of foreign exchange.[1] There is, therefore, a mutual relationship between the foreign exchange rate and the balance of payments; each is both determined by, and a determinant of, the other.

STABLE EXCHANGE RATES

In this section several arguments for stable rates are presented, after which specific techniques of stabilization are discussed.

Arguments for Stable Rates

Exchange rates have seldom been left free to vary with supply and demand. Even before World War I when there was general agreement on the benefits of flexible market prices in merchandise, services, and securities, fluctuating exchange rates were viewed with marked distaste. At this time all of the leading trading nations were firm adherents of the gold standard, which provided fixed rates of exchange. Fluctuating exchange rates, therefore, were considered a mark of failure to remain on the gold standard. Apart from the gold standard, however, there are strong arguments for stable exchange rates; and today, long after the abandonment of the gold standard, most countries maintain either stable or controlled rates that are allowed to change only at official discretion.

It is forcibly argued that the exchange rate is unlike the price of an ordinary commodity, and that it is illogical to view the two in the same light. When the exchange rate varies, the prices of *all* exports are changed for foreign buyers; and, simultaneously, the prices of *all* imports are changed for domestic buyers. These widespread

---

[1] The influence of the exchange rate on the balance of payments is an important means of adjustment to disequilibrium that is taken up in Chapter 11.

price effects unloose a series of repercussions that extend throughout the domestic and foreign economies. This critical nature of the exchange rate, the argument runs, rules out the unlicensed freedom of the unstabilized foreign exchange market. It is also contested that fluctuating rates invite foreign exchange speculation that may intensify balance of payments difficulties. Less fundamental arguments for stable rates spring from considerations of trade and finance. Fluctuating rates provoke uncertainty in foreign payments and investments. The exporter is unable to make a sound calculation of his profit margin since the domestic value of his foreign exchange receipts depends upon an unstable rate of exchange. Lenders and borrowers are also subject to this exchange risk.

We do not intend at this time to evaluate the arguments for stable rates. In all fairness, however, we should point out that most countries still rely on exchange rate adjustments from time to time to remedy balance of payments difficulties, and that one important trading nation, Canada, had a fluctuating rate of exchange in the 1950's. Moreover, with the existence of a forward exchange market, foreign traders and, to a lesser extent, foreign investors are able to hedge against fluctuations in the rate of exchange.[2]

Techniques of Stabilization

Unlike the controlled exchange market, the stabilized market imposes no restraints on private transactions in foreign exchange; the factors of supply and demand are fully operative. How, then, is it possible to prevent fluctuations in the rate of exchange? The answer lies in the open-market operations of government authorities that compensate for movements in the ordinary demand and supply of foreign exchange. Successful stabilization of the rate of exchange requires that the stabilization agency be able to offset movements in market supply and demand to any desired degree. To do so, the agency must possess adequate supplies of domestic and foreign exchange.[3] Under the gold standard, stabilization is assured by the willingness

---

[2] The case for fluctuating rates is presented in Chapter 11.

[3] This may be illustrated by the price stabilization of wheat in the United States. To keep the price of wheat from falling below a minimum level, the stabilization authority (Commodity Credit Corporation) must have enough dollars to buy all the wheat offered at that level; to keep the price of wheat from rising above a maximum level, the authority must have enough wheat to satisfy demand at that level. In practice, the Commodity Credit Corporation has acted to restrain a decline in the price of wheat rather than a rise, that is, it has followed a policy of one-sided stabilization.

of the monetary authorities to buy or sell gold without limit at a fixed price. This *passive* stabilization contrasts with the *active* stabilization practices of today whereby government agencies buy and sell foreign exchange in the market to offset undesired movements in exchange rates.

Passive Stabilization: The Gold Standard. A country is on the gold standard when its basic monetary unit (dollar, pound sterling, franc, etc.) is defined in terms of a specified weight of gold and when its monetary authorities stand ready at all times to buy and sell gold in unlimited quantities at the rate fixed by the legal gold content of the monetary unit. As long as this second condition of unrestricted convertibility is observed, the gold value of the monetary unit cannot vary and the price of gold remains constant. Actually there are several varieties of the gold standard; gold-coin, gold-bullion, qualified gold-bullion, and gold-exchange standards have all existed historically.

The minimum conditions for a true *international* gold standard are two: (1) two or more countries must adopt monetary units with a designated gold content, and (2) the monetary authorities of each country must permit the free, unlimited export and import of gold at a rate fixed by the gold content of the respective monetary unit. Since the gold standard creates fixed exchange rates only between countries on the gold standard, however, it makes its greatest contribution to exchange rate stability when several currencies, particularly key currencies such as the dollar and the pound sterling, are tied to gold.

Gold-standard currencies hold a fixed relationship to each other because they all hold a fixed relationship to gold. Before World War I and during the last half of the twenties, the British pound sterling was defined as 113 grains of gold and the United States dollar as 23.22 grains. The gold content of the pound, therefore, was 4.8665 times greater than the gold content of the dollar. This latter relationship was the *mint parity* of the pound and the dollar at that time —one pound sterling was equivalent to $4.8665. Any holder of 113 grains of gold could obtain one pound sterling from the British monetary authorities, or, alternately, $4.8665 from the American authorities.

Under the gold standard, the mint parity and the exchange rate between two currencies need not be identical. Because of the costs of shipping gold from one country to another (freight, insurance, handling, and interest), the exchange rate is free to vary within narrow limits known as *gold points*. The higher the costs of shipping gold, the greater the spread between mint parity and the gold points. The costs of shipment, when added to mint parity, establish the *gold export point*; the costs of shipment, when subtracted from mint parity, establish the *gold import point*. When the exchange rate rises to the gold export point, gold flows out of the country; conversely, when the exchange rate falls to the gold import point, gold flows into the country. These gold flows provide the compensatory changes in the supply of and the demand for foreign exchange that are necessary to keep the exchange rate from moving beyond the gold points.

This stabilizing function of gold flows under the international gold standard may be illustrated by an example. Let us assume that the mint parity of the pound sterling is $4.8665, and that shipping costs make the gold export point in New York $4.8865 and the gold import point, $4.8465. Now suppose that the rate of exchange in New York rises to the gold export point of $4.8865. The rate will not rise further because foreign exchange dealers can acquire all the pounds sterling they desire at a rate of $4.8865 by purchasing gold for dollars from the American monetary authorities, shipping the gold to London, and then selling the gold for pounds to the British monetary authorities. Thus the supply of foreign exchange becomes perfectly elastic at the gold export point, and the rate of exchange cannot rise beyond it.[4]

Similarly, the gold import point sets a floor below which the rate of exchange cannot fall: exchange dealers will not sell pounds at a rate below $4.8465 because they can obtain that many dollars for each pound sterling by converting pounds into gold in London, shipping the gold to New York, and then converting the gold into dollars. In other words, the demand for foreign exchange becomes perfectly elastic at the gold import point.[5]

When the rate of exchange is between the gold points, there is no longer an option on the part of dealers to acquire foreign exchange by gold exports or to dispose of foreign exchange by gold imports since to do so would involve losses. If, in our example, the sterling exchange rate were $4.8665 (the mint parity), then to acquire or dispose of sterling by gold shipments would mean a loss of two American cents per pound sterling for each transaction (the costs of

---

[4] All the foreign exchange that is demanded at the gold export point will be supplied.

[5] All the foreign exchange that is supplied at the gold import point will be demanded.

shipment). Between the gold points, therefore, the rate of exchange is determined as in a free, unstabilized market. The spread between the gold points, however, is so narrow that we may regard exchange rates under the gold standard as fixed.

It will be noted that this stabilization is achieved without any intervention in the foreign exchange market on the part of the monetary authorities who behave simply as residual buyers and sellers of gold. Gold moves "automatically" from one country to another in response to the supply of and demand for foreign exchange.

Active Stabilization by Monetary Authorities: A true international gold standard has not functioned since the first half of the 1930's, and today exchange rates, unless controlled outright, are stabilized by official compensatory transactions in the foreign exchange market.[6] Actually, most countries of the free world are now committed through membership in the International Monetary Fund to the maintenance of a par value for their currency.[7]

The policy objectives of active stabilization, however, differ considerably from the policy objectives of passive stabilization under the gold standard. Under the old gold standard, the fundamental aim of international monetary policy was to remain on the gold standard and to avoid any change in the gold content of the monetary unit. The almost incidental result of this policy was a fixed exchange rate. As a matter of fact, the exchange rates of the major trading countries were fixed at the same level for several decades preceding World War I. In contrast, contemporary policy seeks to achieve stability in the exchange rate, but allows for occasional adjustments in the rate in order to correct disequilibrium in the balance of payments.[8] This policy of "stable, yet flexible" rates attempts to secure the advantages of stability and, at the same time, to use the exchange rate as an instrument of international adjustment.

---

[6] The first stabilization agency was the British Exchange Equalization Account, which was established in 1932 after the United Kingdom abandoned the gold standard. Upon the devaluation of the dollar in 1934, the United States also established a stabilization agency; and, by the end of the thirties, most countries had adopted a policy of exchange stabilization whether or not implemented by special agencies, central banks, or treasuries.

[7] See Chapter 17 for a discussion of the International Monetary Fund.

[8] In September, 1949, the United Kingdom and several other countries carried through a substantial depreciation of their rates of exchange to meet a widespread dollar shortage. Since then, the Canadian dollar and the French franc have been depreciated, and the German mark and Dutch guilder have been appreciated. Currency depreciations are frequent among the developing nations.

Ch. 8 / Foreign Exchange Rates and Their Determination

We have already briefly described the basic mechanism of exchange rate stabilization; we now look more closely into its actual operation. In order to stabilize the dollar price of sterling between $2.78 and $2.82 (the present range), the United States monetary authorities (Treasury and Federal Reserve System) require two assets: (1) dollars, and (2) sterling exchange, or other foreign exchange freely convertible into sterling or gold. The dollars are needed so that the authorities are able to buy all the sterling that may be offered in New York at $2.78, that is, make the demand for sterling perfectly elastic at that rate. Foreign exchange and gold are needed so that the authorities are able to satisfy any demand for sterling at $2.82, and thereby make the supply of sterling perfectly elastic at that rate.

As part of the government, the monetary authorities have no difficulty in obtaining sufficient dollars for their operations, but the supply of foreign exchange and gold presents a different problem since the government cannot create foreign exchange, and domestic gold production is limited. In the 1950's this country had nothing to worry about on that score—the balance of payments was strong and gold reserves were at a level adequate to meet any foreseeable pressures on the rate of exchange. Today the situation is far different. The persistent deficit in the United States balance of payments has cut into gold reserves to such an extent that some observers believe they are insufficient to insure the stability of the dollar.[9] When stabilization activities are inhibited by inadequate reserves of foreign exchange and gold, governments frequently resort to exchange control.[10]

There is another reason why American monetary authorities need not be concerned over their holdings of dollars. As we have noted, domestic currency is necessary to put a floor under the dollar price of sterling, that is, to avert a depreciation of sterling and a simultaneous appreciation of the dollar. Ordinarily, however, domestic authorities do not support the exchange value of a foreign currency; they are usually interested only in one-sided stabilization, the avoidance of depreciation of the domestic currency. In practice, therefore, the United States authorities impose a ceiling over the dollar price of sterling, while the British authorities place a floor below the dollar price of sterling.[11] This division of labor also occurs

---

[9] See Chapter 22.

[10] An explanation of the role of international reserves in international adjustment is offered in the next chapter.

[11] In other words, the British authorities impose a ceiling over the pound price of dollars in London.

under gold-standard stabilization: gold flows out of a country to maintain an upper price limit (gold export point) on foreign exchange and flows into a country to maintain a lower price limit (gold import point).

CONTROLLED EXCHANGE RATES

Neither the fluctuating rate market nor the stabilized market imposes restrictions on private transactions in foreign exchange. A wide gulf separates these two markets from the controlled foreign exchange market that prohibits private transactions not authorized by the control authority. The controlled exchange rate does not directly respond to shifts in supply and demand; government rationing supersedes the allocating function of the exchange rate and the currency becomes inconvertible. When exchange controls are relaxed, the job of maintaining stable exchange rates is passed on to stabilization agencies or their counterparts.

We shall examine the nature and the effects of exchange control in later chapters. At present we are interested only in the essential mechanism of exchange control—how it works in the foreign exchange market. To simplify our analysis, we assume a completely controlled market in which the control authority is the exclusive buyer (monopsonist) and exclusive seller (monopolist) of foreign exchange. All foreign exchange must be sold to the authority at its stipulated rate, and all foreign exchange must be bought from the authority at its stipulated rate. We further assume that there is only one rate of exchange, although in practice the control agency may charge a much higher rate than it pays for foreign exchange in order to earn a monopoly profit, and/or it may adopt several discriminatory rates.

The supply of foreign exchange is derived from the credit items of the balance of payments, and the control authorities have only a limited influence over it. To raise the supply of foreign exchange, steps must be taken to expand exports, encourage foreign loans, and the like; many of these steps lie beyond the jurisdiction of the control agency. The agency, therefore, considers the supply of foreign exchange as relatively fixed with respect to its own powers, and its main task is the allocation of this fixed supply among those who demand it. This is usually done by an exchange or trade-licensing system—unless a domestic resident can obtain a license he cannot secure foreign exchange. This rationing brings about a "suppressed disequilibrium" between supply and demand by forcibly choking off all excess demand.

The determination of the controlled rate of exchange is shown in Figure 8-5. If the market were free, the equilibrium rate of exchange would be ten pesos for one dollar where the supply and demand schedules intersect. At this equilibrium rate both the amount demanded and the amount supplied would be *O-E* dollars. At the controlled rate of five pesos, however, the amount demanded (*O-F*) exceeds the amount supplied (*O-G*) by an amount of dollars (*G-F*); that is to say, the market is not cleared at the controlled rate. It follows that the control authority must suppress the excess demand (*G-F*) by issuing licenses only for the purchase of *O-G* dollars; otherwise the authority will be unable to maintain the controlled rate.

We can draw the following conclusions from our analysis of the controlled rate of exchange: (1) the controlled rate is less than the equilibrium rate—the controlled rate overvalues the peso in terms of dollars; (2) the amount of dollars supplied the market at the con-

Figure 8-5

THE CONTROLLED RATE OF EXCHANGE: PESO COUNTRY

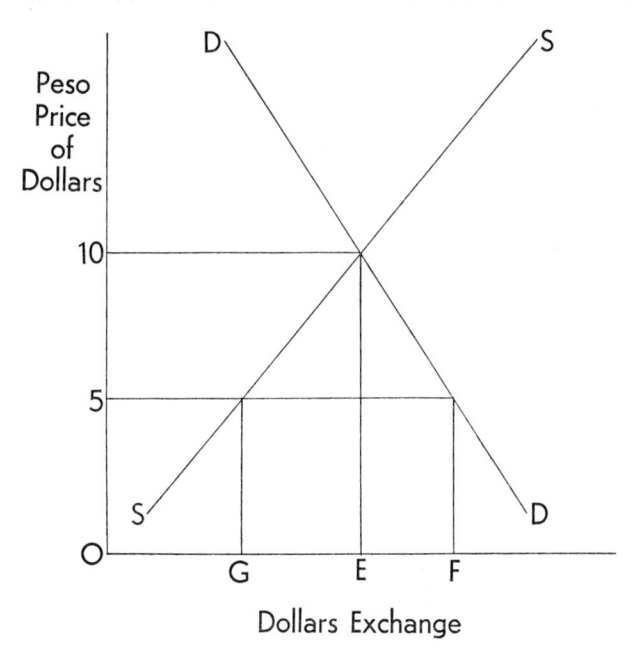

trolled rate is less than the amount supplied at the equilibrium rate (*O-G* compared to *O-E*)—the controlled rate discourages exports by making them more expensive to foreign buyers; (3) the market is not truly cleared—the excess demand (*G-F*) is not satisfied; and (4) the purchase of dollars at the controlled rate is smaller than the purchase at the equilibrium rate (*O-G* compared to *O-E*)—the controlled market cuts imports below the level permitted by the free market.

EXCHANGE ARBITRAGE

We have learned that the rate of exchange is determined by supply and demand in the foreign exchange market or else controlled by monetary authorities. Most of our discussion has focused on the New York market, and we have said nothing about the relationship between rates in that market and rates in the markets of other trading countries. We now explore this topic.

Since it is to be expected that each foreign exchange market will have its own particular supply and demand conditions, does not the rate of exchange, say the price of dollars, differ between markets? The answer is no. Actually, in the absence of exchange control, the price of dollars is identical in all markets no matter where they are located. It is identical because exchange arbitrage conducted by private traders will quickly close any gap existing between markets in the price of dollars or of any other currency.

Definition

Exchange arbitrage involves the simultaneous purchase and sale of a currency in different foreign exchange markets. For example, arbitrage occurs when dollars are bought in New York and simultaneously sold in the same amount in London. Arbitrage becomes profitable whenever the price of a currency in one market differs even slightly from its price in another market. Then, through its effect on the supply of and demand for that currency, arbitrage rapidly erases the discrepancy. Thus exchange arbitrage provides the link between exchange rates in the market of one country and exchange rates in the markets of other countries. In this way arbitrage creates one global foreign exchange market with one rate for each currency.

Arbitrage may require operations in two currencies (bilateral), three currencies (trilateral), or more than three (multilateral). Regardless of the number of currencies, the basic principle of arbitrage must be observed: a sale in one market is offset by a simultaneous purchase in another market. Because of the need for simultaneity, arbitrage is effected through the cooperation of exchange dealers located in separate markets. Bilateral arbitrage in dollars and pounds sterling, for example, is carried out by a dealer in New York and his

Ch. 8 / Foreign Exchange Rates and Their Determination　　　　　167

partner in London. Successful arbitrage rests upon continuous market information, substantial resources, rapid means of communication between markets, and trained minds that are quick to perceive and act upon any discrepancies in rates. For this reason, most arbitrage is done by the large commercial banks that serve as dealers in foreign exchange.

Bilateral Arbitrage

Suppose that sterling is quoted in New York at $4 but is quoted in London at $4.01.[12] Sterling is therefore relatively cheap in New York and relatively expensive in London. Arbitragers will profit by buying sterling in the cheap market and simultaneously selling it in the expensive market. The arbitrager in New York and his partner in London will take the following steps: (1) buy, say, 10,000 pounds sterling in New York for $40,000, (2) sell simultaneously 10,000 pounds sterling in London for $40,100. The pounds purchased in New York will cover the pounds sold in London, while the dollars spent in New York will be covered by the dollars received in London. The profit on these transactions is $100 (minus cable costs), which is split between the two partners.[13]

The effect of these and similar transactions is to wipe out the spread in rates between New York and London. By increasing the amount demanded, the purchase of sterling in New York pushes up its price, and the sale of sterling in London, by increasing the amount supplied, pushes down its dollar price.[14] When the rising price of sterling in New York and the falling price of sterling in London come together, say at $4.005, arbitrage is no longer profitable and it ceases.

Trilateral Arbitrage

Arbitrage in three currencies is more complex than in two, but the principle is the same. Assume that the price of sterling is $4 and

---

[12] Actually the pound price of dollars is quoted in London. In this instance, the price of dollars in London is 1/4.01 times one pound sterling. To simplify matters, we have assumed that the dollar price of sterling is quoted directly in London.

[13] This illustration of bilateral arbitrage has been somewhat simplified. In practice, the New York dealer will buy a sterling cable (draft) while, at the same time, the London dealer will buy a dollar cable (draft). The sterling bought in New York will cover the sterling spent in London, and the dollars bought in London will cover the dollars spent in New York. If the situation is reversed—sterling is cheaper in London than it is in New York—then the New York dealer will sell a sterling cable, while the London dealer will sell a dollar cable.

[14] To the London market the increase in the amount of sterling supplied will appear as an increase in the amount of dollars demanded. See Footnote 12.

the price of francs, $0.02 in New York. In New York, therefore, one pound sterling exchanges for 200 francs via their respective dollar rates; this is the franc-sterling *cross rate*. But now suppose that at the same time it is possible to buy sterling in Paris at a rate of 198 francs while the dollar price of francs in Paris and the dollar price of sterling in London are identical with their prices in New York. Thus, in terms of francs, sterling is more expensive in New York than it is in Paris. Bilateral arbitrage is not profitable but trilateral arbitrage can take advantage of the discrepancy between the franc-sterling cross rate in New York and the franc price of sterling in Paris, the former 200 francs, and the latter, 198 francs.[15] The arbitrager in New York and his partner in Paris will (1) buy, say, 500,000 francs for $10,000 in New York, (2) simultaneously sell 500,000 francs for 2,525.2 pounds sterling in Paris, (3) simultaneously sell 2,525.2 pounds for $10,100.80 in New York. The francs acquired in New York cover the francs sold in Paris while the sterling sold in New York is covered by the sterling purchased in Paris. The resulting profit of $100.80 (minus cable costs) is split between the partners.

The purchase of francs in New York will raise their dollar price, the sale of francs in Paris will raise the franc price of sterling, and the sale of sterling in New York will lower its dollar price. Arbitrage will cease when the franc-sterling cross rate in New York is identical with the franc price of sterling in Paris.[16]

EXCHANGE SPECULATION AND CAPITAL FLIGHT

In the previous pages we have covered many of the factors that determine exchange rates: the ordinary supply of and demand for foreign exchange, gold movements, the compensatory transactions of monetary authorities, exchange controls, and arbitrage. We now turn to a brief description and analysis of exchange speculation and **capital flight that may provoke violent disturbances in the rate of exchange.**

---

[15] If the franc price of sterling is identical in Paris and London, the London rate on francs is also out of line with the New York franc-sterling cross rate. If, on the other hand, the franc price of sterling is *not* identical between Paris and London, then bilateral arbitrage in those two currencies is profitable until an identity is achieved.

[16] As in the case of bilateral arbitrage, the actual transactions consist of cable transfers, namely, the purchase of a franc cable in New York, the purchase of a sterling cable in Paris, and the sale of a sterling cable in New York.

Speculation Proper

The speculator purposely assumes an open position in the foreign exchange market with the intent of making a windfall profit from fluctuations in the rate of exchange. When the speculator expects the exchange rate of a specific currency to rise in the near future, he goes *long* on that currency by buying it. Conversely, when he expects the exchange rate of a currency to fall in the near future, he goes *short* either by selling the currency in the forward market for future delivery or by borrowing the currency on short term and then exchanging it for a currency he considers stable. When the expectations of speculators are not borne out, they suffer windfall losses. Curiously enough, however, if speculation in a currency is strong and one-sided, it may itself force the exchange rate to move in the anticipated direction.

By going long on a currency, speculators sustain its exchange rate—they increase demand and thus help ward off depreciation or even bring about appreciation. For this reason, monetary authorities, anxious to avert depreciation but not concerned about appreciation, tend to view long speculators with less distaste than short speculators. Interwar and postwar currency experiences, however, have made speculators pessimistic, and today they are more apt to undermine a currency by going short than to support it by going long.

Speculation may be *stabilizing* or *destabilizing*. Stabilizing speculation goes *against* the market. When the demand for a currency is falling (or its supply increasing), speculation helps to stabilize the exchange rate by going long and buying the currency. Conversely, when the exchange rate is rising, stabilizing speculation will retard the rise by going short and selling the currency. Stabilizing speculation was common under the gold standard before World War I, when everyone felt certain that the gold points would limit any movements in the exchange rate. Today, however, there is no such assurance; and speculation, by going *with* the market, is predominantly destabilizing.

At times in the past, destabilizing speculation, coupled with capital flight, has swamped the ordinary transactions of the foreign exchange market and has plunged the exchange rate into a dizzy spiral of depreciation. When general confidence in the exchange rate of a currency is shaky, destabilizing speculation may become cumulative: speculation provokes depreciation and this, in turn, provokes further speculation. As was true of the German mark in the early twenties and the Chinese yuan after World War II, this interaction may attain a truly fantastic velocity and bring about a rate of exchange that is below its true value even though domestic inflation may be running rampant.

Capital Flight

Unlike speculation proper, *capital flight* is initiated not by the hope of gain but the fear of loss. When a country faces the prospect of exchange depreciation, the imposition of exchange controls, political instability, or war, domestic and foreign residents who own assets in that country seek safety by transferring funds to a country that is considered stable. The consequence may be a mass flight of capital that seriously weakens the currencies of some countries and brings unneeded foreign exchange and gold to other countries. The greatest capital flight in history occurred during the last half of the thirties when billions of dollars of gold came to the United States from a frightened Europe.

Speculative and flight capital movements continue to take place when there is fear of depreciation. The British pound has been weakened repeatedly by capital flight, and in recent years the United States dollar has also come under attack.[17] In the contemporary international monetary system no country is immune to speculation and capital flight.[18]

THE FORWARD RATE OF EXCHANGE

The markets that we have analyzed deal in foreign exchange bought and sold for immediate delivery. Closely allied to these spot exchange markets are the forward exchange markets that deal not in foreign exchange, but in promises to buy or sell foreign exchange at a specified rate and at a specified time in the future with payment to be made upon delivery. These promises are known as *forward exchange,* and the price at which they are traded is the *forward rate of exchange.*[19]

The forward exchange market resembles the futures markets found in organized commodity exchanges, such as those for wheat

---

[17] Speculation forced at least the timing of the depreciation of the pound sterling in September, 1949.

[18] Chapter 22 discusses this and other aspects of the international monetary system.

[19] The 90-day forward rates for sterling, the German mark, the Swiss franc, and the Canadian dollar are shown in Table 8-1.

and coffee. The primary function of any futures or forward market is to afford protection against the risk of price fluctuations. Forward exchange markets, therefore, are most useful when the rate of exchange is freely fluctuating, and when there are significant exchange risks for those who are committed to make or receive international payments. When the rate of exchange is stabilized, forward exchange is most useful when there is a strong possibility that the exchange rate will be allowed to depreciate in the near future. Since the forward exchange market must be free, it cannot function under exchange control.

The forward exchange market offers protection against the exchange risk by permitting hedging. *Hedging* is the procedure of balancing sales and purchases of an asset so that there is no net open position on the market. Hedging is practiced by the foreign exchange dealer when he covers his exchange risk by balancing sales and purchases of foreign exchange over the trading day. In this instance hedging is done solely in spot exchange, but there are times when hedging is possible only by offsetting spot transactions in foreign exchange with forward transactions.

To illustrate, suppose that an American importer must pay a specified sum in francs to a French exporter two months hence. During those two months the importer is short on the exchange market and he will be hurt by a rise in the dollar price of francs. Of course, he might buy his francs immediately, but this would mean immobilizing his funds for two months; and, in effect, he would be paying cash for his imports despite the two-month credit arrangement. He can avoid this difficulty and still protect himself by purchasing the necessary francs on a two-month forward contract, which specifies the dollar price he will pay when the francs are delivered to him. The importer has now offset his short position on spot francs with an equivalent long position on forward francs; regardless of what happens to the spot rate of exchange, he will obtain the francs he needs at the rate stipulated in the forward contract. When the time comes for payment, the importer will secure the francs on the forward contract and remit them to the French exporter. In this illustration hedging has replaced an indefinite dollar payment with a definite one.

Hedging, however, is not limited to an importer or someone else who is obligated to make a foreign currency payment sometime in the future. Anyone who is to receive payment in a foreign currency at a future time is also exposed to the exchange risk, and he can hedge by selling forward exchange. In this way an American exporter can substitute a definite dollar receipt for an indefinite one.

Hedging also occurs with *interest arbitrage*. For example, when short-term interest rates are higher in London than in New York, there is an incentive for foreign exchange dealers (mainly commercial banks) to borrow in New York and simultaneously lend in London. By so doing, however, they are open to the risk of sterling depreciation which could wipe out any gain from the interest-rate spread. Hence the dealers will cover their open position by selling forward sterling. Whether or not interest arbitrage is profitable depends, therefore, upon (1) the interest-rate spread between the two centers, and (2) the cost of forward sterling. To illustrate, on June 4, 1965, the interest-rate spread on Treasury bills between New York and London was 1.67 percent per annum in favor of London. But at the same time forward sterling was selling at a *discount* from spot sterling equal to an annual rate of 1.82 percent. In these circumstances there was no incentive to borrow in New York in order to lend in London because the cost of forward coverage (1.82 percent) more than wiped out the prospective gain in interest (1.67 percent). It follows that monetary authorities can control the volume of short-term capital flows induced by interest arbitrage either by adjusting short-term interest rates or by intervening in forward markets to influence forward rates of exchange.

Hedging provides complete protection against both speculative gains and losses only when the spot and forward rates of exchange are either equal or move together over the life of the forward contract. The two rates are, however, rarely equal. Forward exchange will usually sell at a discount under, or a premium over, the spot rate of exchange. Normally the forward rate is closely tied to the spread between the short-term interest rates of the relevant financial centers because of interest arbitrage; and, when this is true, hedging will offer a successful, although not necessarily perfect, protection against exchange risks. When, however, forward exchange is used to speculate on the future of the spot rate of exchange, then the forward rate may behave erratically with respect to the spot rate. In such circumstances hedging in the forward market may offer little or no protection.

SUMMARY

1. The exchange rate is the domestic money price of foreign money. The domestic price of cable transfers is the base rate of exchange, and all other

Ch. 8 / Foreign Exchange Rates and Their Determination 173

means of international payment usually sell at a discount from the base rate. Unless otherwise specified, we assume the exchange rate to be one rate, namely, the base rate. The behavior of the exchange rate will depend upon the nature of the foreign exchange market. We can distinguish three sorts of behavior: freely fluctuating rates, stable rates, and controlled rates.

2. Freely fluctuating rates result when the rate of exchange is free to respond to the movements of supply and demand. The rate of exchange is then determined by the intersection of the supply and demand schedules which, in turn, are determined by the credit and debit items of the balance of payments respectively. The rate of exchange, however, also affects the balance of payments, and there is, therefore, a mutual interdependence between them.

3. There are several arguments in favor of stable exchange rates. Under the gold standard, international gold movements prevent any variation in the exchange rate outside the narrow limits of the gold points. Exchange rates may also be stabilized by compensatory purchases and sales of foreign exchange on the part of government agencies. Today most countries seek to stabilize their exchange rate by official compensatory transactions in foreign exchange, but many of them also rely on exchange control.

4. Controlled rates result from the monopoly purchase and sale of foreign exchange by a government agency. The available foreign exchange is distributed by a rationing system; and, because the controlled rate is maintained below the equilibrium rate, there is an excess demand that is not satisfied. The exchange rate is determined by bureaucratic decision rather than supply and demand.

5. Exchange arbitrage involves the simultaneous purchase and sale of foreign exchange in different foreign exchange markets. When arbitrage is permitted, the price of a currency inevitably becomes the same in all foreign exchange markets. Arbitrage may operate in two, three, or more currencies.

6. Exchange speculation and capital flight also influence exchange rates. Because these short-term capital movements usually undermine the exchange rate and weaken the balance of payments, monetary authorities view them with marked distaste.

7. Forward exchange consists of promises to buy or sell foreign exchange at a specified price and at a specified time in the future. Forward exchange permits hedging to protect against fluctuations in the exchange rate.

QUESTIONS AND APPLICATIONS

1. What is the base rate of exchange?
2. What are the three kinds of exchange rate behavior?
3. (a) How is the exchange rate determined when it is freely fluctuating?
   (b) What is the mutual relationship between the exchange rate and the balance of payments?

4. Using graphs, show the effects on the exchange rate of the following shifts:
   (a) Decrease in demand.
   (b) Increase in supply.
5. (a) What are the minimum conditions of an international gold standard?
   (b) Explain how the international gold standard prevents fluctuations of the exchange rate beyond the gold points.
6. What is the function of a stabilization agency? How does it perform this function?
7. Using a graph, show how exchange control determines the rate of exchange. Why is the market not cleared under exchange control?
8. Suppose the price of pounds sterling in New York is $4 while the price of dollars in London is £0.26. Is exchange arbitrage feasible? If so, how? What is the effect of arbitrage on exchange rates?
9. (a) Distinguish between stabilizing and destabilizing speculations.
   (b) What is capital flight?
10. (a) How does forward exchange differ from spot exchange?
    (b) Explain how forward exchange makes hedging possible.

SELECTED READINGS

Hawtrey, R. G. *The Gold Standard in Theory and Practice*, 4h ed. London: Longmans, Green & Company, 1939. Chapter 2.

International Monetary Fund. *Report on Exchange Restrictions*. Washington, D. C., annual.

Machlup, Fritz. "The Theory of Foreign Exchanges," *Economica*, Vol. VI (New Series) (November, 1939), pp. 375-97, and (February, 1940), pp. 23-49. Reprinted in Ellis, Howard S., and Lloyd D. Metzler (eds.). *Readings in the Theory of International Trade*. Philadelphia: The Blakiston Co., 1949.

Marsh, Donald B. *World Trade and Investment*. New York: Harcourt, Brace & Co., 1951. Chapter 14.

Stein, Jerome L. *The Nature and Efficiency of the Foreign Exchange Market*, Essays in International Finance, No. 40. Princeton: Department of Economics in Princeton University, 1962.

CHAPTER 9

INTERNATIONAL PAYMENTS DISEQUILIBRIUM AND ADJUSTMENT

In Chapter 3 two fundamental questions were raised: (1) Why does international trade take place? (2) What are the gains from international trade? We now raise a third important question: How do nations adjust to disequilibrium in foreign trade or, more broadly, in the balance of payments and foreign exchange market?

The achievement and maintenance of equilibrium in international payments is a key objective of national economic policy. No country is immune to changes that can upset its external payments equilibrium. During the late forties and most of the fifties, Americans grew accustomed to a strong balance of payments at home and weak balances of payments abroad. The conventional wisdom of the times implied that balance of payments troubles happened only to others, not to Americans. But the sharp deterioration of the United States balance of payments in 1958 marked the end of this era. Since then, the restoration of external payments equilibrium has been the most pressing and bothersome international economic problem confronting the United States government. In a later chapter we shall describe and evaluate the steps taken by the United States to improve its balance of payments. First, however, we must understand the theory of international payments adjustment which will give us the concepts and other intellectual tools needed to assess balance of payments policy in the actual world economy.

The essence of international payments equilibrium is a stable, enduring relationship between the domestic economy and the economies of other trading nations. In equilibrium, a nation is paying its way (and no more) on a sustainable, long-term basis out of current income or other receipts. In other words, it is paying its way without resorting to reserves of gold and foreign exchange or to funds borrowed from other countries on a short-term basis.

Equilibrium in external payments implies equilibrium in the foreign exchange market. The amounts of foreign exchange in supply and demand are equal, and thus there is no need for compensatory movements of gold and short-term capital or for adjustments in the exchange rate. Equilibrium further implies the absence of government measures to adjust international payments by restricting imports or by artificially promoting exports.[1]

When equilibrium conditions are no longer present, the result is disequilibrium in international payments. The symptoms of disequilibrium, however, do not always appear in the same way. When exchange rates are held stable either through adherence to the gold standard or through the actions of a stabilization authority, disequilibrium usually appears as a one-way movement of gold and/or short-term capital. When, on the other hand, the exchange rate is free to respond to fluctuations in supply and demand, disequilibrium shows up as a one-way movement of the exchange rate. In that event net movements of gold and short-term capital are absent or minor; and, consequently, disequilibrium does not appear in the balance of payments. At times disequilibrium may be "suppressed" by exchange control and other restrictive devices so that it appears neither in the balance of payments nor in the foreign exchange market.

BALANCE OF PAYMENTS DISEQUILIBRIUM

International payments equilibrium is most likely to appear first in the balance of payments because nations usually insist upon the maintenance of stable exchange rates.

Narrowly conceived, the balance of payments is in disequilibrium when the net balance on current account is not fully offset by an opposing balance on long-term capital account. Disequilibrium prevails, therefore, when there is a net balance on short-term capital and monetary gold in the balance of payments. The reasoning behind this definition is straightforward. Insofar as a net balance on merchandise and services is not financed by a net balance on a long-term capital, it must be financed either by short-term capital or gold or a combination of these two items. But the availability of short-term

---

[1] Many economists would also add that equilibrium in international payments is inconsistent with the presence of widespread unemployment. The latter is hardly an element of stability.

capital (foreign exchange) and gold to a nation is limited—they can provide only a temporary "stopgap" financing of the other items in the balance of payments. When a nation's supply of short-term capital and gold runs out, the net balance on merchandise, services, and long-term capital must be eliminated since it can no longer be financed. The burden of this elimination, or adjustment, is usually borne by the current account and it involves a decrease in imports and/or an increase in exports. In short, the presence of net one-way movements of gold and short-term capital is a sign of instability in a nation's international payments that calls for adjustment.

Compensatory and Autonomous Items

The most comprehensive definition of disequilibrium in the balance of payments is based on the distinction between *compensatory* and *autonomous* items. Compensatory items are called into existence to finance autonomous items which, in contrast, are independent of other items in the balance of payments.[2] To illustrate, the export of merchandise is autonomous because it depends on factors such as prices, quality, and other market conditions rather than on the presence or absence of other items in the balance of payments. The export of merchandise, however, requires payment by foreign residents that appears in the balance of payments as a short-term capital outflow. Thus the short-term capital outflow in this instance is compensatory because it has been induced by another item in the balance of payments.

Most international movements of short-term capital are compensatory, occurring in response to the need to finance autonomous transactions between countries. Capital flight and many speculative capital movements, however, are autonomous: they do not finance other items in the balance of payments, but rather create the need for compensatory financing.

Unilateral transfers may also be either autonomous or compensatory. Private unilateral transfers and government unilateral transfers made for such specific purposes as relief, economic development projects, military aid, and reparations are autonomous. On the other hand, government unilateral transfers intended to help a recip-

---

[2] In practice, the distinction between compensatory and autonomous items depends partly on the purpose of one's analysis. For this reason there may be more than one measure of disequilibrium in a particular balance of payments, as we shall discover in Chapter 22. Here, however, we are interested only in the fundamental concept of payments disequilibrium.

ient country finance autonomous imports in its balance of payments are compensatory. Most of the foreign aid grants of the United States government in the early postwar years were compensatory in nature.

Most long-term capital movements are autonomous because they are motivated by expectations of profit or other income from productive investment. Occasionally, however, a government may extend a long-term stabilization loan to another government to provide funds for compensatory financing in the balance of payments. The Anglo-American loan of 1946 was of this sort.

Merchandise and service transactions on current account are always autonomous; they are not induced by any other items in the balance of payments. In contrast, exports and imports of monetary gold are always compensatory; they occur only to finance other items in the balance of payments.

Disequilibrium prevails in a nation's balance of payments when a net balance of compensatory items is needed to finance an opposing net balance of autonomous items. In these circumstances, the balance of payments is unstable because the supply of compensatory financing is limited and cannot continue indefinitely. Net compensatory financing is temporary "stopgap" financing. No nation has unlimited supplies of monetary gold and foreign exchange nor unlimited access to compensatory unilateral transfers or compensatory loans. If disequilibrium persists in the balance of payments, then sooner or later the sources of compensatory financing will become depleted. The net balance of compensatory items must then be eliminated through long-run adjustment in the current account, involving a decrease in imports and/or an increase in exports, together with suitable changes in other autonomous items such as long-term capital. When autonomous items fully offset each other, long-run adjustment is complete, and the balance of payments is in equilibrium.

This last statement needs qualification. Capital flight and destabilizing speculative capital movements are autonomous in that they provoke or worsen disequilibrium in the balance of payments rather than supply compensatory financing. Because of their inherent volatility and the fact that they reflect disturbances in the international economy, it is best to consider any large-scale movements of flight and destabilizing speculative capital as symptoms of disequilibrium. Accordingly, we amend our statement to read: Equilibrium in the balance of payments occurs when autonomous items fully offset each other, *and there are no substantial movements of flight and speculative capital of the destabilizing variety.*

International Reserves

Another measure of balance of payments disequilibrium is the net change that occurs in a country's reserves of gold and foreign exchange over a period. Reserves decline when they are used to finance a net autonomous import balance, and they must eventually give out unless the balance is eliminated. Reserves rise when there is a net autonomous export balance, but this rise must also end when the loss of reserves forces other countries to make adjustments.

When international reserves are influenced by compensatory foreign lending or borrowing, by compensatory unilateral transfers, or by government controls, they become a less satisfactory measure of balance of payments equilibrium. For example, in the early postwar period many European countries experienced a rise in their reserves that was due to compensatory unilateral transfers from the United States rather than to an autonomous export balance in their balance of payments.

Surplus and Deficit Disequilibrium

Disequilibrium in the balance of payments may be *surplus* or *deficit*.[3] Surplus disequilibrium usually appears in a country's balance of payments when its exports exceed imports on current account (merchandise and services), and this net credit balance is not offset by an autonomous export of long-term capital or by autonomous unilateral transfers. Instead, the net autonomous balance is financed by a compensatory export of capital, a compensatory import of gold, or by compensatory unilateral transfers to foreign countries. However, an export balance on current account is not a necessary condition of surplus disequilibrium. When an *import* balance on current account is less than an autonomous inflow of long-term capital, then the balance of payments is also in surplus disequilibrium. In recent years Switzerland, and at times other European countries, has exhibited this sort of surplus disequilibrium.[4]

Surplus disequilibrium adds to the international reserves of the surplus country unless that country is willing to finance the surplus

---

[3] A balance of payments in surplus disequilibrium is often called "favorable," and one in deficit disequilibrium, "unfavorable."

[4] At times, Switzerland has also received substantial amounts of flight and speculative capital which, as noted, are symptoms of disequilibrium. Although adding to Switzerland's monetary reserves, these kinds of capital can leave as suddenly as they arrive, posing a potential threat to the Swiss balance of payments. For this reason and to combat domestic inflation, the Swiss monetary authorities moved in 1963 to restrain short-term capital imports.

in its balance of payments by furnishing compensatory aid to deficit countries.

Conversely, deficit disequilibrium occurs when a country's autonomous debit transactions are greater than its autonomous credit transactions. The resulting net balance is financed in whole or in part by a compensatory import of short-term capital, a compensatory export of gold, or, less commonly, a receipt of compensatory unilateral transfers. In most cases, a deficit disequilibrium originates in the current account where imports are running ahead of exports and the resulting net debit balance is greater than any net autonomous long-term capital inflow. But deficit disequilibrium may also originate in the long-term capital account or, less likely, in the unilateral transfer account. During the first half of the 1960's the United States achieved a very strong surplus on current account, but its balance of payments nevertheless stayed in deficit disequilibrium because this surplus was exceeded by net debit balances on other autonomous items.

Deficit disequilibrium causes a nation to lose reserves of gold and foreign exchange unless the deficit is financed by a net inflow of foreign short-term capital or compensatory aid from abroad.

Surplus disequilibrium, accompanied by rising international reserves, seldom causes concern in the surplus country. An exception occurs, as observed in the case of Switzerland, when reserves are swollen by large-scale inflows of speculative and flight capital that threaten future payments stability and (possibly) intensify domestic inflation. Deficit disequilibrium is another matter. Falling reserves must be checked if the exchange rate is to be held at its current level without the imposition of controls. Autonomous debit transactions must be contracted; autonomous credit transactions expanded. This involves income and price adjustments and/or direct government action to curtail imports, raise exports, discourage long-term capital outflows, stop capital flight or speculative capital outflows, and so on. In short, deficit disequilibrium compels adjustment—one way or another.

Surplus disequilibrium in one country's balance of payments is only possible if there is deficit disequilibrium in the balance of payments of one or more other countries. Even though a country may seek to preserve a surplus in its balance of payments, therefore, the surplus cannot endure any longer than the deficits that are its counterparts in the balance of payments of foreign countries. Actually, the surplus country has everything to gain by facilitating adjustments toward equilibrium in its balance of payments. Otherwise, one day its exports may face a barrier of discriminatory restrictions imposed by deficit nations.

MAJOR SOURCES OF DISEQUILIBRIUM

As a consolidated account of a nation's international transactions, the balance of payments is related to the domestic and foreign economies by a complex pattern of interdependence. Similarly, the supply and demand of foreign exchange is dependent on all the credit and debit transactions of the balance of payments, respectively. Fundamentally, then, equilibrium in the balance of payments and the foreign exchange market demands a stable, mutual adjustment among national incomes, prices, interest rates, money supplies, wages, and other economic variables at home and abroad, as mediated by the rate of exchange. Payments equilibrium does not rule out a change in any one of these variables as long as its effects are neutralized by a change or changes in one or more other variables. Thus, for example, equilibrium will be sustained if a rise in exports, stimulated (say) by higher incomes abroad, is matched by an equal rise in net long-term capital outflows, attracted (say) by higher interest rates abroad. That is to say, equilibrium can be dynamic; indeed, it must be so in a world of continuing movement. When, however, changes in economic variables at home or abroad are not neutralized by changes in other variables, they will cause disequilibrium in the balance of payments mainly by altering the size and direction of money expenditures, by altering prices (including the exchange rate) or by altering both expenditures and prices.

Despite the large number of potential sources of disequilibrium, however, it is possible to classify them into the following relatively few broad categories:

1. Seasonal and random disequilibrium.
2. Cyclical disequilibrium.
3. Structural disequilibrium.
4. Destabilizing speculation and capital flight.
5. Other sources of disequilibrium.

We shall discuss these categories as sources of *deficit* disequilibrium, but since a deficit disequilibrium in one country implies a surplus disequilibrium in one or more other countries, it should be clear that they are also sources of surplus disequilibrium.

Seasonal and Random Disequilibrium

A nation's exports and imports vary seasonally due to seasonal changes in production and consumption, but usually this seasonal variation is not the same for both. The result is seasonal disequilibrium in the balance of payments. Seasonal disequilibrium is ordinarily of little consequence since it is short-lived and self-reversible—a deficit in one season offsetting a surplus in another.

Seasonal disequilibrium is likely to be most visible in the balance of payments of less-developed countries that depend on agricultural products for the bulk of their exports. Seasonal import variations may also be substantial for these countries when the agricultural sector depends on imports of fertilizers, mechanical equipment, and fuels for its seasonal requirements, or when food must be imported to meet consumption needs in the period preceding domestic harvests. Seasonal variations in trade are less prominent in the balance of payments of industrial countries although they are never entirely absent.

Irregular, nonsystematic, short-lived disturbances may also cause disequilibrium in the balance of payments. The traditional example of this kind of disequilibrium is a crop failure that curtails exports or forces a nation to import foodstuffs. The most striking example of this phenomenon in recent years was the crop failure in the Soviet Union that led to large purchases of wheat from Canada and the United States in 1963 and 1964. Labor strikes that tie up transportation or immobilize industries can also affect exports or imports and thus the balance of payments. The long steel strike in the United States in 1959 not only cut back steel exports but also brought about a sharp increase in steel imports. Other sources of random disequilibrium include natural disasters such as floods and earthquakes. The foregoing random disturbances have a once-for-all impact on the balance of payments; they cause only a *temporary* disequilibrium. When disturbances are of such a magnitude as to have pervasive and lasting effects on the economy and trade of a nation (war, revolution, civil strife, etc.), then they are not random in the sense that we are using the term.

Although seasonal disequilibrium is largely predictable and random disequilibrium is not, both are short-lived and do not call for equilibrating adjustments in incomes, prices, or exchange rates. Seasonal deficits should be financed out of seasonal surpluses; random deficits should be financed out of international reserves which are maintained in part for this very purpose.

Cyclical Disequilibrium

Variations in the national incomes of trading countries, whether involving changes in price levels, changes in the levels of production and employment, or both, may lead to cyclical disequilibrium in the balance of payments.

In the early 1930's massive deflations in real income and production (accompanied by widespread unemployment) occurred in the industrial countries of North America and Western Europe. In the nonindustrial countries where the agricultural sector accounted for the bulk of national income, deflation mainly took the form of a catastrophic fall in prices, wages, and terms of trade, rather than in production and employment. This global deflation caused enormous payments disequilibria, wrecked the international monetary system, and forced nations into competitive depreciations and the wholesale use of trade and payments restrictions.

Since the end of World War II the industrial countries have avoided deflation; by and large they have been able to achieve steady growth at full-employment levels. But they have been far less successful in avoiding inflation generated by an effective demand running ahead of production. Since the Korean War in the early 1950's, most industrial countries have experienced a "creeping" inflation averaging one or two percent a year. The situation in many developing countries has been far worse: "runaway" inflation of 50 percent or more in a single year is not uncommon. Brazil and Indonesia may be cited as examples. We can fairly say that inflation has been the single most important source of payments disequilibrium in the post war years.[5]

Cyclical disequilibrium may be a misnomer to denote payments disequilibrium caused by deflationary and inflationary movements in national income and price levels because at most it is only roughly periodic. It can be regarded as temporary or persistent depending on whether the responsible change in national income is self-corrective or can be corrected by monetary and fiscal measures within (say) two years or so.

Structural Disequilibrium

Shifts in the demand for *specific* export goods, whether brought about by changing tastes, a new distribution of income in export

---

[5] Whether the United States balance of payments deficit should be attributed to domestic inflation is touched on in Chapter 22.

markets, or by changes in the availability or prices of competitive products offered by foreign suppliers, are common events in foreign trade. Shifts in the demand for import goods also occur for similar reasons. When a national economy is slow to adapt to these shifts, persistent structural disequilibrium appears in its balance of payments. We were referring to this kind of disequilibrium in earlier chapters dealing with comparative costs when we observed that in a dynamic world a nation cannot reasonably expect its comparative cost advantages to last indefinitely. On the contrary, continuing movements (big and small) in the direction and composition of a nation's exports and imports are a normal condition of world trade.

What is needed to remedy structural disequilibrium is a reallocation of production to conform to new patterns of demand and supply. Persistent structural disequilibrium may be viewed as a failure of the price system which is supposed to guide and encourage reallocation in a market economy. Reallocation is sluggish when prices respond only slowly, if at all, to shifting market conditions because of monopoly, administrative pricing, price agreements, or other arrangements that limit price competition.

Adjustments in production usually demand a reallocation in the use of factors of production. In the export sector, for example, labor and other factors must move out of lines of production no longer in demand in foreign markets and into lines that enjoy a comparative advantage. When wages and the prices of other factors employed in declining export industries are hard to lower (sticky downwards), the reallocating function of factor prices is crippled and must depend on the attraction of higher factor rewards in growing industries in the export sector or elsewhere in the economy. A more serious deterrent to a prompt reallocation of factors is low factor mobility, especially labor. This creates the problem of structural unemployment.

To conclude, a wide variety of forces operating at home and abroad, such as technological and product innovations, new competition, changes in tastes, improvements in productivity, growing populations, and so on, may cause shifts in the supply and demand of individual exports and imports that result in a structural disequilibrium in the balance of payments.

Destabilizing Speculation and Capital Flight

These two phenomena (described in Chapter 8) constitute another source of payments disequilibrium. Although conceptually distinct, these autonomous short-term capital movements tend to occur together. Both intensify an existing disequilibrium, and capital flight may actually create one since it is motivated by fears of safety which sometimes originate in conditions unrelated to the balance of payments, notably the prospect of war or revolution.

In the postwar years the primary stimulus of destabilizing speculation and capital flight has been the possibility of depreciation in a major currency already weakened by a balance of payments deficit. Great Britain has suffered from heavy outflows of speculative and flight capital that have exacerbated its balance of payments troubles since the late 1940's, and in the fall of 1960 similar outflows intensified pressure on the dollar.

Other Sources of Disequilibrium

The preceding four categories cover the main sources of disequilibrium, but they are not exhaustive. As we shall discover later, the United States payments deficit does not fit neatly into any one of these categories. In particular, we should recognize that a huge sustained outflow of long-term investment capital can also create a payments deficit that calls for adjustment.[6] Disequilibrium may also originate in an unrealistic exchange rate, not uncommon when there is exchange control. Some economists also speak of *secular* disequilibrium that arises from technological and other changes that occur slowly as an economy moves from one stage of growth to another over a period of decades.

THE NEED FOR ADJUSTMENT

No nation can continue indefinitely to experience an excess of autonomous imports over autonomous exports or, for that matter, an excess of autonomous exports over autonomous imports. Foreign exchange required to pay for imports cannot be manufactured at home; over the long run it must be earned by exports of merchandise and services or obtained through an inflow of long-term investment capital. In the end, adjustment to a persistent deficit in the balance of payments involves a reorientation of domestic production and consumption—more resources must be devoted to exports and/or there must be a lower consumption of imports.

---

[6] This is the foreign investment transfer problem. See Chapter 21.

Market Versus Nonmarket Adjustment

Basically, a nation may adjust to a *persistent* deficit in its balance of payments in one of three ways: (1) through an internal deflation of prices and incomes relative to foreign prices and incomes, (2) through a depreciation of its rate of exchange, or (3) through an imposition of exchange and trade controls.

The first two methods of adjustment work through market processes involving changes in income, prices, exchange rates, money supplies, interest rates, and other economic phenomena. Market adjustment, however, does not imply the absence of governmental action. Indeed, successful market adjustment to an external deficit depends upon government fiscal and monetary policies directed toward reinforcing equilibrating market forces. Otherwise, government monetary and fiscal policies, while not controlling or supplanting market adjustment, may counteract its equilibrating effects on the balance of payments by introducing disequilibrating changes in income, prices, and the like. Generally, exchange depreciation involves a government decision because most nations seek to stabilize their exchange rates.

Nonmarket adjustment stands in sharp contrast to market adjustment. Government controls and regulatory devices replace the market in order to supress an external deficit. Controlled adjustment is not true adjustment. Although the symptoms of disequilibrium (net compensatory items in the balance of payments or depreciation of the exchange rate) are removed by direct controls, the causes of disequilibrium (cyclical, structural, etc.) are left untouched. The result is *suppressed disequilibrium.* Suppressed disequilibrium generally results from the widespread use of import quotas and exchange restrictions. But restrictive measures and direct controls may take any number of particular forms: tied loans and foreign assistance, discriminatory taxation to inhibit private long-term capital outflows and merchandise imports or to encourage merchandise exports, generalized tariff surcharges, domestic buying preferences, restrictions on the purchase of foreign bonds and on bank loans to foreigners, to name only the more prominent. As we shall see, many of these restrictions have been imposed by the United States government in an effort to eliminate the United States payments deficit.

Varieties of Market Adjustment

Market adjustment to persistent disequilibrium takes two different paths depending upon whether exchange rates are stable or free to vary. When exchange rates are held stable either through adherence to the gold standard or through official stabilization agencies, adjustment occurs mainly via changes in incomes and prices *within* the domestic and foreign economies. On the other hand, when exchange rates are free to vary, adjustment mainly occurs within the foreign exchange market (with repercussions on domestic and foreign income and prices) where the exchange rate moves until an equality is established between the amounts of foreign exchange supplied and demanded as a result of autonomous transactions.

It follows that in a stable-rate system the domestic economy is closely linked to foreign economies, whereas in a fluctuating-rate system the domestic economy is insulated to some extent from foreign economic influences (and vice versa) by the foreign exchange market. The contemporary international monetary system is often termed an "adjustable-peg" system because, although exchange rates are normally held stable, adjustment to balance of payments disequilibrium is made at times by varying the exchange rate. When this happens adjustment substantially agrees with that in a fluctuating-rate system.

In the next chapter we trace the path of adjustment in a stable-rate system and in Chapter 11 look at adjustment in a variable-rate system. Although differences between these two systems are often stressed (and debated) by economists, we shall find that adjustment to deficit disequilibrium in both systems involves a shift of resources to the export sector and a drop in expenditures on imports brought about by income and price changes.

SUMMARY

1. The achievement and maintenance of equilibrium in international payments is a key objective of national economic policy. The essence of international payments equilibrium is a stable, enduring relationship between the domestic economy and the economies of other trading nations.
2. When equilibrium conditions are no longer present, the result is disequilibrium in international payments. In a stable-rate system disequilibrium appears as a net, one-way movement of gold and short-term capital. In a variable-rate system disequilibrium shows up as a one-way movement of the exchange rate.
3. The most comprehensive definition of disequilibrium in the balance of payments is based on the distinction between *compensatory* and *autonomous* items. Compensatory items are called into existence to finance autonomous items which, in contrast, are independent of other items in the balance of payments. Disequilibrium prevails in a nation's balance of payments when a net balance of compensatory items is needed to

finance an opposing net balance of autonomous items. Another, but less satisfactory, measure of disequilibrium is the net change that occurs in a country's reserves of gold and foreign exchange over a period.

4. *Deficit* disequilibrium arises when a net autonomous import or debit balance is financed by a net compensatory export or credit balance. Conversely, a net autonomous export or credit balance financed by a net compensatory import or debit balance indicates a *surplus* equilibrium.

5. The presence of substantial movements of flight and speculative capital of the destabilizing variety is always a sign of disequilibrium even in the unlikely event they are fully offset by other autonomous items.

6. Despite the large number of potential sources of disequilibrium, it is possible to classify them into a relatively few broad categories: seasonal and random, cyclical, structural, destabilizing speculation and capital flight, and other. The most important distinction is between temporary and persistent disequilibrium.

7. Adjustment to international payments disequilibrium is necessary because no nation can continue indefinitely to import more than it exports in autonomous items, or conversely. Adjustments may occur through market processes (income, prices, exchange rate, etc.) or be suppressed by government controls. When exchange rates are stable, market adjustment to a persistent disequilibrium is effected mainly through income and price changes within the domestic and foreign economies. Otherwise, it occurs mainly through variations in the exchange rate.

QUESTIONS AND APPLICATIONS

1. In looking at a balance of payments how would you decide which items were autonomous and which items were compensatory?
2. Define balance of payments equilibrium and disequilibrium in terms of compensatory and autonomous items.
3. (a) What is the function of international reserves?
   (b) Why are reserves compensatory in nature?
4. Distinguish between surplus and deficit disequilibrium.
5. Describe the major sources of disequilibrium.
6. Why does disequilibrium, especially deficit disequilibrium, call for adjustment?
7. Explain the difference between market and nonmarket adjustments.

SELECTED READINGS

See the list of readings given at the end of Chapter 11.

CHAPTER 10

INTERNATIONAL ADJUSTMENT
IN A STABLE-RATE SYSTEM

In this chapter we are interested in market adjustment to *persistent* disequilibrium occurring in a stable-rate system. First, however, we need to say something about the *initial* response to disequilibrium in the balance of payments when exchange rates are fixed or stable.

SHORT-RUN ADJUSTMENT

In a stable-rate system such as the international gold standard, the initial response to disequilibrium in the balance of payments takes the form of compensatory movements of short-term capital and gold. This *short-run* adjustment may be adequate when the disequilibrium is *temporary* (seasonal, random, some cyclical).

Compensatory Financing

Compensatory movements of short-term capital and gold are symptoms of disequilibrium in the balance of payments, but they also serve as the instruments of short-run adjustment to disequilibrium in a stable-rate system by performing two functions. First, compensatory items are the means of financing the net autonomous debit or credit in the balance of payments. Second, compensatory items transfer purchasing power from the deficit to the surplus country and thereby initiate changes in income and prices that eventually lead to adjustment when disequilibrium is persistent.

Short-run adjustment occurs quickly in the capital account of the balance of payments, whereas income and price adjustment works slowly in the current account. Hence short-run adjustment affords the necessary time as well as the stimulus for long-run adjustment—

equilibrating changes in exports and imports of merchandise and services that eliminate the net balance (debit or credit) on autonomous items.

The compensatory items that finance a net autonomous balance in the balance of payments may come from a number of sources. A few of these sources are:

1. The deficit country experiences an inflow of short-term capital when its foreign exchange dealers draw down their foreign balances to finance the excess of imports.

2. Short-term capital may move from the surplus to the deficit country because short-term interest rates rise in the latter country and fall in the former.

These opposing shifts in interest rates are brought about by the net monetary effects of international payments. The greater supply of money in the surplus country tends to lower its short-term interest rate, while the smaller supply of money in the deficit country tends to raise its short-term interest rate. To gain a higher rate of return, therefore, funds move from the surplus to the deficit country.

3. Stabilizing speculation may supply compensatory short-term capital to the deficit country. When the rate of exchange of the deficit country's currency rises toward its gold export point or toward the ceiling maintained by a stabilization authority, speculators may buy that currency in anticipation of a subsequent decline in its rate. Such speculation supplies foreign exchange (short-term capital) to the deficit country.

4. Compensatory short-term capital may also come from the deficit country's stabilization agency when it uses foreign exchange reserves to restrain a rise in the rate of exchange.

5. Compensatory short-term capital may be provided by unilateral transfers and stabilization loans from a surplus to the deficit country.

6. Finally, compensatory financing may come from gold exports of the deficit country.

Importance of Short-Term Capital Movements

The viability of a stable-rate system depends upon large equilibrating flows of short-term capital because most countries have only a small supply of gold. Otherwise, short-run adjustment is unable to provide the financing that may be needed to ride out a temporary disequilibrium or to afford the time required for long-run adjustment in income and prices if the disequilibrium is persistent. When the supply of short-term capital is meager, most countries are forced to adjust through exchange depreciation unless they decide to suppress the disequilibrium with controls.

Before World War I, compensatory movements of short-term capital were encouraged by the adherence of countries to the gold standard "rules of the game." In conformity with these informal rules, the central bank of a deficit country raised its rediscount rate while the central bank of a surplus country lowered its rate. These actions reinforced the interest rate changes brought about by the net monetary effects of international payments.[1] Another unspoken rule made it mandatory that a country alter the gold content of its currency only as a last extremity. Stabilizing speculation was thereby encouraged by a well-founded belief in the fixity of exchange rates.

In the 1920's the gold standard rules were less influential over the conduct of monetary authorities. The rediscount rate was increasingly regarded as an instrument of domestic stabilization rather than international adjustment.[2] Moreover, the general abandonment of the gold standard during the war and the subsequent difficulties encountered in returning to it during the twenties caused a loss of faith in the ability of countries to maintain fixed exchange rates. As a consequence, movements of short-term capital and gold in the twenties were often disequilibrating rather than equilibrating.

Today the bulk of compensatory movements of short-term capital and gold is initiated by governments and their central banks. In the postwar period compensatory financing has come mainly from intergovernment stabilization loans and unilateral transfers, official gold and foreign exchange reserves, the International Monetary Fund, and credit arrangements negotiated by central banks. In general, therefore, national governments now decide on the nature and degree of short-run adjustment.

When compensatory financing is not forthcoming, short-run adjustment with stable rates is not possible; and the deficit nation must either impose or tighten controls over its international trade

---

[1] During this period the rediscount rate of the Bank of England was of primary importance. The power of the interest rate to attract funds from abroad is attested by the saying, common in London at the time, that "8 percent would bring gold from the moon."

[2] After studying the period 1880-1914, Bloomfield concluded that the differences between the pre-1914 gold standard and after World War I were essentially "differences of degree rather than of kind." Before 1914 central banks were not indifferent to the effects of discount policy on domestic economic activity, and did not respond automatically to payments disequilibrium. However, in the period studied, convertibility was the dominant objective of central banks and they "invariably acted decisively in one way or another when the standard was threatened." See Arthur I. Bloomfield, *Monetary Policy under the International Gold Standard: 1880-1914* (New York: Federal Reserve Bank of New York, 1959).

and payments, depreciate its exchange rate, or (if there is time) bring about equilibrating changes in its national income and price level.

Transfer of Purchasing Power

In addition to financing a temporary disequilibrium in the balance of payments, gold and short-term capital movements also act to transfer purchasing power from the deficit to the surplus country. This transfer initiates price and income changes in both countries that bring about equilibrating changes in the exports and imports of merchandise and services. In this way short-run adjustment prepares the ground for long-run adjustment to persistent disequilibrium, to which we now turn.

THE CLASSICAL THEORY OF ADJUSTMENT

The first coherent theory of international payments adjustment was devised by David Hume (1711-76), British philosopher and economist extraordinary.[3] In opposition to the dominant mercantilist thought of the age, Hume asserted the impossibility of maintaining a chronic "favorable balance of trade" in order to acquire gold and silver (specie) from foreign countries.

The Price-Specie Flow Mechanism

Hume's theory of adjustment has come down to us as the *price-specie flow mechanism*. It asserts that an inflow of specie resulting from an excess of exports over imports increases the nation's money supply, and that the latter, in turn, increases domestic prices. These higher prices then curtail exports. At the same time there occurs a fall in the money supply and prices of foreign countries experiencing an outflow of specie. This decline in prices stimulates the exports of those countries, including exports to the country receiving specie. In this way international specie movements eliminate any disequilibrium in the balance of payments—higher prices in the surplus country cause its exports to fall and its imports to rise while lower prices in the deficit country or countries cause exports to rise and imports to fall. International specie movements are, therefore, symptoms of payments disequilibrium, and they will continue until the money supplies and price levels of the trading nations achieve an equality between the exports and imports of each country.

---

[3] This theory appeared in Hume's *Political Discourses* published in Edinburgh in 1752.

Critique of Price-Specie Flow Mechanism

Succeeding generations of classical and neoclassical economists (Ricardo, Mill, Marshall, Taussig, and others) added refinements to Hume's price-specie flow mechanism, but made no basic changes in it. The theory was modified to take account of service or "invisible" items in the balance of payments; short-term capital movements; the fractional reserve system of banking; and the differential price behavior of export goods, import-competing goods, and domestic goods. However, the underlying assumptions of the theory—the quantity theory of money and the effect of price changes on exports and imports—were not effectively challenged until the Keynesian revolution in economic thinking of the late 1930's.

The price-specie flow mechanism is open to all the criticisms that have been leveled against the quantity theory of money. This theory assumes that a change in the quantity of money will bring about a proportionate change in the price level. A change in the quantity of money will, however, affect prices only if it affects spending, and the change in spending induced by a given change in the money supply may be relatively large or small depending on the latter's velocity of turnover. Moreover, the influence of a given change in spending on prices will vary according to the general level of employment and output and the degree of price flexibility in the economy. Hence there is no direct or certain price response to a change in the money supply, and, under conditions of excess productive capacity and unemployment or of imperfect competition, there may be little or no response.

The main criticism of the price-specie flow mechanism, however, is its emphasis upon price adjustment to the almost complete neglect of income adjustment. Classical and neoclassical economists realized that the deficit country underwent a decline in its purchasing power relative to the surplus country, and that this decline, along with the adverse shift in its terms of trade, brought about adjustment by raising its exports and lowering its imports. But this purchasing power or income effect was viewed as the incidental accompaniment of price changes, which were the main instruments of international adjustment. There was no conception of an *autonomous* change in income unrelated to a change in prices. In the classical world of full employment and purely competitive markets, this oversight was almost inevitable for under such conditions a change in spending will cause a change in prices and there are no income effects unaccompanied by price changes.

Writing in 1928, Taussig, the foremost neoclassical economist in America, felt that something was missing in the price-specie flow explanation of international payments adjustment although he was unable to lay his finger on it. In speaking of adjustment to a movement of long-term investment capital, he wrote as follows:

> What is puzzling is the rapidity, almost simultaneity, of the commodity movements. The presumable intermediate state of gold flow and price changes is hard to discern, and certainly extremely short.[4]

At another point he remarked:

> It must be confessed that here we have phenomena not fully understood. In part our information is insufficient; in part our understanding of other connected topics is also inadequate.[5]

Income adjustment is the key to this puzzle. Along with price adjustment it makes up the modern theory of long-run adjustment to balance of payments disequilibrium.

NATIONAL INCOME AND FOREIGN TRADE

When exchange rates are held stable, either through adherence to the gold standard or through official stabilization agencies, short-run adjustment to a balance of payments disequilibrium occurs through the movement of compensatory items in the balance of payments, principally gold and short-term capital. Long-run adjustment to a persistent disequilibrium involves an internal deflation of income and prices in the deficit country and, simultaneously, an internal inflation of income and prices in the surplus country.

The modern theory of long-run adjustment places great emphasis on the role of income changes, both in the deficit and the surplus countries, in effecting adjustment to balance of payments disequilibrium. It does not neglect, however, the equilibrating price movements that may accompany the changes in income.

The modern theory states that a persistent disequilibrium in the balance of payments will cause a cumulative deflation of income in the deficit country and, simultaneously, a cumulative inflation of income in the surplus country. Declining income in the deficit country will lessen the external deficit by inducing a decline in imports and by releasing goods from domestic consumption for export. Rising

---

[4] Frank W. Taussig, *International Trade* (New York: MacMillan Co., 1928), p. 260.

[5] *Ibid.*, p. 239.

Ch. 10 / International Adjustment in a Stable-Rate System

income in the surplus country will lessen the external surplus by inducing a rise in imports and by drawing export goods into domestic consumption.

Falling prices in the deficit country and rising prices in the surplus country will also aid adjustment. In the former, imports will become less attractive to buyers, while in the latter, imports will become more attractive.

In this section we examine the relationships between national income and foreign trade, and in the next section, the mechanism of income adjustment to a balance of payments disequilibrium. Price adjustment is described in the final section of the chapter.

The Gross National Product and Income Equations

The *gross national product* (GNP) of a nation is the market value of all goods and services produced by the national economy over a period of time which is usually a year. In practice, the GNP is estimated by aggregating the total expenditures on goods and services of individuals, business, government, and foreigners in the markets of the nation over the year. Since these are final expenditures, no single good or service is counted more than once.

In a *closed* economy with no foreign trade all expenditures are domestic and GNP may be expressed as follows:

$$GNP = C + I + G$$

where C represents expenditures by individuals for consumption; I, expenditures by business for gross investment (capital equipment, construction, and net additions to inventories); and G, expenditures by government for both consumption and investment.

In an *open* economy, however, GNP is affected by the exports and imports of goods and services that make up the current account of the nation's balance of payments. Exports measure the expenditures by foreigners in domestic markets and therefore are part of GNP. Imports, on the other hand, measure expenditures by domestic individuals, business, and government for goods and services produced by *other* nations, and therefore must be *deducted* from total expenditures to get the *domestic* gross national product.

Hence in an open economy GNP assumes this form:

$$(1) \quad GNP = C + I + G + X - M$$

where X represents expenditures on exports and M, expenditures on imports. The expression $X - M$ links gross national product to the balance of payments because this expression is the net balance on current account which is also the net foreign investment of the nation.

To show this, we can rewrite (1) as follows:

(2) $GNP = C + I_d + G + (X - M)$

where I_d represents *domestic* gross investment and $(X - M)$, net foreign investment.

The production of the goods and services making up the gross national product generates an equal flow of income to the factors which contribute their productive services. Some of this income is spent by individuals on consumption and some is saved by them, some is saved by business as depreciation and "retained corporate profits," and the rest is taxed away by government. Thus we can define *gross national income* (GNI) as follows:

(3) $GNI = C + S_p + S_b + T$

where C represents income spent on consumption; S_p and S_b, personal and business saving, respectively; and T, income taxed away by government.

Since GNP is equal to GNI we now have this identity:

(4) $C + I_d + G + (X - M) = C + S_p + S_b + T$

Simplifying and transposing we get:

(5) $I_d + G + (X - M) = S_p + S_b + T$
(6) $S_p + S_b + (T - G) - I_d = X - M$

since $(T - G)$ is the excess of tax revenue over government expenditure, or *government saving*, $S_p + S_b + (T - G) = S$, where S represents *total* domestic saving. Thus:

(7) $S - I_d = X - M$

This is a basic equation relating gross national income (or product) to foreign trade. It states that any excess of exports over imports (current account surplus) is matched by an excess of domestic saving over domestic investment. Conversely, an excess of imports over exports (current account deficit) is matched by an excess of domestic investment over domestic saving. If domestic saving equals domestic investment, then exports also equals imports.

This discussion of gross national income and product may take on more meaning for readers if we end it with a presentation of those two accounts for the United States in 1964. (Table 10-1.)

Table 10-1
GROSS NATIONAL INCOME AND PRODUCT OF THE UNITED STATES IN 1964
(Billions of Dollars)

GNP		GNI	
C	399.3	C	399.3
I_d	87.7	S_p	32.5
G	128.6	S_b	65.2
X	35.2	T	127.6 *
M	—28.2	Statistical Discrepancy	—2.0
GNP	622.6	GNI	622.6

* Net of government transfer payments, net interest paid by the government, contributions to social insurance, and subsidies less current surplus of government enterprises which together amounted to $17.1 billion.

SOURCE: Adapted from *Federal Reserve Bulletin*, May, 1965, pp. 746-47.

Readers may find it instructive to insert these figures into the gross national product and income equations. In so doing, do not forget the statistical discrepancy on the income side!

Determination of National Income

How do *changes* in gross national income (product) affect the balance of payments? How do *changes* in foreign trade affect gross national income? To answer these questions, we must understand how national income is determined.[6]

Let us return to:

$$(4) \quad C + I_d + G + (X - M) = C + S_p + S_b + T$$

This can be rewritten as follows:

$$(8) \quad \underbrace{C + I_d + G + X}_{\text{Income Injections}} = \underbrace{C + S_p + S_b + T + M}_{\text{Income Leakages}}$$

Simply put, all increases (decreases) in expenditures on domestic goods and services will increase (decrease) national income. The different expenditures, however, do not play the same role in *initiating* changes in national income. Basically, changes in domestic

---

[6] We can offer here only a very condensed version of the theory of income determination. For a fuller treatment see any introductory text on economics.

investment and government and export expenditures are *autonomous* with respect to national income. That is to say, they are not dependent on any prior change in income but rather cause changes in income. On the other hand, changes in consumption expenditure are *induced* by prior changes in national income and do not *initiate* changes in it. In other words, consumption expenditures do not determine national income but instead are determined by national income. Henceforth, we shall refer to autonomous expenditures (domestic investment, government, and exports) as *income injections*.

In contrast to expenditures, domestic saving, taxes, and imports act to *depress* national income. Saving is a decision not to spend, taxes lower spendable income in the hands of individuals and business, and imports divert expenditures away from domestic goods and services to foreign output. For this reason we shall call them *income leakages*.

National income is in equilibrium when the expenditures that consumers, business, government, and foreigners want, or *intend*, to make in domestic markets are equal to *intended* saving, taxation and imports. That is to say, when

$$(9)\ G + I_d + X = S_p + S_b + T + M$$

To simplify matters we can view $(T - G)$ as part of domestic saving (S) along with S_p and S_b, reducing (9) to

$$(10)\ I_d + X = S + M$$

This equation resembles (7), but it is not the same because in our present discussion we are speaking of *intended* expenditures, saving, and imports. Equation (7) always holds, but (10) holds *only* when national income is in equilibrium. If, for example, businessmen end up the year with unwanted, or unintended, additions to their inventories, then they will take steps to reduce them and thus lower income in the following year. Only when intended income injections are equal to intended income leakages is national income "determined," that is, stable. We can draw here an analogy with the balance of payments. As we have seen, the balance of payments is always in accounting balance, but it is in equilibrium only when autonomous items cancel out to a zero balance.

Functional Relationship of Expenditures, Saving, and Imports to Real Domestic Income

In discussing the relationships between changes in expenditures, saving, and imports, on the one hand, and changes in national

Ch. 10 / International Adjustment in a Stable-Rate System

income, on the other, we shall be talking of *real* income changes, that is, income changes that are *not* accompanied by price changes. The assumptions underlying this condition are indicated later on in the chapter.

As discussed above, changes in domestic investment and exports are independent of changes in domestic national income.[7] Investment expenditure depends on the expected return on capital (marginal efficiency of capital) interacting with the cost of capital (interest rate). Changes in exports depend upon changes in tastes and real income in foreign countries. Consumption, saving, and imports, however, are all dependent on income.

The relation between consumption and income is known as the *marginal propensity to consume* (MPC) which is expressed as dC/dY, where dY is a change in national income and dC is the change in consumption induced by the change in income. If, for example, the MPC is 0.8, then a $100 change (increase or decrease) in national income will induce an $80 change in consumption. In brief, the marginal propensity to consume is the fraction or percentage of new income that is spent on consumption.

Some of the consumption expenditure goes to buy imports. Thus the marginal propensity to consume includes the *marginal propensity to import* (MPM). The latter is expressed as dM/dY. The marginal propensity to import, then, is the percentage of new income that is spent on imports. If the MPM is 0.2, then a $100 change in national income will induce a $20 change in imports.

The expression dS/dY is the *marginal propensity to save* (MPS) which relates a change in national income to the change in saving induced by the former. Since income is either spent or saved, the MPC and MPS together always add up to one. If the MPC is 0.8, then the MPS must be 0.2.

The marginal propensities are not necessarily the same at different levels of national income. For example, as family incomes rise beyond a subsistence level, the marginal propensity to consume may decline or, to say the same thing, the marginal propensity to save may increase. For the sake of simplicity, however, we shall assume in this and later discussions that the marginal propensities are constant.

---

[7] This is generally true, but at times changes in investment may be induced by changes in consumption (accelerator principle) and changes in domestic income may alter the supply of export goods and services. Basically, however, investment and exports are autonomous.

Domestic and Foreign Trade Income Multipliers

Reverting to Equation (10), an autonomous shift in domestic investment or in exports will cause a change in national income in the same direction. Increases in these expenditures will raise national income; decreases will lower it. Furthermore, the resulting change in national income will be a *multiple* of the autonomous change in investment or exports. This is because the income first generated by the autonomous expenditure will be respent by its recipients which, in turn, will generate another change in income, and so on. This process of income change (expansion or contraction) will come to a stop when the income leakages induced by the income change become equal to the autonomous income injection. As we have noted, this is when $I_d + X = S + M$.

The relationship between an autonomous change in domestic investment and the subsequent change in national income that it induces is called the *domestic income multiplier*, or dY/dI_d. If the domestic multiplier is 2, then a $100 increase (decrease) in domestic investment will cause a $200 increase (decrease) in national income. We may derive the *domestic* income multiplier as follows:

(a) $I_d + X = S + M$

Now introduce a change in domestic investment (dI) which will induce a change in domestic saving (dS) and imports (dM) via an induced change in national income. Since exports will not change, we can rewrite (a):

(b) $dI_d = dS + dM$

Dividing both sides of (b) into the induced change in national income (dY), we have

(c) $dY/dI_d = dY/dS + dY/dM$, or

(d) $dY/dI_d = \dfrac{1}{dS/dY} + \dfrac{1}{dM/dY} = \dfrac{1}{dS/dY + dM/dY}$

This last equation tells us that the domestic income multiplier (dY/dI_d) equals the *reciprocal of the sum of the marginal propensities to save and import*. If MPS is 0.1 and MPM is 0.1, then the multiplier is 1/0.2, or 5. Thus an autonomous change in domestic investment of (say) $50 would cause a change of $250 in national income. In mathematical terms:

(e) $dY = (dY/dI_d)\, dI_d$

which says that the change in income equals the multiplier *times* the autonomous change in domestic investment.

The relationship between an autonomous change in exports (dX) and the induced change in national income (dY) is known as the *foreign trade multiplier*. We can derive the foreign trade multiplier in exactly the same way we derived the domestic multiplier, and it assumes the same form: $dY/dX = 1/MPS + MPM$. The induced change in national income will be the autonomous change in exports *times* the multiplier.

We may summarize this exposition by saying that changes in national income are induced by autonomous changes in domestic investment or exports. The resulting change in national income will be the product of the autonomous change in investment or exports *times* the income multiplier. Both the domestic and foreign trade multipliers may be expressed as the reciprocal of the sum of the marginal propensities to save and import, or the reciprocal of the sum of the *income leakages*.[8] National income will reach a new equilibrium position (and cease to change) when intended expenditures (income injections) equal the income leakages, that is, $I_d + X = S + M$.

PAYMENTS ADJUSTMENT VIA THE FOREIGN TRADE MULTIPLIER

We are now prepared to see how the foreign trade multiplier helps to bring about adjustment to a persistent disequilibrium in the balance of payments. But first, some general remarks about the relationship between payments adjustment and national income.

Adjustment and Domestic Expenditure

Let us rewrite (1) as follows:

(11) $X - M = GNP - C - I - G$, or
(12) $X - M = GNP - (C + I + G)$

This tells us that when exports are greater than imports, GNP (GNI) is greater than *domestic* expenditures on goods and services $(C + I + G)$ by the same amount. Conversely, when imports are greater than exports, GNP is less than domestic expenditure by the same amount.

---

[8] An alternative formulation of the multiplier uses the marginal propensity to consume which, as we have noted, is equal to $1 - MPS$. Thus MPS is equal to $1 - MPC$. Substituting this expression for MPS in the multiplier, we have $1/1 - MPC + MPM$, or $1/1 - (MPC - MPM)$.

Let us now suppose that M is greater than X, and that this net import balance on current account is financed by a compensatory inflow of short-term capital and/or an export of gold. Clearly, the balance of payments is in deficit disequilibrium. We now see that a current account deficit disequilibrium in terms of national income means that domestic expenditure is greater than gross national product. Payments adjustment requires, therefore, either (1) an increase in GNP in real terms, that is, an increase in physical output, or (2) a decrease in domestic expenditure (whether in C, I, G, or all three) in real terms, that is, a decrease in the domestic "absorption" of goods and services.

The period of time allowed for adjustment to a persistent payments deficit is limited by the availability of compensatory financing, and for most countries it is probably not more than two or three years. When an economy is fully employed, further growth in gross national product must depend mainly upon an improvement in productivity which seldom goes beyond 5 percent a year and is often less. Under full-employment conditions, therefore, it is usually not possible to raise GNP to any significant degree during the period allowed for payments adjustment. Thus adjustment under full-employment conditions calls for *a reduction in domestic expenditure in real terms*, a smaller allocation of goods and services to domestic use. *This is true whether adjustment takes place in a stable-rate or in a variable-rate system.*

When the economy is functioning at less than full employment and has unused productive capacity, it may be possible to adjust to a payments deficit through a rise in GNP with no necessary contraction in domestic expenditure. But this would require expansionary fiscal and monetary policies on the part of the government because the payments deficit acting alone would cause a decline in domestic expenditure. However, today (unlike the 1930's) full-employment conditions are the rule, and adjustment to deficit disequilibrium demands a contraction in domestic real expenditure.[9]

Operation of the Foreign Trade Multiplier

How does the foreign trade multiplier function to bring about an adjustment to persistent deficit disequilibrium in the balance of payments?

---

[9] We are talking here of a deficit disequilibrium that originates in the current account of the balance of payments. Thus this statement does not necessarily apply to a persistent deficit that originates in the unilateral transfer of long-term capital accounts. This unusual kind of deficit has characterized the United States balance of payments in recent years. See Chapter 22.

We can best grasp the essentials of the income adjustment process by means of a hypothetical example. Let us assume that exports of the domestic country fall $100 because of lower foreign demand and that this fall is permanent. Supposing a prior equilibrium, the balance of payments now has a persistent deficit, and long-run adjustment is necessary. We further assume the following marginal propensities in the deficit country: MPC = 1, MPM = 0.4, and MPS = 0. Thus all new income is spent on consumption—0.4 on imports and 0.6 on domestic output. In the same way, a drop in income induces an equal decrease in consumption spread over imports and domestic output. There is no domestic savings leakage.

We now trace the equilibrating income effects of this permanent fall in exports as they occur over income periods. An income period is the time necessary to spend the income earned in the preceding income period and to earn the income that will be spent in the next income period. (It has been estimated that an income period in the United States economy has a duration of about three months.) Turning now to Table 10-2, we observe that there is no change in the level of exports in Income Period 0 and consequently there are no induced changes in imports, domestic consumption, or domestic income. In Income Period 1, however, exports drop $100 to a new level that is sustained throughout our example. This causes a decline of $100 in the income received by those domestic residents who produce and sell the merchandise and services comprising the $100 drop in exports.

Table 10-2

INCOME ADJUSTMENT TO A PAYMENTS DEFICIT
WITH NO SAVINGS LEAKAGE

Income Period	Export Income Injection (dX)	Import Income Leakage (dM)	Decrease in Domestic Consumption (dC)	Decrease in Domestic Income (dY)
0	$ 0	$ 0	$ 0	$ 0
1	—$100	$ 0	$ 0	—$100
2	—$100	—$ 40	—$ 60	—$160
3	—$100	—$ 64	—$ 96	—$196
n	—$100	—$100	—$150	—$250

In Income Period 2, these residents cut their spending on imports by $40 (0.4 *times* —$100) and their spending on domestic output by $60 (0.6 *times* —$100). As a result, a second group of residents who produces and sells domestic goods going to the first group of residents now suffers an income loss of $60. (What is spending to the buyer is income to the seller.) The $40 drop in imports reduces foreign income, but not domestic income. Thus in Income Period 2 domestic income falls by $160—an induced decline in domestic consumption ($60) plus the continuing negative export injection ($100). This process of income deflation continues into Income Period 3, and domestic income falls $196 below its level in Period 0.

As we know, the overall contraction in domestic income is determined by the foreign trade multiplier. In this case the multiplier is the reciprocal of the marginal propensity to import because the marginal propensity to save is zero. Thus the multiplier is 2.5 and domestic income will fall by 2.5 *times* $100, or $250, in Income Period n after all the multiplier effects have taken place. This decline in domestic income induces a $100 fall in imports which exactly matches the autonomous fall in exports, thereby restoring equilibrium in the balance of payments. The process of income contraction comes to a halt in Income Period n because the autonomous fall in export expenditure is fully offset by an induced decline in the import leakage, that is, $dM = dX$.

The Savings Leakage. When spending on imports is the only income leakage, then adjustment to a balance of payments deficit (surplus) is complete—imports fall (rise) until they exactly offset the autonomous decrease (increase) in exports. Income, however, is rarely spent entirely on consumption; part of it is generally saved and this saving, as we have observed, constitutes a second income leakage. Because of the savings leakage the foreign trade multiplier is too small to effect a full adjustment in the balance of payments—the induced change in imports is less than the autonomous change in exports.

Table 10-3 demonstrates this incomplete adjustment by assuming MPC = 0.9, MPM = 0.4, and MPS = 0.1.

Because the combined marginal leakage propensities (marginal import propensity plus marginal savings propensity) are 0.5, the multiplier is only 2 (1/0.5), and domestic income does not contract sufficiently to induce a fall in imports equal to the autonomous fall in exports. Actually, imports fall only $80 and thus there remains a $20 deficit (equal to the savings leakage) in the balance of payments. It is apparent, then, that the foreign trade multiplier will not effect full adjustment to disequilibrium when there is a domestic savings leakage.

Table 10-3
INCOME ADJUSTMENT TO A PAYMENTS DEFICIT WITH SAVINGS LEAKAGE

Income Period	Export Income Injection (dX)	Import Income Leakage (dM)	Savings Leakage (dS)	Decrease in Domestic Consumption (dC)	Decrease in Domestic Income (dY)
0	$ 0	$ 0	$ 0	$ 0	$ 0
1	—$100	$ 0	$ 0	$ 0	—$100
2	—$100	—$ 40	—$ 10	—$ 50	—$150
3	—$100	—$ 60	—$ 15	—$ 75	—$175
n	—$100	—$ 80	—$ 20	—$100	—$200

The Foreign Repercussion Effect. The conclusion reached in the last paragraph is true, but incomplete. To get a complete picture of income adjustment to payments disequilibrium we must take note not only of domestic income changes induced by the balance of payments but of income changes induced in foreign countries as well.

The autonomous fall in domestic exports appears to the rest of the world as a $100 fall in its imports which creates a *surplus* disequilibrium in its balance of payments. Now the foreign trade multiplier functions as soon as there is disequilibrium in the balance of payments regardless of whether the disequilibrium results from a change in exports or a change in imports. Thus the surplus disequilibrium in the rest of the world starts a cumulative expansive movement in foreign incomes which, in turn, induces an increase in imports from the deficit country via the foreign marginal propensity to import. This complicated interaction between the foreign trade multipliers of different countries restrains the decline in income in the deficit country and the rise in income in the surplus country.

The foreign repercussion effect depends on foreign propensities to import and save. Returning to our previous example, let us now assume that the foreign propensity to import is 0.3 and the foreign propensity to save is 0.1. Then the foreign trade multiplier for the domestic country would be 1.25 rather than 2 and domestic income would fall only $125.[10] Because in this instance we are assuming that the domestic and foreign propensities to save are both 0.1, foreign income would rise $125. Thus the rest of the world would increase its imports from the domestic country by $37.5 (0.3 *times* $125) or, to

---

[10] The foreign trade multiplier that takes account of this interaction, or foreign repercussion effect, is $1/MPSd + MPMd + MPMf (MPSd/MPSf)$, where $MPSd$ and $MPMd$ are the marginal propensities to save and import, respectively, of the domestic country, and $MPSf$ and $MPMf$ are the marginal propensities to save and import, respectively, of the rest of the world.

say the same thing, the domestic country's *exports* would increase by $37.5. At the same time, the domestic country would reduce its imports by $50 (0.4 *times* $125). The end result of these income adjustments would be to decrease the domestic country's deficit from $100 to $12.5 because of a foreign repercussion effect of $37.5 and an induced import leakage of $50. Note that the deficit would be less than in our previous example ($12.5 compared to $20) but that adjustment would remain incomplete. This will always be the case unless the domestic savings leakage is offset by a change in domestic investment expenditure *induced* by the change in domestic income.

The foreign repercussion effect will be insignificant for a country whose exports and imports are only a small part of world trade. However, for major trading countries like the United States and Great Britain the foreign repercussion effect must be taken into account in estimating the foreign trade multiplier.

The Domestic Income Multiplier. We have now examined long-run adjustment via the foreign trade multiplier, noting how income changes originating in the balance of payments work toward the establishment of a new equilibrium. But all changes in income do not proceed from disequilibrium in the balance of payments. New income may also be created (or old income extinguished) by independent shifts in domestic investment (construction, capital equipment, inventories) or domestic government expenditures. These shifts in domestic expenditure cause a multiple expansion (or contraction) of domestic income via the *domestic* income multiplier. The change in domestic income then affects the level of imports through the marginal propensity to import, and the result, assuming a prior equilibrium, is a cyclical disequilibrium in the balance of payments.

The fact that income changes originating within the domestic economy will induce changes in domestic imports and thereby provoke disequilibrium in the balance of payments explains why inflation has been the leading cause of deficit disequilibrium in the balance of payments of many nations during the postwar period. It also explains the rapid spread of deflation from one country to another during the early thirties. Because of the domestic income multiplier, government fiscal and monetary policies become key instruments of balance of payments adjustment. By the same token, however, these policies may delay international adjustment by bringing about changes in domestic income that counteract the equilibrating income changes of the foreign trade multiplier. This situation often occurs since nations usually place the objectives of domestic full employment and rapid economic development above that of balance of payments equilibrium.

THE ROLE OF PRICE ADJUSTMENT

In our treatment of the foreign trade multiplier, we concluded that income adjustment to a payments deficit (or surplus) is incomplete when there is a domestic savings leakage. Since a positive marginal propensity to save is a normal condition what, then, acts to complete adjustment? The answer is changes in price levels and in relative prices within the deficit and surplus countries.[11]

The relative importance of income and price adjustment in a particular instance will depend upon the degree of unemployment and excess capacity, the degree of flexibility in wages and prices, and the price elasticities of supply and demand in the economies of trading nations. When (1) prices and wages are inflexible downwards and (2) unemployment and excess capacity prevail throughout an economy, then an autonomous change in expenditure (domestic investment or exports) will cause changes in *real* income with only modest, or no, changes in wages and prices. That is to say, a fall in expenditure will initiate a decrease in production and employment rather than a decrease in prices and wages, and a rise in expenditure will initiate an increase in production and employment rather than an increase in prices and wages. We assumed the existence of these two conditions in our presentation of income adjustment because we wanted to focus on income changes alone, unaccompanied by price changes.

It is unlikely that these conditions would ever exist in the actual world to such a degree as to rule out *all* equilibrating price adjustments. Nor can we accept the empirical validity of another set of conditions that would rule out all equilibrating *income* adjustments: (1) full employment, (2) highly flexible wages and prices both downwards and upwards, and (3) high price elasticities of supply and demand.[12] To conclude, neither the assumptions behind the income adjustment model nor those behind the classical model ever fully

---

[11] This assumes, of course, that the exchange rate is not altered. When income adjustment is incomplete and, for one reason or another, domestic price adjustment is not possible or desirable, then depreciation is necessary to complete the process of *market* adjustment to a deficit disequilibrium.

[12] These are the implicit assumptions of the classical theory of adjustment.

match actual conditions. In periods of massive unemployment, the income-adjustment model becomes a more valid explanation of the actual adjustment process; in periods of full employment and inflation, the classical model gains in relevance. In both situations, however, income and price changes interact to bring about adjustment to payments disequilibrium.

Let us now trace through the price adjustments that will accompany, to a small or large degree, income adjustment to a deficit in the balance of payments. Again we start with an autonomous fall in exports. This will induce a decline in money income and spending in the deficit country that will cause a general fall in prices, although the fall may be spotty and somewhat retarded because of market imperfections. In addition to this fall in the price level, there will also occur changes in the *relative* prices of export, import, and domestic (nontraded) goods. Since the impact of the autonomous fall in export demand is concentrated on specific export goods, they are likely to suffer the greatest price declines. On the other hand, as domestic residents switch from imports (whose prices are rising) to domestic import-competitive goods, the latter experience a rise in demand that will moderate (or even reverse) any price declines. Price declines in other goods will be somewhere between these two extremes: smaller than the decline in specific export prices, greater than the decline in import-competitive prices.

The effect of the general price deflation in the deficit country is to encourage exports by making them cheaper to foreign buyers and to discourage imports by making them more expensive to domestic buyers relative to domestic substitutes. The effect of the relative price changes is to encourage a reallocation of production more in conformity with the new conditions of export demand. Relatively low wages and prices in the specific export sector experiencing an autonomous fall in demand stimulate a movement of labor and capital to other export sectors and to the domestic sector, including import-competing industries where wages and prices are now relatively high. Factors may also move from other domestic industries to the import-competing industries. Both price deflation and shifts in relative prices, therefore, help eliminate the deficit in the balance of payments.

Simultaneously, surplus countries will experience an expansion of money income and spending. This will cause a general rise in the price level (unless there is widespread unemployment and excess capacity) and shifts in relative prices that will encourage imports and discourage exports.

In effect, general price adjustment works through a shift in the terms of trade of both the surplus and deficit countries. The surplus country enjoys an improvement in its terms of trade as its import prices fall and its export prices rise, while the deficit country suffers a deterioration in its terms of trade as its import prices rise and its export prices fall.[13]

Price Elasticities [14]

The degree to which the terms of trade must shift in favor of the surplus country in order to remove disequilibrium in the balance of payments will depend upon the price elasticities of supply and demand of both exports and imports. When elasticities are high, a relatively small change in prices calls forth a relatively large response in the quantity of exports and imports, and the terms of trade need change little to effect adjustment. With low elasticities, however, relatively large price changes will stimulate only relatively small changes in the quantity of exports and imports, and there must be a wide swing in the terms of trade to effect adjustment.

The price elasticities of export and import supply will depend upon the mobility of productive factors within both the surplus and deficit countries. When labor and other resources are induced by only slight variations in relative wages and other factor prices to move from one industry to another, the supply of goods is elastic—the amount supplied can be adjusted to changing demand with relatively small changes in the supply price. When, however, productive resources are relatively immobile, supply elasticities are low; and any adjustment to balance of payments disequilibrium is impeded. In a many-nation world the price elasticity of import supply for a specific country will also depend on whether foreign suppliers have alternative markets. When the domestic demand for import goods is small

---

[13] Hence the surplus country obtains a greater share of the gains from trade as a result of price adjustment. See Chapter 3.

[14] Price elasticities measure the response in the amount demanded or supplied to a given change in price. The price elasticity of demand assumes this expression: $\frac{dD/D}{dP/P}$, where D is the original amount demanded, P is the original price, and dD and dP are the changes in the amount demanded and price, respectively. This may be more simply expressed as the ratio: percentage change in amount demanded/percentage change in price. Similarly, the price elasticity of supply is $\frac{dS/S}{dP/P}$, where S and dS are the original amount supplied and the change in amount supplied, respectively. Or more simply: percentage change in amount supplied/percentage change in price.

compared to the world demand, it will have little or no influence over import prices and import supply will appear highly elastic to the domestic country.

The price elasticities of export and import demand will depend on the nature of the export and import goods and the availability of domestic substitutes. Thus the demand for luxury imports is more elastic than the demand for essential imports; and, other things being equal, the demand for imports with close domestic substitutes is more elastic than the demand for imports with only distant or no domestic substitutes. In a many-nation world substitutes for imports from a given country may also be found in imports from other countries. Hence the demand facing the exports of a country is apt to be less elastic than otherwise when that country supplies most of the world market, that is, when foreign customers have little opportunity to obtain similar goods elsewhere. Conversely, export demand is likely to be more elastic than otherwise when the exporting country supplies only a small portion of the world market.

Obstacles to Price Adjustment

Fundamentally, international adjustment requires shifts in the level and composition of both supply and demand in the surplus and deficit countries. Equilibrating changes in prices are effective in bringing about such shifts when the price elasticities of supply and demand are high. Anything that lowers price elasticities, therefore, hinders price adjustment to balance of payments disequilibrium.

Price adjustment is undoubtedly less effective today than before World War I. As we observed in Chapter 4, few contemporary markets are close to pure competition. Markets for agricultural staples, such as wheat, cotton, and coffee, are usually subject to price stabilization by government agencies, while the majority of markets for manufactured goods have monopolistic elements that allow the seller (or, in the case of monopsony, the buyer) some control over price. Administered pricing by large-scale oligopolistic industries and the enforcement of wage floors by powerful labor unions are common examples of price inflexibility in today's economies. Of special importance is the international cartel that outlaws price competition and fixes the pattern of foreign trade in its products. The widespread abandonment of price competition in favor of nonprice competition in quality, style, and services; government schemes to control production and marketing; and the innumerable devices used by governments to insulate the domestic economy from foreign economic influences have all diminished the importance of price adjustment.

Despite these developments, however, equilibrating changes in prices remain a significant instrument of international adjustment. The prices of many raw materials and foodstuffs in international trade remain uncontrolled and respond quickly to changes in supply and demand. Moreover, all international goods show plenty of price flexibility upward as the postwar inflation has demonstrated time and again. We can conclude that price adjustment, when permitted, is an effective ally of income adjustment and that both are required in a stable exchange rate system if exchange depreciation or suppressed disequilibrium is to be avoided.

SUMMARY

1. When exchange rates are held stable, short-run adjustment to balance of payments disequilibrium comprises international movements of gold and short-term capital, which are also the symptoms of disequilibrium. These movements provide compensatory financing of the autonomous deficit in the balance of payments; and, in doing so they also transfer purchasing power from the deficit to the surplus country. The latter initiates changes in income and prices that lead to long-run adjustment. Short-run adjustment is adequate to meet temporary disequilibrium. When disequilibrium persists from one period to the next, however, long-run adjustment is necessary—the equilibration of exports and imports of merchandise and services.

2. The viability of a stable-rate system depends upon large equilibrating movements of short-term capital since most countries have only a small supply of gold. When compensatory financing is not forthcoming, short-run adjustment is not possible; and the deficit nation must either impose or tighten controls over its international trade and payments, depreciate its exchange rate, or (if there is time) bring about equilibrating changes in its national income and price level.

3. The classical theory of adjustment in a stable exchange rate system (the gold standard) is the price-specie flow mechanism, which stresses the equilibrating role of price changes but ignores changes in income.

4. The gross national product (GNP) is the market value of all goods and services produced by the national economy over the year; it is equal to gross national income (GNI). $S - I_d = X - M$ is a basic equation relating gross national income (or product) to foreign trade.

5. National income is in equilibrium when intended expenditures are equal to the income leakages, that is, $I_d + X = S + M$. The foreign trade multiplier equals the reciprocal of the marginal propensities to save and import, or $dY/dX = 1/MPS + MPM$.

6. Under full-employment conditions, adjustment calls for a contraction of expenditure in real terms. When there is a savings leakage, adjustment to a payments disequilibrium via the foreign trade multiplier is incomplete even when allowance is made for the foreign repercussion effect.
7. The actual process of adjustment in a stable-rate system involves equilibrating changes in both income and prices. In effect, price adjustment works through a shift in the terms of trade of both the surplus and deficit countries.

QUESTIONS AND APPLICATIONS

1. (a) How is short-run adjustment accomplished with stable exchange rates?
   (b) What is the major limitation of short-run adjustment?
2. (a) When is long-run adjustment necessary?
   (b) Describe and evaluate the price-specie flow mechanism.
3. (a) What are the components of gross national product and gross national income?
   (b) Why is GNP equal to GNI?
   (c) Derive the equation, $I_d + X = S + M$, from the gross national product and income equations.
4. (a) What are the equilibrium conditions of national income?
   (b) Derive both the domestic and foreign trade multipliers from the equation $I_d + X = S + M$.
5. (a) How does the foreign trade multiplier explain income adjustment to a disequilibrium in the balance of payments?
   (b) When is income adjustment complete? incomplete?
6. (a) What determines the effectiveness of a shift in the terms of trade in bringing about adjustment in the balance of payments?
   (b) What are the obstacles to price adjustment?
7. Under what conditions is income adjustment likely to dominate adjustment in a stable-rate system? Under what conditions is price adjustment likely to dominate?

SELECTED READINGS

See list of readings at end of Chapter 11.

CHAPTER 11

INTERNATIONAL ADJUSTMENT IN A VARIABLE-RATE SYSTEM

In a variable-rate system adjustment to a payments disequilibrium occurs through an alteration in the rate of exchange.

There are many possible kinds of variable-rate systems. At one extreme is the system of fluctuating rates in which the rate of exchange is determined solely by supply and demand in the foreign exchange market with no attempt by government authorities to limit or moderate fluctuations.[1] At the other extreme is the "adjustable-peg" system in which rates are stabilized by government authorities in the short run and then adjusted once-for-all to a new stabilized level. This system is followed by many countries today.[2] In between these two extremes there are any number of variant systems which have more rate variability than the adjustable-peg system but less variability than the fluctuating-rate system. We shall call these "middle" variants "floating-rate" systems because the rate of exchange may vary beyond the limits imposed on stable rates, but is constrained within wider limits decided by monetary authorities which may or may not change in line with market trends. In all of these systems, however, the rate of exchange continuously or occasionally varies and, in so doing, influences the balance of payments. This variability distinguishes them from a stable-rate system.

---

[1] The determination of freely fluctuating rates was examined in Chapter 8.
[2] Since the adjustable-peg system involves both stable and variable exchange rates, it may be considered as a variant of either the stable-rate or variable-rate systems. In Chapter 8 we described briefly the adjustable-peg system in our treatment of active stabilization. In this chapter our interest lies in the variable-rate element of the adjustable-peg system.

ADJUSTMENT THROUGH VARIABLE RATES

We now examine payments adjustment in the fluctuating-rate and adjustable-peg systems. Later we shall analyze the effects of depreciation in *any* variable-rate system.

Adjustment through Fluctuating Rates

When exchange rates are stable, compensatory movements of short-term capital and gold provide a short-run adjustment to balance of payments disequilibrium. Such movements, however, are small or nonexistent when exchange rates are freely fluctuating—international flows of short-term capital and gold are then exposed to the exchange risk. Under these circumstances, foreign exchange dealers are unwilling to maintain large foreign balances, and any possible gain from higher interest rates in the deficit country is outweighed by the prospect of an exchange loss. Again, there is no reason why speculation should be preponderantly stabilizing when there are no limits to variations in the exchange rate. Furthermore, when the exchange rate is freely fluctuating there is no official stabilization agency to supply compensatory short-term capital, and gold has lost its fixed value and is just another commodity. Hence, movements of short-term capital and gold can be expected to afford little or no short-run adjustment to disequilibrium when exchange rates are freely fluctuating.

Short-run adjustment (as well as long-run adjustment) must, then, occur through variations in the rate of exchange. When exporters supply bills of exchange, they must be sold immediately to importers who wish to make foreign payments since dealers are unwilling to hold them. An increase in the supply of bills (foreign exchange) will force down the rate of exchange until the bills are taken up by those who wish to buy from abroad. In this way exports are offset by imports and there is no net compensatory movement of short-term capital. Similarly, a higher demand for bills will push up the exchange rate until sufficient bills are supplied the market and imports are financed by concurrent exports. This absence of any net movement of compensatory short-term capital or gold in a fluctuating-rate system also means that there is no net transfer of purchasing power from one country to another. In consequence, income and price adjustments do not occur.

In a fluctuating-rate system, therefore, movements in the exchange rate achieve a continuing equilibrium in the balance of payments. At the equilibrium rate of exchange the amounts of foreign exchange in supply and demand that derive from autonomous items in the balance of payments (excluding disequilibrating movements of speculative and flight capital) are equal and the foreign exchange market is fully cleared. Disequilibrium does not show up in the balance of payments because there are no compensatory items to finance a deficit or surplus. The equilibrium rate of exchange is shown as *O-E'* in Figure 11-1 on page 219.

Adjustment through Occasional Depreciation

What we have said above applies to a system in which exchange rates are *always* free to respond to changes in supply and demand. It does not apply to the contemporary payments system in which exchange rates are *occasionally* varied from one stable level to another stable level. In this system, short-run adjustment occurs as under a stable-rate system, while a planned and limited variation in the exchange rate effects a long-run adjustment. Under these conditions a variation in the exchange rate will have income and price effects since it is closing a gap in the balance of payments—a gap that could not exist in a fluctuating-rate system due to the lack of any compensatory financing. In this adjustable-peg system, adjustment to persistent deficit disequilibrium takes the form of *exchange depreciation*—a limited increase in the domestic price of foreign money.

In a freely fluctuating-rate system, the equilibrium rate is determined by the impersonal tug and pull of supply and demand. When, however, a nation that normally stabilizes its exchange rate decides to depreciate in order to correct a deficit disequilibrium, the equilibrium rate of exchange is not known in advance, and yet successful depreciation requires depreciation to the equilibrium rate. The exchange rate will, otherwise, continue to be too low, with domestic currency overvalued; or too high, with domestic currency undervalued.[3]

One solution to this difficulty is to set loose the exchange rate to find its equilibrium rate in the market and then, when equilibrium is restored, to stabilize the rate at the new level. Official fears of destabilizing speculation and capital flight, whether well-founded or not, usually rule out this approach to the problem, however.

---

[3] At times a nation may deliberately seek to overvalue or undervalue its currency, but even this policy presumes a knowledge of the equilibrium rate. See pp. 216-217.

When exchange controls are in existence, either the illegal black-market rate or the official "free" rate is sometimes taken to be the equilibrium rate of exchange. Although these rates will usually reveal whether the domestic currency is overvalued or not, they are apt to be unreliable indicators of the equilibrium rate, since the forces of supply and demand acting to determine them often diverge widely from the forces that would act in a freely fluctuating-rate market.

The Purchasing-Power Parity Doctrine. During World War I and in the early twenties when most countries were off the gold standard, there was widespread discussion as to the exchange rates at which they should return to the gold standard. Gustav Cassel, a Swedish economist, argued that the new rates of exchange should reflect the relative purchasing powers of the different currencies. This proposition is the well-known *purchasing-power parity doctrine.* It states that the equilibrium rate of exchange between two currencies is the ratio of their respective domestic purchasing powers. Thus, if the general price level in the United States is double that in the United Kingdom, then the purchasing power of the dollar is one half that of the pound and the equilibrium exchange rate of the pound is $2.

When this absolute version of the doctrine proved inconsistent with the facts, it was replaced by an explanation of the role of the purchasing-power parity in determining the exchange rate with respect to a base period when the exchange rate was in equilibrium. Suppose that the equilibrium rate of the pound was $4.86 (the gold mint parity) in 1913, but that during the period 1913-20 the price level rose four times in the United Kingdom and two times in the United States. Then, according to the relative version of the purchasing-power parity doctrine, the equilibrium rate of exchange for the pound in 1920 was $2.43, since the decline in its purchasing power relative to 1913 had been twice the decline in the purchasing power of the dollar.

We do not have the space for a full critique of the purchasing-power parity doctrine and shall only mention its main inadequacies. The principal drawback of the doctrine lies in its inadequate coverage of the transactions that determine the rate of exchange. Only the commodity price level is used to determine the purchasing-power parities, whereas the exchange rate is determined by service and capital transactions in addition to merchandise transactions. Furthermore, the doctrine does not distinguish between domestic and international goods and does not account for the demand and supply elasticities of exports and imports. Nor does it take cognizance of the fact that a shift in buyers' preferences or in income may affect the exchange rate independently of any change in price levels and thus the purchasing-power parity.

For these reasons, the purchasing-power parity between two currencies cannot serve as an indication of the equilibrium rate of exchange. The purchasing-power parity doctrine does, however, make a contribution by stressing the influence that may be exerted on exchange rates by divergent movements of the price levels in different countries, and its greatest usefulness is during periods of inflation and deflation when such movements may be extremely large.

Deciding on the Equilibrium Rate. If the purchasing-power parity doctrine, black-market rates, and official free rates are not reliable indications of the equilibrium rate of exchange, how, then, may a government—intent on depreciation but unwilling to set free the exchange rate—discover the equilibrium rate of exchange? The best that can be done is to evaluate the many factors that determine the rate of exchange, including the likely responses of those same factors to a variation in the exchange rate itself.

We learned in Chapter 8 that there is a mutual interdependence between the exchange rate and the balance of payments. When changes in the balance of payments place it in deficit disequilibrium, exchange depreciation is successful only if it reverses those changes or induces new compensating changes. An intelligent policy of depreciation, therefore, depends upon a careful appraisal of the sources of disequilibrium in the balance of payments and of the conditions (supply and demand elasticities, income and price effects, etc.) that will determine the efficacy of a given depreciation in overcoming a specific disequilibrium. Even then, the dynamic nature of economic phenomena makes impossible any certain discovery of the equilibrium rate of exchange and any firm guarantee of successful depreciation. Deciding upon the equilibrium rate of exchange is partly economic analysis and partly hunch.

Competitive Depreciation and Overvaluation. Depreciation stimulates exports and simultaneously deters imports. During the 1930's many countries took advantage of this fact by depreciating their currencies beyond the equilibrium rate of exchange. Their purpose was to create a surplus in the balance of payments and thereby foster greater income and employment in the domestic economy. Since this policy required a deficit disequilibrium in the balance of payments of other countries that also faced depression, it amounted to exporting unemployment. For this reason, the attempt to depreciate more than other countries—*competitive depreciation*—has received the uncomplimentary designation of "beggar-my-neighbor policy." Competitive depreciation is not likely to be effective in the long run since other countries will also depreciate in retaliation, and the end result for a country is usually a disruption of its foreign trade rather than any improvement in the domestic economy.

Competitive depreciation developed out of the rigors of international depression. In our own day widespread inflation has led to *overvaluation* of the exchange rate through exchange control, especially in developing countries. Depreciation is feared for its inflationary impact on the domestic economy, and it is avoided even when overvaluation of the currency perpetuates a deficit in the balance of payments. A more complete explanation of this policy and its effects is undertaken in Chapter 13.

THE EFFECTS OF EXCHANGE DEPRECIATION

The primary effect of depreciation upon the balance of payments depends upon the responses made by the supply and demand of foreign exchange to the new higher price of foreign exchange. When supply and demand are sensitive to depreciation, or highly elastic, then depreciation is very effective in removing a deficit disequilibrium; but when elasticities are low, depreciation must be severe to wipe out even a small deficit.

This effect of exchange depreciation is shown in Figures 11-1 and 11-2. Suppose that the French government decides to depreciate the franc in order to remove a deficit in the balance of payments. If, as in Figure 11-1, the elasticities of the demand and supply of foreign exchange (dollars) are high, then the depreciation will be very effective and will not need to be great. In Figure 11-1 the exchange rate before depreciation is O-E and the deficit is F-G. This deficit is closed by a relatively slight depreciation from O-E to O-E'. On the other hand, when elasticities are low, a considerable depreciation is needed to bring about adjustment. In Figure 11-2, the exchange rate before depreciation is O-P and the deficit, M-N. To wipe out this deficit, the franc must be depreciated from O-P to O-P'. It will be noted that, despite the fact that the deficit in Figure 11-2 is equal to the deficit in Figure 11-1, the exchange depreciation is much larger in the former case.

Ch. 11 / International Adjustment in a Variable-Rate System   **219**

Figure 11-1

EXCHANGE DEPRECIATION WITH HIGH DEMAND AND SUPPLY ELASTICITIES

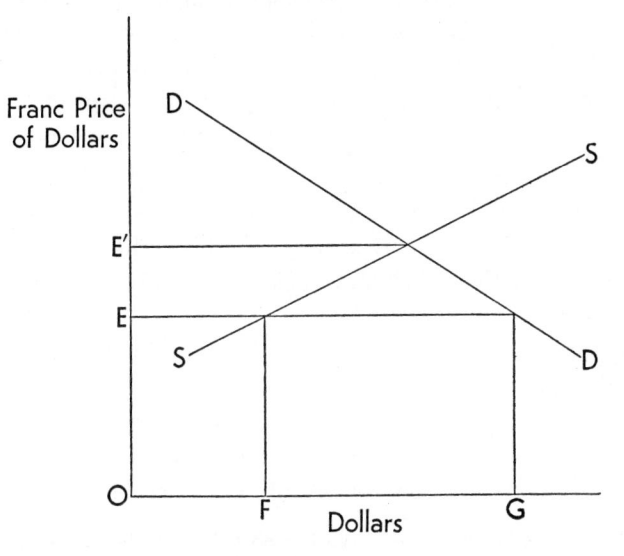

Figure 11-2

EXCHANGE DEPRECIATION WITH LOW DEMAND AND SUPPLY ELASTICITIES

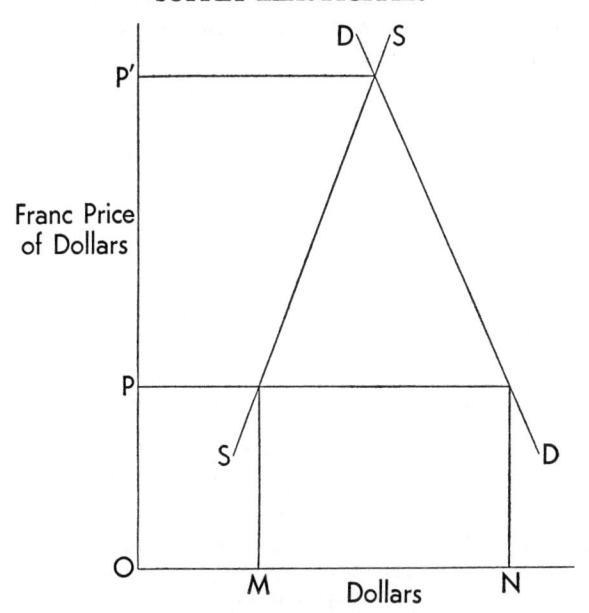

The Elasticity of Foreign Exchange Supply

The elasticity of the supply of foreign exchange is mainly dependent on the elasticity of foreign demand for domestic exports. Upon depreciation the foreign exchange price of exports falls. When foreign demand is elastic, this decline in export prices will stimulate an expansion in the quantity exported that will be sufficient to enlarge total receipts of foreign exchange despite the lower prices in terms of foreign exchange. On the other hand, when the elasticity of foreign demand is low, total receipts of foreign exchange may even be smaller after depreciation. In this unlikely event, depreciation will widen the deficit insofar as the supply of foreign exchange is concerned.

We can distinguish three cases that describe the influence of the elasticity of export demand on the elasticity of foreign exchange supply. (When *domestic* export prices do not change after depreciation because export *supply* is perfectly elastic, then the export demand elasticity *fully* determines the supply elasticity of foreign exchange.)

1. When the elasticity of export demand has a value of *one* (unit elastic), then a 10 percent depreciation causes a 10 percent increase in the quantity of exports.[4] Hence the receipts of foreign exchange are the same before and after depreciation. The elasticity of *foreign exchange supply*, therefore, is zero—foreign exchange receipts do not respond to a variation in the exchange rate—and the effect of depreciation on the supply of foreign exchange is neutral.

2. When the elasticity of export demand is greater than one, then a 10 percent depreciation causes a greater than 10 percent increase in the quantity of exports. Receipts of foreign exchange, therefore, increase and help close the deficit in the balance of payments. In this case the elasticity of foreign exchange supply is greater than zero—

---

[4] We earlier defined the price elasticity of demand as the ratio: percentage change in amount demanded/percentage change in price. (Algebraically speaking, this ratio carries a minus sign since the amount demanded and price are inversely related. However, following common practice we shall ignore the sign.) When demand elasticity is one, then the percentage changes in amount demanded and price are the same, and the amount spent on the product in question stays the same after a price change. When elasticity is greater than one, total expenditure increases (decreases) with a fall (rise) in price. When elasticity lies between one and zero, then total expenditure decreases with a fall in price. When elasticity is zero, then total expenditure decreases the same percentage as the fall in price. Similarly, the quantity supplied changes the same, a greater or lesser percentage than the percentage change in price, depending on whether the elasticity of supply is one, greater than one, or less than one. It should be noted that the amount supplied and price are positively related: they change in the same direction. The use of percentages to define elasticities is a crude simplification and an approximation only. Mathematically, elasticity is $(dQ/dP)(P/Q)$ where dQ/dP is the rate of change (derivative) of Q with respect to P.

foreign exchange receipts respond positively to a higher domestic price of foreign money.

3. When the elasticity of export demand is zero, then a 10 percent depreciation causes no increase in the quantity of exports and foreign exchange receipts fall by 10 percent. When the elasticity lies between zero and one, then the percentage increase in the quantity of exports is less than the percentage depreciation. In both instances depreciation causes a fall in the receipts of foreign exchange that worsens the deficit. Thus the elasticity of foreign exchange supply is less than zero or negative—on a graph the supply schedule slopes *downward* from left to right, unlike the normal supply schedule.

In summary, when the elasticity of export demand is greater than one (elastic), then depreciation causes an increase in the receipts of foreign exchange and helps close the deficit. When, on the other hand, the elasticity of export demand is less than one or zero (inelastic), then depreciation lowers foreign exchange receipts and insofar as the supply of foreign exchange is concerned, worsens the deficit. The elasticities of foreign exchange supply that we have discussed are shown in Figure 11-3 where e_s is the appropriate elasticity.

Figure 11-3
ELASTICITIES OF FOREIGN EXCHANGE SUPPLY

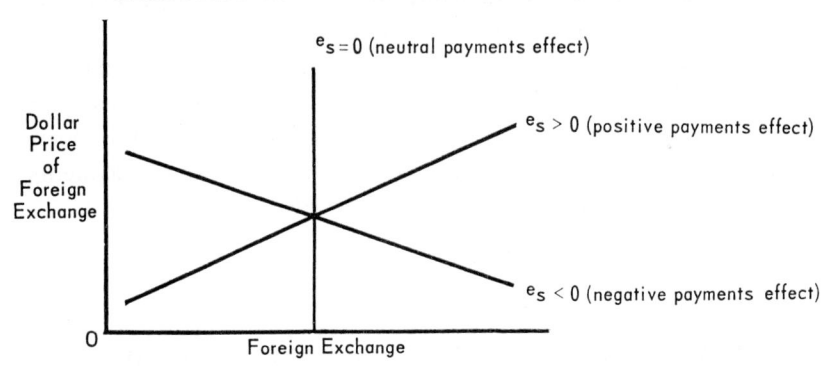

[Graph: Dollar Price of Foreign Exchange on vertical axis, Foreign Exchange on horizontal axis, showing three curves: $e_s = 0$ (neutral payments effect) vertical line; $e_s > 0$ (positive payments effect) upward sloping; $e_s < 0$ (negative payments effect) downward sloping.]

Under what conditions is export demand likely to be elastic? We can make only a few pertinent comments relating to the composition of exports, the relative importance of a nation's exports in world trade, and the presence of trade restrictions.[5] Generally speaking, the demand for manufactured products (especially "luxury-type" products) is more elastic than the demand for agricultural and other primary products which is often inelastic. Many primary products

---
[5] See also pp. 209-210 in Chapter 10.

satisfy basic needs and their consumption is relatively insensitive to price changes. The same is true of intermediate goods that are purchased as raw materials, semimanufactures, and the like when these goods contribute only a small share to total costs of production. Such products face a derived demand that tends to be inelastic.

The demand facing a product with many substitutes is likely to be more elastic than a product with few or no substitutes. That is why a country whose exports are only a small fraction of world exports experiences a more elastic demand (other things equal) than a country like the United States whose exports bulk large in world trade. There is a greater opportunity for substitution between a country's exports and the competitive exports of other countries when the former holds only a modest share of foreign markets.

One final point. Tariffs, quotas, cartels, and other restrictions that inhibit the free play of competition in world markets act to lower effective demand elasticities by limiting the role of price in buying decisions. Trade in agricultural products is particularly restricted in the contemporary world economy.

The Elasticity of Foreign Exchange Demand

The elasticity of the demand for foreign exchange depends mainly on the elasticity of the domestic demand for imports. When higher import prices in domestic currency cause a fall in the quantity of imports, then depreciation improves the balance of payments on the demand side. At the very worst when the quantity of imports stays the same, depreciation has no effect on the balance of payments as far as foreign exchange demand is concerned.

Figure 11-4 illustrates these two cases.

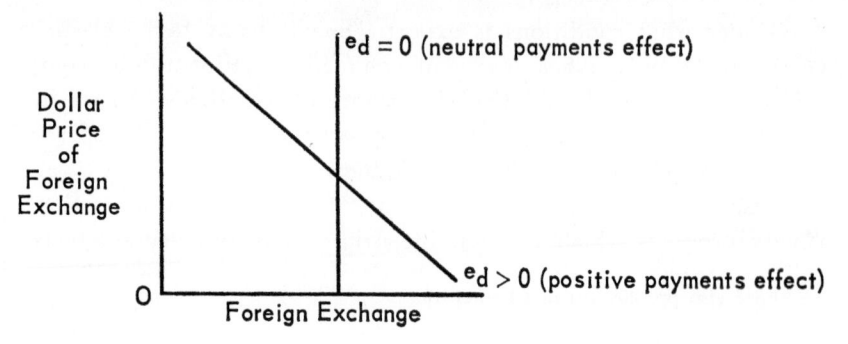

Figure 11-4
ELASTICITIES OF FOREIGN EXCHANGE DEMAND

$e_d = 0$ (neutral payments effect)

Dollar Price of Foreign Exchange

$e_d > 0$ (positive payments effect)

Foreign Exchange

Ch. 11 / International Adjustment in a Variable-Rate System

When the *foreign exchange* price of imports does not change after depreciation (import *supply* is perfectly elastic), then the elasticity of import demand *fully* determines the demand elasticity of foreign exchange. We can distinguish two important cases.

> 1. When the import demand elasticity is *greater than zero*, then the quantity of imports decreases after depreciation, and therefore (given an unchanged foreign exchange price of imports) the quantity of foreign exchange demanded also decreases. The higher the import elasticity, the greater the decline in the amount of foreign exchange in demand. In this case depreciation improves the balance of payments on the demand side.
>
> 2. When the elasticity of import demand is *zero*, then the quantity of imports does not change after depreciation and the *foreign exchange* value of imports is constant. In this case the demand for foreign exchange is perfectly inelastic (zero), and depreciation neither helps nor worsens the balance of payments on the demand side.

The elasticity of import demand will tend to be high when the composition of imports is heavily weighted with luxury-type consumer goods (such as automobiles and household equipment) and expensive capital goods (such as heavy machinery and transport equipment). Conversely, elasticity will tend to be low when most imports are raw materials, foodstuffs, and semimanufactures such as characterize United States imports. Another factor is the degree of substitutability between import goods and domestic goods. When domestic substitutes are widely available at reasonable prices, then higher domestic prices for imports after depreciation will cause a switch to domestic sources of supply, thereby increasing the elasticity of import demand.

Elasticities of Export and Import Supply

In our analysis of the demand elasticities of exports and imports, we assumed that export and import *supply* elasticities were infinite or perfectly elastic. Thus the domestic price of exports and the foreign exchange price of imports did not respond to depreciation. This is an unrealistic assumption and we must now take account of less-than-perfect elasticities of export and import supply.

The significance of supply elasticities may be understood if we make another unrealistic assumption, namely, perfectly inelastic (zero) export and import supplies. In that event depreciation has *no effect* on the balance of payments *regardless* of the demand elasticities. An export supply of zero elasticity means that the quantity of exports cannot be increased. Hence a depreciation of 10 percent is promptly offset by a 10 percent *increase* in the domestic export price as foreign buyers bid for the same quantity of export goods. Thus the *foreign exchange* price of exports remains the same and there is no change in foreign exchange receipts. Similarly, an import supply of zero elasticity means that a 10 percent depreciation is promptly matched by a 10 percent cut in the foreign exchange price of imports as foreign suppliers strive to maintain sales in the depreciating country. Thus the domestic price of imports stays the same after depreciation and there is no effect on foreign exchange expenditures.

It would be tedious to recount the many combinations of demand and supply elasticities and their effects on the balance of payments. Suffice it to say that when demand elasticities are high, the effects of depreciation are most beneficial if supply elasticities are also high. Then lower foreign exchange export prices can expand exports and higher domestic import prices can contract imports. On the other hand, when demand elasticities are low, depreciation is most beneficial (or least harmful) if supply elasticities are low, for then foreign exchange export prices fall less and domestic import prices rise less than otherwise.

When Is Exchange Depreciation Successful?

If the foreign exchange market is in stable equilibrium, then depreciation lessens or eliminates a deficit in the balance of payments as shown in Figures 11-1 and 11-2. But if the foreign exchange market is in *unstable* equilibrium, then depreciation hurts rather than helps the balance of payments in deficit. Figure 11-5 shows that unstable equilibrium occurs when the supply schedule cuts the demand schedule from *above*.[6]

At the exchange rate O-R, foreign exchange demanded exceeds foreign exchange supplied by F-H. In the attempt to wipe out this deficit the exchange rate is depreciated to O-R'. But this only makes matters worse as the deficit increases in size to E-G.

What, then, is the requirement for stable equilibrium in terms of export and import elasticities? Depreciation *always* helps to lessen a deficit in the balance of payments if the sum of the export and import demand elasticities is greater than one, that is, $e_x + e_m > 1$.

---

[6] In that event the sum of the supply and demand elasticities is negative. See Figures 11-3 and 11-4.

Figure 11-5
UNSTABLE EQUILIBRIUM IN THE FOREIGN EXCHANGE MARKET

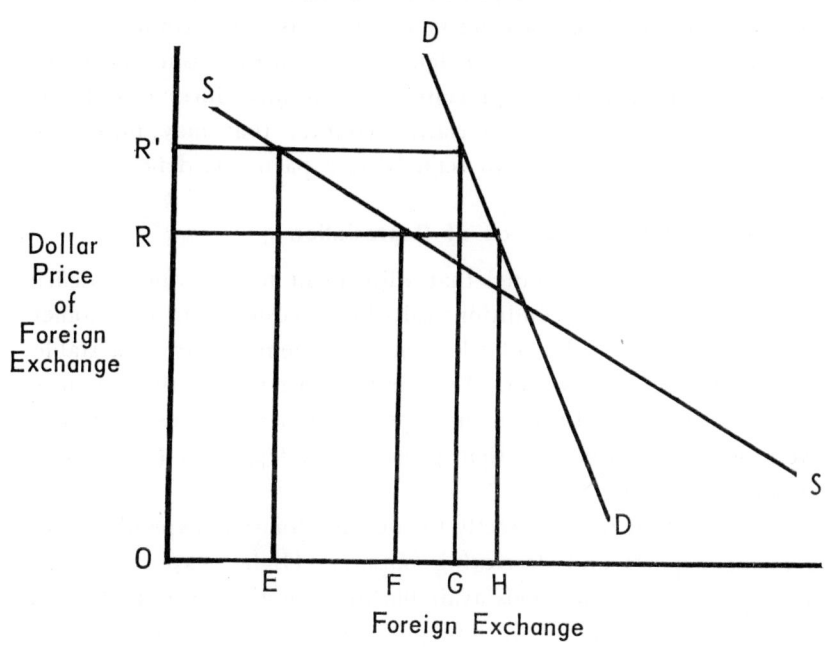

This is known as the Marshall-Lerner condition and we may demonstrate its validity by citing two extreme examples. (The Marshall-Lerner condition assumes perfect elasticities of export and import *supply*.) Suppose the elasticity of export demand is zero and there is a 10 percent depreciation. Then foreign exchange receipts drop 10 percent, but if import demand elasticity is greater than one, foreign exchange expenditures decrease by more than 10 percent. Thus the deficit becomes less. Again, suppose the elasticity of import demand is zero. Then foreign exchange expenditures do not change after depreciation, but if export demand elasticity is greater than one, a 10 percent depreciation leads to a greater than 10 percent increase in the quantity of exports and consequently an increase in foreign exchange receipts. Once again, the balance of payments improves.

When we introduce supply elasticities we discover that the Marshall-Lerner condition is sufficient but not necessary. Even if the sum of demand elasticities is somewhat below one, the balance of payments can improve provided that the supply elasticities are small **enough**.

What is the probability that the demand elasticities of exports and imports of a country will add to a sum greater than one? Today most economists believe the probability is high. As far as elasticities are concerned, therefore, a country can be reasonably confident that depreciation will improve its balance of payments. But elasticities are not the whole story. Depreciation also induces income and general price effects in the depreciating country that may nullify or compromise its effectiveness in remedying a payments deficit.

Income and Price Effects of Depreciation

In Chapter 10 we stated that adjustment to a payments deficit under full-employment conditions calls for a reduction in *real* domestic expenditure regardless of whether adjustment occurs in a stable-rate or a variable-rate system. When imports are greater than exports, then domestic expenditure (consumption, domestic investment, and government) is also greater than gross national product (income) by the same amount.[7]

Depreciation works directly to contract domestic expenditure by increasing exports and decreasing imports. Higher exports depress the supply of domestic goods available to domestic buyers and lower imports depress the supply of foreign goods available to them. Hence the supply of goods absorbed by domestic residents (real domestic expenditure) is cut back by depreciation through its direct impact on exports and imports via demand and supply elasticities.

Depreciation, however, also has *indirect* effects that may lower its effectiveness in contracting real domestic expenditure. When depreciation raises exports and lowers imports, it injects income into the domestic economy and starts a cumulative expansion of domestic money income through the operation of the foreign trade multiplier. This higher money income stimulates higher expenditures on domestic goods and imports and thereby threatens to reverse the contraction in real expenditure resulting from the direct effects of depreciation on exports and imports.

When the domestic economy has substantial unemployment (excess capacity), then the rise in money income and expenditure causes an expansion of production and real gross national product. In this situation it may be possible to have one's cake and eat it too, that is, to achieve an improvement in the balance of payments and

---

[7] See Equation (12) in Chapter 10.

an increase in real domestic expenditure at the same time. But this does not necessarily happen because some of the increase in real expenditure induces higher imports via the marginal propensity to import. Thus government action is required to restrict imports in some way if the direct effect of depreciation on imports is to be sustained. As noted earlier, governments tried to utilize the "employment effect" of depreciation by overdepreciating their currencies in the 1930's.

When the domestic economy is functioning at full employment (allowing for "frictional" unemployment amounting to 3 or 4 percent of the labor force), then rising money expenditure induced by depreciation results mainly in a general rise in prices (inflation) rather than an increase in real output. If this general price rise is of the same order as the depreciation (say 10 percent), then the direct effects of depreciation are completely vitiated and the payments deficit remains the same. Depreciation may also stimulate a general price rise in other ways. Higher domestic prices paid for imports of raw materials, capital equipment, and the like may impose an upward pressure on domestic costs of production and the price level. The higher prices of imported consumer goods may encourage labor unions to ask for higher wages; and, in countries where the wages of most workers are linked to a consumer price index, higher wages inevitably result when there is a substantial dependence upon such imports.[8]

To conclude, under full-employment conditions the income and price effects of depreciation limit its effectiveness; and, in some instances, they may destroy it entirely. Unless government policy firmly restrains inflation, depreciation only leads to further depreciation or to tighter exchange control. Even under conditions of widespread unemployment and excess capacity, depreciation must be buttressed by government action to restrict imports through higher tariffs, quotas, or other devices, unless the marginal propensity to import is very low or the depreciation is excessive in terms of export and import elasticities. Successful depreciation demands, therefore, more than a manipulation of the exchange rate; it must be part of a broader policy of international adjustment.

---

[8] In addition to general price effects, depreciation causes shifts in *relative* prices such as occur in a stable-rate system. Briefly, the domestic prices of exports and imports rise relative to the prices of domestic goods. This stimulates a movement of resources into the export and import-competing sectors of the economy. Unlike the general price effects, these relative price effects are part of the adjustment process.

The Effect of Depreciation on the Terms of Trade

Exchange depreciation improves the balance of payments if its direct effects are not neutralized by income and price effects that prevent a decline in domestic real expenditure. However, the effects of depreciation on the commodity terms of trade are uncertain.[9]

It may seem obvious that depreciation *worsens* the terms of trade of the depreciating country: the foreign exchange price of its exports drops while the foreign exchange price of its imports stays the same. But this price behavior is by no means certain. We can see why if we understand that an exchange depreciation of (say) 10 percent is equivalent to a *duty* of 10 percent on all imports and a *subsidy* of 10 percent on all exports. An import tariff tends to *improve* the terms of trade by lowering the foreign exchange price of imports, but an export subsidy tends to *worsen* the terms of trade by lowering the foreign exchange price of exports. The *net* effect of *both* duty and subsidy on the terms of trade depends on the interaction of the supply and demand elasticities of both imports and exports.

The general rule states that a depreciation worsens the terms of trade if the product of the two supply elasticities is *greater* than the product of the two demand elasticities, or $(e_{sx})(e_{sm}) > (e_{dx})(e_{dm})$. Otherwise, the terms of trade remain unchanged (the two products are equal) or improve (the product of the two supply elasticities is *less* than the product of the two demand elasticities).

THE ARGUMENT FOR FLEXIBLE EXCHANGE RATES

In Chapter 8 we noted some of the arguments for stable exchange rates. We now turn the tables and present the argument for variable or flexible exchange rates.

There is a strong theoretical case for fluctuating exchange rates. In highly simplified terms, it assumes this form. In a stable-rate system, adjustment to a deficit is carried out by deflationary movements in domestic income and prices that contract real expenditure. All goes well if wages and prices are flexible downwards, for then employment and output are sustained at their previous levels. But if wages and prices are *inflexible downwards*, then a contraction in real expenditure involves a fall in employment and output. There is abundant evidence indicating that the second course of events is the more likely to happen in contemporary national economies.

---

[9] For a definition of the commodity terms of trade, see Footnote 18 in Chapter 3.

Unions set floors under wages that are supplemented by official minimum wage policies; oligopolistic industries set administered prices that do not respond to a decline in effective demand which is met instead by a cutback in production. Under these conditions long-run adjustment in a stable-rate system will cause a downward spiral in employment and output. On the other hand, governments are pledged to the maintenance of a fully employed economy. Hence they will act to frustrate any deflation induced by a deficit in the balance of payments by adopting expansionary fiscal and monetary policies that sustain the level of real expenditure necessary to full employment.

Given contemporary government policies with respect to employment and economic stability, then, long-run adjustment in a stable-rate system is not likely to be effective. There are two ways out of this impasse: (1) impose controls on trade and payments, (2) depreciate the rate of exchange. Controls, however, are incompatible with a market economy and they provoke hostility and retaliation in foreign countries. We are left, then, with depreciation or, more comprehensively, variable exchange rates as the only mode of payments adjustment that is compatible both with domestic full-employment policies and the principle of free competition in world markets. Free exchange rates respond to disequilibrating forces and achieve a continuous adjustment in the balance of payments. This gives governments the freedom to follow domestic policies of full employment and growth without worrying about payments deficits.

The theoretical argument for an adjustable-peg system is less strong because adjustment in the exchange rate is apt to be delayed, and the degree of rate variation is determined by a government under circumstances that make the choice of the correct equilibrium rate a very difficult one. Delay in depreciating the exchange rate to correct a deficit is likely to occur in an adjustable-peg system for several reasons. The government often demonstrates a "stable-rate complex" and makes the mistake of identifying its prestige with the maintenance of the existing rate. Or the government may repeatedly postpone rate adjustment in the renewed expectation that the disequilibrium will prove to be "temporary" after all. Or, having decided in principle on depreciation, the government may take a long time to reach a political consensus on the appropriate amount of depreciation. All this adds up to the fact that there is a strong probability that a government will put off depreciation until it is forced to act because its reserves of gold and foreign exchange are running out and its international credit is exhausted. By that time it is clear to everyone that depreciation (or controls) is imminent, and this will stimulate a massive capital flight and destabilizing speculation which will intensify the drain on reserves. In these circumstances a government may feel compelled to undertake a very large depreciation in order to put a stop to speculative activity. In the end the government depreciates the exchange rate and blames the speculators for its troubles.

To sum up, in an adjustable-peg system depreciation to eliminate a deficit is likely to come too late and be too big. Moreover, the deficit country must do most of the adjusting because there is little or no incentive for surplus countries to *appreciate* their exchange rates. These drawbacks do not appear in a fluctuating-rate system shared by several countries: the exchange rates of all countries respond quickly to disturbances, and these prompt adjustments sustain a continuing equilibrium in international payments.

Despite the strong theoretical case for flexible exchange rates, governments and central bankers are almost universally hostile to a fluctuating-rate system.[10] Unfortunately, the reputation of fluctuating rates has suffered from bad company in the past. In this century fluctuating rates involving several major currencies have appeared two times but only by default: in the period following World War I before European countries returned to the gold standard in the middle twenties, and in the 1930's when global depression forced the wholesale abandonment of the international gold standard. Grave instability in international trade and payments characterized both periods. Not surprisingly, speculation and capital flight were rife; exchange rates behaved erratically, making sharp and sudden movements. Thus fluctuating exchange rates came to be associated with instability, speculation, and generally bad times.

The rebuttal of this presumed association is that there is here a confusion of symptom and cause. When underlying conditions are very unstable, then exchange rates will mirror this instability. The same conditions will provoke capital flight and unwanted shifts in domestic income and prices in a stable-rate system. When underlying

---

[10] During the period 1950-62 Canada had a floating exchange rate that was free to vary several percentage points above and below par value, in contrast with the one percentage point variation permitted by the rules of the International Monetary Fund. In May, 1962, the Canadian authorities depreciated the Canadian dollar to a par value of 92.5 United States cents, and since that time they have stabilized the exchange rate within one percentage point of par, thereby getting back into the good graces of the Fund.

conditions are only moderately unstable, then fluctuations in exchange rates will also be moderate.

There is also a widespread belief that fluctuating rates introduce exchange risks that hinder international trade and investment. The rebuttal argument is that forward exchange markets quickly develop in a fluctuating-rate system, making possible the hedging of foreign exchange risks. Moreover, there are trading risks of another kind in a stable-rate system caused by income and price adjustments, to say nothing of trade restrictions stemming from a failure, or rather frustration, of the market adjustment process.

The deep-seated opposition of monetary authorities prevents any general adoption of fluctuating or floating rates by the major trading countries. At present, these countries adhere to an adjustable-peg system sponsored by the International Monetary Fund with the backing of the United States. However, there is a marked reluctance to use depreciation as a means of adjustment, especially on the part of the two key currency countries, the United States and Great Britain.

SUMMARY

1. There are many possible kinds of variable-rate systems, ranging from a fluctuating-rate system to an adjustable-peg system. In a fluctuating-rate system movements in the exchange rate achieve a continuing equilibrium in the balance of payments. In the adjustable-peg system exchange rates are occasionally varied by government action from one stable level to another, and the choice of a new equilibrium rate is difficult. In the latter, the purchasing-power parity doctrine is of limited usefulness.
2. The direct effects of depreciation on the balance of payments depend on the elasticities of demand and supply of both exports and imports. Depreciation *always* improves the balance of payments when the sum of export and import demand elasticities is greater than one (Marshall-Lerner condition). Even if this sum is below one, depreciation improves the balance of payments provided supply elasticities are small enough.
3. Depreciation also has indirect effects on domestic income and prices that tend to counteract its direct effects by sustaining the level of domestic real expenditure. Unless government policy firmly restrains inflation in a fully employed economy, depreciation only leads to further depreciation or to tighter controls. Even under conditions of widespread unemployment, depreciation must be buttressed by government action to restrain imports.
4. The effect of depreciation on the commodity terms of trade is uncertain. It depends on the size of the product of the two supply elasticities of exports and imports as compared with the product of their demand elasticities.
5. The basic argument for fluctuating exchange rates is that they are the most effective means of market adjustment to balance of payments

disequilibrium in the kind of world we live in. It is alleged by proponents of fluctuating rates that long-run adjustment in a stable-rate system is likely to be vitiated by domestic government policies of full employment and stability. The theoretical argument for an adjustable-peg system is less strong because exchange rate adjustment is apt to come too late and be too big. Despite the case for flexible exchange rates, governments and central bankers vigorously oppose them. This prevents any general adoption of fluctuating or floating rates by the major trading countries.

QUESTIONS AND APPLICATIONS

1. (a) How do short- and long-run adjustments occur in a fluctuating-rate system? (b) How do they occur in an adjustable-peg system?
2. (a) Assuming infinite supply elasticities, construct a graph to show the effects of depreciation when the elasticity of export demand is zero and the elasticity of import demand is zero. Does depreciation improve the balance of payments?
   (b) Using graphs, show how the effectiveness of exchange depreciation is determined by the elasticities of the supply and demand of foreign exchange.
   (c) What is the Marshall-Lerner condition?
3. (a) Trace the indirect effects of depreciation on domestic income and prices under both full-employment and less-than-full-employment conditions.
   (b) Why do these indirect effects call for government action? What kind?
4. "The effect of depreciation on the commodity terms of trade is uncertain." Explain.
5. What is the basic argument for flexible exchange rates? Why do governments oppose flexible exchange rates?

SELECTED READINGS

Corden, W. M. *Recent Developments in the Theory of International Trade*, Special Papers in International Economics No. 7. Princeton: Princeton University Press, 1965. Chapter I.

Friedman, Milton. "The Case for Flexible Exchange Rates," *Essays in Positive Economics*. Chicago: The University of Chicago Press, 1953, pp. 157-87.

Haberler, Gottfried. *A Survey of International Trade Theory*, Special Papers in International Economics No. 1. Princeton: Princeton University Press, 1961. Chapter V.

Kindleberger, Charles P. *International Economics*. Homewood, Illinois: Richard D. Irwin, Inc. Chapters 4, 9, 10, and 11.

Nurske, Ragnar. *Conditions of International Monetary Equilibrium*, Essays in International Finance, No. 4. Princeton: Princeton University Press, 1945. Reprinted in Ellis, Howard S., and Lloyd D. Metzler (eds.). *Readings in the Theory of International Trade*. Philadelphia: The Blakiston Co., 1949.

PART 2

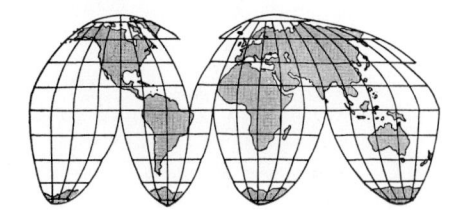

POLICY

The theory of comparative costs reveals the advantages of international specialization and trade. Nonetheless, governments are inclined to treat international economic problems in a spirit of nationalism that often ignores the interests of the community of nations. Unfortunately, this approach to economic policy creates more problems than it pretends to solve. In Part 2 we shall explore the causes of this reluctance to adjust policy to theory, and appraise the consequences of national restrictive measures. We shall also evaluate efforts to liberalize and strengthen international trade and payments through many forms of international cooperation. In doing this, we shall pay special attention to United States policies in the fields of international trade, assistance to developing countries, the balance of payments, and private foreign investment.

PART 2

CHAPTER 21

THE MEANS AND ENDS OF INTERNATIONAL ECONOMIC POLICY

The international economic policy of governments is pervasive; it affects the lives of all of us in a number of ways—as consumers, as producers, and as citizens of a nation which itself is a member of the community of nations. Restrictive government policy forces us as consumers to pay a higher price for many imported goods and, at times, to do without them. On the other hand, liberal government policy enables us to reap the advantages of international specialization. As producers we may be benefited or hurt by specific aspects of foreign economic policy depending upon our place in the economy. The international economic policy of our government may earn us the goodwill and support of other nations, or it may provoke mistrust and retaliation.

Although we cannot escape the impact upon our lives and fortunes of the international economic policy of our own and other governments, we are usually ignorant of its source. The bearing of international economic policy on our interests as consumers is ordinarily indirect and can be traced only by careful economic analysis. Certainly the man on the street is unaware of the relation between international economic policy and the availability and prices of the goods and services that comprise his standard of living— particularly in the United States. Consequently, most of us care little about the foreign economic policy of our own government and few of us seek to change it.

The situation is far different for business enterprises that are directly engaged in international trade or face competition from imports. They well know that government actions in the international economy may spell the difference between profit and loss. Hence they take steps to influence international economic policy in the direction that best accords with their interests. Because of the apathy of the general public, the individuals and groups that have an obvious **financial stake in** the foreign economic policy of their governments have been able to exert an extraordinary influence on policy formation. The effectiveness of protectionist lobbies in Washington and elsewhere is a good example.

The excessive weight given to private vested interests in the formulation and execution of international economic policy not only is undemocratic but also represents a yielding of the national interest to the individual interest. Above our own individual welfare lies the welfare of the nation and the welfare of the community of nations, and, in the last analysis, they are inseparable. Enlightened self-interest demands, therefore, that we take full account of national and international interests in the formulation of international economic policy. To do so we must learn to evaluate international economic policy in the light of these broad perspectives.

THE DEFINITION AND SCOPE OF INTERNATIONAL ECONOMIC POLICY

International economic policy may be both broadly and narrowly conceived.

A Broad Definition

Broadly conceived, international economic policy embraces all **of the varied** economic activities of governments that bear, directly or **indirectly, upon** the composition, direction, and magnitude of **international trade** and finance. This conception of international economic **policy covers** not only such obvious examples as tariff policy, but also domestic governmental measures, such as monetary and fiscal policy, which have an impact upon foreign trade. Since economic activity is characterized by a mutual interdependence, there are few, if any, economic policies of government that have only domestic effects.

Because of the signal importance of the American economy in the world, the economic policies of the United States government, whether ostensibly domestic or foreign, are of particular significance to the well-being of the international economy. The greatest single contribution that our government can make toward the promotion and development of world trade is the pursuit of policies at home that insure the stable growth of the American economy. In this sense the fiscal and monetary policies of the government are more basic to United States foreign economic policy than, for example, its much touted actions in the field of tariff negotiation.

This interdependence of domestic and foreign economic policy works in the other direction as well. For example, should the military expenditures now allocated to the United States foreign aid budget be allocated instead to the budget of the Defense Department? Since these expenditures are intended to strengthen the defense of the United States by building up the defenses of our allies, there is as much justification for including them in our domestic defense budget as in foreign aid. Aware of these and other matters, the Joint Committee on the Economic Report has provided a definition of United States foreign economic policy that is even more inclusive than our own broad definition:

> Our foreign economic policy is broadly conceived to include not only specific government measures in such fields as tariffs and foreign economic aid, but also all American economic behavior, public and private, foreign and domestic, which has its repercussions on the rest of the world.[1]

A Narrower Definition

The interdependence of domestic and foreign economic policy is a truth that must be kept in mind throughout our study of international trade. Unfortunately for the peace of mind of those people who like to think in watertight compartments, the political boundary of a nation cannot serve to demarcate domestic and foreign interests. For reasons of space and analytical convenience, however, in Part 2 we are compelled to limit foreign economic policy to the activities of government that seek *directly* to regulate, restrict, promote, or otherwise interfere with the conduct of international trade and finance. While employing this narrower definition in our subsequent description and analysis of international economic policy, we do not intend to neglect its close relationship with domestic economic policy.

THE MEANS OF INTERNATIONAL ECONOMIC POLICY

International economic policy involves both means and ends, although at times it may be difficult to distinguish between them. In accordance with our decision to use a narrow interpretation of the

---

[1] United States Congress, Joint Committee on the Economic Report, Subcommittee on Foreign Economic Policy, *Foreign Economic Policy* (January, 1956), p. 4.

scope of international economic policy, we shall take the means of policy to signify the methods and practices that are utilized by governments to influence *directly* the course of international trade and finance.

Much of the foreign economic policy of a nation is effected through agreements and treaties with other nations. For the most part, the legal rights that individuals and business enterprises enjoy in a foreign country are those spelled out in treaties and agreements previously negotiated by their own government. Thus international treaties and agreements determine the treatment to be accorded foreigners and foreign interests. Generally speaking, this treatment is either *national* or *most-favored-nation* treatment. Under national treatment, foreigners possess the same rights as nationals. National treatment extends chiefly to the protection of life and property; no Mexican policeman, for instance, would ask for a birth certificate before coming to the rescue of a person in trouble. Most-favored-nation treatment is based on a different concept of equity; it means that a nation treats a second nation as favorably as it treats any third nation. The main purpose of most-favored-nation treatment is to eliminate national discrimination. Its greatest application is in the field of tariffs and other measures of commercial policy.[2]

The means of international economic policy exhibit a wide variety, and it will prove helpful to examine them in terms of three broad policy areas, each of which deals with different items of the balance of payments.

Commercial Policy

Commercial policy refers to the government measures that bear directly on the current account of the balance of payments, especially trade in merchandise. Historically, the main instrument of commercial policy has been the tariff on imports; but today quantitative trade restrictions, bilateral trade agreements, state-trading, and other techniques of control are often of equal or of greater importance.

Financial Policy

Financial policy covers the actions of governments with respect to the capital account of the balance of payments.

There are, first, the many government policies to achieve and maintain equilibrium in the balance of payments. The nature of

---

[2] The most-favored-nation principle is discussed further in Chapters 17-18.

these policies is determined primarily by whether a nation adheres to a stable-rate, variable-rate, or controlled-rate system. Fiscal and monetary policies, exchange rate adjustments, exchange control, and many special measures to influence or restrict the movements of short-term capital and gold may all play a role in balance of payments policy.

Second, financial policy deals with foreign investment or the movement of long-term capital. When properly employed, foreign investments help to develop the productive capacity of the borrowing country and provide the lending country with a profitable outlet for its capital. Despite these merits, governments of both borrowing and lending nations often raise obstacles to the free movement of investment funds; although, strangely enough, the deterrents imposed by governments of borrowing nations are usually the more potent.

Foreign Aid Policy

Foreign aid policy includes all of the activities involved in the field of intergovernmental loans and grants that are intended to aid in the reconstruction, economic development, or military defense of the recipient country. Compared to commercial and financial policy, foreign aid policy is a newcomer; it was born out of the vicissitudes of the early postwar period when Europe lay economically prostrate. Later a recognition of the obligation to help in the development of **the economically backward countries of the world** provided another stimulus to foreign aid policy. Simultaneously, the threat of the **cold war gave rise to large-scale programs of military and economic** aid that sought to buttress the free world against internal and external Communist aggression. Most of the foreign aid of the free world has come from the United States, although Canada and the western European countries have also extended aid to certain countries and all members of the United Nations contribute to the technical aid program of that organization. The United States, however, stands unmatched in the scope and variety of its foreign aid to the other nations of the free world.

Foreign aid involves a host of problems for both the donor and recipient nations. When foreign aid consists of grants, the donor nation must decide such issues as how much to give, to whom to give, and how to control the use of the gift. Recipient nations must, at the very least, decide whether to accept foreign aid and how far they should go in cooperating with the donor nation as to its use. Considerations of national prestige and international politics complicate these matters; some nations have refused United States grants on the grounds that it would ally them with the United States against the Communist bloc. Similar issues arise out of international government loans.

THE ENDS OF INTERNATIONAL ECONOMIC POLICY

There are several ways to classify the objectives that nations may follow in their foreign economic policy, and few classifications are apt to be exhaustive or mutually exclusive. We do not intend to catalog the many ends of international economic policy; but, in order to illustrate their rich diversity, we have chosen for discussion seven of the most fundamental objectives. At this time we are not interested in an analysis of these ends; our purpose is simply one of identification.

Autarky

At one extreme is the objective of *autarky* or national self-sufficiency. A full autarkic policy aims to rid the nation of all dependence on international trade because this dependence is feared for economic, political, or military reasons. Autarky is clearly inconsistent with the continuance of foreign trade; its political counterpart is isolationism.

Actually, most nations do not possess the domestic resources that are required to practice any significant degree of autarky, and in contemporary times this objective has been dominant only in the foreign economic policy of Soviet Russia. More common is a qualified autarkic policy that seeks self-sufficiency in only certain articles of trade, generally of a strategic military value.

Economic Welfare

At the opposite extreme to autarky lies the end of economic welfare that springs from a conception of international trade as an opportunity to reap the gains of international specialization. In Chapter 3 we presented the cogent economic reasoning that underlies this conception of trade. International economic policy in which the objective of economic welfare plays a leading role strives to expand international trade by lowering or eliminating tariffs and other barriers to the free exchange of goods, services, and capital. This liberal philosophy of trade was most dominant in the half century preceding World War I, when the United Kingdom, the paramount trading nation, espoused a policy of free trade and most other nations used only the tariff in controlling trade.

Protectionism

Between the two extremes—autarky, which would regulate foreign trade out of existence, and free trade, which would impose no restrictions whatsoever—there are a number of other ends that serve to motivate international economic policy. Chief among them is protectionism, the protection of domestic producers against the free competition of imports by regulating their volume through tariffs, quotas, and the like. Identification of a specific international economic policy as protectionist is sometimes difficult, since any policy, and there are several kinds, that restricts imports has protectionist effects regardless of its objective. Protectionism, therefore, has many guises and it shows a remarkable ability to adjust to new circumstances by employing arguments and stratagems suited to the times.

Full-Employment Stability

Since the 1930's, stability of the economy at full-employment levels has been among the most important objectives of national economic policy. Contemporary governments have committed themselves in many ways to chart safely the national economy between the Charybdis of inflation, on the one hand, and the Scylla of deflation and unemployment, on the other. When the aim of full-employment stability dominates the foreign economic policy of a nation, international trade is both a source of disturbances to the domestic economy and a means of compensating for disturbances originating within the economy. Whether foreign trade is restricted or encouraged depends mostly upon current levels of domestic economic activity.

Balance of Payments Equilibrium

Sooner or later, all nations are compelled to remedy deficits in their balance of payments whether through market adjustments or controls. When a nation's reserves are low and its balance of payments is weak, the objective of payments equilibrium may come to dominate other objectives of its foreign economic policy and even of its domestic policy. In the decade following World War II the elimination of the dollar shortage occupied first place among the foreign economic policy objectives of western European countries.

In more recent years the United States balance of payments problem has come to overshadow the other foreign economic issues of this country. As we observed in Chapter 11, balance of payments policy may conflict with domestic policies of full employment and growth.

Economic Development

Today the nonindustrial countries of Asia, Africa, and Latin America are desperately striving to accelerate their economic growth and to raise the living standards of their peoples. The pressing concern of these nations with the mammoth problem of economic development has led their governments to regard international trade as an instrument to achieve such development to the exclusion of other ends. Thus, tariffs and other restrictive devices are employed to protect "infant industries" or to keep out "nonessential" consumer goods. On the other hand, capital goods and other "essential" imports are encouraged by subsidies or favorable exchange quotas. Exports may also be regulated in an attempt to promote economic development. Aside from these direct measures of control, economic development programs are likely to provoke disequilibrium in the balance of payments because of their inflationary impact on domestic income and price levels. Further controls may then be imposed to suppress the disequilibrium.

Economic Warfare

During periods of actual warfare the international economic policies of nations are directed toward the overriding objective of winning the war. Even in the absence of armed conflict, however, economic warfare is often among the ends of international economic policy. We live in a time of political tensions between great powers, and it is to be expected that these powers should use foreign trade to further their own political and military advantages and to limit the advantages of those opposed to their vital interests. Thus the United States and its allies impose strategic controls on trade with the Communist countries, and the latter follow a similar course of action against the United States. Foreign aid programs are also used to implement political objectives; indeed, the full range of foreign economic policy comes under the influence of this political contest among nations.

The injection of political and military considerations into international economic policy is nothing new. After all, international economic policy is part of the foreign policy of the nation and it is

Ch. 12 / The Means and Ends of International Economic Policy

inevitably colored to some degree by national political aims. But the degree of coloring is important, and after the comparatively liberal international economic policy of the nineteenth century, the emergence of economic warfare in our own century appears as an abnormal state of affairs to many observers.

THE DIVERSITY AND CONFLICT OF ENDS

In this section we see that the ends of international economic policy are diverse, that the means to achieve these ends are inadequate, that the ends are often in conflict from within and without, and that the international economic policy of a nation must aim to alleviate the internal and external conflict of its objectives.

The Diversity of Ends

The ends of international economic policy are diverse on two counts: (1) each nation usually pursues simultaneously a number of ends in its own foreign economic policy, and (2) the constellation of ends pursued by one nation does not necessarily correspond to the constellation of ends pursued by other nations. If this diversity of ends could be successfully attained by each and every nation, there would be no need for our present analysis of economic policy. As is true of all human affairs, however, no single nation nor group of nations can fully echieve the many objectives that comprise the ends of international economic policy. This failure stems from both an inadequacy of means and a conflict of ends.

The Inadequacy of Means

Even if a nation sought only one end in its foreign economic policy, it might not command the resources necessary to attain that end. Although Brazil might attempt to achieve a stabilization of the price of its major export—coffee—and neglect all other objectives in its international economic policy, the attempt would fail, for Brazil controls only a part of the world supply of coffee and a much smaller fraction of the world demand. An increase in the availability of resources required to implement a policy will, other things being equal, assure a greater success or lesser failure. Thus, if not only Brazil but all the coffee-producing countries would agree among themselves to stabilize the price of coffee, they would be more successful than Brazil acting alone. Still, complete success would elude them because world demand for coffee would remain largely beyond their control. Another addition of resources, the cooperation of all the coffee-consuming countries, would probably insure a very successful policy of price stabilization, but even then control over all the relevant factors would be incomplete as long as consumers were free, say, to switch from coffee to tea.

A nation such as the United States has a much larger capacity to implement a specific international economic policy than a smaller economic power, but even its capacity is limited and many goals of policy will not be fully attainable for that reason. When we introduce the conflict of ends that is internal to a nation's international economic policy and the external conflict of ends that exists between the policies of different nations, the obstacles to satisfactory fulfillment of ends become much more formidable.

The Internal Conflict of Ends

Except possibly during a war when the issue of national survival is paramount, no nation pursues a single objective in its international economic policy; rather, it is confronted with a number of objectives that are often in real conflict. This diversity of ends and the consequent conflict between them are bound to occur since they reflect the diverse and often contradictory economic goals of the nation itself.

The nation is made up of individuals and groups that occupy different positions in the economy, who do not equally benefit from the same economic events and government policies and who have, therefore, diverse economic views and interests. A persistent illustration is the phenomenon of inflation. Rising prices injure the interests of salaried employees and others on a relatively fixed income, whereas businessmen are benefited by a sellers' market and the opportunities for windfall profits when selling prices rise faster than costs. Unionized workers may be able to keep up with inflation by linking wages to a cost-of-living index or even, in some instances, to stay ahead by anticipating price increases in their wage demands. All consumers are hurt by inflation. Inflationary pressures may create disequilibrium in the balance of payments by lowering exports and stimulating a rise in imports. What, then, should be the policy of government with respect to inflation? Who should be the principal beneficiary of this policy—the laborer, the businessman, the consumer, the government, the nation, or the world economy? This conflict of interests is not easily resolved, and often it is resolved in a way that satisfies one or another vested interest while the national interest is sacrificed on the altar of political expediency. Many instances of this internal conflict of ends in the field of international economic policy will be encountered in subsequent chapters.

The External Conflict of Ends

Some countries are extremely dependent upon international trade for their economic livelihood; other countries approach varying degrees of self-sufficiency. Some countries are industrialized and enjoy a high standard of living; other countries are in the early stages of economic development and most of their peoples live close to starvation. Some national economies are organized on a private-enterprise basis; others have a feudalistic or socialistic basis of production. Some countries have strong balances of payments; others are hard pressed to meet their international obligations. These, and the many other differences which distinguish one nation from another, generate different attitudes and policies toward international trade that are often in conflict. One nation may seek to take advantage of the gains from trade by lowering tariffs and other barriers, while other nations are raising barriers in order to protect domestic industry or to meet a drain on international reserves. Such conflicts of national interest abound in the historical and contemporary economic policies of nations.

Lessening the Conflict of Ends

A great deal of international economic policy is made up of efforts to alleviate both the internal and external conflict of ends. Persuasion and compromise are the hallmarks of these efforts.

A nation must introduce order into its own international economic policy if it is to cooperate fruitfully with other nations. There must be a substantial measure of agreement by the government and the people (presumably the need for agreement by the people is not true of totalitarian governments) as to the relative importance of the competing objectives of foreign economic policy if effective action is to be taken. Otherwise an objective may be sacrificed willy-nilly in the attempt to attain a lesser one. This agreement, of course, is never complete; and even if it were, it would not guarantee a wise policy. Agreement must flow from the continuous processes of persuasion, education, and the spirit of compromise that lifts men out of the narrow vision of selfish interests.

Although the ends of international economic policy must be ordered into a hierarchy of priorities and degrees of importance in order to insure the minimum of coherence that is required of a successful program, there still remain the tasks of adjusting one end to another, and the policy that results from this process is bound to displease the partisans of any specific end. A successful international economic policy recognizes the principle that a number of half loaves is probably better, and certainly more attainable, than a single loaf.

The international economic policy of a nation must also be flexible in the constellation of its ends if there is to be fruitful cooperation with other nations. Without this cooperation the external conflict of ends will doom any foreign economic policy except possibly that of sheer economic warfare or outright self-sufficiency. Nations must be prepared to compromise a lesser end in order to achieve a greater end. The United States government has long held firmly to the principle of nondiscrimination in international trade, but the United States has not criticized the discriminatory practices of other nations when it has felt that those practices were an alternative to economic collapse or a crisis in the balance of payments.

International agreements, like the General Agreement for Tariffs and Trade, are replete with exceptions that permit national behavior that is contradictory to the basic principles of the agreement. Without these compromises international treaties and agreements would be impossible, and critics of such compromises must disavow any possibility of agreement if they honestly face the issues. Today, it is clear that the external conflict of ends will not be lessened except through understanding and compromise among nations, buttressed by formal treaties and agreements. If one accepts the belief that some lessening of this conflict is better than no lessening at all, he must also accept the spirit of compromise that is necessary to achieve it.

SUMMARY

1. The international economic policies of governments affect the lives and fortunes of all of us although we are usually unaware of this fact. Business enterprises engaged in international trade or faced with competition from imports, however, realize that foreign economic policies may spell the difference between profit and loss. Accordingly, they take steps to influence the adoption of those policies in a direction that benefits

Ch. 12 / The Means and Ends of International Economic Policy **245**

them; and, because of the apathy of the general public, they are often successful. Hence, international economic policies often represent a sacrifice of the national interest to the individual interest. Enlightened self-interest demands that we take full account of national and international interests in the development of international economic policy.

2. We shall consider international economic policy as all the activities of government that seek *directly* to regulate, restrict, promote, or otherwise interfere with the conduct of international trade and finance. International economic policy and domestic economic policy have a close relationship with each other.

3. An examination of the means of international economic policy in terms of commercial policy, financial policy, and foreign aid policy is helpful. Although interdependent, these three policies deal with separate items of the balance of payments.

4. There are many ends of international economic policy. Seven of the most fundamental objectives are: autarky, economic welfare, protectionism, full-employment stability, balance of payments equilibrium, economic development, and economic warfare.

5. The ends of international economic policy are diverse on two counts: (1) each nation usually pursues simultaneously a number of ends in its own foreign economic policy, and (2) the constellation of ends pursued by one nation does not necessarily correspond to the constellation of ends pursued by other nations.

6. No nation can fully achieve the many objectives of its international economic policy because of an inadequacy of means, an internal conflict of ends in its own policy, and an external conflict of ends between its policy and the policies of other nations. The internal conflict of ends may be alleviated by ordering the ends of foreign economic policy into a hierarchy of importance. In a democracy this requires continuous processes of persuasion, education, and compromise that enable men to see beyond their own selfish interests. The external conflict of ends may be lessened through understanding and compromise among nations, buttressed by formal treaties and agreements.

QUESTIONS AND APPLICATIONS

1. What are the implications of a broad definition of international economic policy?
2. What is the **narrower definition** of international economic policy that is to be used in Part 2?
3. What is meant by the *means* of international economic policy?
4. (a) Describe the three broad areas of international economic policy.
   (b) Evaluate the interdependence of these policy areas in terms of the balance of payments.

5. Identify and discuss the ends of international economic policy.
6. (a) What factors explain the diversity of ends pursued by international economic policy?
   (b) Why do nations fail to achieve all the ends of their international economic policies?
7. (a) Discuss the nature of the internal conflict of ends.
   (b) How does it differ from the external conflict of ends?
8. What steps may be taken to alleviate both the internal and external conflict of ends?

SELECTED READINGS

Boulding, Kenneth E. *Principles of Economic Policy.* Englewood Cliffs, N. J.: Prentice-Hall, Inc., 1958. Chapters 6 and 11.

CHAPTER 13

INTERNATIONAL TRADE AND PAYMENTS RESTRICTIONS

In earlier chapters we have seen that an international environment free of man-made obstacles to trade will afford the best allocation of the factors of production on a world-wide scale and will tend to maximize international economic welfare. Despite the theoretical evidence of greater benefits of unhindered international economic intercourse, governments, more often than not, have interfered with the free movement of goods and services between nations by resorting to restrictive measures in order to achieve certain national objectives. These restrictive measures consist chiefly of (1) *tariffs,* which impose a tax or a customs duty on merchandise crossing the boundaries of a nation, (2) *quantitative trade restrictions,* which, by means of quotas, limit the physical quantities or value of goods that may be imported or exported, and (3) *exchange control,* which, by the denial or allocation of the means of payment for international transactions, achieves the same objectives of quantitative limitation as quotas.

There are also private and governmental institutions that tend to regulate or inhibit international trade such as *cartels, state-trading systems,* and *international commodity agreements* which will be investigated in Chapter 16. In this chapter we shall examine the nature of tariffs, quotas, and exchange control; and in Chapter 14 we shall investigate some of the economic effects of these restrictive measures.

TARIFFS AND TARIFF SYSTEMS

The systematic arrangement or schedule indicating the different customs duties to be levied is known as a *tariff.*[1]

---

[1] The word "tariff" is also used to refer to customs duties that are applicable to a product or a group of products: the tariff on sugar, the tariff on wool, etc. It is also used in reference to the law that establishes schedules of duties, for example, a tariff law or a tariff act.

The Nature of Tariffs

The taxation of trade is probably as old as trade itself and it has been resorted to as a source of revenue under such different appellations as tolls, duties, dues, customs, and tariffs. The reference to such a tax as a tariff appeared only after the Crusades and has been in more or less constant usage ever since. The Mercantilists of the eighteenth century were probably the first to make tariffs more an instrument of national control of international trade than a source of revenue. Tariffs have been used extensively ever since as a protective measure against foreign competition.

Customs Areas. A *customs area* is a geographical region within which goods may move freely without being subjected to customs duties. It generally, but not necessarily, coincides with national boundaries. When a customs area embraces more than one national area, it is known as a *customs union*.

The economic significance of a customs area lies essentially in the movement of goods within the area without payment of tariffs or duties, thus permitting greater efficiency in production under more favorable conditions of specialization and trade with a consequent rise of the standard of living within the area. As powerful as these economic inducements may be, they are often superseded by political considerations born of fear, suspicion, or ambition, feeding on the inevitable short-run difficulties of readjustment.

The customs area of the United States includes all territories under its sovereignty with the exception of American Samoa, Guam, the Virgin Islands, and the Panama Canal Zone; whereas, the customs area of the United Kingdom includes only England, Scotland, Wales, and Northern Ireland. A modern example of a customs union is the Central American Common Market which includes Honduras, El Salvador, Nicaragua, Guatemala, and Costa Rica.

The most dramatic customs union development in history is undoubtedly the creation of the European Economic Community—also known as the European Common Market—which includes six countries of France, Italy, West Germany, Belgium, the Netherlands, and Luxembourg. The Community, which started in 1957, is expected to achieve a full-scale customs union within the next few years. While this experiment has already contributed tremendous benefits to the entire area, it has also created new problems and difficulties for its member as well as nonmember countries.[2]

---

[2] See Chapter 19.

Scope of Customs Duties. There are three general classes of customs duties:

  1. Transit duties, levied by a country on goods passing through its territories, but destined for another country.
  2. Export duties, levied on goods destined for a foreign country.
  3. Import duties, levied on goods coming from a foreign country.

TRANSIT DUTIES. Duties imposed on goods originating in a foreign country and destined for another foreign country are called *transit duties.* They have practically disappeared from the international scene since the Barcelona Statute on Freedom of Transit in 1921. In earlier periods, however, they were used as a source of revenue by cities and states located along strategic trade routes.

EXPORT DUTIES. This class of duty is levied on goods leaving a country for a foreign destination. Export duties, most popular in ancient times, have continued to be applied down through the ages for revenue purposes. With the advent of the Industrial Revolution and the development of freer trade in the nineteenth century, there came the realization that this practice tended to restrict trade; and thus, export duties became less popular. Since World War I, and more specifically since the onset of the great depression of the 1930's, however, export duties have been widely used once again. Export duties are used not only for revenue purposes and to protect rapidly diminishing national raw material reserves but also to induce domestic industrialization in the developing countries. In the United States, export duties are prohibited by the Constitution; but in many countries of the world, especially in Central and South American republics, they are used rather extensively. Export duties may yield considerable revenue that is often used on harbor improvements and the building of roads, for civilian relief, or in connection with price-control plans.

IMPORT DUTIES. By far the most common form of customs duties is the import duty. Before World War I, import duties constituted the most formidable obstacle to international trade, and they continue to occupy a central position in the commercial policies of nations. Designed as a revenue measure, import duties are used more and more as protection against foreign competition, particularly in the developing countries of Asia, Africa, and Latin America.

Kinds of Customs Duties. There are two basic kinds of customs duties—ad valorem and specific. An *ad valorem* duty is stated in terms of a percentage of the value of an imported article, such as 10 percent or 20 percent ad valorem. A *specific duty,* on the other hand, is expressed in terms of an amount of money per quantity of goods, such as 20 cents per pound or per gallon. A combination of an ad valorem and a specific duty is called a *compound duty.*

Ad valorem duties generally lend themselves more satisfactorily to manufactured products, while specific duties are more adaptable to standardized and staple products. This is by no means true under all circumstances. Ad valorem duties on higher priced manufactured goods are, however, considered more effective than specific duties because a single ad valorem rate can usually maintain a more appropriate degree of protection, especially under conditions of rising prices. A specific rate, on the other hand, has the advantage of being more protective in a declining market or in a business recession when cheaper goods are favored. A specific rate will, moreover, discourage imports of the cheaper grade within a class of products as compared to the more expensive variety. For example, a specific rate of $2 per pair on shoes will discourage imports valued at $5 a pair to a greater extent than those valued at $10 a pair.

Compound duties frequently apply to manufactured goods containing raw materials that are on the dutiable list. In such cases the specific portion of the duty—known as a compensatory duty—is levied to offset the duty that grants protection to the raw material industry, while the ad valorem portion of the duty affords protection to the finished goods industry. In the United States, for example, the wool tariff provides for compound duties on worsteds to compensate domestic worsted producers for protection afforded the raw wool industry as well as to provide protection for their own woolen industry.

Sometimes a mixed ad valorem and specific duty is provided for a given product with the provision that the heavier of the two shall apply. This is not a true compound duty; it is an *alternative duty* since only one of the two duties is actually levied.

The United States uses ad valorem as well as compound duties rather extensively, while continental European countries tend to favor specific duties. Great Britain and the other Commonwealth countries usually base their tariffs on the ad valorem type of duty.

Tariff Classifications

There are countless articles of commerce that move in international trade and their number is constantly growing as newly developed products are added every day. For manageable tariff administration, some kind of comprehensive classification or "customs nomenclature" is necessary. Different countries need different types of classification according to the economic framework in which they function. One country's approach to classification may be totally inadequate for another, and the same country may also find its traditional method becoming obsolete with changing internal and external conditions.

As a rule most countries have two major lists in their tariffs: (1) a dutiable list for goods subject to customs duties, and (2) a free list for goods permitted to enter free of duty. Classification in the dutiable list may be made according to: (1) an alphabetical arrangement, (2) the height of the duty, or (3) the attributes of the goods. Each of these methods has its advantages and its drawbacks. The alphabetical and the height-of-the-duty methods are simple in form, but they tend to make reference to any particular product or group of related products difficult. The attribute method of classification is more logical and more widely used in modern tariff systems. Under the attribute approach, classification may be made on the basis of the physical substance from which products are derived, the end-use of the products, or the degree of processing. Sometimes a country may use any one of these broad classifications and provide in addition detailed schedules based on other methods.

Classification for tariff purposes has been growing in complexity throughout the world and has become a source of administrative misinterpretation. Under the auspices of the League of Nations, the World Economic Conference of 1927 made a study of customs classifications in an attempt to standardize customs nomenclatures. Today, almost forty years later, only partial response to the findings of this study is in evidence in the classification methods being used. More definite steps have been taken, however, by various nations individually and collectively toward the simplification of tariffs and tariff administration.

Tariff Systems

Tariff schedules may have one, two, or three different duties for each dutiable article. A nation is said to have a "single-column," a "double-column," or a "triple-column" tariff system, according to the number of different duties appearing on its schedules for each product. When customs duties are established by law they are called *autonomous,* but when they are the result of treaty agreements with other countries they are called *conventional*. Single-column schedules are, as a rule, autonomous, but multiple-column schedules may be either autonomous or partly autonomous and partly conventional.

Single-Column Tariff Schedule. A single-column schedule is essentially autonomous and nondiscriminatory since it provides only one duty for each product, whatever the country of origin.[3] It is not subject to change by negotiation unless legislative permission is afforded. A single-column schedule is best suited for a country whose purpose is either a tariff purely for revenue or purely for protection with no intention of bargaining.

Under present international commercial relations, the rigidity of a single-column tariff system is a handicap when dealing with other nations to resolve mutual trade problems, the supply of which is plentiful. Multiple-column systems, on the other hand, lend themselves more readily to the present needs of international bargaining.

Double-Column Tariff Schedule. This type of schedule has two levels of duties for each product. When both levels are established by law and are not subject to modification by international agreements, there is an autonomous tariff system of a "maximum-minimum form." When only the higher level of duties is established by law and the lower level is a composite of all the reduced duties granted to other nations by negotiation, it is partly autonomous and partly conventional, and is said to be of a "general and conventional form."

When under the maximum-minimum form, the maximum scale is used for normal duties, the minimum scale is extended only to imports from nations that have signed reciprocal agreements to that effect. When the minimum scale is used for normal duties, however, the maximum scale becomes either a weapon resorted to in retaliation against the discriminatory practices of other nations or a threat to induce bargaining and concessions.

Under the general and conventional form, the autonomous higher scale is always used for normal duties; the lower scale is extended to imports from nations that have signed reciprocal agreements entitling them to its benefits. These reduced duties may, however, also be extended to third nations, either conditionally or unconditionally, under most-favored-nation treatment treaties or other expressed policies.

---

[3] A single-column tariff schedule may, however, be conceived on the basis of discrimination if the duties therein are purposely chosen to affect imports from particular countries.

Triple-Column Tariff Schedule. A triple-column schedule is generally used by countries with colonial possessions or with close political affiliations with other countries. It is an extension of the double-column schedule by the addition of a third lower scale that is reserved for intragroup application. This is known as a "preferential system" and it is designed to encourage trade between the different members of the system. The British Commonwealth falls into this category. A triple-column system is sometimes used by smaller countries seeking refinements in their discriminatory policies, generally for political reasons.

Mitigation of Tariffs

The cost of a dutiable article to an importer is always higher than the foreign purchase price by at least the amount of the duty paid.[4] When dutiable raw materials and semifinished products are used in production by domestic industries, the final costs must reflect directly or indirectly the burden of this duty since it is an actual expenditure at some point in the channel of distribution. When goods so produced are reexported, the increased costs due to the tariff may become a serious handicap to trade without serving any protective purpose at home. Transit trade may be similarly affected by the imposition of a transit duty.

Under certain circumstances, tariff laws provide ways of mitigating this unwelcome effect in order to harmonize the conflicting aims of protection and the promotion of exports. This is achieved by either refunding the duty paid in the form of a drawback or by permitting imports to enter free of duty when they are destined for reexport.

Drawbacks. A *drawback* is a refund made by the government to the exporter, in whole or in part, of the tariff duties and taxes paid by the importer upon satisfactory proof of evidence of exportation. The United States refunds 99 percent of the original tariff duties as drawback. Occasionally a drawback is used in lieu of a compensatory duty by reimbursing a domestic manufacturer who uses the imported materials in the production of goods that are in competition with imports made of similar materials not otherwise dutiable. Canada had such a provision in 1935 for the silk that was used in the production of lining caps or other articles for domestic consumption.

---

[4] This statement is consistent with the fact that under some circumstances the imposition of a duty may induce a lower foreign purchase price. See Chapter 14.

Bonded Warehouses. Dutiable imports may be brought into a customs territory and left in *bonded warehouses* free of duty. Under strict governmental supervision, imported goods may be stored, repacked, manipulated, or further processed in bonded warehouses according to the laws of the particular country. The goods may be later reexported free of duty or withdrawn for domestic consumption upon payment of customs duties. When such goods have been processed in a bonded warehouse with additional domestic materials and later entered for consumption, only the import portion of the finished product is subject to duty.

The postponement of payment of the duty is an important consideration especially when large-scale operations are involved, since working capital need not be immobilized. This advantage, however, is often outweighed by the complex regulations and strict customs supervision of operations within a bonded warehouse.

Free Zones and Free Ports. A *free zone* is an isolated, enclosed area with no resident population (generally adjacent to a port) that offers extensive facilities for handling, storing, mixing, and manufacturing imported and domestic goods and materials without customs intervention or immediate disbursement of customs duties. The purpose of a free zone is to enlarge the benefits of a bonded warehouse by the elimination of the restrictive aspects of customs supervision and by offering more suitable manufacturing facilities.

Sometimes, a free zone is referred to as a *free port,* but a true free port is a whole city, or section of a city, isolated from the rest of the country for customs purposes. There are very few free ports left in the world where the population may enjoy the benefit of relatively free trade. Hong Kong, Singapore, and Gibraltar are among the most important of such ports. In medieval Europe, however, free ports abounded along the Mediterranean and northern seas. Venice, Genoa, Naples, Marseilles, Hamburg, and Bremen were prosperous free ports and leading centers of trade for a long period of time.

In the United States, free zones are commonly known as "foreign-trade zones" and are governed by an act of Congress passed in 1934, which provided for their establishment and operation. In 1937, the first foreign-trade zone was opened on Staten Island in New York, followed in 1947 by another in New Orleans, and later in other ports of the country. The history of foreign-trade zones in the United States tends to discourage their development; most of them have operated at a loss, mainly because the geographical position of the United States does not lend itself well to transit and reexport trade.[5]

QUANTITATIVE TRADE RESTRICTIONS

The depression that followed the Wall Street crash of 1929 led to disorganized production and trade and caused widespread unemployment and unrest throughout the world. Prices fell precipitously, affecting primary commodities most severely. In 1931, Great Britain, the pillar of international finance and a clearinghouse for international transactions, was forced to abandon the gold standard as well as its long-standing liberal trade policy and to adopt soon after a general protective tariff. Many nations bound to the pound sterling by political or economic ties were forced into similar action. The result was a wholesale withdrawal from the historic international gold standard.

The disorganization of markets and international economic relations resulted in widespread disequilibrium in balance of payments accounts. The inadequacy of tariff measures to cope with this emergency forced one country after another to resort, in despair, to new instruments of control in order to bring about some order in their chaotic economies. In this trying period of the interwar years, the more refined control measures, such as quotas, exchange controls, and intricate bilateral agreements, were developed to meet individual situations between pairs of countries. In some instances, state-trading and intergovernmental commodity agreements were used.

Quantitative measures of restriction, like tariffs, are tools of national economic policy designed to regulate the international trade of a nation. Unlike tariffs, however, they impose absolute quantitative limitations upon foreign trade and inhibit market responses; this makes them extremely effective under distressed economic conditions such as existed in the depression years. The quantitative trade restrictions are used chiefly to regulate trade in commodities in order to afford protection to domestic producers and/or to bring about the necessary adjustment to a disturbed balance of international payments. As a result, they affect the commercial and industrial activities of a country, as well as its international economic relations.[6]

---

[5] William A. Dymsza, *Foreign Trade Zones and International Trade* (New Jersey Department of Conservation and Economic Development, Trenton, New Jersey, 1964), pp. 229 ff.

[6] Heinrich Heuser, *Control of International Trade* (Philadelphia: The Blackiston Co., 1939), pp. 3 ff. See also Chapter 14.

The most prevalent of the new instruments of trade restriction are direct controls consisting of *quotas* and *exchange control*. Most of the nations of the world, including the United States, use quotas, chiefly import quotas, as an integral part of their protective policy mostly because of the greater effectiveness of this device as compared with others for checking imports.

Many nations are often faced with shortages of foreign exchange resulting in highly disturbing balance of payments problems. They need a system of control that covers not only the physical movement of goods but also the movement of intangible service transactions and capital flows. For this purpose, they resort to the more comprehensive and all-inclusive system of *exchange control* which puts in the hands of the authorities an absolute power over the means of payments for all international transactions.

Quota Systems

Quotas are quantitative restrictions imposed upon dutiable or duty-free commodities entering the country during a given period of time. They are expressed in terms of physical quantities or value, thus restricting within absolute limits the total volume of trade in these commodities regardless of the market forces of supply and demand.

Import Quotas. There are four major types of import quotas in use throughout the world:

1. Absolute or unilateral quota.
2. Negotiated bilateral or multilateral quota.
3. Tariff quota.
4. Mixing quotas.

Each of these four types has its particular advantages and drawbacks; but they all have one thing in common—positive control of the volume of international trade.

UNILATERAL QUOTA. This is a fixed quota that is adopted without prior consultation or negotiation with other countries. It is imposed and administered solely by the importing or exporting country. Because of its unilateral aspect, this type of quota tends to create friction, antagonism, and retaliation abroad that undermine its ultimate success.

A unilateral quota may be *global* or *allocated* depending upon whether or not the fixed volume of imports is specifically assigned by shares to different exporting countries and/or to individual domestic importers or foreign exporters.

A *global quota* restricts the total volume without reference to countries of origin or to established importers and exporters engaged in this trade. In practice, the global quota becomes unwieldy because of the rush of both importers and exporters to secure as large a share as possible before the quota is exhausted. The result is frequently an excess of shipments over the quota, and charges of favoritism may be raised against traders fortunate enough to be the first to seize a lion's share of the business. To avoid the difficulties of a global quota system, a quota may be allocated by countries and by private traders on the basis of a prior representative period. This type of import quota is known as an *allocated quota.*

The period of time during which a given quota remains in effect has generally been short, frequently three months. No country has succeeded in placing its entire import trade under quota. A unilateral quota, whether global or allocated, lends itself to discrimination and mismanagement by the importing country and opens the door to abuse, corruption, and graft. A country may adopt an import quota to restrict imports in general rather than to discriminate between the different sources of such imports, to exact preferential treatment from other countries, or to retaliate against discrimination by other nations against its own exports.

The administration of quotas is fraught with technical difficulties. Foreign traders feel encouraged to misrepresent their products in order to exempt them from quota classification or to resort to methods ranging from simple persuasion to outright graft and corruption of government officials in charge of enforcement. In order to overcome some of the difficulties of the unilateral quota system, an improved plan was developed that tended to replace this type of quota by a less objectionable negotiated bilateral quota.

NEGOTIATED QUOTA. Under the system of a *negotiated bilateral* or *multilateral quota,* the importing country negotiates with supplying countries, or with groups of exporters in those countries, before deciding the allotment of the quota by definite shares. Often the administration of licensing under a bilateral quota is left in the hands of the exporting countries.

A bilateral or multilateral quota tends to minimize pressure by domestic importers upon their own government and to increase cooperation by foreign exporters, thus enhancing the successful operation of the system. When licensing is entrusted to foreign private agencies, however, it often results in the bulk of trade falling into the hands of larger firms or of well-organized international cartels that are in a position to squeeze out most of the monopoly-like profit induced by the restriction of supply relative to demand in the quota country. Hence, domestic importers are deprived of this source of income, and their government, of the opportunity to tax such income.

TARIFF QUOTA. Under a *tariff quota* a specified quantity of a product is permitted to enter the country at a given rate of duty—or even duty free. Any additional quantity that may be imported, however, must pay a higher duty. Thus, a tariff quota combines the features of both a tariff and a quota.

On the surface a tariff quota seems fair and reasonable. It is flexible enough to permit the importation, at a favorable rate of duty, of a limited quantity of a product that is necessary to meet the minimum requirements of the country without closing the gates to additional imports at a higher rate to satisfy those who are willing and able to afford the extra cost.

In practice, however, a tariff quota does not work out exactly that way. If the import needs of a country do not exceed the minimum quantities permitted to enter under the lower rates of duty, the quantities demanded and supplied are not materially affected by the quota and no quota profits are possible. The first rush to import in the early part of a quota period may, however, raise prices abroad and the benefits of the lower duty will then accrue largely to foreign exporters. On the other hand, if domestic needs exceed the quantities permitted by the quota under the lower rates of duty, the lure of a likely quota profit will encourage importers to acquire larger quantities to maximize their share before the exhaustion of the quota. Their action will tend to raise foreign supply prices as well as to glut the domestic market at the beginning of each quota period, thus depressing domestic prices to their own disadvantage. True, domestic prices after the first rush will tend to rise, but further imports that are subject to a higher rate of duty can only take place if the differential between domestic and external prices equals the amount of the duty. Even then, price instability is likely to minimize the possibility of a quota profit. Moreover, highly unstable prices are incompatible with orderly distribution and are hardly beneficial to importers and exporters in the long run.

Tariff quotas have been utilized for a long time to facilitate **border-town** trade between closely interdependent communities of **adjacent countries**. In recent decades, however, tariff quotas have been more frequently used as a vehicle for preferential treatment to encourage trade in particular commodities with certain countries.

MIXING QUOTAS. A number of countries have domestic regulations limiting the proportion of foreign raw materials permitted to be used in the production of certain domestic products. These nominally domestic measures have serious repercussions upon imports and are, in effect, a form of import quotas.

Mixing quotas, known also as *linked-usage regulations,* are used extensively by various countries to promote domestic production of commodities that have a competitive disadvantage with the same or similar foreign products. Mixing quotas, or regulations, even though strictly domestic measures, are nevertheless protective in effect since they encourage high-cost domestic producers to enter the market. Besides, once established, new producers tend to become vested interests and a source of pressure for even greater protection. Mixing quotas tend to compromise the quality of a product and raise its cost of production. They divert the use of the factors of production from their most efficient economic utilization, and their cost burden falls heaviest on the consumer of the country adopting such regulations.

Export Quotas. Exports may be subjected to quantitative restrictions by government action. Quantitative export controls are intended to accomplish one or more of the following objectives:

1. To prevent strategic goods from reaching the hands of unfriendly powers.

2. To assure all or a significant proportion of certain products in short supply for the home market.

3. To permit the control of surpluses on a national or an international basis in order to achieve production and price stability.

These objectives can be attained more positively and with greater ease by the use of quotas than by the use of tariff measures. Like import quotas, export quotas may be unilateral when they are established without prior agreement with other nations, and bilateral or multilateral, when they are the result of agreements. They are administered chiefly by licensing.

Export and production control measures have featured many schemes to improve the market and the price of certain raw materials. Such plans, pertaining to rubber, sugar, tin, wheat, and a number of other commodities, are of long standing. Export quotas are widely used for these commodities, usually under international supervision. The quotas are generally announced in advance with a fixed export price range for each quota period. These controls are usually identified with the international commodity agreements that are discussed in Chapter 16.

Exchange Control

Direct interference of governments in the foreign exchange market is known as *exchange control*. In effect, exchange control replaces the free operation of the market with official decisions that determine the uses and availabilities of foreign exchange.

The Origins of Exchange Control. Exchange control was initially adopted by many governments during World War I when it became necessary to conserve scarce supplies of gold and foreign exchange for the financing of imports vital to the national economy. Following the war, however, exchange control was abandoned everywhere; and by the second half of the 1920's most nations had returned to the gold standard and the full convertibility that characterized the prewar system of international payments. At that time is was widely believed that only the exigencies of war justified the use of exchange control, and few observers expected to witness its revival in a period of peace. Yet within a few years several governments had resurrected exchange control in the face of an event that was almost as convulsive as war in the suddenness of its impact on the international payments system—the international financial crisis of 1931.

The first peacetime use of exchange control by industrial countries arose as a response to the international financial crisis of 1931 that unloosed a panicky run on the gold and foreign exchange reserves of one country after another.[7] The crisis began inconspicuously when the Credit-Anstalt bank in Vienna was declared insolvent in the summer of 1931. This caused a loss of confidence in the ability of Austria to honor its international short-term obligations and there was an immediate large-scale withdrawal of funds from that country. Upon the failure of a large German bank in early July, the run by foreign creditors spread to Germany and to many eastern European countries that had borrowed heavily on short term during the 1920's. Fearful of an exhaustion of its reserves, the German government stopped the flight of capital funds by introducing exchange control in August. By the end of the year, most countries in eastern Europe, as well as Denmark and Iceland, had also applied exchange control

---

[7] In 1929 and 1930 a number of raw material exporting nations imposed exchange control to meet current account deficits brought on by the onset of depression in the industrial countries.

to halt an outflow of capital. Foreign-owned balances in the exchange control countries were now "frozen" and could no longer be freely transferred into gold or convertible foreign exchange. Similarly, residents of the exchange control countries were no longer able to send capital abroad.

The institution of exchange control in Germany next started a run on the British pound sterling. The large short-term loans that the United Kingdom had made to Germany were now immobilized by exchange control, and this created a doubt as to the capacity of the United Kingdom to liquidate its own heavy short-term international indebtedness. The panic rapidly depleted British reserves; but, instead of following the example of Germany, the United Kingdom went off the gold standard in September, 1931, and allowed the pound sterling to depreciate. In June of the following year, the British government established the Exchange Equalization Fund to stabilize the pound at a level below its former gold parity. A number of other countries allowed their currencies to depreciate along with the pound sterling, and in this way gave birth to the Sterling Area.

By 1935 the international financial crisis and the global depression had split the international payments system into five groups:[8]

1. The *Sterling Area,* comprising principally the British Commonwealth and Scandanavian countries.

2. The *Dollar Area,* comprising the United States and most of the countries of Central America and northern South America.

3. The *Gold Bloc* countries of Western Europe.

4. The *Yen Area,* comprising Japan and her possessions.

5. The *Exchange Control Area* of central and southeastern Europe, dominated by Germany.

Some countries, such as Canada, Argentina, Brazil, and Chile, did not fall completely into any one currency area. The Canadian dollar was depreciated about 10 percent against the United States dollar but remained convertible. The other three countries also depreciated but adopted exchange control that rendered their currencies inconvertible.

Exchange control was practiced by Germany, the eastern European countries, and many countries in Latin America throughout the 1930's, long after the international financial crisis of 1931 had become history. Many new uses were found for exchange control and this served to perpetuate its existence. The currencies of the

---

[8] League of Nations, *International Currency Experience* (Geneva: League of Nations, 1944), p. 198.

Dollar Area, the Sterling Area, the Yen Area, and the principal countries of Western Europe (excluding Germany and Italy) remained fully convertible, however, up to the outbreak of World War II. During the war, all countries exercised tight control over their economies and exchange control was only one of several instruments employed for that purpose.

Exchange Control after World War II. In the period following World War II, the countries of the free world gradually dismantled direct controls over the domestic economy and today these controls are largely a thing of the past. As for exchange control, in 1958 only eleven countries—all located in the Western Hemisphere—had *fully* convertible currencies that any holder could transfer freely into other currencies. All other currencies were inconvertible, although the degree of inconvertibility differed greatly between countries.[9]

The widespread use of exchange control after World War II had profound effects upon international trade and payments. It sharply limited the scope of multilateral trade and divided the free world into distinct currency areas. To the individual trader, exchange control meant that he could no longer buy in the low-price market and sell in the high-price market without permission of the authorities. At times this permission was denied outright, and it was almost always limited in some way.

Because of a general improvement in the international financial picture since 1958, many countries have reverted to either full or partial convertibility of their currencies. Restrictions on trade and payments have become on the whole less than they had been in the past, even in the face of balance of payments difficulties. This is especially true of the countries of Western Europe and other industrial nations.

While exchange controls have not been completely eliminated, they have consistently been on the decline so that they no longer play the major restrictive role they once did, except in the new and developing countries where, on balance, they remain a major tool of economic policy.[10]

The Objectives of Exchange Control. The principal objectives of contemporary exchange control systems include:

---

[9] These countries were the United States, Canada, Mexico, Guatemala, El Salvador, Honduras, Panama, Venezuela, Haiti, the Dominican Republic, and Cuba.

[10] International Monetary Fund, *Exchange Control,* Fifteenth Annual Report (Washington, D. C., 1964), pp. 1 ff.

1. The suppression of balance of payments disequilibrium (including the prevention of capital flight).
2. The facilitation of national planning.
3. The protection of domestic industries.
4. The creation of government revenue.

Usually an exchange control system is adapted to pursue two or more of these objectives and it is sometimes difficult to decide which objective is the dominant one. In addition to these basic objectives, exchange control may be used for a number of other purposes, such as strengthening the nation's bargaining position in trade negotiations and expanding exports to other exchange control countries.

THE SUPPRESSION OF BALANCE OF PAYMENTS DISEQUILIBRIUM. When a nation is unwilling or unable to adjust to a persistent deficit in its balance of payments by deflating the domestic economy or by depreciating its rate of exchange or by any other domestic measure of a fiscal or monetary nature, it must suppress the deficit by imposing direct controls over its international transactions. The most important direct control utilized by contemporary governments is exchange control that regulates the acquisition and disposition of foreign exchange. Other forms of direct control—import quotas and import licenses—usually supplement exchange control, although at times they may be used as substitutes.

Exchange control was first used in peacetime mainly for suppression of the unique sort of disequilibrium that is provoked by a flight of capital. When exchange control is used solely for this purpose, there is no reason to restrict imports of merchandise and services because the trouble is not in the current account. Moreover, exchange control need only be temporary, for once the panic has subsided, it may be lifted and most of the capital will return of its own accord. This last statement presupposes, however, a widespread belief that exchange control will not be reimposed. If there is doubt on this score, the cessation of exchange control will itself renew the capital flight. In this way, exchange control may perpetuate the loss of confidence and the speculative attitudes that engendered the original flight of capital. Fearing this consequence, governments tend to maintain exchange control long after the danger of capital flight is past.

There is another reason why exchange control that is imposed to restrain a capital flight may continue as a permanent feature of a nation's foreign economic policy. Exchange control may itself create a current account deficit in the balance of payments and induce further disequilibrium in the balance of payments. This is why many nations, once they have adopted exchange control, dare not abandon it.

THE FACILITATION OF NATIONAL PLANNING. Exchange control has been employed since the war to help governments of the free world achieve certain national economic objectives. In the Communist countries the economy is directed toward specific goals by a comprehensive set of controls that decide the allocation of all productive factors as well as the allocation of the national product. Since private enterprise is forbidden, Communist governments carry on all production and thereby execute the national plans they have drawn up. Under these circumstances exchange control is not necessary to regulate international transactions—all international transactions are conducted by state-trading agencies that behave in accordance with the dictates of the current national plans.

National planning in the private enterprise economies of the free world differs significantly from planning in the Communist economies. In the former, production rests largely in the hands of private entrepreneurs, and the price system is the main instrument in deciding the allocation of production and consumption. Consequently, governments in the free world depend principally (although not exclusively) on fiscal and monetary policies instead of direct controls to implement their national economic programs. But, since these programs are conceived in national terms, they sometimes demand an insulation of the national economy from the world economy. To achieve this insulation governments may impose exchange and trade controls on the private conduct of foreign trade that are supplemented, at times, by state trading in specific commodities.

Since World War II, two objectives have dominated economic planning in the free world countries. Governments of the industrial countries in Europe and North America have sought to maintain full employment, while governments of the underdeveloped economies in Latin America and elsewhere have tried to speed up economic development. The policies associated with these objectives have tended to create inflationary pressures that have, in turn, induced deficits in the balance of payments. Lacking adequate reserves, many countries have been forced to make immediate adjustments to these external deficits. Because of the objectives of national planning, however, the choice of methods of adjustment has been narrowly circumscribed. Deflation has been avoided because it would endanger full employment or slow down the rate of economic growth. Similarly, exchange depreciation has promised little help because any subsequent domestic inflation would offset its effects on international payments. Rather than moderate the goals of national planning, governments, therefore, have used exchange control and other direct measures to insulate the domestic economy from international repercussions.

THE PROTECTION OF DOMESTIC INDUSTRIES. By restricting imports, exchange control inevitably protects domestic producers against foreign competition. Hence, exchange control will be supported by protectionist groups, and they will seek to enhance its protective features. When exchange control is not consciously oriented toward protection, but is set up simply to suppress an external deficit, it will not discriminate against those imports that have close domestic substitutes. All imports will be viewed indiscriminately as a drain on foreign exchange and they will be restricted only to stop that drain. When, however, exchange control also has a protectionist purpose, it will curtail imports of competitive products more stringently than imports of products not produced at home or in sufficient quantities. Once exchange control is established, it usually evolves in the direction of greater protection as a result of the lobbying activities of vested interests. This is also true of the import quotas and licenses that ordinarily accompany exchange control.

THE CREATION OF GOVERNMENT REVENUE. Exchange control is used in some countries to collect revenue for the government. In most instances this occurs where the exchange control authority sets the price at which it will buy foreign exchange below the price at which it will sell foreign exchange. For example, if the authority forces exporters to surrender dollar exchange at a rate of 10 pesos to the dollar and then sells dollar exchange to importers at a rate of 15 pesos to the dollar, it pockets 5 pesos for each dollar that it buys and sells.

Exchange control is used as a source of revenue mainly by developing countries in Latin America, Africa, and Asia. The reliance of nonindustrial countries on exchange control to provide government revenue is largely due to the difficulty of collecting income and other direct taxes. Most of these countries do not have the personnel and skills required to administer direct taxes, and often it is politically impossible to impose such taxes on wealthy individuals. By way of contrast, an exchange control system offers a ready-made apparatus for the collection of revenue with only slight additional administrative expense. Moreover, the tight regulations of exchange control make it difficult to avoid the tax whether in the form of a penalty exchange rate or an exchange tax.[11]

Rate Systems of Exchange Control. No two nations have identical systems of exchange control. Some systems are lenient with almost fully convertible currencies, while others carefully police all uses of foreign exchange and may strongly discriminate against certain currencies. Many other variations in systems of exchange control are attributable to differences in objectives, differences in administrative competence, and differences in economic conditions. It is possible, however, to classify exchange control systems into two broad categories depending upon whether they employ one or several exchange rates.

Single rate systems are administered by an exchange control authority that is the sole buyer and seller of foreign exchange. All foreign exchange transactions are carried on at one official rate of exchange. Exporters and others who receive foreign exchange from foreign residents are compelled to surrender it to the control authority at the official rate. Importers and others who must make payments to foreign residents must obtain permission to buy foreign exchange from the control authority at the official rate. The control authority also regulates the use of domestic currency (bank accounts) owned by foreign residents. Commercial banks are usually authorized to act as buying and selling agents of the exchange control authority. The key to the system of control is the requirement that all foreign exchange transactions involving domestic or foreign residents must pass through authorized banking channels.

In a single rate system of exchange control, the exchange rate itself plays no role in the allocation of foreign exchange among transactions, applicants, currencies, and countries. Indeed, the overvaluation of the exchange rate intensifies the task of allocation by diminishing the amount of foreign exchange in supply and, at the same time, increasing the amount of foreign exchange in demand.

In the *multiple rate systems* of exchange control, however, two or more exchange rates are used to effect the allocation of foreign exchange, although they are usually used in conjunction with exchange licenses and direct trade controls. Because the task of allocation is at least partially carried out by differential exchange rates, multiple rate systems rely far less upon administrative action than do

---

[11] An exchange tax is a charge levied on transactions in foreign exchange.

single rate systems. It is not surprising, therefore, that multiple rate systems are characteristic of many developing countries where it is often difficult to achieve competent administration. But perhaps an even more important reason for the use of multiple rates in those areas is their suitability as devices to raise revenue.

Multiple rate systems exhibit a bewildering variety. At one extreme are the systems that depend upon two or more "free" markets to allocate foreign exchange with few direct controls of any kind. At the other extreme are the systems that use two or more fixed official rates that are supplemented by exchange licenses, import quotas, and other quantitative controls characteristic of single rate systems.

SPECIAL MEASURES OF RESTRICTION

In addition to tariffs and quantitative restrictions, many countries resort to a variety of additional devices that have restrictive effects on trade.

Subsidies, Duties, and Taxes

Many national governments are anxious to see a greater development of certain domestic industries and they frequently pay *subsidies* or bounties to domestic producers or exporters to stimulate the expansion of such industries. Subsidies may be extended in the form of outright cash disbursements, tax exemptions, preferential exchange rates, governmental contracts with special privileges, or some other favorable treatment. The granting of subsidies or bounties results in a cost advantage to the recipient, and for all intents and purposes, they are tantamount to an indirect form of protection.

Goods that are produced under a subsidy or a bounty system and that move in international trade tend to nullify the protective aspect of a tariff in the importing country. To reinstate the intended level of protection, the importing country may impose, in addition to the regular tariff duties, a special surtax or *countervailing duty* generally equal to the amount of the foreign subsidy or bounty. In this manner, the landed cost to the domestic importer is raised by the amount of the subsidy granted to the foreign producer or exporter by his government.

Dumping consists of selling a product in one market at a lower price than it is sold in another. This practice may be justifiable under certain market conditions; but when it is used by foreign producers to undermine or to drive out competition in other countries, the importing country may deem such a practice undesirable and may provide for a remedial or punitive additional duty known as *antidumping duty*. This duty nullifies the effect of the lower price and/or discourages the practice altogether.

Besides the basic customs duties prescribed in tariff schedules, certain imports may be subjected to excise taxes and processing taxes. *Excise taxes* are collectible upon the entry of the goods through customs, while *processing taxes* are payable upon the first domestic processing in the case of certain raw material and semifinished commodities.

The purpose of these special import taxes is generally to compensate for similar taxation of domestic goods. Very often, however, excise and processing taxes are levied exclusively on imports without corresponding levies on similar domestic products, or when similar or competing products are not produced in the domestic market. When excise and processing taxes are assessed exclusively on imports, they become protective measures concealed under less obvious identification, but no less a part of a protective tariff system.

In the United States, excise and processing taxes are levied on a great number of imported articles. Certain inedible animal fats, oils, greases, petroleum products, and lumber are subject to excise taxes, while fatty acids, coconut oils, and other products are the object of a processing tax.

Excise and processing taxes are sometimes preferred to tariffs because they are easier to legislate and administer and because they are not likely to create as much suspicion in the mind of the public. On economic grounds, however, they are no less objectionable than tariffs for they are being used for precisely the same reason.

Administrative Protection

Sovereign states possess the unquestioned right to protect the health and welfare of their citizens, to promote legitimate and desirable social ends, and to regulate competition within their borders when such action is deemed desirable. In the performance of these functions, the state must legislate and, through its police powers, adopt a variety of administrative devices to accomplish its purpose. Of course, it is also necessary and quite legitimate to extend the application of these measures to import activities that fall into the same range. When this type of measure, however, is adopted with discriminatory intentions or is enforced in a manner intended to achieve the restriction or prohibition of imports, it becomes a disguised tool of protection and constitutes, in effect, an *invisible tariff*.[12] In recent decades there has been a marked increase in governmental activities in the control, regulation, and supervision of industry and commerce. As a result, a creeping, insidious, and most oppressive form of protectionism, known as *administrative protection,* has become prevalent.

The most fertile sources of administrative protection are found in the arbitrary enforcement of health and sanitary regulations affecting imports of plants and animal products; labeling and marks of origin requirements; oppressive customs formalities; arbitrary customs valuations; and "Buy American" or "Buy British" and other forms of similar nationalistic legislation or practices.

Nationalistic legislation that makes mandatory the procurement of goods for public use from domestic production, or statutory provisions that set quotas or price differential limitations for the same purpose, are strictly uneconomic practices and are a roundabout method of extending additional protection to domestic producers.

An extreme example of the use of the sanitary approach to protection is the classical hoof-and-mouth disease provision of the United States Tariff Act of 1930. This Act makes mandatory the embargo of all animal and fresh-meat products from a country where such disease exists. In the opinion of the Department of Agriculture during the hearings that preceded the adoption of this legislation, this provision was unnecessary in view of other existing sanitary controls. It was, nevertheless, incorporated into the tariff. Argentina was the main country affected by this measure, in spite of the fact that her lambs and sheep—raised hundreds of miles from the nearest hoof-and-mouth disease area—are free of the infection.[13]

A major attempt is now being made in the Kennedy Round to eliminate or moderate the many forms of administrative protection.[14]

Licensing Systems

Licensing systems were devised to improve upon the methods of allocation and operation of quota and exchange control systems and to eliminate some of the objectionable practices of a global quota. Under a *licensing system,* an importer is required to obtain an official permit or authorization in advance of actual importation of a specified

---

[12] Percy W. Bidwell, *The Invisible Tariff: A Study in the Control of Imports into the United States* (New York: Council of Foreign Relations, 1939).
[13] Commission of Foreign Economic Policy, *Staff Papers* (Washington, D. C.: Government Printing Office, February, 1954), pp. 320-23.
[14] See Chapter 19.

quantity of foreign goods. In this way, equal treatment can be meted out to importers on the basis of their share of the market in a prior representative period. Big firms with extensive financial facilities are prevented from importing large quantities in the early part of a quota period and squeezing out the less fortunate, smaller firms from their fair share of the quota.

Licensing, however, is not without its shortcomings. Licenses tend to bestow upon their holders a privilege akin to a monopoly power with monopoly-like benefits that may create a speculative market in licenses and distort their original legitimate purpose. Such speculation generally results in higher costs to ultimate importers and consumers. Moreover, since licenses are generally issued to established importers and exporters with prior participation in the market, they tend to discriminate against newcomers.[15]

Licensing is not a quota system; it is rather an administrative method of enforcement. Licensing may, however, achieve the same results if the granting of licenses is governed and guided by the same objectives as quantitative restrictions. Because of their versatility, licensing systems are also used in conjunction with the enforcement of foreign exchange control.

SUMMARY

1. Despite the theoretical benefits of free trade, interference with the flow of goods in the form of restrictive measures has always been the rule rather than the exception.
2. Customs duties may be ad valorem, specific, or a combination of both, and may be supplemented by additional taxation of a nontariff character, such as excise and processing taxes.
3. Three major tariff systems are in operation, consisting of either single-, double-, or triple-column schedules, depending upon the number of rates of duties provided for each product in the tariff schedules.
4. Drawbacks, bonded warehouses, and free zones are designated to mitigate the unnecessary protective aspect of tariffs on imports that are destined for reexport.
5. Quantitative restrictions found their greatest development in the interwar period when the world economy underwent economic ordeal. Because of their suitability for emergency action to restrict trade, the use of quantitative restrictions quickly spread throughout the world. Today, practically every nation has some restrictive quotas.

---

[15] Export licenses are also used to compel the surrender of foreign exchange receipts.

Ch. 13 / International Trade and Payments Restrictions   271

6. There are several types of quotas, all of them restrictive. They are generally used to control imports of agricultural, raw material, and semimanufactured commodities for which they are particularly suited.

7. Early quotas were autonomous and global; they created difficult problems of administration and caused other nations to resort to retaliation. They were replaced by the negotiated bilateral quotas with licensing by shares to importers or to exporters on the basis of participation during a prior representative period.

8. The tariff quota antedates other forms of quotas and was used occasionally in the past to promote border-town trade between adjacent countries. It is now applied on a broader scale for the purpose of import control. The tariff quota is the least restrictive of quotas since its use permits additional imports at higher rates of duties beyond the limited quantities allowed under the lower rates.

9. Mixing quotas are special types of domestic regulations that allow a limited quantity of imported materials to be used with similar materials of domestic origin in the production of specified products. Mixing quotas, however, restrict imports and are therefore tools of protection.

10. Quotas separate markets pricewise and create monopoly-like profits that accrue to either importers or exporters to the ultimate disadvantage of domestic consumers.

11. Quotas and tariffs have much in common as measures of control; quotas, however, are more effective than tariffs, especially when quick action is needed in periods of emergency. Because they are more effective than tariffs as tools of restriction, retaliation, and bargaining, quotas have become an integral part of the commercial policy of all important trading nations to the detriment of international specialization and trade.

12. The direct interference of governments in the foreign exchange market is known as exchange control. Exchange control restricts the right of holders of a currency to exchange it for other currencies. It thereby renders a currency inconvertible.

13. Aside from its use during World War I, the first peacetime application of exchange control by industrial countries occurred in response to the capital flight unloosed by the international financial crisis of 1931. During the 1930's, the exchange control area was centered in Germany and eastern Europe although several countries in Latin America also adopted exchange restrictions in the face of balance of payments difficulties. After World War II, exchange control was utilized by all countries outside the Dollar Area.

14. There are many objectives of exchange control. Foremost among them are the suppression of balance of payments disequilibrium, the facilitation of national planning, the protection of domestic industries, and the creation of government revenue. The versatility of ends that may be

served by exchange control is an important factor behind its continued use in contemporary international trade.

15. A useful distinction may be made between single rate systems of exchange control and multiple rate systems. In single rate systems, all foreign exchange transactions are carried on at one official rate of exchange. All foreign exchange receipts are surrendered to an exchange control authority that allocates foreign exchange expenditures by types of import transactions, by countries and currency areas, and by applicants. Single rate systems usually make use of import licenses and quotas in allocating foreign exchange.

16. In a multiple rate system of exchange control, two or more legal exchange rates apply to different foreign exchange transactions. Because at least part of the task of allocating foreign exchange to different uses is carried out by differential exchange rates, multiple rate systems rely on administrative action far less than do single rate systems.

17. Special measures of restriction include subsidies or bounties, countervailing duties, antidumping duties, excise and processing taxes, and administrative protective measures. Administrative measures, such as health and sanitary regulations, are often used oppressively as more of a tool for economic protection than for the biological protection for which they are intended.

QUESTIONS AND APPLICATIONS

1. What is meant by a tariff?
2. (a) What is the difference between a customs area and a customs union?
   (b) How would you classify the United States in this respect?
3. Differentiate between the purposes of transit duties, export duties, and import duties.
4. List the different types of import duties and explain the function of each.
5. (a) What is meant by tariff classification?
   (b) What is the attribute approach to such classification?
6. "Tariffs provide revenue for the government and protection for domestic industries. Therefore, the higher the rates of duties, the greater the revenue and the more protection." Discuss the validity of this statement.
7. Explain the purpose of drawbacks.
8. Differentiate between a bonded warehouse and a free zone or a foreign trade zone.
9. (a) What is a free port?
   (b) How does a tariff system apply on imports through a free port?
10. What is a quantitative measure of restriction?

Ch. 13 / International Trade and Payments Restrictions 273

11. What are the different types of import quotas and in what particular way or ways do they differ?
12. What are the different purposes of export quotas and under what particular conditions are they best suited as control measures?
13. What is exchange control?
14. (a) Trace the origins of exchange control in the 1930's.
    (b) What is the present situation in the world economy with regard to exchange control?
15. (a) What are the principal objectives of contemporary exchange control systems?
    (b) How does exchange control serve these objectives?

SELECTED READINGS

See the list of readings given at the end of Chapter 14.

CHAPTER 14

ECONOMIC EFFECTS OF TRADE AND PAYMENTS RESTRICTIONS

Tariffs, quantitative restrictions, and exchange control are artificial impediments to the free movement of goods and services between nations, and as such they interfere with the free play of economic forces. The extent, intensity, and direction of this interference will vary with the conditions under which they operate. The economic literature on this subject is one of the most extensive in the annals of economics; but it may safely be said that the battle for freer trade has been won in the academic halls of the world, while in the legislative halls it has been honored more in the breach than in the observance.

TARIFF MAKING AND TARIFF FUNCTIONS

When a country is faced with fiscal or other problems of maladjustment in its economy that are of either domestic or foreign origin or when it is in need of new or additional protection for domestic industries, it often resorts to tariff measures.

Depending upon the specific problems to be solved, decisions must be made about the kinds of goods to tax, the types of customs duties to levy, and the heights of the different rates of duties. It must also be decided whether to adopt a unilateral nondiscriminating single-column tariff or a multiple-column system that could be modified later by international agreements. Further, the possible use of more subtle indirect means of protection, such as subsidies, prohibitions, or special extra-tariff measures may be explored.

Legislators who translate these decisions into law are seldom sufficiently conversant with the perplexities of the problems involved. Moreover, they are under great pressure from their constituents who are motivated by the immediate and the local aspects of national problems. As a group, legislators are pressured by highly organized lobbies representing entrenched interests that are seeking a more favorable outcome of such legislation for their own activities regardless of national interest. As a result of the combination of the conflicting influences faced by legislators, a tariff is seldom, if ever, a true picture of the overall needs of a country; it is rather the fruit of compromise and patchwork and the result of the forces at work behind the scene. It is not uncommon, therefore, to find in any tariff legislation a mixture of provisions sometimes incongruent and often incompatible with either logic or theory.

Taxation is a means by which different levels of government acquire the necessary income to finance their numerous activities. Taxation of international trade is generally reserved to the highest or national level, and it is put into effect through a variety of measures of which tariffs are the most widespread.

National governments are also entrusted with the promotion and protection of the economic well-being of their countries. Thus, they use tariffs to regulate and control the flow of international commerce either for protection or for balance of payments adjustments or for purposes extraneous to trade, such as the promotion of greater domestic employment, diversification of production, and a host of other national desiderata.

Irrespective of the merits of tariff-making procedures, tariffs, when adopted, perform certain functions that may or may not be fully as intended; but they do produce revenues and/or afford protection depending on their structure and the conditions under which they operate. Therefore, tariffs may be constructed to perform a revenue function or protection function as the case may be, or a combination of both depending upon the desired ultimate purposes. In addition, tariffs may be used to bring about an adjustment in the balance of international payments of a country or an improvement in its terms of trade.

Revenue Function

In order to perform best their revenue function, tariff duties are applied to commodities of wide consumption; and the rates of these duties are kept low enough to maximize customs collections without unduly restricting trade. The same objective may also be attained by the imposition of a uniform low rate of duty on all merchandise crossing the border either as exports, imports, or in transit.

Because of the generally low rates of duties, tariffs for revenue do not substantially affect prices, production, or consumption. Whatever little influence they exert in these directions is reflected in a diminutive but similar fashion as that of protective tariffs which carry more substantial rates of duties.

The income accruing to the state is practically the only important economic effect of tariffs for revenue. Depending upon the number and kinds of products subjected to the tariff as well as upon the ultimate disposition of the customs revenues derived therefrom by the state, the ultimate effect will be reflected in the distribution of the national income. If the state diverts this income into additional or new expenditures of a civic or security character, additional employment may be effected in the domestic economy; but if this revenue is used to relieve other existing taxation, it will have only a diversionary effect due to the shifting of the tax burden to the consumers and/or the foreign suppliers of the products affected by the tariff.

The revenue function of a duty, therefore, is a relative concept. No matter how it is defined to perform its intended function, a duty is always characterized by an element of protection, however small or unimportant, except, of course, when the taxed product is not domestically produced, and the tariff serves a purely revenue function.

Protection Function

A tariff designed for protection must provide rates of duties high enough to achieve one or more of the following aims predetermined by national policies:

> 1. The encouragement of additional domestic production which could not take place without tariff duties because of prevailing cost disadvantages.
>
> 2. The reduction or elimination of domestic consumption of an imported commodity, thereby diverting expenditure to alternative goods of domestic or even foreign origin.
>
> 3. The development of new, or "infant" industries, which from the start could not compete with entrenched foreign producers without the benefit of protection.

The protection function of the tariff depends upon a partial or complete restriction of imports; this may be accomplished by the height of the relevant duties. When complete protection is desired, a given duty must be high enough to cover at least the difference in the cost of production between domestic and *all* foreign producers, including transportation and incidental expenses of importing. If the tariff is to be only partially protective, the duty must remain below this difference. Under partial protection, goods will continue to be imported but in smaller quantities and the state will collect customs duties. The protection function, therefore—like the revenue function—will usually afford both protection and revenue, although its purpose is primarily one of protection.

The seeming incompatibility of the two functions in the same duty does not necessarily disqualify its adoption since most countries generally desire both protection and revenue. In the tariff schedules of nations, however, a tendency exists to provide a certain number of generally low rates of duties designed essentially for revenue and other higher duties for protection.

The United States is considered to have been a protective tariff country almost since its independence, in spite of the fact that the early tariff acts provided over 85 percent of the total income of the federal government.[1] Today, however, less than 1 percent of the federal revenue is derived from customs revenues, and tariffs are regarded as being designed primarily for protective purposes. Many foreign countries, however, resort to tariffs primarily for revenue.

Especially since World War II, the developing nations have embarked on economic development programs to encourage domestic production and industrialization and have adopted restrictive measures designed to promote new home industries or the partial processing of their raw-material exports.

Balance of Payments Function

The adoption of a new tariff or changes in an existing one will tend to disturb the balance of trade of a country and, therefore, the equilibrium of its balance of international payments. The imposition of tariff duties will, moreover, start in motion economic forces of readjustment at home and abroad that will affect, among other things, prices, production, incomes, and employment. Sometimes nations try to reverse the process and resort to tariffs in order to correct existing maladjustments in their balance of payments. When they do so, however, they are not attacking the fundamental causes of disequilibrium that may lie in other areas of their disturbed economies; nor

---

[1] See Chapter 18.

are they likely to achieve their goals since other countries can, and often do, resort to similar action either in retaliation or self-defense. In any event, they forego some of the economic benefits of international specialization and trade, and they are more likely than not to end up with new problems of a more complex and intractable nature.

The functional use of tariffs for balance of payments adjustment, even though pragmatically effective when it does not invite retaliation, is undesirable nevertheless. It does not correct the fundamental causes of the disequilibrium and, in the absence of retaliation, it is purely a beggar-my-neighbor policy.

ECONOMIC EFFECTS OF TARIFFS

The immediate effects of tariffs are those reflected in price changes and consequent adjustments in production and consumption. Because of the fact that tariffs for revenue have effects similar to those of protective tariffs, but to a lesser degree, we shall confine our discussion to protective tariffs, leaving it to the reader to make the appropriate application to revenue tariffs.

Price Changes Induced by an Import Duty

The incidence of an import duty is a cost burden to the importer of the taxed product which is passed on to the consumer in the normal conduct of business. Depending on the interplay of supply and demand elasticities reflected in price changes and subsequent adjustments in consumption and production, the ultimate effect of a tariff duty may take different forms.

An import duty may affect the market price of the protected commodity in four different ways depending upon the condition of the market and the balance of elasticities of supply and demand at home and abroad of the protected product. This price effect may involve:

1. No price change at all.
2. A price rise of less than the amount of the duty.
3. A price rise equal to the amount of the duty.
4. A price rise greater than the amount of the duty.

No Price Change. When a country is an exporter of the protected product on balance, the imposition of a duty will be meaningless as far as the domestic price is concerned. If the domestic price rises

Ch. 14 / Economic Effects of Trade and Payments Restrictions   279

above the world price behind the tariff wall, the entire supply will be offered in the home market and will tend to depress prices back to the world price level. This actually happened in the United States shortly after World War I, when the government attempted unsuccessfully to raise the domestic price of wheat above the world price to improve the farmers' purchasing power.

In a situation where the import demand is perfectly elastic and the import supply is less than perfectly elastic (most likely when the tariff country is an important market or even a monopsonist) the full amount of the duty will be absorbed by the foreign producer, leaving the cost to the domestic consumer unchanged.[2] When the foreign producer is a monopolist, he may try to maximize his total revenues by dumping into the protected market rather than maintaining a less-profitable uniform world price.

Price Rise of Less than the Amount of Duty. When the dutiable product is manufactured abroad under conditions of increasing costs, and the importing country is an important buyer, the price rise will be less than the amount of the duty, provided that a condition of less-than-perfect elasticity of demand exists in the duty-imposing country, and a condition of less-than-perfect elasticity of supply exists in the exporting country or countries—a condition that may be regarded as normal in large trading countries such as the United States or the European nations. The nature of adjustment may be clarified by the diagrammatic presentation in Figure 14-1.

The total supply and demand schedules of the world for a given product are indicated in Figure 14-1 by Sw-Sw and Dw-Dw respectively, intersecting at the world equilibrium price, O-P, for quantity, O-Qw, which clears the market. In the absence of domestic production, country A imports its entire supply, O-Qa, which is determined by the intersection of its own demand schedule, Da-Da, with the world price, O-P. Upon the adoption of a tariff by country A, the domestic price for the protected article rises because of the customs duty. This price rise reduces the effective total demand for the product at the pretariff equilibrium world price, O-P, thus shifting the world demand schedule from Dw-Dw to $D'w$-$D'w$, since the quantity O-Qw can no longer be absorbed at price O-P.

After the world demand schedule, Dw-Dw, shifts to the left to $D'w$-$D'w$, a smaller total quantity, O-$Q'w$, clears the market at a lower

---

[2] See Chapter 11 for a discussion of price elasticities.

Figure 14-1
PRICE RISE LESS THAN AMOUNT OF DUTY

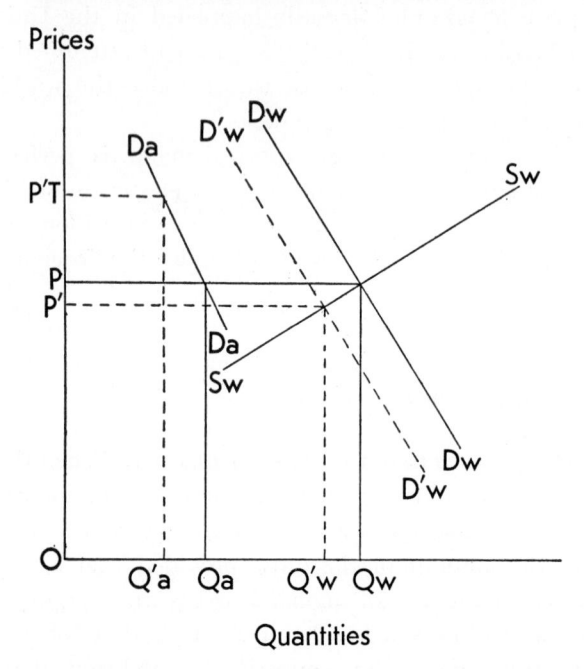

world equilibrium price, $O\text{-}P'$. Under this new equilibrium condition, country A will import a smaller quantity, $O\text{-}Q'a$, at a price, $O\text{-}P'T$ (composed of the new world price, $O\text{-}P'$, plus the duty, $P'\text{-}P'T$), determined by its unchanged demand schedule, $Da\text{-}Da$. The price rise, therefore, will be less than the amount of the duty by $P'\text{-}P$ due to a lower world price, $O\text{-}P'$. When the tariff-imposing country is also a producer of the protected commodity, somewhat similar effects will be obtained if the tariff is not prohibitive. Domestic producers, however, will be in a position to increase their own production because of prevailing higher domestic prices induced by the tariff.[3]

Price Rise Equal to the Amount of Duty. A tariff will tend to increase the price of the protected product by the full amount of the duty under conditions of perfect elasticity of import supply and less-than-perfect elasticity of import demand. The perfect elasticity of import supply may derive from constant costs of production or more commonly because the tariff country is too small to influence the world price of the product by the size of its demand.

---
[3] See Figure 14-2.

Price Rise Greater than the Amount of Duty. A tariff may raise the price to the consumer by more than the amount of the duty when the channel of distribution at home is lengthy and the different middlemen add their individual profit margins, or markups, at each step of the marketing process. The pyramiding of the multiple markups on the duty may force a rise in price substantially greater than the original duty.

The cumulative effect of markups would also occur under the prior assumptions of price increases of less than, or equal to, the amount of the duty whenever importers are not themselves the ultimate consumers, and whenever their goods must flow through extended domestic marketing channels.

The Nature of Tariff Adjustments

In addition to the direct price effect of an import duty, multiple ulterior consequences that are far too intricate to trace here at length occur within the economy. Their nature may be suggested, however, by the mention of the fact that any alteration in the quantity demanded of an imported commodity will start a chain reaction involving a change in the demand for the factors of production. This change will affect the relative costs of the factors of production and their employment in accordance with the principle of opportunity cost. This, in turn, will alter the pattern of production, consumption, and international trade in a variety of products via price and income changes. These changes will disturb the pattern of international payments and set in motion monetary and foreign exchange mechanisms and possibly alter the rate of exchange between currencies. The effect of the changes could bring about a realignment of comparative cost conditions between different nations that could further affect the pattern of international trade. Finally, these changes may also be influenced by the way in which the additional customs revenues are expended by the tariff-imposing country.

All these possible influences may or may not be fully cumulative in their ultimate consequences; but if an import duty is worth adopting, its incidence does generally affect an existing equilibrium in the tariff-imposing country in one or more of the following ways:

1. It will tend to reduce the imports and, indirectly, the exports of the country in the long run.

2. It will usually raise the price to the domestic consumer.

3. It will sometimes lower the price received by foreign producers, thus reducing the cost to the importer.

4. It will raise prices and sales of domestic production, if there is any production.

5. It may improve the terms of trade of the nation by reducing the foreign cost of imports; maintaining or increasing domestic prices; or both.

6. It may create extra revenues for the government that can be used to reduce other taxes.

Although an import duty will induce a variety of changes in the importing and the exporting countries, the more significant of these changes are those affecting domestic prices, consumption, production, and imports—assuming that no significant effect on income and its distribution takes place.

If the country is not itself a producer of the protected commodity, the incidence of an import duty may, if high enough, induce domestic production behind the new tariff wall—a policy often adopted to promote new domestic industries. Otherwise, imports will continue and the final cost to the domestic consumer will be usually higher in either case, although some of the duty may be absorbed by foreign suppliers. Consumption will decrease, and prices abroad will tend to drop or remain unchanged, depending on supply elasticities.

If the country is also a producer of the imported product, the incidence of the tariff will tend to affect not only foreign prices and imported quantities but also the domestic price of the protected product as well as production and consumption at home and abroad. Figure 14-2 on the following page will clarify some of these effects upon the importing country under the simplifying assumption of perfectly elastic foreign supply.

At the prevailing price, *O-P*, the quantity demanded of a given product by country A is *O-Q*, determined by its domestic demand schedule, *D-D*, of which the portion *O-Q1* is domestically produced (determined by the intersection of price, *O-P*, and the domestic supply schedule, *S-S*) and the remaining part, *Q1-Q*, is imported.

Upon the introduction of a tariff by country A, a customs duty of, say, *P-PT* is levied, raising the cost to domestic users from *O-P* to *O-PT*. At this higher cost, the quantities demanded of the protected product are reduced from *O-Q* to *O-Q2*, of which *O-Q3* is domestically supplied, and the remaining portion, *Q3-Q2*, is imported. The effects of such a duty upon the domestic economy are fourfold:

Figure 14-2
EFFECTS OF AN IMPORT DUTY

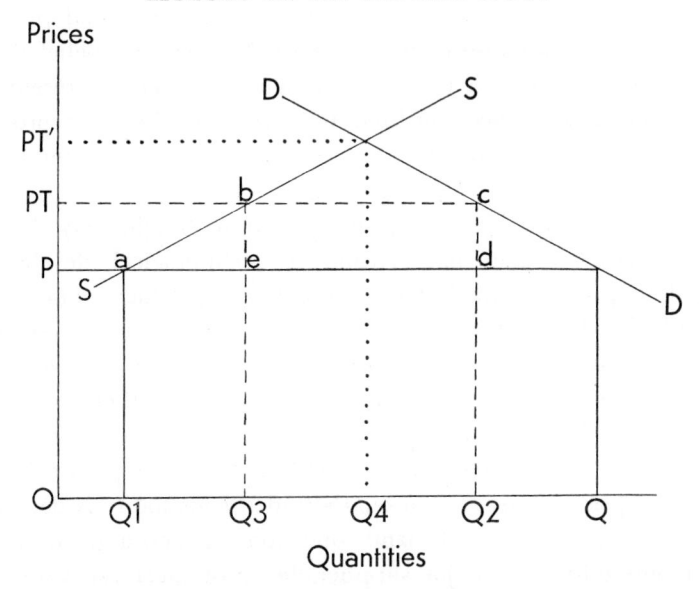

1. A price effect, reflected by the higher cost to domestic users of the taxed product by the full amount of the duty, *P-PT*, which is represented by the rectangle *P-PT-c-d*.

2. A revenue effect, resulting from customs collections accruing to the government, represented by the rectangle *b-c-d-e*.

3. An income-redistribution effect, caused by the extra revenue, or pure rent, paid by consumers to domestic producers over and above their costs of production, represented by the quadrangle *P-PT-b-a*.

4. A protective effect, afforded to domestic producers by the tariff resulting in increased domestic production from *O-Q1* to *O-Q3*, which reduces imports by *Q1-Q3* plus *Q2-Q* and also reduces consumption by *Q2-Q*.

If the duty is high enough to reach *PT'*, there will be no imports —and the entire quantity demanded, *O-Q4*, will be supplied by the domestic producers at price *O-PT'*.

The removal of our assumption of a constant foreign price, *O-P*, would complicate further the impact of a tariff without, however, invalidating our analysis. With less-than-infinite supply elasticity, the price effect would be somewhat less restrictive of imports and consumption since foreign prices would tend to drop, as already established earlier in this chapter. This is especially likely if the importing country is an important consumer of the product.

The Effects of Export Duties

Export duties are relatively easy to administer, and are commonly used as a revenue measure, especially by the raw-material producing countries. They are also used because of the prevalent belief that the burden of the duty falls upon the foreign consumer. In recent times export duties have been utilized to encourage domestic processing and industrial development in order to create additional employment opportunities.

The incidence of an export duty, if too high, may defeat its revenue purpose and may encourage technological developments abroad to provide substitutes for the taxed product. The classical example is Chile with its natural nitrate—at one time exercising a virtual monopoly. A high export duty, instituted in Chile in 1919, further encouraged the manufacture abroad of synthetic substitutes. As a result, Chile lost most of its markets; and in spite of its changed tariff policy, it never recovered its former dominant position.

The price of an internationally traded commodity is determined by the world supply and demand conditions. Unless a given producer is a monopolist or a major supplier, he must meet the world price to dispose of his product. Hence, an export duty puts a competitive producer at a disadvantage and forces him to absorb the duty in order to remain in business. If the producer is a monopolist or a major supplier, and, therefore, in a position to shift the burden of the export duty in some degree to the foreign consumer, the increased price of his product will reduce his total revenues unless foreign demand is inelastic. If the duty is too high, he may lose much of his market.

Measurement of Tariffs

Several methods have been devised to measure the extent of protection afforded by a given tariff by using the height of the duty as a basis. These methods of measurement have proved to be unsatisfactory because of statistical inaccuracies and the lack of adequate data.

The American Tariff League,[4] an organization interested in protection, approached this problem of measurement in an ingenious but somewhat misleading manner. Percentage indices were constructed by dividing the amount of customs revenues by the total value of dutiable and duty-free imports of the different nations for a given

---

[4] Now known as the Trade Relations Council of the United States.

period. The resulting percentages were used as a measurement of the relative height of the different tariffs. The objectionable aspect of this method lies in the fact that high tariffs reduce dutiable imports and, consequently, customs revenues, while at the same time duty-free imports are magnified out of proportion to total imports. Percentage indices are thus reduced in exactly the opposite direction. If the rates of duties become high enough to exclude all dutiable imports, these indices become zero—clearly an absurd conclusion. Conversely, a nation with a very liberal trade policy and a very low revenue tariff would appear to be highly restrictive under this method of measurement—surely a misleading conclusion.

Another method, which includes dutiable imports only, has also been used. Under this approach an equivalent ad valorem rate of duty is obtained by the ratio of total customs collections to the value of total dutiable imports in a given period. This is not truly a measurement of the height of a tariff since specific products subject to high rates of duty are either imported in reduced quantities or not imported at all—a fact not reflected in this method of measurement that is based on actual imports only.

As we have seen, the truly protective effects of a duty are determined by the specific import demand and supply price elasticities that pertain to the product subjected to that duty.

ECONOMIC EFFECTS OF QUOTAS

The economic effects of import quotas upon the domestic economy and the rest of the world are many and complex and vary between the short and the long run. For our present purpose, the discussion will be confined to the more salient effects of quotas upon prices and the balance of payments of the quota country and their relation to international trade.

Quotas as a Source of Monopoly Profits

The immediate effect of an import quota is to restrict the supply of an imported product to a level below that of the prequota level while the domestic demand remains unchanged. In the absence of domestic production, other things being equal, the price of the frozen short supply will be bid up by the forces of demand. If the country is a producer, the fact that it is also an importer implies that domestic production is taking place under conditions of increasing costs. A reduction in the quantities imported tends to increase domestic production and prices rise with additional output. Whether the country is a producer or not, a quota raises domestic prices above foreign prices and separates pricewise the domestic market from the world market.

Figure 14-3 illustrates the incidence of a quota and its effect upon the price of a product subject to this quota under the simplifying assumptions of: (1) increasing foreign costs of production; (2) no domestic production; and (3) no income or secondary effects.

The domestic demand schedule and the import supply schedule of country A are represented by *Da-Da* and *Si-Si* respectively, with quantity *O-Q* imported at the equilibrium price *O-P*. Upon the introduction of a quota, *O-Q'*, by country A, foreign suppliers are willing to accept the price *O-P'* for the quantity *O-Q'* as indicated by the supply schedule *Si-Si*, while domestic users are willing to pay the price *O-P''* for this same quantity on the basis of their demand schedule *Da-Da*. The price differential gives rise to quota profits *P'-P''-L-K*, that is, the excess of the selling price over the supply price (*P'-P''*) times the amount imported (*O-Q'*).

What happens to the quota profits under our assumptions depends upon whether or not domestic importers and foreign

Figure 14-3

PRICE EFFECTS OF A QUOTA

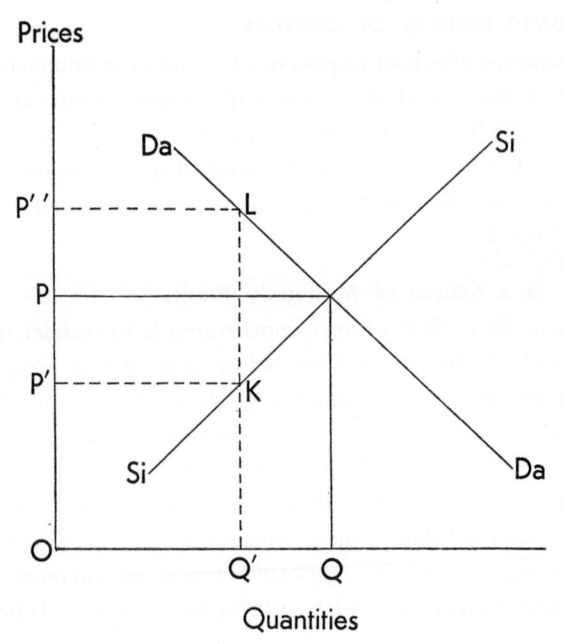

exporters, as separate groups, are freely competing among themselves and with each other, or whether they are separately organized as monopsonists and monopolists. When importers and exporters as separate groups are freely competing in their respective markets with no licensing system in operation, then they will rush to supply the quota country before the quota becomes exhausted. Under such circumstances, quota profits will probably be shared by both importers and exporters depending on the competitive relations between them. If, however, these importers hold import licenses that put them in a monopoly position, they will reap the full benefits of the quota profits. Conversely, if the exporters rather than the importers are the holders of the licenses, or if they are organized and in full control of the market, they will reap the full benefits of the quota profits themselves. Finally, if the government auctions licenses, the quota profits are shared between the state and the licensees. The consumer, however, always pays the difference between the world price and the monopoly price charged him.

A tariff quota will tend to have a somewhat less pronounced effect as far as quota profits are concerned since additional imports may be secured that limit the extent of the monopoly-like increase in the price to the consumer.

When the country is also a producer, the size of the monopoly profit will be reduced subject to the price relationship between domestic costs of production and the higher quota price. Domestic producers will also be in a position to enjoy a windfall profit under these circumstances, especially in the short run.

Quotas and the Balance of Payments

As we have already discovered, quantitative restrictions are quick and positive measures that are used to reduce imports. When a country experiences a trade deficit in its balance of international payments, it can quickly suppress such a deficit by the use of quotas. But the artificial reduction of imports disrupts trade patterns and trade relations, and other countries may be forced to adopt similar policies in self-protection.

Furthermore, once quantitative restrictions are adopted, they tend to create a new class of vested interests that will oppose changes even when the immediate usefulness of these restrictions has long ceased to exist. Quotas, therefore, tend to perpetuate themselves in artificial restraint of competition and trade.

Quotas and Domestic Employment

It is sometimes argued that the reduction of the volume of imports will cause a substantial portion of the country's money expenditures previously channeled into foreign hands to be diverted into the domestic stream. Thus, expenditures on domestic goods will be increased and the expansion of production and employment will be encouraged. The validity of this argument is open to question on the grounds that a reduction of imports reduces the means of payment for the exports of a country, and that, in order for that country to derive any material economic benefit from a quota, it must be a large consumer of the product. If that is the case, the reduction of imports will also induce foreign repercussions. Other things being equal, the exporting countries whose international payments accounts are being threatened with imbalance as a result of reduced exports to the quota country are forced to adopt measures of adjustment. They may resort to import quotas or other restrictive measures either in self-protection or in retaliation. Moreover, quotas inflate domestic prices, money incomes, and purchasing power, which will reduce general exports; tourist business, if there is any; the earnings of merchant marines; and, in turn, the economic activity of other domestic industries dependent upon such services. Therefore, the expected expansion of domestic production and employment must be measured against the full deflationary effects of all the other factors combined.

To conclude, although it is not certain that quotas will generate economic expansion or additional net employment, they are a sure way to damage international specialization and trade.

Quotas and Tariffs Compared

Quotas and tariffs are both tools of protection. As such, they affect prices, income, and the balance of payments. Either may be used for discriminatory purposes in international economic relations.

Quotas, however, are absolute and inflexible irrespective of prices and elasticities. In contrast, the degree of protection afforded by tariffs is relative since it is subject to market responses and to price changes as well as to the height of the duties and to the comparative costs of production. Quotas separate markets pricewise and tend to raise domestic prices to a level inconsistent with world prices by freezing import supply relative to domestic demand. On the other hand, the price influence of tariffs is limited, and prices remain subject to market conditions of production and consumption.

Quotas attempt to correct balance of trade maladjustments by means of government fiat, which, however, is subject to misjudgment and inconsistency. The use of tariffs can bring about similar adjustments, but still leave the door open for market readjustment. Quotas are not conducive to meting out equal treatment to different countries; tariffs, on the other hand, are more amenable to such treatment under the most-favored-nation concept.

Several other differences between quotas and tariffs are noteworthy:

1. Quotas are better suited for quick emergency application by administrative action. Tariffs require statutory legislation, which is too slow for immediate action.

2. Quotas are a direct source of monopoly profits and raise prices unduly to consumers. Tariffs do not necessarily induce monopolistic practices, and they are ordinarily less burdensome to consumers.

3. Quotas invariably stifle competition. Tariffs usually allow some competition.

4. Quotas are simpler and easier to manage than tariffs, but they deprive the government of the revenues that accrue from customs duties (unless, of course, the state auctions import licenses).

5. Because quotas are a more effective tool of restriction than tariffs, they are also a more potent weapon for retaliation and bargaining.

The best that can be said about quotas is that under extreme deflationary conditions at home and abroad, when neither tariffs nor currency depreciation can be satisfactorily used to bring about balance of payments equilibrium, quotas are quick and positive measures that can achieve the desired results and spare an economy from an otherwise slow and painful internal adjustment. The economic merits of quantitative controls, therefore, are dubious on the whole; and, in the long run, there is nothing that they can do that monetary and fiscal domestic policies cannot do better and at a lower national cost.

THE ECONOMIC EFFECTS OF EXCHANGE CONTROL

In Chapter 13, we investigated the origins, objectives, and nature of exchange control. What of its effects? The answer to this question is not simple. For one thing, the effects are manifold; for another, the effects vary greatly in intensity depending upon the severity and comprehensiveness of exchange control. Considering the limitations of space, we can only briefly evaluate the principal effects of exchange control on international trade.

Inconvertibility and Bilateralism

We also observed in Chapter 13 that exchange control renders a currency inconvertible. It therefore strikes at the heart of multilateral settlement, which permits a country to offset its deficit in one direction with a surplus in another direction.

To illustrate, suppose that country A has traditionally run a deficit with country B that has been financed by a surplus with country C. But now country C imposes exchange control and no longer allows residents of country A to use its currency to buy the currency of country B. The effect is to force country A to balance its trade *bilaterally* with country B either by cutting its imports from, or raising its exports to, the latter. Usually the first alternative is adopted; and, as a result, country B suffers a loss of exports to country A that may force it to restrict imports from a third country. Thus exchange control, by disrupting the pattern of multilateral settlement, may compel other countries, one after another, to restrict imports and even to adopt exchange control in turn. A lower volume of trade is not the only consequence of this train of events. The *quality* of trade is also worsened because it is no longer possible for the exporter to sell in the most profitable market or for the importer to buy in the least expensive market. The truth of this remark becomes clearer when we consider bilateral payments agreements.

Bilateral Payments Agreements

When several countries employ exchange control, there is an accumulation of blocked balances, and convertible currencies tend to become scarce. In order to liquidate blocked balances and to avoid as much as possible the use of convertible currencies in the financing of trade, countries enter into bilateral payments agreements. In one postwar study of bilateral payments agreements, it was pointed out that in the early 1950's there were almost 400 bilateral payments agreements embracing most of the nondollar world.[5] The majority of trade between nondollar countries was carried on in accordance with these agreements which were often supplemented by trade agreements that specified the merchandise and services to be traded.

In the words of one authority, a bilateral payments agreement "provides a general method of financing current trade between two countries, giving rise to credits which are freely available for use by one country in making payments for goods and services imported from

---

[5] M. N. Trued and Raymond F. Mikesell, *Postwar Bilateral Payments Agreements*, Princeton Studies in International Finance No. 4 (1955), p. 3.

the other."[6] Bilateral payments agreements contain provisions relating to the unit or units of account that are to be used to record foreign exchange transactions, the amounts and the kinds of credit to be used to finance the net balances of either country, the settlement of balances not covered by credits and the settlement of final balances at the conclusion of the agreement, the tenure of the agreement, and the transferability of balances. The credit and transferability provisions are of particular importance.

Most bilateral payments agreements establish reciprocal credits known as *swing credits*. These credits permit each country to have a deficit in its trade with the partner country up to a specified limit before settlement must be made in gold, dollars, or other agreed manner. At the conclusion of the agreement (it may run for several years), any outstanding balances must be settled in similar fashion. The presence of swing credits lessens the need of the partner countries to achieve an exact balance in their mutual trade, but it may expose the deficit country to a loss of gold or convertible currencies.

All bilateral payments agreements restrict in one way or another the transferability of domestic currency held by residents of the other partner country. This must be done if the agreement is to achieve its main function: the financing of trade with inconvertible currencies. The degree of transferability, however, may vary significantly in different agreements.

At one extreme are the restrictive *bilateral offset agreements* that allow no transferability to third currencies. Under this sort of agreement, usually found only between Communist countries, any net balances are settled by an export of goods from the debtor country. Bilateral offset agreements, like barter, effectively prevent any multilateral settlement by destroying its very basis.

Exchange settlement agreements, as their name implies, allow for the settlement of final balances, and of balances beyond the swing credit, in gold, convertible currencies, or other agreed currencies Although these agreements do not rigidly bilateralize trade, they do encourage bilateral settlement since each partner country seeks to avoid having to pay gold or third currencies to the other.

Automatic transferability agreements allow the automatic transferability of domestic balances held by residents of the partner country to third countries or to a clearing union. These agreements do

---

[6] Raymond F. Mikesell, *Foreign Exchange in the Postwar World* (New York: Twentieth Century Fund, 1954), p. 86.

not attempt to balance trade bilaterally, but rather to extend the advantages of partial convertibility to many countries. Prior to making sterling convertible for all nonresidents at the end of 1958, the United Kingdom had negotiated automatic transferability agreements with most nondollar countries that enabled the latter to use sterling balances to settle trade debts with one another. The European Payments Union also involved such agreements between its member countries.[7]

The adoption of nonresident, current-account convertibility by the important trading nations of Europe at the close of 1958 led to the dissolution of many payments agreements with automatic transferability provisions, notably the European Payments Union. Thus, there is now a considerable degree of multilateral settlement and international competition in free world trade. Further progress toward the dismantling of payments agreements is largely dependent on the abandonment of exchange controls by the nonindustrial and Communist countries.

The Redistribution of Money Incomes

The redistribution of money incomes that results from exchange control will vary depending upon the circumstances. Money income is diverted to the government by high selling rates of exchange, exchange taxes, exchange auctions, and the like. On the other hand, exporters and other sellers of foreign exchange may reap windfall profits when they are allowed to sell their exchange in fluctuating rate markets.[8] In contrast, importers are apt to enjoy windfall profits in a single rate system because the restriction of imports will push up their domestic prices. In the last analysis, the consumer is likely to bear the incidence of exchange control in the form of higher prices for the goods and services that he buys, both domestic and imported. In the administration of exchange control, the government must make every effort to tax away the windfall gains of exporters or importers if it is to discharge properly its public responsibilities.

The Evasion of Exchange Control

Exchange control encourages widespread evasion on the part of residents and nonresidents alike. Evasion of exchange regulations

---

[7] See Chapter 17.

[8] At times multiple exchange control countries may allow certain transactions (usually service and capital items) to be cleared in a "free" foreign exchange market, thus creating a freely fluctuating rate of exchange for an otherwise controlled currency.

by residents is criminal, since it flouts domestic law. The exchange control country, however, has no jurisdiction over nonresidents who are located outside its boundaries and who may also evade its exchange regulations.

Bilateral payments agreements are often designed to lessen evasion of the exchange control of one partner country by residents of the other partner country, but the success of payments agreements in this respect depends upon the willingness and the ability of the government of the latter country to fulfill its obligations. The residents of free exchange countries, such as the United States, are able to evade the exchange regulations of other countries without violating domestic laws, since their governments are usually unwilling to enter into bilateral payments agreements with an evasion clause. Even if exchange control were fully effective in regulating all foreign exchange transactions within the exchange control country, it would not restrain much of the evasion practiced by nonresidents located abroad.

The number of evasion techniques is legion including bribery and corruption of officials, false invoicing of exports and imports, and black-market operations at home and abroad.

False invoicing may involve the underinvoicing of exports so that part of the actual foreign exchange receipts is withheld from the control authority and placed by the importer or other agent in a foreign bank to the account of the exporter. The same thing may be accomplished through the overinvoicing of imports so that the importer obtains more foreign exchange than is needed to pay for his imports, the excess ending up in the importer's private bank account in a foreign country.

The Proper Use of Exchange Control

The principal argument against exchange control is that its use raises obstacles to gainful international trade by restricting the convertibility of currencies, by distorting price and cost relationships, by discriminating between countries and currency areas, by perpetuating balance of payments disequilibrium, and by creating uncertainty and confusion. Hence exchange control interferes with international specialization and trade in accordance with comparative costs.

The main explanation for the continued resort to exchange control is that, although most nations pay lip service to the objective of free multilateral trade, they are unwilling to accept the monetary and fiscal disciplines necessary to sustain the convertibility of their currencies. Other objectives—full employment, economic development, national planning, etc.—are placed ahead of the attainment of international equilibrium. Exchange control then becomes a mechanism to defend national policies against international repercussions.

The achievement of a multilateral trading system does not require the abandonment of all forms of exchange control. Currencies used to finance current transactions in merchandise and services as well as in investment capital must be fully convertible. Exchange control, however, may be used to restrain an occasional capital flight without endangering multilateral trade. Another legitimate use of exchange control is its *temporary* employment to allow a nation enough time to make a fundamental adjustment to a persistent deficit in its balance of payments, assuming that its reserves are inadequate to perform the same task.

In the next chapter, we appraise the many arguments for protection that are used to justify restrictions on trade; but protectionists do not always have it their own way. In Chapter 17, we shall examine the many steps that have been taken since World War II to liberalize trade and payments from the shackles of tariffs, quotas, and exchange control.

SUMMARY

1. When a country adopts a new tariff or revises an existing one upward, it creates an economic disturbance of vast ramifications.
2. An import duty affects the domestic economy and, to some degree, the world economy; it disturbs an existing equilibrium in the balance of payments and creates problems of readjustments. Most of all, however, a tariff affects prices at home and abroad by contracting consumption and reorienting production under less favorable conditions.
3. Although prices abroad may tend to drop somewhat as a result of a tariff, the price benefits derived are outweighed in the long run by the shift in the use of resources from the more productive export industries to the less productive import-displacing industries. The burden of import duties may be said to fall more heavily on the tariff-imposing country as a rule.
4. Export duties are generally used by less advanced countries as a source of revenue; the domestic producer must usually absorb their cost in order to meet foreign competition. Besides, the ever present danger of alternative substitutes abroad renders such a tax a most unwise form of revenue unless it is kept low enough to minimize this risk.
5. The measurement of the height of a tariff would be desirable if feasible; but the various attempts at such measurements have been, so far, logically unacceptable.

6. Quotas, the same as tariffs, create economic disturbances. Their effects on trade are quick and certain and for these reasons they are preferred for positive emergency action. Quotas have the disadvantage, however, of separating pricewise the domestic market from the world market, giving rise to monopolistic quota profits to the ultimate detriment of domestic consumers.

7. The most important effect of exchange control is its disruption of multilateral settlement and the forcing of international trade into bilateral channels. Exchange control thus limits the advantages to be gained from international specialization in a competitive world market. When several countries practice exchange control, blocked balances and the scarcity of convertible currencies raise formidable obstacles to trade. In order to liquidate blocked balances and to avoid the use of convertible currencies in the financing of mutual trade, exchange control countries negotiate bilateral payments agreements.

8. Exchange control also redistributes money incomes since exporters, importers, or the government are able to enjoy monopoly profits depending upon the nature of the system.

9. Exchange control is evaded by both residents and nonresidents in a variety of ways: bribery and corruption of exchange officials, false invoicing, black markets, etc.

10. The main indictment of exchange control is that it interferes with international specialization and trade in accordance with comparative costs. The achievement of a multilateral trading system, however, is compatible with the use of exchange control to stop a capital flight and with its temporary employment to provide time for fundamental adjustment to an external deficit.

QUESTIONS AND APPLICATIONS

1. Explain how tariffs interfere with the interplay of economic forces.
2. What are the different functions that may be performed by a tariff?
3. When is a tariff for revenue also a protective tariff?
4. A nation using a tariff is said to forego some of the benefits of international specialization. Discuss.
5. In what different ways does a customs duty affect the ultimate price to the consumer in the tariff-levying country? Explain.
6. What are the likely effects of an import duty upon the economy of the tariff-levying country?
7. It is sometimes contended that the foreigner pays the duty. Discuss the validity of this contention.
8. (a) What is an export duty?
   (b) How does an export duty generally affect the price received by the exporter?
9. Why and how do import quotas create monopoly profits?

10. Quotas are said to increase domestic employment. Discuss the validity of this statement.
11. Compare quotas with tariffs and appraise their similarities and differences.
12. If you were a Congressman trained in economic theory, and you were debating a bill on the floor of the House dealing with legislation intended to eliminate the use of quotas by this country, what would your major arguments be in support of such a bill?
13. An allocated bilateral quota is an open invitation to monopolistic abuses by exporters or importers. Explain.
14. "Quotas are positive regulations of international trade while the results of tariffs are uncertain. Since a country must know where it is heading, the use of quotas is therefore preferable to that of tariffs." Evaluate this statement.
15. Enumerate the principal effects of exchange control on the conduct of international trade.
16. Describe the purpose and nature of bilateral payments agreements. Comment specifically on their credit and transferability provisions.
17. What is the proper use of exchange control?

SELECTED READINGS

Beveridge, Sir William. *Tariffs: The Case Examined,* 2d ed. London: Longmans, Green & Company, 1932.

Bidwell, Percy W. *The Invisible Tariff: A Study of the Control of Imports into the United States.* New York: Council of Foreign Relations, 1939.

Bloomfield, Arthur I. *Speculative and Flight Movements of Capital in Postwar International Finance.* Princeton: Princeton University Press, 1954.

Dietrich, Ethel B. *World Trade.* New York: Henry Holt & Co., Inc., 1939. Chapter 6.

Dymsza, Wm. A. *Foreign Trade Zones and International Trade* (New Jersey Department of Conservation and Economic Development, Trenton, New Jersey, 1964).

Ellsworth, Paul T. *The International Economy.* New York: Macmillan Co., 1964. Chapters 13, 17, and 18.

Heuser, Heinrich. *Control of International Trade.* Philadelphia: The Blakiston Co., 1939. Chapters 7, 8, 9, and 13.

Humphrey, Don D. *The United States and the Common Market,* New York: Frederick A. Praeger, 1964. Chapters 2 and 4.

International Monetary Fund, *Exchange Control, Fifteenth Annual Report,* (Washington, D. C., 1964).

Kindleberger, Charles P. *International Economics.* Homewood, Ill.: Richard D. Irwin, Inc., 1963, Chapters 3, 15, and 16.

League of Nations. *International Currency Experience.* Geneva: League of Nations, 1944. Chapter 7.

Mikesell, Raymond F. *Foreign Exchange in the Postwar World*. New York: Twentieth Century Fund, 1954.

Taussig, F. W. *Some Aspects of the Tariff Question*, 3d ed. Cambridge: Harvard University Press, 1931.

Towle, Lawrence W. *International Trade and Commercial Policy*, 2d ed. New York: Harper & Brothers, 1956. Chapters 13, 17, 18, 21, and 24.

Wasserman, M. J., and Chas. W. Hultman. *Modern International Economics*. New York: Simmons Boardman Publishing Corp., 1962. Chapter 19.

CHAPTER 15

ARGUMENTS FOR PROTECTION

International trade restrictions are man-made impediments to the free movement of goods and services among nations. They interfere with international specialization and the allocation of the natural, human, and capital resources of the world to their most productive uses. The extent, intensity, and direction of this interference vary with the conditions under which they operate.

The issue of "free trade" versus "protection" has been in dispute ever since the eighteenth century; the literature on this controversy is one of the most extensive in the annals of political economy. The arguments are often complex and subtle, although the controversy itself is rather very simple. The economists, as a rule, have lined themselves on the side of free trade, while the businessman and the politicians have supported protectionism, especially in the present century.

THE CASE FOR FREE TRADE

The case for free trade rests essentially on the theory of international specialization and trade that was developed in Chapters 3, 4, and 5. There it was shown that an unhampered price mechanism operating in competitive markets brings about the optimum allocation of resources among nations. Under conditions of free trade, each nation is enabled to take full advantage of international specialization and thereby to maximize its productivity and real income to the mutual benefit of all. On the assumption that it is unwise, if not foolish, for an individual to attempt to produce for himself all his needs and to do without what he cannot possibly make, so also it is for a nation. Furthermore, no one, including the most ardent protectionists, would oppose specialization and trade between the different regions of the same country; yet, the bases of interregional and international trade are identical. Without domestic specialization, the American market, so vigorous and productive, would be frustrated and wasteful of its resources. The denial of the advantages of international trade can only stem from ignorance or misguided nationalism in blatant disregard of the overall national welfare.

The case for free trade, therefore, is the same as the case for regional specialization and trade with its full benefits optimized in a competitive world market via the price mechanism.

THE CASE FOR PROTECTION

Although Great Britain prospered under a policy of free trade during the nineteenth century, free trade has seldom been adopted by other trading nations. Since World War I all countries have resorted to varying degrees of protection. The prevalence and the strength of protection in international trade stem from a host of economic, political, and social factors. For one thing, protection benefits directly the individual producers engaged in activities that are sheltered from foreign competition. Hence, any attempt to reduce or eliminate existing protection is stubbornly resisted, and persistent pressure is applied to national governments to initiate new protection or to raise existing restrictions. Any adverse implications for the domestic economy as a whole or for the welfare of other countries tend to be disregarded.

The basic assumptions of competitive markets, full employment, and an efficient price mechanism that are necessary to optimize the benefits of free trade are seldom fully satisfied in the real world where monopolistically competitive pricing, labor unions, and other institutional rigidities are the rule rather than the exception. Furthermore, the economic benefits of free trade may not be evenly distributed within a single nation and they may be even less so between different nations.

The arguments against free trade try to show that (1) its advantages are outweighed by its shortcomings; (2) the interdependence of nations implicit in free trade subjects national economies to uncertainties inherent in sudden changes in the policies of other nations that often cause serious dislocations, if not losses, far greater than the benefits to be derived from a free-trade policy; and (3) the price system and free competition underlying the theoretical assumptions for free trade are, at best, only partially valid in the real world where prices and production are subjected to controls and rigidities from many quarters that contribute to what has been referred to as a *disequilibrium system* under which restrictions on consumers and/or producers are the tools of adjustment rather than price.[1]

It is sometimes emphasized that even an inefficient domestic industry may make it possible for a nation to achieve a more balanced growth—if not a greater or faster growth—with more diversified domestic industries. Most of these arguments find their greatest proponents in the developing countries; and they have given rise to the adherence to the more formalized arguments for protection based on the concepts of (1) national security, (2) infant industry, (3) diversification for economic stability, and (4) improvement of the terms of trade of a nation.

When a country is faced with disturbing or threatening economic maladjustments, the internal and external conflict of ends may incline national authorities to regard the tenets of the free-trade theory as more of a distant goal to be hoped for than as a rule of behavior to abide by in formulating their national economic policy. Periods of widespread unemployment generate new appeals for protection. Although employment can be stimulated at a lower national cost through internal fiscal and monetary policies, legislators may succumb to the immediate pressure of their constituencies and groups with special economic interests and curb imports by imposing higher tariffs and other restrictions.

In the course of time many ingenious pleas have been advanced in direct support of protection. The pleas have been based on a variety of arguments, none of which possess unqualified economic validity. A few of these arguments rationalize short-term gains at the expense of long-term national benefits; others follow exactly the opposite approach; while most of the remaining arguments have only partial economic validity or are completely fallacious, drawing their strength mainly from their engaging emotional mass appeal.

The diversity and multiplicity of the arguments for protection will not permit an exhaustive analysis within this chapter. We shall, however, review the most widely used arguments in order to acquire a proper perspective of the case for protection and to understand the

---

[1] J. K. Galbraith, "The Disequilibrium System," *American Economic Review,* 37, 1947, pp. 287-302.

reasons for its persistence as a means of implementing national economic policies.

The long series of arguments for protection may be classified in terms of their relative validity within three major categories:

1. Arguments with qualified validity.
2. Questionable arguments.
3. Fallacious arguments.

ARGUMENTS WITH QUALIFIED VALIDITY

These arguments find their justification either in noneconomic considerations such as the fear of war, or in the expectation of future long-term economic benefits at the sacrifice of the immediate gains from international specialization and trade, such as the protection of inefficient domestic industries. In this category there are three time-honored arguments:

1. National security argument.
2. Infant-industry argument.
3. Diversification for economic stability argument.

National Security Argument

It is often argued that in time of war a nation must have within its borders the essential industries for national defense, irrespective of the economic sacrifices that may be entailed in the process. Adam Smith, the venerable father of free trade, emphatically declared that "defense is more important than opulence." Assuming the validity of this argument, a case can be made for self-sufficiency. Consequently, protection of almost any industry can be justified on the grounds of either direct military necessity or indirect contribution to the morale of a population during a conflict.

A program of self-sufficiency may, however, turn out to be wasteful of the scarce resources of a country in peacetime. Hardly any country can achieve complete self-sufficiency either in war or in peace since the natural resources of the world are not distributed in harmony with national political frontiers. The United States and Russia, both highly self-sufficient nations, found the attainment of self-sufficiency to be an impossible task in wartime. The early experience of Communist Russia in peacetime self-sufficiency has been somewhat modified in the light of actual experience.

The problem of national security can and is being solved in part by methods other than self-sufficiency. Stockpiling is resorted to without the unnecessary sacrifice of the benefits of international specialization. The same end may also be achieved by subsidization of basic industries at a lower and more equitable cost to the ultimate consumer.

While no one disagrees with the necessity to maintain adequate national defense, it is difficult, if not impossible, to define national security in concrete and lasting terms for legislative purposes. Since most producers are inclined to consider their activities essential to the security of their country, the national security argument lends itself particularly to abuses.

In the United States since World War II, many domestic producers have been clamoring for protection on the grounds of national security. Congress has responded to their claims by including in the 1955 and 1958 extensions of the Reciprocal Trade Agreements Act a defense-essentiality amendment, which curtails the authority of the President to reduce tariff rates on items declared essential to national security regardless of other more compelling foreign policy considerations.[2] Besides, imports can contribute measurably to the national security of the United States by strengthening the American economy and the economies of friendly trading nations. Lower rates, rather than higher rates, of duties may help conserve certain national resources that can be invaluable to this country in time of war.

It is sometimes argued that war itself is caused by economic conditions. Further, it is stated that a world free of trade barriers is more conducive to peaceful pursuits and is less likely to engage in armed conflicts since national aims become closely identified with those of other nations. Besides, the wisdom of protection for national security purposes seems open to doubt. Military experts are inclined to view future wars in terms of "adequate strength in a constant state of readiness" to meet an all-out thermonuclear attack rather than in terms of "potential production capacity." If true, the best allocation of the resources of the free world, rather than the restrictions of imports, appears to be in the best interests of the United States.

---

[2] The Reciprocal Trade Agreements Act and its successor, The Trade Expansion Act of 1962, are discussed in Chapter 18.

Furthermore, "there is reason to believe that attempts have been made to use the defense-essentiality amendment as an excuse to raise import barriers." [3] Increases in tariff rates on cheese products, Swiss watches, English bicycles, and quotas on lead and petroleum and other items of trade are suspicious examples of uneconomic measures that are conveniently wrapped in the sanctity of the flag.

On the positive side of the national security argument, at times it may be realistic to sacrifice partial welfare benefits for political considerations in a world of uneasy peace conditions. But the needs of a synthetic rubber industry that is incapable of survival under free trade may be better served by subsidization rather than by high tariffs. Such is the case of the American merchant marine and the aviation industry, which are both heavily subsidized.

Infant-Industry Argument

When a new industry can be started under generally favorable conditions for growth and ultimate competitive efficiency, it is argued that temporary protection is needed to allow the new industry to acquire the necessary experience, the know-how, and the economies of scale that are already possessed by foreign industries because of an earlier start. If the assumed favorable conditions for growth and efficiency can be ascertained in advance, this line of reasoning offers a valid excuse, rather than an argument, for protection. It is felt that a well-conceived *temporary* protection, whose end result is free trade under more favorable national conditions of production, would contribute greater aggregate benefits in the end.

The infant-industry argument is, however, not without its critics who maintain that comparable conditions occur constantly within a country in which new enterprises are started in competition with well-entrenched older establishments without benefit of protection. Often many of the new domestic ventures succeed in displacing less-dynamic older ones on the basis of greater ingenuity, advantages of location or improved conditions of production, and other benefits of internal and external economies. This type of competition is of vital importance to keep an economy from becoming static or retrogressive. It is also pointed out that tariff protection, once granted to nurture an infant industry, tends to become a permanent device, whether or

---

[3] Howard S. Piquet, *The Trade Agreements Act and the National Interest* (Washington, D. C.: The Brookings Institution, 1958), p. 48.

not the young industry comes of age. Sheltered producers become vested interests and are reluctant to give up the privileged position that reduces foreign competition and affords them higher profit margins. In this process the consumer is condemned to continue subsidizing the producer without just compensation.

The infant-industry argument is associated with Alexander Hamilton, the first Secretary of the Treasury of the United States, and Frederick List, a German economist who lived in this country as a political refugee. Alexander Hamilton published his famous *Report on Manufactures* in 1791, urging the use of tariffs to foster the growth of manufacturing and to strengthen the American economy that was then predominantly agricultural. He contended that the vast resources of the country could be advantageously developed to compete with foreign industries that held a vast lead due to a prior start; that even though time and ingenuity could ultimately bring about such a development, governmental aid and promotion would speed up the process; that the need for governmental assistance would constitute only a temporary departure from the free-trade doctrine in order to bring about a speedier, more secure, and steadier demand for the surplus produce of the soil.[4]

Frederick List's historical approach to the question of free trade versus protection led him to the general conclusion that free trade is a cosmopolitan concept that is not necessarily in the best interest of a country in an intermediate stage of economic development.[5] Such a developing country could not readily develop new industries without temporary protection—a view held by the more modern framers of the General Agreement on Tariffs and Trade (GATT).[6]

The real problem of the infant-industry argument does not lie in its theoretical validity, but rather in its practical application, for it is almost impossible to distinguish in advance the exact nature of a new industry and whether or not it will become competitive. Moreover, once a new industry is protected, the pressure from vested interests prevents the removal of protection, especially when the new industry proves to be incapable of ever becoming self-sustaining. The American woolen-worsted industry falls in this category. This industry started in the early years of this country as an infant

---

[4] Isaac Asher, *International Trade, Tariff and Commercial Policies* (Homewood, Ill.: Richard D. Irwin, Inc., 1948), Chapter 4.

[5] Frederick List, *The National System of Political Economy* (London: Longmans, Green & Company, 1922).

[6] See Chapter 17 for a discussion of GATT.

industry and has been protected ever since. It is still very sensitive to import competition and does not show symptoms of being able to overcome its comparative disadvantage.

Diversification for Economic Stability Argument

This argument is closely related to the infant-industry argument, but it applies more specifically to countries that are heavily engaged in the production of one or a few agricultural or mineral products. These so-called one-crop countries may lose heavily if there is a crop failure or a drop in world demand for their few products. Moreover, cyclical price fluctuations are extremely wide for such products. It is easy to sympathize with the desire of one-crop countries to diversify their economic activities to free themselves from overdependence upon outside forces even though it may be uneconomic to do so. Brazil, Chile, Venezuela, and many other developing countries that fall in this category have initiated economic programs for diversification in recent decades.[7]

Unless diversification is introduced with extreme care, the national loss of the benefits of international specialization may turn out to be greater than the realized gains of diversification. Selective diversification will help somewhat, but international efforts directed toward the stabilization of prices and markets for primary products are more likely to alleviate instability and are more in the interest of importing nations. After World War II, during the rush for industrialization by a number of developing countries, ill-advised diversification ended in complete factory equipment, purchased abroad at a tremendous sacrifice of scarce foreign exchange, remaining in warehouses due to a lack of capital, raw materials, or know-how to put such equipment into production.

QUESTIONABLE ARGUMENTS

Some arguments for protection may be justified under certain conditions for a short period of time; better and more lasting results may be achieved, however, by means of domestic measures without sacrificing the benefits of international specialization. The questionable logic of such arguments militates against their make-shift validity. The more popular of these arguments are:

1. The employment argument.
2. The terms-of-trade argument.
3. The bargaining and retaliation argument.

---

[7] The trading problems of the developing nations are explored in Chapter 20.

Employment Argument

The basis for this argument is that the imposition of a tariff or some other form of import restriction in periods of unemployment will reduce imports and generate increased home production. Increased domestic production in turn will increase employment and national income. Since import expenditures, like savings, create a leakage in the domestic income stream that is further magnified by the effect of the foreign trade multiplier, the reduction of imports will tend to generate an even greater measure of domestic expenditures and employment.

This argument carries tremendous appeal in periods of depression and especially under conditions of less than full employment in the domestic economy. Its validity, however, is not so evident as it appears on the surface.

Curtailment of domestic imports reduces the availability to foreign countries of foreign exchange that is needed in payment for domestic exports and, in time, tends to decrease those exports. A small country may successfully combat unemployment by decreasing its imports if other countries do not retaliate. Major countries that resort to this method would tend to spread unemployment abroad, since one country's imports are other countries' exports, and all countries cannot possibly reduce imports and maintain exports at the same time. Therefore, the employment created by the shift in demand from goods previously imported to domestic goods must be measured in terms of the consequent unemployment in the contracting export industries. The net gain in employment, if any, may be only temporary since other nations will most likely adopt countermeasures in self-defense. A policy of protection designed to alleviate unemployment is therefore likely to result in no more than a shift of employment from the more productive export industries to the less efficient import-displacing industries. Even if an actual gain in employment were achieved, its social cost would probably involve a reduction in real income and a lower standard of living. This situation is hardly desirable except under extreme emergencies and only when no other alternative policy is available.

The experience of the United States during the great depression of the early 1930's under the highly protective Hawley-Smoot tariff is a historic example of the ineffectiveness of the employment argument.

Terms-of-Trade Argument

The terms of trade are expressed by the ratio of export prices over import prices of the international merchandise transactions of a country. An increase in export prices and/or a decrease in import prices of a country would result in a higher ratio and, therefore, in an improvement of the terms of trade of that country.

The terms-of-trade argument for protection asserts that higher tariffs will force a reduction in the price of imports. Foreign suppliers who are faced with a falling demand will cut the prices of their goods in order to maintain sales in the tariff-levying country. In this way the same amount of foreign exchange will buy more imports, that is, the tariff country's terms of trade will improve.

Indeed, a country that imports a significant proportion of a product, the supply of which is inelastic, may very well succeed in forcing the world price of its imports downward and may alter the distribution of the world income in its favor, thus improving its terms of trade. But what the protectionist fails to consider in this argument is the secondary effect of the tariff action in lowering the total volume of trade—also a source of national gain—and the fact that other nations can also play the game either in retaliation or for the same shortsighted purpose. The conjectural gains from the improved terms of trade must be contrasted with the obvious and certain loss of a reduced volume of trade and the higher national costs induced by the tariff action. Any step away from the full economic benefits of international specialization is a step toward less efficient production and is, therefore, a negative step unless justified on other grounds—which is not the premise of this argument.

Bargaining and Retaliation Argument

It has been argued that a country with a protective tariff is in a better position to bargain with other countries for concessions on its exports than is a country that has nothing to offer in return. It follows, therefore, that a free-trade (or low-tariff) country should adopt some form of protection in order to be in a bargaining position.

The logic of this argument is strong and such a policy may work out in actual practice. It does not, however, necessarily follow that the argument has economic validity. A free-trade country that resorts to protection for the purpose of bargaining sacrifices the benefits of international specialization on its imports, in addition to losing the benefits on its exports by foreign tariff action. Furthermore, once protection is introduced, domestic industries develop behind its shield and become entrenched, exerting pressures upon their government when the time comes to give up such protection. Experience proves that this kind of pressure is usually most successful in preventing the return to freer trade and, therefore, the country will, in all probability, become permanently committed to protection. Similarly, a country adopting a tariff for retaliation purposes is, so to speak, adding insult to injury by depriving itself of the benefits of free trade derived from unhindered imports.

FALLACIOUS ARGUMENTS

Most of the other arguments for protection fall into the category of purely fallacious arguments that rely on their mass emotional appeal or plausibility to enhance the self-interest of groups that are in a position to influence the passage of protective legislation. The most prevalent of the fallacious arguments are:

1. The antidumping argument.
2. The keep-money-at-home argument.
3. The low-wage argument.
4. The home-market argument.
5. The equalization-of-costs-of-production argument.
6. The prevention-of-injury argument.

Antidumping Argument

The dumping of goods in an importing country at prices below those prevailing in the exporting country may be beneficial or harmful depending upon circumstances. If dumping is persistent, buyers in the importing country reap a continuous benefit that results from lower prices for foreign goods. If the importing country has no domestic industry competing with the dumped product, there is, of course, no argument for protection. If, on the other hand, such an industry exists, domestic producers are in no different position than if the dumping price resulted from a normal cost advantage in the exporting country. The fact that there is an element of unfairness to domestic producers in the situation is not a valid reason for protection since the nation as a whole is benefited.

When dumping is sporadic and is intended to harass and to put a competing domestic industry out of business in order to raise prices afterwards, dumping becomes undesirable. To prevent such *predatory dumping,* action is necessary. High protection that precludes the possibility of predatory dumping, however, inflicts upon the domestic economy a permanent higher cost that is totally unjustified. By administrative action or by antidumping duties, predatory dumping can be prevented if and when it occurs since its practice becomes costly and ineffective.

Keep-Money-at-Home Argument

The proponents of this argument claim that when domestic residents buy imported goods, the country gets the goods and the foreigner gets the money. When, on the other hand, the residents buy domestic goods, it is argued that the country keeps both the goods and the money, and that the country which prevents imports is richer for doing so.

The utter fallacy of this argument is rooted in the crudest form of mercantilistic theory, long since discarded, which maintained that money is wealth in itself. Money, as such, is a means of exchange. When the foreign seller gets the money, unless he can purchase something useful with it, he is simply making a present of his goods to the buyer. Money paid for imports sooner or later must return either in payments for exports or as investment, since it has no redemption value except in the country of its issue.

Low-Wage Argument

Some protectionists claim that a high-wage country cannot afford to trade with low-wage or "pauper-labor" countries without risking a reduction in its own wages through competition with the low foreign wage level and thereby jeopardizing its standard of living. They assert further that, to protect its workers from the competition of low-paid foreign workers, a high-wage country must impose a tariff duty on cheap goods that are imported from the low-wage countries.

This sort of reasoning discloses a complete misunderstanding of the cause and effect of price and wage determination. The cost of a product is not the result of the cost of any one factor of production —labor, in this instance—but the result of the sum total of all the factors used in its production, namely, land, labor, capital, and management. There is, therefore, no guarantee that a low-cost labor input is cheap in terms of output if its productivity is, in comparison, lower than that of a higher cost labor input. Nor does labor alone determine the ultimate cost of a product if its higher or lower cost is offset by the combined difference in costs of the other factors used in conjunction with labor.[8]

Economic theory teaches us that wages tend to equal the value of their marginal product and that high wages are therefore the result of high productivity. Although institutional rigidities, such as strong labor unions and minimum wage laws, modify somewhat these basic principles, there is ample evidence in practice to support their general validity. It is no secret that the United States—a high-wage country—outproduces and outsells low-wage countries like India and Japan in many areas of production. This is due to the superior efficiency and productivity of its labor that is made possible by the greater use of capital in the form of machinery and by the more judicious utilization of its land resources, to say nothing of its more advanced management. Moreover, wages are the effect rather than the cause of productivity. If they indicate anything, it is the relative efficiency of labor in production. Wages are, therefore, a rough measure of productivity. In Japan, output per capita is about one quarter of the output per capita of the United States, indicating a lower productivity per worker for Japan. In the United States, the highest wages are found generally in the export industries that have a high productivity per worker and a low unit cost. How, then, could anyone explain the existence of American exports if lower wage rates were the sole index of absolute advantage?

It is further argued that a low-wage country like Japan, which has access to both capital and technology, could flood the world markets with her cheaper products unless adequate tariff protection were used to prevent such a danger. A broad rebuttal to this argument is that Japan's merchandise exports since World War II have been running consistently below her imports indicating a persistent deficit in her international balance of trade. This is due to the fact that the economy of this country is heavily dependent upon imported raw materials and foodstuffs. The ability of Japan to import depends upon the degree of acceptance of her exports by the outside world. Since trade is a two-way street, the rest of the world must either accept Japanese goods or forego sales to Japan.

If we assume that Japan's exports will exceed her imports in the future as a result of low wages, the balance of her international payments, other things being equal, will be in "surplus disequilib-

---

[8] When wages are the determining cost factor, as in the case of hand embroidery or artwork, the comparative advantage becomes one of low wages and such work should be left to countries having this advantage.

rium." [9] In such an event, readjustments will take place affecting income, prices, production, and employment in that country. Labor costs will tend to rise further than they already have in the past and many existing comparative advantages will disappear.

Unchecked cheap Japanese imports would undoubtedly create round-the-world economic readjustments that would force out less efficient producers competing with Japanese industries. This would cause heavy losses in fixed investments and create temporary structural unemployment before a new equilibrium were reached. It is the fear of this admittedly difficult period of transition that really motivates the proponents of the low-wage argument to clamor for tariff restriction rather than face the unlikely danger of a deterioration of the standard of living. Tariff restrictions, however, are neither the most desirable nor the only solution to this problem. What is really needed is a gradual readjustment period to permit orderly and less-painful reorientation of production and redeployment of workers to minimize losses and to preserve the benefits of international specialization.[10]

Home-Market Argument

This argument claims that the domestic producer has a right to the domestic market and that by reducing or eliminating imports, more goods will be produced at home, more jobs will be created, and increased domestic activity will be the result.

The fallacy of this argument stems from the fact that when imports are replaced by domestic production, increased domestic activity represents a shift in demand from foreign to domestic suppliers of the protected commodities, not an increase in total demand. Besides, there is bound to be elsewhere in the economy a contraction of production of export goods as a result of the reduced means for payments available to foreigners due to the reduction or elimination of imports.

It is sometimes argued that exports need not be financed by imports since, in the balance of international payments of a country, compensatory transactions might serve this purpose. As we have

---

[9] See Chapter 9.

[10] In order to stave off undesirable tariff action abroad, Japan has adopted a policy of self-restraint by setting voluntary export quotas for its textiles and textile apparels that are causing resentment and concern abroad. In addition, she has realigned her production for exports by shifting from the highly competitive cheap textiles to the more selective production goods and higher-quality consumer goods.

seen in Chapter 9, it is true that such items may actually be used to finance exports in the absence of sufficient imports. Gold inflow, however, can be used only in a limited way. Bank reserves and short-term investments must sooner or later be repatriated and cannot be counted upon for a lasting solution. Long-term capital outflow on a continuous basis would in time create a need for the transfer back to the lending country of vast interest and dividend charges, and the repayment of the principal itself which could only take place in the form of imports. Of course, a country may be willing to finance its exports with gifts and grants and thus reduce its domestic supply of goods and services relative to its money income year after year, thereby probably subjecting its economy to "creeping inflation"; but sooner or later this method of financing could prove to be a far more serious problem than the one it is trying to cure.

The home-market argument is a fallacious argument. The shift from foreign to domestic sources of supply does not in any way increase real purchasing power. Moreover, protection on the basis of the home-market argument can only encourage inefficiency in the domestic market at the expense of the consumer. Since the cost of the scarce factors of production tends to rise with the added demand emanating from the new import-displacing industries, the efficient producer, behind a tariff wall, becomes less efficient in comparison with his previous operations.

Equalization-of-Costs-of-Production Argument

Some protectionists have favored the so-called "scientific method of tariff making" that is intended to equalize the costs of production between foreign and domestic producers and to neutralize any advantage the foreigner may have over the domestic producer in lower taxes, cheaper labor, or other costs. This argument allegedly implies a spirit of "fair competition," not the exclusion of imports. When, however, by reason of actual cost structure or artificial measures, costs of production become identical, the very basis of international trade disappears. The logical consequence of this pseudo-scientific method is the elimination of trade between nations. Thus the equalization-of-costs-of-production argument is utterly fallacious and is one of the most deceitful ever advanced in support of protection.

A close examination of the equalization-of-costs argument reveals the presence of many problems. Producers in any country have different and constantly changing costs for the same products. Whose costs are to serve as a frame of reference?

If we aim for protection of all domestic producers against all foreign producers, we must equalize the lowest foreign costs with the highest costs of the least efficient domestic producer. To accomplish this, a very high duty is required to overcome the extreme cost differential. Domestic prices to the consumer must rise to the high level of the domestic marginal producer's cost. The efficient domestic producer will reap an extra monopoly profit, and the domestic consumer will be forced to subsidize the highest form of inefficiency.

On the other hand, if the lower costs of the efficient domestic producer are to serve as the basis for cost equalization, this producer may engage in additional less efficient production in the absence of foreign competition. So long as he keeps his costs below those of his domestic competitors, he can force them out of business and capture the domestic market all for himself—a clear case of monopoly by legislative action with its attendant disadvantages to the economy.

In addition, the literal enforcement of such a policy entails considerable administrative difficulties in the collection of the necessary cost information for duty adjustments. This seems to be hardly worthwhile when the end result can only be the total prevention of imports and the ultimate reduction of the volume of trade as well as the impairment of the country's standard of living—surely a misconception of the scientific approach, to say the least.

Despite these objections, a tariff provision to equalize the costs of production was actually incorporated in the United States Tariff Acts of 1922 and 1930. This provision, however, has only been enforced in certain instances.

Prevention-of-Injury Argument

The prevention-of-injury argument is a relatively new argument designed to safeguard the vulnerability of an economy to increased imports subsequent to contemplated tariff concessions, or to concessions already granted under trade agreements. The advocates of this argument proclaim their willingness to reduce and maintain low tariffs, provided that in so doing no domestic industry or producer is threatened by excessive imports which result from such low rates of duties. Any contemplated concession must not reduce an existing rate to a preestimated low point, or *peril point,* that would jeopardize domestic producers. In addition, when previously reduced rates begin to threaten domestic producers, there should be an escape mechanism, or *escape clause,* to permit the restoration of higher rates or the tightening of quota controls.

On the surface, this argument sounds reasonable and implies an attitude of moderation. What this argument means in actual practice, however, is the elimination of international competition under comparative advantage when such competition threatens to divert a portion of the home market away from domestic producers, regardless of changed market conditions in the use of resources and technology at home and abroad.

The prevention-of-injury argument is closely related to the home-market and the equalization-of-costs-of-production arguments. It is an argument in denial of progress that is likely to encourage the preservation of static and regressive economies.

The United States has incorporated in its tariff legislation peril-point and escape-clause provisions in the extensions of its Reciprocal Trade Agreements Act to prevent excessive imports, even though the balance of its international trade has long been one of excess exports. In 1962, however, the Trade Expansion Act eliminated the peril-point provision and liberalized somewhat the enforcement of the escape clause.

PERSISTENCE OF PROTECTION

Our examination of the specific arguments for protection has revealed little if any justification for its support and has established instead the vulnerability of these arguments to economic analysis. In the few instances where protection may be successful in performing therapeutic functions, we have discovered that other devices such as public works, liberal credit, and employment policies can bring about superior results with less injury to the national economy.

Whatever merits may prevail in selective protection, as in the case of infant industries and diversification of production, the uncertainties and pitfalls inherent in its practice make it difficult to condone. In the light of historical experience, protection once established usually becomes a permanent institution under the relentless pressure of the vested interests it creates, even when it outgrows its original usefulness.

If so little can be said in its favor, why is protection so persistent? Why do all the nations of the world cling to it and inflict upon themselves such a malignant malpractice? Why is it that in the last century protection has grown so much in strength while liberal or free-trade policies have steadily given ground in spite of their economic and intellectual justification?

The answers to these perplexing questions are not to be found in the realm of logic or economics. The answers, deeply embedded in human nature and in human behavior, are the result of selfishness and fear that feed on ignorance and prejudice and that find their highest expression in the political arenas of the world. Furthermore, the stresses and strains of international relations cause some nations to support programs of self-sufficiency and others to seek self-contained economies for the nationalistic and the demagogic appeals that are also influential factors in the persistence of protection.

SUMMARY

1. The case for freer trade has been well established in theory, but in practice no nation in the world today adheres to it. Protection is rampant in spite of the shaky foundations upon which it rests as evidenced by the lack of validity of most of the arguments advanced in its support.
2. Pleas for protection, more often than not, are based on weak arguments. The national security and the infant-industry arguments possess some justification and command qualified acceptance. The argument for diversification of economic activity, even though weak, has its advantages for one-crop countries, which are often at the mercy of wide price fluctuations.
3. Other arguments are either allegations or downright misrepresentations for protection, with the equalization-of-costs-of-production argument the most flagrant example of all.
4. The persistence of protection, however, stems from the natural inclination of individuals and groups whose interests are directly at stake to pressure their representatives in government for legislation that is favorable to their immediate interests. These representatives are motivated by their individual political aspirations and are often prone to submerge the wider national interest and to legislate in favor of pressure groups.

QUESTIONS AND APPLICATIONS

1. What are the reasons, in practice, for the widespread disregard of the established theoretical validity of the case for freer trade?
2. Discuss the arguments for protection that, in your opinion, have the most validity.
3. Choose the arguments for protection that, in your opinion, are the most fallacious and discuss their basic weaknesses.
4. What are the reasons for the preponderance of arguments for protection?

5. "Imports are said to pay for exports. Yet, most governments spend a great deal of effort promoting their export trade while, at the same time, they impose all kinds of restrictions on their import trade." Discuss.

6. Define a truly infant industry. On the basis of your definition, are there any American industries that may be justified as infant industries?

7. Frederick List said that only the least-developed countries and the most highly industrialized countries can afford the practice of free trade. Discuss.

8. Why are internal fiscal measures preferable to tariffs for the creation of additional domestic employment?

9. "For reasons of national security, the United States should produce all the wool it needs. Therefore, a high tariff to prevent wool imports would be in the national interest." Evaluate these statements.

10. "Imports of cheap Japanese textiles made out of American cotton are undermining the domestic market for United States textiles. The United States should impose an export tax on raw cotton to compensate for the wage rate differential between Japanese and American textile workers." Discuss the economic aspects of such a solution.

SELECTED READINGS

Beveridge, Sir William. *Tariffs: The Case Examined.* London: Longmans, Green & Company, 1932.

Buchanan, N. S. "Deliberate Industrialization for High Incomes," *Economic Journal,* Vol. LVI (1946), pp. 533 ff.

Ellsworth, P. T. *The International Economy,* Rev. ed. New York: Macmillan Co., 1964. Chapter 13.

Galbraith, J. K. "The Disequilibrium System," *American Economic Review,* 37, 1947, pp. 287-302.

Haberler, Gottfried von. *The Theory of International Trade.* New York: Macmillan Co., 1937. Chapters 14, 16, and 17.

League of Nations. *Industrialization and Foreign Trade.* Geneva: League of Nations, 1945.

Taussig, Frank W. *Some Aspects of the Tariff Question,* 3d ed. Cambridge: Harvard University Press, 1931.

Towle, Lawrence W. *International Trade and Commercial Policy,* 2d ed. New York: Harper & Brothers, 1956. Chapter 20.

CHAPTER 16

CARTELS, STATE TRADING, AND COMMODITY AGREEMENTS

In addition to the tariffs, quotas, and exchange controls that are used by national governments to regulate international trade, a variety of other forms of restrictions is employed by both private business and governments. These restrictions encompass the monopolistic practices of cartels, state-trading systems, and international commodity agreements, which may be far more obstructive to the normal flow of commerce between nations than the usual official measures of control.

In this chapter we shall investigate several types of private and governmental monopoly-like activities and appraise their roles in international commercial policies.

INTERNATIONAL CARTELS

A *cartel* is said to exist when two or more independent enterprises in the same or affiliated fields of economic activity join together for the purpose of exerting control over a market. When the members of a cartel are located in different countries and operate beyond national borders, their association is referred to as an *international cartel*.

Nature of Cartels

Cartels vary in form and in organization. They may operate as:

1. Loose association memberships with informal understandings; straight agreements; patent, license, and trademark arrangements; joint selling agencies, etc.

2. Strict association memberships with provision for penalties or fines.

3. Arrangements with government participation.

Any given cartel may operate simultaneously under one or more of these arrangements.[1] From the point of view of their operation, however, cartels may be classified into the *association* and the *patents and processes* forms.

The Association. The *association* form of cartel is characterized by the fact that its independent members agree to pursue certain defined group policies with respect to levels of production, prices, and marketing arrangements, as well as other common or specific policies pertaining to industrial or trade activities.

The Patent and Processes. The *patent and processes* form is distinguished by the fact that the right to the exclusive use of the patents and processes of the several members is confined solely to the members and only in their respective markets and/or by common agreement in other defined markets. Thus, outside competition is excluded and competition between members is regulated.

There is another form of arrangement whereby several various producers join together in a single organization under common ownership and management in which autonomous units surrender their independent corporate status. This form of arrangement is called a *combine*. It is not a cartel in the strict sense of our definition, even though the economic behavior of this type of organization may be and often is similar to that of a cartel.[2]

Whatever the organizational form or setup of a cartel, the individual members are most likely to have enjoyed, prior to its formation, a certain measure of monopolistic control in their respective markets. By joining together, nationally or internationally, their combined strength under a common policy can wield tremendous monopoly power that may be used to enhance their own best interests to the detriment of the ultimate consumer and the public welfare.

Objectives of Cartels

As a rule, the primary objective of a cartel is to maximize profits for its members. This objective may be directly or indirectly achieved by:

1. Control over prices.
2. Allocation of markets.
3. Restriction of supply.

---

[1] Corwin D. Edwards, *A Cartel Policy for the United States* (New York: Columbia University Press, 1945), p. 7.

[2] Corwin D. Edwards, "International Cartels as Obstacles to International Trade," *American Economic Review*, Supplement (March, 1944), pp. 330-31.

4. Control over technological changes and other activities of its members.

5. Elimination of external competition.

Control over Prices. Many cartels are formed in time of severe competition when economic survival leads to unprofitable cutthroat price competition in the market. Under these conditions, price stability can be restored by mutual agreement of competing producers under a cartel arrangement. Once prices are stabilized, however, cartels usually move in the direction of price increases greater than those that are likely to prevail under free competition with or without cutthroat competition. On the other hand, in times of declining prices, resistance to the general decline may be accomplished more readily by cartels with control over the volume of production of its members. Cartels often support stable prices in their major markets and dump excess inventories in other markets where they are in competition with nonmembers.

A classic example of price control and gouging by a cartel is the case of General Electric of the United States and Krupp of Germany who entered into a patent-pooling agreement in 1928. As a result of this agreement, the price of tungsten-carbide rose from $50 to $450 a pound. Even in the depression years that followed, the price never dropped below $225 a pound. An indictment by the United States government under the antitrust laws in 1941,[3] however, brought the price down to less than $50 almost overnight. By 1942 this price had fallen to a low of $27 per pound.[4]

Allocation of Markets. A common cartel practice is the allocation and distribution of production among its members by means of well-defined geographic market areas. Under this type of arrangement, the members of a cartel agree not to invade one another's territory. In some instances nonallocated markets are left open to all members under prescribed conditions of competitive practices.

An example of this type of cartel agreement is that of the chemical industry which operated in the 1930's. The duPont Company was granted the exclusive rights in the United States and Central America for the production of certain chemical products, and the Imperial Chemical Industries of Great Britain was given the

---

[3] *General Electric et al.* v. *Industrial Diamond Co. et al.,* 33 F. Supp., p. 969.

[4] Corwin D. Edwards, *Economic and Political Aspects of International Cartels,* Monograph No. 1 (Washington, D. C.: United States Senate, Subcommittee on War Mobilization of the Committee on Military Affairs, 1944), pp. 12-13.

exclusive rights in the British Empire, except Canada. The two companies agreed to exploit the Canadian market and the Brazilian and Argentine markets through joint ownership of subsidiaries.[5]

Restriction of Supply. This is one of the most common methods of control used by cartels. By creating an artificial scarcity for a given product, the members of a cartel are able to exact a higher price from the public. The limitation of supply, however, is often difficult to enforce in spite of the punitive measures that may be provided for this purpose. Particularly is this true in times of depression when there is a tendency on the part of individual members to break away from cartel-imposed restrictions. Moreover, it is also difficult in boom periods to prevent entry into the market of new independent producers who are unwilling to cooperate with cartels. Thus, cartels often resort to price-cutting devices and other pressure tactics in order to induce collaboration.

A most amazing case of the restriction of production capacity took place in the United States prior to World War II. As a result of a cartel agreement between the Aluminum Company of America (Alcoa), the Dow Company, and I. G. Farbenindustrie of Germany, Alcoa agreed to pool its magnesium patents and to cease production; the Dow Company agreed to limit its production of magnesium to 4,000 tons a year to be marketed only in the United States at controlled prices; and the Farbenindustrie of Germany—which had an international monopoly—agreed to purchase any unsold American magnesium produced by Dow in the United States. As a result, Alcoa prevented magnesium from becoming a substitute for aluminum in the United States; the Dow Company avoided domestic competition in magnesium; and the Farbenindustrie insured its monopolistic position throughout the world. With the outbreak of World War II, the United States found itself in the uncomfortable position of having inadequate production facilities for magnesium production while Germany possessed a production capacity of this very important war metal which was at least five times greater than that of the United States.[6]

Control over Technological Changes. Changes in the arts make possible new, superior processes and substitute products. Unless a

---

[5] *Ibid.,* p. 13.

[6] Joseph Borkin and Charles Welsh, *Germany's Master Plan* (New York: Duell, Sloan, & Pierce, Inc., 1943), Chapter 16.

cartel is in control of technological changes, its hold on the market may be lost to nonmembers who possess the new technology.

To discard costly existing facilities every time a superior process or a substitute product is discovered that requires new investment may not be in the immediate interest of the cartel, however.

This problem is often overcome by extensive research facilities maintained by cartels to find ways in which their basic patents may be modified just enough to prolong their legal validity and to prevent nonmembers from the use of such patents. On the other hand, when substitute products are discovered or the patent rights to such products are obtained through purchase, cartels may delay the industrial application of the new discoveries or even keep them completely out of production. By this action cartels succeed in maintaining their hold on the market, but they also deprive the public of the benefits of technological improvements.

Elimination of External Competition. In order to improve or maintain its monopolistic hold on the market a cartel may impinge or harass a recalcitrant or unwanted competitor by denying him access to necessary production factors or even its own established outlets.

To achieve such an objective, a cartel or combination may resort to a price war within the territory of operation of the competitor. In this struggle, the ensuing losses can be offset by profits from other operations or simply allocated to the members of the cartel.

If a cartel decides to deprive competitors of the means of production or access to production factors, it will either deny them the benefits of its pooled patents and processes or make them subject to discriminatory terms and conditions of use and so put such competitors at a distinct disadvantage.

In the marketing sector, a cartel may try to keep out competitors by offering special terms and conditions of representation to distributors or even by dictation if not by simple persuasion, thus keeping out unwanted competitors in their own established territories.

Areas of Cartel Activities

The success of a cartel is a function of the monopoly hold that it can exert over the market. Consequently, cartels tend to develop in those industries in which concentration of ownership is feasible or in which patents and trademarks play an important role. Cartel arrangements are now generally found in mining, chemical, ceramics, metals, textile, and staple-food industries, as well as in transportation and communication service industries. In the raw material field, the production and distribution of diamonds and natural rubber are dominated by cartels. The European steel and aluminum industries are likewise highly cartelized, especially for export activity. The dyestuff and rayon industries, as well as the incandescent lamp industry, have a high degree of cartel activity. Steamship transportation is well known for its conferences that act in a cartel-like manner.

A study made by the United States Department of Justice revealed that in 1939 the number of international cartels was 179, of which 109 included American enterprises. Of the 179 cartels, 133 were engaged in the production of manufactured and semimanufactured goods; 32 covered minerals; 8 involved agricultural products; and the remaining 6 were in various forms of services.[7] A publication by the United Nations indicated that in the interwar period 40 percent of world trade was subject to control by international cartels.[8]

Benefits and Drawbacks of Cartels

In their operations, cartels may bring about certain alleged benefits that are of value to consumers. On the other hand, however, cartels possess serious drawbacks since they usually exact higher prices from consumers as a result of reducing supply and protecting inefficient production.

Alleged Benefits. It is argued that cartels decrease inefficiency in production and distribution and thereby contribute to the public welfare. It is further stated that specific gains are derived from the cooperation of cartel members as a result of

> 1. The reduction of the costs of production due to standardization, exchange of patents and processes, avoidance of overexpansion and reduction of inventories.
>
> 2. The elimination of competitive advertising and selling, and wasteful duplication of cross-freight charges.
>
> 3. The centralization of research and trade information that helps to regulate supply with changing demand, to smooth out the effect of cyclical variations, and to reduce technological unemployment.

While these claims may possess some validity with reference to large-scale operations and effective management principles, international cartels cannot possibly realize all of these benefits since their

---

[7] "International Cartels as Obstacles to International Trade," *op. cit.*, p. 330.
[8] United Nations, Department of Economic Affairs, *International Cartels* (New York: United Nations, 1947), pp. 28-29.

individual members remain independent, especially in management. Even under the combine, the separate plants must operate under a decentralized system because of the vast geographical distances and the dissimilar operating conditions of the separate units.

Drawbacks. The cartel form of organization is subject to serious limitations and drawbacks. The independence enjoyed by the members of a cartel gives rise to differences of opinion that often result in dissension and internal conflict. It has been said that, during the interwar period, the German cartels were riddled with dissension and inconsistencies that constantly threatened their existence. When such conditions are extended into the international field, they become even more accentuated because of the different economic conditions prevailing in the constituent countries.

During the interwar period, the International Steel Cartel, for example, had to contend with continuous overproduction by its German members who were dissatisfied with their individual quotas. In spite of the punitive measures in the form of fines that are generally provided in cartel agreements to curb overproduction, individual members may have greater incentive to produce in excess of allotments in order to support a contention for a larger quota in a subsequent period.

The difficulties inherent in the loose form of cartel arrangements may be further intensified by the different economic conditions in the allotted markets of the individual members and also by the varying national economic policies. Protective tariffs, for example, which are established to encourage the development of infant industries, may also be supplemented by special legislation that forbids foreign affiliation of domestic producers in order to prevent outside influences from defeating the purposes of national economic policies.

It seems, therefore, that by their very nature cartel associations are essentially negative arrangements created to protect producers from the consequences of industrial maladjustment and competitive growing pains rather than organizations for positive measures to promote industrial expansion and economic development.[9]

Cartels and International Trade

The fundamental objectives of cartels—the control over prices, markets, supply, and technological changes—are deterrents to speciali-

---
[9] George W. Stocking and Myron W. Watkins, *Cartels in Action* (New York: Twentieth Century Fund, 1947), pp. 9-10.

zation and trade not only in the products directly under control, but also in other products manufactured in part from cartelized materials. These practices represent a clear departure from free competition and are, therefore, inimical to the development and growth of international trade on the basis of comparative costs. They constitute, in fact, a step backward.

Furthermore, cartels are prone to pressure governments into the adoption of national tariff and other protective measures for the products under their control in order to insure more favorable domestic markets for their individual members. When international cartels become widespread, their aggregate influence results in a reduced volume of international trade and in a less efficient utilization of the world resources, both material and human.

Public Policy toward Cartels

Cartels have been condemned not only for interfering with free competition and public policy, but even more because they

> . . . favor the rich against the poor, large corporations against the small, producers against consumers. It is rather that, in its ultimate tendencies, cartelization is restrictive of much more than just freedom to compete. By interfering with freedom of access and entry, cartelization at the same time interferes with expansionist influences in the determination of output, capacity, and survival of the fittest producers. It is this inclusive and far-reaching restrictionism which is so thoroughly inimical to the national interest.[10]

Because of this galaxy of unfavorable consequences, a great deal of public agitation against cartels has developed throughout the world. National attitudes, however, are not always a reflection of public sentiment as much as they are an expression of the national interest that is held by policy makers.

In prewar Nazi Germany and Japan, for example, cartels were the instrument of the state and a strong helping hand in shaping the governmental policies of industrialization and development in preparation for war. In underdeveloped countries, cartels are looked upon favorably when they assist in the stabilization of staple commodity prices or in raising these prices when their economies are heavily dependent on such commodities. The same countries, however, may also view with alarm the power of international cartels to interfere

---

[10] Charles R. Whittlesey, *National Interest and International Cartels* (New York: Macmillan Co., 1946), p. 159.

with their industrialization and economic planning when these plans do not coincide with the self-interests of the members of the cartels that are sometimes located in the planning country itself.

A national cartel policy, therefore, varies according to the economic necessities and the philosophy of each individual country. It is embodied in unilateral legislation that reflects the national attitude of a country at a given period of time toward monopolistic or oligopolistic practices. The arm of the law, however, cannot reach beyond political jurisdiction. This task is made even more difficult by the fact that cartel arrangements are surrounded by a great deal of secrecy which often makes it impossible to gather information or valid evidence against participating residents who are acting in violation of the law. As a result, international cartels may become almost supranational private institutions that are practically immune to national regulation or control.

United States Cartel Policy. The antitrust laws of the United States, starting with the Sherman Act of 1890, make all forms of monopoly and collusion in restraint of trade illegal, unless exempted by specific legislation. Since the restriction of supply, price fixing, and the allocation of markets restrain trade, cartels are illegal in the United States.

The widespread control of international trade after World War I tended to interfere with and to constrict the foreign commerce of the United States at a time when this country needed additional markets for its vastly increased production capacity. To assist American exporters, Congress passed the Webb-Pomerene Act of 1918, exempting Webb-Pomerene associations of exporters from the antitrust laws. As a result, American exporters can act like export cartels as long as they do not restrain domestic trade or unduly affect prices and competition in the United States.[11]

The opposition of the United States government to international cartels and the vigilance of the Department of Justice against violations of the antitrust laws of this country have helped to break up monopolistic tendencies and overt participation by American firms in international combinations in restraint of trade. There is, however, ample evidence that American firms have not always lived up to the spirit of the law as evidenced by the numerous indictments

---

[11] Further discussion of Webb-Pomerene associations will be found in Chapter 29.

brought against individual producers as well as against Webb-Pomerene associations for illegal participation in international cartel activities and for restraining United States domestic trade.

Policies of Other Countries. The traditional attitude toward combinations in trade and industry has been generally more tolerant outside the United States. Germany was the cradle of cartels and a leader in concentration movements. The German government encouraged and occasionally participated officially in restrictive agreements. After World War II, the decartelization directives of the Allied High Commission in Germany broke up certain German cartels to prevent that country from ever becoming once again a threat to its neighbors and a danger to world peace.

In 1958 a new "Law against Restriction on Competitive Trade" became effective in West Germany. This law, which is intended to be the regulating factor of competition in the German economy, provides that agreements made by enterprises in restraint of competition are invalid. Exceptions are provided, however, for a few sectors of the economy, such as agriculture, banking, insurance, and ocean shipping. An escape-clause provision in the law authorizes the Federal Economics Minister to permit the formation of a cartel if such action is required by overwhelming considerations of public welfare and the general economy. As a member of the EEC, Germany is now subject to the antitrust laws of that organization. This policy is discussed in Chapter 19 where it is noted that, unlike the United States, the EEC makes a distinction between "good" and "bad" cartels.

In Great Britain, the common law limits freedom to combine by declaring null and void all contracts and agreements in restraint of trade. Such understandings, however, are not actually illegal unless they involve an illegal act. A contract that is technically in restraint of trade has long been regarded by the courts as valid and enforceable when it involves a particular restraint which is not greater than the protection that is reasonably required by the party with whom the contract is made.

The policy of the United Kingdom, as expressed in the Restrictive Practices Acts of 1948, 1953, and 1956, prohibits acts or agreements found to be detrimental to the public interest. In determining whether an act or agreement is detrimental to the public interest, consideration is given to the need to (a) achieve production and distribution of goods of such types and qualities and of such volume and prices by the most efficient and economical means that will best serve the home and foreign markets; (b) encourage efficiency and new enterprises; (c) make the fullest use of manpower, materials, and industrial capacity; and (d) bring about the development of technical expansion and the opening up of markets. The law requires that restrictive trade agreements be registered and, in time, considered by a special Restrictive Practices Court which decides whether or not they are in the public interest. The British attitude toward monopolies is, therefore, typically empirical. There is no outright assumption that cartels are necessarily evil, but they are prevented from acting against the public interest.

Other European and Latin American countries look upon cartels in the light of their own economic conditions and industrial development, and, in principle, they do not consider them indiscriminately either good or evil.

International Regulation of Cartels

The control of international cartels can be successfully undertaken only by a concerted action that is based on full international cooperation by the participating countries. The divergent national viewpoints regarding the necessity for such action and the complexity of the problem of effective enforcement, however, render unlikely any subjection of cartels to international regulation and control in the foreseeable future.

In 1945, the United States submitted to other governments its "Proposals for the Expansion of World Trade and Employment." Among other things, cooperative action to curb the restrictive activities of international cartels was suggested in that document. As a result of the various meetings subsequently held in preparation of a charter for an International Trade Organization (ITO), an article was devoted to this problem in the final draft of the charter, which was ratified in Havana in 1947.[12] The refusal of the United States Congress to ratify the ITO resulted in a death blow to this proposed international organization to the dismay of its friends and to the satisfaction of devotees of international cartels.

Even though the control and/or regulation of international cartels since World War II attest to some progress, this has been confined to national measures, except for the EEC where it is regional and by no means international in scope and effect.

---

[12] Havana Charter for the International Trade Organization, Article 46, Paragraph 2.

The literature on this subject is vast, complex, and too technical for useful analysis here. This is due to the many imponderables such as sovereignty, jurisdiction, immunities, absence of conspirators, and many other considerations. But, above all, the lack of positive means of enforcement of judicial decisions is the most frustrating for a hopeful solution to this problem.

The experience of the United States in this area is rich in controversies that have reached the highest courts of the country for decision. The Timken Roller Bearing case, the The Imperial Chemical Industries, Ltd.; the National Lead Co.; and the Watchmakers of Switzerland are a few examples of a very long list of cases in restraint of United States trade. The decisions by the courts give no definite pattern as to make binding precedents for future judicial references.[13]

An idealistic approach to the solution of the cartel problem based on a full-employment program designed to prevent the depressions that foster cartels has been suggested. Such a program would require the major industrial nations to assume a key role by maintaining full employment and prosperity in their own countries and by assisting other nations technologically and financially in their pursuit of economic growth and development. Steps in this direction have been taken under the United States foreign aid program, the British Colombo Plan, and United Nations programs of economic assistance. Whether these efforts will curb or prevent cartel activities is rather doubtful in the light of experience.

STATE TRADING

When a government engages in actual commercial operations, directly or through agencies under its control, either to the exclusion of or in addition to private traders, it is said to practice *state trading*.

Nature and Significance of State Trading

In the nineteenth century national or local governments engaged in numerous activities that were not necessarily an essential function of the state, such as: (1) charitable enterprises, like milk distribution and cheap lodging for the underprivileged; (2) the ownership and operation of public services and utilities and other similar natural monopolies; (3) commercial undertakings for the control and pro-

---

[13] See Kingman Brewster, Jr., *Antitrust and American Business Abroad* (New York: McGraw-Hill Book Co., 1958); and General Agreement on Tariffs and Trade, *Restrictive Business Practices* (Geneva: 1959).

Ch. 16 / Cartels, State Trading, and Commodity Agreements

motion of public health, such as the production and/or distribution of liquor and spirits; and (4) production and/or distribution of articles of wide consumption for revenue purposes under a system of legally instituted monopolies. The entry of the state into these various activities was generally motivated by a desire for internal control or for revenue rather than for the regulation of trade or for protection from foreign competition.

In recent decades, however, national governments have performed specific tasks of procuring and distributing strategic materials and commodities in short supply during wars and national emergencies. This intrusion upon private enterprise has spread to other areas of commercial activity since World War II and has become an integral part of domestic planning schemes in many countries. As a consequence, international trade has been the object of a great deal of state trading.

The institution of a state-trading system affords the government monopoly powers that may be used to regulate international trade far more effectively than tariffs or any of the other measures of control we have studied so far, with the possible exception of foreign exchange control. These powers are inherent in the system itself when the state becomes the exclusive buyer and seller of a given commodity. The imports and exports of a country may thus be timed and directed unilaterally to achieve discrimination between different nations or to exert economic pressure to exact political advantages. The state may even choose to ignore cost and price relationship in order to realize its end in the process. When so utilized, state trading constitutes the ultimate weapon of economic warfare and a tool for good or evil at the discretion of the state.

Theoretically, commercial transactions may be carried on by the state and by private enterprise either in conformity or in contradiction to the basic principles of international trade and comparative advantage. In practice, private enterprise is more likely to be influenced by, and conform to, market forces in order to insure profitable operation and economic survival. The state, on the other hand, may ignore the profit motive for political considerations; and the tremendous powers centered in the government may be ill-advised, misdirected, or even misapplied. The resulting distortion of the market leads to a poor utilization of the resources of the world, particularly those of the state-trading country. Furthermore, whatever discrimination may develop is likely to create ill feeling and concern abroad and to give rise to retaliation that jeopardizes international efforts toward trade liberalization.

Objectives of State Trading

The Union of Soviet Socialist Republics and the other Communist countries control and regulate all domestic and foreign trade as an integral part of their ideological system. In the capitalist countries, state trading is an extraneous activity of the state, generally used to achieve one or more of the following objectives:

1. To protect domestic planning programs from being disrupted by outside economic forces.
2. To dispose of accumulated surpluses under price-support schemes.
3. To obtain more favorable prices and terms with large-scale purchasing.
4. To gain access to specific commodities in short supply at home and/or abroad.
5. To afford protection to domestic industries against higher or lower foreign prices.
6. To acquire strategic materials or prevent them from reaching potential enemies.

Even though the above objectives may be desirable under certain conditions, resorting to state trading to achieve these objectives is, nevertheless, in contradiction to the basic philosophy and principles of private enterprise.

Extent of State Trading

In the Communist countries, which control almost one third of the population of the world, all economic activities are dictated in one way or another by state agencies. In the capitalistic countries, state trading has been practiced on a limited or incidental basis by almost every country since World War II.

State Trading in the Soviet Union. After the Russian Revolution of 1917, all economic activities, including foreign trade, fell under the control of the government. Before 1928, Soviet foreign trade remained inactive because of internal difficulties and readjustments. The first significant international transactions by the Soviet government took place in the midst of the world depression in 1930 and 1931. Soviet products, even though they were in short supply at home, were dumped abroad, ostensibly to weaken even further the already shaky structure of the capitalistic markets.

International trade can be just as beneficial to Russia as it is to the rest of the world, but the Russian leaders have looked upon such trade with suspicion and have regarded it as a form of dependence upon an unfriendly and unreliable outside world. Soviet planners have tried to insulate the economy of their country from the consequences of what they consider to be insecure capitalistic markets doomed to cyclical depressions. Moreover, they feel that they must achieve autarky and military preparedness at any cost. Consequently, they look upon imports as a necessary evil to be minimized and to be paid for with gold or with whatever domestic products can be sacrificed in the form of exports. Under this philosophy, Soviet trade with the capitalistic world has been reduced to a minimum in spite of the vastly improved productivity of the Soviet economy and a large increase in population. About 90 percent of the foreign trade of Soviet Russia was oriented in the direction of the satellite countries and away from the West in the mid 1940's. The present pattern has been estimated to run around 70 percent to the satellites and 30 percent to the outside world indicating some change in the early attitude towards international trade by that country.

State Trading in Communist China. The international trade of Communist China, like that of Soviet Russia, is governed by similar ideological considerations. It is state induced and state directed for political ends and security as well as for economic reasons. Its volume, extent, and direction are restricted and well below their true potentials. The volume of this trade in 1964 was about ½ of 1 percent of world trade and less than one third of Soviet trade with the West.

State Trading in Great Britain. During World War II, Great Britain initiated a program of "bulk-buying" contracts with other governments to insure a supply of foodstuffs and raw materials under difficult wartime conditions. Bulk buying or bulk purchasing by the British government from other governments or private groups in foreign countries consisted of bilateral arrangements that specified the volume of commodities and the terms and conditions of importation and exportation over a certain period of time. With the advent of the Labor government after the war, this type of state trading was expanded as a device to direct trade toward the Sterling Area, presumably in accord with the socialistic philosophy of the government at the time. At the end of the 1950's, however, Britain had no such arrangements in actual operation.

State Trading in France. During World War II France, like Great Britain and the United States, had its state-trading program. After the War, this system was gradually relinquished. France, however, has separate peacetime state-trading *regies,* or fiscal monopolies, on such products as tobacco, matches, and playing cards that produce special revenues for the state.

State Trading in the United States. Trading by the state is regarded as an improper function of the government in the United States, except under special circumstances. When resorted to, state trading is usually performed indirectly through private channels for the account of the government for:

1. The disposal of surplus agricultural products that accumulate as a result of the price-support program of the country.

2. The acquisition of strategic materials, such as tin and rubber, to be held for national emergency purposes.

3. The purchase of goods and services outside the United States under the offshore procurement program for purposes of military and economic assistance to other countries.

These operations are not intended to be a departure from the overall philosophy of noninterference with private enterprise. Even though these operations are sizable at times, they represent only a small part of the total volume of United States international trade. Nevertheless, they have been viewed with concern, especially by domestic traders, in spite of the fact that they are not intended for revenue or protection purposes.

Regulation of State Trading

Regardless of intent or motives, a state-trading system creates monopoly powers by the mere size of the purchases and sales that are centered in government hands. The existence of such powers influences prices and is, therefore, a source of conflict between state trading and private trading that is difficult to reconcile. In addition, when monopoly powers are actually exercised for economic or political advantages, the problem becomes most significant in international relations and is of great concern to the world. Since the interwar period, attempts have been made to solve this problem by agreements between different nations on either a bilateral or a multilateral basis. These efforts, however, have generally failed.

The United States approach to the solution of discrimination under state trading has been met chiefly by reciprocal agreements under the Reciprocal Trade Agreements (RTA) program. In these agreements, special provisions have been included as safeguards against state-trading discrimination that might affect United States trade. Since 1947, when the General Agreement on Tariffs and Trade (GATT) became operative, other nations have followed the United States example and have included in their agreements provisions to the same effect. These provisions stipulate that in case a government monopoly exists it shall be influenced in its foreign purchases only by such considerations as price, quality, terms of sales, and other market factors that would normally be taken into account by private traders.

These considerations represent a step in the right direction, but they are hardly a guarantee for unqualified satisfactory performance. They are broad enough to permit differing interpretations and vague enough to invite elusive action, especially since they do not deny to the state the right to maximize economic gains, a right that is normally exercised by private traders in the choice of sources of purchase and destination of sales. On the other hand, the many intangibles involved in economic decisions do not lend themselves to a more definite formula that is applicable under all circumstances and that would permit, at the same time, the establishment of clear evidence in the event of nonconformity.

INTERGOVERNMENTAL COMMODITY AGREEMENTS

Intergovernmental commodity agreements are arrangements between leading producing countries or between leading producing and consuming countries to control and regulate production, prices, international trade, and certain marketing practices of specific primary commodities, such as wheat, cotton, coffee, rubber, and tin. In the past there also have been international commodity agreements between private producers, with or without government participation. Commodity agreements are similar to cartels, since they are generally concerned with the control of production and exports to stabilize or raise prices.

Most intergovernmental commodity agreements tend to be arrangements between consuming as well as producing countries. They are initiated by governments or by private associations that seek governmental sponsorship and support to widen market coverage, to strengthen control, and to insure compliance. The participation of consuming countries is intended to safeguard the interests of all concerned and to insure cooperation that will enhance the ultimate success of these agreements.

Unlike cartel arrangements, which protect the interests of a few already large and influential producers, intergovernmental commodity agreements seek to protect the interests of consumers as well as those of a large number of generally small producers who cannot individually influence the market by their separate actions.

Types of Intergovernmental Commodity Agreements

According to the distinct purposes for which they are organized, intergovernmental commodity agreements fall into two major types: (1) those motivated by international socio-economic and political objectives; and (2) those seeking remedies to the problems of excess production capacity and price instability in specific primary products.

Intergovernmental commodity agreements of the socio-economic and political type have been usually used for:

> 1. The protection of international health and morals, such as the organization for the regulation of opium traffic and other narcotics.
> 2. The conservation of international resources as in the case of fishing on the high seas.
> 3. The conservation of strategic raw materials for international security reasons.

The second type of intergovernmental commodity agreements is concerned essentially with the control and adjustment of excess productive capacity and the management of existing or potential surpluses in given commodities. This type of problem has been the subject of a growing number of agreements throughout the world.

Effects of Intergovernmental Commodity Agreements

The urge for organized action regarding certain primary products is due mainly to the fact that the supply of and the demand for these products are highly inelastic relative to price changes. As a result, a rise or a fall in price will bring about only slight or even perverse adjustments in the quantities supplied or demanded, causing wide and erratic price fluctuations. The price mechanism in a competitive market, therefore, is inadequate since it does not satisfactorily perform its equilibrating function. Moreover, higher prices induce individual producers to expand production in order to increase income and profits while price deterioration may also induce producers to increase production to maintain income. Therefore, whether prices rise or fall, they may generate long-term tendencies for excess capacity and overproduction. Surpluses that accumulate distress the market and darken the outlook; the value of exports declines, especially in countries that are heavily dependent upon agricultural and extractive industries; and purchasing power declines, reducing imports. In this process, international trade suffers and the distressed local conditions soon become an international problem.

When such conditions develop, producers may form a private raw material cartel to deal with the situation. Since cartels usually try to set high prices, however, they encourage expansion of production by outsiders without materially reducing the capacity of their members. Moreover, cartels do not usually possess the necessary financial resources to withhold existing surpluses from the market. This sometimes induces a few of their members to break away from their allotted quotas for economic survival; thus the very foundation of the cartel is threatened. Experience has shown that private cartels in primary products are inadequate to deal with the situation, especially when excess capacity is at the root of the problem. Consequently, the state is often induced to take a hand in support of a private cartel or to resort to independent unilateral action. In either case, the benefits of competition and free enterprise are likely to be sacrificed to the immediate necessity of economic relief to alleviate existing distressed conditions.

Before World War I, national schemes of control of agricultural and raw material exports were attempted without much success. In some instances, the schemes met with utter failure, as in the case of Brazil with its early coffee valorization plans that resulted in the expansion of production in contiguous countries, and in the case of Chile with its natural nitrates that encouraged the development of synthetic substitutes abroad.

The failure of unilateral private and national schemes emphasized the need for a multilateral approach to the problem of the price and market stability for the products of agricultural and extractive industries of the world and opened the way for intergovernmental commodity agreements.

In the 1920's and the 1930's, governments entered into several commodity agreements covering such items as wheat, coffee, sugar, rubber, petroleum, copper, tin, and many other primary commodities. These agreements, however, were mostly directed toward maintaining prices high enough to protect existing producers by keeping surpluses off the market and by allocating markets to reduce competition. They did not generally include all producing or consuming countries and did not provide for an adjustment of existing excess capacity. Consequently, importing countries shifted their demand from controlled to uncontrolled sources of supply. New suppliers entered the field in the uncontrolled countries and thereby increased the already excessive world productive capacity.

Intergovernmental commodity agreements, especially since World War II, have attempted to overcome the weaknesses of prior agreements by including consuming countries, by assuring producers and consumers minimum sales and purchases within agreed-upon quotas and price ranges, and by providing for limitation of production within the confines of export quotas and domestic consumption, or by creating a buffer stock with a fund and a governing body that may intervene in the market to prevent violent price fluctuations. Every commodity agreement does not necessarily include all these provisions even though they are not mutually exclusive.

United States Policy

On the grounds that intergovernmental commodity agreements, like private international cartels, promote monopolistic practices and restrain trade, the United States has been historically opposed to such arrangements except when they were intended for the promotion of public health and morals or for the conservation of natural resources. The attitude of the United States government, however, has since undergone some change in this respect mainly as a result of American experience with government-held surpluses and of the realization that such surpluses, as well as excess capacity, are problems that cannot readily be solved by unilateral action.

The Agricultural Adjustment Act of 1933, as amended, requires that the United States government subsidize farm income by supporting agricultural prices. To accomplish this purpose, the government may buy specified farm products and hold them off the market and/or use production controls and loans (with commodities as collateral) to guarantee minimum prices. Although this program is largely confined to commodities of which the United States is an exporter, it covers a long and growing list of agricultural products—practically all

Ch. 16 / Cartels, State Trading, and Commodity Agreements

major agricultural crops, ranging from "King Cotton" to the lowly peanut.

The repercussions of the United States agricultural price support program have widespread ramifications and affect the world's markets, as well as total world supplies. When the world price of a supported item falls below the United States market price (which cannot fall below the support price), excess production cannot be disposed of abroad and it is sold to the government. American farmers are thus encouraged to overproduce within the limits of their allotted acreage and total world supplies are increased. Accumulated government-held stocks can only be disposed of in a manner that does not interfere with private enterprise. Therefore, American exporters have to be subsidized when foreign prices fall below United States support prices, and imports have to be either excluded or subjected to strict quotas in order to achieve domestic price support. Thus, the means employed to carry out this program are in direct contradiction to established United States international trade policy and are incompatible with the official opposition of the United States to international trade barriers.

Since World War II, the United States has participated in and championed international efforts toward a more orderly and stable production and distribution of primary commodities. It has given its temporary support to commodity agreements under the proposed International Trade Organization and has participated in the International Tin Study Group, the Wool Study Group, the International Cotton Advisory Committee, the Coffee Study Group, and the Rubber Study Group. The United States has also become a member of an international wheat agreement, a sugar agreement, a coffee agreement, a tin agreement and others. Its attitude towards international commodity agreements has changed from early hostility, through benevolent neutrality, to acceptance and participation. It has even expressed interest in an international fund for the stabilization of export receipts in favor of primary-producing countries.

Commodity agreements are now subject to increasing attention by many governments. The European Economic Community has shown a strong desire to negotiate such agreements at the Kennedy Round, and the developing countries pressed hard for more commodity agreements at the United Nations Conference on Trade and Development in 1964.

SUMMARY

1. Cartels, state trading, and intergovernmental commodity agreements are private or public institutions created for the common objective of artificial manipulation of supply and demand in interference with the forces of the market for purposes varying from the maximization of monopolistic profits to the stabilization of prices and markets in the public interest. Their common denominator is a departure from competition, and their ultimate effect is often a misallocation of the scarce resources of the world.

2. Cartels are associations of private competitive producers, with or without government sponsorship, designed to control production and distribution of given products toward the end of increasing profits. They are found mainly in industrial production. Generally they are formed in periods of declining demand characterized by excess productive capacity.

3. The major activities of cartels are: (1) control over prices, (2) allocation of markets, (3) restriction of supply, (4) control over technological changes, and (5) elimination of outside competition.

4. Although cartels may use their economic power to reduce costs of production and distribution and to lower prices to consumers, they usually reduce supply, protect inefficient production, and exact higher prices from the public.

5. International cartels may control the movement of world trade far more skillfully and positively than tariffs, quotas, and possibly exchange controls instituted by national authorities, and thwart national and international economic policies whenever their own interests do not coincide with such policies.

6. International cartels are regarded more or less unfavorably by different nations for different reasons, which makes international control and regulation of their activities a difficult problem.

7. State trading exists when a national government takes over, in part or in whole, directly or through official agencies, the actual trading of the country, especially foreign trading and generally in specific commodities.

8. Under extreme socialism or communism, state trading is an integral part of the economic structure; but, under capitalism, it is ordinarily used as a measure of control during national emergencies and wars. During World War II, state trading was extensively applied by the free world as a security measure. After the War it was utilized as a source of revenue, or as a means for trade control and discrimination, or for protection of domestic industries.

9. Intergovernmental commodity agreements are multilateral arrangements between producing countries or between producing and consuming countries. They are generally aimed at the control and regulation of production and trade in primary commodities. The purpose of these agreements is to overcome the wide and erratic price fluctuations in primary com-

modities that are due to their high inelasticity relative to price changes. Unlike private international cartels, which also attempt to perform this function for the protection of producers, intergovernmental commodity agreements try to protect consumers as well as producers by equilibrating supply with demand at equitable prices.

10. Because cartels, state trading, and intergovernmental commodity agreements are in restraint of trade, the United States has been traditionally opposed to their activities. But American experience with agricultural price-support has led to the realization that excess capacity and price stability in the agricultural sector cannot be solved by unilateral action. As a result, the United States has developed a more conciliatory attitude toward these problems in recent years. Since World War II, the United States has cooperated with a number of international study groups dealing with different commodities and has become a participant in several intergovernmental commodity agreements.

QUESTIONS AND APPLICATIONS

1. Differentiate between a cartel and a combine.
2. What are the various objectives of cartels?
3. Contrast the economic benefits and drawbacks of international cartels.
4. Since the United States government is opposed to international cartels, why has it legalized cartelization in export trade?
5. If international cartels eliminate free competition, why are they favored by many foreign countries?
6. (a) Should cartels be controlled by international means?
   (b) If so, what particular problems would be involved in such control?
7. How does state trading lend itself to trade discrimination? Explain.
8. State trading is used by the Soviets as a political instrument. Discuss.
9. State trading by the Soviets lends itself to monopsony, but the same cannot be true of American state trading. Explain.
10. In what ways may state trading be used to defeat foreign monopolistic practices?
11. Intergovernmental commodity agreements are a departure from free competition. Nevertheless, the United States is now a party to several such agreements, without having renounced its official opposition to restraint of trade. Discuss.

SELECTED READINGS

Borkin, Joseph, and Charles A. Welsh. *Germany's Master Plan.* New York: Duell, Sloan & Pearce, 1933. Chapter 16.

Brewster, Kingman, Jr. *Antitrust and American Business Abroad.* New York: McGraw-Hill Book Co., 1958.

Edwards, Corwin D. "International Cartels as Obstacles to International Trade," *American Economic Review,* Supplement (March, 1944).

Edwards, Corwin D. et al. *A Cartel Policy for the United States.* New York: Columbia University Press, 1945.

Hexner, Erwin. *International Cartels.* Chapel Hill: University of North Carolina Press, 1946.

Mason, Edward S. *Controlling World Trade: Cartels and Commodity Agreements.* New York: McGraw-Hill Book Company, Inc., 1946. Part I deals with cartels and Part II with intergovernmental commodity agreements.

Stockings, George W. and Myron W. Watkins. *Cartels in Action.* New York: Twentieth Century Fund, 1947.

——————————. *Monopoly and Free Enterprise.* New York: Twentieth Century Fund, 1951.

Towle, Lawrence W. *International Trade and Commercial Policy,* 2d ed. New York: Harper & Brothers, 1956. Chapter 27 deals with international cartels, Chapter 24 with state trading, and Chapter 28 with international commodity agreements.

United Nations. *Restrictive Business Practices.* Supplements No. 11 and 11A. New York: United Nations, 1953.

Wasserman, M. J., and Chas. W. Hultman. *Modern International Economics.* New York: Simmons-Boardman Publishing Corporation, 1962. Chapter 20.

CHAPTER 17

INTERNATIONAL ARRANGEMENTS TO
LIBERALIZE TRADE AND PAYMENTS

Since World War II, several international measures have been undertaken to liberalize trade and payments between nations. Plans for the creation of a liberal, multilateral system of world trade were started while the war was still in progress. Initiated for the most part by the United States, these plans envisaged the close economic cooperation of all nations in the fields of international trade, payments, and investment. At the time, it was widely believed that such cooperation, formalized by agreements and implemented by international organizations, would avoid the mistakes of the past and lay the cornerstones for a progressive world economy. The two notable achievements of this wartime planning were the International Monetary Fund and the International Bank for Reconstruction and Development. The first institution was to insure the free convertibility of currencies; the second was to supplement and stimulate the international flow of private capital.

Once the war had ended, it soon became apparent that the difficulties of postwar reconstruction in Europe and elsewhere had been greatly underestimated. The weakness of the United Kingdom was dramatically highlighted by its failure to restore the convertibility of the pound in the summer of 1947, despite the assistance of the Anglo-American loan negotiated the previous year. Attention shifted from the now distant goal of a global system of multilateral trade to the immediate threat posed by Western Europe's economic distress and by the spread of communism. The end of ambitious international planning was symbolized by the refusal of the United States Congress in 1950 to ratify the treaty establishing an International Trade Organization (ITO). As we shall see, the failure of the ITO was offset somewhat by the existence of the General Agreement on Tariffs and Trade. In the 1950's and 1960's new arrangements to liberalize trade and payments have been regional in nature and have focused on Europe.

In this chapter we shall examine the General Agreement on Tariffs and Trade, the International Monetary Fund, and the several regional arrangements intended to liberalize trade and payments. The International Bank for Reconstruction and Development, which is not primarily concerned with the liberalization of trade and payments, is treated in Chapter 20.

GENERAL AGREEMENT ON TARIFFS AND TRADE

The effects of the failure of the ITO on international cooperation in commercial policy were considerably softened by the rise to prominence of the *General Agreement on Tariffs and Trade,* known as GATT.[1] GATT was an almost casual offshoot of the international conference held at Geneva in 1947 to consider a draft charter for the ITO. There the United States initiated six months of continual negotiations with 22 other countries that led to commitments to bind or lower 45,000 different tariff rates within the framework of principles and rules of procedure laid down by GATT.

Technically, GATT was viewed by the United States administration as a trade agreement that came under the provisions of the Reciprocal Trade Agreements Act and, hence, did not require the approval of Congress. It was considered a provisional agreement that would lapse when the ITO was established to take over its functions. In the interim, GATT was to serve as a token of America's willingness to implement a liberal trade policy and thereby gain the adherence of other countries to the projected ITO. GATT began its "provisional" existence on January 1, 1948, when eight of its contracting parties, including the United States, put into effect the tariff concessions negotiated at Geneva.[2]

---

[1] The ITO Charter was signed by representatives of 54 countries at Havana, Cuba, on March 24, 1948. The Charter was an ambitious document covering not only commercial policy but also such topics as employment, economic development, state trading, cartels, and intergovernmental commodity agreements. The Charter has never been ratified by the signatory states; late in 1950, the United States Department of State announced that it would no longer press for Congressional approval.

[2] A signatory of GATT is known as a *contracting party*. When the signatories act collectively in affairs of GATT, they are referred to as *contracting parties* since, legally, GATT is not an organization. For convenience of exposition, however, we shall frequently use the term "member" to refer to participation in GATT.

Major Provisions of GATT

The General Agreement is a lengthy document containing 38 articles and numerous annexes. The tariff schedules listing the thousands of concessions that have been negotiated by the contracting parties are also part of the Agreement. Despite its complexity, GATT comprises four basic elements:

1. The rule of nondiscrimination in trade relations between the participating countries.
2. Commitments to observe the negotiated tariff concessions.
3. Prohibitions against the use of quantitative restrictions (quotas) on exports and imports.
4. Special provisions to promote the trade of developing countries.

The remaining provisions of GATT are concerned with exceptions to these general principles, trade measures other than tariffs and quotas, and sundry procedural matters.

Tariffs. GATT obligates each contracting party to accord nondiscriminatory, most-favored-nation treatment to all other contracting parties with respect to import and export duties (including allied charges), customs regulations, and internal taxes and regulations. An exception to the rule of nondiscrimination is made in the case of well-known tariff preferences, such as those between the countries of the British Commonwealth. No new preferences may be created, however, and existing preferences may not be increased. Frontier traffic, customs unions, and free trade areas are exempted from the general rule of nondiscrimination.

GATT legalizes the schedules of tariff concessions negotiated by the contracting parties and commits each contracting party to their observance. An escape clause, however, allows any contracting party to withdraw or modify a tariff concession (or other obligation) if, as a result of the tariff concession (or obligation), there is such an increase in imports as to cause, or threaten to cause, serious injury to domestic producers of like or directly competitive products. When a member country uses the escape clause, it must consult with other member countries as to remedies; if agreement is not reached, those countries may withdraw equivalent concessions.

Quantitative Restrictions. GATT sets forth a general rule prohibiting the use of quantitative import and export restrictions. There are, however, several exceptions to this rule. The four most important exceptions pertain to agriculture, the balance of payments, economic development, and national security.

The Agreement sanctions the use of import restrictions on any agricultural or fisheries product where restrictions are necessary for the enforcement of government programs in marketing, production control, or the removal of surpluses. This exception is especially important to the United States which has placed import quotas on several agricultural products.

GATT also permits a member to apply import restrictions in order to safeguard its balance of payments when there is an imminent threat, or actual occurrence, of a serious decline in its monetary reserves or when its monetary reserves are very low. The member must consult with the contracting parties with respect to the continuation or intensification of such restrictions. Representatives of GATT must also consult with the International Monetary Fund when dealing with problems of monetary reserves, the balance of payments, and foreign exchange practices. Members of GATT are not to frustrate the intent of GATT by exchange action nor the intent of the Fund Agreement by trade restrictions. A country that adheres to GATT but is not a member of the Fund must conclude a special exchange agreement with the *contracting parties.*

GATT recognizes the special position of the developing countries and allows such countries to use nondiscriminatory import quotas to encourage infant industries. Prior approval, however, must be obtained from the collective GATT membership.

A member of GATT may use trade controls for purposes of national security. The strategic controls over United States exports (including the embargo on trade with Communist China) come under this exception.

In addition to these four major exceptions, there are many of lesser importance. For example, members may use trade restrictions to protect public morals, to implement sanitary regulations, to prevent deceptive trade practices, and to protect patents and copyrights.

All quantitative restrictions permitted by GATT are to be applied in accordance with the most-favored-nation principle. Import licenses may not specify that goods be imported from a certain country.

Special Provisions to Promote the Trade of Developing Countries. In 1965 the contracting parties added a new Part IV—Trade and Development—to the General Agreement in recognition of the need for a rapid and sustained expansion of the export earnings of the less-developed member countries. Under the terms of the three articles comprising Part IV, the developed countries agree to undertake the following positive action "to the fullest extent possible": (1) give high priority to the reduction and elimination of barriers to products currently or potentially of particular export interest to less-developed contracting parties; (2) refrain from introducing or increasing customs duties or nontariff import barriers on such products; and (3) refrain from imposing new internal taxes that hamper significantly the consumption of primary products produced in the developing countries, and accord high priority to the reduction or elimination of such taxes. In addition, the developed countries agree not to expect reciprocity for commitments made by them in trade negotiations to reduce or remove tariffs or other barriers to the trade of less-developed contracting parties.

In return, the developing countries commit themselves to take "appropriate action" to implement the provisions of Part IV for the benefit of the trade of other less-developed contracting parties.

The concluding article, Article XXXVIII, pledges the contracting parties to collaborate jointly to take action in a number of ways to further the objectives of Part IV. A new Committee on Trade and Development is charged with keeping under review the implementation of the provisions of Part IV.

Other Provisions. Many other substantive matters are covered by the provisions of GATT: national treatment of internal taxation and regulation, motion picture films, antidumping and countervailing duties, customs valuation, customs formalities, marks of origin, subsidies, state trading, and the publication and administration of trade regulations. The intention of most of these provisions is to eliminate concealed protection and/or discrimination in international trade.

Several articles of GATT deal with procedural matters. In meetings, each member is entitled to one vote; and, unless otherwise specified, decisions are to be taken by majority vote. A two-thirds majority vote is required to waive any obligation imposed on a member by the General Agreement. Articles also cover consultation procedures and the settlement of disputes between members.

Activities of GATT

The members of GATT meet in regular annual sessions and special tariff conferences. An Intersessional Committee deals with matters between sessions and prepares the agenda for each session.

In addition, intersessional working groups have been appointed at regular sessions to report on specific topics at subsequent sessions.

Adding further to the continuous influence of GATT has been the practice of member governments to consult with each other before the regular sessions. The membership has obtained a secretariat from the United Nations that, among other things, publishes an annual report. In these and other ways, GATT has behaved like an international organization and, as a matter of fact, has been more effective than some legitimate organizations.

The main activities of GATT fall into three categories: (1) tariff bargaining, (2) quantitative restrictions, and (3) settlement of disputes.

Tariff Bargaining. The parties to GATT have participated in six tariff conferences to negotiate mutual tariff concessions.[3] Most of these conferences have lasted about six months and have involved scores of bilateral agreements and thousands of tariff concessions. The initial conference at Geneva negotiated 45,000 different tariff rates, and today the schedules of GATT include well over 60,000 rates on products that make up more than half the world's trade. All of these rates have been either reduced or bound against any increase in the future.

The magnitude of this accomplishment is unprecedented in tariff history; it represents a new approach to the task of lowering tariff barriers. Before World War II the most successful attempt to reduce tariffs by reciprocal bargaining was the trade agreements program of the United States. That program was limited, however, by its bilateral nature. GATT has overcome this disability by applying multilaterally the same principles and procedures that underlay the bilateral trade agreements of the 1930's.

Briefly, tariff negotiations at a GATT conference are conducted along the following lines. Each participating country prepares beforehand lists of products whose duties it is prepared to negotiate with other members of the conference. Actual negotiations are carrried on by *pairs* of countries in accordance with the "chief supplier" principle, that is, each country negotiates with another country on tariff

---

[3] GATT launched its seventh, and most ambitious, tariff conference in May, 1964, after an entire year of preliminary negotiations. Known familiarly as the "Kennedy Round," this conference intends to negotiate not only on industrial tariffs (as did previous conferences) but also on nontariff trade barriers, agricultural products, and the products of less-developed countries. The goal of the Conference is a 50 percent across-the-board, linear reduction of tariff levels.

rates for those products that are mainly supplied by the latter country. Thus there is a great number of bilateral negotiations at each conference. For example, at Geneva in 1947 there were 123 pairs of nations that completed negotiations, and at Annecy, 147.[4]

The results of the round of tariff negotiations at each conference are not finalized until all of them are gathered into a single master agreement signed by the participating countries. The concessions in the master agreement then apply to trade between all members of GATT. In this way, each member receives the benefits of every tariff concession and becomes a party to every tariff agreement.

GATT has brilliantly overcome the difficulties of a purely bilateral trade agreements program—the reluctance of nations to lower or bind tariff duties unless a large number of their trading partners are taking similar action; and the time-consuming negotiation of individual trade agreements, each containing its own code of conduct and other provisions.[5] While it is negotiating, each member knows that other members are also negotiating and that the results of those negotiations will accrue to its benefit. Countries are, therefore, apt to be more generous because the prospects of gain are greater. Moreover, one set of rules applies to every tariff concession and it is much more comprehensive in scope than would be possible in the case of individual bilateral agreements. GATT has also created an environment conducive to tariff bargaining, and it has often induced countries to bargain when they preferred to stand pat.

The superior effectiveness of the multilateral approach of GATT to the bilateral approach of the 1930's is clearly observable in the experience of the United States. Between 1934 and 1945 this country negotiated trade agreements with 29 countries; but, in a single GATT conference, that at Geneva in 1947, it completed negotiations with 22 other countries. Negotiations under GATT have brought about a more rapid and deeper percentage cut in American tariff rates than negotiations in the 1930's. The United States Tariff Commission has estimated that trade agreements have lowered the ad valorem equivalent of the American tariff from 24.4 percent to 17.9 percent over

---

[4] The number of possible pairs at most of the later conferences was 561 since there were 34 countries in GATT. In 1955 Japan was admitted on a qualified basis and, in the fall of 1957, Ghana and Malaya entered GATT to raise the total membership to 37. Since then, membership has grown rapidly: in 1965 there were 66 contracting parties plus 13 countries linked to GATT by provisional accession or other forms of association. Most of the new members are developing countries.

[5] The experience of the 1930's showed that the abandonment of protective import quotas though bilateral bargaining was virtually impossible.

the period 1934 to 1945 and from 17.9 percent to 12.2 percent over the period 1945 to 1953.[6] The drastic fall in rates during the second period was due entirely to negotiations under GATT.

GATT has been extremely successful in lowering and binding tariff duties. Because of GATT, there has been no repetition of the tariff wars that followed World War I. To be sure, the most recent tariff conferences have not accomplished as much as the earlier ones. This reflects the revival of protectionism in many countries, and the fact that with a lessening of other restrictions tariffs have become more important in the regulation of trade. When all things are considered, however, the achievements of GATT in this field are without parallel in the long checkered history of commercial policy.

Quantitative Restrictions. Until 1959 GATT made only slow progress toward the elimination of import restrictions (quotas). The majority of GATT members took advantage of the balance of payments exception to the general prohibition of import quotas. The restoration of currency convertibility by western European countries at the very end of 1958 broke this logjam. At the Tokyo session of GATT in November, 1959, member governments reaffirmed their intention to abolish balance of payments restrictions as soon as possible. Since then, all the major trading countries have abandoned quantitative import restrictions that were previously justified on grounds of a weak balance of payments or low monetary reserves. The problem has, therefore, shifted to the elimination of residual import restrictions no longer justified under the provisions of GATT, particularly those related to agricultural products.

Countries that continue to apply import restrictions for balance of payments reasons are required to hold periodical consultations with GATT. As a result, many countries have lowered or eliminated their restrictions or have removed objectionable features. Consultations are also mandatory when a member country introduces new restrictions or substantially modifies existing restrictions.[7]

Perhaps the greatest contribution of GATT toward liberalizing import restrictions lies in its role as a forum for frank discussion

---

[6] United States Tariff Commission, *Effect of Trade Agreement Concessions on United States Tariff Levels Based on Imports in 1952* (Washington, D. C.: Government Printing Office, September, 1953).

[7] In October, 1964, Great Britain imposed a 15 percent surcharge on imports from all sources, with certain specified exceptions. This measure violated the General Agreement which allows the use of import quotas for balance of payments reasons but not the use of tariffs. In subsequent consultations with Great Britain, GATT pressed for the early removal of the surtax without discrimination. In April, 1965, the British government lowered the surtax to 10 percent.

between member countries. National measures in the field of commercial policy are now open to public scrutiny and criticism. Moreover, the close contact brought about by regular meetings, tariff conferences, and intersessional activities has helped to breed a common international viewpoint on trade policy. Hence member governments take GATT into account when contemplating measures to protect their balance of payments and feel it necessary to explain and justify any action that is not in accord with the spirit of the Agreement.

Settlement of Disputes. One of the most striking but least publicized of GATT's accomplishments is the settlement of trade disputes between members. Historically, trade disputes have been matters strictly between the disputants; there was no third party to which they might appeal for a just solution. As a consequence, trade disputes often went unresolved for years, all the while embittering international relations. When disputes were settled in the past, it was usually a case of the weaker country giving way to the stronger. GATT has improved matters tremendously by adopting complaint procedures and by affording through its periodic meetings a world stage on which an aggrieved nation may voice its complaint.

A large number of disputes has been resolved by bilateral consultations without ever coming before the collective membership. The mere presence of GATT was probably helpful in these instances. Thus the British government repealed a requirement forbidding the manufacture of pure Virginia cigarettes when the United States protested the requirement as a violation of GATT.

When a dispute is not settled bilaterally, it may be taken by the complainant country to the collective membership at the next regular meeting on the ground that the treatment accorded to the commerce of the complainant country by the other disputant is impairing or nullifying benefits received under the Agreement. A panel on complaints hears the disputants, deliberates, and drafts a report. The report is then acted upon by the membership. In this way GATT resolved an extremely bitter disagreement between Pakistan and India.

In the event that the GATT recommendation is not observed, the aggrieved party may be authorized to suspend the application of certain of its obligations to the trade of the other party. Thus the Netherlands was allowed to place a limitation on wheat flour from the United States because of the damage caused its exports by United States dairy quotas.

The most dramatic trade dispute erupted in 1963 between the United States and the European Economic Community. In the middle of 1962 the EEC countries sharply raised their duties on poultry imports which came mostly from the United States. In Germany, the biggest United States poultry market, the duty was increased from 5 cents to 12.5 cents per pound. As a result United States poultry exports to the EEC tumbled 64 percent in 1963. The charges and countercharges between this country and the EEC became known as the "chicken war." When bilateral negotiations between the two parties ended in a deadlock, a special panel of GATT experts was asked to arbitrate the question of damages to United States poultry exports. In October, 1963, the panel ruled that the United States had experienced a loss of $26 million (the United States had claimed damages of $46 million while the EEC put the figure at $19 million) and could withdraw concessions to the EEC of that amount if the parties could not reach a settlement. Both sides accepted the ruling but were unable to resolve the chicken war. In January, 1965, the United States imposed the high 1930 duties on imports of brandy, trucks, dextrine, and potato starch in retaliation for the EEC poultry import duties. This action affected EEC exports to the United States valued at $25.4 million in 1962. (Compensatory tariff concessions were later made to third countries which also exported these products to this country.) In this instance the GATT settlement machinery did not succeed in modifying the EEC duties on poultry, but it did limit the United States retaliation and prevent any counter-retaliation by the EEC.

Organization for Trade Cooperation (OTC)

Notwithstanding its significant accomplishments, GATT suffers from a serious drawback—it is a provisional agreement that may be dissolved at any time. Concerned over this weakness, the member countries in 1955 negotiated an agreement on an Organization for Trade Cooperation (OTC) that would administer GATT. The object of the OTC is to place GATT on a permanent footing. As an international organization with its own secretariat and facilities, the OTC would carry on the business of GATT more expeditiously than the present makeshift arrangements. It would sponsor tariff negotiations, consult with members on their use of quantitative restrictions, help settle trade disputes, and serve as a forum for the discussion of problems arising out of international trade.

Facing the determined opposition of protectionist interests, the establishment of the OTC still awaits the approval of the United States Congress.[8] Passage of the OTC by Congress would go far to convince other nations that the United States sincerely desires a liberal, multilateral trading system embracing the entire free world. In the meantime, GATT continues to expand its activities, most notably in the field of trade and economic development.

INTERNATIONAL MONETARY FUND

The Articles of Agreement of the International Monetary Fund (IMF) and those of the International Bank for Reconstruction and Development (IBRD) were signed by 44 nations on July 22, 1944, at Bretton Woods, New Hampshire. The Fund began operations on March 1, 1947.[9]

Purposes of IMF

The purposes of IMF are clearly set forth in Aritcle I of its Articles of Agreement:

> 1. To promote international monetary cooperation through a permanent institution which provides the machinery for consultation and collaboration on international monetary problems.
>
> 2. To facilitate the expansion and balanced growth of international trade, and to contribute thereby to the promotion and maintenance of high levels of employment and real income and to the development of the productive resources of all members as primary objectives of economic policy.
>
> 3. To promote exchange stability, to maintain orderly exchange arrangements among members, and to avoid competitive exchange depreciation.
>
> 4. To assist in the establishment of a multilateral system of payments in respect of current transactions between members and in the elimination of foreign exchange restrictions which hamper the growth of world trade.
>
> 5. To give confidence to members by making the Fund's resources available to them under adequate safeguards, thus providing them with opportunity to correct maladjustments in their balance of payments without resorting to measures destructive of national or international balance of payments of members.

---

[8] Technically, the OTC cannot come into existence without the approval of the United States since the OTC agreement must be ratified by contracting parties accounting for 85 percent of the external trade of contracting parties and the United States accounts for more than 15 percent.

[9] The IBRD is discussed in Chapter 20.

Resources of the Fund

The resources of the IMF come from the gold and currency subscriptions of its hundred-odd member countries.[10] Upon entering the Fund each country is allotted a quota in accordance with its relative economic importance. Twenty-five percent of a country's quota must be paid to the Fund in gold and the remainder in the country's own currency.[11] In April, 1958, the quotas of all member countries aggregated $9.09 billion, of which $1.72 billion had been paid to the Fund in gold. In 1959 the need for more liquidity in a rapidly expanding world economy led to a general increase of 50 percent in the size of quotas. In 1964 Fund quotas aggregated about $16 billion, and the Fund's gold holdings (including claims on gold) amounted to $3.1 billion.[12] The largest quota is subscribed by the United States (over $4.1 billion); the next largest, by the United Kingdom (almost $2 billion).

The size of a country's quota is significant in two respects. First, it determines, approximately, the voting power of a member's executive director. Thus, the executive director of the United States has 23.1 percent of the voting power of the Executive Directors; the executive director of the United Kingdom, 11 percent. This gives these two countries a dominant voice in the operation of the Fund. Second, as explained in the following section, the size of a country's quota determines the overall amount that it may draw from the resources of the Fund.

Use of the Fund's Resources

A member country is entitled to buy from the Fund, with its own currency, the currency of another member subject to the following conditions:

---

[10] Almost all countries of the free world are now members of the Fund. No country in the Soviet bloc is presently a member, however, although there are no restrictions on entry. Czechoslovakia joined the Fund before that country was taken over by a Communist regime in 1948, but withdrew from membership in December, 1954. Cuba withdrew from membership in 1964. In 1963-64, 18 countries became members of the Fund, bringing total membership to 102 countries.

[11] When a country's gold reserves are low, it is permitted to join the Fund without full payment of its gold subscription, using its own currency as a substitute. Full payment is expected, however, when the country's gold reserves become adequate.

[12] Quotas are calculated in United States dollars. The dollar equivalents of nondollar currencies are determined by their respective par values. In 1965 the member countries agreed to raise quotas by a further 25 percent, with larger increases for certain countries, such as West Germany. When finally approved, this will expand the Fund's resources to about $21 billion.

1. The member desires to buy a currency in order to make currency payments consistent with the provisions of the Articles of Agreement.

2. The Fund has not given notice that its holdings of the desired currency are scarce.

3. The proposed purchase does not cause the Fund's holdings of the purchasing member's currency to increase by over 25 percent of its quota during the twelve-month period ending on the date of such purchase nor to exceed 200 percent of its basic quota.

4. The Fund has not previously declared that the member desiring to purchase is ineligible to use the resources of the Fund.

To illustrate, suppose that Norway wishes to buy dollars from the Fund against its own currency and has not yet utilized any of its drawing rights. Assuming the conditions outlined above are met, Norway will be permitted to buy dollars up to 25 percent of its quota, that is, 25 percent of $100 million, or $25 million. If Norway takes full advantage of this drawing right, the Fund will then hold Norwegian currency equal to 100 percent of Norway's quota—the original subscription equal to 75 percent of its quota plus the 25 percent now sold to the Fund for dollars. Providing the drawing conditions continue to be met, Norway will be able to purchase from the Fund an additional 100 million United States dollars (or the equivalent in other currencies) over the next four years. At that point Norway's drawing rights will be exhausted, since the Fund will hold Norwegian currency equal to 200 per cent of Norway's quota.[13]

In practice, the Fund has freely allowed member countries to purchase other currencies up to the first 25 percent of their quotas (often called the *gold tranche*). It has also waived the twelve-month requirement in many instances. The Fund will not permit a country to draw beyond 25 percent of its quota, however, unless convinced that the country in question is following policies directed toward the eventual achievement of convertibility or the avoidance of exchange restrictions. Convertibility is a principal objective of the Fund and it attempts to employ its resources accordingly.

The IMF also encourages liberal exchange policies by negotiating *stand-by agreements* with interested member countries. Through these

---

[13] This assumes that no other member country has purchased Norwegian currency from the Fund. If, for example, the Fund has sold Norwegian currency equal to 10 percent of Norway's quota, then Norway will be permitted to purchase additional dollars equal to 10 percent of its quota. Then the Fund will hold Norwegian currency equal to 200 percent of Norway's quota and drawing rights will be exhausted.

agreements, member countries receive the Fund's guarantee that they will be allowed to draw on the Fund for the currency or currencies covered by the agreement within a specified period of time. To qualify for a stand-by agreement, a country must satisfy the usual drawing conditions. By enabling a member to count definitely on aid from the Fund, if it proves necessary at sometime in the future, stand-by agreements lend strength to national policies consistent with the Fund's purposes.

In addition to drawings under these general arrangements, a country may apply for a special drawing to obtain compensatory financing for a temporary decline in its export earnings. Intended to assist developing countries, such special drawings will not normally exceed 25 percent of a country's quota, but they may bring the Fund's holdings of a country's currency over the limit of twice its quota.

Revolving Nature of the Fund's Resources

The resources of the Fund are intended to supplement the reserves of a country when it is faced with a temporary deficit in the balance of payments. Hence the Fund is supposed to provide only *short-term* financial assistance that will be repaid by the borrowing country within the near future. Only if the Fund's resources revolve rapidly, can they fulfill their function as an international reserve; if they become frozen through long-term arrangements between the Fund and member countries, they will not be available to meet new demands. The Fund is not a source of capital like the International Bank, and no member country should look to it for more than stop-gap compensatory financing of an external deficit.

The IMF has adopted the rule that currency purchased from it by member countries should not remain outstanding for more than three to five years. A schedule of charges on the use of the Fund's resources puts teeth into this rule. The Fund also places pressure on a country to repurchase its currency with gold or an acceptable currency through a system of mandatory consultations.

Exchange Rates

Besides providing short-term financial assistance to its members, the Fund is also concerned with exchange rate policies. Upon entering the Fund, a country must submit a par value of its currency expressed in terms of gold or in terms of the United States dollar of the weight and fineness in effect on July 1, 1944. All exchange transactions between member countries are to be effected at a rate that diverges not more than 1 percent from the par value of the respective currencies.

A member may change the par value of its currency only to correct a *fundamental* disequilibrium in its balance of payments and only after consultation with the Fund. If the Fund objects to the change but the member nevertheless goes ahead with it, the Fund may declare that member ineligible to use its resources.[14] Although the Fund may object to a proposed change in the par value of a currency, it cannot formally propose a change of its own accord. These provisions envisage, therefore, a system of stable exchange rates with an occasional depreciation (or possibly appreciation) to remove a persistent disequilibrium in the balance of payments.

Exchange Control

Article VIII of the Agreement forbids members to restrict current (account) payments or to discriminate in their currency practices without the approval of the Fund. Members are also obligated to maintain the convertibility of foreign-held balances acquired or used in connection with current transactions. Thus Article VIII clearly outlaws exchange control over international payments for merchandise and services. On the other hand, Article VI allows members to control capital movements as long as current transactions remain unaffected.

There are two exceptions to the provisions of Article VIII. One exception occurs when the Fund declares a currency to be scarce because the demand for the currency in question threatens the Fund's ability to supply it. A scarce currency declaration authorizes member countries to impose exchange control over all transactions in the scarce currency. The scarce currency provision explicitly recognizes that free convertibility cannot be sustained if most countries have persistent deficits with the same surplus country for, in that event, multilateral settlement of the deficits is out of the question. This provision also applies pressure on the surplus country to take remedial measures in order to avoid discrimination against its trade.

The most important exception to the provisions of Article VIII, however, is found in the provisions of Article XIV. This article allows

---

[14] If the proposed change, together with all previous changes, whether increases or decreases, does not exceed 10 percent of the initial par value of the member's currency, the Fund shall raise no objection.

a member country to retain exchange restrictions on current international transactions in effect when that country entered the Fund. Moreover, these restrictions may be adapted to changing circumstances in order to deal with balance of payments difficulties. The decision to abandon exchange restrictions permitted under Article XIV is left to the member country, but it is supposed to occur when such restrictions are no longer necessary to settle the balance of payments without undue dependence on the Fund's resources. Once a member abolishes its exchange control over current payments and accepts the obligations of Article VIII, it cannot reimpose similar exchange restrictions without the approval of the Fund.

Article XIV was conceived as a "transitional arrangement" that would not be necessary once the member countries had overcome the problems of readjustment immediately following the War. Events turned out otherwise, however, and it was not until 1961 that the major countries in Western Europe were able to accept the obligations of Article VIII. The last big trading country, Japan, came under Article VIII in 1964. The remaining Article XIV countries are obliged to consult annually with the Fund on the continuance of exchange restrictions; but, as we noted earlier, the Fund has no power to decree their abolition. Nor do the Articles of Agreement specify the duration of the transitional period.

Activities of the Fund

From the start of its operations on March 1, 1947, through the fiscal year ending April 30, 1964, the IMF sold $7.47 billion of currencies to 54 member countries, and unused standby credits amounted to more than $6 billion. During the same period member countries repurchased $5.76 billion of their own currencies, leaving $1.71 billion of currency sales (drawings) outstanding at the end of April, 1964.[15]

Most of the Fund's lending activity has been crowded into the years since 1956-57 when the Suez crisis compelled many countries to come to the Fund for drawings and standby credits.[16] The United Kingdom obtained an immediate drawing of $561 million and a stand-by credit of $738 million—a total of more than 100 percent of its quota at that time. Total purchases by member countries in 1957

---

[15] International Monetary Fund, *Annual Report* (1964), pp. 16-18.

[16] In 1947 eight European countries drew a total of $467 million from the Fund; then the Marshall Plan took over the job of compensatory financing. In the five years 1951-55, repurchases exceeded new drawings in every year, and at the end of 1955 the net amount of outstanding drawings was only $234 million.

amounted to $1.1 billion. In the fiscal year ending April 30, 1964, total purchases reached the extraordinary sum of $2.2 billion plus almost $2 billion in stand-by credits.

Before May, 1958, over nine tenths of the drawings were made in United States dollars, but in the three years 1961-63 this fraction dropped to about one third. Indeed, during those years dollar repayments exceeded new dollar drawings by $300 million. These changes reflected, of course, the passing of the "dollar shortage" and the arrival of the "dollar glut" created by big United States payments deficits.

After a long period of relative quiescence, therefore, the Fund has become an important source of short-term compensatory financing for its member countries. The expansion of its resources has allowed the Fund to continue this active role in international finance.

In addition to acting as an international reserve, the Fund has also kept close watch over the exchange practices of its members. Since 1952, it has consulted annually with all Article XIV countries on the relaxation of exchange controls. It has sought to persuade countries to relax restrictions whenever conditions warranted, to abandon discriminatory currency practices, and to unify multiple exchange rates into a single rate. Toward these ends the Fund has given technical advice and assistance whenever requested, and its missions have visited many member countries. Through its publications and the speeches of its officials, the Fund has persistently warned against inflation and other sources of balance of payments disequilibrium and has urged member countries to adopt corrective policies consistent with the Fund's purposes.

Evaluation of the Fund

The International Monetary Fund was originally intended to carry out its functions in a world economy enjoying a substantial degree of overall equilibrium and free of any persistent maladjustments, such as the dollar shortage. In such an economy, countries would adjust to temporary deficits in their balance of payments by resorting to their own reserves and, if necessary, to the resources of the Fund. Free convertibility would be maintained by all countries and exchange rates would be altered, after consultation with the Fund, only to correct a fundamental disequilibrium. In this way, the advantages of the gold standard—convertibility and stable exchange rates—would be gained while an occasional exchange depreciation would maintain equilibrium without the disadvantage of internal deflation. More specifically, the Fund was conceived as an antidote to the conditions of the 1930's. In those years convertibility was maintained between the dollar and the pound sterling (the key trading currencies), but its effects were compromised by disorderly exchange practices, such as competitive depreciation and the spread of exchange control to central and eastern Europe and to Latin America.

In the light of these observations, it is not surprising that the Fund could not fulfill its intended functions in the first decade of its existence. During those years nondollar countries showed persistent payments deficits and continued to restrict dollar payments. Moreover, unlike the 1930's, inflation rather than depression was the principal obstacle to external stability after the War; and, with few exceptions, exchange rates were controlled to avert depreciation. During this period of restrictions and nonconvertibility the Fund was mostly a bystander and little use was made of its resources. This passive role ended abruptly with the Suez crisis in 1956-57.

We can now see in retrospect that the Suez crisis coincided with the end of the dollar shortage—in 1958 the United States balance of payments suffered the first of a continuing series of big deficits which replaced the dollar shortage with a dollar glut. When called upon at the end of 1956, the Fund quickly responded with compensatory financial assistance that was needed to overcome the trade disruptions and fears of the time. The resumption of convertibility by western European countries at the end of 1958 carried with it the widespread abandonment of exchange controls on current transactions and later, on capital transactions. With the accession of Japan to Article VIII in 1964, the Fund came close to achieving one of its basic purposes—the elimination of exchange controls for the bulk of world trade.

The return of convertibility, however, brought another problem in its wake—sudden, massive movements of speculative and flight capital among the financial centers of North America and Western Europe. In the 1960's such capital movements have exacerbated international payments disequilibrium (notably in the case of Great Britain) and at times have strained the Fund's resources. To meet this problem the Fund has increased its resources and has made arrangements (known as the General Arrangements to Borrow) to borrow some $6 billion in the currencies of the ten major trading countries, if and when needed. Despite these welcome additions to international reserves, there has arisen a spirited controversy regarding the present adequacy of the international monetary system and the plans for its reform. We shall look at this controversy and the international financial role of the Fund in Chapter 22.

In the past decade the International Monetary Fund has contributed mightily to the stability and growth of international trade and finance. Apart from its signal successes in the promotion of currency convertibility and in compensatory financing, the Fund has also provided a meeting place for the monetary authorities of the free world that has encouraged international consultation and an understanding of each other's problems. Perhaps of greater importance than anything else, the International Monetary Fund has become the conscience of its members in matters pertaining to international monetary relations. Increasingly, nations feel compelled to justify any actions incompatible with the objectives of the Fund. It is doubtful that this attitude would have developed in the absence of the Fund; it is a hopeful sign for the future.

REGIONAL TRADE AND PAYMENTS ARRANGEMENTS

GATT and the IMF are global measures to liberalize trade and payments; they are open to the membership of all nations; and, as we have observed, they actually embrace all the important trading nations of the free world. Alongside of these global attempts to restore a multilateral system of world trade characterized by currency convertibility, orderly exchange rates, low tariffs, and the absence of trade restrictions, there are a variety of regional trade and payments arrangements that involve, in one way or another, efforts to remove obstacles to trade among nations. The motivations behind the creation of these regional institutions and the full range of their purposes vary widely, but in all cases the participating countries believe they can attain their common objectives only through regional action.

Regional trade and payments arrangements have borne fruit mainly in Western Europe where a high degree of economic interdependence and many common trade and payments relationships with the rest of the world have stimulated intimate forms of economic cooperation and even economic integration. The most important of these arrangements are the Sterling Area, the Organization for European Economic Cooperation (OEEC), the European Economic Community (EEC), and the European Free Trade Association (EFTA). In 1961 the OEEC was transformed into the Organization of Economic Cooperation and Development (OECD) that embraces not only the former OEEC members but the United States, Canada, and Japan as well.

Latin America has also developed regional trading arrangements although their economic basis is much less favorable than in Western Europe. In 1958 five countries started a Central American Common Market (CACM), and in 1961 nine other countries set up the Latin American Free Trade Association (LAFTA). Discussions of economic integration have occurred in the Middle East, Africa, and Asia, but no important steps have been taken to that end.

The United States has supported regional arrangements in Western Europe for both political and economic reasons. Political support is based on the assumption that economic cooperation and integration in Western Europe will strengthen the free world in its struggle with the Communist powers. Economic support comes from the assumption that European regional arrangements contribute to the evolution of the global trade and payments system envisaged by GATT and the IMF. Both assumptions were unquestioned by United States officials in the 1950's, but events in the 1960's have introduced some doubts, particularly with respect to the European Economic Community. United States support for trade associations in Latin America derives mainly from the belief that they will accelerate the economic development of the member countries, together with the expectation that these associations will shun shortsighted autarkic policies and instead realize their objectives within a global trading system.

In this chapter we are interested in the influence of regional arrangements on the liberalization of international trade and payments. For that reason we offer only a brief description of their organizational structure and ignore activities unrelated to liberalization.

The Sterling Area

The contemporary Sterling Area is a remnant of the global sterling area that centered on the United Kingdom before World War I.[17] The abandonment of the gold standard by the United Kingdom in 1931 struck a heavy blow against the supremacy of the London financial center in world trade and payments, and many countries ceased to maintain their reserves in that center because of the uncertainty of sterling vis-à-vis gold and the dollar. Other countries, how-

---

[17] See Chapter 6 for a brief description of the early global sterling area.

ever, continued to link their currencies to sterling because of the close dependence of their exports on British markets; the importance of London as a source of both short- and long-term capital; and, in some instances, because of traditional political and sentimental ties. These countries comprised the Sterling Area in the 1930's.[18]

The Sterling Area in the 1930's had no formal organization; it was simply a loose grouping of countries that pegged its currencies to sterling and maintained its reserves in London. It did not represent an effort to liberalize trade and payments since the pound was fully convertible into the dollar. The stability of exchange rates, however, probably facilitated trade within the area, and the British preferential tariff system, which was devised at the Ottawa Conference in 1932, further promoted trade between the Commonwealth countries.

Features of the Sterling Area. The Sterling Area as we know it today may be traced to the outbreak of World War II. Its main features during the War and until the resumption of sterling convertibility at the end of 1958 were as follows:

   1. Free interconvertibility of all currencies within the area.

   2. Exchange controls in each member country that restricted convertibility between Sterling Area currencies, on the one hand, and gold and dollars, on the other.

   3. The centralization of reserves in London, in particular the pooling of dollars and gold for the entire area.

   4. Tariff systems and import restrictions that discriminated against countries outside the Sterling Area, notably against dollar countries.

   5. A membership comprising the Commonwealth countries (excluding Canada), the British possessions, Iceland, Ireland, Iraq, and Burma.

Today the Sterling Area has dropped the second and fourth features since the pound sterling is now freely convertible into dollars and other currencies. The membership is also somewhat different, but is still basically the Commonwealth countries (excluding Canada) and the British possessions.

Briefly, the Sterling Area functions in this fashion. Each independent member retains full control over its trade and payments

---

[18] At one time or another during the 1930's, the Sterling Area included the British Commonwealth countries (except Canada), the British possessions, Egypt, Estonia, Iraq, Latvia, Portugal, Thailand, the Scandinavian countries, Argentina, Greece, Iran, Japan, and just before the war, France. See League of Nations, *International Currency Experience* (Geneva: League of Nations, 1944), **p. 51.**

policies but pegs its currency to sterling and holds its foreign exchange reserves in the form of deposits and securities in London. Payments between members of the Sterling Area, therefore, are channeled through London banks. Each member transfers to London (in exchange for sterling balances) any gold or foreign exchange it earns from exports to countries outside the area in excess of its own immediate needs. By the same token, when a member country requires foreign exchange or gold to finance its imports, it is able to draw on the British reserves in exchange for its sterling balances. Thus, the United Kingdom is the central banker for the entire area and its reserves must buttress the area's trade with the rest of the world.

The Future of the Sterling Area. The future of the Sterling Area hinges upon Britain's capacity to develop a dynamic economy and a strong balance of payments that will sustain sterling convertibility at a stable exchange rate and, at the same time, will finance a large outflow of capital to the other member countries. Otherwise, the independent members of the Sterling Area are likely to question the wisdom of linking their currencies to the pound and will look increasingly outside the area for capital. On the other hand, the Sterling Area is now less important to Great Britain because of its greater participation in European economic affairs and the return of convertibility among the major currencies. The outlook for the Sterling Area, then, is a smaller role in international trade and payments. In the decade following the War the Sterling Area provided a multilateral trading system for its members and thereby contributed to the liberalization of trade and payments. In the 1960's this function disappeared as the Sterling Area was absorbed into a global system of multilateral trade.

Organization for European Economic Cooperation

The Organization for European Economic Cooperation (OEEC) was established in April, 1948, by the 16 European countries receiving Marshall Plan aid from the United States.[19] These countries pledged themselves

> to combine their economic strength, to join together to make the fullest collective use of their individual capacities and potentialities, to increase their production, develop and modernize their industrial and agricultural equipment, expand their commerce, reduce progressively

---

[19] See p. 365 for country membership of the OEEC. Although it did not receive dollar aid, the adherence of Switzerland to the OEEC brought the total membership to seventeen.

barriers to trade among themselves, promote full employment, and restore or maintain the stability of their economies and general confidence in their national currencies.[20]

OEEC representatives met daily in Paris to work toward these objectives. Although the United States and Canada were not members of the OEEC, they participated in its activities.

Initially, the OEEC was chiefly concerned with the coordination of national plans for economic reconstruction and the allocation of Marshall Plan aid. As reconstruction programs began, however, the OEEC intensified its efforts to liberalize intra-European trade and payments. Somewhat later, after Europe had surpassed prewar levels of production and trade, the OEEC addressed its energies to the liberalization of Europe's trade with the United States, Canada, and the other dollar countries. The signal achievements of the OEEC in liberalizing trade and payments were the creation of the European Payments Union (EPU) and the progressive relaxation of import restrictions between member countries.

European Payments Union. By the end of 1947, over 200 trade and payments agreements had been negotiated between the countries of Europe.[21] The bulk of these payments agreements was of the exchange settlement type providing for the settlement in gold or dollars of bilateral balances beyond a "swing" credit. At first such agreements made possible some trade that might otherwise not have occurred; but as the swing credits became rapidly exhausted, deficit countries sought to balance their trade with surplus partners to avoid the loss of gold or dollars. Hence, intra-European trade was forced into bilateral channels and its volume was kept down to a level that could be financed by the exports of the deficit partners of the many payments agreements.

The obvious solution to this impasse was to make European currencies freely convertible into each other. As early as October, 1948, an Intra-European Payments Scheme was devised to promote the multilateral clearing of trade balances in intra-European trade. Subsequently, other payments schemes were introduced; but it was not until the creation of the European Payments Union in mid-1950 that intra-European payments were placed on a fully multilateral footing.

---

[20] Organization for European Economic Cooperation, *7th Report of the OEEC* (Paris: February, 1956), p. 4.

[21] William Diebold, Jr., *Trade and Payments in Western Europe* (New York: Harper & Brothers, 1952), p. 19.

Essentially, the EPU was a clearing house for the central banks of the OEEC countries. At the end of each month central banks reported to the clearing agent of the EPU (the Bank for International Settlements at Geneva) the surpluses and deficits that arose out of that month's trade between their respective countries and each of the other member countries. These surpluses and deficits were then consolidated or cleared by the agent so that each country ended up with a net surplus or deficit for the month with the entire EPU area. Net surpluses were settled partly through payment of gold by the EPU to the surplus countries and partly through an extension of credit to the EPU by these same countries. Similarly, the net deficits were settled partly through the payment of gold to the EPU by the deficit countries and partly through an extension of credit by the EPU to those countries.[22]

The EPU was not an inexhaustible source of credit for debtor countries. Each member had a quota that equalled approximately 15 percent of its trade with the other members in 1949. Outstanding surpluses and deficits with the EPU (those settled in credit rather than in gold) were cumulated from one month to the next. When a country's net *surplus* rose above its quota, the EPU settled that excess with a 100 percent gold payment to the surplus country. Conversely, when a country's net *deficit* rose above its quota, that country settled the excess with a 100 percent gold payment to the EPU. This arrangement exerted pressure on EPU members to avoid net deficits with the rest of the EPU area that exceeded their respective quotas, but it did not encourage members to reduce net surpluses that exceeded quotas.

The EPU achieved the free interconvertibility of its members' currencies by making all currencies equally acceptable in the settlement of balances on intra-European trade.[23] Each country was able to offset trade deficits in one part of the EPU area with trade surpluses in another part. Exports to any country in the EPU area provided credits with the EPU that were available to finance imports from any other country in the EPU area. Thus a country needed to

---

[22] The ratio of gold to credit in the settlement of net surpluses and deficits was altered several times in the direction of a larger proportion of gold and a smaller proportion of credit. At the end of 1958 when the EPU was dissolved, the settlement arrangement was 75 percent in gold and 25 percent in credit.

[23] The membership of the United Kingdom in the EPU made EPU currencies also freely convertible into Sterling Area currencies. Moreover, the European dependencies in Africa and elsewhere were included in the EPU area. Hence the establishment of the EPU created convertibility conditions for well over half the world's trade.

concern itself only with its overall surplus or deficit position with the EPU.

At the close of 1958, ten countries of Western Europe took measures to establish the *nonresident* convertibility of their currencies on *current* account. This new convertibility ended the EPU. As a regional substitute for global convertibility, the EPU lost its function when many of its members adopted nonresident global convertibility. This development was foreseen in 1955 when the EPU members drew up the European Monetary Agreement, which replaced the EPU. Since all inter-European balances must now be cleared entirely in gold, dollars, or other convertible currencies, the European Monetary Agreement does not involve clearinghouse activities.

The Code of Liberalization. The liberalization of intra-European payments was accompanied by an OEEC program directed toward the progressive relaxation of intra-European trade restrictions. Otherwise, the beneficial effects of interconvertibility might have been nullified by discriminatory import quotas and the like. Trade liberalization started in July, 1949, when the OEEC set forth as a goal the abolition of quantitative restrictions on 50 percent of intra-European trade using 1948 as a base year. By the end of 1950 liberalization had attained 67 percent and by the end of 1955, almost 86 percent. In the early sixties liberalization was extended to imports from the United States and other third countries.

The Organization for Economic Cooperation and Development

The OEEC had largely achieved its objectives by the end of the 1950's. After a decade of rapid economic growth, Western Europe had restored currency convertibility and was dismantling exchange restrictions and import quotas. At the same time, increasing economic and financial interdependence between Western Europe and North America was creating a need for a new form of economic cooperation. Thus in 1960 the United States initiated discussions that led to the formation in 1961 of the Organization for Economic Cooperation and Development (OECD) as a successor to the OEEC.[24]

The purposes of the OECD are set forth in Article I of its *Convention*:

---

[24] Initially, the OECD included 20 countries: the 17 original OEEC countries (Austria, Belgium, Denmark, France, Germany, Greece, Iceland, Ireland, Italy, Luxembourg, the Netherlands, Norway, Portugal, Sweden, Switzerland, Turkey, and the United Kingdom), Spain, Canada, and the United States. In 1965 Japan joined the OECD as a full member.

The aims of the Organization for Economic Cooperation and Development shall be to promote policies designed:

(a) to achieve the highest sustainable economic growth and employment and a rising standard of living in Member countries, while maintaining financial stability, and thus to contribute to the development of the world economy;

(b) to contribute to sound economic expansion in Member as well as nonmember countries in the process of economic development; and

(c) to contribute to the expansion of world trade on a multilateral, nondiscriminatory basis in accordance with international obligations.[25]

Unlike the OEEC, which concentrated on the problems of Western Europe, the OECD is outward-looking and assumes responsibilities for the well-being of the entire free world.

Key concepts in the operation of the OECD are consultation, cooperation, and coordination. Its Development Assistance Committee has worked to establish common objectives in the field of foreign assistance to developing countries and to coordinate national aid programs. Other committees are active in economic policy; trade and payments; agriculture and fisheries; industry and energy; science, technology, and education; manpower and social affairs; and nuclear energy. The OECD now includes all of the industrial countries of the free world who collectively generate almost two thirds of the free world's exports and are the main source of its development capital. Its potential influence on world trade and development is correspondingly great.

Economic Integration in Western Europe

In the 1950's many Europeans, as well as Americans, considered economic cooperation under the auspices of the OEEC inadequate to cope with Europe's problems. They argued that only economic integration that transcends national boundaries would enable Europe to match the continental economies of the United States and the Soviet Union. Economic integration would create the large competitive markets that are the necessary counterparts of mass production and economies of scale, and it would stimulate a more efficient allocation of labor, materials, and capital.

---

[25] *Convention on the Organization for Economic Cooperation and Development.*

Supported by the United States, the drive toward European economic unity gained strength in the 1950's despite widespread doubts as to its ultimate success. Its first notable success was the establishment of the European Coal and Steel Community (ECSC) in 1952 to create a common market in coal, steel, and iron ore covering France, Germany, Italy, Belgium, the Netherlands, and Luxembourg. The second big step toward economic unity was the negotiation and approval by these same countries of a *Treaty Establishing the European Economic Community* in 1957. The failure of negotiations for an OEEC-wide free trade area led to the formation of the European Free Trade Association in 1960 by the United Kingdom, the three Scandinavian countries, Switzerland, and Portugal. Since then, Western Europe has remained at sixes and sevens.

The European Economic Community. The six nations forming the European Economic Community (EEC) are striving to achieve a full integration of their economies by the end of the 1960's. (The ultimate goal is *political* unity.) Since 1958 the EEC has steadily advanced towards integration. Consider only these accomplishments: (1) tariffs on trade among the Six are now only 20 percent of their 1958 levels and are scheduled for complete removal by the end of 1966; (2) all agricultural products are now covered by an agreement to set up a common market with free trade among the Six; (3) a common external tariff system vis-à-vis outside countries is substantially in place and the EEC countries now negotiate as a single entity in GATT tariff conferences.

The EEC is a major new force in world trade and a powerful influence on United States trade policy. Its importance is so great to an understanding of contemporary international economic policies that we shall devote all of Chapter 19 to this regional organization.

The European Free Trade Association. The European Free Trade Association (EFTA) is an industrial *free trade area* which is planned for full completion by the end of 1966. At that time, member countries will impose no restrictions on their mutual trade in industrial products. Unlike the EEC (which is a *customs union*) there is no common EFTA tariff system vis-à-vis third countries—each member country retains its own tariff system and follows its own trade policy with regard to nonmember countries.

The principal motivation behind the formation of EFTA in 1960 was to set the stage for later negotiations with EEC to work towards a regional trading arrangement that would cover the whole of Western Europe. Because of the remarkable success of EEC, the United Kingdom opened up negotiations in 1961 to enter EEC as a full member. By 1962 all EFTA members had expressed their willingness to join EEC or enter into an association with it. However, this was not to be—negotiations came to a sudden halt in January, 1963, when President Charles de Gaulle declared France's opposition to British entry. Following this rebuff, EFTA's energies turned towards strengthening its own activities.

There are now two regional arrangements in Western Europe. Both have made remarkable progress in liberalizing trade among their members. But there is also a split that separates Western Europe into two trading blocs, a split that violates both economic and political common sense. The big question is whether EEC and EFTA can overcome this split and work together towards the liberalization of *global* trade.

Economic Integration in Latin America

To round out this discussion of regional trade and payments arrangements, we offer a brief description of efforts towards economic integration in Latin America. The examples of EEC and EFTA have undoubtedly stimulated these efforts.

The Central American Common Market. Five countries in Central America—Honduras, El Salvador, Nicaragua, Guatemala, and Costa Rica—have established the Central American Common Market (CACM). The weight of CACM in world trade is minimal; the member countries have a total population of less than 12 million, a per capita annual income of around $200, and an area about the size of France. Their economic problems are poverty, rapid population growth, overdependence on agriculture (about 75 percent of their exports consist of coffee, bananas, and cotton), and a dearth of development capital. CACM is expected to accelerate economic development by widening market opportunities, increasing specialization, making possible economies of scale in industry, and by attracting foreign capital.

The Treaty of Managua, which created CACM in 1961, provides for the immediate removal of restrictions on one half the products in mutual trade and the progressive elimination of remaining restrictions by 1966. The Treaty also envisages the promotion of regional industries, common finance and payments agencies, and other steps leading to eventual economic union with a common monetary system.

CACM has made a good start. Agreement has been reached on the location of new industries such as the production of tires in Guatemala and of copper wire in El Salvador. Mutual trade is now almost entirely liberalized and work is going forward in transportation, agriculture, and labor mobility. But much remains to be done. One measure of the task ahead is the fact that internal trade is still less than 10 percent of CACM's exports to foreign markets.

The Latin American Free Trade Association. The nine member countries of the Latin American Free Trade Association (LAFTA) are engaged in creating a free trade area: they have agreed to remove all restrictions on mutual trade (with some exceptions) by 1973. These nine countries—Argentina, Brazil, Chile, Colombia, Ecuador, Mexico, Paraguay, Peru, and Uruguay—account for 85 percent of Latin America's population, almost 75 percent of its output, and over 60 percent of its trade. In the first four years of LAFTA's existence (1961-65) several rounds of negotiations resulted in tariff and other concessions on more than 5,000 products, reducing the weighted average of previous duties about 40 percent.

LAFTA does not have automatic tariff reductions such as EFTA. Each round of tariff concessions depends on negotiations and members can select the products they are willing to bargain on. Since the easy concessions have already been granted, negotiations are becoming increasingly arduous and less fruitful, especially for manufactured products where protectionism is strong. Thus there is a very real doubt that internal trade will be substantially freed by 1973. Furthermore, LAFTA has made little progress in coordinating its members' monetary and fiscal policies or in promoting industrial integration. Unless LAFTA adopts automatic tariff cuts and is strengthened in other ways, its future contribution to the liberalization of Latin American trade will remain dubious.

Advantages and Disadvantages of Regional Arrangements

The principal advantage of regional arrangements lies in their demonstrated capacity to achieve certain objectives that for one reason or another are not obtainable on a wider scale. The Sterling Area and the EPU established free convertibility among the currencies of their member countries at a time when the IMF was unable to bring about free convertibility between dollar and nondollar currencies. The EEC is well on the way towards economic union, and EFTA is approaching complete liberalization of industrial trade among its members. In contrast, GATT—although markedly successful in lowering tariffs—has not achieved a general abandonment of trade restrictions and is not likely to do so in the foreseeable future.

The principal disadvantages of regional arrangements are two. First, they do not achieve multilateral trade on a worldwide scale. And yet, no region in the free world is self-sufficient; each region must continue to depend upon other regions both as markets and sources of supply. This is obvious in the case of CACM and LAFTA, but it is also true of EEC and EFTA.

Second, regional arrangements inevitably discriminate against outside countries. The EEC is abolishing internal restrictions but raising an external tariff system directed against imports from third countries. EFTA countries retain their tariffs for nonmember trade while removing them for member trade. The same discrimination can be said about CACM and LAFTA.

It is impossible to reach a final judgment on regional trade and payments arrangements for they are capable of an evolution that may be antagonistic or sympathetic to the creation of a system of multilateral trade covering the entire free world. For this reason, the existence of regional arrangements makes the IMF and GATT more important than ever. Without the IMF and GATT, there would be far less chance to merge eventually the many regional arrangements into a wider system of trade and payments. Thus strong support of the IMF and GATT, particularly by the United States, is necessary if we are to avert a world of regional trading blocs discriminating against each other. This demands, however, that the United States convince the other countries of the free world that it is fully committed to a global trading system based on full convertibility of currencies and the free movement of goods, services, and capital. This takes deeds rather than words.

SUMMARY

1. Since World War II several international and regional measures have been undertaken to liberalize trade and payments between nations. The International Montary Fund and the General Agreement on Tariffs and Trade arose out of war and early postwar planning for the creation of a liberal, multilateral system of world trade. In the 1950's and 1960's new measures to liberalize trade and payments have been regional in nature and have occurred in Western Europe and Latin America.

2. GATT comprises four basic elements: (1) the rule of nondiscrimination in trade relations between the participating countries, (2) commitments to observe negotiated tariff concessions, (3) prohibitions against the use

of quantitative restrictions on exports and imports, and (4) special provisions to promote the trade of developing countries.
3. GATT has fostered widespread tariff reductions and has exerted steady pressure on member countries to abandon or relax quantitative restrictions. GATT has also developed machinery for the settlement of international trade disputes.
4. The principal function of the IMF is to promote currency convertibility and stable exchange rates by making its resources of gold and currencies available to its member nations. These resources come from the quota subscriptions of the member nations; each member is able to draw foreign currencies from the Fund equal to 200 percent of its quota subject to certain conditions. Since the start of its operations in 1947, the Fund has contributed financial assistance to members in balance of payments difficulties and has sought to eliminate exchange restrictions. The Fund has brought about a high degree of international monetary cooperation that is a hopeful sign for the future.
5. GATT and the IMF, which are open to membership for all nations, are global measures to liberalize trade and payments. In contrast, the Sterling Area, OEEC, EPU, OECD, EEC, EFTA, CACM, and LAFTA are (or were) regional in nature. The main advantage of regional arrangements is their demonstrated ability to achieve interconvertibility and lower trade barriers on the mutual trade of their member countries. Their principal disadvantages are that they do not solve the problem of multilateral trade and that they discriminate against the trade of outside countries.
6. Because of regional arrangements, the IMF and GATT are more important than ever; without these two global organizations there would be far less chance to bring the many regional arrangements into a wider system of trade and payments. Unless GATT and the IMF are given strong support, especially by the United States, we may face in the future a world of regional trading blocs, each discriminating against the other.

QUESTIONS AND APPLICATIONS

1. What are the four basic elements of GATT?
2. (a) List the exceptions to the GATT rule of nondiscrimination.
   (b) How does the escape clause function?
3. (a) Discuss the exceptions to the GATT rule prohibiting the use of quantitative import and export restrictions.
   (b) Why does GATT permit the use of discriminatory import restrictions for balance of payments reasons?
4. (a) Evaluate the accomplishments of GATT in the field of tariff bargaining.
   (b) How are tariff negotiations conducted at a GATT conference?
   (c) What advantages does GATT bring to tariff negotiations?

5. How has GATT helped solve trade disputes?
6. Explain the significance of the proposed Organization for Trade Co-operation.
7. What are the purposes of the International Monetary Fund?
8. (a) What are the resources of the International Monetary Fund?
   (b) How are these resources made available to member countries?
   (c) What are stand-by agreements?
   (d) What is meant by the revolving nature of the Fund's resources?
9. What are the implications of the International Monetary Fund's rules regarding exchange rates?
10. What have been the positive contributions of the Fund to the liberalization of trade and payments?
11. (a) Trace the origins of the Sterling Area.
    (b) What are its major characteristics today?
    (c) How does it function?
12. Describe the purpose and operation of the European Payments Union.
13. (a) Distinguish between EEC and EFTA.
    (b) Compare CACM and LAFTA to EEC and EFTA, noting any similarities or differences.
14. (a) What are the advantages and disadvantages of regional arrangements as compared with global arrangements like GATT and the IMF?
    (b) What are the implications of regional arrangements for United States foreign economic policy?

SELECTED READINGS

Committee for Economic Development. *Economic Development of Central America.* New York: 1964.

European Community Information Service. *The Facts.* Washington, D. C.

————. *Treaty Establishing the European Economic Community and Connected Documents.* Brussels: 1962.

European Free Trade Association. *Annual Report.* Geneva.

————. *Convention Establishing the European Free Trade Association.* Geneva.

General Agreement on Tariffs and Trade. *The Activities of GATT.* Geneva: annual.

International Monetary Fund. *Annual Report.* Washington, D. C.

————. *Articles of Agreement.* Washington, D. C.

————. *Summary Proceedings.* Washington, D. C.: annual meeting.

Organization for Economic Cooperation and Development. *The OECD.* Paris: undated.

Wionczek, Miguel S. "Latin American Free Trade Association," *International Conciliation.* New York: Carnegie Endowment for International Peace, 1965.

CHAPTER 18

THE COMMERCIAL POLICY
OF THE UNITED STATES

The economic policy of a country reflects the official attitude of that country toward its own commercial and financial problems at a given period of time. Since economic activity is characterized by a high degree of interdependence among the different nations of the world, a policy in the best interests of a nation must take into account such interdependence since it affects and, in turn, is affected by the policies of other nations. Consequently, a wise national economic policy must be conceived within a broad international frame of reference, especially when the nation involved holds a dominant position in world affairs and when its conduct is apt to have important repercussions abroad.

Unfortunately, most nations, large and small, are inclined to disregard this dual aspect of their economic policies and to ignore the fact that by building roadblocks of interference on one side of the international highway of commerce, they block the other side as well. Whether those artificial fences consist of tariffs, quantitative or other restrictive measures, they tend to reduce trade in both directions to the detriment of everyone concerned. The United States, like other nations, has been guilty of this shortsighted approach to economic policy at various periods of its history, although in the past its action has been largely confined to tariff measures.

Today the United States holds a dominant position in the world economy. With only 6 percent of the world's population, this country produces some 40 percent of the world's goods and services and accounts for about 15 percent of all international trade.[1] Thus the economic behavior of the United States can do much harm or

---

[1] For a more complete picture of the international trading position of the United States, see Chapter 2.

good, depending upon the stability of its economy and the direction of its foreign commercial policy. A liberal United States trade policy will promote world economic growth and will help free nations to become strong and in a better position to meet the menace of communism. Lower tariffs benefit the United States in many ways. They enlarge the volume and the variety of goods and services that are available to consumers at lower prices and they contribute to lower costs of production as well. The expansion of American imports also benefits the rest of the world by increasing dollar earnings abroad and by making other countries better able to afford American products in greater quantities.

United States commercial policy is a major component of a broader foreign economic policy that, in turn, is an integral part of the overall foreign policy of the nation. The success or failure of any of its constituent parts is reflected in the effectiveness of the whole. United States foreign policy aims to promote economic strength at home and abroad, and to build and maintain cohesion in the free world. To accomplish these objectives, the United States has followed three basic economic policies:

    1. A commercial policy for trade liberalization and trade expansion.
    2. A financial policy for the promotion of United States private foreign investments, especially in developing countries.
    3. A foreign economic assistance policy for the economic growth and development of friendly nations.

In this chapter we shall deal with the trade or commercial policy of the United States. The financial and foreign economic assistance policies will be treated in subsequent chapters.[2]

EVOLUTION OF THE UNITED STATES TARIFF POLICY BEFORE 1934

The evolution of the United States tariff policy has been intimately related to the economic development of the country. The Constitution of the United States specifically vested in Congress the responsibility for regulating the foreign commerce of the nation. On March 4, 1789, a week before the inauguration of George Washington as President, a bill that was to become the first Tariff Act of 1789 was introduced by James Madison. Since then, over 1,000 laws have been enacted to regulate American foreign trade. In the early years, customs duties provided from 80 to 90 percent of the federal govern-

---

[2] See Chapters 20, 21, and 22.

ment's income. Subsequently, this high ratio declined, but proceeds from customs duties continued to be an important source of federal revenue until World War I.

The history of the American tariff policy during this long period shows many swings reflecting the changing internal and external conditions of the time. After the War of 1812, however, there was a marked tendency for a high level of protectionism to dominate the picture, although there were short-lived periods of tariff reductions that temporarily interrupted the upward trend in protection.

After World War I, the United States emerged into a position of world dominance, but the country was prevented from assuming effective world leadership because of the powerful forces of isolationism and protectionism at home. In the first half of the interwar period, the United States tariff resumed its upward climb to reach its highest level with the Tariff Act of 1930. It was not until the collapse of the world economy—including that of the United States—as a result of the great depression of the early 1930's that freer trade became the avowed policy of the United States as embodied in its Reciprocal Trade Agreements program of 1934.

After 1934, the United States gradually began to exercise its international responsibilities, but it was only after World War II that active world leadership was fully assumed and utilized to bring other nations along the road of more liberal trade.

Tariff Act of 1789

The Tariff Act of 1789 was the first expression of United States commercial policy. This Act was inspired by Alexander Hamilton, then Secretary of the Treasury, who favored a mildly protective policy to encourage the development of infant industries that would create a greater domestic market for agricultural production and would achieve some degree of self-sufficiency for national security. A sharp cleavage occurred over this first tariff act between the North, which was anxious to grow industrially, and the South, which was unequipped for industrialization but was interested in maintaining its high exports of cotton. The overwhelming agricultural character of the American economy, however, and the wide popular interest in the traditional imports at the time did not encourage new domestic manufactures under the relatively mild protection afforded by the first tariff act. As a consequence, the tariff issue remained more or less in the background for a while even though alterations and increases took place in succeeding years.

Tariff of 1816

In the early nineteenth century, the Napoleonic Wars, which caused England to blockade the European mainland, led to an American embargo in 1807 that was followed by the Nonintercourse Act of 1809 and the War with Britain in 1812. As a result, a large number of new industries was established in this country in order to supply the needs of the national economy. When peace with Britain was concluded in 1814, imports glutted the American market. Domestic producers were hard hit by the sudden inflow of cheaper imported goods that spelled disaster or ruin for many of them. Concern in Washington led to the enactment of the highly protective Tariff of 1816, the first protective measure of real consequence. Succeeding acts continued the upward trend in protection; and, by 1832, the situation had become so distasteful that it created a great deal of popular resentment and a threat of secession from the Union by South Carolina whose legislature declared the tariff unconstitutional.

After 1832, the tariff issue was dominated by two contending schools of thought that became firmly established in the political affairs of the country. On the one side were the protectionists—identified with the Whigs and later with the Republican Party—and on the other side were the partisans of a tariff for revenue—represented by the Democratic Party. As a result, the tariff policy of the country vacillated with the political fortunes of either party, making the tariff issue a political football. Tariff revisions thus became the inevitable consequence of every change in administration in Washington.

Effects of World War I upon Tariff Policy

World War I stimulated the development of new industries in the United States and caused a vast expansion of industrial and agricultural activities. When peace came, the enlarged production facilities looked to markets abroad in addition to the domestic market. Nevertheless, trade liberalism was viewed as a threat to the economy. The forces of protectionism returned to power and remained in control of the government for twelve crucial years. During this period the world experienced unprecedented political and economic trials, culminating in a worldwide depression, the extent and intensity of which have never been equaled before or since. The new place of the United States in the concert of nations was not fully appreciated at home and the duties of a leading nation were assumed either hesitantly or not at all.

In the commercial policy area, the United States was decidedly reluctant to adjust to its new role of a creditor nation and to accept payment in goods and services for the vastly increased income from its foreign investments. Instead, it resorted to unprecedentedly high protectionism and isolationism. The Fordney-McCumber Act, enacted in 1922, marked a return to the high protectionist policy that had been temporarily interrupted in 1913. Some 2,400 changes in rates were made and the so-called "flexible provision" was added authorizing the President to revise rates up or down by 50 percent when existing rates failed to equalize costs of production between domestic and foreign producers.

Hawley-Smoot Act of 1930

Conceived at the beginning of an unprecedented world economic crisis, the Hawley-Smoot Act of 1930 was the crowning achievement of protectionism in this country. While the bill was still in the Senate, it brought protests from foreign nations and pleas from a group of American economists who opposed the unwarranted attempts by the government to embark upon an economic policy fraught with disaster to the economy of this country and to the rest of the world. These economists pointed out that the contemplated action was unjustified either in principle or in practice and was bound to invite retaliation and to threaten world peace. In spite of these warnings, the Act was passed by Congress and signed by President Hoover, unleashing a worldwide movement of retaliatory measures.[3]

In the opinion of a noted scholar and a student of United States financial policy:

> Few actions of the United States have been more detrimental to the foreign relations of this country than the Hawley-Smoot Tariff of 1930. Almost none of the rates could be justified in terms of the infant-industries argument or on grounds of national security. Many of the items on which tariffs were imposed or the rates raised were not in direct competition with any American product.[4]

---

[3] According to the League of Nation's Economic Survey of 1932-33, the Hawley-Smoot Tariff Act of 1930 was the signal for an outburst of tariff-making activity in other countries, partly, at least, by way of reprisals. Extensive increases in duties were made almost immediately by Canada, Cuba, Mexico, France, Italy, and Spain, followed by many other nations; and it was generally considered to be an unwarranted and unfriendly act of a creditor and powerful nation. See Asher Isaacs, *International Trade, Tariff and Commercial Policies* (Chicago: Richard D. Irwin, Inc., 1948), pp. 234-35.

[4] Raymond F. Mikesell, *United States Economic Policy and International Relations* (New York: McGraw-Hill Book Company, Inc., 1952), p. 62.

Such inordinate action could not long endure without giving rise to countervailing forces for redress. After two years of the Hawley-Smoot tariff, the shrinkage of trade and the deterioration of the American economy were instrumental in convincing influential groups of the mutual relationship between imports and exports and of the effects of the American tariff policy upon the level of world trade. Their voices found more sympathetic ears in the new administration that took the reins of the government in 1932. Under the stewardship of President Roosevelt and his able and vigorous Secretary of State, Cordell Hull, brighter horizons were in sight.

THE RECIPROCAL TRADE AGREEMENTS PROGRAM, 1934-62

In 1934, Congress passed the Reciprocal Trade Agreements Act (RTA)—now superseded by the Trade Expansion Act of 1962 discussed later in this chapter—as an amendment to the Hawley-Smoot Tariff Act of 1930. The RTA ushered in an era of commercial liberalism in this country and paved the way for similar trends abroad that culminated after World War II in the General Agreements on Tariffs and Trade (GATT)—an international organization for the promotion and practice of commercial liberalism.

Reciprocal Trade Agreements Act of 1934

The RTA Act of 1934 recognized the relationship between imports and exports and authorized the reduction of our tariff rates up to 50 percent by means of bilateral trade agreements with foreign countries. The objectives of this program were clearly expressed in the preamble to the law itself which said that the Act was established:

> For the purpose of expanding foreign markets for the products of the United States (as a means of assisting in the present emergency in restoring the American standard of living, in overcoming domestic unemployment and the present economic depression, in increasing the purchasing power of the American public, and in establishing and maintaining a better relationship among various branches of American agriculture, industry, mining, and commerce) by regulating the admission of foreign goods into the United States in accordance with the characteristics and needs of various branches of American production so that foreign markets will be made available to those branches of American production which require and are capable of developing such outlets by affording corresponding market opportunities for foreign products in the United States. . . .[5]

---

[5] Public Law 316, 73d Congress, Sec. 350 (a).

Authority Granted to the President. To accomplish this purpose the Act authorized the President to negotiate bilateral agreements with other countries (not subject to Senate ratification) by offering tariff reductions in return for concessions. Each agreement was to contain an unconditional most-favored-nation treatment clause so that all concessions made by either party to third countries would freely and automatically apply to the trade of the other party to an agreement. Thus, the United States would receive always most-favored-nation treatment of its exports from every agreement country. The United States would grant the concessions it gave to *all* countries, whether parties to the agreement or not.

Under this Act, the President was authorized to raise as well as to lower the basic rates of the Tariff Act of 1930 by not more than 50 percent. The prevailing rates were the highest in United States history and offered, therefore, the best bargaining position for obtaining concessions.

Limitations Placed upon the President. The limitations on the President's powers were also prescribed in the original Act as follows:

1. The customs duties or other import restrictions provided for by the United States in any trade agreement, with the exception of the Cuban agreement, are "generalized" or freely extended to similar products of all other countries.

2. No article may be transferred between the dutiable and free lists.

3. The indebtedness of any foreign country to the United States may not be cancelled or reduced in any manner in a trade agreement.

4. Reasonable public notice of the intention to negotiate an agreement must be given so that an interested party may have an opportunity to present his views to the President or to such agency as the President may designate.

5. Before concluding a trade agreement, the President is required to seek information and advice from the United States Tariff Commission, the Departments of State, Agriculture, and Commerce and from such other sources as he may deem appropriate.

6. Trade agreements are to run for periods generally of three years, and if continued in effect for a longer period, may be terminated upon six months' notice.

During the prosperous war years, the extension of the RTA Act evoked little concern or opposition. After the war, however, Congressional attitude toward the program was mixed and, at times, uncertain. Periodic renewals met with increased opposition. While additional authority to reduce tariff rates was granted the President, other provisions were adopted to prevent contemplated reductions from inflicting harmful effects upon domestic industries, and to retract concessions already extended.

Postwar Extensions of the RTA Act

The RTA Act was extended eleven times after its passage in 1934. The most significant changes occurred after World War II in the extensions of 1945, 1955, and 1958. These changes involved:

> 1. New authority for further reductions and increases in the rates of duties and, under certain conditions, the imposition of a duty on duty-free items.
>
> 2. The adoption of the so-called *peril-point provision,* which required the Tariff Commission [6] to set minimum rates for contemplated concessions below which domestic industries might be harmed by imports.
>
> 3. The adoption of an *escape-clause provision* to be included in every agreement to permit the withdrawal of extended concessions that subsequently might prove harmful to domestic industries.
>
> 4. The adoption of a *defense-essentiality amendment* to adjust imports of a product whenever such imports threaten to impair the national security.

Authority to Lower or Raise Duties. In 1945 the authority to reduce rates up to 50 percent was extended and was made to apply on rates existing as of January 1, 1945, which, in many instances, were already reduced under the original authority granted in 1934.

In 1955 the authority to reduce rates up to 50 percent was abolished, but new authority was granted to reduce rates existing as of January 1, 1955, by a maximum of 15 percent with the provision that no more than a 5 percent reduction each year for three years could be made. The President was also granted authority to cut existing rates that were above 50 percent ad valorem to 50 percent, with no more than one third of the cut to be made in any one year.

In 1958 the authority of the President to revise the tariff was modified in several respects. Under the Trade Agreements Extension Act of 1958, the President was empowered to:

---

[6] The Tariff Commission is a nonpolitical agency of the government whose function is the investigation, study, and submission of recommendations to the President on tariffs and other matters pertaining to the foreign trade of the United States.

1. Reduce the rates of duties existing as of July 1, 1958, **by either 20 percent or 2 percentage points**, with not more than half the reduction to be made in any one year.

2. Lower to 50 percent duty rates exceeding this rate, with not more than one third of the total reduction to be made in any one year.

3. Raise duties as much as 50 percent of the ad valorem equivalent of the rates existing on July 1, 1934, under the Hawley-Smoot Act of 1930—the highest tariff in the history of the United States.

4. Impose, in escape-clause cases, a duty as high as 50 percent ad valorem on duty-free items previously bound in trade agreements.

5. In defense-essentiality cases, restrict such imports that are found to threaten the national security, but not decrease the duties.

The Peril Point. The peril-point clause was first incorporated in the 1948 extension of the RTA Act. It was deleted in 1949, and reincorporated in 1951.

Before entering into negotiations with a foreign country, the President had to furnish a list of contemplated tariff concessions to the United States Tariff Commission for investigation, study, and recommendation. The findings of the Tariff Commission indicated what it considered to be the lowest rate of duty, or *peril point,* for each product below which tariff reduction would cause or threaten serious injury to the domestic industry producing similar or competitive goods. If the President subsequently permitted reduction beyond the peril points, his action remained valid.

The peril-point provision, therefore, was not binding upon the President and did not prohibit reductions beyond the limits set by the Tariff Commission, but it did constitute a restraining influence that was likely to carry weight during the negotiation of an agreement. Under the 1958 extension of the RTA Act, moreover, the Tariff Commission was directed to institute an escape-clause investigation whenever it found that a tariff concession had been granted that ignored the peril point so that an "increase in duty or additional import restriction was required to avoid serious injury to the domestic industry producing like or directly competitive articles." Thus, an unheeded peril point became an escape-clause subjecting a concession to revision and possible reversal by Congress.

The Escape Clause.[7] The escape clause was used occasionally in trade agreements as early as 1941, but more extensively after an

---

[7] For a further discussion of the escape clause, see Irving B. Kravis, "The Trade Agreements Escape Clause," *American Economic Review* (June, 1954), pp. 319-38, and J. M. Letiche, "United States Foreign Trade Policy," *American Economic Review* (December, 1958), pp. 955-56.

executive order in 1947. In 1951 the escape clause became a statutory provision when it was incorporated into the extension of the RTA Act of that year. It provided that no concession in any trade agreement

> ... shall be permitted to continue in effect when the product on which the concession has been granted is, as a result, in whole or in part, of the duty or other customs treatment reflecting such concession, being imported into the United States in such increased quantities ... as to cause or threaten serious injury to the domestic industry producing like or directly competitive products.[8]

The escape clause could be invoked by request of the President; by resolution of either house of Congress or of the House Committee on Ways and Means; by motion of the Tariff Commission; or by application of any interested party. When an application was made, the Tariff Commission was required to make a prompt investigation and to report its findings, or to hold public hearings if so directed by the Senate Committee on Finance or by the House Committee on Ways and Means. The Commission was further required to recommend to the President the withdrawal, modification, or suspension of the concession in whole or in part, or the establishment of import quotas necessary to remedy the situation. If the President rejected the Tariff Commission's recommendations, his action could be reversed by a two thirds' majority vote in both houses of Congress under the 1958 extension of the RTA Act.

In arriving at a determination as to whether imports were causing or threatening injury, the Tariff Commission was directed to consider, among other factors, "a downward trend of production, employment, prices, profits, or wages in the domestic industry concerned, or a decline in sales, an increase in imports, either actual or relative to domestic production, a higher or growing inventory, or a decline in the proportion of the domestic market supplied by domestic producers."

The RTA Act extension of 1955 defined *domestic industry,* for escape-clause purposes, as an industry producing like or directly competitive products. Under this definition, a prosperous domestic industry that produced more than one product—as is generally the case in the United States—could plead injury under the escape-clause provision if any one of its segments was adversely affected by foreign competition. If the rate of growth of one segment of a multiproduct industry in competition with imports was increasing at a decreasing

---

[8] Public Law 50, 82nd Congress, 1st Session, and Public Law 85, 85th Congress, 2d Session.

rate in comparison with other segments producing goods for domestic consumption or export, claims could possibly be sustained under escape-clause criteria. Even if an industry was experiencing business difficulties from causes extraneous to foreign competition, redress under the escape-clause provision could be invoked.

It was rather incongruous for a law to provide for increased imports as a means for expanding exports and at the same time decree that the effectiveness of these means constituted proper criteria for their discard. Conceptually, therefore, the escape-clause and the peril-point provisions of the 1955 extension were in contradiction to the spirit and objectives of the RTA Act. They constituted a class legislation that championed the exclusive interests of producers to the detriment of consumers. Indirectly, these provisions also discouraged development of imports since foreign producers, faced with the possible sudden alteration or withdrawal of a concession granted under a reciprocal agreement, were naturally fearful of making the necessary investments to develop products for the American market or for more suitable distribution facilities in this country.

Action on escape-clause applications rested essentially with the President. So far, the broader considerations of American foreign economic policy—also a Presidential function—have prevailed in arriving at the final disposition of these cases. Of a total of 135 applications filed by industry as of October 4, 1963, 41 reached the President for consideration, of which only 15 received favorable action. This relatively small percentage of successful applications had a retarding effect on the number of applications filed. It is quite conceivable, however, that the future course of Presidential action could very well be reversed in the event of a domestic recession or depression that would also tend to increase the claims by industry.

Defense-Essentiality Amendment. The extensions of the RTA Act in 1954, 1955, and in 1958, directed the President to use import restrictions to protect the industrial mobilization base of the country from injurious import competition whenever in his opinion, and upon the advice of the Director of the Office of Defense and Civilian Mobilization (ODCM)—now the Office of Emergency Planning—such action was deemed necessary for national defense purposes. Subsequently, the President requested the ODCM to designate a representative to serve as an observer on the Trade Agreements Committee.

The role of the ODCM as an adviser and in charge of defense-essentiality matters opened another avenue through which domestic producers could seek relief from foreign competition in addition to the escape-clause and the peril-point provisions, which were under the jurisdiction of the United States Tariff Commission.

The RTA and the GATT [9]

Participation of the United States in the General Agreement on Tariffs and Trade was achieved under the authority granted the President by the RTA Act, as amended. By this authority the United States entered into GATT in 1947. This action combined in one agreement the major features of United States trade agreements previously negotiated with 29 countries. This procedure also offered the prospect of greater benefits through negotiations with many trading nations at one time instead of by the separate bilateral agreements that prevailed before GATT.

Nontariff Restrictive Policy

In addition to protective tariffs, the United States employs a variety of other restrictive measures in its commercial policy:

1. Import quotas.
2. Embargoes.
3. Strategic export controls.
4. Buy-American regulations.
5. Shipping restrictions and subsidies.
6. Administrative restrictions and other measures.

Import Quotas. As was pointed out in Chapter 13, the United States uses various kinds of quotas to limit the importation of certain products in conformity with its commitments under international commodity agreements, or when the unrestricted importation of these products interferes with domestic economic policies, such as the price-support program for agriculture.

Absolute quotas have been established for domestic price-support purposes under Section 22 of the Agricultural Adjustment Act. Certain types of cheese, butter, peanuts, wheat and wheat flour, certain types of cotton, cotton waste, and other agricultural products have absolute import quotas.

Tariff quotas are applied to certain types of cattle, white potatoes, and woolen fabrics.

---

[9] See Chapter 17 for treatment of GATT.

Quota controls discriminate particularly against the small importers who are not financially able to maintain large inventories in bonded warehouses or foreign-trade zones for quick withdrawals at the beginning of a quota period. As we observed earlier, quotas restrict trade, interfere with supply, and tend to raise or maintain high consumer prices.

The use of import quotas by the United States is incompatible with its policy of trade liberalization and has been a source of embarrassment in its international efforts to reduce the trade barriers of other nations. Since its agricultural quotas violate GATT, the United States was forced to ask for a special waiver of GATT rules.

Embargoes. Foreign products may be denied entry into the United States if they fall into any of the following categories:

1. Goods prohibited by reason of health or moral considerations.

2. Goods produced abroad wholly or in part by convict or forced labor, except where domestic supply is inadequate for consumption.

3. Goods that tend to impair or reduce domestic production or interfere with storing and marketing facilities or the operation of the domestic price-support program as provided by the Defense Production Act of 1950, as amended.

4. Goods that originate in countries that persist in discriminating directly or indirectly against American commerce.

The most prevalent of these different kinds of prohibitions are: (1) the classical embargo on certain beef and beef products of Argentina because of hoof-and-mouth disease allegedly prevalent in certain areas of that country; (2) subversive or obscene literature, lottery tickets, and pornographic pictures or films; (3) certain types of birds and wild animals; and (4) agricultural products that are likely to carry harmful insects or the importation of which would jeopardize our price-support program.

Strategic Export Controls. Starting in the early 1950's the United States has applied export controls in order to prevent the Communist bloc countries from obtaining strategic goods likely to strengthen their war potential. In this effort, the United States has received only limited cooperation from other nations of the free world.

Today this country still maintains strict controls over its exports to Communist countries, including an absolute prohibition of trade with Communist China, North Korea, North Viet Nam, and Cuba. The marked weakening of strategic export controls in Western Europe, growing opportunities for East-West trade, the sale of United States wheat to the Soviet Union in 1963, and a slackening of the Cold War have led to demands by American businessmen and others that the United States take steps to liberalize its export controls and bring them more in line with those in Western Europe.

Buy-American Regulations. Buy-American legislation aims to afford legal priority rights to domestic suppliers over their foreign competitors for the large quantities of goods purchased by the official agencies of the government. An amendment to the Treasury and Post Office Department Appropriation Act in 1933, provided that:

> . . . only such unmanufactured articles, materials, and supplies as have been mined or produced in the United States, and only such manufactured articles, materials and supplies as have been manufactured in the United States substantially all from articles, materials or supplies, mined, produced or manufactured . . . in the United States, shall be acquired for public use.

Exceptions are permitted under this amendment when the cost of the domestic product is considered "unreasonable," or when procurement from domestic sources is deemed inconsistent with public interest.

It has been argued that domestic purchasing preference by the government at a higher cost is justified on the ground that the domestic producer who pays domestic taxes indirectly compensates the government for the immediate additional cost involved. Of course, this argument ignores the fact that imports and exports are related, and that the government will also fail to collect taxes on the profits from unrealized exports. When purchasing preferences are not confined to industries essential to national defense, they constitute a special form of protection to individual producers supplying goods to the government.

Shipping Restrictions and Subsidies. In 1934 Public Resolution No. 17, passed by the 73d Congress, provided that goods acquired with funds lent by any United States government agency should be shipped in American bottoms whenever possible. In practice, the interpretation of this "rule of guidance" has been to reserve 50 percent or more to American carriers whenever possible.

Since American vessels on most ocean routes outside the continental shores of the United States are subsidized by the United States government to equalize domestic and foreign construction and operation cost differentials, this is a form of preferential treatment tantamount to a tariff on foreign shipping services.

Administrative Restrictions and Other Measures. With changes in technology, business conditions, and economic policies, tariff provisions and administrative practices of the United States have had a tendency to become archaic and superfluous or even contrary to the purposes for which they were intended. Many practices that discourage imports and that unnecessarily increase their ultimate cost are the result of special directives and regulations issued by the Customs Administration in interpretation of the law or by overzealous customs officials in the performance of their duties, sometimes called "invisible tariffs."

Among the most obstructive practices of this type are the compulsory labeling and mark-of-origin requirements, the uncertain results of product classification and of final clearance of customs entries, and especially the complex and uncertain operation of the system of valuation of imports under the law as applicable prior to 1958.

These complexities have created numerous problems of customs administration and have led to the revision and simplification of the United States tariff in order to make its structure commercially realistic.

After World War II, frequent complaints from importers and shippers led to the realization that trade impediments were working at cross-purposes with the aims of the RTA program. In order to harmonize the means with the ends of United States commercial policy, legislative action was sought to streamline the procedural aspects of customs administration and to simplify the cumbersome structure of statutory tariff provisions.

To remedy the situation, Congress passed the Customs Simplifications Acts of 1954, 1956, and 1962. This brought about some significant improvements such as the reclassification of schedules for imports from fifteen to the present eight schedules, and a new basis for customs valuation (put into effect in 1956) which eliminated some of the controversial and cumbersome provisions of the previous method.

The new basis for customs valuation is as follows:

> 1. The *export value*—the price at the foreign export point of the imported or similar merchandise in the usual wholesale quantities offered for exportation to the United States and including all incidental expenses for placing the goods in condition ready for shipment.

2. If the export value cannot be determined satisfactorily, the *United States value*—the price of the imported or similar merchandise in the usual wholesale quantities in the principal markets of the United States, excluding the usual markups, commission, transportation, insurance costs, and customs' duties.

3. If neither the export value nor the United States value can be determined satisfactorily, then the *constructed value*—the total cost abroad of materials and manufacturing of the imported or similar merchandise at the time preceding exportation to the United States plus the usual expenses incidental to exportation.

4. The *American selling price* in the case of an imported article with respect to which there is in effect a rate of duty based upon the American selling price (certain organic chemicals and a few other products). The American selling price is the usual wholesale price of an American article, similar to the imported article, at the time of exportation of the imported article.

Although the simplifications acts eliminated some of the complexities of customs administration, other provisions still remain that need to be brought into line with the philosophy of trade liberalization and trade expansion. Certain internal import taxes, prohibitively high rates of duty, and Buy-American and embargo provisions, as well as some aspects of the escape clause, require reconsideration in light of the objectives of United States commercial policy. Even though the United States is no worse than many other nations in this regard, there is little excuse or justification for the continuance of unnecessary burdens on international trade that serve no valid purpose.

The Impact of the RTA Program

The consequences of any specific aspect of a general policy upon an economy as complex as that of the United States are impossible of exact measurement. They are the result of the balance of many forces that, at times, work at cross-purposes. Some of these forces are known; others are hard to detect; and still others have roundabout effects that can only be conjectured. Because of this complexity, the results of the RTA program cannot be clearly isolated and appraised. Some indications of the results of this program after thirty years may be determined, however, by the comparison of available data, even though the data and their interpretation must be highly qualified.

The ad valorem equivalent of United States tariff rates has fallen under the RTA program from an average of 51.5 percent for dutiable imports in 1934 to 11.1 percent in 1962, as indicated in

Table 18-1

AVERAGE AD VALOREM RATES OF DUTY ON IMPORTS FOR CONSUMPTION UNDER UNITED STATES TARIFF ACT OF 1930, AS AMENDED

Period	Ratio of Dutiable to Total Imports	Ratio of Duties Collected to Value of Dutiable Imports
1931-1935	37.6	51.4
1936-1940	39.5	39.4
1941-1945	34.0	33.0
1946-1950	41.6	17.1
1951-1955	44.6	12.2
1956-1960	56.9	11.6
1961-1962	61.6	11.1 *

* Estimated.

SOURCE: Arranged from data in United States Department of the Treasury, *Annual Reports of the Treasury on the State of the Finances* (1930-1964).

Table 18-1. Of course, such comparisons are statistically debatable because of the inherent limitations in their calculation. But the comparisons do point out, nevertheless, the long distance traveled along the line of liberalization of our basic tariff law, the Hawley-Smoot Act of 1930.

Also during the life of the RTA program, a relative increase in the percentage of dutiable to nondutiable imports has taken place that indicates a rising trend in the volume of imports at the reduced tariff rates. This increase might have been even more pronounced during the period were it not for the growing dependence of the United States economy upon foreign sources for essential raw materials—a type of import that is generally duty-free.

Deterioration of the RTA Program

Developments in the 1950's indicated a strong tendency in favor of moderation and even of reversal of the liberal trade policy of the country under the RTA program as evidenced by (1) the stiffening attacks upon this program in general, (2) the opposition to specific rate reductions already effected, and (3) the implications of recent escape-clause and peril-point legislation.

In the 1950's, Congress curtailed the power of the President to reduce the tariff. The adoption of the peril-point, the escape-clause, the defense-essentiality amendments, and the new provision to reverse the President by Congressional action, demonstrated a growing difference in views between the Administration and the Congress as to whether the RTA program was to remain the vehicle for a liberal international trade policy or was to become a means for the protection of domestic producers, collectively and individually, against injury from foreign competition. Whenever consideration had been given to a renewal of the RTA, vigorous opposition in Congress forced a further curtailment of the President's powers by means of restrictive amendments undermining the effectiveness as well as the very philosophy of the program.

Moreover, the item-by-item approach to bargaining under the RTA and GATT procedures coupled with the principal-supplier concept as the basis for negotiation resulted in a proliferation of tariff subclassifications for many products in order to confine the benefits of the lower duties to the negotiating parties. Otherwise, these benefits would have accrued to third countries producing similar but not identical products without reciprocal concessions because of the *unconditional-most-favored-nation (MFN)* treatment principle.[10]

Furthermore, after thirty years of tariff reductions under the RTA and GATT, over 400 United States industrial products remained unaffected by negotiations and subject to the high tariff rates of the Hawley-Smoot tariff of 1930—an inherent weakness of the item-by-item bargaining system which tends to retain high protection whenever and wherever pressure by entrenched interests prevails.

In addition to these domestic protectionist policies that weakened the original intent of the RTA Act, international developments in the late 1950's, such as (1) the abandonment by EEC in 1960-61 of the item-by-item approach to negotiations, and (2) the built-in preferential treatment within the EEC and EFTA—sanctioned by GATT but discriminatory nevertheless against the outside world—were creating a new situation, putting the United States at a distinct disadvantage.

To meet the new international challenges and to reverse the internal creeping forces of deterioration in the international commercial policy of this country, the Congress of the United States under the leadership of the late President Kennedy passed the *Trade Expansion Act of 1962 (TEA).*

---

[10] Under the MFN policy any reduction in the tariff of a nation is automatically extended to all nations, except, at times, to those considered politically or economically inimical.

THE TRADE EXPANSION ACT OF 1962

On October 11, 1962, the late President Kennedy signed into law the Trade Expansion Act of 1962 (TEA).[11] This Act is considered as the most important tariff legislation since the RTA in 1934, and is held in many quarters as a landmark in United States commercial policy.

Unlike the previous eleven extensions of the original RTA of 1934, the TEA of 1962 is a totally new statute and provides authorities and tools of implementation which, in some instances, are unprecedented for the United States.

In the language of the Act itself the purposes of the TEA are:

> 1. To stimulate the economic growth of the United States and maintain and enlarge foreign markets for the products of United States agriculture, industry, mining, and commerce;
>
> 2. To strengthen economic relations with foreign countries through the development of open and nondiscriminatory trading in the free world; and
>
> 3. To prevent Communist economic penetration.

To achieve these objectives the law provides three major avenues for action:

> 1. Negotiating authority,
> 2. Restriction authority,
> 3. Adjustment assistance authority.

Negotiating Authority

During the five-year period from July 1, 1962, to June 30, 1967—the life of the new Act—the President is authorized to do any of the following:

> 1. To reduce by as much as 50 percent the rates of duties existing as of July 1, 1962;
>
> 2. To reduce up to 100 percent the tariff rates on the products of industries where the United States and the European Economic Community (EEC) combined represent 80 percent or more of the free-world trade;
>
> 3. To reduce to zero tariff duties of 5 percent or less existing as of July, 1962;
>
> 4. To eliminate tariffs on tropical products by agreement with the EEC subject to their extending comparable treatment and without

---

[11] Public Law 87-794, 87th Congress, H.R. 11970.

discrimination as to source of supply of these products, but only if such products are not produced in the United States in significant quantities;

5. To eliminate tariffs on certain farm products if in the opinion of the President such action would tend to assure the maintenance or expansion of United States exports of like articles.

Except for the tropical-products authority, which may be applied when proclaimed, the Act requires that all other negotiable cuts be put into effect in at least five installments a year apart—(the first when concessions are proclaimed) to allow domestic producers time to adjust to foreign competition.

Restrictive Authority

The President is authorized to impose restrictive measures in the form of higher duties or quantitative limitations whenever the interests of the United States are, or may be, in jeopardy by inimical action by a foreign country or as a result of injury to the United States economy which, in his judgment, requires redress. These restrictive powers fall into the following three categories:

1. Retaliation and discrimination.
2. National security requirements.
3. Escape-clause action.

Retaliation and Discrimination. The President is given broad powers to cope with foreign import restrictions that unjustifiably or unreasonably burden United States commerce or prevent the expansion of trade on a mutually advantageous basis. Where tariff relief is used the increase in the duty may be as high as 50 percent above the rate existing on July 1, 1934, or up to 50 percent ad valorem where the product is not dutiable otherwise. The President may also withdraw concessions, deny MFN treatment, or withhold action having due regard to the international obligations of the United States and/or those of the offending country.

National Security Requirements. Essentially, the national security provisions of the RTA Act, as amended, remain the same as under TEA, leaving the President with complete discretion in the disposition of such proceedings in this area.

Escape Clause. Unlike its predecessors, the new escape clause requires that injury or threat of injury to an industry be traceable to actual competitive imports caused by a concession and not by causes such as an increase in the national income or the population of the United States or possibly a change in technology—all related to the dynamics of growth rather than to the granting of the concession itself.

The new law also draws the line between partial and total injury (by reason of a concession) to an *establishment* within an industry producing several products. For a company to qualify for redress, it is necessary to prove its case on the basis of its overall activities. Thus, a partial injury within an otherwise profitable whole operation is expected to be absorbed by the company, even though the industry as such may qualify for redress.

In a case of a proven injury, the President may decide to maintain the concession for reasons of superseding foreign policy considerations and certify the company and/or the displaced workers of that company for compensation under the *Adjustment Assistance* provision of the TEA—an important innovation in American tariff policy.

The law provides also that the Congress may overrule the President's decision not to invoke the escape clause by a simple majority of both Houses—a provision regarded as controversial and probably unconstitutional, since decisions pertaining to the foreign policy of the country are the province of the executive rather than the legislative branch of the government.

The peril-point provision as it existed before the TEA has been abandoned for all practical purposes, but the Tariff Commission is given the task of advising the President of the likely economic effects of lower duties upon *firms* and *workers* in industries producing directly competitive products with imports under consideration for tariff concessions.

Reservations are made in the new Act to maintain the existing status of products on which action has already been taken under the escape clause, the National Security Amendment and the Orderly Marketing provision for agricultural products.

The no-injury concept under the RTA, as amended, has been modified in the sense that although the TEA recognizes that tariff concessions are bound to increase imports and to cause hardship for industries and workers, such hardship is not to be remedied by an upward readjustment of duty rates (except in extreme instances), but is to be compensated for by technological, financial, and/or tax assistance to the injured in order to help them meet the new import competition.

Adjustment Assistance

When injury is established and no escape-clause action is taken, the President may initiate negotiations towards agreements with foreign countries to voluntarily limit exports to the United States, either individually or as a group, thus giving relief to injured United States industries. If only the less efficient firms within a given industry are affected by the increased imports, the law provides for governmental assistance to them in a variety of forms.

Assistance to Firms. An injured firm that has been certified as such by the Tariff Commission may apply to the Secretary of Commerce for relief under the adjustment-assistance provision of the TEA. The various forms of assistance which may be extended singly or in combination are:

1. Technological aid at governmental expense,
2. Financial assistance in the form of partial or outright loans or government guarantee for same,
3. Tax relief in the form of a five-year carry-back loss privilege instead of the normal three-year provision of the general tax laws.

Assistance to Workers. Displaced workers, because of tariff concessions, are eligible under the law for various forms of assistance ranging from retraining, relocation, and hardship allowances to prolonged periods of unemployment compensation with additional benefits above the prevailing rates.

The law also provides, among other things, for prenegotiation and administrative procedures as well as for a more precise definition of terms such as injury, industry, firm, and other key terminologies, in order to preclude subsequent interpretations that may distort the original intent of the law and, in time, its very spirit.

APPRAISAL OF UNITED STATES COMMERCIAL POLICY

The present world's disorders reflect the disintegration of a past system of relationships that no longer provides the necessary measure of political and economic stability among nations. The social and economic conditions that were taken for granted have become intolerable under the present conditions of the world's revolution of expectations.

The challenge of a peaceful and equitable solution to these new problems can only be met successfully by the industrial nations of the world, particularly by the United States whose example is most likely to invite emulation by other like-minded nations. Action to liberalize trade between nations on an equitable basis can provide the necessary spark to set off a higher production of goods and services—the ultimate source of economic affluence.

The comparison of the objectives of the original RTA program of 1934 with those of the new TEA of 1962 points to a basic change in the philosophy underlying United States foreign commercial policy. The RTA was born in the great depression when the foreign trade of the United States and the domestic economic activity of the country were at a very low ebb. The objectives of the RTA program reflected the hopes and needs of this country. In the language of the Act itself, they were intended to benefit the various depressed sectors of the United States economy.

In contrast, the TEA came into being at a time when the foreign trade as well as the domestic economic activity of the country were at an all-time high in a dynamic world economy. The objectives of the new Act reflected these conditions and the desire of this country to strengthen its politico-economic relations with the free world, especially with the fast-growing European Common Market, to assist the developing nations, and to prevent economic penetration by the Communist bloc.

This is a remarkable change from a relatively inward-looking policy under the RTA to an outward-looking, truly international policy under the TEA. In this perspective, the TEA is, indeed, a landmark in United States international commercial policy.

The new and the revised methods of implementation of the TEA are essentially:

> 1. The rejection of the no-injury concept and the provision of adjustment assistance to hardship cases consequent to tariff concessions,
>
> 2. The linear across-the-board approach to tariff negotiations with other countries, including customs unions such as the EEC, and
>
> 3. The total elimination of rates of duty of 5 percent or less, and under certain conditions, those on tropical and industrial products that require no protection.

Overprotection, unnecessary protection, and protection by subclassification are all sources of friction and reasons for hesitation on the part of domestic and foreign exporters to invest in long-term activities for trade expansion. The new law provides avenues for the removal of such roadblocks towards a harmonization of the needs of the United States economy with those of other nations.

By accepting domestic injury and providing for remedial assistance to the injured, the TEA furnishes an alternative to high-cost domestic production at the expense of more efficient production for export. Thus, the United States is contributing towards the better allocation of its own as well as the world's resources—a step in harmony with the theory of comparative costs.

In a broad sense, the new international commercial policy of the United States, as reflected in the TEA, is a foundation for a new era of global thinking at the governmental level. If emulated by other industrial nations, this policy would stimulate economic growth for the benefit of all nations, including the developing nations of the free world. However, the benefits of the new United States policy under TEA are contingent upon the consummation of actual tariff negotiations; otherwise the President's tariff-cutting authority will lapse in mid-1967 and the TEA will be barren of results. The impact of the new United States policy in liberalizing the world's trade at this time hinges mainly upon the course of action and the extent of cooperation of the EEC countries and the United States. In the following chapter, we examine the confrontation of the United States and the EEC in the Kennedy Round after looking at the EEC itself and its bearing on world trade.

SUMMARY

1. The history of the commercial policy of the United States is essentially the history of its tariff. Before 1934, tariff measures were relied upon for both revenue and protection. Tariff rates grew higher with the economic development and industrialization of the country.

2. The present basic tariff law is the Hawley-Smoot Tariff of 1930, the highest tariff in the history of the United States. However, the RTA program, introduced in 1934, permitted numerous reductions in rates by executive action; and today the United States tariff is among the lowest in the world.

3. From 1934 to 1962, the RTA program became the core of United States commercial policy which is part of the broader overall foreign economic policy of the nation. The success of this policy has been justified by its beneficial contribution to the United States and to the rest of the free world.

4. In the 1950's stiffening opposition to the RTA program became evident, threatening its further development if not its very existence. A reversal of United States liberal trade policy would have adverse international repercussions likely to lead the world back to isolationism and bilateralism, the bane of the 1930's.

5. Today a strong position in favor of continuation and expansion of the benefits of the liberal trade policy of this country is the expressed official

attitude of the United States government at the executive level. This attitude finds its support in the concept that liberal international trade policies are at the very foundation of the peace and security of the free world.
6. The Trade Expansion Act of 1962, as passed by the United States Congress, may usher in a new era in this country's foreign commercial policy more in harmony with the theory of comparative costs.

QUESTIONS AND APPLICATIONS

1. The United States tariff policy has been marked by a high tendency toward protectionism. Appraise.
2. What is the background for the liberalization of United States commercial policy since 1934?
3. What were the purposes of the RTA program, and in what way or ways were they implemented?
4. Explain the purpose and operation of the TEA of 1962.
5. Evaluate the escape clause in terms of the purposes of the TEA.
6. Is the use of quotas by the United States justified in light of the basic premise of the RTA program and/or the TEA?
7. Under what different conditions are embargoes used by the United States?
8. How does "Buy-American" legislation influence United States imports?
9. (a) What are the major problems created by a United States administrative protectionism?
   (b) What steps have been taken by the United States Congress to mitigate and/or to eliminate administrative protectionism?
10. Discuss the bases of customs valuation by the United States after 1958.
11. Why is the United States commercial policy considered to be of vast influence on the economic and political conditions of the world? Discuss.
12. "United States industry is geared for mass production for a vast domestic market. Therefore, the country needs a policy of protection, not a liberal trade policy." Evaluate.
13. "The combination of a protective tariff in the international trade of the United States and free trade in domestic trade has made this country the most productive and prosperous in the world." Discuss.

SELECTED READINGS

Barber, J. (ed.). *Foreign Trade and the United States Tariff Policy.* New York: Council of Foreign Relations, 1953.

Committee for Economic Development. *Trade Negotiations for a Better Free World Economy.* New York: 1964.

Humphrey, D. D. *American Imports.* New York: Twentieth Century Fund, 1955.

——————. *The United States and the Common Market.* New York: Frederick A. Praeger, 1964.

Krause, Lawrence B. "United States Imports and the Tariff," *American Economic Review* (May, 1959), pp. 542-58.

Letiche, J. M. "United States Foreign Trade Policy," *American Economic Review* (December, 1958), pp. 955-66.

Piquet, H. S. *Aid, Trade and the Tariff.* New York: Thomas Y. Crowell Co., 1953.

——————. *The Trade Agreements Act and the National Interest.* Washington, D. C.: The Brookings Institution, 1958.

Smith, R. Elbertson. *Customs Valuation in the United States.* Chicago: University of Chicago Press, 1948.

Tasca, H. J. *The Reciprocal Trade Policy of the United States.* Philadelphia: University of Pennsylvania Press, 1937.

Taussig, Frank W. *The Tariff History of the United States.* 8th ed. New York: G. P. Putnam's Sons, 1931.

CHAPTER 19

THE EUROPEAN ECONOMIC COMMUNITY AND WORLD TRADE

Postwar European economic cooperation began with the establishment of the Organization for European Economic Cooperation in 1948 to allocate Marshall Plan aid and accelerate the recovery of Western Europe. In the 1950's, quotas and payments restrictions on intra-OEEC trade were rapidly dismantled, and European countries grew accustomed to close cooperation on trade and other economic matters.

In 1952 six countries—France, West Germany, Italy, Belgium, Luxembourg, and the Netherlands—moved from economic cooperation towards economic integration in the coal and steel sectors by setting up the European Coal and Steel Community. For one reason or another, the remaining OEEC countries did not join this enterprise.

The Coal and Steel Community proved to be a forerunner of the European Economic Community (EEC) which was established by the same six countries in 1957. The main feature of the EEC is the creation in planned stages of a *customs union* for both industrial and agricultural goods, involving the abolition of all restrictions on trade among member countries and the erection of a common external tariff. But EEC goes much further than this. A second objective is a full *economic union* with free movement of persons, services and capital, and progressive harmonization of social, fiscal and monetary policies. The ultimate objective is a *political union* of the Six.

The formation of the EEC has introduced a new force to world trade and has provoked a major attempt by the United States to negotiate with the EEC to lower tariffs and other trade barriers. In this chapter we shall describe the principal features of EEC and its progress towards the creation of both a customs and economic union. Next we shall examine the policies of EEC towards the outside world, including the common external tariff and agricultural protection. Finally, we shall consider trade relationships and policy issues between the United States and EEC which have been revealed most vividly in the GATT Tariff Conference known as the Kennedy Round.

THE DEVELOPMENT OF THE EUROPEAN ECONOMIC COMMUNITY

The Treaty establishing the European Economic Community is a lengthy document comprising over 200 articles.[1] The Treaty lays down a timetable for the progressive development of a customs union but goes far beyond this goal—it contains numerous provisions relating to the free movement of persons, services and capital, transportation, rules governing competition, the harmonization of laws, economic policies, social policies, and the organs of the Community.

Institutions of the Community

The basic institutions, or organs, of the Community are four in number: Commission, Council of Ministers, European Parliament, and Court of Justice.

The nine-member Commission is the executive body of the EEC and has two main functions. First, it administers the Treaty and other Community policies. Second, it initiates new policies by making proposals to the Council. The Commission represents the Community rather than the member states, and it is the driving force in the EEC.

Each of the six members of the Council of Ministers represents his own national government. For the most part, the Council makes final policy decisions but can do so only on proposals by the Commission. During the first two stages Council decisions require a unanimous vote but then shift to a majority vote basis.[2] It is through the Council that national governments influence and control the evolution of the EEC by approving, amending, or rejecting Commission proposals.

---

[1] The Treaty was signed in Rome on March 25, 1957, and was then ratified by the six countries. A separate treaty setting up a European Atomic Energy Community (Euratom) was signed and ratified at the same time. Both the EEC and Euratom treaties went into effect on January 1, 1958. Fusion of the three Communities (EEC, ECSC, and Euratom) into a single European Community is to be accomplished by 1970.

[2] Votes are weighted for majority decisions: France, Germany, and Italy have four votes each; Belgium and the Netherlands, two each; and Luxembourg, one. The third stage began in 1966.

The 142-man European Parliament draws its members from the legislatures of the member countries. However, the Parliament does not pass laws and is not a true legislature since this function is performed jointly by the Commission and Council. The Commission must report to the Parliament annually and the latter must be consulted before certain specific decisions are taken. But the only important power of the Parliament is the right to remove the Commission by a motion of censure voted by a two-thirds majority.

The Court of Justice has the sole power to decide on the constitutionality of acts performed by the Commission and Council. The Court's judgments have the force of law throughout the Community and they are binding on all parties whether individuals, business firms, national governments or other Community institutions.

Towards a Customs Union—Free Trade in Industrial Products

To form a customs union the EEC must (1) abolish all restrictions on trade among its member countries and (2) establish a common tariff and commercial policy vis-à-vis nonmember countries. We look first at the *internal* development of the customs union: the creation of free trade among the six member countries. The Treaty calls for a transition to complete free trade in three stages which may take from 12 to 15 years, that is, until 1970 or 1973.

The EEC has made impressive progress in lowering internal barriers on industrial trade and is about three years ahead of the Treaty schedule. By 1966 industrial tariffs were only 20 percent of their 1957 levels and there were no quotas on internal trade. The Commission has proposed the full elimination of internal tariffs by mid-1967. Together with high rates of economic growth in the member countries, this rapid movement towards free trade has greatly stimulated intra-Community commerce. The value of internal trade among the Six in 1964 was 166 percent higher than in 1958.[3]

The Commission is now working on proposals that would harmonize customs legislation and eliminate licenses, visas, permits, and other export-import formalities so that the common market will have the same characteristics as a domestic market.

Towards a Customs Union—Free Trade in Agricultural Products

Each of the EEC countries has a domestic farm program involving price supports and import restrictions. This situation calls

---

[3] European Information Service, *Summary of the Commission's Eighth General Report,* June, 1965, p. 6.

for a different approach to free trade in agricultural products, namely, the establishment of a common agricultural policy that will free intra-Community trade but, at the same time, improve the economic position of Community farmers.

Negotiations for a Common Agricultural Policy. The EEC Treaty does not spell out the details of a common agricultural policy; they have had to be worked out in a series of laborious negotiations that at times have threatened the very existence of the Community. In 1965, a dispute over agricultural policy once again provoked a crisis in the EEC.

The EEC took its first big step towards a common agricultural policy in January, 1962, when the Council of Ministers (after a marathon session ending at 5 A.M.) agreed on the basic features of that policy and on regulations for grains, pork, eggs, poultry, fruit, vegetables, and wine. These regulations went into effect on July 30, 1962.[4] The second big step was taken at the end of 1963 (the "Christmas eve" marathon) when the Council agreed on a common policy for rice, beef, veal, dairy products, vegetable oil, and oilseeds. By November, 1964, when regulations covering these products went into effect, 85 percent of the agricultural output of the Community was under common organization.

These first two agreements did not extend to the common prices that would rule once a single agricultural market was fully established in the Community. This was the next order of business and it proved exceptionally arduous. The key factor was the common price of grain. Germany, the high-cost producer, tried to stall agreement on a common grain price while France, the low-cost producer, pressed hard for its early establishment. The issue was finally resolved in December, 1964 (in another marathon conference that ended at 5:15 A.M.), when the Council agreed on a common grain price—closer to the French than to the German price—applicable to member countries no later than mid-1967.

The adoption of a common grain price broke a logjam; it was then possible to start negotiations on other common agricultural prices. But this was not the end of troubles in establishing a common agricultural policy—in mid-1965 a new crisis erupted which once again put a question mark over the future of the EEC. Because of its political implications we shall describe this crisis in a later section.

---

[4] At that time imports of all these products except fruit, vegetables, and wine became subject to variable levies. This precipitated the "chicken war" with the United States. See Chapter 17, p. 350.

Structure of the Common Agricultural Policy. Americans should not find it difficult to understand the basic farm problem in the EEC because it is very much like the United States farm problem. A technical revolution is now sweeping European agriculture such as the one experienced by the United States during the 1940's. Productivity on farms in the EEC is increasing at a rate faster than industrial productivity; farmers are leaving the land in hordes (one fourth left in the decade 1952-62); and per capita farm income is lagging behind that in other sectors of the economy. Production is almost equalling and, in some instances, surpassing the consumption of many commodities. The EEC is now fully self-sufficient in potatoes, sugar, pork, milk, butter, and vegetables; 99 percent self-sufficient in cheese; 93 percent in beef, veal, and poultry; 91 percent in wheat; and 78 percent in feed grains. The degree of self-sufficiency will most likely rise in the future—with or without a common agricultural policy.

Although the farm problems in the EEC and the United States have many common features, their impact on international trade is very different. The EEC is still the world's largest importer of farm products while this country is the world's largest exporter. Because it is a net exporter of temperate farm products, agricultural policy in the United States involves production controls, storage of surplus commodities, and the subsidization of exports, with import restrictions playing only a modest role except in dairy products. In contrast, agricultural policy in the EEC—a net importer of farm products—is based primarily on the restriction of imports. In this way the EEC hopes to avoid production controls and surpluses (so troublesome in this country) by placing the burden of adjustment on third country suppliers, notably the United States.

The structure of the common agricultural policy in the EEC is best illustrated by the common grain policy. First, there is a *target price*. This is the base price for grains to be established annually at the market of the region in the Community with the least adequate supplies. Farmers will receive subsidies in order to sell their crops at prices as close as possible to the target price.

Second, there is an *intervention price*. This is the price (between 5 and 10 percent below the target price) at which the Community will buy from producers. It is the guaranteed minimum selling price.

Third, there is a *threshold price*. This is the price used to calculate the variable levy on imported grains. The threshold price is fixed at a level that will bring the selling price of imported grains up to the level of the target price in the region of the Community with the least adequate supplies.

Fourth, the *variable import levy* is a tariff imposed on grain imports from countries outside the Community. It is determined daily and is equal to the difference between the world price for grain imports and the Community threshold price, taking any quality differences into account.

The following hypothetical illustration may help to clarify the price structure of the common grain policy and the determination of the variable import levy:

		PER BUSHEL
1. Target price		$2.80
2. Intervention price		$2.60
3. Threshold price:		
Target price	$2.80	
Less transportation and marketing costs	.10	$2.70
4. Variable import levy:		
Threshold price	$2.70	
Less adjusted world price	$1.50	$1.20

At the present time these prices differ among the six Community countries and variable levies are imposed on intra-Community trade. If all goes well, however, by mid-1967 there will be a common grain price throughout the Community and all intra-Community levies will disappear. When this happens for grain and other farm products there will be a single agricultural market matching the common market in industrial products.

In conclusion, two points need stressing. First, there are no production controls: the Community must buy any quantity of a commodity offered at the intervention price. Second, variable import levies make third countries residual suppliers of farm products; imports are allowed only when EEC producers fail to meet Community requirements. Consequently, the target prices are a key concern of the United States and other outside suppliers. High target prices will encourage EEC production and cut down on imports; low target prices will greatly mitigate this effect.

Towards a Customs Union—Free Movement of Persons, Business Enterprises, and Services

In addition to free trade in industrial and agricultural products, the EEC common market involves the free movement of persons, business enterprise, and services.

Workers can now move freely among the six countries in response to employment opportunities. Labor laws and social legislation are being harmonized so that workers will enjoy the same rights and protection throughout the Community.

By the end of the transition period (1970) business firms in one member country will be free to establish branches or other enterprises anywhere in the Community without fear of discriminatory restrictions. Already mergers, expansions, and acquisitions are crossing national boundaries as EEC companies adapt to Community-wide market opportunities and competition.

Progress is also being made to eliminate restrictions on the movement of services in insurance, banking, law, and other fields. The Commission is working towards the mutual recognition of diplomas and the right of professional people, such as lawyers and physicians, to practice freely anywhere in the Community.

Towards an Economic Union

The EEC is much more than a customs union; it seeks to integrate all facets of the national member economies. The end result would be an economic union—a single economic system embracing the entire EEC. It was recognized from the start that a truly successful customs union would not be possible if each member country were free to choose its own policies without regard to the others.

"Harmonization" is a key word in the evolution of the economic union. Harmonization calls for the gradual elimination of differences in national legislation, administrative practices and policies, and their eventual integration to form a Community-wide policy carried out by common institutions. Since economic integration involves all aspects of the national economies, harmonization must proceed simultaneously on many fronts: antitrust policy, transportation and energy policy, trade policy, monetary and fiscal policy, wage and social policy, and so on. Actual progress towards economic union of the EEC countries has been very uneven—substantial in those areas where the Rome Treaty makes specific provision, but only modest in those areas where economic integration has to be negotiated in the Council of Ministers. Here is a brief description of accomplishments and the work to be done.

Rules Governing Competition. The Rome Treaty gives to the Commission specific powers to prevent the formation of, or to break up, cartels and monopolies that lessen competition in the common market. The overriding purpose of this antitrust policy is to prevent private business agreements and industrial concentrations from nullifying Community-wide competition—private restrictions are not to be allowed to replace the disappearing tariffs and other restrictions.

Although the EEC antitrust provisions (Articles 85 and 86) have been influenced by United States antitrust legislation, there is a fundamental difference in philosophy between the two. Under United States law *all* "unreasonable" restraints on trade are illegal, and agreements to fix prices, allocate markets, etc., are per se illegal regardless of their effects. In contrast, the EEC distinguishes between "good" and "bad" cartels and monopolies. Business agreements and concentrations that help improve the production or distribution of goods or promote technical and economic progress are legal in the EEC provided that they do not eliminate competition in a "substantial" part of the market.

The administration of antitrust policy in the EEC also differs from that in the United States. All cartels must register with the Commission, and to become legal they must be granted a dispensation. Failure to register makes a private agreement null and void and the Commission may impose retroactive penalties on the guilty parties. In this country there is no prior registration because all cartels are illegal by their very nature; instead each case is decided on its merits and the parties involved are presumed innocent until proved guilty.

How effective is EEC antitrust policy likely to be? Certainly the Commission has ample authority to dismantle or regulate cartels and monopolies. The Commission has very sharp teeth: it may impose fines ranging up to $1 million, or 10 percent of annual sales, on companies that willfully violate or ignore its antitrust directives. The effectiveness of antitrust policy in the EEC depends, therefore, mainly on how the Commission uses its powers. So far the Commission has compelled the registration of all private restrictive agreements, but it is still processing the nearly 40,000 agreements and has made very few decisions. Rather than arbitrating each application for antitrust clearance, the Commission is trying to make key decisions affecting broad classes of agreements.[5]

---

[5] By mid-1965 the Commission had published only five decisions on restraints of competition. The first important antitrust decision came in 1964 when the Commission prevented the German electronics firm, Grundig, from operating under an agreement giving a French firm, Consten, exclusive rights to Grundig sales in France. Since some 6,000 of the agreements registered with the Commission are exclusive agency agreements similar to the Grundig-Consten agreement, it is expected that many firms will amend their agreements to conform to Commission policy.

We can reasonably expect severe treatment of arrangements that nullify, or threaten to nullify, any liberalizing effects of the customs union, but there is little prospect of an antimonopoly drive in the EEC. The Commission is unlikely to prohibit mergers or to dissolve existing concentrations. Quite the contrary. There is a strong belief in the EEC that European firms are too small to compete effectively against United States firms. It is pointed out, for example, that of the 500 largest companies in the world, 306 are American and only 74 belong to EEC countries. The sales of General Motors alone exceed the German federal budget and equal the combined sales of Germany's 13 largest companies.[6]

Viewed broadly, the EEC's antitrust policy represents a radical break with the past. Although this policy is limited to trade among the six countries and does not apply to purely domestic trade or to trade with nonmember countries, the Commission has already gone a long way towards establishing a common policy on competition in the EEC that is an indispensable part of economic union.

Common Policies for Transportation and Energy. Together with the European Coal and Steel Community and Euratom, the EEC is seeking to develop common policies in transportation and energy.

The common policy in transportation would create a market free of any national discriminations. This involves the elimination of double taxation on motor vehicles, common rules for international passenger traffic, coordination of investment in transportation facilities, the standardization of procedures for issuing trucking licenses, a common rate-bracket system, the application of rules of competition for road, rail, and inland waterway transportation, as well as many other matters in this very complex field. It is expected that air and sea transportation will also eventually come under a common policy.

The first important step towards an integration of energy in the EEC was taken in 1964 when the member governments agreed to carry out a common energy policy. However, aside from Euratom which is restricted to nuclear energy and ECSC which is restricted to coal, no substantial progress has been made in this field.

Harmonization of Economic and Social Policies. Already the EEC is progressing toward a *common trade policy*. It is establishing a common external tariff and it negotiates as one body at the GATT

---

[6] "United States-European Competitive Positions Compared," *European Community*, No. 81, May, 1965, pp. 12-13.

tariff conferences. In accordance with the Treaty, by 1970 a common commercial policy will be effected to cover trade relations with nonmember countries (especially the Communist countries), anti-dumping regulations, export credit, and all other elements comprising the commercial conduct of a nation.

The EEC is still a long way from a *common fiscal and monetary* policy. In 1964 a small start was made in this direction when the Council agreed on measures to halt inflation and adopted procedures to coordinate medium-term economic policy and strengthen the structure of monetary and financial cooperation. However, real progress towards a common economic policy (including exchange rates and balance of payments policies) is presently thwarted by the refusal of member countries (notably France) to give up monetary and fiscal sovereignty. Control over the monetary system and over government taxation and expenditure lies at the very core of national sovereignty. Hence a true integration in these areas depends on concomitant progress towards political union.

The Commission is pushing integration in *social policy* by developing common policies in vocational training, social security, industrial safety, and labor regulations. It is also engaged in removing national restrictions on the movement and residence of workers and in supporting measures to harmonize living and working conditions throughout the Community.

Towards a Political Union?

From the beginning the ultimate objective of the EEC has been political union—the establishment of a United States of Europe. Attempts in the early postwar years to move directly towards political union in Western Europe were frustrated by national jealousies and ambitions. It was then that men like Maurice Schuman and Jean Monnet turned towards economic integration as a means to achieve eventual political integration. The first concrete success in this direction was the creation of the European Coal and Steel Community in 1952 which pooled the coal and steel resources of the six countries. (Other countries, notably Great Britain, stayed out of the ECSC precisely because of its political implications.) In the early 1950's a new attempt to bring about political union by direct means was thwarted when in 1954 the French Assembly rejected the European Defense Community Treaty. Meanwhile, to the surprise of many, the ECSC got off to a strong start and progressively demonstrated that economic integration was not an illusion but a practical achievement. Its success led to the more ambitious EEC Treaty in 1957. The statesmen who drafted and negotiated the Rome Treaty firmly believed that they were building a new Europe, that gradual economic integration over the transitional period would be crowned by a political federation of the member countries.

It can be argued that the Community is already a political union in specific areas of economic and social policy. Certainly the member countries have given up much of their sovereignty in international trade and agriculture. On the other hand, it is also true that the national governments still retain control: the Commission proposes but the Council of Ministers disposes. The Community institutions are supranational only to a limited degree; real power remains with the national governments. As long as this situation prevails, political union is a distant goal and it is even doubtful whether full economic union can be brought about because it will demand enhanced powers for Community institutions to the detriment of national powers.

In 1961 the Six solemnly reaffirmed in Bonn their determination to establish a political union and give it statutory form. It soon became evident, however, that France, in the person of President Charles de Gaulle, wanted no more than a loose confederation of national states while the other member governments (particularly the Netherlands and Belgium) wanted a supranational federal government. Then in January, 1963, the drive for political union was struck a possibly fatal blow when De Gaulle unilaterally rejected Britain's bid for membership without any prior consultation with the other EEC countries. In mid-1965 another crisis paralyzed EEC because of French opposition to any strengthening of the Commission and the European Parliament. The Commission had proposed that it be given the authority to finance its budget by collecting the revenues generated by the external common tariff and the variable import levies. At the same time, the Commission also proposed that the European Parliament be given power over the Community budget. If approved by the Council, these proposals would have given fiscal autonomy to the Community and made it much less dependent on the national governments. The French government vigorously opposed this initiative and then recalled its EEC minister, thereby halting the decision-making machinery of the EEC.[7]

---

[7] After a seven-month boycott, France agreed to participate in the Council of Ministers at the end of January, 1966. Although this broke the deadlock that had paralyzed the EEC, it did not resolve the basic dispute about the EEC's political evolution.

In the middle of the 1960's, therefore, the Community was brought to a standstill by diametrically opposed ideas of what the Community should be. France wanted a Commission of administrators and technicians that would simply execute the decisions made by the national governments in the Council of Ministers. The other five governments (although disagreeing somewhat on details and timing) wanted a strengthening of the Commission and Parliament and their eventual transformation into a supranational federal government.

In brief, the outlook for political union is bleak. Not only will diplomacy and defense remain outside the EEC, but it is doubtful that plans for further economic integration, such as a common monetary system, will come to fruition in the foreseeable future. However, this does not mean that the EEC can be written off as a complete failure. Far from it. As we have seen, the EEC has nearly completed its customs union and this achievement alone has had, and is continuing to have, profound effects on Europe's role in the world economy. The likelihood is that EEC will continue to be a powerful force in international trade even if its higher objectives of full economic and political union are not realized.

PLACE OF THE COMMUNITY IN WORLD TRADE

The European Economic Community and the United States are the two giants of world trade. Excluding trade among its members, the Community accounts for about 15 percent of the free world's exports, approximately the same as the United States. All the EEC countries (counting Belgium-Luxembourg as a single trading unit) belong to the ten principal trading countries shown in Table 2-2 in Chapter 2. Furthermore, with the exception of Japan, the EEC has been growing more rapidly than the other industrial areas. In the decade 1953-63 the average annual increase in the Community's gross national product was 5.5 percent compared to 2.7 percent for the United Kingdom and 2.9 percent for the United States. Because of its economic size and dynamism, the external commercial policies of the EEC have a pervasive influence on the composition, direction, and volume of international trade.

This section describes the basic policy of the EEC towards third countries, its relations with countries that have been granted preferential status, and the split between the European Economic Community and the European Free Trade Association.

The Common External Tariff and Variable Import Levies

The basic policy of the EEC towards third countries is expressed by the common external tariff and the variable import levies on agricultural products.

When fully erected, the common external tariff is to be a simple arithmetic average of the national tariffs levied by the member countries in 1957. Since the Netherlands, Belgium, and Luxembourg had already formed a customs union (Benelux) this means an averaging of four duties for each item imported by the EEC. The Rome Treaty stipulates a movement towards the common tariff in three steps over the transition period—two alignments of 30 percent and a final alignment of 40 percent. The first two steps were accomplished by mid-1963, and the Commission has proposed the full establishment of the common tariff by mid-1967 coincident with the establishment of complete free trade within the Community.[8] At that time the member countries will no longer have national tariff systems; zero tariffs will prevail within the common market and the Community will levy duties on imports from outside countries. Generally, the erection of the common tariff has involved reductions in French and Italian duties and increases in Benelux and German duties.

Although the common tariff will most probably be lower than an average of the 1957 rates, it will have a greater protective effect because it discriminates against nonmember countries. Before the formation of EEC, for example, both German and American manufacturers of (say) machine tools paid the same duties in exporting to France. But when the common tariff is in full operation, the German manufacturers will be able to ship duty-free exports to France while the American manufacturers will have to pay the common tariff. When competition is close, tariff discrimination can be decisive in shutting out imports from third countries.

In analyzing the effects of a customs union on trade, economists speak of *trade diversion* and *trade creation*. Diversion occurs when member countries now buy from each other what they formerly bought from third countries. Trade creation occurs when the elimination of internal tariffs and other barriers stimulates *new* trade among the

---

[8] Actually the EEC is closer to the common external tariff than this statement suggests because the EEC is adjusting towards a common tariff that is 20 percent *below* the average of the 1957 rates. This lower common tariff is contingent, however, upon reciprocal concessions from third countries. If such concessions are not forthcoming in the Kennedy Round, then the EEC will revert to the original common tariff.

member countries that does not displace third-country imports. Trade creation is most likely to be substantial when the economies of the member countries are competitive (as is true of the EEC countries) because then there is considerable scope for shifts from high-cost to low-cost suppliers *within* the customs union. Even in this case, however, trade diversion will occur when the lowest-cost suppliers are located outside the union.

These *allocation effects* of a customs union are not the whole story, however. Insofar as a customs union stimulates internal economic growth by providing opportunities for large-scale production (economies of scale), by intensifying competition, by encouraging higher capital investment, and in other ways, then these *growth effects* will induce more imports from third countries that may offset, or possibly more than offset, any diversion effects. This seems to have been true of the EEC, at least up to the mid-1960's; since 1958 EEC imports from third countries have risen by more than half despite the progressive discrimination introduced by the simultaneous elimination of internal and the erection of the common external tariffs.

We have already described the variable import levies imposed by the EEC on imports of temperate agricultural products. These levies are much more protectionist than the common external tariff levied on imports of industrial and tropical agricultural products. Their diversion effects are likely to be especially serious for low-cost suppliers like the United States. Also the comparatively slow growth in food consumption in the EEC offers little prospect that growth effects will neutralize diversion effects.

The discrimination inherent in the common tariff and variable levies is a cause of concern to all third countries. This concern is behind the efforts to bargain down the EEC tariffs in the Kennedy Round.

Countries Accorded Preferential Status by the EEC

The Community has an *Association Convention* with 18 independent African states that gives these developing countries free access to the common market under the same conditions as the six EEC countries.[9] In return, the 18 countries are obligated to abolish quotas and lower tariffs by 15 percent annually on imports from the Community, but they retain the right to maintain old tariffs and

---

[9] When the Rome Treaty was signed in 1957 most of these African states were French colonies.

quotas, or create new ones, in order to protect infant industries. In addition, the EEC's European Development Fund for Overseas grants development assistance to the associated states which amounted to $581 million in the period 1958-63 and is expected to reach $730 million in the period 1963-68.

The preferential status of the 18 African countries has raised problems for other tropical countries in Africa, Latin America, and elsewhere that export the same products to the EEC, such as coffee, bananas, peanuts, cocoa, and cotton. Four Commonwealth countries in Africa—Nigeria, Kenya, Tanzania, and Uganda—have expressed an interest in concluding with the EEC an agreement similar to the Association Convention.

Greece and Turkey were accorded preferential status when they became associated members of the Community in 1962 and 1963 respectively. The agreements with these countries call for eventual full membership in the Community, but because of their low levels of industrialization they are allowed 12 to 25 years to eliminate duties and quotas on imports from the EEC while enjoying free access to the common market.[10] The Community is also negotiating trade agreements with a number of countries; by mid-1965 it had concluded agreements with Israel and Lebanon.

So far the extension of the Community beyond the six original members has not included the other industrial countries in Western Europe. Negotiations that would have broadened EEC to include most of Western Europe were broken off in January, 1963, when France rejected the membership bid of the United Kingdom. This has prolonged the split in Europe between the EEC and EFTA.

The Split in Western Europe—EEC and EFTA

In Chapter 17 we offered a brief description of the European Free Trade Association (EFTA), pointing out that the motivation behind its establishment in 1960 was to facilitate later negotiations with the EEC towards a regional trading arrangement that would comprise the whole of Western Europe. The dramatic failure of Britain to enter the EEC provoked a crisis in EFTA out of which evolved a determination to strengthen its own operations and a frank recognition that a solution of the European trading problem was not feasible in the present political circumstances. Since then, EFTA has continued to make rapid progress towards an industrial free trade area;

---

[10] Austria and Spain have also applied for association with the EEC.

the seven members have agreed to remove all tariffs on their mutual trade in industrial goods by the end of 1966.[11]

Today EFTA's policy towards EEC is focused on the Kennedy Round of tariff negotiations. EFTA countries fully support the United States effort to reduce the EEC common tariff and moderate the effects of the variable import levies. A successful outcome to these negotiations would do a great deal to mitigate the present cleavage in Europe and would make it easier to ameliorate at some time in the future. But it would not remove the rift between EEC and EFTA which violates both economic and political common sense.[12]

THE UNITED STATES AND THE COMMUNITY

The Trade Expansion Act of 1962 was a direct response to the progressive establishment of a customs union by the European Economic Community. The provisions of this Act, which were described in the previous chapter, give to the President sweeping authority to reduce or eliminate United States import duties in return for similar concessions from the EEC and third countries. The focus on prospective negotiations with the EEC animates all of the President's tariff-cutting authority, and it is explicit in the "80-percent" authority and the authority to go to zero on agricultural duties.[13]

The EEC has become the most dynamic export market for the United States, taking about one fifth of total United States exports in the first half of the 1960's. But this attractive picture is shadowed by fears of the future. United States-EEC trade prospects are threatened by several developments:

1. The degree of EEC discrimination on industrial products will increase sharply in the future: there will be zero duties on industrial trade among the Six while outsiders will pay the common tariff.

2. The common external tariff appears to be more protective than the national tariffs it is displacing because in most instances it

---

[11] Because it is a free trade area and not a customs union, EFTA involves the abolition of barriers to internal trade, but not the erection of a common external tariff. Each member country (the United Kingdom, Sweden, Norway, Denmark, Portugal, Austria, and Switzerland) maintains its own tariff system for trade with third countries and negotiates on its own at tariff conferences. Finland is an associate member of EFTA. For a fuller description of EFTA see Franklin R. Root, "EFTA and the EEC," *International Trade Review*, March, 1965, pp. 29-35.

[12] The EEC and EFTA are the best customers of each other, and the members of both groups cooperated intimately in OEEC and today belong to OECD.

[13] The 80-percent authority has been rendered almost useless by the failure of Britain to enter the EEC.

is higher than the former German tariff. This means that German manufacturers—the major suppliers of most industrial products in the EEC—will enjoy greater protection than before, apart from the tariff advantages they are gaining within the EEC.

3. The common agricultural policy is very protectionist, limiting third countries to the role of residual suppliers and stimulating agricultural self-sufficiency in the EEC.

4. The economic growth of EEC countries has slackened in recent years, and it is expected that growth effects on imports will be less significant in the 1960's than in the 1950's.

This combination of factors points to a substantial diversion of trade, a substitution of intra-EEC trade for trade with third countries. One study estimates that this diversion will cost the United States an export loss of $650 million by 1968: $200 million in manufactures, $100 million in nonagricultural raw materials, and $350 million in agricultural products.[14] As a result, it is expected that United States exports to the EEC will rise only $1.2 billion (instead of $1.85 billion) in the period 1962-68.

The key importance of EEC markets to the United States and the threat that these markets would become limited by protectionist policies convinced the new Kennedy administration that the United States must make a strong effort to bargain down EEC trade barriers and prevent, or mitigate, the trade diversion that menaced the export interests of countries outside the Community. The persisting United States balance of payments deficit lent urgency to this decision.

The Kennedy Round

Backed by the Trade Expansion Act, the United States called for a new GATT Tariff Conference, and in May, 1963, the ministers of the GATT countries met in Geneva to decide on the basic principles that would guide negotiations scheduled to start in May, 1964. United States and EEC representatives clashed on several points, but compromises on both sides led finally to an apparent agreement on general principles:

1. Negotiations would cover all classes of products, including agricultural and other primary products. (The United States insisted on coverage of agricultural products which had been neglected in previous GATT negotiations.)

2. Negotiations would deal with nontariff trade barriers as well as tariffs.

---

[14] Walter S. Salant, *et al.*, *The United States Balance of Payments in 1968* (Washington, D. C.: The Brookings Institution, 1963) p. 112.

3. Negotiations would be based on a plan of substantial and equal linear reductions with a bare minimum of exceptions which would be subject to confrontation and justification. However, in those cases where there were "significant disparities" in tariff levels, the tariff reductions would be based on special rules of general and automatic application. (This principle was a direct compromise between the United States and the EEC, the former fighting for substantial linear cuts, the latter holding out for special treatment of tariff disparities.)

4. Negotiations should provide for acceptable conditions of access to world markets for agricultural products.

5. Every effort should be made to reduce barriers to exports of the developing countries, and the developed countries should not expect to receive reciprocity from the developing countries.

Agreement on these principles did not resolve the differences between the United States and the EEC. As Ludwig Erhard remarked at the time: "We have agreed on the shell of the egg, but what the egg will contain we do not yet know." [15] The job of hammering out agreement on the contents of the "egg" was handed over to a newly created Trade Negotiations Committee. One issue bogged down the work of the Committee from the start—the question of tariff disparities. It so occupied the attention of negotiators that discussions on agriculture, nontariff trade barriers, and trade with developing countries had scarcely begun by May, 1964, when the Tariff Conference, popularly known as the Kennedy Round, opened officially.

Issues between the United States and the Community

A brief description of the major issues in the Kennedy Round negotiations will help us understand why agreement is so difficult and why the grand objective of the Kennedy Round—an across-the-board 50 percent reduction in tariff duties—is in jeopardy.

Tariff Disparities. Both the United States and the EEC agree that the average height of their respective tariffs (as measured by the ratio of duties collected over the value of dutiable imports) is about the same, around 12 percent. But the EEC tariff is very homogeneous with most rates falling between 10 and 20 percent because the EEC tariff is an arithmetical average of its members' tariffs. In contrast, the United States tariff has some very high duties as well as some very low ones.[16]

---

[15] European Community Information (London), *European Community*, June, 1963, p. 2.

[16] For example, 14.7 percent of United States tariff rates are over 25 percent

The United States wants a 50 percent linear cut in tariff rates with a minimum of exceptions, a position supported by the EFTA countries. In opposition, the EEC contends that a 50 percent cut would not be fair because it would still leave some United States duties at a high level. In the case of United States rates and low EEC rates, the EEC wants to cut its own duties by (say) 25 percent in return for 50 percent cuts by the United States. After more than a year of fierce argument, the GATT negotiators decided to circumvent the issue by permitting each country to place products subject to disparities on its exceptions lists. This did not solve the disparities problem but it did prevent an impasse in negotiations.

Exceptions Lists. In November, 1964, the United States, EEC, and other industrial countries submitted lists of products that they wanted to be excepted from linear cuts. The size of these lists (about 20 percent of dutiable imports for both the United States and EEC) is higher than expected and it is now doubtful that the Kennedy Round will accomplish an overall tariff cut of 50 percent. Negotiations on exception-list products will involve item-by-item bargaining with only modest concessions in prospect.

The Agricultural Issue. The United States insists that any tariff-and-trade package it negotiates in the Kennedy Round must provide an access to EEC markets for United States agricultural products. The United States negotiating plan contains these elements: (1) substantial reductions in any *fixed* import duties on agricultural products in line with reductions in industrial duties; (2) the inclusion of variable import levies in negotiations in a meaningful way and, in particular, agreement on market-sharing arrangements in the EEC for both domestic and foreign producers involving nondiscriminatory global quotas; (3) the removal of quantitative restrictions or state-trading activities that impede trade in agricultural products.

The EEC has steadfastly refused to negotiate on target prices and has rejected any market-sharing arrangements. Instead, the Community proposes a "freeze" on the amount of domestic price support (the difference between the world price and the domestic price) in the Community, the United States, and other countries. The United States views this proposal as a binding of higher levels of protection

---

compared to 3.6 percent of the EEC rates. On the other hand, 26.6 percent of United States rates lie in the 0-5 percent range compared to only 16.2 percent of the EEC rates. See Committee for Economic Development, *Trade Negotiations for a Better Free World Economy,* May, 1964, pp. 46 ff.

in the EEC rather than as a reduction in trade barriers. The Community also subscribes to the negotiation of global commodity agreements, and has submitted plans for a worldwide grain covenant to include binding support levels, an established world-reference price, and special provisions for developing countries.

Nontariff Trade Barriers. For the first time a GATT Tariff Conference is addressing itself to the problem of nontariff trade barriers. These arise from a broad variety of national laws, regulations, and administrative procedures, and they are often more restrictive than tariffs. Both the United States and the EEC have many nontariff barriers that frustrate traders on both sides of the Atlantic.

Europeans are particularly annoyed by the United States customs valuation based on the American selling price. Most United States imports are valued f.o.b. the foreign port of export; but organic chemicals and some other products are valued at the wholesale price in the United States of the competing American products, including distribution costs and profits. Europeans allege that the use of the American selling price can double or even triple the effective tariff rate, and they are demanding its abolition. Strong criticism is also directed against the United States Anti-Dumping Act and the "Buy-American" Act.

In turn, the United States charges the EEC with special taxes that discriminate against United States automobiles and other products, the practice of basing tariff rates and some taxes on high c.i.f. valuations, and many other barriers such as the French prohibition on advertising grain liquors.[17]

The Developing Countries. All the concessions made in trade negotiations among the industrial countries will be extended to the 40-odd developing countries that belong to GATT without the need for reciprocal concessions on their part. The United States is also willing to eliminate completely tariffs on tropical products in return for similar action by the EEC. But the EEC is reluctant to move in that direction because it would destroy much of the preferential treatment now accorded the associated African states. Instead, the EEC favors the negotiation of global commodity agreements that would stabilize prices and insure orderly markets. The United Nations

---

[17] In 1963 the Italian road tax was $170 for a United States compact car, $44 for a Volkswagen, and only $17 for a Fiat. In France there is a surtax of $60 on a two-gallon container of grain spirits, a product not produced in France.

Conference on Trade and Development (UNCTAD) in June, 1964, highlighted the needs of developing countries for more generous treatment of their trade by the industrial countries. Both the United States and EEC are experiencing mounting pressures to negotiate tariff concessions and adopt other policies that will enhance significantly the trading prospects of developing nations.

The Significance of the Kennedy Round

Progress in the Kennedy Round has been painfully slow—in part because the issues are so many and so complex and in part because the EEC has not fully completed its customs union and must reconcile the often divergent interests of its members before it can negotiate effectively with the United States.

Only a very brave (or foolish) person would predict the eventual outcome of the Kennedy Round. But whatever the outcome may be —good or bad—it will do much to shape the structure of world trade in the 1970's.[18] The stakes are very high. If negotiations should utterly fail, it could mean a protectionist, inward-looking Community, the collapse of GATT, a widening split between EFTA and EEC, a tariff war between EEC and the United States, and a disruption of the Atlantic Alliance.

In the final analysis, the Kennedy Round is an acid test of the willingness of the Atlantic nations to strengthen economic cooperation and build the kind of partnership that is the essential basis for a better world. It is a test that the United States, the EFTA countries, and the EEC can ill afford to fail.

SUMMARY

1. The European Economic Community started its official existence at the beginning of 1958. The main feature of the EEC is the creation in planned stages of a *customs union* for both industrial and agricultural goods. A second objective is a full *economic union* with free movement of persons, services and capital, and progressive harmonization of social, fiscal, and monetary policies. The ultimate objective is a *political union* of the Six.
2. The basic institutions of the Community are four in number: Commission, Council of Ministers, European Parliament, and Court of Justice.

---

[18] Negotiations are expected to continue until the end of 1966, with the final package agreed upon early in 1967 before the Trade Expansion Act authority expires on June 30, 1967. Thus tariff concessions are not likely to be put into effect before the middle of 1967 and they are due to be staggered over a five-year period.

3. The EEC has made impressive progress in lowering internal barriers on industrial trade. By 1966 industrial tariffs were only 20 percent of their 1957 levels, and the Commission has proposed their full removal by mid-1967. This rapid movement toward internal free trade has greatly stimulated intra-Community commerce.

4. Through a series of laborious negotiations the EEC has developed a common agricultural policy involving target, intervention, and threshold prices, and variable import levies. Two points need stressing: there are no production controls, and the variable import levies make third countries, such as the United States, residual suppliers of farm products.

5. The EEC is much more than a customs union; it seeks to integrate all facets of the national member economies. Harmonization is a key word in the evolution of the economic union. Its objectives are the gradual elimination of differences in national legislation, administrative practices, and policies, and their eventual integration to form a Community-wide policy carried out by common institutions. Actual progress towards an economic union has been substantial in the fields of antitrust policy, trade policy, and some aspects of social policy; progress has been slow in the fields of transportation, energy, and fiscal and monetary policy.

6. It can be argued that the Community is already a political union in specific areas of economic and social policy. But it is also true that the Community institutions are supranational only to a limited degree and that real power remains with the national governments. As long as this situation prevails, political union is a distant goal; and it is even doubtful whether full economic union can be brought about because it will demand enhanced powers for Community institutions at the expense of national powers. In the second half of 1965 a crisis paralyzed the EEC because of French opposition to any strengthening of the Commission and the European Parliament.

7. The EEC and the United States are the two giants of world trade. The basic policy of the EEC towards third countries is expressed by the common external tariff and the variable import levies on agricultural products. As a customs union, the EEC inevitably discriminates against third countries. In analyzing the effects of a customs union on trade, economists speak of *trade diversion* and *trade creation*. In addition to these allocation effects, there may be positive *growth effects* insofar as a customs union stimulates internal economic growth. The discrimination inherent in the EEC common tariff and variable levies is a cause of concern to all nonmember countries.

8. The EEC has accorded preferential status to 18 African countries, and Greece and Turkey have become associated members of the Community. But the EEC has not extended membership to other industrial countries in Western Europe. In January, 1963, France rejected the membership

bid of the United Kingdom, thereby prolonging the cleavage in Europe between EEC and EFTA.
9. The EEC has become the most dynamic United States export market, but the United States is concerned about the effects of EEC discrimination in future years. This country is now attempting in the Kennedy Round to lessen discrimination by bargaining down EEC tariffs and other obstacles to trade. The Kennedy Round is the most ambitious GATT Tariff Conference ever held, comprising negotiations on industrial tariffs, restrictions on agricultural trade, nontariff trade barriers, and the trade of developing countries. Several issues between the United States and the Community have slowed negotiations: tariff disparities, exceptions lists, agriculture, and nontariff trade barriers. The goal of a 50 percent across-the-board reduction in tariffs now appears unlikely.
10. Whatever the outcome of the Kennedy Round may be—good or bad—it will do much to shape the structure of world trade in the 1970's.

QUESTIONS AND APPLICATIONS

1. Identify the institutions of the EEC and describe their functions.
2. (a) What is a customs union? How does it differ from a free trade area?
   (b) Discuss the progress of the EEC in setting up a customs union for industrial products.
3. (a) Why is the EEC approaching a common market in agriculture differently from a common market in industrial products?
   (b) What is the structure of the common agricultural policy? How does this structure affect EEC imports of farm products?
4. (a) What is an economic union?
   (b) Describe the progress of the EEC towards the formation of an economic union.
   (c) Is full economic union possible without political union? Explain.
5. (a) What is the common external tariff?
   (b) What is the meaning of trade diversion, trade creation, and growth effects?
   (c) Appraise the effects of the EEC on United States trade in terms of these three concepts. (This will require an analysis of relevant trade and other economic data.)
6. Does the preferential status accorded by the EEC to 18 African countries have any bearing on Latin America's trade with the EEC? How?
7. How did the cleavage in Europe between EEC and EFTA come about?
8. (a) Describe the scope of the Kennedy Round.
   (b) What are the issues between the United States and the Community in the Kennedy Round?
   (c) Why is the United States pressing so hard for a successful outcome of the Kennedy Round?

SELECTED READINGS

Benoit, E. *Europe at Sixes and Sevens.* New York: Columbia University Press, 1963.

Committee for Economic Development. *Trade Negotiations for a Better Free World.* New York: May, 1964.

Dewhurst, J. F. and Associates. *Europe's Needs and Resources.* New York: Twentieth Century Fund, 1961.

European Community Information Service. *European Community.* Washington, D. C.: monthly.

——————. *General Report of the Activities of the Community,* annual.

Krause, Lawrence B. (ed.) *The Common Market, Progress and Controversy.* Englewood Cliffs, New Jersey: Prentice-Hall, Inc., 1964.

CHAPTER 20

THE DEVELOPING NATIONS AND WORLD TRADE

Seventy percent of the people that inhabit the non-Communist free world live a daily round of grinding poverty. More than one hundred nations have annual per capita incomes that are barely one twentieth of the United States level. Occupying the vast stretches of Asia, Africa, and Latin America, these poor nations are now committed to programs of economic development that seek to break the vicious circle of poverty. Industrialization has become the supreme national goal; it dominates the economic policies of the developing nations and will probably continue to do so for generations to come. In particular, the drive for economic development shapes the attitudes, policies, and expectations of the poor nations in the area of international trade and finance.

In this chapter we shall examine the problems that developing nations encounter in international trade and the policies they advocate to overcome them. We shall also look at the response that the developed nations of the free world are making to the needs and demands of the developing nations. But before taking up these international subjects, we must comprehend the economic situation of the poor nations and the major obstacles to a betterment of their low standards of living. For it is this situation that generates the drive for development and the policies the developing nations follow in dealing with the developed nations.

THE DEVELOPING NATIONS AND THEIR POTENTIAL TRADE GAP

Which are the developing nations? What is their stage of economic development? What are the major obstacles to further development? What is their potential trade gap? These questions occupy our attention in this opening section.

Which Are the Developing Nations?

The developing nations include all the countries of non-Communist Asia (except Japan), Latin America, and Africa (except South Africa).[1] Although different in many respects, these nations have several common features, such as low per capita incomes, high illiteracy rates, a predominance of agriculture and other primary production, and a dependence on commodity exports, that set them off from the economically advanced countries located mainly in Western Europe and North America.

Tables 20-1 and 20-2 reveal the wide and growing gap between the rich and poor nations.

Table 20-1

GROSS DOMESTIC PRODUCT AND POPULATION BY MAJOR REGIONS OF THE FREE WORLD, 1950 AND 1960

	Gross Domestic Product (Billions of 1960 Dollars) 1950	1960	Average Annual Compound Rate of Growth (%) 1950-1960	Population (Millions) 1950	1960	Average Annual Compound Rate of Growth (%) 1950-1960
Developed Economies:	621.8	920.1	4.0	575.6	652.6	1.2
North America	388.5	539.8	3.3	166.0	198.6	1.8
W. Europe *	199.2	314.3	4.7	303.9	332.3	0.9
Japan	16.1	39.0	9.3	83.1	93.2	1.1
Oceania and South Africa	18.0	27.0	4.1	22.6	28.5	2.3
Developing Economies:	110.3	169.8	4.4	1046.2	1300.6	2.2
Latin American Republics	39.1	61.4	4.6	155.6	204.9	2.8
Africa †	18.1	27.0	4.1	193.5	239.3	2.2
Far East ‡	45.2	68.3	4.2	652.9	800.5	2.1
West Asia §	6.6	10.9	5.2	40.4	51.2	2.4
Others ¶	1.2	2.2	6.2	3.8	4.7	2.1

* Including Turkey.
† Excluding South Africa.
‡ Excluding Japan.
§ Excluding Turkey.
¶ Consists mainly of countries and dependent territories in the Caribbean.

SOURCE: Adapted from United Nations Conference on Trade and Development, *A Review of World Trends in Gross Domestic Product*, E/Conf. 46/67, March, 1964, Table 1, p. 7 and Table 2, p. 10.

---

[1] This is the classification used by the United Nations and we shall adopt it in this chapter. We shall use the terms "developing," "poor," and "nonindustrial" interchangeably to denote these nations. This classification excludes low-income countries in southern Europe (Portugal, Spain, Greece, and Turkey) that are also badly in need of economic development.

For the decade 1950-60, the developing nations taken together recorded an average annual compound rate of growth of 4.4 percent, higher than the 4.0 percent rate achieved by the industrial, developed nations. Although this rate of growth was probably the highest ever accomplished by the developing regions over a ten-year period, its effects on per capita income were vitiated by a rapid rise in population averaging 2.2 percent annually. Thus Table 20-2 shows that per capita income (the best single index of living standards) grew only 2.2 percent annually in the developing countries during the 1950's while it rose at an annual rate of 2.7 percent in the developed countries where the population growth rate was much lower. In Latin America where population expanded at an annual rate of 2.8 percent, per capita income grew at a rate of only 1.8 percent a year.

It is evident that the per capita income gap between the developed and developing nations *widened* during the 1950's. In 1950 per capita income in the developed nations was about ten times as large as in the developing nations; by 1960, it was eleven times as large. If these trends continue, it would take thirty-three years for the developing regions to double per capita income, and the gap

Table 20-2

PER CAPITA GROSS DOMESTIC PRODUCT BY MAJOR REGIONS OF THE FREE WORLD, 1950 AND 1960

	Amount in 1960 Dollars 1950	1960	Average Annual Compound Rate of Growth (%) 1950-1960
Developed Economies:	1,080	1,410	2.7
North America	2,340	2,718	1.5
W. Europe	655	946	3.7
Japan	193	418	8.0
Oceania and S. Africa	800	948	1.7
Developing Economies:	105	130	2.2
Latin American Republics	252	300	1.8
Africa	93	113	1.9
Far East	69	85	2.1
West Asia	164	214	2.7
Other	319	472	4.0

GENERAL NOTE: Territorial coverage is the same as in Table 20-1.
SOURCE: Adapted from United Nations Conference on Trade and Development, *A Review of World Trends in Gross Domestic Product,* E/Conf. 46/47, March, 1964, Table 3, p. 11.

between the two groups of countries would widen steadily. Given these trends, the developing nations would need several generations to achieve the *1960* per capita income levels of the developed nations in Western Europe and North America.

The size of the income gap is enormous. By the end of the 1950's per capita income was less than $100 per annum for 46 percent of the free world's population that contributed only 7 percent to the gross domestic product of the free world. At the other end of the scale, more than half of the free world's gross domestic product was produced by only 10 percent of the population, located mainly in North America.

The poverty of the developing nations is not new; it has been a way of life for untold generations. What is new is the bitter awareness of poverty, the knowledge that it is not inevitable, and the determination to raise living standards one way or another. Many of the countries of Asia and Africa have recently emerged from a colonial status to full political independence and others are moving in that direction. Independence has been accompanied by a virulent nationalism, high expectations, and, in many cases, antagonism towards the West.

What has been called "the revolution of rising expectations" is cause for both hope and fear. Of hope, for after centuries of stagnation the developing countries are now striving to create the conditions essential to economic and social progress. Of fear, for the frustration of their high expectations may turn these peoples towards undemocratic solutions (as it has already done in some instances) and against the West. This fear is accentuated by the persistent efforts of the Communist powers to destroy Western influence in the developing countries through ceaseless propaganda, internal subversion, and calculated programs of economic penetration.

The Stages of Economic Growth

How did the income gap arise? How do economies develop? In his highly influential book, W. W. Rostow identifies five stages of growth that characterize all societies.[2]

The Traditional Society. The traditional society is grounded on pre-Newtonian science and technology and pre-Newtonian conceptions of the physical world. Although some change must and does occur

---

[2] W. W. Rostow, *The Stages of Economic Growth* (Cambridge, Massachusetts: Cambridge University Press, 1960).

in such a society (*ad hoc* technical innovations, fluctuations in population, political and social movements, etc.), there is a ceiling on per capita output and income because of the absence of modern science and technology. The early civilizations of the Middle East and the Mediterranean, the dynasties of China, and Medieval Europe belonged to the traditional stage of economic growth.

The Preconditions for Takeoff. This is a transitional stage when societies develop the conditions necessary for the next stage. These preconditions were created first in Western Europe (led by Great Britain) in the late seventeenth and early eighteenth centuries when modern scientific discoveries were applied to agriculture and manufacturing.

Outside Western Europe the preconditions stage was initiated by the impact of another more advanced society, notably the European. The spread of European political and economic power throughout the world in the eighteenth and nineteenth centuries disrupted traditional societies in Asia, Latin America, and Africa, introducing by actual demonstration the revolutionary idea that economic progress is both possible and desirable.

Because they are transitional, precondition societies are a mixture of the traditional and the new. A few enterprising persons take up the new ways, mobilizing capital and investing it in modern production facilities; but the masses of people remain peasants clinging to the traditional ways that spell low productivity and stagnation. A decisive factor in this stage is political—the building up of a centralized national state. The majority of poor nations now occupy this stage of economic development.

The Takeoff. This is the stage of the great watershed of economic growth: traditional resistances weaken and are finally overcome as the society enters upon a process of cumulative growth. Modern technology, modern organization, and modern attitudes come to dominate economic activity. The rate of new investment rises to 10 percent or more of national income; new industries are born, stimulating the birth of ancillary industries in widening ripples of influence. As agriculture becomes commercialized and more productive, peasants leave the land *en masse* to supply the expanding need for industrial labor. Over a decade or two, these new forces so transform the political, social, and economic structure of society that steady, sustainable growth becomes possible.

Rostow assigns the takeoff of Britain to the two decades after 1783; of France and the United States to the several decades preceding 1860; of Germany, the third quarter of the nineteenth century; of Japan, the fourth quarter of the nineteenth century; of Russia and Canada, the quarter century preceding World War I.

Since World War II a number of developing countries appear to have reached the takeoff stage. Notable examples include Mexico and Brazil in Latin America, Egypt and Ghana in Africa, Israel and Lebanon in the Middle East, and India and Taiwan in Asia.

The Drive to Maturity. In this stage of growth, the economy moves beyond the industries that originally gave impetus to its takeoff, such as textiles and steel. The society now has the capacity and technology to produce anything it chooses to produce, although it would be uneconomic to do so given the advantages of international specialization. Industrial processes become progressively more sophisticated; new industries, such as electronics and chemicals, come to the fore. The economy assumes a different role in world trade as shifts occur in its comparative cost structure: earlier import goods are now produced at home, new import requirements arise, and modern technology creates new export products.[3]

Historically, about sixty years were required for a society to move from the beginning of takeoff to maturity. Britain, the United States, Germany, and France had passed into this stage about the end of the nineteenth century. None of the developing countries has yet reached this stage.

The Age of Mass Consumption. In this stage the society develops affluent standards of living and an emphasis on the production of durable consumers' goods and services. The key symbol of this stage is the mass production and consumption of automobiles with their pervasive influence on life styles. The United States first entered this stage just before World War I; Western Europe and Japan did so in the 1950's.

Rostow acknowledges that his five-stage model of economic growth is necessarily an arbitrary and limited way of looking at the sequence of modern history. No historical model can take account of the many accidents and events that distinguish the evolution of

---

[3] See the discussion of changes in the United States composition of trade in Chapter 2.

one society from that of all the others, giving it a unique flavor. Another limitation of Rostow's model is its appearance of inevitability —each stage follows logically the preceding stage. We must recognize, however, that a society may stagnate indefinitely in the precondition stage, or early phase of the takeoff stage, because of (say) a population explosion that prevents improvements in the standard of living. Indeed, it is this possibility (or even likelihood) of stagnation that haunts the spokesmen of many developing nations today. These qualifications in no way minimize the value of Rostow's contribution; his model illuminates a great deal of the history of economic development in the modern world. Rostow also offers us a broad understanding of how the income gap between the developed and developing nations first arose, and how it one day may be closed.

The majority of the developing nations is still building the preconditions for takeoff; a minority has entered takeoff; none has become a mature economy. Further progress requires a continuing modernization of economic, social, and political institutions. A key factor in this modernization is capital formation and its accompanying technology which constitute the very heart of the development process.

The Development Process: Capital Formation

Capital formation—the creation of transportation, communications, and power facilities; the construction of factories; the acquisition of machines, tools, and other instruments of production—is an essential condition of economic growth. The harnessing of mechanical energies, the organization of mass production, the utilization of modern technology, the education and training of workers—all of these are dependent on the formation of capital. The developed nations are rich because their capital resources per capita are high; the developing nations are poor because their capital resources per capita are low.

To increase its stock of capital a nation must invest a part of its national product.[4] Investment reduces the resources available to satisfy immediate consumption, but it raises the level of consumption in the future by enhancing economic productivity. The relationship between new investment and output depends on the marginal productivity of capital that may be expressed as the *marginal product-capital ratio*. Suppose, for example, that a nation is making a net

---

[4] More precisely, a nation must invest an amount beyond that needed to maintain its existing capital stock (depreciation) if it is to make a net addition to capital stock.

annual investment (after depreciation) equal to 15 percent of its net national product (national income) and that the marginal product-capital ratio is 0.5, then national income will increase at an annual rate of 7½ percent.[5] If the annual population growth is 2 percent, then per capita income will rise about 5½ percent.

Domestic investment (capital formation) must be financed out of domestic saving or net borrowing from abroad. We can illustrate this truism by means of the national income equations that were introduced in Chapter 10. There we showed that $I_d + X = S + M$.[6] Thus: $I_d = S + (M - X)$. This tells us that new domestic investment (capital formation) is equal to the resources provided by domestic saving plus those provided by net borrowing from abroad (the excess of imports of goods and services over exports). Hence a nation may step up its rate of investment either by increasing domestic saving (which means lowering domestic consumption) or by borrowing more from abroad to finance a bigger deficit on current account.

Because the rate of saving is low in a poor economy and is difficult to increase by restricting consumption, the developing nations are highly dependent on the developed nations for funds to finance their capital formation. There is also another reason for this dependence. Even if their domestic saving were adequate to sustain desired levels of investment, the developing countries would still need foreign exchange to pay for imports of capital goods that can be obtained only from the advanced economies. As we shall observe later, the developing nations are now facing a potential shortage of foreign exchange—a deficiency of foreign exchange relative to their expected need for imports to achieve development goals.

Obstacles to Economic Development

The developing nations must overcome many obstacles to achieve a rate of investment that will provide a satisfactory rate of economic growth, especially in per capita terms. These obstacles comprise a

---

[5] A marginal product-capital ratio of 0.5 implies that $1 of new investment will generate 50 cents of new product. Thus investment equal to 15 percent of national income generates a rise in production of 0.5 (15 percent) or 7½ percent. There is, of course, a lag between the time new investment is initiated and the time it is ready to contribute to production. For a detailed explanation of the product-capital ratio and its use in projections of economic growth, see United Nations, *Analyses and Projections of Economic Development*, Part I (New York: 1955).

[6] See Equation (10) on page 198. In our present discussion I_d is *net* domestic investment and S is *net* domestic saving. This does not alter the equality.

complex set of both internal and external factors. Although it is widely agreed that the basic restraints on growth derive from the very structure of the poor societies, external conditions that hinder the exports of developing nations or limit the availability of financial assistance from abroad also can restrain growth. To become mature economies, the developing nations must undertake a massive transformation of their societies, and this can be accomplished only by their own peoples and national leaders. To do so, however, they need the capital goods and technology of the developed, industrial countries. This section looks at major obstacles to growth *within* the developing countries themselves; international trade and financial conditions that limit growth are taken up later in the chapter.

The situation of developing countries has been aptly described as interlocking sets of vicious circles that perpetuate economic stagnation and poverty. We have already alluded to one of these vicious circles: (1) productivity is low because investment is low; (2) investment is low because saving is low; (3) saving is low because income is low; (4) income is low bceause productivity is low. Thus in a very real sense the poor nations are poor because they are poor.

Lack of Social Overhead Capital. Social overhead capital supplies the services—power, transportation, storage, communications, education, etc.—that are indispensable to modern industry and agriculture. The lack of this capital in the poor nations is a bottleneck to economic development. Inadequate transportation and communication facilities block the exploitation of attractive resources located in the interior regions of many countries in Latin America, Asia, and Africa. A food-deficit country like India may lose up to one third of its agricultural output because it lacks storage facilities to protect against spoilage, rodents, and other wastage. The absence of electrical power thwarts the establishment of the many industries dependent on it, as well as impeding community and urban development.

Educational facilities are a vital element of social overhead capital. The majority of the population of developing nations is illiterate. Lacking the basic skills and training necessary to industrial production or modern agriculture, these people can make little contribution to economic development. The developing countries must stamp out illiteracy mainly by educating the new generation of their peoples; unless this is done, there is little hope for the future.

Lack of Business Managers and Government Administrators. The efforts of countless, mostly private entrepreneurs gave Western

Europe and North America the momentum to move into and beyond the takeoff stage of economic growth. Eagerly searching for new profit opportunities, these men combined factors of production in new ways and on a broader scale than ever before in history in order to produce new products for emerging markets. Later a large class of business managers arose to promote and administer the expanding private enterprise sectors of these economies. Today the professional preparation for careers in business is commonplace in the United States and is gaining recognition in Western Europe and Japan.

In contrast, the developing nations generally lack a business class that is willing to invest in new industrial enterprises and has the know-how to manage them. Their businessmen are likely to be traders and merchants engaging in foreign trade, wholesaling, and retailing rather than in manufacturing; they tend to be speculative, looking for quick profits in real estate or monopoly market situations. Frequently the upper class in the poor societies disapproves of business, preferring to invest in land and rearing their sons to be land-owning aristocrats, soldiers, lawyers, and diplomats instead of business executives. Partly owing to this class prejudice against business, foreigners dominate the commercial activity of many developing countries, such as the Chinese in Malaysia and the Philippines and the European Jews in Latin America.

Lacking private entrepreneurs, the governments of the developing nations must take the lead in formulating and implementing national development plans. Here another problem arises: the shortage of trained government administrators. The result is often incompetence, worsened by endemic bribery and favoritism. Ineffective systems of taxation fail to mobilize financial resources for capital formation; investment is allocated in ways that do not promote economic growth; public enterprises are operated inefficiently at a loss, draining off scarce capital rather than creating it.

Cultural Blocks to Economic Growth. Old ways and new ways live side by side in the developing societies and in many, the old ways remain dominant. Preindustrial attitudes towards work and belief in traditional ways are very hard to change. And yet they must be changed if the economy is ever to achieve takeoff: workers must develop the motivations and discipline essential to industrial production; peasants must become commercial farmers, open to technological innovations in agriculture.

Poor motivation, high turnover, absenteeism, and a generally sloppy performance characterize the industrial workers of many developing nations. In the early stage of industrialization, an increase in wages may actually cause absenteeism because people work only to maintain a traditional standard of living, having no conception of a rising standard.[7] Undoubtedly, however, the peasant offers the most stubborn resistance to changing his ways. Getting him to use commercial fertilizers, improved seed strains, crop rotation schemes, etc. requires a time-consuming education process that is likely to be only partially successful, as witnessed by the community-development programs in India and Latin America.

Cultural blocks are often elusive and hard to identify. Once identified, they are hard to change. Nevertheless, they must be overcome because prescientific, traditional attitudes and beliefs act to reinforce the vicious circles of poverty that plague the developing nations.

The Population Explosion. Table 20-1 indicates that the population of the developing nations grew at an average annual rate of 2.2 percent during the 1950's. (In Latin America the rate was 2.8 percent.) Moreover, in recent years this overall rate has been rising; it was 2.4 percent for the period 1955-60 compared with 2.1 percent for the period 1950-55. These high growth rates—unprecedented in history for such a large part of the globe—added over 250 million people to the developing countries during the 1950's decade. During the 1960's decade the population of the developing countries is estimated to increase from 1,301 to 1,642 million, or an annual rate of 2.4 percent.

This vast upsurge of population—aptly called the population explosion—is the single greatest obstacle to economic development, threatening to undo even the modest progress of the past. As we have previously noted, while the gross domestic product of the developing countries rose at an annual rate of 4.4 percent during the 1950's, the per capita growth rate was only 2.2 percent because of the population explosion.

Fundamentally, the population explosion is a consequence of the "public health" revolution in the poor nations. The introduction of modern medicine has cut death rates drastically (especially in the early years of life), but has had no influence on birth rates which

---

[7] This causes a "backward sloping supply schedule" for labor. This situation is not likely to last very long, particularly in urban areas where newly arrived workers are exposed to examples of higher standards of living.

remain at the traditional, high levels. Ironically, modern medicine by saving lives is making it increasingly difficult to lift those lives out of poverty. In the 1950's economic growth barely kept ahead of a rising population in several developing countries—for 13 percent of the population of the poor regions, per capita income either fell or rose at annual rates of less than 1 percent.

Only recently have the governments of developing nations officially recognized the need to control their population explosion. But so far their programs have failed to slow down the birth rate.[8] Increasingly, these nations are looking for technical and financial assistance from the developed nations. This is a hopeful sign, but the time is already late. Until the population explosion is checked, much (if not all) of the increase in the production of the poor nations will be literally consumed by babies.

The Potential Trade Gap of the Developing Nations

In December, 1961, the United Nations General Assembly set a target to be achieved by all developing nations by 1970. The target of this Development Decade is a minimum annual rate of growth of 5 percent, not much higher than the 4.2 percent reached during the 1950's. What are the implications of this growth target for the balance of payments of the developing nations in 1970? Based on the relationships that existed in the 1950's, experts at the United Nations offer the estimates shown in Table 20-3.

These estimates assume that a 5 percent annual growth in the gross domestic product of the poor nations will require a 6 percent increase in imports: a higher rate of capital formation will generate bigger imports of machinery, equipment, and raw materials. Thus the developing nations will have to raise their exports by 6 percent each year in order to maintain balance of payments equilibrium, a rate significantly higher than the 4 percent recorded in the 1950's. Since the opportunity for export expansion is mainly dependent on the growth rate of the rich, industrial nations, the outlook is for a deepening of the poor nations' trade deficit if the growth rate of the rich nations experienced in the 1950's (a *trend* rate of 3.7 percent annually) continues into the 1960's. As shown in Table 20-3, a current account deficit of $20 billion is projected for the developing nations by 1970. If past trends continue, only $9 billion of this deficit will be

---

[8] Since World War II the only successful population control has been carried out in Japan—an industrial nation.

Table 20-3
PROJECTION OF THE BALANCE OF PAYMENTS OF THE DEVELOPING NATIONS FOR 1970
(Billions of Dollars in 1960 Prices and Exchange Rates)

	1960 (Actual)	1970 (Projected)
Gross domestic product	170.0	277 *
Commodity imports from rest of world	22.5	42 †
Commodity exports from rest of world	21.0	31 ‡
Payments for investment income and other services (net)	3.3	9 §
Initial gap on current account	4.9	20 ¶
Net inflow of long-term capital and grants		9 **
Projected gap on current and capital accounts		11

* Assumes an average annual compound rate of growth of 5 percent for period 1960-70.

† Based on relationships prevailing in period 1950-60 between imports and gross domestic product of the developing countries.

‡ Assumes the gross domestic product of the developed economies will increase at the same *trend* rate as in the period 1950-60 (3.7 percent annually).

§ Assumed to be related to commodity exports and imports.

¶ Projected deficit on current account based on historical relationships between trade and gross domestic product.

** Assumes the flows of public and private funds will follow same trends as in 1950's.

SOURCE: Adapted from Table 1 on page 6 and Table 2 on page 14 of United Nations Conference on Trade and Development, *Trade Needs of Developing Countries for Their Accelerated Economic Growth,* E/Conf. 46/58, March, 1964.

financed by a net inflow of long-term capital and grants. Hence the prospect is a shortage of foreign exchange aggregating $11 billion for the developing nations as a group. Because this shortage will arise out of the disparate growth rates of exports and imports, it may be referred to as the *potential trade gap* of the developing nations in the 1960's decade.

The potential trade gap is, of course, a hypothetical figure only. A change in any of the assumptions upon which it is based would also change the size of the gap. If, for example, the developed economies were to grow in the 1960's at an average annual rate of 4.2 percent (the target set by the OECD) instead of the assumed 3.7 percent, then the exports of the developing countries would be $2 billion higher, making the potential trade gap $9 billion rather than $11 billion. The potential trade gap would also be smaller if we assumed larger inflows of long-term capital and grants. All in all, however, the assumptions used by the United Nations experts appear reasonable in the light of the past. It is a fact that the trade position of the developing countries steadily worsened during the 1950's, moving from a merchandise *surplus* of $1.8 billion in 1950 to a merchandise *deficit* of $2.6 billion in 1960. Although it is possible to disagree, therefore, on the size of the potential trade gap, there is a general agreement on the need of the developing nations to increase their receipts of foreign exchange by a substantial amount if they are to achieve the growth target of the Development Decade.

How can the developing nations eliminate their potential trade gap? Private foreign capital and foreign government assistance cannot be counted on to do the job.[9] This leaves only exports.[10] Somehow the developing nations must find ways to increase their exports so as to finance the imports needed for economic growth. To do so, however, they must overcome many obstacles that now limit export expansion.

EXPORT PROBLEMS OF THE DEVELOPING NATIONS

It was pointed out in Chapter 2 that the share of the non-industrial areas in world trade has been declining since 1950. In that year the developing countries accounted for 32 percent of the free world's exports; in 1962, only 21 percent.[11] In the 1950's exports from the developing countries grew at less than half the rate of exports from the industrial, developed countries.

Table 20-4 reveals that the divergent export experience of the poor and rich nations is explained mainly by dissimilar increases in the volume (quantum) of exports, but has been accentuated by dissimilar price behavior. The 151 percent growth in the exports of the developed economies over the period 1950-62 was accounted for by a volume increase of 112 percent and a price (unit value) increase of 19 percent. In contrast, the exports of the developing economies grew

---

[9] In the period 1961-63, the foreign exchange receipts of the developing nations from these two sources actually *fell* by $600 million.

[10] In estimating the potential trade gap, account was taken of the opportunity for import substitution in the developing countries. Any further reduction in imports would lessen the availability of capital and other goods needed to reach the 5 percent growth target.

[11] These percentages are lower than those shown in Table 2-4 in Chapter 2 because the latter include the exports of Oceania and South Africa.

Ch. 20 / The Developing Nations and World Trade

Table 20-4

INDEXES OF VALUE, QUANTUM, AND UNIT VALUE OF EXPORTS AND IMPORTS, 1962
(1950 = 100)

	Value	Quantum	Unit Value
Exports:			
Developed Economies	251	212	119
Developing Economies	150	157	96
Imports:			
Developed Economies	240	220	108
Developing Economies	179	167	108

GENERAL NOTE: Exports are valued f.o.b.; imports, c.i.f.

SOURCE: Adapted from United Nations Conference on Trade and Development, E/Conf. 46/12, February, 1964, Table 2, p. 8.

only 50 percent, less than the 57 percent growth in the volume of their exports because of a 4 percent decline in unit value.

Table 20-4 shows also that the imports of the developing countries grew more than their exports in this period. Not only did import volume go up 67 percent, but import unit value also rose 8 percent. The growth in the volume of their imports relative to their exports plus the 12 percent deterioration in their commodity terms of trade caused a marked worsening in their trade balance with the rest of the world.[12] This balance changed from a $1.8 billion surplus in 1950 to a $0.6 billion deficit in 1955 and a $2.3 billion deficit in 1962.

The most fundamental explanation of these divergent trends in the exports of the rich and poor nations is found in the changing composition of world trade. In this period manufactures have been by far the most dynamic element in international trade, their share rising from 41 percent in 1955 to 47 percent in 1961. On the other hand, exports of primary products have performed sluggishly, rising at less than half the rate of manufactures and suffering a steady decline in their share of world exports.[13]

The developing nations have been badly hurt by these shifts in the composition of trade because nine tenths of their exports are primary products. To make matters worse, the primary exports of the

---

[12] See Footnote 18 on page 65 for a definition of the commodity terms of trade.

[13] For further details see Table 2-6 and the discussion of trade composition in Chapter 2.

developing nations have expanded more slowly than those of the developed nations: technological innovations have greatly improved the productive capacities of primary industries (especially agriculture) in the latter while the population explosion in the former has absorbed more of their primary output, leaving less for export. As a consequence the industrial nations have increased their share of primary exports. Adding further to the troubles of the developing nations is the tendency in recent years for the export prices of primary products to fall relative to those of industrial products.

The export problems of the developing nations center, therefore, on two features of international trade in primary commodities: (1) the comparatively slow growth of commodity exports, and (2) the decline of commodity prices relative to industrial prices. A third feature, the short-run instability of commodity prices, is also injurious to the trading interests of the developing countries. After a closer examination of these phenomena, we shall take a look at the new trade policies and reforms advocated by the developing nations to resolve their export problems.

The Slow Growth of Commodity Exports

The export problems of the developing countries relate mainly to agricultural commodities. As shown in Table 20-5, such commodities account for six tenths of all their primary exports. The importance of agriculture to the nonindustrial nations is further

Table 20-5

EXPORTS OF THE DEVELOPING NATIONS TO THE REST OF THE WORLD, 1959-61 AVERAGES
(Billions of Dollars)

	Value	%
Agricultural commodities	10.9	54
Nonagricultural raw materials	2.3	11
Petroleum	5.0	25
All primary commodities	18.2	90
Manufactures	2.1	10
Total exports	20.3 *	100

* Only 5 percent of the developing nations' exports go to Communist countries, consisting mostly of primary commodities.

SOURCE: Adapted from "Commodity Export Earnings and Economic Growth" by Gerda Blau in United Nations Conference on Trade and Development, E/Conf. 46/61, March, 1964, Table 1/II, p. 22.

emphasized when we recall that agriculture generates more than half the national product of many of those nations compared with one fifth or less in the industrial nations. In several poor nations agricultural exports make up 80 percent or more of their total exports and are concentrated in only a few commodities. In 1958-59 the figures for Brazil were 90 percent (64 percent in coffee and cocoa); the United Arab Republic, 80 percent (75 percent in cotton and rice); Ceylon, 98 percent (82 percent in tea and rubber); and Thailand, 88 percent (66 percent in rice and rubber).

Although petroleum exports are responsible for one quarter of the primary exports, they originate in only a few developing countries, which for the most part have relatively small populations, such as Libya, Saudi Arabia, and Kuwait. Hence petroleum exports do not benefit the vast majority of poor nations, an unfortunate situation, because unlike agricultural commodities they face a buoyant demand in the industrial areas. In the period 1955-61 exports of petroleum from the developing countries expanded at an annual rate of 5.5 percent compared with only 0.7 percent for foodstuffs and 0.9 percent for agricultural raw materials and ores. Nonagricultural raw materials, such as bauxite, copper, lead, and tin, also have better market prospects than agricultural commodities because of the exhaustion of these minerals in the industrial countries. But here again only a minority of the poor nations has significant mineral endowments.

Summing up, the export problems of the developing nations revolve mainly around agricultural commodities. The following discussion applies to them in particular.

Why does the volume of commodity exports grow less rapidly than the volume of industrial exports? A full answer to this question would involve an examination of the specific supply and demand factors that influence the production and consumption of each of the many individual commodities. Such an examination is out of the question here. Instead we shall look at the main features of the demand for primary commodities in the industrial areas, and their effects on the primary exports of the developing areas. It is widely agreed that the slow, long-term growth of primary exports is traceable mainly to market conditions in the industrial areas rather than to supply conditions in the developing areas, although (as we have noted) the latter should not be ignored.[14]

---

[14] Variations in supply conditions (such as crop yields) play a more important role in the *short-run* fluctuations of commodity exports.

Low Income Elasticities. The income elasticity of demand for primary products tends to be low, taking on values below one.[15] This contrasts with the higher income elasticities for manufactured goods that seldom fall below unity. To illustrate, a 4 percent rise in national income may cause only a 2 percent rise in the consumption of agricultural products (income elasticity equal to 0.5), but a 6 percent rise in the consumption of manufactured goods (income elasticity equal to 1.5). The consumption of primary products in the industrial areas, therefore, does not keep pace with their general economic growth. For example, while production in the industrial countries rose 77 percent between 1938 and 1954, their consumption of foodstuffs (both domestic and imported) rose only 35 percent.[16] Low income elasticities for foodstuffs reflect family spending patterns. As far back as 1857 Ernst Engel observed that a poor family spends a higher proportion of its income on food than a family better off. Once a household has satisfied its needs for the basic necessities of food, shelter, and clothing, it spends additional income on durable consumer goods, personal services, travel, education, and the like.

Displacement by Synthetics. The depressing effects of low income elasticities on the consumption of primary commodities in the developed nations have been reinforced by a continuing stream of synthetic, manufactured materials that replace natural materials. Starting before World War I with rayon and manufactured nitrates, the development of synthetics has now reached flood proportions in the industrial nations. After World War II synthetic fibers, artificial rubber, and detergents strongly challenged cotton, wool, jute, abaca, oils, fats, natural rubber, and other commodities. Today, for example, most of the rubber used in the manufacture of passenger automobile tires in the United States is synthetic. As a result of this substitution in tires and other products, United States imports of natural rubber fell from 803 thousand long tons in 1952 to 413 thousand long tons in 1962. To conclude, synthetics have cut deeply into the consumption of agricultural raw materials and are partly responsible for the relatively slow growth of commodity exports from the developing to the

---

[15] Income elasticity of demand measures the response in the amount demanded to a change in income, assuming the mathematic expression: $\frac{dQ/Q}{dY/Y}$ We can interpret this as the percentage change in amount demanded divided by the percentage change in income.

[16] General Agreement on Tariffs and Trade, *Trends in International Trade*, (Geneva: 1958) Table 13, p. 40.

industrial countries. This is not to say that natural materials are doomed to be entirely replaced by synthetics. It does mean that they must compete in quality and price with manufactured substitutes.

Primary Production in the Industrial Countries. The primary exports of the developing nations have not even kept pace with the slow-growing consumption of primary commodities in the industrial areas. Increasingly, the developed countries have been meeting their needs for foodstuffs and agricultural raw materials out of domestic production and imports from other industrial countries. They have been able to do so because the application of modern technology to agriculture has multiplied productivity to such an extent that production frequently outruns home consumption to generate export surpluses. As noted earlier, the developed countries have increased their share of world primary trade in recent years. (At the same time, the population explosion has compelled many developing countries to become large importers of foodstuffs.) Thus agricultural imports from the developing areas are being displaced by the technologically advanced agricultural industries of North America and Western Europe. The displacement is greatest in temperate products, but the United States—the world's leading primary exporter—also exports large quantities of "tropical" products, notably cotton and tobacco.

Import Restriction by the Industrial Countries. All of the industrial countries have agricultural programs that protect their farmers from competition in the open market. Most frequently, this involves the maintenance of domestic agricultural prices at levels higher than those prevailing in world markets. To prevent foreign producers from capitalizing on this situation, imports are restricted by tariffs or quotas. The variable import levies of the European Economic Community are an example of such restriction.

In addition to import restrictions that are by-products of agricultural support programs, many European countries impose revenue duties or taxes on tropical agricultural products they do not produce at home. Mineral interests may also be protected against import competition; import quotas on petroleum, lead, and zinc in the United States and on coal in Western Europe fall into that category.

Deterioration in the Terms of Trade of Developing Nations

The detrimental effect of stagnant commodity exports on the import capacity of the developing countries has been magnified by worsening terms of trade. As indicated in Table 20-4, the overall terms of trade of the developing nations deteriorated 12 percent in the period 1950-62; that is to say, the same amount of exports paid for 12 percent less of imports in 1962 than in 1950. This deterioration in terms of trade offset a substantial part of the foreign aid and private investment received by the developing countries over those years. One estimate places the cumulative loss in external purchasing power resulting from changes in the terms of trade of the developing countries during the years 1951-62 at $16.7 billion or over one third of the net inflow of long-term capital and grants recorded in that period ($45.9 billion).[17]

Some economists, notably those associated with the United Nations, believe there is a persistent, long-run tendency for the terms of trade of the developing countries to deteriorate. Raul Prebisch explains this alleged tendency along the following lines.[18] Because of the slow growth in demand for primary commodities, only a declining proportion of the labor force in the developing countries can be absorbed in their production. Improvements in the productivity of primary activities cause an even further drop in that proportion. Thus the labor force has to be shifted to industrial production, but this takes a very long time and in the meantime the surplus labor exerts a downward pressure on the real level of wages in the developing countries. Higher productivity in the primary export industries, therefore, is reflected in lower prices rather than in higher wages. In this way, the fruits of technical advance in the developing countries are passed on to the industrial countries. In the latter countries, on the other hand, the relative shortage of labor and strong labor unions keep wages rising in step with rising productivity, preventing any fall in prices. Hence a persistent deterioration of the terms of trade of the developing countries is the result of fundamental structural differences between the industrial centers and the peripheral, developing countries.

Although the Prebisch model is plausible, it is hardly proof of a built-in, secular tendency for terms of trade to turn against the developing countries. The historical record is ambiguous because of a

---

[17] United Nations Conference on Trade and Development, *Financing for an Expansion of International Trade*, E/Conf. 46/9, March, 1964, Table 15, p. 26.

[18] For a detailed presentation of his views see Raul Prebisch, "Commercial Policy in the Underdeveloped Countries," *American Economic Review*, May, 1959, pp. 251-73. Similar views are expressed by Gunnar Myrdal in *Rich Lands and Poor* (New York: Harper and Row, 1957).

lack of data and all the well-known difficulties of index number construction. We do know that periods of worsening terms of trade have alternated with periods of improving terms of trade. In the 1930's the terms of trade of the developing nations sharply deteriorated; in the decade following World War II they improved beyond the level registered in 1913; in the last half of the 1950's they worsened once again. Regardless of the validity of the Prebisch model, it is indisputable that the developing countries were badly hurt by the deterioration of their terms of trade in the 1950's. As we shall see, they are actively seeking ways to minimize the effects of any future deterioration.

Short-Run Price Instability of Commodity Exports

In addition to slow growth, the commodity exports of the developing countries are subject to frequent and sudden price changes that cause unpredictable, short-run fluctuations in export earnings. This instability is detrimental to economic growth because it disrupts development programs when the actual supply of foreign exchange falls short of the projected supply.

In the period 1953-61, the average variation in price from year to year of the major agricultural commodity exports was 8 percent, ranging from 22.3 percent for cocoa to 2.7 percent for bananas.[19] Price changes are often extremely rapid. The price of sugar fell from 8.5 cents a pound in 1963 to 3.4 cents in November, 1964—a drop of 70 percent. During the same time the price of tin *rose* 52 percent. The importance of these short-run price changes is shown by the case of coffee. In 1964 world trade in coffee amounted to 6.4 billion pounds; a one cent per pound decline in price, therefore, would involve a loss of income to all exporting nations of about $64 million.[20] Because of falling prices in the period 1957-62, total export earnings from coffee went down about one quarter ($600 million a year) in spite of an *increase* of one quarter in the volume of coffee exports.[21]

The price volatility of commodities in world trade results from low *price* elasticities of supply and demand. Cyclical and random

---

[19] United Nations Conference on Trade and Development, *Trade in Agricultural Commodities in the United Nations Development Decade*, E/Conf. 46/57, March, 1964, Table 1.2/V, p. I-17.

[20] Sidney Weintraub, *The Foreign-Exchange Gap of the Developing Countries*, Essays in International Finance, No. 48 (Princeton, New Jersey: Princeton University Press, 1965), p. 7.

[21] International Bank for Reconstruction and Development, *Annual Report 1964-65* (Washington, D. C.: 1965), p. 55.

shifts in demand in the industrial countries cause sharp price responses because the supply of commodities is relatively fixed in the short run. Prices also react violently to shifts in supply, such as crop yield fluctuations, because the consumption of primary commodities in the industrial countries is insensitive to price changes (price elasticity is below unity).

New Trade Policies and Reforms Advocated by the Developing Nations

A widespread recognition among the developing nations that the slow growth in their export earnings imposes a critical restraint on domestic economic development has stimulated a rising crescendo of complaints and demands for new trade policies that would restructure the world trading system. This crescendo reached a climax at the United Nations Conference on Trade and Development (UNCTAD) held in Geneva in 1964. There the spokesmen of over seventy developing nations called upon the industrial nations for action on a broad front. The new trade policies advocated by the developing countries had been ably presented by Raul Prebisch, the Secretary-General of UNCTAD, in an earlier report that set the tone of the conference.[22] These policies are directed towards improving commodity exports, expanding exports of manufactures, and neutralizing a deterioration in the terms of trade.

Improving Commodity Exports. The developing nations view *international commodity agreements* as an effective way to sustain the demand for their primary exports at remunerative prices that are protected against short-run fluctuations.[23] They want a substantial increase in the number of commodities regulated by international agreement and a broadening of their scope, including provisions for promoting consumption. These agreements would involve the regulation of supply, export quotas by the developing nations, and minimum import commitments by the industrial nations.

To increase further their access to primary markets, the developing countries are pressing the industrial countries to remove tariffs, quotas, and internal consumption taxes that are now levied on primary imports. They are also asking the developed countries to revise their

---

[22] United Nations, *Towards a New Trade Policy for Development*, Report by the Secretary-General of the United Nations Conference on Trade and Development (New York: 1964). This section borrows heavily from this report.

[23] See Chapter 16 for a discussion of international commodity agreements.

domestic agricultural programs so that high cost production is not subsidized to the detriment of imports.

Expansion of Industrial Exports. The many difficulties encountered by primary exports (notably low income elasticities and synthetic substitutes) have convinced the developing nations that they must depend increasingly on industrial products to obtain a satisfactory, long-term growth in their exports. They are seeking a new pattern of international specialization whereby the industrial nations would export manufactures requiring advanced levels of technology while importing older and less complex manufactures from the developing nations.

Manufactures now account for only 10 percent of the exports of the developing countries, and four areas—the countries of India, Israel, and Mexico, and the British Crown Colony of Hong Kong— are responsible for over half of them. To improve this situation, the developing countries propose that *preferential treatment* be given to their exports of manufactures by the industrial countries, and that the developing countries accord preferential treatment to each other (but not to the industrial countries). Spokesmen of the developing countries assert that the most-favored-nations policy is suitable between economies on the same level, but not between rich and poor economies. They argue that preferential treatment for their industrial exports would be a logical extension of the infant industry argument: if the infant industry needs protection in the domestic market, it needs even more protection in foreign markets in the form of preferences. The form of preferential treatment would have to be worked out in negotiations between the developing and industrial nations. But for the time being the developing nations are asking for free access (no import restrictions of any kind) to the industrial markets of the developed areas.

Even with free access, the developing countries will not find it easy to expand their exports of manufactures to the industrial countries. Unlike commodities, manufactures require a comprehensive export marketing program based on up-to-date market research. Manufacturers in the developing countries must develop the capacity to compete in foreign markets not only in price but also in quality, promotion, channels of distribution, and in the other areas of export marketing that are described in Part 3.

Compensatory Financing to Offset Deteriorating Terms of Trade. Spokesmen of the developing nations are advocating a compensatory scheme that would automatically transfer financial resources to a developing country in order to offset a loss of foreign exchange resulting from worsening terms of trade. They argue that this would simply be an international extension of the compensatory programs that the industrial nations already offer their own agricultural producers.

Basically, a compensatory scheme would sustain the import capacity of a developing country by matching any decline in its external purchasing power due to worsening terms of trade with an equal amount of external financial assistance. Several technical problems would have to be overcome to set up such an arrangement. Initially, from what base year should the terms of trade be calculated? That is, to what degree (if any) should compensation be granted for a past deterioration in the terms of trade? Once the scheme is in operation, should compensatory financing be based on yearly changes in the terms of trade, or on some other time period? Suppose the terms of trade of a developing nation improved. Should the scheme compensate industrial countries whose terms of trade have deteriorated? How would the financing be shared by the industrial countries? These and similar questions suggest the difficulties in designing a workable mechanism that would be acceptable to the participating governments. However, technical problems can be solved if there is political agreement. The most important question, therefore, is whether the developed countries will agree to this radical proposal that would break new ground in the economic relations between the rich and poor nations.

EXTERNAL ASSISTANCE TO THE DEVELOPING NATIONS: PRIVATE INVESTMENT AND GOVERNMENT AID PROGRAMS

The sluggish growth in commodity exports and worsening terms of trade in the past decade have made the developing countries more dependent on external assistance to finance their development programs. Although the new policy measures outlined above would improve the outlook for the developing nations' exports, they cannot be counted on to close fully the trade gap projected for 1970. It is amply evident that the foreign exchange earned by exports must be supplemented by external financial assistance if the developing countries are to have the import capacity essential to a 5 percent

Ch. 20 / The Developing Nations and World Trade   447

growth target. Even in the unlikely event that the poor nations' exports were to rise at the 6 percent rate of the projected import requirements, they would still need external assistance to finance a current account deficit in order to supplement low domestic savings.[24]

The industrial nations have responded to the growing requirements of the developing nations by increasing the flow of long-term capital to the latter. In the period 1951-55, the net flow of long-term capital from the industrial countries and international agencies to the poor nations averaged $2.6 billion a year. During the 1950's this flow more than doubled, and in the period 1960-62 it averaged $6 billion a year, of which private investment contributed $1.2 billion.[25] The outlook for the 1960's, however, is less attractive; in recent years the volume of external financing received by the developing countries has stabilized around the $6 billion level reached at the start of the decade.

External Assistance by the United States

More than half the financial assistance extended by governments of the industrial nations to the developing nations has come from the United States.[26]

Foreign aid has been a dominant factor in American foreign economic policy since World War II. During the early postwar years United States government assistance was directed mainly towards the rehabilitation and recovery of Western Europe—the Marshall Plan era. At the start of the 1950's United States foreign aid became oriented towards rearmament of the free world, emphasizing military and defense support assistance. It was not until 1957 that United States foreign assistance turned definitely towards the developing countries. In that year Congress approved the creation of the Development Loan Fund to finance projects in the developing countries. Formal recognition of this turn in United States foreign aid occurred in 1961 when a new agency—the Agency for International Development (AID)—was set up to administer economic and technical assistance programs. That year also saw the birth of the Alliance for Progress—an ambitious program to accelerate economic growth in

---

[24] They would also need external assistance to help finance their mounting external debt burden. See p. 450.

[25] United Nations Conference on Trade and Development, *Financing for an Expansion of International Trade,* E/Conf. 46/9, March, 1964, Table 1, p. 6.

[26] The United States contribution was 54 percent for 1950-55 and 57 percent for 1960-62.

Latin America in close cooperation with the Latin American governments.

The AID program now falls into three major categories: development loans, technical assistance grants, and supporting assistance. *Development loans* (including Alliance for Progress funds), accounting for more than 60 percent of the program, are intended to finance social and economic projects essential to the economic growth of developing nations. All AID development loans are repayable in dollars with minimum terms of ¾ of 1 percent service charge during the initial ten-year grace period and 2 percent interest thereafter. *Technical assistance grants* stress the development of human resources by technical aid in health, education, public administration, community development, housing, industry, and agriculture. *Supporting assistance* is economic aid directed primarily towards immediate political and security objectives. Most supporting assistance goes to only four countries: Viet Nam, Laos, Korea, and Jordan.

For the fiscal year 1966 the President requested $1.5 billion for development assistance, about $300 million for technical assistance, and $380 million for supporting assistance.[27] This appropriation request (totalling $3.4 billion including military aid) was the lowest in the history of American foreign aid. It was less than ½ of 1 percent of the United States gross national product compared with 1¾ percent at the peak of the Marshall Plan. The percentage attributable to development assistance alone was, of course, considerably smaller.[28]

The flow of United States private investment funds to Latin America, Asia, and Africa has been very small compared with the flows of such funds to Canada and Western Europe. Although the United States government is seeking to promote private investment in the developing countries, United States investors have found better opportunities and fewer obstacles in the other industrial countries. The following chapter examines United States foreign investment and

---

[27] The President also requested $1.2 billion for military assistance to foreign countries. See Agency for International Development, *Questions and Answers about the Foreign Aid Program for Fiscal Year 1966* (Washington, D. C.: 1965). AID also administers the Agricultural Trade Development and Assistance Act (P.L. 480) under which the United States government ships surplus agricultural commodities to developing countries in return for payment in local currencies. In fiscal 1964 these shipments amounted to around $1.5 billion.

[28] In 1961 the bilateral government aid of France to the developing countries was 1.38 percent of its gross national product compared to 0.62 percent for the United States, 0.54 percent for the United Kingdom, and 0.41 percent for West Germany. See United Nations Conference on Trade and Development, *Financing for an Expansion of International Trade*, E/Conf. 46/9, 1964, p. 34.

government policy, and nothing further will be said about them here. The many obstacles that may confront the private investor (particularly in developing countries) are treated in Chapter 26.

International Agencies Providing External Assistance

Although the bulk of external assistance has been provided by the governments of the developed nations directly to the governments of the developing nations, the former have also contributed funds to international agencies that finance economic development. The most prominent international lending agencies make up the World Bank Group, comprising the International Bank for Reconstruction and Development (IBRD), the International Development Association (IDA), and the International Finance Corporation (IFC).[29] In 1965 the IBRD lent more than $1 billion (to 27 countries) for the first time in its history. That same year the IDA extended assistance of over $300 million while the IFC invested $26 million. Most IBRD and IDA funds go to finance basic public utilities in the developing countries, but increasingly they are also supporting agriculture and education.

Each of the World Bank agencies has its own lending terms and policies. The IBRD is essentially an international investment bank: it finances projects on long term (ranging up to 35 years or so) charging a substantial interest rate of $5\frac{1}{2}$ percent. The inability of many developing countries to qualify projects for IBRD loans and the high interest costs led to the formation of the IDA. The IDA extends credits to developing countries for fifty years that are repayable in easy stages after a ten-year grace period and with no interest except for a service charge of $\frac{3}{4}$ of 1 percent. The IDA is frequently described as a "soft loan" agency while the IBRD is a "hard loan" agency. The IFC, unlike the IBRD and IDA, does not make loans to governments; instead it participates in industrial projects along with private investors. In 1964-65, for example, the IFC lent $2.5 million to a manufacturer of industrial paper in Argentina, $1.95 million to a jute company in Pakistan, and made investments in several other industrial and development finance companies.[30]

Other important international agencies engaged in development financing include the Inter-American Development Bank (IDB), the

---

[29] The IBRD came into being as a sister organization of the IMF and began operations in 1946. The IFC was set up in 1956, and the IDA was started in 1961. Almost all the countries of the free world are members of the World Bank Group.

[30] International Finance Corporation, *Annual Report 1964-1965* (Washington, D. C.: 1965), pp. 13-19.

United Nations Expanded Program of Technical Assistance, and the United Nations Special Fund. Altogether, the international development agencies made disbursements in 1962 totalling $560 million—about one twelfth of the total flow of financial assistance to the developing countries.

The Debt Service Burden of the Developing Nations

The outstanding external government debt (including government-guaranteed debt) of the developing nations amounted to $24 billion at the end of 1962. Servicing that debt required payments of $900 million for interest and $2.1 billion for amortization. This "debt service burden" of $3 billion was equal to over 10 percent of the developing nations' export receipts in 1962.[31] The steep rise of the debt service burden in the past decade is expected to continue in the foreseeable future. In addition to the servicing of public external debts, the developing countries are also faced with income and amortization payments on private foreign investment.

The growing debt service burden threatens to check the economic development of the poor countries by absorbing foreign exchange vitally needed to finance imports. It means that a substantial portion of their external assistance is being offset by interest, dividend, and amortization payments to the lending nations. Several steps can be taken to alleviate the burden of debt repayment. In the short run, credits can be consolidated to lengthen repayment periods. In the longer run, external assistance can be extended on more favorable terms such as grants instead of loans, longer loan maturities, longer grace periods, etc. Moreover, the developing countries can improve their investment planning so as to avoid making unwise borrowing, bunching their borrowings at one time, relying excessively on short-term credits, and the like.

Changes in External Assistance Advocated by the Developing Nations

Representatives of the developing nations are unhappy at the failure of external financial assistance to keep pace with their development requirements. At the UNCTAD meeting, the industrial countries agreed that each of them should try to give *net* financial assistance to

---

[31] United Nations Conference on Trade and Development, *Financing for an Expansion of International Trade*, E/Conf. 46/9, 1964, pp. 71-72. The percentage rose to 12 percent in 1964 and was about 4 percent in the mid-1950's. See IBRD, *Annual Report 1964-65* (Washington, D. C.: 1965), p. 58.

the developing countries approaching as nearly as possible 1 percent of its national income. As we have noted, today only France has reached (and gone beyond) that percentage, while the United States percentage has been dropping in the 1960's. Moreover, these percentages are *gross* (although they do not cover private investment) because amortization, interest, and dividend payments have not been deducted from financial assistance. If current trends continue, even gross external assistance will increase to only $9 billion by 1970—some $3 billion more than the early 1960's level. In addition to a step-up in the flow of external assistance, the developing countries want compensatory financing to offset any worsening of their terms of trade, a subject we have discussed earlier.

Spokesmen of the developing nations also advocate that more external assistance be channelled through international agencies. They point to the fact that bilateral funds must often be spent in the donor country (true of AID funds), a practice that may raise development costs. Also bilateral assistance is subject to the political policies of the donor nations and may be interrupted at any time. They want external assistance to be related to development plans with aid commitments covering the entire planning period of four to five years. Finally, the developing nations are pressing for action to relieve their external debt burdens.

A Final Note

This chapter has described the drive for development now proceeding in the poor countries of the free world and its bearing on their international trade, including the potential trade gap. We have discussed a series of mounting pressures and unresolved problems. It should now be evident that these pressures and problems are the concern of the entire free world, the rich, industrial nations as well as the poor, developing ones. What is called for is international action on a broad scale, involving, among other things, a transformation of the pattern of international specialization and trade. Nothing less than the political stability of the free world is at stake; nothing less than an all-out effort can promise success.

SUMMARY

1. The drive for economic development shapes the attitudes, policies, and expectations of the poor, developing nations in the area of international trade and finance. These nations include all the countries of non-Communist Asia (except Japan), Latin America, and Africa (except

South Africa). The size of the income gap separating the developing and developed economies is enormous—by the end of the 1950's per capita income was less than $100 per annum for 46 percent of the free world's population.
2. Rostow identifies five stages of economic growth: the traditional society, preconditions for takeoff, takeoff, the drive to maturity, and the age of mass consumption. The majority of the developing nations is still building the preconditions for takeoff; a minority has entered takeoff; none has become a mature economy.
3. Capital formation is an essential condition of economic growth. To increase its stock of capital a nation must invest a part of its national product. Domestic investment must be financed out of domestic saving or net borrowing from abroad. Because of low savings levels, the developing countries are highly dependent on the industrial nations for funds to finance their capital formation. They also need foreign exchange to pay for imports of capital goods that can be obtained only from the advanced economies.
4. The developing countries must overcome many obstacles to achieve a rate of investment that will provide a satisfactory rate of economic growth, especially in per capita terms. The situation of the developing countries has been aptly described as interlocking sets of vicious circles that perpetuate economic stagnation and poverty. Major obstacles to economic development include lack of social overhead capital, lack of business managers and administrators, cultural blocks, and the population explosion.
5. If the developing countries are to achieve a growth rate of 5 percent during the 1960's, United Nations experts estimate a potential gap in current and capital accounts in their balance of payments amounting to $11 billion by 1970. How can the developing nations eliminate their potential trade gap? Major reliance must be placed on an expansion of their exports.
6. Nine tenths of the developing nations' exports are primary commodities that have experienced a sluggish growth in the past decade or more. Four factors are mainly responsible for this slow growth: low income elasticities, displacement by synthetics, primary production in the industrial countries, and import restriction by the industrial countries.
7. In addition to stagnant exports, the developing countries have suffered from worsening terms of trade. A third export problem is the short-run price instability of commodity exports.
8. The developing nations are now demanding new trade policies and reforms in the international economic system. They advocate more commodity agreements and the complete abolition of restrictions on commodity imports of the industrial nations. To promote exports of manufactures the developing countries want free access to the markets of the industrial countries, including preferential treatment. They also ask for a compensatory financing scheme that will offset a loss of foreign exchange resulting from a worsening of their terms of trade.

Ch. 20 / The Developing Nations and World Trade 453

9. The developing countries have become more dependent on external assistance to finance their development programs because of the poor performance of their exports. In recent years, however, the volume of external financing received by the developing countries has stabilized around the $6 billion level reached at the start of the 1960's.
10. More than half the financial assistance extended by governments of the industrial nations to the developing nations has come from the United States. However, in the 1960's United States foreign aid has been declining as a percentage of United States gross national product. Many international agencies also provide external assistance: the World Bank Group, the Inter-American Development Bank, and United Nations agencies. They contribute about one twelfth of the flow of financial assistance to the developing countries.
11. The developing nations are now facing a debt service burden because of their large external debts. This threatens to check their economic development by absorbing foreign exchange vitally needed to finance imports.
12. The developing nations are asking for more external assistance during the 1960's, at least an amount equal to 1 percent of the national incomes of the industrial countries. They also want more aid channeled through international agencies, and they are pressing for action to relieve their external debt burden.

QUESTIONS AND APPLICATIONS

1. Which are the developing nations? How do they differ from the developed nations?
2. Why did the per capita income gap between the developing and the developed countries *widen* during the 1950's?
3. What are Rostow's five stages of economic growth? Why is the takeoff stage so important? Choose five developing countries. At what stage of growth are they? Defend your answer.
4. Explain the implications of the following national income equation: $I_d + X = S + M$. What is the marginal product-capital ratio?
5. What is meant by this statement: "The situation of developing countries has been aptly described as interlocking sets of vicious circles...."?
6. What is the potential trade gap? How can the developing nations eliminate their potential trade gap?
7. Why does the volume of commodity exports grow less rapidly than the volume of industrial exports?
8. What are the commodity terms of trade? How does Prebisch explain the deterioration in the terms of trade of the developing countries? Do you agree with his explanation? Why or why not?
9. What factors cause the short-run price instability of commodity exports?
10. The new trade policies advocated by the developing nations are controversial. What do you think of commodity agreements, preferential treatment for manufactures, and compensatory financing? Should the United States government support these arrangements?

11. In what ways can external assistance help the developing countries?
12. Undertake research to answer the following question: Why has United States foreign aid dropped off in the 1960's compared with the 1950's?

SELECTED READINGS

Gill, Richard T. *Economic Development: Past and Present.* Englewood, Cliffs, New Jersey: Prentice-Hall, Inc., 1964.

General Agreement on Tariffs and Trade. *Trends in International Trade.* Geneva: 1958.

International Bank for Reconstruction and Development. *World Bank and IDA.* Washington, D. C.: Annual Report.

Millikan, Max F. and Donald L. M. Blackmer. *The Emerging Nations.* Boston: Little, Brown and Company, 1961.

Myrdal, Gunnar. *Rich Lands and Poor.* New York: Harper and Row, 1957.

Rostow, W. W. *The Stages of Economic Growth.* New York: Cambridge University Press, 1960.

United Nations. *Proceedings of the United Nations Conference on Trade and Development,* Volume I-VIII. New York: 1965.

———. *Towards a New Trade Policy for Development.* New York: 1964.

Weintraub, Sidney. *The Foreign-Exchange Gap of the Developing Countries,* Essays in International Finance, No. 48. Princeton, New Jersey: Princeton University Press, September, 1965.

CHAPTER 21

FOREIGN INVESTMENT OF THE UNITED STATES

The export of long-term investment capital from capital-rich to capital-poor nations is vital to the progress of the free world. Foreign investment directly finances a large volume of international trade; and, more significantly, it provides much of the capital and the managerial and technical know-how necessary to raise the productivity of developing economies. Thus foreign investment today contributes to the growth of incomes and production that, in turn, will stimulate greater international trade in the future.

The United States is now the leading exporter of long-term capital, and foreign investment enters into its economic relations with the rest of the world in a number of ways. Foreign investment by Americans finances a considerable fraction of United States exports; it is responsible for many United States imports; and it earns large amounts of dividends and interest. Moreover, foreign investment offers to many United States firms the opportunity to continue or accelerate their growth by establishing operations abroad, thereby benefiting both themselves and foreign countries.

In this chapter, we are primarily concerned with *private* foreign investment, but much of what we have to say will be true of foreign investment in general whether private or public. Although we emphasize the private investment experience and policy of the United States, our discussion of the nature of private foreign investment is pertinent to all private foreign investment regardless of source.

THE NATURE OF FOREIGN INVESTMENT

After looking at the transfer and repayment problems that accompany foreign investment, we shall also distinguish between portfolio and direct investment.

The Transfer Problem

A net export of capital from one nation to the rest of the world involves both a financial transfer and a real transfer. The *financial transfer* occurs when residents of the lending country transfer purchasing power (usually in the form of bank balances) to residents of the borrowing country. This financial transfer does not make the lending country a *net* exporter of capital because its export of long-term capital (the original loan) is exactly offset in the balance of payments by an import of short-term capital, namely, the funds acquired and not yet spent by the foreign borrowers.[1]

A *net* export of capital occurs only when the borrowed funds are spent, directly or indirectly, on goods and services of the lending country. Then the export of long-term capital is no longer offset in the balance of payments by an import of short-term capital but, instead, by exports on current account. These exports of merchandise and services that are financed by the export of long-term capital represent the *real transfer* of capital from the lending country to the borrowing country.

Thus, a nation can be a net exporter of capital only when it has a net surplus on current account. Similarly, a nation can be a net importer of capital only when it experiences a net deficit on current account. Hence, to invest abroad, a nation must develop a net export balance on current account (inclusive of unilateral transfers) while the borrowing nation must have a net import balance. This necessity for adjustments in the current account in order to effect a net movement of capital between nations comprises the transfer problem.

When a long-term foreign investment is "tied," the transfer problem is easily solved. The proceeds of a tied loan must be spent in the lending country; and, when the spending occurs, it shows up as exports on current account from the lending to the borrowing country. But suppose the loan is not tied and, further, that the loan funds are not spent in the lending country. How then is the real transfer of the loan brought about? The answer is found in the processes of adjustment to disequilibrium that were examined in Chapters 10 and 11.

---

[1] Residents of the borrowing country acquire from residents of the lending country bank balances that are located in the lending country, the borrowing country, or elsewhere. In the first instance, the short-term international liabilities of the lending country are increased while, in the second and third instances, its short-term international assets are decreased. Hence, in all instances the lending country experiences a short-term capital inflow (credit) that offsets its autonomous long-term capital outflow (debit). See Chapter 7, p. 138.

Briefly, an export of long-term capital creates a deficit in the balance of payments of the lending country and a surplus in the balance of payments of the borrowing country. When exchange rates are free to vary, this disequilibrium causes a depreciation in the investing country's currency and an appreciation in the borrowing country's currency. These adjustments in the exchange rate cease when the lending country develops a surplus on current account that exactly offsets its export of long-term capital and the converse occurs in the borrowing country.

When exchange rates are held stable, the real transfer of a long-term capital movement is mainly effected by an inflation of incomes and prices in the country or countries in which the borrowed funds are spent, that is, in our example, in the borrowing country and/or a third country. Some deflation of incomes and prices may also occur in the lending country if the outflow of purchasing power brought about by the capital export leads to a decline in domestic spending.[2] These income and price effects would then restore equilibrium along the lines discussed in Chapter 10. The end result would be a surplus on current account in the lending country equal to its long-term capital export and an equivalent deficit on current account in the borrowing country that stems directly from trade with the lending country or multilaterally from trade with other countries.

The Repayment Problem

We have seen that foreign investment involves a real transfer of goods and services from the lending country to the borrowing country, either directly or indirectly. Similarly, the payment of income earned on foreign investments as well as their eventual amortization also involves a real transfer of goods and services but, in this instance, from the borrowing country to the lending country.

Consideration of the repayment problem reveals a distinction between "productive" and "unproductive" foreign investment. In most economic contexts, a productive investment is one that increases the capacity of a nation to produce whereas an unproductive investment is one used for purposes that do not measurably raise productive capacity although it may be desirable for other reasons. When related to foreign investment, however, these terms take on a more

---

[2] This would occur, for example, if foreign investment diverted funds from domestic investment or if the decline in the domestic money supply caused a decline in spending.

precise meaning. Specifically, a *productive foreign investment* is one that creates the supply of foreign exchange necessary to service it and repay it either directly by increasing exports or indirectly by reducing the need for imports in the borrowing country. An *unproductive foreign investment* is not self-liquidating in this sense; it neither earns foreign exchange through exports nor saves it by lowering imports.[3] Today, many nations define productive foreign investment even more narrowly, namely, investment that will earn, directly or indirectly, the currency of the lending country or, as is often more desirable, convertible currencies.

The point of this discussion is that productive foreign investments cause no repayment problem while unproductive foreign investments may cause severe problems of adjustment to achieve a real transfer of investment earnings and amortization. Today this distinction underlies the foreign investment policies of most developing nations because of their great concern over the repayment problem. This conception of productive and unproductive investment often causes borrowing countries to inhibit foreign investment that may be productive in the usual sense but that is not clearly self-liquidating in terms of the balance of payments.

The repayment problem also concerns the lending country. If the lending country adopts high tariffs and other policies that restrict its imports, foreign countries will find it difficult or impossible to service and repay its loans. For a time the repayment problem may be postponed by a continuous outflow of new capital from the lending country that supplies foreign countries with the foreign exchange required to service and amortize loans made in the past. When, however, the outflow of new capital is interrupted or fails to keep pace with receipts of interest, dividends, and amortizations, the lending country must develop a deficit on current account (inclusive of investment income) in order to solve the repayment problem. The unwillingness of a lending country to make this adjustment may cause widespread defaults and restrictive policies in the borrowing countries that, in turn, will deter new capital exports by the lending country and will lower its exports on current account. This sequence of events took place in the interwar period when the outflow of capital from the United States abruptly declined at the end of the 1920's and this country adopted the highly protectionist Hawley-Smoot tariff.

---

[3] Foreign loans to finance the construction of public monuments or to help a government meet a general budget deficit are examples of "unproductive" foreign investments.

In considering the effects of foreign investment on the balance of payments of lending and borrowing countries, we must not lose sight of the fact that the fundamental contribution of foreign investment lies in the development of and superior allocation of productive resources that are brought about by the movement of capital from countries where its marginal productivity is relatively low to countries where its marginal productivity is higher. The international flow of investment capital may also be accompanied by managerial and technological skills that are essential to the economic growth of less-developed economies. This is the true economic function of international investment and it is unfortunate that balance of payments considerations at times raise obstacles to its fulfillment.

Portfolio and Direct Investment

Private foreign investment may be classified in a number of ways: by maturity, by the currency in which the investment is made, by the purpose of the investment, by geographical location, etc. Probably the most important classification is the distinction between portfolio and direct private investments. The criterion of this distinction is *managerial control.*

When the private investor has no managerial control over his investment, it is a *portfolio investment.* The investor either holds bonds and other nonequity securities or he does not hold an amount of stock or other equities sufficient to give him managerial control of a foreign enterprise.

When the private investor does have managerial control over his foreign investment, it is a *direct investment.* Although ownership of 51 percent of the voting stock is technically required to exercise the right of management, a lesser percentage may be adequate when the stock is widely scattered in small holdings. Moreover, at times, a large stockholder may be reluctant to use his power to select management. Thus there is no clear-cut distinction between portfolio and direct investment in terms of stock or equity claims; the distinction rests on the absence or presence of managerial control by the investor. Direct investment by Americans is generally represented by the overseas branches and subsidiaries of United States companies.

Portfolio and direct investments differ in several respects. Generally speaking, direct investment has less formidable transfer and repayment problems than does portfolio investment. The income and amortization of most portfolio investments (bonds) are contractually

Table 21-1
INTERNATIONAL INVESTMENT POSITION OF THE UNITED STATES IN SELECTED YEARS
(Billions of Dollars)

	1914*	1919	1930	1939	1946	1953	1957	1963
United States investments abroad	3.5	7.0	17.2	11.4	18.7	39.6	54.2	88.2
Private	3.5	7.0	17.2	11.4	13.5	23.8	36.8	66.4
Long-term	3.5	6.5	15.2	10.8	12.3	22.3	33.6	58.3
Direct	2.6	3.9	8.0	7.0	7.2	16.3	25.3	40.6
Portfolio	0.9	2.6	7.2	3.8	5.1	6.0	8.3	17.6
Short-term	na	0.5	2.0	0.6	1.3	1.6	3.2	8.1
United States government †	...	...	...	...	5.2	15.7	17.4	21.8
Foreign investments in the United States	7.2	4.0	8.4	9.6	15.9	23.6	31.4	51.5
Long-term	6.7	3.2	5.7	6.3	7.0	9.2	12.8	22.8
Direct	1.3	0.9	1.4	2.0	2.5	3.8	4.8	7.9
Portfolio	5.4	2.3	4.3	4.3	4.5	5.4	8.0	14.9
Short-term	0.5	0.8	2.7	3.3	8.9	14.4	18.5	28.7
United States net creditor position	—3.7	3.0	8.8	1.8	2.8	16.0	22.8	36.7
Net long-term	—3.2	3.3	9.5	4.5	10.3	28.5	36.3	52.6
Net short-term	—0.5	—0.3	—0.7	—2.7	—7.4	—12.5	—13.5	—15.9

* At June 30
† Excludes World War I loans; includes some short-term assets ($4.7 billion in 1963).
na Not available.
GENERAL NOTE: Data for various years are not wholly comparable because of different sources and methods, but the data are adequate to show main trends over the period.
SOURCE: United States Department of Commerce, *Survey of Current Business*, various issues.

arranged in advance, and thus they represent a fixed foreign exchange obligation on the part of the borrowing country that does not vary with economic circumstances.[4] In contrast, the income from direct investments is usually in the form of dividends that tend to vary with the profitability of business operations and frequently with the foreign exchange earnings of the debtor country. Also, direct investments are not tied to any fixed amortization schedule.

Direct investments ease the transfer problem because they often involve the shipment of capital equipment and supplies from the investing country to foreign branches and subsidiaries rather than the movement of funds. Portfolio investments, on the other hand, place funds in the hands of foreign borrowers who may spend them outside the lending country. In that event, real transfer calls for adjustments in trade that may be difficult. Another difference between the two is that direct investment normally contributes managerial skills and technology as well as capital to foreign economies.

THE INVESTMENT EXPERIENCE OF THE UNITED STATES

The investment experience of the United States will be analyzed in this section by considering the overall international investment position, and then by breaking down the investment experience for specific areas, major industries, and in terms of net capital outflow and investment income. Finally, we shall look at the production, employment, and sales generated by United States business investments in foreign countries.

International Investment Position of the United States

Table 21-1 shows the international investment position of the United States in selected years over the period 1914-63. A close examination of this table reveals many of the features of United States investment experience.

United States Investment Abroad. The foreign investment of the United States rose from $3.5 billion in 1914 to $88.2 billion in 1963. This growth, however, was not steady. After reaching a peak of $17.2 billion in 1930, foreign investment in general declined greatly in the 1930's as Americans ceased making new investments and liquidated old investments. In addition, many portfolio investments were defaulted by nations that were sorely pressed by the collapse of export

---

[4] When bonds are issued in the currency of the borrowing country, there is no fixed obligation in foreign exchange. Most bonds, however, are issued in the currency of the lending country.

markets. The global depression also caused a precipitous drop in the earnings on direct investment and thus discouraged new ventures.

This situation changed, however, with the coming of World War II. During the war, United States foreign investment grew noticeably, but largely because of United States foreign government loans rather than because of private investment. In the period 1946-57, foreign investment increased by over $35 billion, government loans accounting for about one third of the increment, and private investment for the remainder. Private investment has been responsible for most of the growth since 1957.

Most United States foreign investment, both private and government, has been long term rather than short term. It has been used primarily to finance investments in mines, plantations, factories, public utilities, and trading establishments that have added to the productive capacities of the recipient nations.

The relative shares of portfolio and direct investments in United States private foreign investment have altered greatly over the period 1914-63. Portfolio investment expanded remarkably during the 1920's, and, in 1930, it almost equalled direct investment. Among the most important factors behind this growth were the intense demand for capital in Europe and elsewhere that could not be met by the United Kingdom and other traditional sources; the general restoration of the gold standard after the middle of the decade; the optimism of American investors; the attractive rates of interest paid on foreign securities; and, last but not least, the aggressive salesmanship of the American investment houses that floated foreign bond issues.

United States portfolio investments fared badly during the 1930's. Most of the foreign securities held by American investors were payable in dollars; and, when the dollar receipts of foreign countries fell abruptly in the early 1930's, these fixed dollar commitments could be met only with great difficulty or not at all. Outright defaults ensued in many countries; and, in others, exchange control made it impossible to liquidate portfolio investments except at a very heavy loss. This unfortunate investment experience has left a lasting imprint on the character of American foreign investment.

Portfolio investment rose very slowly after World War II, and not until 1955 did United States holdings of foreign portfolio securities exceed the level of 1930. In the early postwar period, Americans restricted their purchases of foreign portfolio securities, for the most part, to those issued by Canada, the International Bank for Reconstruction and Development, and certain countries in Western Europe. The resumption of convertibility by European countries at the end of 1958 created more favorable conditions, and in the early 1960's United States portfolio investment moved up sharply as Europeans, Japanese, and Canadians floated new bond issues in New York. As will be noted in the next chapter, the United States government in 1963 imposed an "equalization tax" on the purchase of foreign securities to lessen the outflow of portfolio capital. Political and economic instability, inconvertibility, hostile attitudes, and other factors continue to obstruct the resumption of large-scale United States private portfolio investment in other areas of the world.

Unlike portfolio investment, United States private direct investment remains subject to the control of American investors. For this and other reasons, direct investment is less sensitive to the uncertainties and restrictions that characterize the contemporary world economy. During the 1930's, United States direct investment fell only from $8 billion to $7 billion; and, since the war, it has grown at a much faster pace than private portfolio investment. In 1963, direct investment accounted for almost seven tenths of United States private long-term investment compared to little more than one half in 1930.

Foreign Investment in the United States. The character of foreign investment in the United States differs in many respects from United States investment abroad. In 1963, in contrast to the situation before the war, foreign short-term investment in the United States exceeded by a considerable margin foreign long-term investment. By and large, this short-term investment represents the dollar reserves of foreign countries, reflecting the position of the United States as an international financial center.[5]

Long-term investment in the United States declined during World War I as European creditors liquidated their investments to finance war expenditures. Unlike the experience of the United States abroad, however, foreign investments in the United States rose during the 1930's largely because of an influx of flight capital from Europe.

Another difference is also significant: during the entire period 1914-63, portfolio outranked direct investment by large amounts.

United States Net Creditor Position. World War I transformed the United States into a net creditor nation. In 1914 this country

---

[5] The role that the United States plays as an international financial center is discussed in Chapter 22.

held foreign investments that aggregated $3.5 billion, but this amount was less than one half of the $7.2 billion of foreign investments in the United States. This relationship was reversed during the war by a simultaneous increase in United States investments abroad and a decline in foreign investments in the United States. In 1919 United States investments abroad were 75 percent greater than foreign investments in the United States. Since that time, the United States has never relinquished its net creditor position.

It is noteworthy that although the United States is a net international creditor, it has consistently been a net debtor on short-term capital account. This state of affairs is a natural one, and it parallels the earlier investment experience of the United Kingdom whose position as the world's dominant long-term investor and financial center has now been assumed by the United States. The much higher short-term indebtedness of the United States after World War II as compared to previous years reflects the greatly enhanced role of the dollar in international trade and finance. Nevertheless, as will be observed in Chapter 22, the rapid increase in short-term liabilities to foreigners since 1957 has raised doubts about the international liquidity of the United States.

Foreign Investment by Area

Table 21-2 presents United States private long-term investment abroad by area in selected years of the postwar period. The area distribution of United States private foreign investment is derived from historical, political, economic, social, and other factors. Americans

Table 21-2

UNITED STATES PRIVATE LONG-TERM INVESTMENT ABROAD BY AREA IN SELECTED YEARS

(Billions of Dollars)

Area	1946	1950	1953	1957	1963
Total	12.3	17.5	22.3	33.6	58.3
Canada	5.4	7.0	8.6	12.5	20.3
Latin American Republics	3.6	5.1	6.4	9.7	10.4
Western Europe	2.3	3.1	3.7	5.8	15.4
All Others *	1.0	2.3	3.6	5.6	12.2

* Includes international institutions.
SOURCE: United States Department of Commerce, *Survey of Current Business*, various issues.

have invested in Western Europe to take advantage of the world's second largest industrial market; they have invested in Latin America chiefly for the production of the minerals and agricultural products required by the United States economy; and they have invested in Canada because of its rapidly growing domestic market and its rich natural resources. These economic motivations have been reinforced by the many political and cultural ties between these areas and the United States.

On the other hand, many countries in Asia have had neither the domestic markets nor the accessible natural resources to attract large amounts of United States private investment. Also, some Asian countries and most of Africa have been colonial wards of Western Europe and did not welcome United States capital. Distance, lack of knowledge, and a host of other conditions have also limited the flow of United States private capital to areas outside the Western Hemisphere and Western Europe.

Direct Investment by Major Industries

Over 70 percent of the postwar growth in United States private long-term investment abroad has been in the form of direct investment. Table 21-3 shows the value of United States direct investments abroad by major industries. Several points should be noted:

Table 21-3

VALUE OF UNITED STATES DIRECT INVESTMENT ABROAD BY REGION AND MAJOR INDUSTRY IN 1963

(Millions of Dollars)

Region	Total	Mining and Smelting	Petroleum	Manufacturing	Public Utilities	Trade	Other
All Areas	40,645	3,350	13,698	14,890	2,051	3,305	3,351
Canada	13,016	1,540	3,133	5,746	460	747	1,390
Latin America	9,875	1,303	3,627	2,211	758	963	1,014
Europe	10,351	55	2,828	5,610	40	1,234	585
Far East	1,510	31	718	387	35	191	149
Oceania	1,463	70	496	728	1	81	88
Africa	1,423	351	701	176	9	81	105
Middle East	1,274	1	1,207	33	3	10	21
Other	1,732	—	988	—	745	—	—

SOURCE: United States Department of Commerce, *Survey of Current Business*, August, 1964.

1. Investment in the petroleum industry is about one third of total direct investment. In the nonindustrial regions petroleum investment mainly takes the form of facilities and equipment to produce crude oil while in Europe most of the investment is in refineries, pipelines, and marketing outlets. In the Middle East petroleum accounts for nearly all United States investments.

2. Investments in mining and smelting depend on the presence of the proper ores; most of this investment is in Canada and Latin America.

3. The bulk of investment in manufacturing is attracted by sizable, growing markets which are principally found in industrial regions. This is why Canada and Europe account for almost four fifths of all manufacturing investment. Investment in trade is also closely associated with market size and growth.

4. Investment in public utilities is now much less important than it used to be. The negative attitude of developing countries towards the foreign ownership of public utilities makes such investment risky and unattractive.

5. Over half of all United States direct investment is in the Western Hemisphere, and over three quarters is in Canada, Latin America, and Europe.

Net Capital Outflow and Investment Income

The figures given for United States foreign investment in the previous tables are book values, and their annual changes are the sums of net United States capital outflows, undistributed subsidiary earnings of American companies abroad, and minor accounting adjustments. A fair measure of the net United States capital outflow for a given year, therefore, is the increase in United States investment abroad minus undistributed subsidiary earnings during the same year.[6] This is the procedure used to estimate net United States capital outflow for the period 1950-63 in Table 21-4.

The net United States capital outflow is the movement of investment funds from the United States to the rest of the world less any liquidations of United States foreign investment. It indicates, therefore, the net flow of new investment dollars to foreign countries; it is the positive contribution of United States foreign investment to foreign dollar receipts.[7] In 1956 the net United States capital outflow rose sharply to reach over $3.5 billion after remaining between $1.36

---

[6] This estimate of net capital outflow does not agree precisely with the figure that appears in the United States balance of payments because of the aforementioned accounting adjustments.

[7] As previously mentioned, some of the United States capital outflow, par-

billion and $1.84 billion during each of the previous six years. This initiated a remarkable outflow of capital in succeeding years as American businessmen eagerly expanded foreign operations and foreign bond issues rose in New York. In 1963 United States capital outflow reached over $6 billion.

The rapid growth in United States investment abroad since 1956 has been nearly matched by the increase in income received on investment. Note, in particular, the jump in portfolio income between 1957 and 1963. However, the bulk of income *generated* by United States foreign investment comes from direct investment—undistributed earnings of $1,565 million and dividends of $3,059 million in 1963.

Although the role of private foreign investment in the United States balance of payments is an important one, the real contribution

Table 21-4

UNITED STATES FOREIGN INVESTMENT: NET CAPITAL OUTFLOW AND INVESTMENT INCOME

(Millions of Dollars)

	1950	1953	1955	1957	1963
Increase in United States investment abroad	2,179	2,201	2,738	4,739	7,811
Undistributed subsidiary earnings	475	776	898	1,017	1,565
Net United States capital outflow *	1,704	1,425	1,840	3,722	6,246
Income received on investment †	1,593	1,910	2,444	2,881	4,565
Direct	1,294	1,442	1,912	2,313	3,059
Portfolio	190	216	258	363	1,008
United States government	109	252	274	205	498

* Increase in United States investment abroad minus undistributed subsidiary earnings.
† Earnings on investment minus undistributed subsidiary earnings.
Source: Derived from data in United States Department of Commerce, *Survey of Current Business*, various issues.

ticularly direct investment capital, does not supply "free" dollars to foreign countries since it takes the form of merchandise and service exports that are shipped directly from the United States parent company to its overseas branches or subsidiaries. The effect on the balance of payments, however, is the same.

of foreign investment is found in the economic growth that it stimulates by bringing capital, managerial skills, and technical know-how into combination with the labor and resources of the borrowing country. Some aspects of this contribution are brought to light in the following section.

The Contribution of United States Investment to Foreign Economies

Data on book value, net capital flows, and earnings afford only a partial understanding of the contribution of United States investment to foreign economies. To improve its knowledge of the economic impact of United States foreign investment, the United States Department of Commerce carried out a comprehensive survey of the operations of American companies abroad in 1957.[8] Response to this survey was mandatory, and coverage was virtually complete. About 2,800 United States companies reported on direct investments abroad which involved over 10,000 direct-investment enterprises. Here are some highlights of the survey:

1. Total assets employed by United States owned companies abroad amounted to $42 billion at the end of 1957, not including financial concerns.

2. Aggregate sales of these companies producing manufactures, petroleum, mineral, and agricultural commodities totaled about $32 billion in 1957 (excluding intercorporate petroleum sales).

3. Manufacturing sales from United States foreign plants were over $18 billion in 1957, with over 40 percent in Canada, about one third in Western Europe, and about 13 percent in Latin America. Largest sales were reported for automotive products, chemicals, food products, and electrical machinery. Overall, production abroad was 50 percent greater than exports of comparable manufactures from the United States. Exports from United States foreign plants to the United States were $1 billion in 1957.

4. Aggregate production outlays abroad and foreign taxes paid by direct-investment companies were $30 billion in 1957 (exclusive of goods purchased by trading companies, imports from the United States, intercorporate petroleum sales, and depreciation charges). Wages and salaries totaled almost $7 billion; purchases of materials and services, $17 billion; and other costs, $1.7 billion. Imports by these companies from the United States, as reported as supplementary data (not mandatory), were $2.6 billion. However, total imports were much larger.

---

[8] U.S. Department of Commerce, *U.S. Business Investments in Foreign Countries* (Washington, D. C.: Government Printing Office, 1960).

5. Companies responding to the supplementary inquiry on employment reported about two million foreign employees, of whom less than 1 percent were sent from the United States. Estimated total employment by all United States companies abroad was 3.2 million in 1957.

6. Nearly three quarters of total direct investment ($25 billion) was in enterprises owned 95 percent or more by United States parent companies. United States ownership was less than 50 percent in only 5 percent of the enterprises. Forty-five United States companies had holdings of over $100 million each, accounting for 57 percent of the book value of all United States direct investment.

7. The economic impact of United States direct-investment enterprises is very great in some foreign areas. Total sales of United States owned companies in Latin America in 1957 (about $8 billion) after deducting imports and profit remittances were equal to roughly one tenth of the gross product of the area as a whole. Approximately one third of all Latin American exports come from United States owned companies, and over 40 percent of all Latin American exports, excluding coffee. Tax payments by direct-investment enterprises accounted for one fifth of all Latin American tax revenues. In another area, Canada, gross sales of United States owned companies in 1957 were $11 billion, of which about $2 billion was exported from Canada, mainly to the United States.

Table 21-5

SALES, CURRENT EXPENDITURES, AND EARNINGS OF UNITED STATES DIRECT-INVESTMENT ENTERPRISES ABROAD IN 1957

(Billions of Dollars)

	All Industries	Petroleum	Manufacturing
Total Sales	38.2	14.5	18.3
Exports to U.S.	3.8	1.4	1.1
Other Exports	6.7	3.5	1.8
Local Sales	27.7	9.5	15.4
Current Expenditures	32.3	12.9	17.5
Materials and Services	22.0	8.0	11.2
Wages and Salaries	6.9	1.2	3.7
Indirect Taxes	2.1	1.6	0.3
Income Taxes	2.4	1.0	0.8
Depreciation and Depletion	1.7	0.7	0.6
Other	2.2	0.4	0.9
U.S. Share in Net Earnings	3.6	1.7	0.9

SOURCE: U.S. Department of Commerce, *U.S. Business Investments in Foreign Countries* (Washington, D. C.: Government Printing Office, 1960).

Table 21-5 offers a summary statement of the activities of United States direct-investment enterprise abroad in 1957.

In conclusion, this survey forcefully demonstrates the vital contribution that United States direct investment is making to the economies of foreign countries. It reveals that United States private investment abroad is far more significant than is suggested by mere book values, net capital flows, and net earnings. We shall look again at United States investment abroad in Chapter 26 when we describe the foreign operations of American business, including obstacles to private foreign investment.

THE FOREIGN INVESTMENT POLICY OF THE UNITED STATES

Until the late 1950's the United States government encouraged American investment in all countries of the free world. This policy was based on a number of considerations involving the economic welfare of both the United States and the nations receiving American capital. It was recognized that private foreign investment creates export markets for United States products and develops foreign sources of supply to meet the growing needs of American industry, as well as affording a profitable employment of American capital. Foreign investment was also supported because it alleviated the dollar shortage, and strengthened United States foreign economic assistance to developing countries. Finally, private foreign investment was viewed as a positive element in the struggle to gain the adherence of the underdeveloped areas of the free world and to invigorate the free world in general.

The onset of the United States balance of payments troubles in 1958 marked the end of this investment policy. Once promoted as a means of relieving the "dollar shortage," private foreign investment was now accused of intensifying the "dollar glut." The capital outflow to Western Europe drew special criticism from government authorities who argued that Western Europe was no longer in need of foreign investment and, indeed, should increase its own foreign assistance and investment in the developing countries. Starting in 1963, the United States government undertook special measures to lessen the outflow of investment capital to other industrial nations, especially in Western Europe. We shall describe these measures (the interest-equalization tax and the voluntary restraint program) in the next chapter. In this section we shall mention certain features of the 1962 Revenue Act that are directed towards the same end.

The restraint of new American investment in Western Europe (and, to a lesser extent, in Canada and Japan) has been accompanied by active encouragement of American investment in the less-developed areas of the free world. It is believed that United States private investment in Latin America, Asia, and Africa can make a unique contribution to economic development, not only by bringing capital to poor nations, but also by transferring technical and managerial skills and by demonstrating the effectiveness of private enterprise in ways that cannot be matched by government foreign assistance.

In sum, today United States investment policy is split into two parts. On the one hand, the United States government opposes new American investment in Western Europe because of its alleged damage to the balance of payments. This switch in policy has come about as a reaction to a current situation rather than from any disavowal of the traditional arguments favoring American investment *anywhere* in the free world. On the other hand, these traditional arguments are used to support an active promotion of private American investment in less-developed countries. American foreign investment is welcomed by the United States government when directed towards Latin America, Asia, and Africa, not only for its own sake but also because of the strength it lends to government foreign assistance.

We now consider specific features of United States investment policy.

Investment Treaties

The traditional policy of the United States with respect to private foreign investment has involved treaties of Friendship, Commerce, and Navigation with many countries; diplomatic assistance to American investors abroad; insistence on most-favored-nation treatment of American investments; and, at times in the past, the military protection of American-owned property abroad, notably in Central American and Caribbean countries.

Since World War II, however, the United States government has sought to encourage private foreign investment by negotiating treaties that deal more specifically with the conditions that affect investment abroad. These treaties have included provisions that protect the right of American investors to engage freely in business activities in a foreign country, including freedom from restrictions on the ownership or management of business enterprise. Other provisions may guarantee national or most-favored-nation treatment in taxation and other matters; reasonable requirements regarding the employment of local workers; the unrestricted remittance of earnings and repatriation of capital; and freedom from expropriation, or prompt, adequate compensation in the event of expropriation.

The negotiation and ratification of investment treaties is a very slow process; treaties are noticeably lacking with countries in which the investment climate is most unfavorable. It has proved extremely difficult, for example, to reach agreement with developing nations on the free transfer of earnings and capital. Investment treaties, therefore, have had only a limited success in lowering obstacles to United States capital abroad. There have been frequent suggestions for the negotiation of an international investment code among nations of the free world that would enunciate principles of international law applicable to private foreign investment. However, the gap between the capital-exporting nations and the developing nations in this regard makes very doubtful the negotiation of an agreement satisfactory to all parties. Prospects are better for the adoption of international machinery for the settlement of investment disputes along the lines proposed by the International Bank.[9]

Tax Incentives and Disincentives

The strongest incentives the United States government can offer Americans to invest abroad are found in the field of taxation. Too, United States tax policy can deter private foreign investment.

In general, the United States government does not distinguish between income earned at home and income earned abroad. In order to avoid double taxation, however, the government does permit American investors to credit their tax obligations in the United States with income taxes paid to foreign governments. A major tax concession is granted to United States companies that qualify as a Western Hemisphere Corporation. Such companies must do all their

---

[9] This proposal involves creation of an autonomous International Center for Settlement of Investment Disputes that would make available facilities for conciliation and arbitration. Use of these facilities by a country would be entirely voluntary, but once a government and a foreign investor had agreed to use them, they would be required to carry out their agreement, including compliance with any arbitral award. Moreover, all contracting States would be bound to recognize such an award.

business in the Western Hemisphere, receive 95 percent of their income from sources outside the United States, and earn 90 percent of their income from the active conduct of a trade or business. Western Hemisphere Corporations are granted a reduction of 14 percentage points in the normal United States corporate income tax rate.[10] Investment income earned in United States possessions also qualifies for certain tax exemptions. Over the years many bills have been introduced in Congress to afford additional tax relief to foreign investment income, but so far they have all come to nought.

Until the 1962 Revenue Act, the tax treatment of United States branches and subsidiaries (United States owned foreign corporations) was basically different. Considered a part of the domestic United States company, the branch was (and is) taxed by the United States government on its current earnings along with the rest of the domestic company's income. Earnings of subsidiaries, however, were taxable by the United States government only when *received* by the United States parent company as dividends, royalties, or other forms of income. This made possible the avoidance (or better, postponement) of United States taxes on foreign-source income earned by subsidiaries operating abroad when that income was retained abroad rather than sent home to the parent company. Often this tax avoidance (which was perfectly legal) was facilitated by the parent company's establishment of a nonoperating subsidiary in a "tax haven" country, such as Panama or Switzerland, where taxes on foreign-source income were low or nonexistent. Earnings from operating subsidiaries were then fed into the tax-haven company and were available for reinvestment elsewhere in the world without payment of any United States taxes.

The 1962 Act struck hard at tax-haven arrangements by making the income of tax-haven companies subject to United States taxation when it was *earned,* regardless of whether or not it was repatriated to the United States. The intent of this new tax treatment was to help the balance of payments and also slow down new American investment in the industrial countries.[11] The 1962 Act is exceedingly complex; its ultimate effects on foreign investment are impossible to gauge at this time. But the Act has forced United States parent companies to dissolve tax-haven arrangements, and has introduced

---

[10] Western Hemisphere Corporations are predominantly involved in exporting; their effects on foreign investment have been minimal.

[11] Investments in underdeveloped countries are exempted from many of the 1962 tax provisions.

onerous reporting requirements. Furthermore, it has put United States business investors in foreign operations on the defensive, and has made United States taxation a major factor in international business decisions.

Apart from its own tax laws, the United States government has negotiated tax treaties with several countries to eliminate double taxation and prevent tax avoidance. These treaties define the tax jurisdiction of the signatories and the tax credits that are allowable against taxes paid in one country by residents of the other country.

The Investment Guarantee Program

To stimulate United States private investment in developing countries the Agency for International Development (AID) offers guaranties against the political risks of inconvertibility, expropriation or confiscation, and loss from damage to physical assets caused by war, revolution, and insurrection. To be eligible for such guaranties: (1) the investor must be a United States citizen, a United States corporation at least 51 percent owned by United States interests, or a wholly owned subsidiary (foreign or domestic) of such a corporation; (2) the investment must be a new project, including expansion of an existing foreign operation; (3) the application for risk coverage must be specifically approved by the foreign host government in writing; and (4) the investment must be in a developing country that has signed an agreement with the United States government.

AID charges 0.5 percent per year on the current amount of the investment for each of the three risks covered. Guarantees run for twenty years and are nonrenewable The protection against inconvertibility suggests the nature of the AID guarantees. In the event earnings or capital are blocked by exchange restrictions (or repatriation is made too expensive), the guarantee gives the investor 95 percent of the United States dollars he would otherwise have obtained for local currency at the exchange rate current at the time he tried to repatriate the earnings or capital. The investor is *not* protected against the risk of exchange depreciation. When payment occurs under a guarantee, the United States government assumes all the rights and claims of the private investor in accordance with the terms of its bilateral agreement with the host government.

In 1961 AID introduced an extended-risk guarantee which covers *all* losses (including those originating in ordinary business risks) up to 75 percent of an investment. The cost is 1.75 percent a year, but this coverage is available only for high-priority, risky projects in certain countries. AID has also started an extended-risk housing program to encourage home construction in developing countries.

How effective is the guarantee program? Apparently, quite effective. At least, private investors think it important to get guarantees—in 1965 there was over $5 billion of new applications awaiting action by AID. Undoubtedly, the expropriations in Cuba (where United States investors did not bother to obtain guarantees) have intensified the demand for coverage now available in over sixty developing countries. Perhaps the effectiveness of the program is owing mainly to the fact that participating host governments have granted the United States government the right to assume all the private investor's claims once he is paid for a loss covered by a guarantee. The reluctance to deal directly with the United States government in an investment dispute probably induces respect for the rights of United States investors. In other words, the program has been effective because so few investors have had to ask AID for loss compensation. Since the start of the program in 1947 through 1964, the United States government has collected $21 million in premiums, but has paid out only $70,000 in claims.[12]

AID also promotes United States private investment in developing countries in other ways. It identifies and publicizes investment opportunities, going as far as to solicit United States businessmen, and pays up to one half the cost of investment surveys undertaken by prospective investors. (If actual investment follows, the investors pay the full costs.) Mention should also be made of the funds available from AID and the Export-Import Bank to help finance United States private investment in developing countries.

Private Investment and Foreign Aid

It is appropriate to close this chapter with a brief consideration of the relationship between private foreign investment, on the one hand, and United States government loans and grants for economic development abroad, on the other.

American businessmen and others have charged that loans and grants by the United States government have discouraged private investment for one or all of the following reasons:

---

[12] Irving Trust Company, *The Irving International Letter,* March, 1965, p. 1.

1. Foreign countries are not interested in borrowing private capital when they can obtain public capital on better terms.

2. Government loans and grants encourage foreign government enterprise that is adverse to private interests.

3. In the absence of United States government aid, foreign governments would seek to improve investment climates and thereby attract private capital.

These charges probably have some validity in particular instances, but a number of considerations justifies the use of public loans and grants to promote development of the poor economies of the free world. For one thing, public funds are necessary to *supplement* the flow of private capital to the developing countries. As we have seen, private investment has fallen short of the needs of those countries for the external capital required to initiate and sustain a satisfactory rate of economic growth. When adjusted for price changes, the net United States private long-term capital outflow (including reinvested earnings) did not exceed the level of 1928 until 1956. Moreover, the bulk of the private capital outflow since the war has gone to Canada, Latin America, and Europe, while many developing countries in Africa, the Middle East, and Asia have received only small amounts.

It is true that an improvement of the investment climate in many of those countries would stimulate an inflow of private American capital, but many of the obstacles to private foreign investment stem from unstable social, economic, and political conditions and nationalistic attitudes that can be altered only over the long run. In the meantime, these countries seek desperately to raise the standard of living of their peoples and they look to the United States to help them. If the United States refuses economic assistance, it must face the risk of losing the allegiance of many underdeveloped countries to the principles that this country strives to uphold in its global struggle with communism.

Government loans and grants may also *complement* private foreign investment. A rapid rate of economic growth in the underdeveloped countries requires capital for transportation facilities, power, communications, irrigation, harbors, etc., as well as for technical assistance in agriculture, education, public administration, and public health. All this capital cannot be financed out of local savings, and it is unlikely to be supplied by private foreign investors in view of the low rates of return and the risks that attach to investments of a public utility nature. Thus loans, grants, and technical assistance by governments and international agencies are particularly helpful to developing countries in the creation of the "social overhead capital" that is often the prerequisite of private investment.

The complementary relationship of private and public investment works both ways. Private direct investment brings to foreign economies much more than capital. Its greatest contribution probably lies in the entrepreneurial spirit and the advanced managerial and industrial technology that it puts to work in countries that are notably lacking in those intangible economic assets. The example of a dynamic foreign-owned business firm often leads to emulation by local enterprises. These advantages of direct private investment cannot be duplicated by government loans and grants, and they should not be overlooked in assessing the significance of private foreign investment to the growth and welfare of developing economies.

SUMMARY

1. A net export of capital from one nation to the rest of the world involves both a financial transfer and a real transfer. A nation is a net exporter of capital only when it has a net surplus on current account. This net surplus represents the real transfer of capital. Similarly, a net import of capital involves a net deficit on current account.

2. The amortization or repayment of foreign investments calls for the creation of a surplus on current account in the balance of payments of the debtor country and a deficit on current account in the balance of payments of the creditor country. These adjustments in the current account may be brought about by any of the processes analyzed in Chapters 10 and 11, depending upon the relevant circumstances.

3. When a foreign investment involves managerial control of foreign operations, it is a *direct* investment. When, on the other hand, a foreign investment does not give the investor a voice in management, it is a *portfolio* investment.

4. The foreign investment of the United States, both private and public, rose from $3.5 billion in 1914 to $88.2 billion in 1963. United States private long-term investment aggregated $58.3 billion in 1963, $40.6 billion of which was direct. The bulk of this private investment is located in Canada, Western Europe, and Latin America, in order of importance. Three major industries—petroleum, manufacturing, and mining and smelting—have accounted for the major share of United States direct investment since the War. Book values, net capital flows, and net earnings underestimate the contribution of United States private investment to foreign economies. This is demonstrated by a survey conducted by the United States Department of Commerce.

5. The United States government promotes private foreign investment in developing countries through investment treaties, tax incentives, investment guarantees, the acquisition and dissemination of information regarding investment opportunities, and the diplomatic support and protection of United States investments abroad. At the same time, the government seeks to restrain United States private investment in Western Europe and other developed areas in order to alleviate the deficit in the balance of payments.
6. Foreign aid is needed both to supplement and complement private foreign investment. The advantages of direct private investment cannot be duplicated by government loans and grants, and they should not be overlooked in assessing the significance of private foreign investment to the growth and welfare of developing economies.

QUESTIONS AND APPLICATIONS

1. Discuss the ways in which foreign investment enters into the foreign economic relations of the United States.
2. (a) What is the *transfer problem?*
   (b) When is a nation a *net* exporter of capital? a *net* importer?
   (c) What adjustments occur in both the lending and borrowing nations to effect a *real* transfer of capital when exchange rates are held stable? when exchange rates are freely fluctuating?
3. (a) Distinguish between "productive" and "unproductive" foreign investments in terms of the repayment problem.
   (b) What can the creditor country do to ease the repayment problem?
4. Explain the fundamental economic contribution of foreign investment.
5. Distinguish between portfolio and direct investment.
6. Comment on the principal features of the international investment position of the United States over the period 1914-63.
7. (a) Discuss the significance of the *net* United States capital outflow.
   (b) Why do data on net capital flows, book values, and investment earnings afford only a partial understanding of the role of United States investment abroad? Substantiate your answer by reference to the findings of the survey of United States investment abroad made by the Department of Commerce.
8. (a) What specific measures have been undertaken by the United States government to promote private foreign investment in developing countries?
   (b) Why has the United States government sought to promote such investment?
   (c) Why does the United States government act to restrain American investment in Western Europe?
9. (a) Discuss the relationships between United States private investment and the foreign economic aid of the United States government.
   (b) What are the disadvantages of private investment as compared with government foreign aid? the advantages?

SELECTED READINGS

Agency for International Development. *Cumulative Report on Investment Guaranties.* Washington, D.C.: September, 1964.

Fayerweather, John. *Facts and Fallacies of International Business.* New York: Holt, Rinehart and Winston, 1962. Chapters 4 and 10.

Mikesell, R. F. (ed.). *U.S. Private and Government Investment Abroad.* Eugene, Oregon: University of Oregon Books, 1962.

Joint Economic Committee, U.S. Congress. *Private Investment in Latin America.* Washington, D.C.: 1964.

U.S. Department of Commerce. *Investments in* (Name of Country). Washington, D.C., various years.

——————. *U.S. Business Investments in Foreign Countries,* A Supplement to the Survey of Current Business. Washington, D.C.: 1960.

U.S. Department of State. *Expanding Private Investment for Free World Economic Growth* (Straus Report). Washington, D.C.: 1959.

CHAPTER 22

THE UNITED STATES BALANCE OF PAYMENTS AND INTERNATIONAL MONETARY REFORM

Beginning in 1958 the United States has run annual deficits in its balance of payments which have fluctuated between $3 and $4 billion, as measured by the United States Department of Commerce. At first, the tendency was to regard these deficits as temporary in nature and not calling for any extraordinary measures by United States authorities. But by the fall of 1960 it had become obvious that the United States was facing a payments situation that was not self-corrective and showed signs of a disconcerting permanency.

The complexity of the United States balance of payments, the mutual interdependence of its individual items, the many factors—economic and political—that have a causal bearing on international transactions, and, in some instances, the lack of sound quantitative data—all of these circumstances have rendered impossible a precise determination of the cause or causes of the successive United States deficits. This is hardly surprising when we realize that a balance of payments is a summary of *all* the economic transactions between one country and the rest of the world over the year. It is also not surprising that economists should disagree—and sometimes sharply—as to the underlying cause or causes of the United States disequilibrium.

Analytical disagreements have inevitably engendered policy disagreements. All sorts of remedial measures have been urged upon the United States government by American and European economists. These include the "classical medicine" of internal deflation, dollar depreciation, gold appreciation, floating exchange rates, capital issues control, orthodox measures to increase world liquidity, and a basic reform of the international monetary system. These policy recommendations have often been supported by cogent reasoning, but all of them have been controversial in one way or another. In the field of balance of payments analysis and policy, because of their extraordinary complexity, it is easy for highly trained economists to disagree among themselves—which they have done—over what is wrong with the United States balance of payments and what corrective action should be taken.

In this chapter we shall trace the evolution of the United States payments deficit and describe the remedial steps taken by the United States government. We shall then turn to the question of international monetary reform which has been activated by United States payments difficulties.

THE UNITED STATES PAYMENTS DEFICIT

Surplus and deficit are economic concepts rather than accounting concepts, and there is disagreement as to the best way to measure disequilibrium in a balance of payments. Before looking at the United States payments situation, then, it will be instructive to describe briefly the three principal concepts of surplus and deficit.

Concepts of Surplus and Deficit

We pointed out in Chapter 7 that the balance of payments always adds to zero because it is based on the principles of double-entry accounting. Thus any concept of surplus and deficit involves a distinction between different items. In Chapter 9 we discussed the theoretical distinction between autonomous and compensatory items, but in practice this distinction is not self-evident, depending in part on what the analyst is seeking to measure. The method of presenting a measure of surplus or deficit is to place some items "above the line" which are regarded as autonomous and the other items "below the line" which are viewed as financing the surplus or deficit (compensatory items).

Three alternative concepts of surplus and deficit have been used in measuring the international payments position of the United States: (1) *basic transactions* concept, (2) *liquidity* concept, and (3) *official settlements* concept. The key distinction in the basic transactions concept is between short-term and long-term capital while in the official settlements concept it is between transactions by monetary authorities and all other transactions. The liquidity concept employs both distinctions, the classification of foreign assets in the United States as short-term (liquid) or long-term (nonliquid) and the separation of the transactions of monetary authorities from all other transactions.

Until the early 1950's the United States Department of Commerce used the basic transactions concept, but then moved to the liquidity concept. A recent study recommends a new switch to the official settlements concept.[1] Each of these three concepts has its advocates and critics. In analyzing the United States payments position it is important to know which concept is being used, including what it measures and what it does not measure. Table 22-1 illustrates these different concepts in terms of the United States balance of payments for 1964. Note the wide discrepancies among the "basic," "liquidity," and "official" measures of deficits.

The Liquidity Deficit in the United States Balance of Payments

The United States balance of payments is compiled by the Department of Commerce and the United States deficit that we read and hear about is so calculated as to reveal changes in the net international liquidity position of the United States. Simply put, this position is defined as the net difference between the gold and foreign exchange (including the IMF gold tranche, see Footnote 6, page 490) held by the United States monetary authorities, on the one hand, and the United States liquid liabilities (mainly bank deposits, United States Treasury obligations, bankers' acceptances, and other short-term claims on the United States) owing to foreign governments and monetary authorities and to private residents of foreign countries, on the other. A deficit in the United States balance of payments worsens the United States liquidity position, usually by a combination of gold outflows and an increase in short-term liabilities to foreigners (Items 15, 14, and 9 in Table 22-1).[2]

---

[1] *The Balance of Payments Statistics of the United States,* Report of the Review Committee for Balance of Payments Statistics to the Bureau of the Budget (Washington, D. C.: Government Printing Office, April, 1965). Hereafter we shall refer to this document as the "Bernstein Report."

[2] To ease pressure on its gold reserves the United States government has entered into "special transactions" with foreign governments, namely, advance repayments of United States government loans, advances on United States military exports, and the sale of nonmarketable, medium-term securities. There is uncertainty as to whether these items should be placed "above the line" (autonomous) or "below the line" (compensatory). In Table 22-1 they are placed below the line for both the basic and liquidity balances, but in estimating the official balance, advances on military exports and the sale of United States government securities to foreign nonmonetary institutions are treated as autonomous and placed above the line. Thus the liquidity deficit in Table 22-1 is the sum of the changes in liquid liabilities to foreigners and in monetary reserves *plus* the special government transactions.

Table 22-1
UNITED STATES BALANCE OF PAYMENTS IN 1964 SHOWING THE BASIC, LIQUIDITY, AND OFFICIAL DEFICITS
(Millions of Dollars)

1. Net balance on goods and services *	8,209
2. Remittances and pensions, net	— 830
3. U.S. government grants and capital flow, net †	—3,450
4. U.S. and foreign long-term capital, net ‡	—4,100
5. *Balance on "Basic" Transactions* (1, 2, 3, and 4)	— 171
6. U.S. private short-term capital, net	—1,989
7. Net errors and omissions	— 893
8. *"Liquidity" Balance on "Regular" Transactions* § (5, 6, and 7)	—3,053
9. U.S. liquid liabilities to foreign nonmonetary institutions ‖	1,517
10. Advances on U.S. military exports	206
11. U.S. government securities sold to foreign nonmonetary institutions, net **	— 174
12. *"Official" Transactions Balance* (8, 9, 10, and 11)	—1,504
13. Advance repayments on U.S. government loans	122
14. U.S. liabilities to foreign official monetary institutions	1,211
15. U.S. monetary reserve assets (increase —) †† (12, 13, and 14)	171

* Excludes military transfers under grants.

† Excludes military grants, advance repayments of United States government loans, advances on United States military exports, and sales of United States government nonmarketable, medium-term, nonconvertible securities.

‡ Except foreign holdings of marketable United States government bonds and notes.

§ "Regular" transactions exclude "special" government transactions—the last three items in the explanation for (†) above.

‖ Foreign commercial banks, international nonmonetary institutions, and private nonbank foreigners.

** Nonmarketable, medium-term, and nonconvertible.

†† Includes gold, convertible currencies, and IMF position.

GENERAL NOTE: Debit entries are indicated by a *minus* sign.

SOURCES: Adapted from Tables 9.2, 9.3, and 9.5 in *The Balance of Payments Statistics of the United States*, Report of the Review Committee for Balance of Payments Statistics to the Bureau of the Budget (Washington, D. C.: Government Printing Office, April, 1965).

The Department of Commerce focuses on changes in the net United States liquidity position, as defined above, because it is concerned with the capacity of United States monetary authorities to maintain the gold value of the dollar by standing ready at all times to exchange dollars offered by foreign monetary authorities for gold at the rate of $35 per ounce of gold. Therefore, United States liquid assets are so defined as to *exclude* United States private short-term claims against foreigners (Item 6 in Table 22-1) on the grounds that such private claims are not available to United States monetary authorities to finance a payments deficit. Put another way, the Department of Commerce considers all transactions in the balance of payments as autonomous except for monetary gold, official holdings of convertible currencies, special government transactions, and liquid liabilities owing to *all* foreign residents. (The argument for including all foreign residents is that private foreign residents can sell their dollar claims to foreign monetary authorities who, in turn, can demand gold for their dollars.) As noted above, this is the liquidity deficit concept.

What has been the evolution of the liquidity deficit in the United States balance of payments during the 1950's and in recent years? Table 22-2 gives us the data for the years 1950 through 1964. In commenting on the liquidity deficits for those years, we shall indicate the movement of United States merchandise exports and imports. This will be done not to explain the deficits, but rather to demonstrate that there is no simple explanation of them.

Table 22-2

LIQUIDITY, BASIC, AND OFFICIAL SETTLEMENTS DEFICITS IN THE UNITED STATES BALANCE OF PAYMENTS

(Billions of Dollars)

Year	Liquidity Deficit	Basic Deficit	Official Settlements Deficit
1950	—3.6	—3.4	—3.3
1951	—0.3	—0.7	+0.5
1952	—1.0	—1.6	—0.8
1953	—2.2	—2.6	—2.1
1954	—1.5	—1.1	—1.5
1955	—1.1	—1.5	—0.7
1956	—0.9	—1.0	—0.3
1957	+0.5	—0.5	+1.1
1958	—3.5	—3.7	—3.0
1959	—4.2	—4.2	—2.3
1960	—3.9	—1.7	—3.4
1961	—3.1	—0.7	—2.0
1962	—3.6	—1.8	—3.3
1963	—3.3	—2.2	—2.3
1964	—3.1	—0.2	—1.5

SOURCES: For 1950-59, Hal Lary, *Problems of the United States as World Trader and Banker* (New York: National Bureau of Economic Research, 1963), pp. 12-13. For 1960-64, *The Balance of Payments Statistics of the United States*, Report of the Review Committee for Balance of Payments Statistics to the Bureau of the Budget (Washington, D. C.: Government Printing Office, April, 1965), Tables 9.2, 9.3, and 9.5.

Since 1950 the United States has experienced a liquidity deficit in its balance of payments in every year with the single exception of 1957. This nation started the 1950's with a big deficit, particularly in view of the surpluses in preceding years. This deficit was owing mainly to the outbreak of the Korean War in June, 1950, although the European devaluations in September, 1949, probably had some influence. United States merchandise imports rose $2.2 billion over 1949 to feed rearmament and speculative demands while exports fell $2 billion as United States production was diverted to domestic use.

In 1951 the liquidity deficit dropped sharply as United States exports surged ahead by $4 billion, partly in response to European demand provoked by the Korean War. At the same time, imports rose $2 billion. In the succeeding five years, 1952-56, the liquidity deficit averaged $1.66 billion, fluctuating from a high of $2.1 billion in 1953 to a low of $0.9 billion in 1956.

The Suez crisis in 1957 gave the United States its first liquidity surplus since the small surplus ($175 million) in 1949. Exports soared $2 billion while imports rose only $0.5 billion. At the time, fears were voiced about a return of the dollar shortage, but their unreality was demonstrated in the very next year.

In 1958 the respectable surplus of 1957 turned into a whopping deficit of $3.5 billion—almost equal to the 1950 deficit. Exports dropped off $3.1 billion while imports rose $660 million. In retrospect, 1958 marks the end of a period of modest deficits and the start of the United States payments problem. Before that year deficits were viewed by United States officials as a desirable alleviation of the dollar shortage which so plagued the early postwar world.

In 1959 the deficit rose even higher to $4.2 billion—the highest in United States history. Exports stagnated at the low 1958 level, but imports jumped $2.4 billion. In the following year the deficit dropped only marginally to $3.9 billion even though exports shot up $3.2 billion while imports dropped almost $600 million. The *immediate* cause of the deficit was mainly a large, speculative outflow of short-term capital of the order of $2.5 billion (including a switch in net errors and omissions). Speculators were now going short on the dollar.

In the four years 1961-64, the United States achieved the largest surpluses on goods and services (current account) in its peace-time history. Merchandise exports rose from $19.9 billion in 1961 to $25.2 billion in 1964 while imports rose from $14.5 billion to $18.6 billion.

Despite this impressive performance the liquidity deficit remained at over $3 billion. Why? The answer lies in unilateral transfer and capital movements: from 1960 through 1964, net United States government grants and capital increased $0.9 billion, net long-term capital outflow increased $2 billion, and United States private short-term claims on foreigners increased $0.7 billion—an overall increase of $3.6 billion which offset the improvement in the current account balance.

This brief review of liquidity deficits in the United States balance of payments points to certain conclusions:

> 1. Apart from the abnormal years of 1950 and 1957, the United States deficit experience falls into two distinct periods: a period of modest deficits (1951-56) which caused no concern, and a period of high deficits after 1957 which have aroused deep concern both in Washington and elsewhere.
> 2. High deficits have continued into the 1960's despite remedial measures undertaken by the United States government.
> 3. There is no single explanation of the deficit in terms of the balance of payments items. For example, in 1958 the big deficit period was inaugurated by a sharp deterioration in the current account, but in 1964 the current account surplus rose by $2.5 billion over 1963 and the liquidity deficit dropped only $0.2 billion.

The Basic Deficit in the United States Balance of Payments

The liquidity deficit does not measure the basic, or fundamental, deficit in the United States balance of payments because it treats United States private short-term capital movements and net errors and omissions as autonomous items. Both of these items are very sensitive to temporary, short-run factors and they are partly compensatory. To overcome this drawback we can measure the deficit in terms of basic transactions that include trade in merchandise and services (current account), government grants and capital flow (except for special government transactions), and private long-term investment (Items 1, 2, 3, and 4 in Table 22-1). This approach comes much closer to the theoretical concept of deficit that was described in Chapter 9.

It is instructive to compare the basic deficits against the liquidity deficits that are shown in Table 22-2. Any differences between them are attributable to United States private short-term capital movements and shifts in errors and omissions; in years when the deficit is mainly traceable to the current account, United States government grants and capital flow, and/or United States and foreign long-term capital, the basic and liquidity deficits are similar. This was substantially the case from 1950 through 1959, except for the abnormal year of 1957. As we have noted previously, however, the deficits in the 1960's have been fed by large outflows of United States private short-term capital and debit entries for errors and omissions. This has caused a wide divergence between the basic and liquidity deficits. In other words, the large outflows of short-term capital in the early sixties have concealed the marked improvement in the balance on basic transactions over 1958 and 1959. Some of this export of private short-term capital was used to finance United States exports of merchandise and services and, therefore, did not worsen the United States deficit. But much of it was speculative or induced by interest arbitrage, and had little to do with financing United States exports.

The Official Settlements Deficit in the United States Balance of Payments

Table 22-2 also shows the official settlements deficit in the United States balance of payments for the years 1950-64. As indicated in Table 22-1, this deficit (or surplus) concept differs from the liquidity concept in that it places above the line United States liquid liabilities to foreign nonmonetary institutions as well as certain special government transactions (Items 9, 10 and 11). Thus any divergence between these two measures of the United States deficit is explained by these items, especially United States liquid liabilites to foreign nonmonetary institutions which now serve to reduce the official deficit (or increase it in years when such liabilities decrease) rather than to finance it. During most of the 1950's this divergence was modest, but in 1959 the official settlements deficit was $1.9 billion less than the liquidity deficit and in 1964, $1.6 billion less. In each of those years liabilities to foreign commercial banks increased over $1 billion which lowered the official settlements deficit but not the liquidity deficit.

The official settlements approach considers as compensatory only reserve transactions (Items 14 and 15) and advance repayments on United States government loans (Item 13). In short, only transactions between the United States monetary authority (the Federal Reserve System and the Treasury) and foreign monetary authorities are placed below the line.

The main arguments favoring the use of the official settlements concept are as follows: [3]

1. Under the present international monetary system, national monetary authorities—central banks and Treasuries—are charged with the maintenance of stable exchange rates. As we learned in Chapter 8, they do this by providing the compensatory financing needed to equalize autonomous transactions in the foreign exchange market, that is, the amounts of foreign exchange supplied and demanded by persons, business firms, and nonmonetary government agencies.

2. In carrying out this stabilization, the monetary authorities gain or lose reserve assets (gold and foreign exchange) and experience a gain or loss in liabilities to foreign monetary authorities. Thus the size of these reserve transactions is the best measure of the degree of intervention by monetary authorities in the foreign exchange market and hence of payments disequilibria.

3. Only monetary authorities have a responsibility to maintain stable exchange rates. The bulk of private international transactions is motivated by profit expectations which are not shared by monetary authorities. Thus the distinction between monetary authorities, on the one hand, and all other participants in international transactions, on the other, is of greater analytical significance than the distinction between private foreign residents and private domestic residents. (This latter distinction is made by the liquidity concept: Item 6 in Table 22-1 is put above the line while Item 9 is put below the line.)

4. Through the middle 1950's it was defensible to regard both private and official foreign liquid assets in the United States as foreign "reserves" without greatly distorting the facts. Thus the liquidity concept was initially close to the official settlements concept. But today the principal currencies are freely convertible and there is a broad variety of financial transactions between private United States and foreign residents. The volume of liquid dollar assets held by foreign *nonmonetary* institutions has greatly increased primarily because of the need for higher levels of working capital to finance a growing volume of international trade and investment. To regard the increase in these liquid liabilities to foreign nonmonetary institutions as helping to finance a United States deficit is misleading.

These arguments, in our opinion, are sound and favor the substitution of the official settlements concept for the liquidity concept in the compilation of the United States balance of payments by the Department of Commerce. (As a compromise, the Department could use both concepts and publish two deficit [or surplus] estimates.) In particular, the asymetric treatment of United States short-term capital

---

[3] See "Bernstein Report," pp. 110-11.

(above the line) and foreign short-term capital (below the line) in the liquidity concept is hard to defend today. It means, for example, that the deposit of $100 in a French bank by an American goes above the line and adds to a liquidity deficit whereas the deposit of $100 in a United States bank by a foreigner goes below the line and does not affect the size of a liquidity deficit.

The official settlements concept, however, is not a substitute for the basic transactions concept. If our interest is not in the compensatory actions of monetary authorities but rather in the fundamental strength or weakness of the balance of payments, then the basic transactions concept would appear to be superior to the others.

In closing, let us note that the controversy over the best way to measure disequilibrium in the United States balance of payments is not merely academic. The concept used will help shape attitudes towards the balance of payments and thereby influence United States payments policies.

The United States Deficit as a Transfer Problem

Despite its big deficits, the United States has *not* been living beyond its means, internationally speaking. On the contrary, its annual export surplus on goods and services averaged $5.7 billion over the five years 1960-64. (This surplus was generated even though military payments to foreigners averaged over $2.9 billion.) This means that the United States deficit situation is highly unusual; the normal deficit condition involves a deficit on current account such as was experienced by the United Kingdom in the fall of 1964. The United States basic deficit is rather a consequence of United States foreign aid and private long-term capital exports which together have exceeded the United States surplus on goods and services.[4] We view the United States basic deficit, therefore, as fundamentally a real *transfer* problem.[5] The United States has not developed a surplus on *commercial* goods and services big enough to finance fully its military expenditures abroad, its foreign aid, and its private long-term foreign investment. These three items, together with remittances and pensions, averaged over $9 billion annually in the period 1960-64 on a net basis.

---

[4] For the sake of completeness we should also include net remittances and pensions which had an average debit balance of over $700 million in the period 1960-64.

[5] The real transfer problem relating to long-term foreign investment was discussed in Chapter 21 in general terms.

We do not want to suggest that the sum of these items is the magnitude of the transfer problem. Probably about three quarters of United States foreign assistance is now spent directly in the United States and therefore represents no transfer problem. Also a substantial portion of United States direct investment goes abroad as exports of machinery and other capital equipment. Although it is difficult to determine precisely the magnitude of the transfer problem, there is no doubt a transfer problem remains even after all the "feedback effects" of foreign aid and private long-term investment abroad are taken into account. (There is relatively little direct feedback from military expenditures and portfolio investment.)

This transfer problem has been obscured by massive outflows of speculative and other short-term capital which have added greatly to the liquidity deficit. Clearly remedial steps to reduce this outflow are necessary, but the long-run health of the United States balance of payments depends on a solution of the transfer problem.

The fundamental strength of the United States international financial position is demonstrated by the continuing growth in *net* international assets. We saw in Table 21-1 in the last chapter that the net United States *investment* position rose from $22.8 billion in 1957 to $36.7 at the end of 1963, or an improvement of $13.9 billion. During that same period United States gold holdings fell $7.3 billion and the United States IMF position deteriorated $1 billion—an overall decline of $8.3 billion in United States monetary reserves.[6] Thus the net improvement in the United States international financial position (investment position *plus* reserve asset position) from 1957 through 1963 was $5.6 billion. Basically, the United States has been borrowing on short-term and investing on long-term. These short-term borrowings (Items 9 and 14 in Table 22-1) rose $10.2 billion from 1957 to the end of 1963, and they occurred because the dollar is the key reserve currency, financing a large part of world trade and making up a substantial portion of international monetary reserves. Increasingly, however, foreign monetary authorities have been reluctant to add to dollar holdings because of concern about their future

---

[6] The IMF position (or "gold tranche") of a country represents 25 percent of its Fund quota plus its net lending to the Fund (net drawings of its currency from the Fund by foreign countries *minus* its own drawings from the Fund). It is the amount that can be drawn from the Fund automatically. At the end of 1963 the United States quota in the IMF was $4,125 million and its IMF position, $1,035 million.

convertibility into gold. The dollar cannot serve as a key currency unless foreign monetary authorities have confidence in its strength which depends in the first instance on the gold and other reserve assets of the United States. That is why it is so important to stop any further deterioration of United States official reserves. But our concern for liquidity should not blind us to the strong—and growing —net international financial position of the United States.

REMEDIAL MEASURES TAKEN BY THE UNITED STATES GOVERNMENT

Beginning in 1960 the United States government has initiated an extraordinary variety of measures to correct the United States payments deficit. By 1965 these measures encompassed all of the major classes of international transactions making up the balance of payments. In this section we shall delineate the more important remedial measures, describing their main features but avoiding detailed commentary.

Measures to Expand Exports

We have indicated that the United States deficit is fundamentally a transfer problem. Broadly speaking, this problem can be solved (1) by an expansion of United States exports of goods and services; (2) by a restriction of imports, government grants, loans and expenditures abroad, and private capital exports; or (3) by a combination of both expansion and restriction. The first solution—the expansion of United States exports—is the most attractive solution on several counts. By eschewing restrictions on trade and payments, it would conform to the traditional United States policy favoring a liberal multilateral trading system. Expanding exports would also directly benefit the United States economy by raising the levels of production and employment (the export multiplier) and, at the same time, add to the gains from international specialization. This solution would also represent an enduring improvement in the international competitive strength of American industry.

In contrast, the restrictive approach is opposed to the spirit of United States foreign economic policy and may also require the sacrifice of other objectives, such as rapid economic growth in developing countries and the unfettered international movement of capital. If applied in a wholesale fashion, such an approach would undercut United States efforts since the second World War to rid the world economy of obstacles to the movement of trade and the transfer of payments. As we shall see, the United States government has adopted certain restrictive measures, but only reluctantly and after several years of deficit. It has strongly resisted the use of import restrictions, seeking instead to enlarge the surplus on goods and services through a policy of active export promotion.

The Export Expansion Program. In 1960 the United States government launched an Export Expansion Program to reinforce the marketing efforts of existing export enterprises and to induce domestic manufacturers to enter export markets for the first time. Run by the Department of Commerce, the program has many facets: regional export expansion councils composed of businessmen working closely with the regional Commerce offices, the establishment of permanent overseas trade centers for the exhibition of American products, trade mission programs involving trips abroad by businessmen and government officials to seek out new market opportunities, a program to encourage and assist American companies to participate in international trade fairs, as well as many supporting activities.

How effective is the Export Expansion Program? No conclusive answer can be given to this question because of the multiplicity of factors involved in export activity. But there is evidence that the program has encouraged many companies to undertake exporting. By 1965 the number of new exporters recruited under the program was running at a rate of almost 1,000 per year, and the volume of annual exports generated by these new exporters was approaching $500 million.[7] Despite this achievement one survey indicates that the Export Expansion Program has not reached a major part of small and medium-sized manufacturers.[8] Probably everyone would agree that there is a significant export potential in this country that is yet to be tapped.

Export Credit Insurance. Adequate export financing at a reasonable cost is an important factor in making United States products competitive in foreign markets.[9] In recent years the Export-Import Bank has developed programs to provide various kinds of export

---

[7] "Small Concerns Aid Export Drive," *New York Times,* June 20, 1965, p. F-5.

[8] William A. Dymsza, "Export Expansion—An Evaluation," *International Trade Review,* March, 1965, pp. 14-16. Dymsza suggests the possibility of a program similar to the county agent and agricultural extension programs that reach individual farmers at the local level.

[9] Chapter 27 treats the role of financing in international trade.

credit, including long-term financing, medium-term guarantees against both commercial and political risks, and a short and medium-term program operated by the Foreign Credit Insurance Association (FCIA) comprising 70 insurance companies. By insuring exports against non-payment due to political risks and, in some instances, commercial risks as well, the Export-Import Bank and the FCIA make it easier for the exporter to obtain financing from his own bank and thereby sell his goods.

The Trade Expansion Act of 1962. The Trade Expansion Act and the Kennedy Round were discussed in previous chapters, and there is no need to describe them here. Their mention at this point is justified because trade negotiations to lower tariffs and other trade barriers (especially in the European Common Market) are viewed by the United States government as an important way to expand United States exports and thereby alleviate the payments deficit. It is realized, of course, that lower United States import duties will stimulate more imports, but it is believed that lower trade barriers in foreign countries will give a greater boost to United States exports because of the competitive strength of American industry and agriculture.

Domestic Price Stability. In addition to these specific measures to promote exports, the United States government has worked to maintain domestic price stability by keeping wage increases in line with productivity gains. This policy was successful in the first half of the 1960's when United States prices rose appreciably less than prices in Western Europe—the major United States export market and its chief competitor in third markets. Price stability gave American exporters a firm basis for profitable sales at fully competitive prices. In 1965, however, prices started to rise in the United States as the economy approached full employment.

Measures to Reduce Net United States Government Outlays Abroad

United States government outlays abroad—military expenditures and foreign assistance to developing nations—are big debit items in the balance of payments. A sharp cutback in these outlays would go far towards eliminating the payments deficit, but only at the cost of sacrificing other key objectives. This is a concrete illustration of what Chapter 12 called the diversity and conflict of ends and the inadequacy of means.

The decision to station American troops in Western Europe and Japan was made by the United States government in the late

1940's on military and political grounds. To call home these troops because they add to the payments deficit would entail the sacrifice of long-range political objectives, and the United States government has clearly rejected this course of action. Nevertheless, much progress has been made in reducing the *net* effect of military expenditures on the balance of payments. United States troops abroad are now supplied from domestic United States sources to a greater extent than before and this has cut down the foreign exchange cost of their maintenance. More important, the United States has greatly increased military sales (including advances on future sales) to foreign countries as offsets to its own military expenditures abroad. The result of these actions has been to cut *net* military expenditures by $0.9 from 1960 through 1964.[10]

The United States government has also refused to weaken its foreign assistance to developing countries because of payments difficulties. Quite the contrary. Between 1960 and 1964, United States government nonmilitary grants and long-term credits rose from $2.9 billion to $4.3 billion. But the net impact of each dollar of foreign assistance on the United States balance of payments has been significantly reduced by tying government grants and credits to the procurement of United States goods and services. By the mid-1960's all Export-Import Bank loans were tied (a traditional practice) and about four fifths of other government grants and loans to developing countries were used to finance United States exports. Most economists oppose tied grants and loans in principle because they distort the international allocation of goods and services. The tying of United States foreign aid, however, is a relatively mild form of restriction and its economic effects (as opposed to its payments effects) are probably minimal when account is taken of the quality and range of American production. This is not to say that tied assistance should become a permanent United States policy; it should be abandoned once the balance of payments deficit is overcome. Only by following an open policy itself can the United States hope to persuade other nations to stop tying their own foreign assistance.

Measures to Restrain United States Private Capital Exports

In the five years 1960-64 the outflow of United States private long-term capital jumped from $2.6 billion to $4.3 billion, and the

---

[10] In 1960 United States military expenditures were $3 billion; in 1964, $2.8 billion; United States military sales were $0.3 billion and $0.8 billion in the same years. Advance military payments were nonexistent in 1960 and $0.2 billion in 1964.

outflow of short-term capital from $1.4 billion to $2.1 billion. This overall increase of $2.4 billion in United States capital outflows neutralized a good part of the improvement in the current account surplus recorded over the same period. United States officials have watched closely the size and growth of private capital exports, and the 1962 Revenue Act was intended to restrain United States direct investment in Western Europe and Japan. But *direct* action to curtail private capital outflows was not taken until 1963 (portfolio investment) and 1965 (direct investment and bank loans abroad).

The Interest Equalization Tax. The first direct action to lessen the outflow of private capital occurred in mid-1963 when President Kennedy proposed a tax (running as high as 15 percent) on the value of foreign securities bought by United States residents. Although this proposal did not become law until September, 1964, it was retroactive to the time it was proposed and its effects were felt immediately. In the first half of 1963 foreign securities worth $1.2 billion were sold in the United States, but in the second half they dropped to $3.5 million.[11] In 1964 purchases of outstanding foreign securities by American investors were less than their sales of such securities.

It is evident that the interest equalization tax is effective in curbing the outflow of portfolio investment even though Canada, developing nations, and international financial agencies are exempted from the tax. Just after the tax became law, the city of Oslo floated a $15 million issue in New York, but the tax cut the yield for American investors from 5.6 percent to 4.9 percent and as a result European investors took the entire issue. The tax has forced many international borrowers to raise funds in European capital markets, a difficult task because of their relatively small size and restrictions on the purchase of foreign securities.

The Voluntary Restraint Program. The curtailment of United States portfolio investment after mid-1963 was more than offset in 1964 by a big jump in United States bank loans to foreign borrowers and a further growth in United States direct investments. This precipitated a series of measures called the voluntary restraint program.

In a special balance of payments message to the United States Congress in February, 1965, President Johnson proposed a series of new steps to eliminate the payments deficit, including the application

---

[11] "Longer Life Likely for Dollar Gap Tax," *Business Week*, October 10, 1964, p. 162.

of the interest equalization tax to bank loans to foreigners of one year or more (except export credit), the voluntary cooperation of United States banks to limit their lending abroad, and the enlistment of United States business in a national campaign to limit direct investments abroad.[12] Shortly thereafter, the Federal Reserve System and the Department of Commerce issued a set of guidelines to commercial banks and business corporations respectively, requesting them to achieve specified goals in restraining loans and investments abroad.

Commercial banks were asked to limit their credits to foreigners in 1965 to an amount not more than 5 percent of the credits outstanding at the end of 1964. They were to do this without cutting back on export credits or loans to developing countries. In many instances, banks were called upon to cut back their foreign credits because they were already over the 5 percent mark.

In a letter to over 600 corporate executives who were responsible for most United States direct investment overseas, the Secretary of Commerce asked that each company set up a balance of payments ledger (on a simple one-sheet form) and take steps to improve it for 1965 and 1966. How to bring about an improvement was left to each company and any one or several ways was possible: an increase in the company's exports, the postponement of new investments abroad, the repatriation of liquid assets now held abroad, and borrowing more from abroad. The Secretary was hopeful that the average improvement would be 15 to 20 percent over 1964. The companies were asked to submit quarterly reports showing their individual payments forecasts and goals for the year.

The voluntary restraint program is likely to be most effective in reducing the outflow of private capital. Bankers and businessmen know that if the present program does not work, they face the prospect of much tighter government regulations. It must be recognized, however, that this program is only a temporary stop-gap; it is not a real solution of the deficit. Its function is to lessen immediate pressures while an enduring adjustment is achieved in the balance of payments. Restrictions on foreign investment—even though nominally voluntary—are antithetical to the private enterprise system and the traditional goals of United States foreign economic policy.

---

[12] Other important points in the President's message were the extension of the interest equalization tax to the end of 1967, the stepping up of efforts by the Department of Defense and AID to cut overseas dollar costs, a reduction in the duty-free exemptions of returning American tourists, and a redoubling of efforts to promote exports.

Measures Taken by United States Monetary Authorities

The monetary authorities of the United States—the Treasury and Federal Reserve System—have the responsibility of maintaining the gold value of the dollar by standing ready at all times to convert the dollar holdings of foreign central banks into gold at a rate of $35 per ounce.[13] Between the end of 1957 and 1964, $7 billion of gold was used for this purpose, reducing the United States gold stock from $22.9 billion to $15.9 billion. To lessen this gold drain and to forestall speculation the United States monetary authorities have initiated several measures which are often described as the "first line of defense" for the dollar.

Traditionally, the United States has supported the dollar through a policy of passive stabilization.[14] This policy shifted in May, 1961, when the United States Treasury actively intervened in the foreign exchange market for the first time since the early 1930's. Using its Exchange Stabilization Fund, the Treasury's first intervention was limited to sales of forward German marks to prevent excessive speculation in that currency which could lead to a flight from the dollar. Since then, it has extended its operations to other currencies in both spot and forward markets. Active stabilization of the dollar was massively reinforced in March, 1962, when the Federal Reserve System entered the foreign exchange market on its own account (for the first time since the late 1920's) rather than simply acting as an agent of the Treasury. In the ensuing years the United States monetary authorities have engaged in numerous transactions in all the leading currencies, mainly to prevent or moderate speculative capital movements in both the dollar and foreign currencies, especially the pound sterling. To conduct a policy of active stabilization the United States monetary authorities held $432 million in foreign currencies at the end of 1964 compared to none in the years before 1961. In addition, the United States authorities have access to large amounts of foreign central bank credit under bilateral swap agreements.

Bilateral Swap Agreements. As part of its new intervention activity, the Federal Reserve System has entered into a series of reciprocal currency arrangements (commonly called swap agreements)

---

[13] Legally only the Treasury has this responsibility. However, the Federal Reserve System works closely with the Treasury and together they comprise the United States monetary authorities.

[14] See Chapter 8.

with the central banks of Western Europe, Canada, and Japan. Under these bilateral arrangements a foreign central bank provides stand-by credits to the Federal Reserve System in return for an equal amount of stand-by credits. The credits are limited in size and must be liquidated (at the exchange rate prevailing at the time they were drawn) within three to twelve months depending on the individual agreement. At the end of 1964 the total amount of swap stand-by credits was over $2.3 billion, the largest single credit being $750 million with the Bank of England.[15] The swap network has benefited foreign countries, such as Italy and the United Kingdom, by supplementing their reserves with an assured access to dollars. Since the start of the agreements in 1962 through 1964, total drawings by both the United States and foreign central banks amounted to over $3.5 billion of which 88 percent had been repaid.[16] The network has given the United States a buffer to absorb sudden speculative drives on the dollar and has thereby protected its gold reserves.

Sales of Medium-Term Securities. To reduce the "overhang" of United States liquid liabilities owing to foreign central banks, the United States Treasury has issued a series of medium-term bonds payable in dollars or in specified foreign currencies for sale to foreign governments and central banks. Net sales of these bonds (mostly payable in foreign currencies) in 1963 and 1964 were one billion dollars. In effect, these sales of medium-term bonds have relieved pressure on United States gold reserves by giving foreign central banks an opportunity to acquire an earning asset payable in their own currencies.

None of the foregoing measures introduced by the United States monetary authorities have reduced the United States deficit. But they have lessened the gold drain and have dampened speculative capital outflows by influencing spot and forward rates of exchange (especially forward rates), by interposing a buffer of foreign central bank credits, and by converting a part of United States liquid liabilities to a less liquid, more stable form. The skillful management of the United States Treasury and Federal Reserve System has also strengthened the capacity of the international monetary system to deal with the shocks of sudden, massive movements of speculative and flight capital.

---

[15] Board of Governors of the Federal Reserve System, *Annual Report* (Washington, D. C.: March, 1965), p. 163.
[16] *Ibid.*, p. 163.

Constraints Imposed on United States Payments Policy

The fact that we can point to no single dramatic remedial measure underscores the constraints imposed on United States payments policy by the unique role of the United States in the world economy. As leader of the free world, the United States is the major bulwark against Communist aggression and the primary source of aid to the developing countries. It is also guardian of the dollar—the world's principal reserve currency. Persistent unemployment and the low growth rate of the United States economy in the late 1950's added further constraints. Hence the United States has refused to (1) cut back its military forces abroad and its foreign aid because of payments considerations, (2) impose trade or exchange restrictions, (3) devalue the dollar, or (4) deflate its economy.

As we observed in Chapter 10, the "classical medicine" for a deficit is deflation of the domestic economy. But today all governments are pledged to achieve full employment and a rapid rate of economic growth and they reject this solution. However, much can be done to bring about adjustment through the adoption of monetary and fiscal policies that prevent inflation without causing unemployment and a sharp fall in the growth rate. This is true especially when foreign surplus countries pursue less restrictive policies and experience a rise in wage and price levels. Proof of this is found in the monetary and fiscal policies of the United States in the first half of the 1960's. Over the period 1960-64 the United States gross national product grew from $503 billion to $623 billion, and employment rose from 66.7 million to 70.4 million workers, while wholesale prices remained virtually stable.[17] This signal achievement, together with rising prices in Europe and elsewhere, has made possible the remarkable upsurge in United States exports and the substantial correction of the basic deficit in the balance of payments. In short, both income and price adjustments have been operative in the United States balance of payments, but their effects have been obscured by large-scale exports of United States private capital and, at times, speculative and capital-flight movements.

United States officials have consistently rejected proposals to alter the gold value of the dollar, although several academic economists here and in Europe have urged a depreciation of the dollar. The contemporary international monetary system rests upon the link between the dollar and gold, and the United States government

---

[17] *Federal Reserve Bulletin*, June, 1965.

is convinced that any disruption of that link would wreck the system. Given the strong trade surplus and competitive vigor of the United States, it is also questionable whether foreign countries would allow a dollar depreciation without depreciating their own currencies to an equal extent. If they would not, then a dollar depreciation would be fully neutralized and have no effect on the current account while the rash of counter-depreciations would set off an immense speculative activity endangering all countries.

A final note. The elimination of the United States deficit has been made more difficult by the unwillingness of the surplus countries in Europe (with some exceptions) to make equilibrating adjustments. By maintaining high interest rates they have encouraged an inflow of short-term capital and by restricting the flotation of foreign securities in their capital markets they have placed most of the burden of international finance on the New York market. Except for Germany and the Netherlands which appreciated their currencies 5 percent in 1961, no European country has appreciated its currency vis a vis the dollar despite the probably excessive European depreciations in 1949 and in the case of France, in 1957 and 1958 as well. Furthermore, the European Economic Community is raising common tariff and agricultural restrictions that have already harmed some United States exports.

INTERNATIONAL MONETARY REFORM

The persistent deficit in the United States balance of payments has stimulated a tremendous amount of discussion and controversy about the adequacy of the contemporary international monetary system, including a bewildering variety of reform proposals. (Devising international monetary reforms has been the favorite intellectual game of economists and central bankers in recent years.) In this closing section we can only briefly sketch the alleged weaknesses of the present gold-exchange standard and the major kinds of proposals for reform.

The Question of Liquidity

The key to the concern over the international monetary system is the now famous question of international liquidity—the free world's supply of gold and foreign exchange held by national monetary authorities ("owned reserves") and facilities for borrowing them ("borrowed reserves"). Specifically, will international reserves be adequate in the future to finance payments disequilibria in a growing world economy when there is no longer a United States deficit to create new reserves?

The pertinence of this question is revealed by Table 22-3 which shows the importance of United States dollars to the growth of international reserves.

In the ten-year period 1953-63, total reserves grew $15.8 billion but gold contributed only $5.9 billion to this expansion. The major contribution came from the dollar holdings of foreign monetary authorities which grew by $7.7 billion. (These are liquid liabilities of the United States—Item 14 in Table 22-1.) The contribution of sterling—the other reserve currency—was negative, falling $1.6 billion. Without this growth in dollar reserves it is probable that the international economy would have suffered a liquidity shortage sometime ago with all of its unfortunate consequences. Instead, thanks to a continuing series of United States deficits, international liquidity kept pace with world trade which nearly trebled during this period.

But what of the future? The United States deficit cannot endure indefinitely and when it stops dollar reserves will cease to grow. In

Table 22-3

COMPOSITION OF INTERNATIONAL RESERVES OF THE FREE WORLD

(Billions of Dollars; End of Year)

	1953	1958	1963
Gold Reserves	34.3	38.0	40.2
Exchange Reserves			
U.K. Pound Sterling *	8.1	7.0	6.5
U.S. Dollar †	6.0	8.5	13.7
Other ‡	3.0	3.8	4.8
IMF Gold Tranche Position	1.9	2.6	3.9
Total Reserves	53.3	59.9	69.1

* Liquid claims on the United Kingdom held by foreign central banks.
† Liquid claims on the United States held by foreign central banks.
‡ Includes credit balances of national central banks with the Bank of International Settlements and the European Payments Union (liquidated in 1958), and central bank deposits in countries with convertible currencies, other than the United States and United Kingdom.

SOURCE: International Monetary Fund, *International Financial Statistics*, June, 1965. Fritz Machlup, *Plans for the Reform of the International Monetary System* (Princeton, New Jersey: Princeton University, 1962), p. 3. J. Keith Horsefield, "International Liquidity," *Finance and Development*, The Fund and Bank Review, December, 1964.

the event of a United States surplus, dollar reserves will fall. It is widely agreed that the annual increment in gold reserves will be insufficient to maintain international liquidity in an expanding world economy. What, then, should be done? What is wrong with the contemporary system?

Criticism of the Present Gold-Exchange Standard

Under a pure international gold standard, nations would maintain reserves only in gold, while under a pure exchange standard they would hold only reserves of foreign exchange. The contemporary international monetary system is a mixture of both standards and may be described as a gold-exchange standard. Under this system the key currency country—the United States—maintains its reserves in gold while nonreserve countries hold reserves of both gold and dollars.[18] The United States (and only the United States) preserves the link between gold and dollars by freely converting upon request the dollar holdings of foreign monetary authorities into gold at a fixed rate, or vice versa. The gold-exchange standard has served the world well since World War II, but in the early 1960's it came under critical attack.

The present system is criticized on the grounds that the growth of reserves is haphazard. More seriously, the growth of dollar reserves requires that the United States run a deficit. This situation is dangerous both for the United States and the international economy, and now that the United States is closing its deficit, the outlook is for a future liquidity shortage. Further, it is alleged that the system is "fragile." Its functioning depends on the willingness of foreign central banks to hold dollars and this, in turn, rests mainly on their confidence in the gold convertibility of the dollar. A general failure of confidence would cause a massive switch from dollars to gold which would force a rapid decline in international liquidity as dollar reserves were eradicated by conversion into gold. The end result would be a collapse of the international monetary system such as occurred in the early 1930's: the cessation of United States gold sales, the proliferation of exchange restrictions and trade controls, and a catastrophic fall in world trade with depression and unemployment spreading throughout the free world.

---

[18] The United Kingdom, as a secondary reserve center, holds both dollars and gold but favors the latter.

Plans for Reform

Plans for international monetary reform may be grouped under four headings: strengthening the gold-exchange standard, increasing the price of gold, transforming the International Monetary Fund into a central bank, and adopting flexible exchange rates. We shall make no attempt to discuss these plans in detail or pass judgment on them.

Strengthening the Gold-Exchange Standard. Generally, the monetary authorities of the United States and other countries favor a strengthening of the existing system by increasing the availability of borrowed reserves rather than replacing it with a new system. Considerable progress has already been made along these lines: the expansion of IMF quotas, the use of IMF standby credits, the General Arrangements to Borrow which provide $6 billion of supplementary foreign exchange reserves through the IMF,[19] and the United States bilateral swap agreements. There are proposals for increasing the automatic availability of IMF credit beyond the gold tranche, for making the General Arrangements permanent and automatic in operation, and negotiating multilateral swap agreements.

Other proposals suggest the creation of a *multiple-currency* system by the adoption of the German mark and other strong currencies as key reserve currencies in addition to dollars and sterling. This would mean that the United States would hold other currencies as part of its reserves. Actually, the present system appears to be drifting in that direction; as noted above, the United States monetary authorities now hold foreign currencies. If the United States would finance any future payments surpluses by acquiring foreign currencies, then international reserves would continue to rise, thereby averting a potential liquidity shortage. Clearly, any further evolution of a multiple-currency standard would require confidence in all of the key currencies.

Increasing the Price of Gold. The price of gold has remained at $35 an ounce since 1934. A number of proposals recommend an increase in this price to, say, $70 an ounce. At one stroke this would double the dollar value of the free world's gold reserves and would further add to them by encouraging a higher gold production and causing (presumably) the dishoarding of private gold stocks. Raising

---

[19] Participants in the General Arrangements, known as the "Group of Ten," are Belgium, Canada, France, Germany, Italy, Japan, Netherlands, Sweden, United Kingdom, and the United States. In 1964 Switzerland became an associate member.

the price of gold would favor those countries that have kept most of their reserves in the form of gold and penalize those countries that, as good citizens of the gold-exchange system, have refrained from converting their dollar and sterling reserves into gold. It would also benefit the two principal gold producers—the Soviet Union and the Union of South Africa.

To avoid a wild scramble for gold, a price increase would have to be put into effect without any prior indication of such a step. It is hard to conceive how this might be done since a price increase would require the prior agreement of many countries. Even if this hurdle were overcome, speculation might feed on the expectation of future price increases. These points work against the adoption of a higher gold price despite the apparent simplicity of this solution to the liquidity problem.

Making the IMF an International Central Bank. Today all countries have central banks that provide the liquidity needed in the domestic economy. Why not set up an international central bank that would insure an adequate supply of international liquidity at all times? There are several proposals suggesting this solution to the liquidity problem, notably the *Triffin Plan*.[20] This plan would give the IMF the right to create (or destroy) international monetary reserves through open market transactions in member countries in the same way a national central bank creates or destroys commercial bank reserves by buying and selling securities in the open market. In addition, the IMF could create international reserves through advances or rediscounts requested by the central bank of a borrowing country. Each member country would be required to hold at least one fifth (or some other fraction) of its monetary reserves in the form of deposits with the IMF which would be acquired initially by depositing gold and foreign exchange (mainly dollars and sterling). The IMF would convert its dollar and sterling holdings into long-term debts repayable in small annual installments by the United States and the United Kingdom. In this way dollar and sterling reserve assets would be gradually liquidated and as confidence in the new IMF grew, international reserves would come to consist entirely of IMF deposits.

Under the Triffin and similar plans the level of international reserves would be determined by the management of the Fund. It

---

[20] See Robert Triffin, *Gold and the Dollar Crisis* (New Haven: Yale University Press, 1961).

would require, therefore, a transfer of authority from national central banks to a supranational institution. This political factor is probably the single greatest obstacle to its adoption.

Adopting Flexible Exchange Rates. Under the IMF rules the current gold-exchange standard is an adjustable-peg system. In practice, the industrial countries have adjusted their exchange rates reluctantly and only after their reserves have reached dangerously low levels. As the leading key-currency country, the United States has steadfastly refused to depreciate the dollar. This reluctance to make exchange rate adjustments and the avoidance of any domestic deflation have weakened the international adjustment mechanism. As a result the contemporary system has placed increasing reliance on a large supply of international liquidity to provide compensatory financing for deficits.

The foregoing appraisal has led to proposals to substitute a fluctuating-rate system for the present stable-rate system. The arguments in favor of fluctuating rates were covered in Chapter 11, and there is no need to go over them again. Let it be noted that a fluctuating-rate system would dispense with the need for international reserves entirely. For the reasons mentioned in Chapter 11, the chances for its adoption are meager. Other more modest proposals suggest a widening of the spread around the IMF currency par values which is confined to 1 percent on either side by IMF rules and, in practice, is kept to within $\frac{3}{4}$ of 1 percent. It is argued that a wider spread (floating exchange rates) would diminish speculation and also contribute to payments adjustment.

Concluding Note. It is now more than twenty years since the Bretton Woods Agreement set up the International Monetary Fund and shaped the postwar international monetary system. Today there are abundant signs that the time is ripe for a new international monetary conference that will strengthen the monetary structure of the free world to avoid any repetition of the early 1930's or a slowdown in the rapid growth of world trade. Agreement on international monetary reform will not be easy—national jealousies and honest differences of opinion can be frustrating obstacles. But the high degree of international monetary cooperation today compared to anything in the past is a favorable augury for the future.

SUMMARY

1. Beginning in 1958 the United States has run annual deficits in its balance of payments. Different concepts of deficit (and surplus) may be used to

measure the payments position of the United States: the basic transactions concept, the liquidity concept, and the official settlements concept. The Department of Commerce uses the liquidity concept, but the basic transactions concept comes closest to the theoretical concept presented in Chapter 9.

2. **The basic deficit fell sharply in the period 1960-64, but the liquidity deficit was kept above $3 billion by large outflows of United States private short-term capital.** In 1964 the official settlements deficit, which measures only changes in official reserves and official liquid liabilities, was $1.5 billion. There are good arguments for replacing the liquidity concept with the official settlements concept in the balance of payments statistics published by the Department of Commerce.

3. **The United States deficit is fundamentally a transfer problem.** The United States has developed a big surplus on current account and has not been living beyond its means. But this surplus is not big enough to finance military expenditures abroad, foreign aid, and private long-term foreign investment. In effect, the United States has been borrowing on short-term and lending on long-term: since 1958 its net international assets have continued to increase although its net international liquidity position has sharply deteriorated. The transfer problem has been obscured by massive outflows of speculative and other short-term capital which have added greatly to the liquidity deficit.

4. **The United States government has undertaken a broad variety of remedial measures to eliminate its payments deficit:** the Export Expansion Program, the provision of export credit insurance, the Trade Expansion Act of 1962, reductions in net government outlays abroad, the interest equalization tax, the voluntary restraint program, as well as domestic policies to prevent increases in the price level. United States monetary authorities have conserved the United States gold supply and have moderated speculative activity by entering foreign exchange markets, by developing a network of bilateral swap agreements, and by selling medium-term securities to foreign central banks and governments. The United States government has refused to adjust to the deficit by domestic deflation or dollar depreciation. Adjustment would be easier for the United States if the surplus countries in Western Europe demonstrated more willingness to make equilibrating adjustments.

5. **The persistent deficit in the United States balance of payments has stimulated a tremendous amount of discussion and controversy about the adequacy of the contemporary international monetary system, including a bewildering variety of reform proposals.** The key to this concern is the question of international liquidity—the free world's supply of gold and foreign exchange and facilities for borrowing them. Much of the growth in international reserves in the 1950's and 1960's has been generated by the continuing series of United States payments deficits. What will happen when the United States deficit is eradicated, perhaps to be replaced by a surplus?

6. Plans for international monetary reform may be grouped under four headings: strengthening the gold-exchange standard, increasing the price of gold, transforming the International Monetary Fund into a central bank, and adopting flexible exchange rates. The time is now ripe for a new international monetary conference that will fortify the monetary structure of the free world to allow a continued expansion of world trade and investment.

QUESTIONS AND APPLICATIONS

1. Define the three concepts of deficit and surplus presented in this chapter. Which one do you find most attractive? Why?
2. Explain why the three concepts give different results when used to measure United States deficits over the period 1958-64.
3. Has the United States been living beyond its means since 1957? Explain your answer.
4. "We view the United States basic deficit as fundamentally a transfer problem." What is implied by this statement?
5. (a) Describe the remedial measures undertaken by the United States government to overcome the United States payments deficit.
   (b) Why has not the United States adjusted to its payments deficit by deflating the domestic economy? by depreciating the dollar?
6. (a) What is the liquidity problem? How is it related to the United States deficit?
   (b) What are the alleged weaknesses of the present gold-exchange standard?
7. (a) What are the major kinds of proposals for international monetary reform?
   (b) Write a short essay on any one kind of reform proposal, pointing out both its merits and drawbacks.

SELECTED READINGS

Board of Governors of the Federal Reserve System, *Annual Report*.
——————, *Federal Reserve Bulletin*, monthly.
Hansen, Alvin H. *The Dollar and the International Monetary System.* New York: McGraw-Hill, 1965.
International Monetary Fund, *Annual Report*.
Joint Economic Committee, United States Congress. *Factors Affecting the United States Balance of Payments.* Washington, D.C.: Government Printing Office, 1962.
Lary, Hal B. *Problems of the United States as World Trader and Banker.* New York: National Bureau of Economic Research, 1963.
Machlup, Fritz and Burton G. Malkiel (eds.). *International Monetary Arrangements: The Problem of Choice.* Princeton, New Jersey: Princeton University Press, 1964.

Machlup, Fritz. *Plans for Reform of the International Monetary System,* Special Papers in International Economics, No. 3. Princeton, New Jersey: Princeton University Press, 1962.

Salant, Walter S. *et al. The United States Balance of Payments in 1968.* Washington, D.C.: The Brookings Institution, 1963.

The Balance of Payments Statistics of the United States, Report of the Review Committee for Balance of Payments Statistics to the Bureau of the Budget. Washington, D.C.: Government Printing Office, 1955.

Triffin, Robert. *Gold and the Dollar Crisis.* New Haven: Yale University Press, 1961.

PART 3

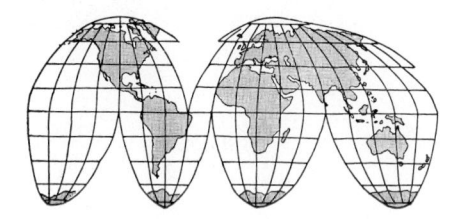

PRACTICE

We now consider the role, the organization, and the operation of the enterprisers who conduct the business that has been treated in the theoretical and national sense in Parts 1 and 2 respectively.

In this section, the flesh and blood of international business will be presented. We shall become acquainted with the organizations, agencies, and facilities that operate in this field. These will include administration, marketing, promotion, and such collateral activities as price quotations, transportation, insurance, banking, credit, and legal matters.

CHAPTER 23

THE NATURE AND SCOPE OF INTERNATIONAL BUSINESS

International business differs from national or domestic business in that it flows over national boundaries. Business between firms in the states of New York and Illinois is domestic; business between Spain and Portugal is international. The difference is that the latter crosses national boundaries and, therefore, involves two sovereign countries. Sovereignty grants each independent nation the authority to make its own laws, rules, and regulations governing the rights and privileges of resident citizens of other sovereignties. Nations surrender a portion of their sovereignty rights in understandings reached with other sovereignties, as set forth in the terms of international treaties and agreements. Therefore, the business firm of one nation has no right to transact business with firms of another nation unless this right has been set forth in agreements and treaties. Indeed, a person or business firm of one country has no rights whatsoever outside his own sovereignty, except as they have been negotiated on his behalf by his own sovereignty. Simply stated, when John Smith, an American or a Britisher, goes abroad, the important thing is that he is an American or a Britisher and, incidentally, has the name of John Smith.

RELATION OF SOVEREIGNTY TO INTERNATIONAL BUSINESS [1]

As discussed in Part 1 of this book, the sovereignty of independent nations leads to the determination of rates of foreign exchange and choice of means of adjusting to disequilibria in the balance of payments. International business firms may find that they cannot collect for obligations incurred by their counterparts in other countries. This, in turn, causes a strain on the credit standing of the foreign customer—

---
[1] See Chapter 1.

as well as his country—and unless this condition is rectified, further credit will not be extended.[2]

In Part 2 we examined the question of protective or liberal trade and payments policies that determine the ability of individual enterprise to participate in international business, and also described the concessions that are granted or withheld in trade and investment negotiations with other nations.

Added to these prerogatives of sovereignty are certain natural factors arising out of conditions in history, geography, philosophy, and customs. People in other countries with whom the international business firm must associate may speak a language foreign to it; may have entirely different scales of values relative to satisfactions derived from the use of material goods or lack thereof. A great gap may exist in the standards of living among various countries; and the philosophy of nations, derived from their religious and philosophical beliefs, may cause entirely different mental and emotional attitudes.

In light of these differences, which the international business firm encounters abroad, it is clear that the firm must be prepared to cope with circumstances and situations that are entirely unlike those experienced in its home country.

It is for these reasons that many firms are reluctant to plunge into international business, particularly if their domestic market is quite satisfactory. The appeal of the domestic market is probably felt more keenly in the United States than in any other country because of the magnitude of the United States domestic market.

WHAT IS AN INTERNATIONAL BUSINESS ENTERPRISE?

When we say that the United States, the United Kingdom, Germany, or Japan exports and imports merchandise and services, we really mean that the individual business enterprises of these countries, in the aggregate, actually perform annually millions of separate transactions.

An international business enterprise may be an individual or a domestic corporation or an international corporation.[3] Many individuals in all countries engage in international trade, usually in specific lines of merchandise and generally within certain limited geographical areas. Domestic corporations engage in international business by means of their own trading facilities or by utilizing the

---

[2] See Chapters 13 and 14.
[3] Also called multinational.

trading facilities available from others. This business enterprise generally looks on its export business as a separate appendage and often subservient to its prior and more important domestic business. In the United States import business, however, such corporations frequently regard the import business as an integral part of their operations. Consider, e.g., sugar refining, coffee roasting, and iron smelting—each of which is, in large part or entirely, dependent upon imports of basic raw materials. Thus, the import business is an **inherent and essential** part of the entire business operation.

The *international corporation* is a relatively new concept that identifies a corporation that is not anchored in any one country but views its world business as a common enterprise. Such a corporation may have its headquarters in any country and has loosened its national moorings, wherever they may have been.

In addition to the business enterprises that engage in what may be called the commodity business, there is a variety of enterprises engaged in what is termed the *service* business. This term envelops transportation lines (air and ocean), communications companies, banks and banking institutions, advertising agencies, travel agencies, consulting firms, and all such who operate for profit.

DECISION MAKING

The most important decision made by a business enterprise initially engaging in international business was the decision that led it into that business in the first place. There must be some appeal, some challenge, or some inspiration that precipitates this move. The decision is rarely, if ever, reached entirely by rational analysis, which, of course, must follow in order to determine where and how to export. Engaging in import trade and producing raw materials abroad, on the other hand, are much more tied to domestic business operations. A business enterprise decides to import a product because it is generally not available in the home market, or because it is cheaper, or in some other way superior as a marketable item to the domestic product. In many instances, there is no domestic product, and unless the foreign product is imported, the demand cannot be satisfied.

There are many ways in which a decision to engage in export is reached. Perhaps an official of a company has traveled abroad and has seen the possibility of markets and profits that had previously been overlooked. Perhaps such an official has read an article or a book or listened to a fine lecture. Any of these could be the motivation for the export effort. Or he has a friend who is successful in international business or sees bright possibilities for the firm in question.

Only after interest has been aroused through one or more of the factors mentioned, will decisions on a rational basis begin to take shape. Now the firm seeks to determine whether its product or service can be successfully marketed abroad; and if so, where?; and if where, how?; and if how, under what price and credit terms?; etc.

The Product

The first of these decisions has to do with the product or service. If it is a movable product (not a bridge nor an acre of real estate), it probably will enjoy a market in other countries. If it is an article for human consumption, it may be unknown in another country. How many readers relish eating prepared shark fins—a delicacy of the South Seas area? If it is bulky and of low value, as building bricks, the expense of shipping far from the place of manufacture probably will exclude the product from foreign markets. If the product is technical in nature, a foreign market may well exist, but some markets may be incapable of utilizing such a technical item. Even as simple a manufactured product as an electric toaster may not find certain markets because the people do not like toasted bread or do not have continuous electricity available. The location of the steering column in an automobile and its gas and oil consumption may be of paramount importance in another market. A prospective exporter adapts to conditions or he does not export.

An interesting and instructive way to consider the subject of product is in terms of imported products you know. If you like your morning coffee, tea, cocoa, or bananas, or your evening Scotch on the rocks, you know that certain delectable products, not available from home production, are available from foreign sources. The discriminating woman who prefers French perfumes and haute couture is aware that some exquisite luxuries must be obtained from foreign sources. All these products illustrate *taste* as a factor affecting the market for a product.

The same is true of American products that are sold throughout the world. Soft drinks, canned and preserved foods, confections, and many others find a foreign market because of taste that is inherent only in such American products. Probably every country has at least one product of taste in which it enjoys a kind of monopoly. This is true of handicrafts, foods, drinks, apparel, and such products that appeal to the appetite or senses.

The commodity network of world trade is such that raw materials and manufactured goods comprise the main categories.[4] Some raw materials, as indicated above, move in world trade because there is no home production. In such cases, the foreign product enjoys what the classical economists called an absolute advantage. Gem diamonds come chiefly from South Africa and there is absolutely no substitute for these gleaming gems. Other raw materials do not enjoy an absolute advantage because they are available from various areas and often in sufficient quantity. These latter raw materials that flow in international trade are deemed most acceptable for the price paid. Such products enjoy a comparative advantage.

For certain manufactured goods, some countries may enjoy an absolute advantage but, generally speaking, the advantage in a particular line of merchandise is more likely to be comparative. Consider automobiles again. The American car essentially is a large vehicle designed for fast travel over wide spaces and good roads. Gasoline is relatively inexpensive in the United States and, with a high standard of living, gas economy is not a compelling sales point. If a customer in another country desires such a car, his best purchase is doubtless the American car. On the other hand, if low cost of operation is sought and if speed is not essential, the smaller European or Japanese (or American compact) car may be the best answer. In either case, the purchaser will have an automobile but the American car offers a comparative advantage for one buyer, and the foreign or United States compact car has a comparative advantage for another buyer.

American home appliances are regarded in the United States as a kind of status symbol. They are flashy, they are efficient, and they are laborsaving. In other countries, the demand may be for an inexpensive device that is not as flashy or efficient and does not offer laborsaving as a feature. If this is the case, the market for the home appliance will be small. We must remember that laborsaving is an attraction when labor is expensive and not when labor is cheap.

Finally, it must be remembered that products sold in export are always or nearly always products that are made for domestic or national consumption. Therefore, an international business enterprise generally has no reason to consider exporting until its capacity produc-

---

[4] See Chapter 2.

tion appears to have exceeded the domestic demand; perhaps it finds that it cannot market all of its production at home due to competition, and decides—perhaps erroneously—that the foreign market may be the answer. While the above statement is true of the United States, it is not necessarily true as it pertains to some European and Japanese firms. It is quite likely that some of them produce a given product solely for export.

As revealed by the kinds of transactions that appear in the balance of payments, there are many services that one country sells to all others and that the same country buys from all others. Steamship and airlines operate all over the world and many nations engage in these operations Whether they all perform their services economically cannot be determined because government subsidies are extensively paid for these services. Banks also engage in international trade and they do so for the profit derived from services they perform. Communications companies, advertising agencies, consulting firms, motion picture companies, and many others find profit in operating to and in other countries. These represent efforts to maximize profits and, in some cases, to hold a business that may no longer be profitable when operated solely in the home market.

Where Can the Product or Service Be Sold?

The second logical question raised by the incipient exporting firm is where the product or service can be sold. This question requires a much more precise answer than the first question pertaining to the exportability of the product or service. The latter information can be obtained from qualified, knowledgeable people. Where the product or service can be exported must be pinpointed to indicate the specific markets where sales may be anticipated. This requires intensive research into specific markets—a subject that will be explored in the succeeding chapter.

How Can the Product or Service Reach the Foreign Market?

Except for certain lines of merchandise where trading channels have become traditional, the decision as to method of exporting is essentially based on trial and error. While some channels of trading are basically preferred for some products and certain foreign markets, these will not always prove to be the most desirable. Succeeding chapters will explain these traditional channels in some detail.

The first and most important of these decisions relates to the nature and degree of executive backing and support for the export venture. Experience has clearly shown that where executive support is lacking, the export venture is likely to be abortive. This is not to say that it may not fail with executive backing; but in that event, lack of executive support will not be responsible for its failure.

The reason for this observation is that in practically every case where the export venture is attempted by a domestic or national company, with an established domestic market and all of the tried-and-proved techniques and procedures developed in connection therewith, the export venture enters the picture as something additional and strange—it frequently has been called a stepchild. Therefore, any changes in production techniques and procedures that may be required for the export market will encounter the opposition of the employees. They are likely to be "set in their ways" and resist any effort to change their time-honored procedures. Unless executive backing is assured, the export venture may die of frustration.

A second important decision relates to the permanence of the export venture. The most successful international business enterprisers declare that when they go into a foreign market, they go in for keeps. With some rare exceptions, the foreign market in this era is not for the hit-and-run firm. It follows, then, that if an export venture is worth trying at all, it is worth backing by management.

What Prices and Credit Terms Should Be Quoted?

While a decision on these subjects is not of immediate importance, it is basic because if the prices and terms are not competitive, the export venture will founder. It is well at the outset to bear in mind that the prices of products entering export are essentially the same as those for domestic markets. The only exception to this principle is provided by raw materials which enjoy a world market and are traded on commodity exchanges; that is, all products of a known quality command the same price at a given time, regardless of their domestic price. The producer (miner, farmer, fisherman) has no control over the price that he receives except, of course, to withhold the product from the market because of low prices—in which event he runs the risk of greater losses, unless circumstances work in his favor.

Other Decisions

While decisions in other areas may be important in certain instances, the foregoing are essential for a firm contemplating export trade—a matter of first things first. There is no merit in seeking customers abroad for a product that has no foreign market, or which is unacceptable or out-of-line pricewise, or available for export only because of a temporary lull in the domestic market. After the preceding decisions have been made, there are additional difficult kinds of decisions that the firm must make as the export venture prospers.

THE STRUCTURE OF INTERNATIONAL BUSINESS

The discussion thus far in this chapter has outlined the steps normally followed by a business firm prior to engaging in export and/or import trade. For American business firms, these are particularly difficult steps because of the tremendous pull of the domestic market. No country has such a great domestic market as has the United States.

On the other hand, a firm that has reached this point in its business evolution does not necessarily stay there; this is merely a beginning for many business firms. As to the structure of international business, a distinction can be made between (1) the conduct of export and import business, and (2) foreign operations. In exporting and importing, the business firm depends upon other business firms to transact this business. The exporter may arrange to have his products exported by foreign market specialists situated in his country; and, more frequently, he will deal with business firms in foreign countries. The importer similarly may acquire his imported products in his own country from business firms that imported the merchandise; or, and also more frequently, he has arrangements with suppliers in the foreign country from which his imports come. In both cases—export and import—other business firms, domestic or foreign, are depended upon to transact the business.

The other element in the structure of international business is foreign operations. Here the business firm, to a greater or less degree, conducts the business through its own facilities abroad or through facilities in which it has some interest. Foreign operations are the final step in international business and are a further extension of exporting and importing which they rarely replace. It is inconceivable for a business firm, starting in international business, to begin with foreign operations, except in the cases of mining and plantation operations abroad. In the latter operations, business firms go directly to the source for the petroleum, copper, nickel, and many minerals that are found abroad; also, they must establish plantations for the cultivation of agricultural products that cannot be grown economically at home, such as coffee, bananas, pineapples, etc. In almost every instance, these operations provide the products needed for the functioning of the business firms themselves. These foreign operations are not generally conducted to supply these minerals and agricultural products to other business firms. Minerals are essential to provide the raw materials for metallurgical and petroleum production and distribution, while agricultural products are processed and sold through the usual wholesale channels. Chapters 25 and 26 will deal specifically with these two elements of international business.

Another course also is available to the company that has never exported and now decides to do so. Instead of exporting, the company may go directly into *licensing* abroad with processes and techniques that it has for this purpose. Thus, it engages in foreign operations without having first tested the market by means of export.

Supporting agencies constitute an important element in the structure of international business; without them it would be impossible to conduct international trade. Supporting agencies include banks, which are essential to most international business firms; transportation services and facilities; communications services and facilities; legal arrangements and provisions; risk-bearing agencies and methods; promotion facilities offered by both government and nongovernmental agencies; and even education. These factors are discussed in Chapters 27 and 28.

It takes little imagination to realize that very little, if any, international commerce could be consummated without using some or all of these facilities. True, some firms handle their own banking and some conduct their own shipping through ownership or chartering of ships; but communications, risk bearing, government promotion and even nongovernmental promotion are essential and beneficial to the firm and cannot be effectively provided by any firm alone; and without education, a firm would have no personnel with which to function.

Thus, the structure of international business rests on a threefold foundation of export-import, foreign operations, and supporting services.

SUMMARY

1. International business is different from domestic business basically because it involves two or more national sovereignties.

2. In addition to sovereignty, international business differs from domestic business because of variations in language, history, geography, philosophy, and customs.
3. While a country is said to export this and import that, the fact is that these transactions are generally performed by business firms. Essentially, these are firms established in and operating out of a specific country, but increasingly business firms are assuming an international stature, affording greater flexability in the context of the world market.
4. An important decision to be made by a business firm is that of engaging in export business. Conversely, engaging in import trade is quite logical, for when a business firm requires a certain product in order to operate, it will naturally seek this product even if it must be obtained abroad.
5. While the foreign market is essentially sought for the product lines of the business firm, adaptations may be required in order to meet the requirements of the foreign market; and some products cannot even then be expected to find a market abroad.
6. Generally speaking, business firms do not consider engaging in international business until the domestic market has been completely or partially exhausted.
7. Where the product can be sold must be determined from a market survey. As to importing, the question is basically where it can be obtained—and the answer essentially is "go and get it."
8. Decisions must also be made as to organization for the conduct of international business. Basic to these decisions is the importance of executive backing to assure the successful permanence of the venture and avoid an ineffectual operation.
9. Another series of decisions that must be made early in the international business venture relate to prices and credit terms.
10. The structure of international business may be classified as export-import on one hand, and foreign operations on the other. In export-import, the business firm generally depends upon other agencies to accomplish its purpose; while in foreign operations, the firm utilizes its own facilities to a greater degree.
11. Another element in the structure of international business is the supporting services without which most business firms would be unable to operate effectively. These include transportation, banking, communications, advertising, and other agencies.

QUESTIONS AND APPLICATIONS

1. Explain the scope of sovereignty as it affects international business.
2. Describe the several kinds of international business transactions reflected in the balance of payments of a country.
3. Describe an international business enterprise.
4. Why is the decision to enter the export business so difficult for most American business firms?
5. How does the decision to enter the import business differ from the decision to enter the export trade?

6. Of what importance is the product or service to be exported?
7. Comment on the division of the structure of international business into export-import and foreign operations. Explain any relation that you may see between these two divisions.
8. Explain why foreign operations in the import business are more logical initially than foreign operations in the export business.
9. Select any one of the National Planning Association's studies of individual business firms engaged in international business. (See Selected Readings.) Write a report on this study.

SELECTED READINGS

Dartnell International Trade Handbook, The. Chicago: The Dartnell Corporation, 1963.

Kramer, Roland L. *International Marketing,* 2d ed. Cincinnati: South-Western Publishing Company, Inc., 1964.

National Planning Association, Case Studies on United States Business Abroad:

    Burgess, E. W. and F. H. Harbison. *Casa Grace in Peru.* Washington, D. C., 1964.

    Lindeman, John. *The Philippine American Life Insurance Company.* Washington, D. C., 1955.

    Taylor, Wayne C. *The Creole Petroleum Corporation of Venezuela.* Washington, D. C., 1955.

    ―――――. *The Firestone Operations in Liberia.* Washington, D. C., 1956.

    Wood, Richardson and Virginia Keyes. *Sears Roebuck de Mexico, S. A.* Washington, D. C., 1953.

Root, Franklin R. *Strategic Planning for Export Marketing.* Scranton: The International Textbook Company, 1966.

CHAPTER 24

RESEARCHING FOREIGN MARKETS

The word *research* connotes classrooms, laboratories, computers, and similar intellectual activity. However, the word antedates these facilities. Indeed, one writer declares that research is search, further search, and additional search, followed by analysis and evaluation. Research is a tool of enterprise, whether it is related to domestic or to foreign activity. Every endeavor in life requires that we see ahead before we go ahead, that we look before we leap.

With capital and resources at stake—to say nothing of reputation—the business firm should be fully aware of the need for research. Indeed, every activity of enterprise is based on research of some sort—not on blind decision.

A survey of foreign markets is the same—as far as research goes—as a domestic market survey, but it is completely different in many respects. This is because of the nature of foreign markets.[1] Some of the differences found in foreign market research have been treated in previous chapters. Comparative costs determine whether and to what extent a product or service may find a market in a foreign country. The transfer of international payments is inherent in all foreign marketing.

The commercial policy of the home country, as well as that of every other country, must be thoroughly analyzed. The preceding chapter made reference to the customs, foreign languages, philosophy, standards of values, etc. With these differences in mind, let us examine the nature of foreign market research.

---

[1] American Marketing Association, celebrating Marketing's Golden Threshold on June 14, 1965, scheduled a subject entitled "International Marketing on the Threshold."

NATURE OF FOREIGN MARKET RESEARCH

Foreign market research is more difficult than domestic market research because of the variety and sometimes paucity of data available. Even when data are available, it behooves the person conducting the research to understand the elements of strength and weakness of such data. Much resourcefulness and imagination go into foreign market research. Information obtained must be checked and verified. Sources must be defined and utilized with care.

These peculiarities are likely to baffle the business firm that is considering the desirability of foreign markets for its products or its services. The chief executive of one such firm has been heard to say:

> This company has made a start in marketing its products in Europe and we expect to do much more exporting in the next year or two. Therefore, the more we can learn on international trade, the better equipped we will be. Before this company enters certain European markets with its products, we should like to have a survey made of those countries.

It is for this reason that consulting firms have expanded into foreign market research, some of which have foreign branches and foreign affiliates.

As noted in Chapter 22, the objective of the Export Expansion Program of the United States Department of Commerce is to encourage more American business firms to engage in export trade. One way of doing this is to conduct foreign trade seminars throughout the country. For a modest fee, business firms may send their representatives to hear lectures and to participate in discussion of the various aspects of international trade.

These efforts are good as far as they go; they provide an inspiration and arouse a curiosity. But they cannot take the place of actual research into foreign markets or of engaging in export trade. The firm itself must perform these activities or employ someone to do so.

CHARACTERISTICS OF SOURCES OF FOREIGN MARKET INFORMATION

While the last subject treated in this chapter presents a wide variety of sources of information for use in connection with foreign market research, some comments about these sources and the nature of the information available will be helpful. As stated earlier, it is important to be able to evaluate information as to its accuracy.

In the first place, it is well to recognize the difference between official data and accurate data. Official data, as every reader doubtlessly knows, are published by government agencies. We usually accept such data as valid and thus we do not question their accuracy.

But we should also recognize that government data depend upon information provided by agencies and business firms. If the latter do not provide accurate data, the final compilations will be inaccurate. As far as United States government foreign trade statistics are concerned, we generally accept these as accurate. They are probably correct as to total figures but they may not be correct as to details. If foreign market research is conducted for a given company, data must be pinpointed as far as possible. It may be that the specific information that is sought is not segregated in statistical compilations but falls within a "basket group." In such case, the research cannot determine the amount and direction of export trade for such a product.

Statistics that are dependent on data provided by business firms, as is true in the United States for exports and imports, may be unreliable as to descriptions and values and even possibly destinations. A study of automobile batteries exported to a South American country was undertaken and not a single battery appeared in the export statistics as going to that country. Nevertheless, it was known that at least three American manufacturers were exporting batteries to that country. Why did they not show up? The steamship freight-rate classification of "Automobile Accessories" carried a lower freight rate than batteries; all batteries were declared as auto accessories—and so they are!

When countries are suffering from a foreign exchange shortage and exchange control is in effect, some importers secretly arrange with cooperating foreign suppliers to bill them at a price higher than the actual figure in order to obtain additional foreign exchange to be left abroad. In order to cover such an arrangement, the export value of such a product will be articifially higher and this higher value is reflected in the export statistics.

Foreign exchange valuations for foreign trade statistics are often not actual but artificial. With the variety of exchange rates prevalent in some countries, the actual United States dollar value is sometimes impossible to determine.[2]

Therefore, when dealing with foreign trade statistics, it is advisable to check them as precisely as is possible. If auto batteries are the subject of research, check the import statistics of the destination country; check the export statistics of every other country that may

---

[2] See Chapter 14.

presumably export auto batteries, such as Canada, European countries, Japan, and some Latin American countries, such as Mexico, Argentina, Brazil, etc.

Finally, one weakness of all foreign trade statistics is that they are not up to date. For the detail needed in a market survey for a given product, this delay is a minimum of six months and up to two years for many countries.

Data regarding a specific commodity that are not generally shown in official statistics can often be obtained from a trade association dealing with such product. Through special channels the association often has more up-to-date statistics on a specific commodity than can be obtained from official sources. For example, during World War II, when the United States government was greatly interested in mahogany for airplane construction, the most accurate and up-to-date information on imports was obtained each month from the Mahogany Association.

Reliable information on the current market situation is available from government reports (United States, Canada, the United Kingdom, Germany, Japan, etc.); from banks that have international divisions; and, sometimes from trade journals and trade associations, particularly those devoted to a particular part of the world or a specific product.

United Nations and International Monetary Fund data are essentially republications of information released by the several governments whose statistics are reproduced. The textual explanatory information in such publications should always be read with an eye to the supporting statistical data.

Finally, businessmen-exporters are reliable sources of foreign market information. This is one of the reasons for joining export trade clubs or associations and, in particular, attending meetings. While valuable information may be given in open meeting, the most intimate and reliable knowledge is often obtained by conferring personally with associates. Friendly relationships often develop into valuable sources of information. Frequently, international business firms are visited by their foreign representatives or personnel and if rapport has been established, these visitors from abroad can provide valid and timely information. Export associations are national, regional, and local in scope and each of them has its own advantages.

TOPICS COVERED IN FOREIGN MARKET SURVEYS

While business firms engaged in international business are constantly making surveys of their markets, an intensive survey is imperative when a specific market is first contemplated. At this prefatory stage it is impossible to obtain too much information.

The Country

An initial foreign market survey requires a preliminary analysis of the country without reference to the special interests of the business firm. This is done not only because the firm and its board of directors or other executives probably know nothing about the market but also because such information has a bearing on the business outlook.

The Location

The location of the market is important, because the nearer the market the more competitive will be the products or services of the business firm. The climate also influences the market situation, if the product or service is in any way seasonal or is such as to encourage or discourage its sale. For example, central heating systems will not find a market in the tropics; summer sportswear will not be appreciated in polar regions; rain gear is not salable in desert and arid areas; hams and bacon are not likely to find a good market in Israel, and so on.

Natural Resources and Economic Activity

The natural resources and economic activity of the market will bear directly on the market outlook for any product or service. Countries that produce chiefly primary products are likely to be uncertain markets because of the unstable and often low price of such primary products in world markets. Significantly, the bulk of world trade is exchanged between the industrial nations, not between the primary-producing countries.

Population and Its Characteristics

Population and its characteristics have a great bearing on any market survey. If the study pertains to a consumer product, this may be the paramount factor. The age, sex, and education of the population may be important. Number of people is less important than purchasing power; a few people with income to spend offer a better market than many people with no income to spend.

Infrastructure

The infrastructure of a country is both a market determinant and an indication of the development of the market. Highways, railways, power systems, hospitals, educational institutions, and such are factors that cannot be ignored. If transportation is inadequate, the resources of the country are not capable of being fully developed and markets are restricted because of the inability to reach all important segments. Lack of medical facilities generally indicates a population that is not healthy; and lack of educational facilities means that the people are not adequately trained.

All of these factors have a bearing on any market survey. As indicated in several examples, some of them influence very directly the market for specific types of products or services. This is where a foreign market survey may stop, having found that the product or service is not salable for any one of a number of reasons revealed by this preliminary analysis. It may have served to ascertain certain limitations or qualifications that have a bearing on further portions of the market survey.

Commercial Policy

The commercial policy of any country has a direct effect upon any foreign market survey. The commercial policy of the home country may, as in the case of the United States, prohibit any business whatsoever with such countries as Cuba, North Viet Nam and North Korea. Market surveys for such countries are useless for an American firm. Limitations are imposed on trade with all Communist countries.

All countries impose some restrictions on freedom of trade.[3] These must be closely examined from the standpoint of the firm for which the survey is undertaken. Such restrictions may be in the nature of tariffs and other taxes that may possibly be surmounted or they may be outright prohibitions that cannot be circumvented legally. There may be a restriction on the marketing or labeling of the product; this usually can be taken care of at small, if any, cost—but it is necessary, nevertheless.

If the market is one that suffers from recurrent balance of payments difficulties, it possibly will be slow in making payments—or it may not pay at all. Clearly no firm strives for a foothold in a market without recovering some of the expenses incurred and, hopefully, also some profit.

Marketing Structure

The marketing structure of the country must be covered in the foreign market survey. As will be pointed out in Chapter 25, every

---

[3] See Chapter 13.

country in the world has some sort of marketing system. For the business firm contemplating a specific market, "some kind" of marketing system may not be sufficient; what it needs may be a particular kind of marketing system.

If the products or services involved call for a sophisticated marketing system, then a primitive marketing system will not suffice. If service is to be supplied along with sales, marketing firms must be available to provide such service. If business can be transacted only with government institutions, the proper channels and techniques must be found to conduct such business. If business is in the hands of firms foreign to the market, as in the case of the developing African countries, the trade buyers will be in such country (in Europe) and not in the country where the market is (in Africa).

Perhaps the product or service can be sold best by means of advertising. In this case, it is necessary in the foreign market survey to determine the methods of advertising available as well as advertising agencies to be found.

The selection of marketing channels and the arrangements made with them call for a complete knowledge of the techniques of international trade. These techniques also vary as among the several industries. Terms of sale, price quotations, weights and measures, units for designating sales, packing, and similar matters are extremely important in trade.

Competition

This is a subject that must be determined and thoroughly analyzed. Competition can come from domestic producers and/or from producers in foreign countries. The nature and extent of domestic competition in the foreign market must be determined because the domestic product may differ substantially from the product under survey. Domestic production in many countries is the signal for excessive restrictions on imports in order to protect the domestic producers. If such restrictions do not exist, it is likely that foreign as well as domestic producers are selling their products in the market. The volume of business and the nature of the products of all these competitors are essential elements in the foreign market survey.

Prices of Competitive Products

Prices of competitive products must be determined in order to establish the possibility of competing on prices. Differences in product value must be analyzed to understand the reasons for legitimate differences in prices. Terms of sale are also important, as competitors may be able to capture business by means of sales terms, particularly long-term credits. If such practices exist in the foreign market, the firm for which the survey is made must determine whether it is in a position to equal such sales terms.

FOREIGN MARKET SURVEY REPORT

With these pointers in mind, let us sketch a foreign market survey report. Let us take, say, canned pet foods (meat) and survey the market in West Germany. The following questions may be asked in connection with such a survey:

1. Is Germany an open market for imported goods?
2. Are canine pets commonly kept by Germans?
3. What is the attitude of Germans toward their pets?
4. What German government regulations will be encountered?
5. If it is possible to import into Germany, what competition will be met?
6. Through what channels of marketing will pet foods go?
7. What are the names and standing of reliable German or other firms who might be interested in importing and distributing these canned pet foods?
8. What prices are charged and what differences occur in the sales appeal or quality of canned pet foods?

Basing our analysis on the subjects treated at the beginning of this chapter, let us now apply them to this particular line of business.

1. Is Germany an open market for imported products? The answer depends upon the countries from which the imports come. Germany is a member of the European Economic Community and under this arrangement eventual free trade will flow among the six members of the Community. Therefore, an American or Canadian or British producer of canned pet foods would, at present, be at a disadvantage compared to producers in all six members of the Community.

2. Are canine pets commonly kept in Germany? The answer is yes. Next to the British, the Germans are most fond of their pets. Moreover, Germany is a breeding ground for canines, chiefly shepherds and dachshunds, which are shipped to other countries. An active Kennel Club exists in Germany.

3. What is the German attitude toward their pets? This question is difficult to answer. As indicated in the preceding question, the Germans are fond of their pets. Whether their attitude is such that they will pay for canned pet foods rather than feed them scraps from the table is another question. Our research does develop, however,

that a number of German firms is engaged in manufacturing canned pet foods, thus establishing a market for such products in Germany.

4. What German government regulations will be encountered? We do know that agricultural trade has been the most difficult subject to deal with under the terms of the European Economic Community. Whether this extends to pet foods must be investigated. Many countries, including Germany, have explicit sanitary laws covering all foods offered for sale. There may be a requirement that canned pet foods pass an official inspection. There may also be a problem of labeling that violates German laws. This information must be determined by examining the official regulations of the German Republic and/or the several states comprising the Republic pertaining to the importation and sale of food and particularly canned pet foods.

5. If it is possible to import into Germany, what competition will be met? We have established that German pet food producers are in business. Just what kinds of pet foods they produce must be ascertained; their products may not be competitive with our product insofar as the kind of pet food is concerned. Canada is known as an exporter of pet foods and perhaps would be a competitor. This subject must be examined thoroughly.

6. Through what channels will pet foods go? In the United States, pet foods generally are marketed through the grocery trade. If the same is true of Germany, our problem is to learn how the grocery business in Germany is conducted. Upon investigation we find that it is very much the same as in the United States, with importing distributors, chain stores, supermarkets, and neighborhood stores. As in the United States, the business is a volume business and this causes pressure on prices.

On the other hand, the German pet owner may be adequately supplied by pet foods manufactured in Germany and more particularly by table scraps. Unless our product can be offered at an appealing price, it will meet severe competition. In this event, it may be possible to establish a kind of quality market for the product, as found in exotic food departments of high-class food retailers and some department stores. The market then will be selective but not large.

Furthermore, reflection points to a market in Germany that should not be overlooked. This is the market created by United States personnel in Germany, both military and civilian. It is likely that these prospective customers have brought with them their pet-feeding practices learned at home which would include the use of prepared and canned commercial pet foods. This market might be tapped; but if the objective is the military market, the product must be purchased by the Quartermaster Corps and sold by Army PX establishments. German importers and distributors would be useless here, as the customer is the United States government.

7. Which German or other firms would be interested in importing and distributing these canned pet foods? These can be determined

from the trade lists published and sold by the United States Department of Commerce. They also can be determined from "food" manufacturers with export operations in Germany—provided they are willing to cooperate. Investigation reveals that there are hundreds of importing distributors and thousands of retail outlets and our task is to select the most desirable importing distributors. This is the procedure, of course, if the firm wishes to handle its own distribution overseas. An alternative would be to employ the services of an exporting firm in the home market, provided one can be found that is engaged in the export grocery line.

8. What are the prices charged and the differences in quality of the various products? Pet foods invariably are sold at low prices for rather obvious reasons. Whether a pound of dry cereal pet food at a given price is equivalent in nutritional value to one-quarter pound of canned pet food (meat) is difficult to establish. After all, medical science has not progressed to this extent on behalf of the animal population. It is obvious that prices must be competitive, and if differences in nutritive value actually exist, it will be expensive to emphasize this point by advertising.

9. Conclusions and recommendations would complete the research.

SOURCES OF INFORMATION FOR FOREIGN MARKET SURVEYS

As stated earlier in this chapter, the foreign market researcher must know not only the sources of information but also how to interpret and apply them. It should be remembered that sources of information generally deal with subjects broadly, or they are technical and sometimes so complex that the researcher must understand clearly what he is about.

Since the United States is paramount in its volume of international trade, the student of this subject should have knowledge of the various kinds of foreign market information available in this country.

Official Sources of Information

United States Department of Commerce. The knowledgeable researcher would begin with this department because it is the agency of the United States government charged with the promotion of both domestic and foreign trade. We are interested only in the latter.

One great advantage of considering this department first is that it has regional offices located in every commercially important city in the United States. Accordingly, most researchers and international business firms have only to locate the address of the nearest regional office which serves as a branch of the main office in Washington, D. C. Not only are government publications available for purchase at these regional offices but also free advice from competently trained international business specialists.

In matters relating to international business the United States Department of Commerce serves as the publishing agent for the United States Department of State, whose reports are prepared in the foreign field by Foreign Service officers. These reports, in addition to the reports prepared by commercial attaches located in most capitals of the world, are available in various kinds of publications. Probably the first of these is *International Commerce*—a weekly journal that provides information on foreign markets as well as a variety of data on matters pertaining to every facet of international business, including profitable opportunities for United States trade expansion.

There is also a series of Overseas Business Reports (OBR's) that deal with such specific subjects as *Basic Data on the Economy of (Country), Market Factors in (Country), Foreign Trade Regulations of (Country), Living Conditions in (Country), Preparing Shipments to (Country), Investment Factors in (Country)*, etc. These reports may be purchased individually for a nominal sum of 15 cents or a subscription for one year may be entered.

Moreover, the Department of Commerce publishes handbooks covering many countries—*Colombia, A Market for United States Products*, for example. *The Survey of Current Business* is a monthly periodical that frequently contains an article or special feature on foreign trade of the United States and the balance of payments and foreign investment position of the United States.

The Department of Commerce also publishes Trade Lists for many hundreds of lines of businesses for most countries. This will be referred to in Chapter 25 as a means of finding possible representatives and customers in foreign markets. Also available from the Department of Commerce are World Trade Directory (WTD) reports that deal with the standing of individual business firms abroad, which will be referred to in that portion of Chapter 27 pertaining to the collection of foreign credit information.

The Bureau of the Census in the Department of Commerce compiles and publishes the official foreign trade statistics of the United States. These are published in several series—monthly, quarterly, and annually—showing countries by commodity and the reverse, that is, commodity by countries.

United States Department of Agriculture. The United States is not only an international trading nation in manufactured goods, but agriculture also is very important in the foreign trade of this country. The United States Department of Agriculture is interested in the problems of the farmer, many of which are concerned with the international market. Just as the United States Department of Commerce publishes *International Commerce,* the Department of Agriculture publishes a weekly entitled *Foreign Agriculture (Including Foreign Crops and Markets).* This magazine provides current information on agricultural developments abroad and the foreign trade and outlook for the future. This department also publishes statistical data entitled *World Agricultural Production and Trade* (monthly).

Other United States Government Agencies. Several other agencies deal with matters important to international business but do not publish many reports. In the Department of the Interior, the Bureau of Mines prepares economic analyses of world production, distribution, and consumption of mineral products. It publishes *Minerals Yearbook.* The United States Tariff Commission publishes many reports on specific products moving in world trade, with special attention to their impact on United States industry and trade. The Federal Reserve Board publishes the monthly *Federal Reserve Bulletin* containing articles dealing with international trade and payments.

Foreign Governments. Practically every government has at least one agency that compiles and publishes information useful for foreign market research. Generally, the main publication is issued by the central bank or by a ministry of finance, both of which are government agencies. In many countries, chiefly the industrial ones, a government department similar to the United States Department of Commerce publishes a bulletin dealing with commercial and economic matters in the international field. In the United Kingdom, for example, the Board of Trade (the Department of Commerce of that country) publishes the *Board of Trade Journal* (weekly), which is particularly good for foreign government regulations. The Dominion of Canada has a Department of Trade and Commerce which publishes the biweekly *Foreign Trade.* This is particularly good for material on specific foreign markets for specific products. Many governments, chiefly in the developing areas, have a department of statistics which compiles and publishes bare statistical data with little interpretation.

United Nations and Related Agencies. Most students of international trade probably are not old enough to remember the statistical and economic work of the prewar League of Nations. The League blazed the trail for cooperation among nations in the publication of statistics, and then worked out some degree of uniformity.

As the successor of the League of Nations, the United Nations has continued and expanded the work performed for over two decades between the wars. As the First National City Bank of New York states in its "Foreign Information Service" report of November, 1964, entitled *A Businessman's Guide to Sources of Foreign Information:*

> A great wealth of current information on world trade, international economic and financial conditions, industrial production in various countries, agriculture, natural resources, and population trends is made available at low cost by the United Nations and related agencies.

United Nations reports cover all countries of the world. The *Statistical Yearbook* (annual) is a large volume covering all phases of the economic activity and social conditions of all countries. Since an annual compilation is usually late, the United Nations also publishes a *Monthly Bulletin of Statistics* treating the same subjects as those that appear in the Yearbook.

Two foreign trade statistical publications are of particular interest since they deal with over 130 countries. The *Yearbook of International Trade Statistics* (annual) gives the data for trade by country and by commodity—which country sells which product to which country. *Commodity Trade Statistics* covers the main trading nations and gives commodity information followed by countries of export and import—which commodity was exported by which country to which importing country.

Other global publications are *Demographic Yearbook* (populations and their characteristics); *Compendium of Social Statistics* (basic statistical indicators of standards of living over a period of time); *The Growth of World Industry* (mining, manufacturing, construction, and public utility industries over several decades for nearly 100 countries); and others covering world energy supplies, vital statistics of population, etc.

In the strictly economic field, the *World Economic Survey* presents in two volumes a global picture of international trade, payments, industrial developments and production by country and region. In accordance with the regional structure of the United Nations regional economic surveys are published. These annual surveys currently appear for Europe, Asia and the Far East, Latin America, the Middle East, and Africa. In addition to these annual economic surveys, monthly statistical bulletins are also published which provide information that is more current.

The Food and Agricultural Organization (FAO) is a specialized agency of the United Nations in the important area denoted by its name. By means of the FAO, worldwide information on agriculture and its problems is readily available. Among its regular publications are two yearbooks. One, the *Production Yearbook,* gives data on output of all agricultural activities as well as on the use of fertilizers, farm machinery, and price trends. The other, the *Trade Yearbook,* presents world trade in agricultural products. To keep the information up to date, a monthly *Bulletin of Agricultural Economics and Statistics* is issued. Other publications relate to forest products and timber and an annual economic review and analysis of world agriculture, including food consumption and per capita caloric intake by country.

The Organization for Economic Cooperation and Development (OECD), composed of 21 countries, including the United States, also publishes data covering all members of the organization, by country. These various series include statistics on industrial production, finance, prices, and manpower; three series on foreign trade; national accounts; individual studies by industrial sectors such as cement, chemicals, engineering, textiles, energy, etc.; and economic surveys of each member country.[4]

The European Economic Community (EEC) releases reports on the six members of the Community, which treat the economic situation, industrial and other statistics, and foreign trade. The European Free Trade Association (EFTA), the so-called outer seven, issues a monthly bulletin and several information series.

The International Monetary Fund (IMF) publishes several outstanding and authoritative reports. Chief among these is its monthly periodical, *International Financial Statistics,* and its annual supplement. It also publishes a monthly *Direction of Trade* and a *Balance of Payments Yearbook.*

Private Sources of Information

In a broad sense, published nongovernmental information is derived from business associations, miscellaneous, area, and commodity sources. There are many organizations and sources of information, particularly in the developed countries, that provide data and advice for international market studies.

---

[4] See also Chapter 17.

Business Associations. Many countries have a national association of businessmen that issues statements on matters pertaining to foreign trade which are packed with considerable authority. In the United States, for example, there are the Chamber of Commerce of the United States and the National Association of Manufacturers; also the National Foreign Trade Council and the National Council of American Importers. The latter two are interested specifically in international trade, and the first two are indirectly concerned but do express views and publish statements and reports. The National Foreign Trade Council sponsors an annual convention drawing thousands of international businessmen. Here prominent speakers address the gathering, and special conferences on specific international business subjects are held. The *Proceedings of the National Foreign Convention* (annual) constitutes an important source from which to obtain the views of international business leaders and policy makers. The National Council of American Importers is concerned with the problems of import trade and is a source of information in this area.

There is also an International Chamber of Commerce with national councils, including one in the United States, which is striving to assemble business opinion of all nations.

Organizations of the nature just described are primarily concerned with topics pertaining to the international business field. True, they usually devote certain sessions of major conventions to area discussions and analyses, but their main interest and effort are directed toward international business.

Regional and local foreign trade associations are in the same category. These provide a forum where information and advice may be obtained from personal acquaintances. Most foreign market surveys require information gleaned from the experiences of international businessmen, and it is through these regional and local foreign trade associations that such personal contacts are most easily developed. In many cities, the Chamber of Commerce represents local foreign trade interests.

Miscellaneous Sources. The most current information is available through electronics and daily newspapers and periodicals. Radio and television may be helpful for certain needs of foreign market research, but the information received may be nebulous at best. The better newspapers and journals that treat international business matters are excellent sources of information; for example, the *Journal of Commerce* and the *New York Times* cover world news; and the *Wall*

Street Journal specializes in markets, commodities, and financial conditions. There are many superior newspapers published abroad, which are generally found in libraries, if not on newsstands. Such publications as *The Times* of London, (London) *Economist, Manchester Guardian,* and *Financial Times* are, of course, published in English, as is also the *Financial Post,* of Toronto. Some of the outstanding newspapers in the Far East are published in English, such as the *Bangkok Post, Dawn* (of Karachi), and a number of Japanese newspapers; but most of the foreign newspapers are in the language of the country as *Handelsblatt* of Düsseldorf, and *El Mercurio,* of Santiago, Chile. These foreign newspapers provide insight into international trade matters that may not be obtained from a survey of national newspapers only. We learn from them how the British, the French, the Germans, the Japanese, the Argentines look at matters of worldwide interest.

Magazines in the international business field are principally identified with a specific kind of business or a specific area. Those that deal with the international field from a topical standpoint are the *American Exporter,* with several editions, and *Business Abroad.* The publishers of *Business Abroad* also publish the *Exporters' Encyclopaedia,* which is a detailed treatment of methods and organizations in the international business field.

Area. From a business standpoint there are many organizations that are interested only in a given geographical area. Chief among these are the chambers of commerce abroad, such as the United States chambers of commerce abroad, and the foreign chambers of commerce in the United States and other countries. The interests of the members of such organizations relate only to business with Germany or France or Mexico or Japan or some other country. Many of them publish a monthly bulletin and also occasional reports.

Magazines are also published that deal with special geographical areas. There is, for example, *Vision* for the Latin American area.

Commodity. In this category, there are trade associations whose members are expert in specific commodities. In a country like the United States, there is scarcely an industry that is not represented by a trade association of some kind, whether local, state, regional, or national. Many of these associations have extensive libraries relating to the commodity and they also publish bulletins and statistical reports.

Another source of information for commodity analysis is the membership of foreign trade associations, since most or all of the members deal in a product that moves in international trade.

Many of the associations and publications cited here and many more that are not may be valuable sources of information required for a foreign market survey.

There are two readily available ways of identifying mercantile publications, namely, by the use of the *Business Periodicals Index* and *Public Information Service*. These guides to commercial literature deal with business journals and government publications respectively.

SUMMARY

1. Research may be defined as search, search, and search, plus analysis and evaluation. In the international marketing area, research is different because of national sovereignty which leads to differences in commercial policy. Also, differences in people, their standards of living, their cultural attitudes, etc.—all have a bearing on foreign market research.
2. The paucity and tardiness of information are major obstacles to foreign market research. Data must be examined with a critical and resourceful attitude. Weaknesses inherent in certain data must be considered and alternative approaches devised when these weaknesses are recognized.
3. Topics to be included in a market survey for a given firm and also a given product (or service) include the overall foreign market, the people, the infrastructure, the commercial policy, the marketing structure, the competition, the price structure, and every other topic that will have a bearing on the market for any product or service.
4. Illustrative of the last point is the survey of the German market for canned pet foods (meat). In a specific situation such as this, the dog population must be determined; the attitude of the people toward their pets must be ascertained; hygienic, sanitary, and labeling regulations must be appraised and adhered to; and, the competitive situation, in addition to the pricing and marketing picture, must be evaluated. Most of these topics, as may be noted, are applicable only to the specific product for which the survey is undertaken.
5. The sources of information for foreign market surveys are extensive but they must be handled with great care. In general, they may be divided among business associations, miscellaneous, area, and commodity.
6. The United States government sources of information are largely in the hands of the United States Department of Commerce. With regional offices maintained by the department, much information is available locally. Publications relate chiefly to areas and products. The Bureau of the Census of the Department of Commerce compiles and publishes the official foreign trade statistics of the United States.

7. The United States Department of Agriculture provides considerable information on international trade in agricultural products.
8. Many governments, particularly those classified as industrial, likewise promote export trade and publish reports and statistics useful for foreign market survey work.
9. The United Nations and its specialized agencies, such as the FAO, publish extensive information on the industry, commerce, finance, and so forth in the areas covered by the respective organizations; the regional groupings, such as the EEC and EFTA, provide published reports covering economic developments of all kinds in the countries included in these groups.
10. The IMF is a particularly useful source for information pertaining to international finance, balance of payments, and foreign trade.
11. Many nongovernmental sources of information are also available. Some of these are topical in nature, such as the NFTC and the Chamber of Commerce of the United States; others are area-oriented and these are chiefly the foreign chambers of commerce in the United States and also United States chambers of commerce in foreign countries.
12. Newspapers and magazines are published that deal essentially with international business and those that are published in other countries provide a basis for a more cosmopolitan point of view.
13. For nongovernmental commodity information, trade associations, generally on a national scale, are paramount in importance.

QUESTIONS AND APPLICATIONS

1. Why is foreign market research different from research in domestic trade?
2. Explain some of the characteristics of the sources of foreign market information.
3. How does the country under study influence the approach of the foreign market survey?
4. In what various ways does the commercial policy of countries affect the survey?
5. How are marketing and competition to be treated in a foreign market survey?
6. Why is the United States Department of Commerce such an important source of information for foreign market surveys and what is the nature of the information to be obtained from that source?
7. Define the nature of information to be obtained from other countries.
8. Discuss the kind of foreign market information to be obtained from United Nations sources, including related agencies.
9. Comment on the nongovernmental sources of foreign market information.
10. Select a product and a country and undertake a market survey for that product. This application will afford good experience in utilizing the sources mentioned in this chapter.
11. Examine any one of the named sources of information listed and write a critical report on it.

SELECTED READINGS

American Management Association, Inc., International Management Division. *Market Research in International Operations* (AMA Management Report No. 53.)New York: 1960.

Dartnell International Trade Handbook, The. Chicago: The Dartnell Corporation, 1963.

Exporters' Encyclopaedia. New York: Dun and Bradstreet, Inc., annual.

International Markets. New York: Dun and Bradstreet, Inc., monthly.

Root, Franklin R. *Strategic Planning for Export Marketing.* Scranton: International Textbook Company, 1966. Chapter 2.

United States Department of Commerce, Bureau of International Commerce: *Investments in (Name of Country).*
(Name of Country), Market for United States Products.

United States, Executive Office of the President, Office of Government Reports. *United States Government Manual.* Washington, D. C.: Government Printing Office, annual.

United States General Services Administration, National Archives and Records Service, Office of the Federal Register. *United States Government Organization Manual.* Washington, D. C.: Government Printing Office, annual.

CHAPTER 25

INTERNATIONAL TRADING CHANNELS

This chapter is the first of two dealing with the organization and conduct of international business in its broadest sense. Some of the arrangements are identical with those used in domestic trade and others are found only in international trade.

This chapter is devoted to the *commercial agencies* that conduct international trade. Since the aim of all distribution is to bring a product or service from the producer to the consumer, these agencies serve in a particular capacity to accomplish this objective. To understand the contribution of each of these agencies to the entire distribution pattern, we shall analyze each of them in an effort to explain exactly what it does and how it fits into the overall channel of distribution.

In marketing literature a channel of distribution is a structured arrangement of intermediaries. In a sense, any specific marketing intermediary can only be a link in a chain. A wholesaler is not a channel—he is an intermediary who has something to sell which he rarely, if ever, produces. There is a producer who establishes the nature of the product, the price and terms at which it is sold, the packaging and packing, sales promotion, and so forth. Then there are the transportation and financing agencies that support the channel, the legal staff that establishes the conditions under which the business may be conducted, the retailer, and finally the consumer. Add all these together and we have in effect a structured arrangement to bring the product of a given producer to a given consumer, the wholesaler being an important, but only one, link in this chain.

Chapter 26 deals with foreign operations which are not isolated marketing facilities. They constitute a part of the marketing channel mix—a structured arrangement of intermediaries. In manufacturing abroad, there is the control and administration that determine initially if manufacturing should be undertaken; the policy decisions that must be made and by whom, apart from the manufacturing operation itself; and the sale of the products by a sales department or subsidiary of the factory.

Thus, the reader should bear in mind that, while each of the international trading agencies is discussed as though it were a self-contained facility that is independent of other facilities, this is not the case; it is an intermediary in the terms explained above.

A discussion of international trading channels may be broken down into three broad topics, *viz.*, (1) organization of the company, (2) channels in the home market, and (3) channels in the foreign market. Each of these topics will be taken up in order.

ORGANIZATION OF THE COMPANY

Following the discussion presented in Chapter 23, the organization of a company for the conduct of its international trade should be assured of executive backing. If this authority is established, the functioning of international trade becomes a matter of logical and effective organization and management.

Export Organization

One method of operation is recognized that does not require a company to establish any organization for the conduct of its export trade: this is to make arrangements with another manufacturer, who has established an export and distribution system including foreign operations, whereby the latter exports the products of the first company through its own organization. This is known as an *allied company* arrangement or as a "mother-hen" concept. It is not extensively practiced, but it is of sufficient importance to justify its mention at this point.

Still another arrangement whereby export sales can be obtained without any company organization is to turn the export effort over to a firm that operates as a *combination export-management* firm. Such a firm contracts with a number of manufacturers to conduct their export trade in the name of the respective manufacturers.

The simplest method of organization for the conduct of international marketing, aside from the aforementioned two methods, is to instruct company personnel to execute the directives of a supervising export manager. This is known in the trade as a *built-in export department.* The supervisor or export manager, of course, must be experienced in export trade and must have the ability to train, encourage, and obtain cooperation from personnel to follow his instructions.

This simple and inexpensive form of company organization is satisfactory as long as it is effective. When successful, this type of operation expands to the degree that it is economically justified to engage employees specifically for export work rather than to utilize domestic employees for this purpose.

As the number of employees engaged solely in export work increases, a point is reached where the export department becomes more or less self-contained and is known in the trade as a *separate export department.*

In many large companies, the separate export department becomes a division that is, in effect, incorporated and identified by its affiliation with the home organization. Examples are General Motors Overseas Corporation; Pfizer International; Western Union International, Inc.; and IBM World Trade Corporation.

Occasionally, a company is organized in such manner as to classify it as an *international* or *global* or *multinational* corporation. Such a company views its worldwide business as an integrated whole, and all of its top management has international responsibilities. It usually has geographical divisions designed to cover the areas where business is conducted including, of course, the home market. This type of organization is probably the most advanced structure to be found at present in the international trading area. It is inconceivable, however, for a company to start out on this basis; it is, in fact, a culmination of the company's efforts to organize and operate in a manner best suited to the several stages through which it has passed.

Import Organization

Import organization, like export organization, can take a variety of forms. It is not unusual for a so-called importer to purchase his imported products through another import organization. In such a case the former is in no sense engaged in the import business. Rather, he simply deals in imported products. Moreover, there are many instances of built-in import departments which may, in effect, constitute an essential part of the purchasing department. This is particularly true of manufacturers who depend in varying degrees on imports of raw materials. The separate import department is generally found in merchandising companies, such as department stores and specialty shops. In the latter, the separate import department is likely to be a service department, i.e., it does not actually engage in the conduct of import trade. This department arranges for buying trips by the several merchandise managers who travel abroad to make selections of foreign merchandise. It may also place orders for goods for which purchase arrangements have already been established. The department may finally be in charge of customs clearance of imported merchandise.

There are many small business firms, and even individuals, who have no need for a special department, because they provide the management that is involved in every phase of the business, including export and import transactions.

INTERNATIONAL TRADING AGENCIES IN THE HOME MARKET

It is not correct to assume that when a business enterprise engages in either export or import trade it must negotiate necessarily with enterprisers located in foreign countries. The portion of Chapter 23 relating to sovereignty discusses those business firms that contract with firms abroad or themselves operate abroad. By employing agencies located in the home market, the problems arising out of direct contact with other sovereignties can be avoided.

There are many trading agencies in the home market through which international trading may be consummated without going abroad or even writing a letter to a firm abroad. These agencies will be discussed under the following categories.

Salesmen and Buyers from Abroad

Business enterprises desiring to purchase foreign merchandise may be visited by salesmen representing foreign producers. These salesmen take orders which they may fill from stocks maintained in the home market, or they may send the orders abroad from where the merchandise will be shipped to the domestic enterprise. Similarly, buyers come from abroad to purchase products in the home market. This is particularly true of raw materials where selection may be of great importance. Raw wool and some grains are examples.

Government Buying Commissions

Some countries maintain buying commissions abroad which place their orders with domestic firms and ship the merchandise by means of their own facilities. Amtorg Trading Corporation, for example, is a New York corporation which purchases almost all the merchandise that Soviet Russia buys in the United States. Similarly, other state-trading nations, as well as those that are not, maintain such buying offices. By this means, they have available all the producers of a country and not just those that are engaged in international trade.

Contractors

A firm that manufactures machinery and equipment may find that it can obtain orders for shipment abroad from contractors who purchase such products for contracting operations abroad. A contractor, engaged in building highways abroad, for example, may wish to purchase earthmoving and other equipment to fulfill his contract obligations. A firm receiving such an order knows that this equipment is being exported, but the contractor is doing the exporting.

Export and Import Merchants

A merchant, by definition, is one who purchases at one price and hopes to sell at a higher price, thus earning a profit. There are many export and import merchants throughout the world. As the definition indicates, they buy and sell on a profit basis. They do not produce any goods; they deal in products produced by others. Therefore, a business enterprise may find its merchandise in export markets via the export merchant route. The latter takes care of the exporting. Similarly, a business enterprise may purchase imported merchandise from an import merchant with the latter taking care of the importing.

Export and Import Brokers

In the raw material trades, particularly in connection with organized commodity markets, the broker is a prominent intermediary. By definition, a broker brings buyer and seller together; he receives a commission from the party for whom he is functioning. Usually, the identity of the producer of the goods handled by commodity brokers is lost, since raw materials are bought and sold on a basis of established grades and not by means of trademarks or trade names. The broker, however, does not transact the actual business; this is left to the parties that he has brought together. Therefore, the buyer or seller may be obliged to import or to export the goods contracted for; only if delivery can be made in the home market can the broker be considered a home-market international trading agency.

Commission Houses—Export and Import

The commission house is a specialized international trading agency which has been in operation for a very long time. By definition, a commission house is a buying agent—not a selling agent. The export commission house buys domestically for foreign customers and the import commission house buys foreign goods for domestic customers. A few examples will illustrate. A school board of a town in a foreign country wishes to purchase textbooks. These are not produced in the foreign country and no foreign publisher has any foreign purchasing connection. Therefore, the school board asks an import commission house to shop around the foreign sources and find the best textbooks to fill its requirements. Upon completing the purchase, the books are shipped to the school board by the commission house and a buying commission is included in the price.

A lumber dealer in the home market seeks to purchase mahogany plywood directly from the Philippine Republic. He wishes to avoid purchasing from importers in the home market in the hope of buying at a lower price. He asks an import commission house with an office in the Philippine Republic to purchase this plywood for him. If the project is successful, the lumber dealer will have the plywood from the Philippines and a buying commission will be included in the price.

Again, a missionary group in Africa requires a variety of supplies. It contacts an export commission house in the United States and outlines its requirements. The commission house shops around to fill the order which it ships at a delivered price including a buying commission.

Trading Houses

This is a term rather than a precise definition of a business enterprise; it combines several of the functions discussed in this section. Historically, merchants and commission houses came first. It is probable that the commission house was an offshoot of the merchant business. At an earlier time, commission houses dominated international trade; they were the specialists in international business and possessed knowledge and experience which, at that time, were unknown to others.

The challenge to the supremacy of these trading houses came when manufacturers believed that they could develop and handle their foreign business better than the trading house. After all, trading houses handle so many lines of merchandise that it is difficult, if not impossible, to give close attention to any one of them. With the growth of manufacturing, it was inevitable that manufacturers would endeavor to develop export markets through their own efforts and facilities.

At the present time, these trading houses are of particular importance in the less-developed areas of the world where manufacturers have not found markets large enough to justify their own sales efforts. They are also paramount in Japan where manufacturers rarely attempt to sell their products abroad. As a result, Japanese trading houses carry on the export business.

Many of these trading houses operate as merchants and commission houses, and many also have agency contracts under which they act as sales representatives for manufacturers.

INTERNATIONAL TRADING AGENCIES IN THE FOREIGN MARKET

In every country there are many trading agencies to and through whom a foreign exporter may sell or a foreign importer may purchase his merchandise.[1] These are independent business firms in that they are in a position to purchase from or sell to whom they choose and also to represent foreign exporters and importers on one of several bases.

The marketing structure of any country depends upon the stage of its economic development. In countries like the United States, Canada, Japan, and those in Western Europe, a marketing structure is fully developed with importers, exporters, wholesalers, jobbers, and retailers. In the less-developed countries, these channels tend to telescope. An importer is likely to be also a wholesaler and, perhaps, a retailer. The jobber function is performed by the wholesaler and even by the retailer. On the other hand, exporters are likely to be the same as in developed countries, and very often they are not nationals of the particular country. The exporters of raw materials from the developing countries are almost invariably business firms that are foreign to these countries. Indeed, many raw materials flowing in international trade from the developing countries are the result of the production and consequent selling efforts of firms from the developed countries, which either have a need for such materials or else a market for them.

---

[1] In addition to these channels, there are also other types of foreign operations which are discussed in the next chapter.

Many exporters in the industrial countries, moreover, are not technically known as exporters because they are manufacturers and not separate merchandising companies. The main exception to this statement is Japan where manufacturers do not export their own products but rather export them through trading companies.

Importers may be discussed in the same terms as exporters; they may be foreign or domestic firms or they may be manufacturers that import their own requirements.

At this point, brief definitions will be given for the trading agencies mentioned so far. *Importers* are business firms that import foreign merchandise either exclusively as a line of business or as a part of the business. *Exporters* are business enterprises that export merchandise either exclusively as a line of business or as a part of a business. *Wholesalers* deal in large volume obtained from producers and supplied to retailers, jobbers, or other outlets. *Jobbers* are essentially subwholesalers and operate in markets where the volume or distance is so great that wholesalers require this additional agency to distribute properly to the retail trade. *Retailers* are at the end of the distribution chain and serve the ultimate consumer. Accordingly, they are found wherever consumers are found. In metropolitan centers, retailers occupy permanent quarters in which their merchandise is on display and for sale. Some of these retail shops are plush and others are shabby; this depends on the class of trade to which the retailer appeals. If volume is sufficiently great, the retailer may specialize in a certain line or lines of trade, e.g., food, women's wear, men's and boys' clothing, hardware, pharmaceuticals, etc. When volume is not great, several lines of merchandise are handled. However, large establishments and large volume go together, as is true of supermarkets and department stores, where either many lines are handled or there is great volume in a narrow line.

On the other hand, when customers are scattered, as in rural areas, the retailer is required to offer a wide variety of products even though sales in any one line may be meager. The so-called country store is found all over the world in rural areas. In some countries, particularly in the Middle and Far East, there are bazaars that sell a great variety of merchandise at retail. In a bazaar, each shop is individually owned, just as some department stores and supermarkets are owned and operated. Some bazaars are traveling bazaars and move about as a circus does.

In some trades, a *factor* is to be found. This is a wholesaler who finances the supplier of the goods that he distributes. This type wholesaler is found in the textile and leather trades particularly. There also is the mail-order method of conducting international as well as domestic trade. Commercial gatherings are a permanent but usually a periodical method of transacting international business. Many of these gatherings are known as trade fairs, some of which have been established in Europe for over 700 years. Merchandise is displayed at these fairs and orders are readily placed.

Almost all of the above-mentioned trading channels are available in all countries for conducting international business. Any merchandise for which there is a market can be moved by or through these channels. Basically, international business is administered at the wholesaler and producer level; a meager portion of it is negotiated at the retail level. This is because export firms prefer to concentrate their sales efforts on one or a few outlets in a particular market; to sell to retailers would greatly complicate their operations and increase their costs.

Since most of the channel intermediaries mentioned above are available for the movement of any marketable commodities, they also are available to serve a specific foreign firm or firms. In acting in such capacity, the intermediary becomes an agent or a distributor.

Agents and Distributors

When an intermediary becomes an *agent*—frequently called foreign representative—the agent's chief activity is to represent the business interests of the principal. The agent solicits orders; when orders are received, he sends them to the principal for acceptance and, if accepted, for execution. By this means, the principal reserves control over prices and terms. When the transaction is consummated, the shipment is made directly to the buyer, not to the agent, and the billing may also be sent directly to the buyer. The agent receives a commission for his services; and if he backs the credit of the buyer, he receives an extra commission and is sometimes called a *del credere* agent.

The *distributor,* on the other hand, is also a representative of a foreign firm, but he purchases the merchandise that he sells. He purchases from the supplier usually at list price less export discount. The distributor stocks merchandise, makes sales, delivers from stock, and assumes responsibility for payment by his customers. In other words, a distributor is a merchant who buys goods and sells them at a profit. He also provides service for the products that he handles and stocks repair and replacement parts.

Agents or distributors may be general, exclusive, or semiexclusive. If *general,* they assume the responsibility described but not for one firm; they are free to accept the same responsibility for other firms even in the same line of business. If *exclusive,* they will not act in the same capacity for any other firm in the same line of business in the same geographical area. Also, under an *exclusive* arrangement, the principal or supplier may not designate any other firm as agent or distributor. In the *semiexclusive* situation, the arrangement can be any variety of the two just mentioned. One usual arrangement that causes an exclusive agreement to become semiexclusive is that all orders obtained from governmental bodies or large industrial or plantation buyers will be handled directly by the supplier. This is because such orders may be in such large volume that special prices and terms may be required to obtain the business. In such cases, the agent or distributor may be allowed a split commission or profit because of the efforts he exerted to obtain the order. Indeed, agents are particularly advisable in lines of merchandise where sales in large volume are made at infrequent intervals to large buyers, including governmental units. In trades of this nature, the agent is exclusive because only large volume business is transacted. Examples would be textbooks for a school board, vehicles for a police or fire department, rolling stock for a railroad, dynamos for power plants, etc.

Terms of Agency and Distributor Contracts

Some business firms prepare formal contracts for their agency and distributor business and others depend on negotiations confirmed by correspondence. Regardless of the form in which the arrangement is made, there are certain matters on which agreement is essential. Among these are the following:

Territory. The agreement stipulates the territory granted to the agent or distributor. This may be an entire country or a section of a country. In the United States market, there are instances in which the entire nation is covered, but usually only some section of the country is designated. The extent of the territory covered in an agreement depends in large part on the scope of the operations of the agent or distributor and, of course, the nature of the product.

Subagents and Subdistributors. Under an exclusive arrangement, the supplier has no right to deal with any firm other than the appointed agent or distributor. However, the latter may be given the right to appoint subagents or subdistributors, who are generally called dealers, as a means of covering the territory assigned.

Quotas. In the case of distributors, there may be a requirement to purchase a certain minimum amount of merchandise within a designated period of time. The quota may be expressed either in terms of units or of value. Quotas may also be found in agency contracts, and shipments within the quota may be made on consignment. When merchandise is shipped on consignment, title remains with the supplier.

Duration. The duration of the contract is, of course, a matter of paramount importance. Initially, both agency and distributor contracts may be written for one, two, or three years, with the right of cancellation within a certain period of time reserved for both parties. There may also be an automatic extension provision.

Direct and Indirect Sales. When a firm holds an agency or distributor contract it naturally expects the full protection of the territory assigned. *Direct sales* refer to sales made directly by the supplier to large buyers and governmental units. Whether the agent or distributor is to participate in such transactions must be stipulated.

Indirect sales occur when goods enter a market through outside channels that have acquired those goods by various and perhaps devious means and then seek to sell them in a foreign area where an exclusive arrangement has already been established. This practice is very difficult to deal with.

Another important aspect is that the agent and distributor agree not to sell in any territory outside of the area assigned.

Price Change. The price-change provision is very important in order to protect both the supplier and the agent or distributor. Since there is an inevitable time lapse between the determination of a new price and the receipt of such information by the foreign representative, explicit understanding must be reached on this point. Usually this problem is solved by specifying a final date of applicability to the quoted price.

Approval of Order. An approval-of-order clause is ordinarily found in foreign agency contracts and even in some distributor contracts in which the supplier insists upon the right to approve all orders that are placed. This is, in part, related to the financial standing of the distributor.

Compensation. Compensation and the method of its determination are set forth in the contract. As stated above, an agent receives a commission and a distributor earns a profit.

Trademarks. These are usually protected in agency and distributor contracts in order to secure the legal rights of the supplier to retain this valuable industrial property for himself.[2]

Advertising. Advertising responsibility is frequently spelled out in agency and distributor contracts. The obligations of the agent and distributor as to advertising expenditures are expressed as well as the extent to which the supplier will furnish advertising materials or defray advertising costs.

Service. A service clause is found in many contracts, particularly those pertaining to merchandise that requires service and maintenance as well as replacement parts. In many lines of mechanical equipment, for example, the sales appeal of a product may depend in large measure on the service that is offered.

The above are the main clauses to be found in agency and distributor contracts. Other factors that are considered in these contracts are the security that is provided by the agent or distributor; maintenance of records and the right to audit accounts of the foreign representative; the amount of stock to be maintained; damaged goods claims; and assignability of the contract on the part of both the representative and the principal or supplier.

SUMMARY

1. This chapter has discussed a wide variety of international trading facilities available, in varying degrees, all over the world. Every country has some kind of marketing structure. Retailers are found from the primitive to the most sophisticated society. Wholesalers of some stature are also widely found, if only to supply retailers that may be scattered over a large territory.
2. Since these international trading facilities are found, in varying degrees, in all countries, they are indicative of the scope and variety of world trade and facilities available to its conduct.
3. Many firms shrink from engaging in international business, particularly the export business, because of the unknown conditions that must be faced. For these, there are many ways to enter and participate in that business without being exposed to bewildering situations in the foreign market. Numerous facilities exist in the home market by which entry

---

[2] For a consideration of trademarks, see Chapter 28.

Ch. 25 / International Trading Channels 551

into international business can be achieved without actually getting into it.
4. Similarly, a firm that chooses to conduct its own exporting and importing will find numerous facilities outside the home market. Arrangements can be made to conduct this business on any one of a variety of bases. Sales and purchases may be made; merchandise may be bought and sold on commission; sales representatives may be appointed on any of several bases of relationship as agents or distributors. And considering all the agencies mentioned in this chapter, there is still another variety under the control of the manufacturer or supplier which is generally known as foreign operations. This is the subject of the next chapter.

QUESTIONS AND APPLICATIONS

1. Define a channel of distribution as considered in marketing literature.
2. Define the allied company or "mother-hen" concept of international marketing; the combination export-management firm; the built-in export department concept; the separate export department; and, the export subsidiary.
3. In what ways does organization for import trade differ from organization for export trade?
4. Name the international trading channels in the home market.
5. Define the role of a government buying commission.
6. How do export and import merchants operate?
7. Define the function of an export or import broker.
8. How does an export and import commission house operate?
9. Why is international trade conducted at the wholesaler and producer level rather than at the retail level?
10. Distinguish between agents and distributors.
11. Define "exclusive" as used in dealing with agents and distributors.
12. Visit a department store and talk to the manager of the merchandising department that deals with imports. Ask how he conducts this business and write a report on your interview.

SELECTED READINGS

Chamber of Commerce of the United States. *Introduction to Doing Export and Import Business,* 5th ed. Rev. Washington, D. C., 1959.
Dartnell International Trade Handbook, The. Chicago: The Dartnell Corporation, 1963.
Economic Cooperation Administration, Office of Small Business. *Guide for the Prospective Exporter.* Washington, D. C.: Government Printing Office, 1949.
Fayerweather, John. *International Marketing.* Englewood Cliffs, New Jersey: Prentice-Hall, Inc., 1965.
Kramer, Roland L. *International Marketing,* 2d ed. Cincinnati: South-Western Publishing Company, 1964, Chapters 8-19.
Root, Franklin R. *Strategic Planning for Export Marketing.* Scranton: International Textbook Company, 1966.

CHAPTER 26

FOREIGN OPERATIONS OF UNITED STATES BUSINESS

"*Foreign operations* is the term now used to embrace all kinds of business conducted in foreign countries by enterprises of a different nationality. From the standpoint of the United States, the term means the operation of businesses in foreign countries by American companies.

"The industrial nations of Western Europe were the first to engage in what we know as foreign operations. Such European business firms built railroads, canals, public utility facilities, water works, and factories. Likewise, plantation and mining operations were commenced by these firms. American companies came on the scene at a later date. In fact, it was not until almost the twentieth century that American companies began to engage in foreign operations. The earliest of these were the meat packers, petroleum companies, plantation companies, mining companies, and a few enterprising manufacturers. Among these was H. J. Heinz—'the pickle people'—whose first effort in foreign operations was the establishment of a factory in Scotland in 1867";[1]

and also the Singer Company, then known as The Singer Sewing Machine Company.

This chapter does not deal with a new subject; in fact, it is a continuation of the preceding chapter that covers international trading channels. Foreign operations are also international trading channels. The difference is that in the preceding chapter these channels were essentially in the hands of business enterprises independent of the home-based company; whereas in foreign operations, the various facilities are generally in the hands and under the control, in varying degrees, of the home-based company.

---

[1] Roland L. Kramer, *International Marketing* (2d ed.; Cincinnati: South-Western Publishing Company, 1964), p. 273.

THE BRANCH OFFICE

The simplest form of foreign operations is to be found when a foreign sales or purchase office or house is established. This does not disturb the previously existing international trading channels in most cases, but rather serves to supplement these channels. A foreign sales office or house, for example, may coordinate the work of the intermediaries already operating in a given market; it may place orders or handle complaints or do a variety of things that enables the existing intermediaries to operate more effectively. A foreign purchase office may do the same type of work as a foreign sales office or house, although it may be the sole purchasing facility in the foreign market and thus displaces facilities that previously had been used. This is less likely to occur where a foreign sales office exists.

FOREIGN BRANCH WAREHOUSE

By taking this step, the business firm moves closer to the trading channels in the foreign market. Normally, warehousing, if necessary, is performed by the distributors and other customers in the foreign market. The business firm may decide to establish a warehouse for any number of reasons—one of these being a need to control large volumes of merchandise for filling orders abroad and for exporting to the home market.

FOREIGN ASSEMBLY

In lieu of a warehouse or in addition to it, a firm may establish an assembly operation. This is a step closer to manufacturing although it may be only an assembly of components, all, or many of which, have been imported.

The progressive steps taken by the home-based firm as it expands into foreign operations continue to reveal the application of the economic and, at times, the political factors that motivate these operations. The assembly function, for example, may be undertaken because steamship rates on completed products are higher than for parts and components. Economics dictate that the product be shipped as parts for assembly and thus move at lower steamship rates. However, if the cost of assembly in the foreign market more than outweighs the savings in steamship rates, this operation will not be economically justified. Or, consider another element such as import duties which are usually higher for completed products than for parts and components. This is a political enigma that requires an economic answer.

Again, the problem is to equate the lower import duties and lower steamship rates with the additional costs entailed in assembling abroad.

In considering these points, it is well to recall the discussion in Chapter 3 concerning the application of the several factors of production and the cost of each of these. By assembly abroad, part of the manufacturing process is now transferred to a foreign location. In so doing, the costs of assembly at the home-based operation are saved and are offset partly or totally by savings in steamship rates, savings in import duties, and cost of assembly abroad. The assembly operation abroad will be performed under a different set of cost factors from those used for assembly in the home market. These must all be evaluated to determine the profitability of assembly abroad.

FOREIGN MANUFACTURING

The next progressive step toward foreign operation occurs when manufacturing is completely or almost completely performed abroad. This is often the next logical step after assembly abroad. While it may be a logical step, it is nonetheless a very large step. In assembling abroad, the parts and components for assembly are probably manufactured in the home country, but if complete manufacture is undertaken abroad, little if any home manufacture may be imported.

To the extent that manufacturing is transferred abroad, this operation is now performed, as stated above, under a set of cost considerations different from those applied to manufacturing at home. Taking each of the four factors of production separately, these questions must be answered:

Land

How much will it cost to acquire the land necessary for the manufacturing operation?

Labor

Since foreign nationals will, no doubt, be employed in the foreign factory, what will be the cost of labor in terms of its effectiveness? If manufacturing operations are relatively simple, the effectiveness of labor will be greater than if the manufacturing functions require skilled labor that may be as expensive as at home or that may not be available at all.

Capital

How much capital must be invested in order to establish the foreign manufacturing facility? If the home-based company has sufficient capital to finance the operation, the cost of this capital will be the same as it is at home. If it is necessary to borrow capital and it can be borrowed at home, this again will entail the same costs; but if it is to be borrowed abroad, the costs will probably be different.

Business Enterprise

Management of the foreign factory must be provided. It may be possible to find a foreign national capable of managing the enterprise. If not, a manager must be transferred from another base, possibly the home base, which is more expensive than employing him at home. The cost of transferring him abroad and perhaps financial inducements to attract him to a foreign location must be weighed.

Careful consideration of these factors only emphasizes that manufacturing abroad is not always economically justified.

HOME MANUFACTURING

Before proceeding further, let us review these same elements in terms of costs incurred in a manufacturing operation in the United States.

Land

There is no reason to expect that land is any cheaper in foreign countries than it is in the United States.

Labor

It is common knowledge that labor is cheaper abroad than in the United States on a basis of comparison of wage rates. But this is not the determining factor. The important consideration is the quality of productivity that may be purchased at lower wage rates abroad. It is by no means certain that foreign labor, in terms of productivity, will be any less expensive than labor in the United States.

Capital

This is probably less expensive in the United States than in most other countries. If an American manufacturer must compete with manufacturers in the foreign market, this lower cost of capital is an advantage to the American manufacturer.

Business Enterprise

Business enterprise is likely to be less expensive in the United States than abroad. This does not mean that foreign businessmen are any less smart than their American counterparts. It does mean, however, that the American has the advantage of having been trained in American business methods which in many ways are different from those abroad. One of these differences is the merchandising ability that the American has learned as a part of the mass-distribution techniques and skills that are typical of the United States market. Other differences resulting from the first are "drive" and the concept that unit profit is not as important as total profits derived from skilled management. It is for such reasons that United States companies often send their own managers abroad rather than employ foreign managers who do not have these concepts of management and merchandising.

A most enlightening study of comparative manufacturing costs in the United States as compared with different foreign areas was published by the National Industrial Conference Board, in 1961, entitled *Costs and Competition: American Experience Abroad*.[2]

In making comparisons of costs between countries, many complications are encountered. The components included in this study are material, labor, plant overhead, selling and distribution, and general and administrative costs. From these components total unit costs are calculated that indicate some surprises. The overall picture, which varies with geographic areas, shows that total costs of manufacturing abroad are lower in 42 percent of the cases and higher than in the United States in 44 percent! The United Kingdom and the European Economic Community countries are the only areas covered in the study where the percentage for costs lower than in the United States is greater than for costs that are higher than in the United States. The labor factor cost abroad is lower than in the United States, except in Australia where it is higher. Material is preponderantly less expensive in the United States; while selling and distribution, plant overhead, and general and administrative costs are usually less expensive abroad. Of course, these are percentage comparisons and not absolute costs but they do show a valid picture.

---

[2] National Industrial Conference Board. *Costs and Competition: American Experience Abroad*, 1961. New York: The Conference Board, Studies in Business Economics, No. 73.

OBSTACLES TO FOREIGN OPERATIONS

When undertaking manufacturing operations abroad, the business concern faces certain obstacles that may add greatly to the ordinary risks of business enterprise. At best, these obstacles simply complicate the management and operation of companies abroad; at worst, they cut deeply into profitability and may even force the loss or failure of an enterprise. However, the situation is not completely dark, since there are also inducements to foreign investment offered by some governments. These will be presented after the following obstacles are discussed:

1. Traditional obstacles.
2. Foreign exchange restrictions and inconvertibility.
3. Economic and political instability.
4. Foreign government intervention.
5. Adverse foreign laws and regulations.
6. Nationalism.

The Decision to Invest Abroad

The decision to invest abroad depends, in the final analysis, upon the answer to the key question: Is the investment likely to be profitable now or in the near future?[3] To determine the likely profitability of a proposed foreign investment, however, is not an easy matter. Many factors must be considered to arrive at a careful decision; a judicious balance must be struck between inducements to invest, on the one hand, and the risks of investment, on the other. Unfortunately, there is no formula or mechanical procedure that will render a wise investment decision. Each foreign investment is unique and must be evaluated on its own merits. Conditions that turn away the portfolio investor may be considered irrelevant by the direct investor. The company that is contemplating investment abroad in an export industry may be able to ignore many factors that must be evaluated by a company planning to manufacture in a foreign country for sale in that country.

When conditions in a foreign country attract foreign investment, that country is said to have a "favorable investment climate." A favorable investment climate results from the presence of sound economic opportunities that are not nullified by government policies, such as

---

[3] The *immediate* motivations behind foreign business investments begin with profit and range from the preservation of overseas markets, competition, the acquisition of raw materials, the expansion of sales, etc., to expected income from portfolio securities.

exchange control, expropriation, or discriminatory taxation. When a country does not generally attract private foreign investment because of its economic and social policies or because its economy does not offer sound investment prospects, its investment climate is considered poor. Today the investment climate is poor in the majority of developing countries in Latin America, Africa, and Asia, despite the fact that many of these countries have ample economic opportunities for profitable investment. This is due to the large number of government policies that discourage private foreign investment.

We must not forget that obstacles to foreign operations are only half the story; the decision to invest abroad also depends on incentives. When incentives are strong enough, investment will take place despite the presence of numerous obstacles. The important point is that obstacles represent negative factors that must be set against positive factors in reaching a decision to invest in a foreign country. At times, the former outweigh the latter and a specific investment is not undertaken; at times, the converse is true. Thus the significance of obstacles is not that they entirely eliminate foreign investment but rather that they restrict foreign investment by preventing investment that would occur in their absence. The investment climate of a country depends upon a combination of obstacles and inducements that is unique with each country, and it is this combination that the private investor must evaluate in deciding whether or not to invest abroad.

Traditional Obstacles

Foreign exchange restrictions, inconvertibility, economic and political instability, foreign government intervention, adverse foreign government laws and regulations, and nationalism are not the only obstacles to private foreign investment. Even if these obstacles were swept away, private capital for the most part would move more freely within a country than between countries. For one thing, opportunities for profitable foreign investment are likely to be less well known than opportunities for investment at home. The distances that often separate one country from another; the differences in languages, customs, and social and political conditions; and the usual ignorance of affairs outside one's own country all conspire to dull the incentive to invest abroad.

Another obstacle is the special risk that attaches to foreign investment. The foreign investor must take cognizance not only of ordinary business risks, but also of the risk that arises from the fact that his investment is subject to foreign laws and regulations. In the event of legal difficulties, the investor may be compelled to seek remedy in a foreign court at considerable expense; and when an action of a foreign government is involved, the investor may have no legal remedy at all.

A further obstacle to private foreign investment is the lack of profitable opportunities. Many countries do not have the transportation and communication facilities and other public utilities that are the prerequisites of many private investments. Investors may turn away from a country because its domestic market is too small to support the economical production of manufactures. The unavailability of skilled labor, raw materials, supply parts, etc. may also deter investment in a foreign country. The absence of exploitable natural resources is an especially important obstacle because it rules out investment in production for export to the industrial countries.

Foreign Exchange Restrictions and Inconvertibility

Foreign exchange restrictions deter private foreign investment by making it difficult or impossible to convert investment earnings or investment capital into the investor's currency.[4] Many countries impose limits (usually expressed as a percentage of the invested capital) on the amount of earnings that can be converted into the investor's currency in a single year. The repatriation of capital may be prohibited for a specified number of years after the investment is made; and, even then, only gradual amortization may be allowed.

Exchange control may also interfere with the shipment of supplies and equipment to overseas branches and subsidiaries and thereby jeopardize their business operations. Even when the authorities place no restraints on the repatriation of earnings and capital, the presence of exchange control enhances the investment risk for there is always a danger that exchange regulations may restrict repatriation sometime in the future.

Economic and Political Instability

Economic and political instability in foreign countries adds greatly to the risks of private investment. Since the war, inflation has

---

[4] Under some circumstances, however, private foreign investment may take place *because* of exchange restrictions. For example, an American company may establish a producing subsidiary in a foreign country because exchange restrictions make it impossible to export to that country. Again, governments may attract specific foreign investments by offering preferential exchange rates for the transfer of investment earnings, etc.

been the principal source of economic instability; at times, it has assumed runaway proportions in many countries of Latin America and Asia. Inflation breeds maladjustments in all walks of economic life by violently disrupting ordinary relationships between costs, prices, and incomes.

The foreign investor is particularly exposed to the consequences of inflation for a number of reasons. Foreign-owned public utilities may find it impossible to obtain permission to increase rates even though costs are being rapidly pushed up by the inflationary spiral. Subsidiaries and branches of foreign parent companies are in a weaker bargaining position than domestic firms in the face of wage demands that are unloosed by the inflationary rise in the cost of living. When foreign firms raise prices after granting an increase in wages, they may be accused of contributing to inflation and blamed for the economic ills confronting the nation. More important, inflation usually places a strain on the balance of payments which, in turn, leads to exchange restrictions that interfere with the repatriation of earnings or with the importation of materials and capital equipment needed in production. Again, the uncertainties introduced by inflation make it extremely difficult for the foreign investor to plan soundly for the future; and they inhibit, in particular, further investment in productive operations.

Much economic instability is caused by political instability. In addition, political instability is an obstacle to private foreign investment because the investor has no assurance that the laws and regulations that govern the conduct of his business will not be subject to a drastic overnight change. A revolutionary government may disavow the policies and obligations of its predecessor regarding foreign investment and may even undertake punitive measures. A weak government may court public favor by attacking foreign investment as imperialistic, and it may go so far as to expropriate foreign properties. Events in Iran, Egypt, Indonesia, Argentina, Cuba, and other countries have cogently illustrated the dangers of political instability to the private foreign investor.

In the past, private investors have sought to influence or even to dominate foreign governments, and at times they have relied on the threats of armed intervention of their own governments. But today the age of "dollar diplomacy" is past, and the private investor can expect little direct help from his government. A wise course of action for foreign-owned companies doing business in politically unstable countries is to keep out of local politics and to refrain scrupulously from asking special favors of local governments.

Foreign Government Intervention

Foreign government intervention in economic affairs often acts as an obstacle to private investment abroad. The most damaging blow that a government may strike against the foreign investor is the expropriation of his properties. Although outright expropriation has occurred only rarely in countries of the free world (in contrast to Communist countries), the underdeveloped nations of Latin America, Asia, and elsewhere assert as a principle their right to expropriate as they see fit. A resolution to this effect was adopted by the United Nations General Assembly late in 1952.[5] This attitude disturbs private investors and multiplies the risks of conducting business in many foreign countries.

More insidious and just as effective as outright expropriation is the harassment of foreign-owned enterprises through government actions that make it increasingly difficult to carry on profitable operations. This "creeping expropriation" has been most common in the public utility industries. Governments may systematically refuse to allow a foreign-owned public utility to charge the rates necessary to earn a proper return on its investment. As a consequence, the properties depreciate in market value and the owners may become anxious to sell. In this way a government may be able to purchase a foreign-owned public utility at bargain rates. Fines, discriminatory exchange rates, and the competition of government enterprises may also be used to force private investors to liquidate their foreign operations.

The establishment of government enterprises often obstructs private foreign investment. Private enterprise may be excluded from certain economic sectors so as to afford an opportunity for government monopoly. For example, the petroleum industry in Brazil and Argentina is in the hands of government enterprises, and foreign capital is effectively excluded.[6] Even when private firms are not prohibited, they may find it difficult to compete against government enterprises that receive subsidies and do not have to pay taxes.

---

[5] The only "nay" vote was cast by the United States representative although there were several abstentions by European representatives.

[6] In recent years, these countries have contracted with foreign petroleum engineers to help them develop these resources.

On the other hand, the home market may discourage or forbid the foreign operation of its national firms on one of several bases. One of these is to prevent the outflow of capital: e.g., in 1965, the voluntary restraint program of the United States government as one of the efforts used to correct its balance of payment problem.

Adverse Foreign Laws and Regulations

Foreign laws and regulations are fertile sources of obstacles to foreign operations. Many foreign countries restrict the foreign ownership and management of business enterprise. For example, in Mexico only Mexicans by birth or naturalization may own lands and waters or may obtain concessions for operating mines or for utilizing waters and mineral fuel. Since July, 1944, the "51 percent law" has decreed that permission to conduct certain lines of business in Mexico may depend on Mexican participation in ownership of capital stock of not less than 51 percent of the total. Such a law is objectionable to foreign investors because it may jeopardize control over their investments. Foreign investors often seek local participation in ownership and management, but they resent being forced to accept local participation where it is unsuitable to their business operations.

Many countries have comprehensive labor and social legislation that imposes a number of obligations on foreign-owned enterprises. Labor laws often provide for minimum wages, paid vacations, profit sharing, insurance of employees against accidents, pension funds financed by the employer and employees, and the payment of indemnities to workers discharged under certain conditions. Usually these provisions do not discriminate against foreign business firms, but they may add greatly to the costs of operation and make it difficult to remove incompetent workers. Labor laws may also specify that a certain percentage of employees must be nationals. In Brazil, two thirds of all employees of business firms must be Brazilians and two thirds of the entire payroll must be paid to Brazilians. In countries where there is no law requiring the use of indigenous labor, the governments may strongly encourage the hiring and training of nationals.

Foreign tax laws must be carefully examined by the private investor. The effect of taxation on foreign investment depends to a large extent upon whether the taxes paid to foreign governments may be credited against the taxes levied by the investor's own government.

Tax laws in some countries discriminate against foreign investors in order to protect competitive domestic firms or to exploit the sometimes relatively weak position of foreign-owned enterprises. Even when there is no discrimination in the tax laws, the foreign-owned enterprises may suffer a competitive disadvantage if there is widespread evasion of taxes by local competitors. The foreign-owned business cannot afford to act illegally in tax matters even though it may be customary for domestic firms to do so.

Another set of laws that may interfere with foreign investment relates to imports. High duties, quotas, uncertainties in tariff classification and appraisal, and excessive fines and penalties for minor violations of customs laws, even when the violations are unintentional, may make it difficult and costly to acquire the raw materials and capital equipment essential for profitable foreign operations. As we have noted, exchange restrictions may have a similar effect.

Nationalism

The developing countries of the world are intensely nationalistic. Many of these countries have recently gained their independence after many decades or centuries of domination by the colonial powers of Europe. The countries of Latin America, although independent for the most part since the early nineteenth century, resent their economic dependence on the United States and Western Europe. All too often, developing countries identify foreign capital with imperialistic exploitation and overlook its positive contribution to their economic growth. Antagonism toward foreign capital is directed in particular toward private direct investment that involves business operations controlled and managed by foreigners. To make matters worse, antiforeign sentiments are often whipped up by demagogues who are intent on gaining political leadership. The consequence of this virulent nationalism is an atmosphere that is hardly conducive to foreign operations.

Nationalism and resentment toward the foreign enterprise are not confined to the developing countries of Latin America, Africa, and Asia. United States investment in Canada has come under sharp attack in recent years. United States capital controls about 45 percent of Canadian manufacturing and mining (including petroleum), and most of the foreign investment in Canada since the war has been American. Canadians complain that American companies do not sell the stock of their Canadian subsidiaries to Canadians. Criticism has also been leveled against the exploitation by American companies of Canada's natural resources and their processing in the United States. It has been pointed out in rebuttal that Canadian investors often do not buy the equities of American subsidiaries when they are offered to them, and that Canada's natural resources would remain largely undeveloped without the assistance of United States capital. Despite these criticisms of American capital, Canada offers by far the best investment climate to United States investors, and this is likely to be true in the foreseeable future. The Canadian case illustrates, however, that the private international investor can seldom overlook the presence of nationalistic attitudes in the formulation of his investment plans.

INCENTIVES TO FOREIGN OPERATIONS

While the obstacles to foreign investment are important, there are other factors to be considered and these are the attractions offered by countries to encourage foreign investment. These are the inducements mentioned at the beginning of this discussion, and they must be weighed in terms of the obstacles in order to arrive at a rational decision.

Among the attractions commonly offered by some countries, despite the obstacles imposed, are the following:

Low or Reduced Import Duties

These may be offered as an inducement for a producer to set up a manufacturing business in a foreign country. When the enterprise needs equipment and sometimes raw materials, the country offers to permit the importation of these supplies at low import duties or even duty free for a period of time. This will be done when a country welcomes a particular kind of manufacturing. Many countries, through their planning agencies, distinguish the kinds of manufacturing that are to be encouraged. If national interests have not engaged in such operations, inducements are extended to foreign (and domestic) manufacturers by lowering duties on imports that are required in order to begin operations.

Tax Inducements

Many countries that may otherwise impose obstacles to foreign investment offer tax inducements to encourage foreign business firms to establish manufacturing operations within their borders. Sometimes this inducement takes the form of lower taxes for a period of time; it may constitute a tax holiday also for a period of time, such as ten years. Since business firms are painfully conscious of the tax burden, inducements of this kind are most appealing.

Land Sites

Another inducement commonly offered to encourage foreign manufacturers to come into a country is the offer of land sites and even structures at low cost or at no cost at all. This is another attraction that is difficult to resist. An excellent example of the effects of such inducements is found in the case of Puerto Rico with its "Operation Bootstrap." Puerto Rico has benefited enormously from the business enterprises it has attracted by this policy. Other countries have also witnessed an expansion of manufacturing because of such attractions.

Repatriation of Capital and Profits

Another incentive is extended by some countries in the form of a guarantee of the repatriation of capital and profits. As stated in the discussion of the obstacles to foreign investment, restrictions are imposed by many countries on such repatriation. Clearly, this is one certain way to discourage foreign investment. However, any country that guarantees repatriation of capital and profits, even though limited to a stated amount, is offering an incentive to a degree. The chief difficulty in responding to such incentives is doubt as to the ability of the country to carry out its offer. Adverse trade factors may occur and the country could be forced to restrict the use of foreign exchange. In that case, the release of precious foreign exchange to permit the repatriation of foreign capital and profits would be most unlikely. Therefore, this kind of incentive is as good as the country that offers it.

It will be noted that these inducements have been extended chiefly to manufacturing. The developing countries are eager to encourage manufacturing, as they see in it a way to escape from the monoculture to which they have heretofore been subject. Sometimes this very monoculture has been induced or promoted by reason of earlier foreign investment, as in petroleum, copper, tin, bananas, rubber, and other such products. Still, the honest observer may wonder where these countries would be today if the foreign enterpriser had not gone in to develop these latent resources.

While it is true that manufacturers generally go abroad to produce as the best of several alternatives, the worst of which is to lose the market completely, there are instances of manufacturers who have gone abroad as a result of planning when they felt no such pressure. These have been manufacturers who saw ahead and anticipated conditions before they materialized. They recognized that their business would expand and that obstacles to export would be encountered, so they established manufacturing operations abroad before they were faced with the ugly alternatives. These are the companies that are alert and are among the world's largest and most successful international business enterprises.

FOREIGN PRIMARY PRODUCTION

This subject is examined at this point as it is a part of foreign operations, but it is entirely different from manufacturing abroad. Foreign primary production usually requires that a company go into a foreign country to produce raw materials, crops or services. It may not be a matter of deciding on alternatives; there may be no alternative.

Mineral Operations

The largest foreign production is in the petroleum field. Why do companies go abroad to find and pump crude oil? Because they require this raw material in order to continue in the petroleum refining and distributing business. The crude oil is not produced to supply the countries in which the oil is located; it is essentially produced to serve world markets. The same may be said of all minerals—copper, lead, bauxite, tin, nitrates, sulphur, gold, iron ore, etc.

The unique feature of production of minerals is that every pound or ton or gallon of a mineral that is mined or pumped is gone forever; there is no replacement. Largely for this reason many countries have refused to permit foreign enterprises to develop their precious and irreplaceable minerals. Or they have stoutly asserted their inalienable right to the ownership of the minerals and, recognizing that foreign companies have the know-how, the capital, and the markets to develop these resources profitably, have granted rights and concessions to these foreign companies. Under these rights, the foreign companies are permitted to prospect a specific geographical area. They pay heavy taxes on their production or on their profits. They may be required to process the minerals in some degree and thus afford the country an industry that will provide employment and also earn a greater amount of foreign exchange, or save the foreign exchange necessary to pay for imported products of such nature.

Agricultural Operations

Another aspect of foreign production is in the agricultural field. Every reader knows that bananas, pineapples, vegetable fibres (sisal, hemp, etc.), crude rubber, coffee, tea, cocoa, and many other agricultural products are produced in foreign countries by enterprisers of a different nationality. Many of these products are produced abroad as a foreign operation by American companies. Perhaps the best known of these companies is the United Fruit Company that has pioneered in banana plantation operations in Central America as a means of supplying the American and other markets with bananas.

Agricultural production, as compared to mineral production, has the attraction that it is self-perpetuating and not exhaustible. Crops can be produced year after year, frequently on the same land, and thus the resources of the country are not depleted. However, agriculture encounters severe risks in the form of weather and diseases so that it is not entirely an unmixed blessing. The point is that agricultural production as a foreign operation is quite different from mineral production. Indeed, it is somewhat akin to manufacturing in that production is continuous, but different, because some agricultural products, as in the case of minerals, are the result of foreign operations that supply the world rather than the national market.

Lest the reader be unaware of the scope of foreign operations in mineral and agricultural production, it is important to realize that nobody, not even a foreign enterpriser, can simply blast a hole in a mountain or in the ground or plant bananas and sugar in a jungle and enjoy the fruits of his work. Plans must be carefully worked out: roads and railroads and shipping facilities must be constructed, transmission and power lines provided, living accommodations for workers, stores, churches, dispensaries, and so forth built—in other words, an entire civilization may be the necessary price for mineral and agricultural production in the developing areas of the world. These facilities are provided to serve the needs of the foreign operation, but as development expands they may become available for use by all the people of the country. Moreover, educational facilities are commonly provided in such foreign primary operations, and the residents of the country derive certain benefits from them. These points should be remembered when criticisms are directed against companies where foreign primary operations have been introduced.

LICENSING FOR FOREIGN OPERATIONS

Finally, we come to a different form of foreign operation which is called licensing. This is not the same as operating a foreign branch office, warehouse, assembly or production facility. *Licensing* in foreign operations entails the utilization of the production facilities of business firms situated in the foreign country.

Licensing is essentially the sale or "rental" of patents, technical know-how, processes, etc. to foreign firms. Let us cite some examples. A manufacturer has a patented process for manufacturing a certain tool. He approaches a foreign manufacturer of tools and negotiates for the use of this patent by the foreign firm. If the negotiations are successful, the foreign company can now produce the tool for which the first manufacturer holds the patent rights. Another example is the sale of know-how, which may include such a wide range of activities as how to establish and operate a mutual savings bank, or a hotel, or a sporting event, or a style show, or raising chicks, etc. Licensing is extensively employed both domestically and internationally. Around 1903, Charles M. Schwab, steel magnate, *bought* the patents of an English inventor which made possible the wide-flanged structural shapes that ushered in the skyscraper era. This was when he was trying desperately to put Bethlehem Steel Company on its feet.[7]

Why license? The instigator of the license—the licensor—possesses something that he has reason to believe will be marketable to another firm (the licensee) from which both will profit. Of course, the impetus may work the other way in that the prospective licensee approaches the anticipated licensor, as in the Charles M. Schwab illustration above. If the licensor has the initiative, he chooses this method of foreign operation because it will provide him with a market abroad for his product or process without necessitating the establishment of his own production facilities abroad. As discussed above, the other methods of foreign operation require capital outlay and perhaps the provision of key personnel, which, in the case of manufacturing and production, can be excessive. The licensee is interested in such a proposition since it affords knowledge of a product or process that he does not possess and will therefore add to his output or effectiveness. Moreover, licensing agreements generally require the licensee to market as well as to produce in the foreign market. Thus, the licensor has surrendered to the licensee the production or performance; and if it is production, the licensee also takes over the marketing.

---

[7] *Forbes Magazine*, March 15, 1965, p. 23.

Risk Inherent in Licensing Agreements

As may be seen from this discussion, licensing demands an unusual amount of good faith on the part of both parties. The licensee has in his possession valuable rights that he has *purchased,* and he is free to improve the information that he has acquired. If the licensing agreement is mutually satisfactory, it may result in an exchange of improvements for the benefit of both parties. On the other hand, the licensee may see an opportunity to proceed on his own and dislodge the licensor, eventually forcing him completely from the market. This is a risk that is inherent in licensing, and good faith is the only safeguard. In the operation of the licensing method, it is generally understood that the licensor should make every effort to improve the methods that are contained in the license, supply these improvements to the licensee, and thus encourage him to continue the agreement and to cooperate.

Licensing has attracted considerable attention since the end of World War II. The main reasons for this have been the increased interest in world markets on the part of United States companies and those of other industrial countries and the increased productive capacity of both developed and developing countries, resulting in improved knowledge and in the ability to accept licensing agreements.

Provisions of Licensing Agreements

Due to the nature of licensing, the agreements reached between licensors and licensees generally cover a variety of subjects, each of which is important. The term of the agreement runs from two or three years to as many as fifteen years, with a longer rather than a shorter term being the rule. In the case of licensing of patents, the agreement should run for the period of years covering the validity of the patent. The matter of quality control and maintenance of standards is of paramount importance when a production facility of some kind is licensed. The licensor does not want his product or process to suffer from a reputation for poor quality. Therefore, measures must be designed to assure that quality will be maintained, and if not that the agreement will be abrogated.

Various provisions are embodied in these agreements to induce a licensee to perform on a basis of some minimum standard. These may be expressed in terms of units of value or production; and if such levels are not maintained, the agreement again can be nullified. If the license is for manufacturing a product that is to be marketed by the licensee, care must be taken not to violate the antitrust laws dealing with exclusive arrangements.

Financial considerations are, of course, of primary importance. They determine if and how much the licensee is to pay to initiate the agreement (a sort of down payment). His payments during the life of the agreement are based on some factor such as volume or value of licensed product sales or of performance, or it may be a fixed fee. How frequently such payments are to be made and in what currency are also important. In this connection, provision must be made for the procedure to be followed in the event of nonpayment because of restrictions on foreign exchange. Another form of payment is to give the licensor the privilege of acquiring stock in the licensee's business.

Patent rights covered in licensing agreements should be carefully reserved to the ownership of the licensor, and the licensor should not relinquish his legal rights to trademarks.

CONTROL OVER FOREIGN OPERATIONS

Regardless of the kind of foreign operation that a company may adopt, there is always the matter of control to be considered. This is not always a question of the desires of the business firm, because governments frequently have something to say with regard to financial control of national enterprises.

In the first place, the typical business firm will prefer to exercise complete control over all of its business operations. This may be expensive but it is usually considered worth the expense in terms of administration. When complete control is in the hands of the business firm, it can move as it chooses without having to consider a partner.

Secondly, such complete control may not be possible in some countries and in certain lines of business. Many countries, including the industrial nations, prefer or require that national interests be represented in foreign business enterprises. As stated earlier in this chapter, a business firm today cannot move into a foreign country and set up business without first considering the policy of the government. For reasons that may be more nationalistic than otherwise, the policy may be to discourage foreign participation in the industry of a country.

A recent statement of this problem is attributed to the chairman of one of the large petroleum companies who said:

> The greatest obstacle to private investment in the developing nations today is not the threat of expropriation and breach of contract, serious as these threats may be in some areas. The greatest obstacle lies in the actions which governments have taken to carve

out large areas of economic endeavor in which private investors are simply not permitted to operate. This is the policy of the closed door.[8]

To combat this policy, the speaker continued,

> United States private investors have acted flexibly to try to gain broader recognition of their potential contribution to the developing areas. In many areas they have joined together to carry out cooperative community action programs.

Examples of such actions are the work of petroleum affiliates in developing a sense of strong private local economy through participation on a minority equity basis in small business ventures. The most important contribution that the affiliates give is technical and managerial know-how, not capital. There is also the Adela Investment Co. in which more than 120 major firms in Japan, Europe, and North America have joined together to provide capital to the private sector of those Latin American countries that offer reasonable security.[9]

From the standpoint of control, the licensing system has nothing to offer. If anything, control is completely lost as the licensee holds a patent or a process which can be developed rapidly. Some companies have sought to buy into or buy out a licensee, but this is not always possible because there may not be any stock available with which to acquire ownership.

JOINT VENTURES

By means of joint venture, a foreign company agrees with a national company to participate in a given venture on a joint basis. This may be evidenced by a division of stock, as 50-50 or some other proportion; or it may be achieved by some agreed contribution of equipment, structures, etc. The objective of the joint venture is to share control as between the foreign and the national participants.

This sharing of control is now frequently required under the law of the country in which the joint venture is located. Some countries specify the percentage of control that is to be allocated to national interests. This is intended to prevent foreign enterprisers from controlling national ventures. Not only the developing countries, where nationalism is so common, but also some industrial countries now operate on this principle.

---

[8] Michael L. Haider, Chairman, Standard Oil Company (New Jersey), address to the Harvard Business School of Washington, D. C. April 28, 1965, and printed in *Congressional Record*, 89th Congress, First Session, May 14, 1965, pp. 776-181-98370.

[9] *Ibid.*

Distinction must be made between a *new* joint venture and a *going* joint venture. In the new joint venture, the characteristics of the enterprise are essentially like those of a newly established, wholly owned subsidiary. Starting anew, this type of joint venture may suffer from some of the disadvantages of lack of experienced personnel, lack of an established national image, and possible risk due to the new foreign partner. Therefore, it is considered a better practice to engage in a joint venture with a going concern with which experience can be associated and a national image established, at least in part.

In summary, to the foreign company the joint venture offers the following advantages:

1. Cash outlay is less than in the case of a wholly owned enterprise.
2. With the reduced amount of capital to be invested, the amount that is saved can be spent in other markets to expand the business.
3. An immediate local market position, local political position, and local industry are created, thus assuring cooperation from government and labor and avoiding popular resentment.
4. Local legal requirements are more easily satisfied and personnel problems are reduced by means of a joint venture with a going concern.

These advantages may be offset by the loss of complete control so that care must be exercised in the choice of partners. Many manufacturing firms that go abroad for production form joint ventures with their export distributor or agent. These distributors or agents make most desirable foreign partners in a joint venture because the business enterprise has had the experience of working with such firms.

Moreover, some companies prefer, as a policy, to go in on a 50-50 equity basis because they do not wish to have complete control. If the law of the country requires that the government be the partner, the situation is vastly different. Government anywhere is politics and politics, particularly abroad, do not mix well with business.

While the joint venture offers a means of escaping some or all of the wrath of nationalism in a country, it does not eliminate the fears of foreign investment and the opposition to it. The foreigner is still in the picture and he is the one against whom nationalism explodes. Again it is important to note that the authority quoted is a representative of the petroleum business which is a giant in the international business field. The same reaction and the same fears are not usually expressed with regard to manufacturing or distribution operations abroad. As previously stated, inducements are even offered to encourage foreign capital to enter these fields.

SUMMARY

Contrasting the various methods of foreign operation broadly, the following points can be made:

1. The foreign branch office or warehouse provides the home-based manufacturer at his own expense a closer contact with more control over the foreign market.
2. The foreign assembly plant offers the possibility of savings in transportation, import tariff rates, and assembly costs. It provides no better control over the market but may offer a lower cost position. This operation is entirely at the expense and risk of the home-based company.
3. The foreign manufacturing plant, which is also conducted at the expense of the home-based company, provides a means of competing more effectively in markets where rival producers for one of several reasons have achieved a competitive advantage. All the costs and risk of the manufacturing enterprise are for the account of the home-based company.
4. The foreign primary-production facility is also at the expense and risk of the home-based company, but it serves essentially the world market rather than the foreign (national) market. By this means, raw materials necessary for manufacturing or consumption are unearthed from foreign sources, chiefly the developing nations, and thus become available in the markets of the world.
5. Licensing for foreign operation is a procedure in which the home-based company has little or no investment or actual participation. The licensee produces the product or service under arrangements made with the licensor. Whether it is a successful agreement depends on the good faith of the parties and on the significance of the patent or process or know-how that is licensed.
6. From the standpoint of control of foreign operations, the following points should be emphasized:
    (a) A wholly owned foreign operation provides complete control, requires more capital, and entails more risk.
    (b) Joint ventures reduce the amount of capital to be invested, reduce the nationalistic risks, but depend on the standing and good faith of the partner.
    (c) Licensing offers no control to speak of; the licensee operates independently under the terms of the agreement and is naturally interested in his own business.

QUESTIONS AND APPLICATIONS

1. Define foreign operations.
2. Explain the functions of a foreign branch office or branch warehouse.
3. Why do business firms establish foreign assembly operations?
4. How does foreign manufacturing differ from foreign assembly?
5. Comment on the statement that manufacturing abroad is not always economically justified.

6. Attempt to justify the obstacles to foreign investment imposed by governments.
7. Also attempt to justify the inducements offered by foreign governments to encourage foreign investments.
8. Why do business firms go abroad for primary production?
9. Define licensing for foreign operations. Why do business firms engage in licensing abroad?
10. Explain the various provisions found in licensing agreements for international trade.
11. Examine one or more of the licensing agreements found in the books listed in the Selected Readings.
12. Compare wholly owned foreign operations with joint ventures.

SELECTED READINGS

Bryson, G. D. *American Management Abroad.* New York: Harper & Row, 1961.

Cardinale, Joseph S. *Manual on the Foreign License and Technical Assistance Agreements.* New York: American Heritage Publishing Co., Inc., 1958.

Dartnell International Trade Handbook, The. Chicago: The Dartnell Corporation, 1963.

Eckstrom, Lawrence J. *Licensing in Foreign Operations.* Essex, Connecticut: Foreign Operations Service, Inc., 1958.

Fayerweather, John. *Management of International Operations,* Text and Cases. New York: McGraw-Hill Book Company, Inc., 1960.

Fenn, Dan J., Jr. *Management Guide to Overseas Operations.* New York: McGraw-Hill Book Company, Inc., 1957.

Foreign Licensing Agreements. Studies in Business Policy No. 86. New York: National Industrial Conference Board, 1958.

Foreign Licensing: Questions and Answers. New York: Pegasus International Corporation (undated).

Gibbons, William J. *Tax Factors in Basing International Business Abroad.* Boston, Massachusetts: Little, Brown & Company, 1957.

Kramer, Roland L. *International Marketing,* 2d ed. Cincinnati: South-Western Publishing Company, 1964.

CHAPTER 27

FINANCING INTERNATIONAL TRADE

Financing is vital to any business and, in international business, its vitality is emphasized by the differences inherent in that business. Many of these differences have been discussed in previous chapters.

MEANING OF FINANCE

Two views must be kept in mind in considering this chapter. The familiar view considers terms of payment on sales, the use of banks and bank documents in connection with such sales, and the whole subject of credit. This phase of financing relates to the sale and purchase of products or services in the international field.

Another view of financing international trade considers the means used by the international business firm to obtain the necessary funds to carry on its operations. It is true that, to a certain extent, methods of financing international sales and purchases afford a basis for financing business operations; but when there are no international sales or purchases, as well may be the case in foreign operations, financing must be of a different kind.

NATURE OF FINANCE

While elementary, it is important to review the basic concept of financing business. At its inception a business firm usually has its own funds since a credit position has yet to be established. With its own funds, the company prospers. Now it can go to a commercial bank and establish what the bank calls a credit line, which means that the commercial bank has evaluated this company as eligible to borrow from the bank up to the limit of the credit line. Now the company has two sources of financing: its own funds and the bank's funds.

After another period of prosperity, the company is in position to go public. It will offer for sale its securities to the general public. Its stock is issued and is offered for sale. Purchasers of such stock provide funds for the operation of the company and this adds a third source of funds.

It must be remembered that the company is a debtor to the bank to the extent of its utilized credit, and is owned to the degree of its stockholdings by other people. Thus, we have three kinds of financing: the company's own funds, borrowed funds, and proprietorship (equity) funds. If the company's own funds are inadequate for the task, the company becomes bankrupt and loses all that it has put into the company. If a bank lends to the company, the bank becomes a creditor and seeks to reclaim its entire advance. If stock has been issued, the stockholders have no financial claim on the company; they are owners and take their chances. If the company fails, they lose their investment and there is no recourse.

When a company is exporting and importing merchandise, it can generally finance its current transactions by means of bank documents and bank financing. When, in addition to or in lieu of exporting and importing, the company goes into foreign operations, it must provide capital and thus we have completed the cycle. The company must now use its own funds, borrowed funds, or funds acquired from the equity owners through the sale of stock.

NEED FOR CREDIT EXTENSION IN INTERNATIONAL TRADE

Credit is commonly extended in business; a buyer has a certain period of time in which payment is expected for merchandise or service. Sometimes a discount is given for prompt payment such as "2 percent 10 days, net 30 days," that is, if the invoice is paid within ten days of receipt, a discount of 2 percent may be deducted. In any event, the full amount of the bill, with or without discount, is payable in thirty days. These are commonly used domestic sales terms.

Consider the use of such terms in international trade. In order to take advantage of any cash discount within ten days, the overseas customer would be obligated to have a paying representative in the exporter's country to effectuate such an arrangement. This underlines the necessity for credit in international trade.

Many reasons are cited for the need to extend credit in international business. Shipping distance, for example, is one reason. If the shipment takes three weeks to reach its foreign destination, the buyer is most reluctant to expend funds at least until the shipment has arrived. Some foreign markets are much farther away than three weeks in terms of time in transit.

Then there is the nature of the economy of the buyer's country. If it is a country that depends chiefly on primary agricultural products for its economic health and international stability, its income is derived at harvest time. If the agriculture of such a country depends, at least to some extent, on foreign seeds, plants, fertilizer, and machinery, as is often the case, the importer of these products cannot hope to be paid for the merchandise until the harvest is reaped. Therefore, it is obvious in this instance that the importer needs as liberal credit as is possible; merchandise he imports will not be converted locally into cash for a period of perhaps four to six months.

Several economic results flow from an economy of the kind just described. One of these is a shortage of local capital for financing business transactions. Another is the high interest rate resulting from the imbalance between supply and demand for capital as well as the risks involved. Under such circumstances it is not difficult to understand why a businessman in such a country will seek to import on long-term credit, willingly paying 6 percent for outside credit, and utilize his own funds locally at interest rates that may be a multiple of 6 percent per year. He borrows at 6 percent and lends at 12, 18, 24, 36, 72 percent per year.

Another circumstance necessitating credit in international trade is the foreign exchange rate situation. There are fluctuations in foreign exchange rates and delays in obtaining foreign exchange to meet foreign obligations. An importer facing such a situation requires credit to handle his business operation in accordance with changes in the foreign exchange situation.[1]

Finally, matters such as custom and competition must not be overlooked. In many trades it is customary to grant credit of a certain length of time—or not to grant credit at all—as generally is traditional in the raw material trades. Competition sometimes is effective because of the credit extended, quite apart from the quality or price of the merchandise or service that is sold.

INTERNATIONAL PRICE QUOTATIONS

Let us now consider the nature of international price quotations which are standardized in two different groups, but the differences

---

[1] See Chapter 8.

between these two groups are minor. The first group is called American Foreign Trade Definitions, Revised, and is sponsored by all the national foreign trade organizations in the United States. The second group is called Incoterms and is sponsored by the International Chamber of Commerce. To reiterate the differences are slight.

All these price quotations establish (1) the inherent costs to a precise point which the exporter includes in the price he quotes and (2) the precise point at which the exporter's responsibility for the shipment ceases and that of the importer begins. These are very technical questions and they are spelled out in great detail in the official descriptions.

These price quotations are cited in symbols or abbreviations. There are several f.o.b. quotations, meaning free on board. Examples would be f.o.b. cars factory, meaning literally the price for the shipment placed on board freight cars (or it could be trucks or barges) at the factory; f.o.b. cars origin point, which would mean the same as f.o.b. cars factory, unless a local transportation charge is made to move the freight cars from the factory to the classification yards or terminals of the carrier. Then there is a quotation f.o.b. cars port of export, under which the price of the shipment would include the transportation charges to the port of export. In many ports, the knowledgeable shipper bills the shipment f.o.b. cars port of export *for export*. The addition of the words *for export* entitles the shipment to be placed in the export port at a place where it will be available for loading on board a vessel. If the words *for export* are not used, the shipment might be delivered at a point miles away from the waterfront and an additional charge would be incurred to move the shipment to the waterfront. The quotation f.o.b. vessel means exactly that—all costs incurred to place the shipment on board the vessel. Finally, there is an f.o.b. destination quotation that includes all costs incurred to deliver the shipment to the destination point indicated. If this is an inland point in a foreign country, all these costs would be included in the price.

In all of the f.o.b. quotations mentioned, the responsibility of the shipper ceases at the same point where his costs end.

These quotations sound simple enough and they may be, except for the vicissitudes inherent in international business. There may be unexpected accidents or delays that interrupt the flow of the shipment and, consequently, increase costs. If such costs have not been anticipated, profit on the transaction will be reduced or actually lost.

Other price quotations common in international trade are f.a.s. vessel port of export and c.i.f. destination port. The f.a.s. vessel quotation requires the exporter to pay all costs and assume all responsibility in placing the shipment alongside the vessel. This means that the shipment must be placed within reach of the ship's tackle—the ship machinery used in loading and discharging cargo.[2] The c.i.f. quotation means a price including cost, insurance, and freight to the destination port, but in this quotation the responsibility of the exporter ceases at the port of export and does not extend to the destination port.

These are the basic export and import price quotations commonly employed in international trade.

SOURCES OF FOREIGN CREDIT INFORMATION

Since financing inevitably involves credit, we must now investigate the sources of foreign credit information. In domestic trade, credit information is easily available through credit reporting organizations and banks. In the international field, these sources are not uniformly available. Credit reporting organizations, such as Dun and Bradstreet, have not succeeded in obtaining financial statements from business firms all over the world. In many countries, business firms refuse to divulge financial information. Moreover, business organization in foreign countries is often the small family-type business which is particularly reluctant to reveal financial information. Banks with international divisions provide foreign credit information but generally it is obtained from correspondent banks abroad, and they are faced with the same reluctance to reveal financial information as are the credit reporting organizations.

In the United States, a unique method of foreign credit reporting is provided by the National Association of Credit Management which operates a Foreign Credit Interchange Bureau. This is a voluntary operation through which United States exporters report their paying experience with foreign customers. These experiences are assembled into a report that is made available to members who inquire about specific foreign business firms. In essence, this is an exchange of ledger experience. The weakness of the system is that it reveals only the experience of United States suppliers.

---

[2] The inquisitive reader may wonder what the difference is between f.o.b. vessel and f.a.s. vessel. If under f.a.s. an accident occurs in loading the vessel, the exporter has no responsibility; the importer has. If the shipment requires extra heavy cranes in order to load the cargo on the vessel, there is considerable difference in cost btween f.a.s. and f.o.b.

Credit information of a kind can be obtained through United States Department of Commerce and Department of State sources. While not technically foreign credit reports, the WTD (World Trade Directory) reports that are prepared by overseas representatives of the two Departments serve to evaluate the commercial position of foreign firms and this is often the only information that can be obtained.

Another source of foreign credit information is experience. Having dealt with a foreign business firm for an extended period of time, an exporter is in position to evaluate that firm's credit standing.

Foreign credit insurance is available in many countries, having started in the United Kingdom in 1926. Under such plans, exporters may purchase insurance against political risks, insolvency, and inconvertibility of currencies on the part of their foreign customers. No plan pays 100 percent of the amount that is lost. In the United States, foreign credit insurance was established in 1962 with the formation of the Foreign Credit Insurance Association. This is a group of private insurance companies with the Export-Import Bank acting as a catalyst and also assuming responsibility for political risks assumed in foreign credit insurance policies. The Export-Import Bank had earlier granted export financing without recourse for certain transactions which was a kind of export credit insurance.

Under the FCIA the exporter must submit two credit reports on each customer for which he seeks to obtain foreign credit insurance. On short-term transactions, all of the exporter's business must be covered, except Canadian sales and letter-of-credit transactions. On long-term sales, individual coverage may be purchased.

In international trade the credit problem, as indicated earlier, is twofold: it is first the credit standing of the individual and, second, it is the financial position of the country in which the individual is located. This second factor is unique to international trade. It is not unusual to know that a customer is perfectly reliable, but credit cannot be extended to him because of the unstable economy of the country. If a customer is unable to obtain foreign exchange to meet his obligation, the exporter will not be paid and the customer cannot be blamed. Therefore, in all foreign credit work, the economic position of the country is as equally important as the standing of the firm.

TERMS OF PAYMENT

Having presented the need for credit in international trade, the nature of international price quotations, and the sources of foreign credit information, we come now to terms of payment. In considering these terms the previous information will be used.

Cash

The term *cash,* commonly used in domestic trade, seldom is used in international trade. Actually, from the standpoint of international trade there is no such thing as cash. United States dollar bills cannot be used as legal tender in many countries—they have their own currency or cash. Therefore, a term of payment that specifies cash with order or cash against shipment requires the foreign customer to obtain United States dollars in order to provide the means of payment. Since he is in another country whose currency is not United States dollars, he must perform a foreign exchange function by converting his currency into United States dollars. This is the only normal way that cash can be provided in the United States by a customer in a foreign country.

However, international payment terms are basically extensions of credit; rarely must a foreign customer provide cash with an order or for a shipment. The most common payment terms within the framework of credit as applied in the international trade are open account, bills of exchange, and letters of credit.

Open Account

Open account is a term of payment frequently used in domestic trade. Under this term of payment the customer pays the bill voluntarily within a designated period of time. The seller trusts the customer to make payment, and obviously has complete confidence in the ability and the willingness of the customer to do just that. Open account payment is also extended to Canadian customers.

Open account is not commonly used in international trade because the exporter's financial resources would be extended and this is not good business. Why would this be the case? A Chicago firm extends open account to a customer in Kansas City or St. Louis or Denver or Los Angeles or Montreal or Winnipeg or any other United States or Canadian city. Terms are 2 percent 10 days, net 30 days. All these customers would have no difficulty in paying the bill within thirty days of shipment and many of them would take advantage of the 2 percent discount for payment within ten days. Now, let us consider customers in London, Berlin, Johannesburg, Buenos Aires, Yokohama, Bombay. The domestic terms of 2 percent 10 days, net 30 days mean nothing to them. The vessel carrying shipments to these destinations may not arrive for thirty or sixty or more days. Regardless of the credit worthiness of the customers, the exporter cannot afford to have his funds tied up for such a long period. To the customers, payment within thirty days of shipment would be no credit at all; in most cases, it would be considered payment in advance. And in international trade, where competition is worldwide and where credit is essential, such terms of payment are unacceptable. No sales could be made on this basis. Now, what do we do? We turn to the bill of exchange. This is the basic document which finances the bulk of all world trade.

Bill of Exchange

A *bill of exchange* is a written demand executed by an exporter and served on an importer.[3] This demand for payment stipulates the amount to be paid, the currency in which to be paid, the party to be paid, and the time that it is to be paid. (The latter is known as tenor or usance.) There are three kinds of bills of exchange—date, sight, and arrival. A *date* bill of exchange demands that payment be made at a designated period of time after date, such as 30, 60 or 90 days. This is fixed. A *sight* bill of exchange is likewise made out for a designated period of time—at sight or after sight. *Sight* means that the importer has been sighted or seen. If drawn at sight, he pays then; if after sight at 30, 60 or 90 days, he *accepts* the obligation to pay at that time. This is accomplished by having the importer write *accepted* across the face of the bill of exchange, sign it, and date it. This document now becomes what is known as a *trade acceptance*. If the bill of exchange has 90 days to run, the importer is not required to pay until 90 days after he has accepted it. Here is where the bill of exchange provides a means of financing international trade from the standpoint of the supplier. This accepted bill of exchange may now be *discounted* in the banking system. This means that the exporter can obtain an advance from a bank on the basis of the trade acceptance. For this accommodation he pays interest which is defined as the *discount*.

The exporter now has an advance, but he still bears the responsibility of the importer paying the bill of exchange after the expiration of the 90-day period. In other words, the funds the exporter obtains from the bank on the basis of the accepted bill of exchange are merely a loan. If the importer fails to pay, the exporter suffers the entire loss. Therefore, under a bill-of-exchange transaction the funds to

---

[3] See also Chapter 6.

the exporter are advanced on the credit rating of the *exporter* and not on the credit standing of the *importer*. Then why the accepted bill of exchange as a basis of financing international trade? This is to meet the requirements of banking laws which are concerned with banks and only indirectly with bank customers.

It is well here to recall the point made at the beginning of this chapter concerning the credit line established by the business firm with its bank—the accepted 90-day sight bill of exchange is now discounted at this same bank by the business firm-exporter. The exporter, therefore, cannot walk into any bank, lay down the trade acceptance, and expect to receive a cash advance. The amount advanced by the bank is charged against the credit line of the exporter. Why could not the exporter receive the same advance without an accepted bill of exchange? He could, and in that case he would sign a promissory note. In other words, the exporter could sell a piece of paper declaring value due to someone: in the promissory note, it is to the bank; in the bill of exchange, it is also to the bank by reason of the endorsement by the exporter on the acceptance.

While these devices provide bases for bank financing for domestic business firms, as well as international business firms, they also provide a facility for the bank, in turn, to obtain cash for these documents in case the bank needs it. The bank is, therefore, always in a liquid position on these transactions. If need be, it can go to the Federal Reserve Bank and obtain advances against these documents. And never forget that if the importer, at the head of the line, fails to pay at the end of 90 days, the exporter bears full responsibility to reimburse the bank.

Another form of bill of exchange is called *arrival*, and it is due on arrival of the merchandise or so many days after arrival. Since the date of arrival is rarely if ever known precisely, there is no way to determine the due date of such a bill of exchange. For this reason it is infrequently used and in many countries it is actually illegal.

Letters of Credit

Another term of payment in international trade is by means of *letters of credit*. The importance of the letter of credit stems from the weakness of the bill of exchange under which the entire risk of payment by the importer is borne by the exporter. This situation underscores the need for adequate credit information, because the terms of sale acceptable to an exporter are determined by his credit evaluation of the customer.

With a letter of credit, the importer's bank assumes the payment responsibility for the importer, and the bills of exchange are delivered against that or some other designated bank and are not drawn on the importer. To induce the bank to open a letter of credit on his behalf, the importer must provide whatever security his bank requires. Having opened the letter of credit, the importer's bank notifies a bank in the exporter's country; and in due course the exporter is advised that the letter of credit has been opened.

The letter of credit spells out the particular transaction for which the funds are being advanced. The shipment is described in detail, the price is given, the documents to be provided by the exporter are stipulated, and an expiration date is given. All of the stated obligations of the exporter must be fulfilled on or before the expiration date; otherwise the funds under the letter of credit are forfeited. Therefore, the protection afforded the importer under a letter of credit may be worth the cost to him of using this instrument. Letters of credit present one problem, though, in that they are not standardized and each such document must be read closely. The funds to be paid under a letter of credit are obtained by a bill of exchange; but here the bill of exchange is drawn on a bank.

Further analysis reveals three major kinds of letters of credit. One is *revocable* which means that the opening bank may revoke its commitment at any time prior to shipment of the merchandise. This is not a very reliable letter of credit. The second is *irrevocable,* under which the opening bank agrees not to revoke its commitment as long as the letter of credit is valid, which means until it expires. This type letter of credit is just as good as the bank that opens it. A third variation introduces what is known as *confirmation.* An irrevocable letter of credit may be and often is confirmed by a bank in the exporter's country. This latter bank, in effect, lends its endorsement to the undertaking of the opening bank. If, for any reason, the opening bank does not pay, the confirming bank will pay. In practice, the bill of exchange drawn under the letter of credit by the exporter is generally drawn against the paying bank in his country. This may be his own or another commercial bank.

A FINANCING PACKAGE

In reviewing the material presented in this chapter we shall assemble a financing package to demonstrate how these various topics merge in an actual international business transaction. After thorough credit investigation, we have decided that our foreign customer is good for 90 days sight draft terms. Our price is f.o.b. vessel port of export. Our quotation then is $X f.o.b. vessel, port of export, 90 days bill of exchange payable after sight. The importer knows that he must pay for ocean freight, marine insurance, and all other costs incurred after the vessel is loaded. He also knows that he has 90 days in which to pay the bill covering the shipment because the date on which he "sights" the bill of exchange will be approximately the date when the shipment arrives. Indeed, if the bill of exchange arrives before the shipment, the importer can easily make himself unavailable to accept it. He will be available when the shipment arrives.

We (the exporter) know that the compensation we will receive will cover the cost of manufacture or acquisition, the profit, packing, and shipping costs until the shipment is on board the vessel in the port of export. We also assume that the importer will accept the bill of exchange when presented to him and that he will also pay at the end of 90 days. Finally, we know that if we are in need of funds, we can easily obtain an advance from our bank with the use of the accepted bill of exchange.

Now we shall review the same transaction but use an irrevocable and confirmed 90-day letter of credit instead of a 90-day sight bill of exchange. The letter of credit is required because the country in which the importer is located has balance of payment problems; and it is too risky to expect the importer, 90 days after acceptance of the bill of exchange, to be able to obtain the United States dollars necessary to pay the bill of exchange. Therefore, a letter of credit is essential. United States dollars are immediately made available by the opening bank and are transmitted to the paying bank in the exporter's country. Everything is the same as in the first transaction, except for the letter of credit. The importer has confidence that the exporter will perform as required and the shipment will be made as stipulated in the letter of credit. The exporter may then present his bill of exchange to the paying bank in his country, drawing it in accordance with the letter of credit, and may obtain an acceptance by this bank. This is known as a *bank acceptance* and is considered more reliable than a trade acceptance. This is not only because a bank is expected to be more reliable than a business firm but because the funds under a letter of credit are already transferred by the opening bank to the paying bank, while the funds to pay a 90-day sight bill of exchange (trade bill) will not be available until the 90 days have been accomplished; and if foreign exchange is not then available, payment cannot be made.

THE BANK'S ROLE

We have been discussing commercial banks—banks that have a foreign or international department or division—but we have not explained how they operate in connection with the financing of international trade. Almost all seaboard banks and some inland banks now have such departments. Banks deal with banks; when the exporter's bank sends documents abroad covering a business transaction of the exporter, these documents go to a *bank* abroad. The connections that banks have domestically and abroad are generally by means of correspondent banks; only a few United States banks operate their own branches abroad, while branch banking domestically is confined to a single state. A correspondent bank exchanges business with its counterpart, whether domestic or international. Each has a deposit of funds (in balance of payments terminology known as short-term capital) in the other. Under the letter of credit the United States correspondent with which the opening bank has a United States dollar deposit debits the opening bank's account immediately. In effect, under a letter of credit, the necessary funds to meet the obligation are already in the exporter's country, but are withheld from the exporter pending fulfillment of the terms of the letter of credit.

Under the 90-day sight bill of exchange (trade bill) the banks perform another helpful function. The foreign correspondent bank of the exporter's bank is asked to present the bill of exchange to the importer for acceptance. How does the foreign bank induce the importer to accept? It is very simple. The importer is eager to receive the shipment, but he cannot claim the shipment without surrendering the endorsed negotiable *ocean bill of lading*. This vital document is one of the papers that the correspondent bank is holding. Therefore, if the importer wishes to claim his shipment he will receive the essential bill of lading from the bank *if* and *when* he accepts the bill of exchange. Thus, the bank acts as a kind of policeman for the financing of international trade.

If anything should go wrong—and it may—the correspondent bank, through the exporter's bank knows what procedure to follow. This is all determined in advance. If the importer, for example, refuses to accept the bill of exchange because certain minor fees or taxes have been added, the correspondent knows whether or not to waive claims for such payment.

This is how the bulk of international trade is financed. The commercial banks of the world play a central role.[4]

GOVERNMENT AND INTERNATIONAL BANKS

In this era, government and international banks exercise an important role in financing international trade, that is, that type of trade not financed by commercial banks with commercial documents. This is international trade that is financed by funds advanced by government and international banks in the form of loans or grants. If loans, the funds must be repaid; if grants, they are gifts. Such financing is for specific purposes, and generally the funds are used to pay for equipment that is provided for such purposes. Such funds rarely are transferred to a borrower or grantee in the form of foreign exchange.

One of the earliest of these banks is the Export-Import Bank of Washington, D. C. This is a United States government bank whose purpose is to provide financing for international trade transactions that commercial banks are not equipped to finance. For example, a South American country plans to build a new airport, a new highway, or a new power system. These are not the kinds of transactions that commercial banks handle. They are long run and are social rather than commercial in nature—sometimes even political.

The International Bank for Reconstruction and Development (IBRD), as the name implies, finances reconstruction and development. However, since reconstruction of Europe and Japan as a result of World War II has been completed, the IBRD is now assisting in the advancement of developing countries which is a keynote of today's international political policy.[5]

The IBRD has spawned several new and different financial institutions: e.g., the International Finance Corporation, which is designed to finance the economic development of the less-developed countries, with emphasis on the role of private enterprise; and the International Development Association, which essentially does the same thing but is more liberal than either the IBRD or the IFC.

In the Western Hemisphere a new bank has been established, also in response to demands of less-developed countries. This is the Inter-American Development Bank, which makes long-term loans to Western Hemisphere countries for accelerating the process of economic

---

[4] See also Chapter 6.
[5] See Chapter 20.

development. Some of these institutions charge low interest rates and one of them, the IDA, charges no interest.

The International Monetary Fund (IMF) is a different kind of financial agency whose purpose is to make foreign exchange available to countries that are short of necessary foreign exchange, which, in turn, keeps international trade flowing. A shortage of foreign exchange is a great obstacle to the flow of that trade and one which must be overcome in the interest of worldwide economic health.[6]

SUMMARY

1. Financing international trade comprises two different concepts. One is the facility of payment extended to the foreign customer. The other is the means used by the supplier to finance his business operations. The finances that business enterprises need can come from their own sources, by borrowings from banks, and by the sale of securities to the public, or by any combination of these.
2. Export and import price quotations are established arrangements to enable suppliers and customers to understand each other regarding all costs included in quoted prices and also to understand the responsibilities of both parties.
3. Since credit is generally granted in international trade, it is necessary to obtain foreign credit information. This is not as readily available or as accurate as it is in United States domestic trade.
4. Terms of payment include the amount of credit extended and also transmission of price quotations. Basic terms of sale are cash, bill of exchange, and letter of credit. In international trade, the bill of exchange is the essential collection document, and when a letter of credit is used it acts as a security document.
5. Banks are the essential intermediaries to permit this system of financing to operate. They handle the documents, police the transaction, and advance funds to assist both suppliers and customers. Foreign credit insurance is also available as a means of protecting the credit risk.
6. Government and international banks also participate in financing international trade. Their role is the long-term, social type of investment or grant, in which a commercial bank is generally not interested.

QUESTIONS AND APPLICATIONS

1. Explain the two meanings of finance.
2. Why is credit often extended in international sales?
3. Explain the meaning of international price quotations. Cite two examples of such quotations.
4. Comment on the sources of foreign credit information.

---

[6] See Chapter 17.

Ch. 27 / Financing International Trade

5. Why would an exporter take out insurance through the Foreign Credit Insurance Association?
6. Explain the twofold nature of international credit.
7. Why is cash a sales term not commonly used in international trade?
8. Why is the open-account term of payment generally unattractive to an exporter?
9. Define the nature and purpose of a bill of exchange.
10. Define the nature and purpose of a letter of credit and include consideration of the several kinds of letters of credit.
11. Compare the risks incurred by an exporter in sales terms of 30 days sight draft as compared with a 30-day irrevocable and confirmed letter of credit.
12. With the great number of private banks equipped to handle international financial transactions, why have governmental and intergovernmental financial institutions been established?
13. Examine the annual report of any one of the governmental or intergovernmental banks and write a report on the nature and extent of its operations.

SELECTED READINGS

American Management Association. *Financing International Operations—A Guide to Sources and Methods.* New York: American Management Association, 1965.

——————, International Management Division. "Sources and Methods of International Financing." American Management Association, Management Report No. 59. New York: American Management Association, 1961, Part 2.

Bankers Trust Company. *Washington Agencies That Help to Finance Foreign Trade.* New York: Bankers Trust Company, 1962.

Dartnell International Trade Handbook, The. Chicago: The Dartnell Corporation, 1963. Part 1, Chapters 3, 5, 9. Part 2, Chapters 2-8.

Henning, Charles N. *International Finance.* New York: Harper & Brothers, 1958.

Loomis, John E. *Public Money Sources for Overseas Trade and Development.* Washington, D. C.: Bureau of National Affairs, 1963.

Rosenthal, Morris. *Techniques of International Trade.* New York: McGraw-Hill Book Company, Inc., 1950. Parts VI and VII.

Wasserman, Max J., Charles W. Hultman, and Laszlo Zsoldos. *International Finance.* New York: Simmons-Boardman Publishing Corporation, 1963.

CHAPTER 28

SUPPORTING AGENCIES IN INTERNATIONAL TRADE

While some of the agencies to be covered in this chapter have been mentioned or inferred in earlier chapters, an attempt will now be made to deal with all of them as a group. This chapter emphasizes the truth that no business firm in either domestic or international trade can conduct its business without the help and cooperation of many outside agencies. The supporting agencies in this chapter are divided into the following categories:

1. Promotion
2. Merchandising
3. Legal
4. Financial
5. Transportation
6. Risk bearing
7. Communications
8. Education

Each of these categories will be treated briefly so that the reader may learn something about these important supporting agencies.

PROMOTION

As explained in Chapter 23, the business firm would have no standing whatsoever in other countries if it were not for the treaty rights arranged by its own country. These pacts are necessary because of sovereignty—the right of each country to make its own decisions in relation to domestic and international commerce. These treaty rights are, therefore, vital and initial supporting agencies.

In pursuit of these rights, the governments of all industrial countries and also some of the developing countries promote their international trade, with special emphasis on exports. This program

Ch. 28 / Supporting Agencies in International Trade

takes various forms based on the principles brought out in Chapters 3, 4, and 5. It is because of the benefits to the country in terms of production, employment, prices, etc. that public funds are spent to promote export trade.

Every nation has an ambassador or a minister accredited to all countries with which diplomatic relations are maintained, and also a consular corps of officers stationed not only in the capital but also in ports and trading centers. Consuls perform a political-commercial-protective role. In the commercial area, their function is to promote good relations and trade with the country in which they are stationed. They prepare commercial reports for the district in which they are located; protect the rights of citizens of their own country who have interests there; and, generally promote the welfare of their home country.

Many countries also maintain at the embassy or legation a number of so-called attaches who represent various interests, such as commercial, financial, agricultural, military, labor, and so on. For our purposes, the first three are noteworthy. These attaches devote their full time to the subject of their assignment and thus provide information useful to the international business firm.

Another method of promoting export trade is by means of trade missions and trade fairs where products are displayed. Inquiries are answered, prices and terms are quoted, and sales contracts are initiated or completed. Floating exhibits also display foreign merchandise from port to port. Both governments and private agencies utilize this method of promotion.

Still another method is the compilation of lists of business firms interested in engaging in international trade, which contain information pertaining to their business operations and their reputation.

While this discussion began with ambassadors and consuls, an international business firm will have little contact with such officials. They are affiliated with the United States Department of State or, as it is usually called in other countries, the Foreign Office. This department concerns itself essentially with countries and not with individuals. Therefore, the business firm confers with the Department of Commerce whose function is to promote the domestic and international trade of the country. In the United States, it is the Department of Commerce that obtains and distributes information and reports prepared by the officers of the Department of State including commercial officers abroad. In every large city in the United States, the Department of Commerce has a regional office which serves as a miniature of and a conduit to the Washington headquarters. All the publications and reports mentioned here are available at or through regional offices which serve as local contacts with the business community.

The Bureau of International Commerce of the United States Department of Commerce performs the trade promotion work, and the Business Defense and Services Administration specializes in commodity lines. The former is primarily concerned with manufactured products, while the latter deals also with some raw materials. However, if the raw materials are of an agricultural nature, the United States Department of Agriculture is the place to get the information; and if they are of a mineral nature, the United States Department of the Interior, Bureau of Mines, is the place to go.

Thus the various departments of the federal government in one way or another influence and support international trade; however, most promotion performed by governments is of a general nature.

There are several areas of government promotion, however, that are specifically designed for individual firms. One of these is providing authoritative information by commercial attaches, consuls, or Washington officials in reply to letters of inquiry from business firms. Another is the Trade Contact Service of the BIC through which a firm, at a nominal fee, may have a comprehensive study made that is useful only to it. This is also done when government financial institutions participate in underwriting business transactions on a long-term basis, since a large part of the aid given by all industrial countries to the developing countries consists of raw materials and manufactured goods that are furnished by business firms who thus engage in international trade through the foreign aid program of their countries.

Private trade-promotion agencies also perform functions that are designed especially for use by international business firms, as we described at length in Chapter 25. Both governments and private trade-promotion agencies publish reports and bulletins that are helpful to international business firms. These may be had on a subscription basis or purchased individually. The same may be said of publications of international agencies, such as the United Nations, the International Monetary Fund, and others.

MERCHANDISING

This category of support is listed separately, although some of the government agencies treated in the preceding section also perform merchandising functions. In this context, reference is made to support for sales and advertising programs of individual business firms. As already mentioned, government promotion is generally not specifically designed for use by a given firm; it requires the firm to make its own application and adaptation of the information received. However, there are private agencies, as explained in Chapter 25, that perform the merchandising functions for a business firm that does not have the knowledge or the personnel to conduct these functions itself.

There are also advertising agencies that perform merchandising and publicity functions. Many of these have expanded to the international field and are equipped to undertake market studies and advertising programs for their clients. Some of them have their own branches abroad but most of them utilize advertising agencies in foreign countries.

Publications that cover the know-how of exporting and importing, as well as foreign operations, are particularly helpful. Their editors and writers are businessmen who travel extensively and who are equipped to help plan merchandising programs for overseas business. The same is true of consulting firms that have expanded their operations to the foreign field. Local, regional, and national foreign trade associations also provide much useful information and many helpful hints that will assist business firms in conducting their merchandising operations.

LEGAL

Among the agencies in support of international trade are those constituting the entire field here designated as legal. Of primary importance is the subject of private commercial law under which business firms must operate. When companies are engaged in business in or with foreign countries, they must be aware of their legal rights and obligations. Despite the nationality of a business firm, it must accept the legal principles that govern each country where it operates. While some of these principles may appear to be onerous, it must be conceded that all laws are designed to benefit, in one way or another, those persons affected by them.

There are two chief bodies of law in force throughout the world. One of these is based on English common law and the other is the code law compiled initially by Napoleon Bonaparte. The English common law principle is applied in many countries as a result of the vast colonial empire that Great Britain established all over the world.

Countries like the United States follow these principles of law because of their inheritance from British rule.

These two systems of law differ basically in one way: common law is predicated essentially on precedents of court decisions, statutes, and government decrees; code law is predicated on the written codes of law—find the applicable article of the particular legal code and the decision is practically automatic.

A business firm established in a common-law jurisdiction is confronted with code law when it engages in international trade and/or operates abroad, and it is incumbent upon the firm unfamiliar with the principles and requirements of code law to determine their effects on company operation. Earlier, mention was made of sovereignty and the exercise thereof. As demonstrated in specific business practices and procedures, some of the differences in law are quite marked. In a code-law country, for example, a merchant or a business firm does not simply open up a business and go to work. Rather, certain stipulations govern. A merchant (or business) must register in the commercial register of the jurisdiction in which he operates. Then, and only then, is he deemed to be a legal entity. Failing to adhere to this procedure, the firm has no standing in court.

Another example is a power of attorney that is often used to authorize one person to perform acts and make decisions on behalf of another person. A general power of attorney is not accepted in a code-law country; it must be specifically drawn and also notarized. In common-law countries the notary is required for certain formal documents such as deeds to property, but in code-law countries nearly everything appears to be formal and the notary is a very important functionary. He certifies all kinds of documents and transactions—even an agreement of marriage.

Consider the numerous patents that protect many products that are exported or manufactured abroad. Whether these patents granted by the home country are valid abroad will depend upon the law and upon international agreements. The subject of trademark rights is even more bewildering. In common-law countries, the rights to a trademark reside in the party who first used the trademark, while in code-law countries the party who first registers the trademark is the legal owner. If a company from a common-law country sells its trademarked products abroad, it may find in some code-law countries that some unscrupulous rogue has registered the trademark in his own name; hence, the only way the real owner of the trademark can regain his rights is to buy off the illegitimate possessor. International agreements to overcome this problem have been signally ineffective.

Legal procedures in international trade disputes are so cumbersome that knowledgeable international business firms "stay out of court." Since disputes are bound to occur, the only other way to settle them is by means of commercial arbitration. This means that the dispute is settled by businessmen who have no particular knowledge of law but who have a sense of good business practice and good judgment. Facilities and rules for the conduct of arbitration are provided by such organizations as the American Arbitration Association and numerous arbitration arrangements established by other countries, including the Soviet Union. However, arbitration will be effective only if the laws of the countries in which it is applied make provision for the legality of arbitration procedure and awards. Many countries have done this so that awards made by arbitration tribunals are enforceable in courts of law in case of a refusal to accept the arbitral award.

Thus, the international business firm receives the support of commercial law when it engages in international trade or operates abroad, but it is mandatory for the firm to be aware of the provisions of these laws, particularly if different from those of his own country.

FINANCIAL

Because of the outstanding support that financial institutions give to the conduct of international trade they have been treated in connection with the financing of that trade. Financial supporting agencies for international trade include banks and credit agencies as was pointed out in Chapter 27.

It will be of interest, especially to American readers, to learn that United States national banks at one time were not permitted to negotiate documents arising out of the international trade of the United States. This narrow restriction was removed with the passage of the Federal Reserve Act of 1913 which authorized all national and other bank members of the Federal Reserve System to finance international business transactions. Prior to that time, American branches of foreign banks, a few state banks, and private bankers financed the international business of the United States. These still do so, but with the great expansion of United States trade and operation overseas, the enabling legislation of 1913 did not come any too early.

Other financial supporting agencies are foreign exchange brokers and dealers who participate in the foreign exchange markets, and by so doing, assist in equating supply and demand of foreign exchange in the short run.

TRANSPORTATION

Transportation agencies provide and supervise the physical services required to move international shipments. These include foreign freight forwarders, customs house brokers, steamship agents, and travel agents.

Foreign freight forwarders are employed in international trade since complicated regulations and complex paper work are inherent in international transactions—problems not encountered in domestic trade. The most important functions of foreign freight forwarders are to book cargo space and prepare the documents necessary for international trade. These papers are required (1) by the government of the country *from* which the shipment is going, (2) by the government of the country *to* which the shipment is going, (3) by shipping companies, and (4) by banks.

For example, on export shipments from the United States, a *shipper's export declaration* is required to describe the shipment, its quantity, its value, its destination, etc. The information obtained from these papers provides the export statistics for the United States, and the document itself serves as a means of exercising export control with regard to the nature of the commodity, the destination, and the consignee as well as the consignor.

For import shipments, an *import declaration* must be made. The shipments are inspected by the Customs service that levies import duties and enforces other regulations governing the import trade. This operation is so complicated that customs house brokers are employed because only they are thoroughly familiar with these regulations.

The country of import also requires certain papers. These may be consular invoices or certificates of origin or quarantine documents. Some commodities are prohibited from being exported or imported, and others may have quotas on the volume that may be imported or exported. Most exasperating of all government regulations are those pertaining to restrictions on foreign exchange. All these regulations are subject to change, and the foreign freight forwarder is expected to be fully cognizant of all changes.

The shipping company also requires certain papers. Chief of these is the ocean *bill of lading* for shipments that are to move by sea.

If going by air, a waybill is used, which is a kind of bill of lading that is not negotiable as is often the case with an ocean bill of lading. Prior to issuance of the bill of lading, a dock receipt may be provided by the shipping company. Almost all of these documents are prepared by the foreign freight forwarder.

Banks issue papers in connection with the financing of international trade and foreign freight forwarders check these papers to determine if all requisites have been met. Many times the forwarder performs the banking transaction for his client, not only by checking the requirements but also by making deposits or advancing funds required in connection with the negotiation.

Thus, the foreign freight forwarder actually performs these functions for his client who prefers the forwarder because of his wide experience, facilities, and knowledge of documentary procedures.

Steamship lines, represented by agents and by their own offices, are important supporting agencies in international trade because they, too, carry shipments to their destinations. The same may be said of airlines and—for trade with Canada, and to some extent with Mexico—of railroads, truck lines, and inland waterways. Most of the international business of the world still moves by sea which brings the steamship agent into the picture.

International shipping is performed by the carriers of many nations. Indeed, the United States, which is the largest international trading nation in the world, carries only about 10 percent of its trade in United States flag vessels. These American steamship lines join with the steamship lines of various nations in what are known as steamship conferences, under which they can agree on rates to charge and rules to govern the freight which they handle.[1] This is not a violation of antitrust law, even in the United States, because these conferences are exempt from that law. However, regulatory agencies supervise the operation of the conferences.

Shipping by sea is completely different from land transportation. In the first place, cargo rates are governed by weight or by volume. In other words, cargo is not only weighed but also measured for sea transportation, and the rate earning the greatest revenue is applicable. Therefore, a ton is not only 2,240 pounds (or 2,000 pounds in Far East trades) but also 40 cubic feet.

A second difference in ocean shipping, where conference rules apply, is that two levels of rates often apply. One of these is known

---

[1] See also Chapter 4.

as the contract rate and the other as the noncontract rate. The contract rate is lower than the noncontract rate by around 10 percent, and it is available to all shippers who sign an agreement to use conference lines for all of their shipments for a year. The international business firm must decide whether it is to its advantage to sign a conference contract. True, it is charged lower rates from the conference, but in some trades, steamship lines do not belong to any conference. In order to obtain traffic, these lines generally quote rates as low as or lower than the conference contract rates. The only difficulty in relying on independent steamship lines for lower rates and paying higher rates for conference vessels when needed is that the independent, as a single line, cannot possibly offer the frequency of service that 4, 6, 8, 10, 12, or 20 lines in a conference can offer.

The entire ocean shipping of the world is not performed by steamship lines. Business firms that have a great volume of shipping may charter vessels to carry their cargo. In the petroleum industry, for example, there is no such thing as a steamship line; all petroleum carriers or tankers are privately owned by petroleum companies or by companies that own tankers and are chartered within the industry. In the dry cargo trades, ores, lumber, grains, sugar, and many other products also move in chartered vessels which are often owned and operated by companies trading in these commodities.

Mention was made earlier of the importance of packing for international transportation. Since cargoes must be packed as compactly and economically as possible to assure safe delivery of the contents, specialized knowledge is required to achieve these goals. Export packing and packaging companies are supporting agencies that determine proper methods of packing certain products and also perform the actual packing operation for many firms. As *containers* come more into common use, packing problems will be minimized because containers are proving their safety and economy. As compared to packing a shipment in a case, barrel, or other outside device, a container is a large device, usually made of steel, in which several or many shipments may be placed with no more immediate protection than inside packing, eliminating the outside heavy casing. For example, in the fiscal year 1962-63, a complete potash plant was moved in 53 containers and cases from an East Coast United States port to Haifa, Israel; and one container carried 36,000 pounds of Florida grapefruit to Basel, Switzerland. In that same fiscal year, approximately 30,000 to 40,000 van containers, more than 250,000 cargo containers, and a large number of pallet containers were used. One problem encountered in this mode of shipping has been the standardization of size of containers. Progress is being made along this line, although eventually many specialized containers for particular jobs will be designed.[2]

To see containers utilized in this manner one should look for a large truck carrying a removable container that has the appearance of a truck trailer, or a railroad train with cars carrying one to three containers, which is known in the trade as riding "piggy-back."

Finally, there are travel agents who facilitate international travel by making reservations, obtaining tickets, and arranging for accommodations. Unlike the foreign freight forwarder, the customs house broker, and the packing companies, travel agents receive no compensation from the client for making reservations and obtaining tickets for travel; they are compensated by the transportation company for bringing the business to them. While the same is true of the foreign freight forwarder relative to steamship bookings, the forwarder still makes a charge for the paperwork and other services that he performs.

RISK BEARING

Other supporting agencies assist in bearing various risks inherent in international trade. These risks fall under three headings: capital risks, physical risks, and credit risks.

Capital risks are inherent in all business and Chapter 27 has explained how banks assist in bearing this risk. However, government financial facilities are sometimes available to guarantee capital investment against political and, in some cases, commercial risks. This government guarantee is made available to private business firms that invest in certain unattractive areas of the world. As a means of encouraging firms to invest in developing countries, the governments of a number of developed countries provide this means of protection.[3]

Physical risks by business firms require private insurance company protection, specifically marine and inland marine insurance. Marine underwriters quote rates to insure against certain declared perils of transportation and certain perils of the market. This is a highly complex profession and the marine broker is needed to work out proper insurance coverage for a business firm.

---

[2] Interstate Commerce Commission, *Annual Report 1962/63*, quoted from United States Steel Corporation, Transportation and Defense Section, Commercial Research Division. *Containerization, The Outlook for Shipping Containers,* June, 1963.

[3] See also Chapter 22.

Foreign credit insurance is another risk-bearing facility that essentially removes the credit hazard from international business. Nearly all foreign credit insurance plans are government operated or supported. They cover the loss sustained by reason of failure or bankruptcy and also the political risk of expropriation or exchange inconvertibility. A premium is charged that measures the risk in terms of country, standing of the foreign business firm, and terms of sale.

COMMUNICATIONS

Communications are considered here as a supporting agency, although some of them are actually sales methods, particularly correspondence, when used for mail-order purposes. However, correspondence serves chiefly as a supporting agency by transmitting information, quotations, orders, etc. established by the export department or international division of the firm.

Correspondence in international business is unavoidably different from domestic correspondence. Language is of great importance; English is widely used but other languages are also necessary. These are chiefly Spanish, French, and German. All correspondence with countries of the Far East is in English. Many American firms follow the practice of writing in English and accepting replies in another language. This procedure has the merit of assuring complete understanding on the part of both firms. It is not difficult, with some knowledge of a language, to determine the meaning of a letter, but it is quite another thing to compose a letter in a foreign language. In foreign operations, correspondence is generally in one language.

The name of a foreign business firm may be difficult to decipher. According to Spanish custom, the mother's name is the last, so that Juan Huerte-Santos would be addressed as Mr. Huerte. Many Far Eastern names are reverse to English speaking people. Thus, Chung Changtsu is Mr. Chung.

With many names so difficult to interpret, the filing of international business correspondence is generally on a geographical basis—accordingly, Santos, Rodriquez, and Chung are properly filed by *location*. The same difficulty occurs in English speaking areas with such names as Smith, Jones, and Cohen.

Correspondence in international business should be less brisk than correspondence in the United States. Businessmen, particularly in non-European countries, appreciate common courtesies that have been practically forgotten in United States and European practice.

Communications are also accomplished by means of cable and radio. These are instantaneous communications methods compared with mail that moves by steamer and by air. Communications companies perform these services and charge for each word used in a message. Moreover, each word is based on fifteen letters and if a word exceeds fifteen letters, it is counted twice. To avoid excessive expense in sending cable and radio messages, code systems have been devised to express entire sentences in one word. However, a chargeable word contains five letters when code is employed. In addition to words, photos, diagrams, and other graphic work can be transmitted by instantaneous cable and radio.

Finally, international telephone communication is available for almost all countries of the world. While the cost of such services has been greatly reduced over the years, it is still used chiefly for urgent information and, of course, for business requiring discussion.

Translation also is included as a supporting service, since it achieves understanding in business relationships. Everyone who knows or speaks a foreign language is not necessarily a good translator. Of course, the gist of a letter or article in a foreign language may be comprehended by anyone who knows something about the language, but this does not necessarily guarantee accurate or complete translation. When technical data are involved, exact translation is even more important.

Experience has proved the wisdom of using personnel who have a thorough knowledge of the business as well as the foreign language requiring translation, since a literal dictionary translation of a foreign language is often ridiculous.

EDUCATION

Education may be considered a supporting agency because it provides training for those who aspire to engage in international business. Probably all practical training must be obtained from special trade schools. Many of these are found in European countries, but very few in the United States and other areas. There are also training institutes that offer instruction that lasts from three or four days to two years. The several-day instruction facilities are generally designed for those already in the international business field and serve as a refresher or for treatment of certain specific topics.

The greatest expansion in international business education in the United States has occurred in colleges and universities. Many of these now have special departments of instruction or have expanded the instruction offered by the economics, marketing, and political science departments. Only a very few universities have developed what might be called a full curriculum in international business. Graduates of these courses are sought by recruitment representatives of the firms engaged in international business.

Finally, as a part of the Export Expansion Program of the United States, special courses have been instituted in many cities to attract new firms to the international field. These latter do not lead to college credits but they have served to arouse the interest of firms that heretofore had no knowledge of nor interest in international markets.

SUMMARY

This chapter has assembled eight types of supporting agencies in the international business area.
1. Promotion is defined as assistance provided by public or private sources and includes information, trade leads, business reports, trade contact services, exhibits, and displays. A department of commerce is generally charged with the promotion of international trade of a country. Generally speaking, private promotion agencies provide a more personal service than that supplied by public services.
2. Merchandising support may be obtained from international advertising agencies, publications, consulting firms, and foreign trade associations.
3. Legal procedures introduce the code-law system as distinguished from the common-law system. Formality is much more pronounced under code law and, consequently, causes many "snares" that astute business firms must know about, namely: what constitutes a merchant? a power of attorney? what, if any, patent rights are assured? how should a trademark be protected? etc. Since legal procedures are time-consuming and costly, commercial arbitration is often used. A worldwide system of arbitration has been established.
4. Financial supporting agencies are for the most part, banks and foreign exchange brokers.
5. Transportation, as a supporting agency, includes foreign freight forwarders, customs house brokers, steamship lines, agents and conferences, and travel agents. The foreign freight forwarder is extensively used because of regulations and complex paper work involved in international business transactions. Steamship line conferences offer contract services at lower rates if the contract is exclusive for the conference. Rates are governed by weight or measurement—the greater derived revenue is the basis of determination. Travel agents arrange for trips and accommodations. Customs house brokers are expert in getting imports through customs.

Ch. 28 / Supporting Agencies in International Trade   603

6. Risk bearing requires the assistance of financial institutions in bearing the capital risk. For marine risks, marine insurance companies provide the protection. For foreign credit risk protection, foreign credit insurance in now widely available.
7. Communications include letters that are written in support of trade and in conduct of trade; cables, radio messages, and international telephones that provide instantaneous transmission; and translation services that are essential to the even and articulate flow of international trade.
8. Education is defined as a supporting service that trains aspiring candidates for the international business field. Trade and service schools prepare them for the practical work; at the college level many courses of study are offered.

QUESTIONS AND APPLICATIONS

1. Explain the nature and variety of international trade promotion techniques pursued by governments.
2. Comment on the nature of private vs. government trade promotion.
3. Define the scope of the agencies discussed under the heading of merchandising.
4. Explain the difference in principles of common law and code law. Illustrate these differences as they relate to the status of a businessman or merchant; rights to industrial property (trademarks).
5. Name and define as many transportation agencies as you can.
6. Name the several kinds of risk bearing in international trade. How can each of these risks be borne by supporting agencies?
7. How does correspondence in international trade differ from domestic?
8. Explain the nature of problems involved in translations into a foreign language.
9. Explain the need for and the use of codes in international communications.
10. Justify the inclusion of education as a supporting agency.
11. Examine and write a report on the foreign trade promotion organization and work of the United States Department of Commerce.
12. Visit the office of a foreign freight forwarder or a steamship company or agency and examine an ocean freight tariff. Write a report describing the contents of this tariff.

SELECTED READINGS

Bonnell's Manual on Packing and Shipping. Plainsfield, New Jersey: Bonnell Publications, Inc.
Bureau of National Affairs, Inc. *Export Shipping Manual.* Washington, D. C., annual.
Dartnell International Trade Handbook, The. Chicago: The Dartnell Corporation, 1963. Part 3.

Exporters' Encyclopaedia. New York: Dun & Bradstreet, Inc., annual.
Insurance Company of North America. *Export Packing.* Philadelphia: Insurance Company of North America, undated.
Kramer, Roland L. *International Marketing,* 2d ed. Cincinnati: South-Western Publishing Company, 1964. Chapters 4-6, 12-13, 20, 24, 31.
Rosenthal, Morris. *Techniques of International Trade.* New York: McGraw-Hill Book Co., Inc., 1960. Parts IV, V, IX.
See also references in connection with Chapters 23, 25, and 27.

CHAPTER 29

MEETING INTERNATIONAL COMPETITION

This is an appropriate title for this concluding chapter. There is scarcely a chapter in the preceding twenty-eight that has not, in one way or other, alluded to some inherent element of competition.

Competition in international business has been growing keener since the close of World War II. Prior to that war, international competition was intense but the factors bearing upon it have changed materially.

Before World War II, the leading international trading nation was the United Kingdom. The export trade of that country was a mixture of reexports of products manufactured or mined in the United Kingdom and exports of other countries that used the United Kingdom as a clearing and transshipping station. This was made possible because of the far-flung international trading facilities of the United Kingdom whereby many of the exports of countries, chiefly those emanating from the colonial areas, were marketed through the United Kingdom. Moreover, this country was a shipping, financing, and insuring center that tended to draw trade from all over the world.

CHANGING FACTORS IN INTERNATIONAL COMPETITION

Since World War II, the United States has become the leading international trading nation. Its exports are almost entirely products of the United States, and its manufactured products are sold abroad using marketing and promotional adaptations of methods pursued in the vast domestic American market. Thus, it may be observed that a new dynamism has ignited international trade competition, fired by service- and promotion-minded United States international business enterprises.

Many other factors have served to change and animate the complexion of international trade competition. The old colonial markets are gone, and now we have independent nations reveling in their sovereignty. They can decide autonomously what they wish to import and also what they are capable of exporting. Another aspect of this evolution is the recognition of the importance of what the United Nations designates as the LDC's (less-developed countries). These emerging nations and some that emerged decades ago are identified as LDC's because they do not possess economic independence, despite the fact that they do have political independence. Efforts are being exerted by the industrial countries and the United Nations organizations to aid in developing the LDC's. International trade is, therefore, promoted by contributions and loans extended to the LDC's. A large part of the capital goods as well as a portion of the primary products imported by the LDC's are acquired by means of such aid. The competition for this business is worldwide, except when loans or aid are "tied" so as to restrict business to a given country.

Another important change in the factors affecting international competition is the present condition of our world map. The Communist area is spread from eastern Europe across Asia and it includes Cuba. Since the ideological concept of trade is at the state level, two effects are apparent. One is that trade must be conducted at the state level, which is abhorrent to democratic nations where business is a private preserve. Owing to this, world competition has diminished because the state decides what will be purchased, and the best salesmanship in this world will not sell something which the state does not approve. Moreover, international business conducted by such state organizations manifests an ideological rather than a commercial attitude.

Moreover, the Communist countries are so controlled that the economic principles of cost and price brought out in Chapters 3, 4, and 5 are ignored. Therefore, competition at any time can be more intense because under state-controlled operations, the price of a product can be set by fiat. Such competition is the more vicious because it may be present for only a short time, and there is no way to determine this at a given moment. It thus disrupts commercial business and causes the most destructive kind of competition.

Another factor—also relating to our changing world map—is the emergence of multinational communities resulting in economic integration. The most outstanding of these is, of course, the European Economic Community, while others under way or in the making are in Latin America and Africa. The effects of such programs on international competition are again twofold. To the extent that barriers are removed from trade, finance, and migration that move within the area, competition for those outside the area is most severe. Before the emergence of such communities, Germany, for example, in selling its products to France, incurred the same import duties as those levied on products shipped from any other country. With the Community in operation, all trade between Germany and France will eventually be free of all barriers. The implications for the outside competitor are obvious.

Further, with economic integration all countries participating should find a significant growth in their economic ability resulting in a greater market for both consumer and capital goods, as well as for primary products. This has already been demonstrated by the tremendous expansion of the market in the European Economic Community. This increase in business causes a greater market for a wider variety of goods in greater quantities, and countries outside the Community have shared in this expansion despite rising barriers.

Concomitant with the emergence of new nations and the economic integration programs, there has been a vast increase in the establishment of foreign branch factories. When the European Common Market (now known as the European Economic Community) was under consideration, there was a rush of foreign manufacturers to establish production facilities within the Community in order to benefit from the free exchange of goods among the several countries, and to avoid the rising barriers to trade from areas outside the Community. This has taken the form of both licensing and foreign production. Developing countries, on the other hand, are trying desperately to free themselves from their former dependence on a single product for economic stability. They are endeavoring to diversify and one way to do this is to restrict and prohibit imports of certain products as a means of inducing manufacturers to establish plants within their borders. With such endeavors frequently arranged on a joint financial basis, the desired manufacture is obtained.

Thus, another factor is affecting international competition by attracting foreign manufacturers to establish their production facilities abroad. To a certain extent, this eliminates former exports, but, as pointed out in Chapter 26, it may also mean an increased market for capital goods and for raw materials. The competition in this instance is, therefore, of a different character; the manufacturer who produces behind a high tariff wall is granted a kind of monopoly and competition is essentially stifled. Manufacturing within the European Economic Community, on the other hand, enables the foreign manufacturer to be on a competitive basis with European producers. If the foreign factory is located in France, for example, it will enjoy the same freedom of trade that French manufacturers will enjoy, when trade among the countries of the Community is entirely free; and, in the meantime, the same lower tariff rates enable it to maintain an equal competitive position.

This changed competitive situation is supported, in some degree, by the technological changes that are occurring in production methods. Such economies or advances as may be provided by these changes afford a strong competitive position whether they are located in the home country or abroad. Technological advances have reached all areas of the world in varying degrees, depending upon the ability of a country to accept and utilize them. The resurgence of the devastated areas in Europe and Japan is an economic miracle, and in the process, the equipment that has been installed in these areas has been of the latest design. This development has also contributed to the change in the nature of international competition.

Not only have these changes occurred in production, but, in addition, many service facilities have also entered the international competitive arena. Among these may be cited banks, advertising agencies, and consulting firms. These also face a new kind of competition, not only by entering the international field but also by encouraging improvement in similar facilities previously located in other countries.

Thus, the new competition is buttressed by these advanced methods and techniques and has caused it to be more intense.

In international trade, the most severe kind of competition is encountered. In a national market, with its established devices to favor domestic or national trade over international trade, as presented in Chapters 13 through 15, the national market is isolated, to a greater or lesser extent, from international competition. Take the United States market, for example. Competition in practically every line of business is intense, but it is essentially among United States producers. A foreign business firm that seeks to market its textiles, electronic appliances, foodstuffs, automobiles or any other product in the United States market usually has import obstacles to surmount—import duties, quotas or any of a bewildering array of restrictions. However, the point is that having surmounted such restrictions, the foreign firm must then contend with established, rigorous, domestic competition.

Similarly, an American producer seeking to export products to a foreign country must overcome comparable import restrictions. Moreover—and this is important—he will likely encounter domestic competition, along with competition from exporters of many other countries, including his own. Thus, in international competition, a business enterprise striving to sell in foreign markets faces this threefold competition which is even more ruthless than domestic competition only.

MEETING INTERNATIONAL COMPETITION

The subject of meeting international competition will be considered under several headings with some illustrations to provide emphasis and reality. These headings are:

1. Product
2. Price
3. Terms
4. Organization
5. Promotion—Government
6. Promotion—Private

Product

Emerson observed that if a man could make a better mousetrap, the world would beat a path to his door. In other words, if a product is superior, there will be no difficulty selling it anywhere in the world. However, it is fairly well established that few, if any, products offer such superiority, although inventions do provide superiority for a time. Consider such well-known products as aspirin, penicillin, harvesting machinery, record players, electric light bulbs—indeed almost any product; at one time, some person or company had a complete monopoly in the production of these items. But this monopoly did not last long—it was lost because someone "built a better mousetrap," or because the secrets involved were released for the use of others to improve these products, or because they, as in the case of aspirin, fell victim to identification as a generic term and the monopoly ceased.

Can the reader name a single product that is the complete monopoly of a person or business firm? There are probably some chemical compounds and drugs that are monopolistic at the moment, but such products are either of no great significance or some competitor is successfully "building a better mousetrap." Even in atomic energy, a widely known subject, monopolies appear here and there as improvements and applications are made but they are short-lived. Space travel offers the best opportunity for a monopoly with only a few competitors—national governments—in the field. But even here, when the Americans or Soviets awe the world with a space accomplishment, either country soon follows with a feat equally astonishing.

Finally a novelty may enjoy a monopoly momentarily, but history has shown that novelties do not last; and if they do, they do not remain novelties.

Consequently, a monopoly that permits a producer to require the world to come to him simply does not exist. Of course, we could cite gem diamonds that come closer to monopoly than any other product. But even here, it is really not the gem diamonds that provide the monopoly but the skillful production and marketing program of the de Beers' interests, which holds this precious diamond at a high price and, in turn, is supported by deeply established sentimental concepts.

In discussing international competition we must recognize that we are considering the availability of a product from any place in the world. Otherwise, one could say that an automobile company would have a complete monopoly in the Congo where no automobiles are manufactured; but automobiles are manufactured and exported by many companies in a number of countries and all of them would offer to sell automobiles in the Congo. Moreover, a textile manufacturer may have a monopoly because imports of textiles are forbidden by government decree. This is an artificial monopoly that would immediately be destroyed if competition were permitted.

The conclusion to which we are forced is, therefore, that products that sell in international markets are competitive, and it is because of superiority of quality or because of sales promotion or financing that each competitor can share in the market.

Did you ever ride a motorcycle? This noisy vehicle, capable of great speed, had become in the United States a mark of the police and of the leather-jacketed young sports enthusiasts. Up until the late 1950's, this business was stagnating in the United States and production was not even keeping up with the increase in population. But now, imports, chiefly from Honda in Japan, have caused a revival of the American industry while imports have not stopped growing. A new wheeled vehicle called the scooter has been introduced, and the imported product is now promoted and sold as a "second car" rather than supplied to police departments and young sports enthusiasts. An increasing number of American families that can afford a second car are buying a scooter or a motorcycle for the run to the store or shopping center.[1] As further evidence of this startling development, it is reported that a grandmother mounts her Harley-Davidson in Detroit and drives to Florida to see her grandchildren; an Episcopalian clergyman in Westchester County, New York, visits his parishioners on a Lambretta motor scooter; a state representative in Connecticut attends sessions of the legislature by traveling on his motorcycle; Mrs. Chet Huntley drives to the supermarket on her lightweight motorcycle; a film producer in New York drives to the studio on his heavyweight cycle; and, in Beverly Hills, California, Dean Martin and his wife drive the Freeway on their motorcycle. The leading seller in the United States is Honda (Japanese), while the biggest United States producer is Harley-Davidson, of Milwaukee. Other strong competitors are Yamaha and Suzuki of Japan, BSA and Triumph and Associated Motors of England, and BMW of Germany.[2]

This is a fascinating example of a foreign product entering a market that, at one time, produced and exported a large number of motorcycles, but that had evidently been satisfied to accept a specialized (and not altogether complimentary) and shrinking market.

Consider also automatic bowling equipment. The American companies (Brunswick Corporation and American Machine and Foundry—AMF) revived an indoor sport by developing automatic pinspotting machines and designing flashy bowling alleys. The reader is fully aware of the appeal of the modern bowling alley as a sports and social center. These companies have disproved the old concept that when doing business abroad local traditions must be scrupulously observed. Starting to export as recently as 1960, these companies have installed equipment in thousands of alleys in Europe, Asia, and Australia. Their skillfully devised advertising program has not only created interest in bowling abroad but has succeeded in bringing women into the bowling alley in countries where women have traditionally stayed at home.[3]

This is an example of a product that is not monopolistic but rather brand new, and by reason of technical excellence and good merchandising, an export market has been successfully established.

---

[1] *Journal of Commerce,* July 2, 1965.
[2] *New York Times,* August 22, 1965, Business and Financial Section, pp. 1 and 3.
[3] *Journal of Commerce,* May 10, 1962.

While the motorcycle, scooter, and bowling equipment represent a new approach to an old market and an opening of a new market respectively, other products are able to deal with competition successfully by means of style or even preeminence. We know that French haute couture is admired and imitated the world over; that champagne is considered the epitome of gourmet wines; that a gem diamond is cherished for bespeaking tender thoughts; that Wedgewood is a unique porcelainware distinguished for its exquisite cameo relief; that an Oriental rug is synonymous with luxury and elegance; and so on. These are products that have established a worldwide reputation for excellence; they do not yield to change in attitude and taste; they are classic in that they are treasured from generation to generation. These and others like them maintain a continuous world market with no change and with little, if any, fanfare. A company, a province or a country that offers such products to the world market is fortunate indeed because it has achieved a reputation for superiority that is not affected by time. These products possess no monopoly and yet they do in that there is no substitute for a Paris gown, champagne, Wedgewood, and Oriental rugs.

Less-renowned products have succeeded in international competition by means of originality or status. United States chinaware is being exported to Japan (which is tantamount to carrying coals to Newcastle); however, it is distinctive and appeals to the Japanese. United States wallpaper manufacturers are expanding their exports in the face of strong competition from a host of long-established foreign producers. They stress quality and original design, including some brand new ideas of materials to be used for wall covering.[4] United States pretzel-baking machines have been exported to Japan, introducing an entirely new food novelty into that market. Vending machines have achieved a prestige reputation all over the world. This is an American triumph; when stocked with American-labeled foods and other merchandise, they have advanced the exportation of such products, as foreign customers have come to appreciate the reliability of the machines and of the products that they dispense. This is now a $100 million export business for the United States.[5] Another product—hi-fi equipment—is now recognized as a status symbol.[6]

---

[4] *Ibid.*, March 4, 1965.
[5] *Ibid.*, June 2, 1964.
[6] *Ibid.*, April 15, 1964.

Merchandise is not alone in the international competitive scene; services are also capable of engaging in international competition. Hostelry is one of the oldest services known to man, dating back thousands of years. Today United States hotel chains build and operate hotels all over the world. The reader will wonder why this is so, since hotels have been in operation for thousands of years. What have American hotel chains to offer that is not already available in foreign countries? The answer is that they have know-how—the techniques and skills to build and operate hotels profitably. The governments of many countries, chiefly in the developing areas of the world, approach American hotel chains with propositions aimed at inducing them to build and operate in their countries as a means of attracting tourist trade. As recently as mid-1965, the countries negotiating with United States hotel chains included Egypt, Tanzania, Kenya, Ethiopa, Libya, Malaysia, the Philippine Republic, Kuwait, Corsica, Sardinia, Malta, and several South and Central American countries.[7]

Thus, a product or service may be of such nature as to command a market, or it can be of such design or technique as to meet international competition successfully.

Price

Price is always a factor in international competition, although price without consideration of quality is meaningless. A gem diamond sells because it is high in price; if it were not, it would lose its symbolic appeal to the market that it enjoys.

Price is a product factor in the comparative advantage principles explained in Chapter 3, 4, and 5. If the factors of production required for a given product or service are such as to permit output at a price lower than that of any other country, this product or service will be competitive in world markets. The numerous staples that comprise a sizable portion of international trade move because of price. Countries that import wheat, cotton, coffee, sugar, rubber, and many other staples cannot produce these products as cheaply as the exporting countries can—and some importing countries cannot produce them at anything like a profitable price. Some of these products are sold on organized commodity exchanges where prices are set by means of grades and competitive bidding. These prices represent what may be called a world price arrived at by bidding of commodity traders as opposed to being "administered" by a business firm.

---

[7] *Ibid.*, June 25, 1965.

This is not true of manufactured and semimanufactured merchandise where the price is established by the business firm. Price quotations were discussed in Chapter 27; however, the price of a product is determined by its supply-demand ratio, with the aggregate costs of factors of production acting as a floor. Thus, the price of an automobile produced in the United States is less than the price of an equivalent automobile in Brazil. This is because raw materials, capital, and business enterprise cost less (or use is greater by reason of mass production dependent on a mass market) than in Brazil. Products that can be best produced with a large labor input tend to be cheapest where the cost of labor is comparatively low, unless low wages are neutralized by low productivity. On the other hand, products that can be best produced with large inputs of capital and enterprise are cheapest in countries where the costs of these inputs are comparatively low, a situation usually found in the industrial countries.

The costs of production factors are constantly changing, as labor costs advance or retrogress, raw material prices increase or decrease, capital becomes more or less expensive, and land shifts in price. It is because of these fluctuations that industries are forced to close or to move to areas where cost factors are more favorable. This is one of the basic reasons for manufacturing abroad or even manufacturing in other areas of the domestic country. Such shifts in manufacturing location are induced by changes in cost factors of production—as well as by shifts in market demand. Whether such changes are effected by social or political legislation is of no importance; the very fact that the cost factors have shifted is sufficient.

This discussion serves to emphasize that prices must cover the costs incurred in production in the long run. Much publicity is given to exorbitant profits that are earned by companies or by industries that charge high prices for their products or services. Competition serves to prevent just such occurrences but an occasional monopolistic position may permit them. Prices, therefore, are related to costs; and competitive strength is dependent on cost positions. The fact that international trade embraces over one hundred countries indicates that every one of these countries has something that it can sell in foreign markets at a price lower than, or equal to, that of any competitor.

A firm engaging in international trade may quote prices that are the same as those charged in domestic trade, lower than these prices or, even in some instances, higher. The usual practice is to charge the domestic price to which, of course, must be added the additional costs

Ch. 29 / Meeting International Competition   **615**

incurred in international sales as described in export and import price quotations discussed in Chapter 27. Sometimes, the export price is lower than the domestic price in an effort to stimulate sales and to meet or eliminate competition. Selling abroad at lower-than-domestic prices is technically known as dumping which some countries, including the United States, penalize. Most countries, however, impose no obstacles to dumping. Only in times of shortage, usually, are prices higher for export than for domestic consumption.

Since the United States is the world's leading exporting and importing nation, it is evident that producers in the United States are able to quote prices attractive enough to maintain this country's leadership. It is also evident that other nations offer products at prices attractive to United States importers, and because of the magnitude of the American market, the volume is so great that it makes this country the world's leading importer also.

Another aspect of pricing to meet international competition is the currency in which prices are quoted. As explained in Chapter 27, the currencies of only a very few countries are actually used in international price quotations. Chief of these are the United States dollar and British pounds sterling. The currencies of most of the other countries of the world are not used—not because they are unreliable but because they do not represent a great volume of trade as is true of the dollar and pounds sterling. Therefore, when a foreign customer asks for a quotation in his own currency, rather than United States dollars and pounds sterling, the exporter is inclined to be dubious. Granted that an importer would greatly prefer to pay in his own currency, as this would not involve a foreign exchange transaction for him, an exporter would be taking a great risk if there were no active foreign exchange market for this local currency.

Nevertheless, it is true that quoting in the currency of the importer is an effective means of competing in international trade; and if the risks are not excessive, the exporter may try this method of competition. One exporter who had been serving a certain foreign firm for several decades was asked by that firm to quote the price for the next order in the currency of its country. All previous business had been quoted in United States dollars and pounds sterling, but the country was running short of both of these world currencies and because of the long history of business relations, the foreign company confidently asked for this favor. After considerable soul-searching, the exporter reluctantly declined to quote in the currency of the foreign country and the order was not forthcoming. As later events revealed, the exporter was wise from a financial standpoint because the currency of that country depreciated rapidly.

Terms

The subject of *terms of sale* is introduced as a factor influencing international competition and, in some situations, terms may be more attractive than price. As explained in Chapter 27, credit is extensively granted in export sales of manufactured goods. Credit is not granted in the private sale of staples; that is a cash transaction. Credit means "terms" and an indeterminate portion of international trade is sold on a basis of terms rather than price alone. If a customer is presently low in financial resources and must purchase stocks of merchandise to recoup his financial standing, he will pay a higher price for terms of six months to avoid sight or thirty days sight payment. The reason is obvious: he has no cash; although if he enjoys good financial standing, he could obtain a loan from his bank. However, the interest on the loan may be such that a quotation at six months is a better proposition. He clearly expects within six months to dispose of his stock of merchandise and make a profit.

Aside from such normal reasons for using credit in lieu of a lower price, there are conditions under which sales can be made only on credit. These conditions arise when foreign exchange and balance of payments problems occur in the foreign market. As explained in Chapter 8, foreign exchange rates may fluctuate and if, at the time shipment is received, the exchange rate is high, the customer is obliged to pay a high rate of exchange in order to cover. Thus, he confidently hopes that if credit is granted, the exchange rate will be more favorable when payment is due.

Balance of payment problems likewise may cause strains on the ability of customers located in such countries to obtain foreign exchange. Restrictions on payments for imports are imposed and no sales may be made at all. However, it is also possible that the balance of payments problem is of relatively short duration, and imports may be permitted if payment can be deferred to a later date when it is anticipated that the problems will have been corrected.

Traditionally, United States exporters have been loathe to compete abroad on a basis of credit; they prefer to compete on the bases of price and service as well as product. However, exporters of some countries, chiefly in Europe, have often used credit as a sales-promotion device and, as mentioned previously, such terms may be used to obtain orders.

The subject of terms will be considered again under government promotion of foreign trade.

Organization

One of the factors influencing international competition is the organization of a business enterprise. Apart from the determination exercised by the management of a firm, the kind of organization used for participating in international trade is an important factor.

As explained in Chapter 25, various types of export departments reveal the magnitude of the international business venture. The built-in department yields to the separate export department which in turn surrenders to the international trading subsidiary. Some firms have gone one step further by organizing on a global or multinational basis. This type of organization speaks eloquently of the business venture because it has obliterated a long-standing distinction between domestic and international trade. The entire organization is geared to the requirements of the world market, including the domestic.

Whether or not a global enterprise, many business firms have established foreign branches for sales or purchase, storage, assembly, or manufacturing. As explained in Chapter 26, such foreign operations have been prompted by competitive conditions and unless such steps were taken, the firm, no doubt, would have lost out in international competition. Proof of this statement is the fact that foreign factories affiliated with American companies now produce twice as much as the annual value of exports from the United States. No one would maintain that had these factories not been established, the export trade of the United States would be three times its present value; practically all this production is for the local foreign market and only a small portion for export. It is useless to argue that this production would have been replaced by exports from this country because, as pointed out in Chapter 26, the problem was one of survival—either establish the facilities in the foreign market or lose out entirely.

Another method of organization intended to aid United States exporters in international competition is the Webb-Pomerene Act of 1918 which permits competing United States companies to combine for the purpose of export trade. Without this law, such operations would violate the antitrust laws. Great results were anticipated for American export trade under the authority of this Act but such has not been the case. The number of organizations has remained almost constant at thirty to forty. The reason for this lack of growth is that manufacturers of competing products sold on a trademark or quality basis lose their identity under such an arrangement. Therefore, the kinds of merchandise represented in the organizations formed under this law are chiefly metals and metal products, followed by products of mines and wells, lumber and wood products, and foodstuffs. The value of business in any one of these lines conducted through the agency of a Webb-Pomerene association is very small. The law is, nevertheless, an effort to increase the competitive standing of United States business firms in world markets.

Promotion—Government

The treatment of government promotion in Chapter 24 had to do with the kinds of information published by and available from government and international agencies for foreign market research purposes. As stated in that chapter, governments promote export trade as a means of stimulating employment and earning foreign exchange. The information provided and the services performed are designed to increase the competitive strength of their exporters.

Through embassies, legations, and consulates that governments maintain in other countries, personal representation establishes a good image and promotes trade and investments. Some of these representatives, as well as others in the agricultural and mineral fields, study the basic economic conditions of the country, contact national business and political interests, discover opportunities for trade, provide lists of possible customers with information on their standing, and recommend the consideration and selection of foreign firms and agencies. They furnish introductions for businessmen from their country and thereby make their foreign business trips more effective.

Apart from these efforts to promote trade and investment, many foreign government representatives also seek to protect the rights of their nationals. These rights are spelled out in treaties and agreements and provide the legal basis without which trade could not be conducted. In addition, they provide the conditions which are paramount in any effort to compete internationally. Such rights as those pertaining to property, residence, movement, etc. also have a direct bearing on the ability of a business firm to compete at all, and are directly based on international law and agreements that are enforced through the cooperation of the foreign country. Earlier in the present century, the strong industrial nations often took such matters into their own hands by means of unilateral action including armed intervention.

Government representatives stationed in foreign countries are on the front line of international competition, devoting their entire efforts to the protection and promotion of the welfare of their nationals and their business and financial interests. Consequently, no country has any particular advantage because every nation has similar goals in all countries where they maintain representation.

National governments seek in other ways to promote their export trade. One of these is to dispatch trade missions to foreign countries where trade and investment opportunities are investigated and promoted. Another way is to maintain trade shows, either floating, temporary or permanent, in foreign countries whereby sample displays of merchandise available for export are exhibited. Facilities for taking orders are usually provided. Such efforts are exerted particularly by the governments of the developed countries whose exports consist of a wide variety of manufactured goods.

Terms of sale were discussed as a means of meeting international competition. Here again the governments of the industrial countries provide the means for exporters to extend long-term credits. These are found in two different types of exports:

> 1. Exporting of primary products by developed nations may be financed by government subsidy or by long-term credits. The United States and Canada, for example, sell enormous quantities of wheat on long-term credits. These are intergovernmental transactions, although private business firms may be called upon to carry out the sale.
>
> 2. The other type of trade for which long-term credit is available from governments is capital goods where credits up to several years are extended. The same is true of construction projects abroad. It is patent that such business as here mentioned would not exist if governments did not provide the necessary financing.

Another type of governmental assistance, foreign credit insurance, that helps exporters to compete more effectively was discussed in Chapter 27. With such backing, exporters are free to extend credit where they may otherwise hesitate or refuse. This activity is conducted by developed countries: the United Kingdom started in 1926; while the United States did not grant foreign credit insurance until 1954, when the Export-Import Bank guaranteed credits up to 60 percent of certain transactions. Export credit insurance for all types of transactions was not issued in this country until 1962.[8]

---

[8] See Chapter 27.

Promotion—Private

Marketing promotion by private business firms is also used to compete in international trade. This differs from the preceding subject in that it is individual promotion by the business firm for its own profit rather than government promotion on behalf of the aggregate exporters of the country. This is the heart of American business philosophy and is one key to the secret of the gigantic American domestic market. The enormous expanse of the domestic market has been made possible in high degree by a policy of advertising, merchandising, and selling for profit.

In Chapter 28 the subject of advertising agencies was treated as one of the supporting agencies for the conduct of international business. While such agencies develop and execute promotion programs for business firms, it is the business firms that take the initiative and provide the funds. Promotion of business does not stop at the water's edge; it is extended to foreign markets, and many of the techniques that business firms use at home are applied abroad.

Let us consider the promotion of automobiles in international trade. United States automobile companies have been marketing their products abroad for many decades. They ship complete cars, trucks and buses; chassis only; disassembled vehicles—and they also manufacture abroad. Their foreign sales promotion has followed the domestic pattern of advertising, display, and financing. They are considered among the strongest of American industries, and they dominate the domestic market and many foreign markets as well.

In view of this situation, what is a newcomer in the automobile business to do? The very thought of competing in this field is frightening.

Not many years ago the European small car began to appear in the United States market. Known as a compact car, it rapidly gained a share, although small, of the United States market. American manufacturers presumably considered this competition to be transitory in the belief that American buyers preferred large and powerful cars. When they realized that the compact car was making headway in the United States market, they produced their own version of such a car. Imports immediately declined and some foreign manufacturing exporters withdrew from the American market. But one foreign manufacturer—Volkswagen—unlike other foreign producers, realized from the beginning that entering the American market meant operating precisely as American companies operate, that is, by means of distributors, dealers, and service facilities. In recent years, this company has strengthened its marketing system by inducing its distributors to sell its automobile line alone, rather than handling a number of imported company car lines. Distributors had been forced into this type of operation because the volume of sales of one particular line was not sufficient to justify the expense of their operation. Now, Volkswagen distributors handle that line only and supplement it with noncompetitive consumer durables. Thus, this German manufacturer has established a position in the United States market by an improved marketing system.

Also in response to competition of the compact car and before United States manufacturers had produced their own versions, the Rambler made its appearance in the American market. This is produced by American Motors and, like the other American manufacturers, the company decided to enter foreign markets. This was viewed in the trade as folly because it was thought that the American compact was too big for the foreign compact market where only standard American automobiles have been sold for many decades. Despite these forebodings, the company proceeded on the basis of assembly facilities on a joint venture plan. The president of the company announced that the company believed "that to be partners rather than bosses in foreign lands is not only the best practical way to operate but the best moral way to operate as well." [9] As a result, the company's export market has grown from 9,000 cars in 1958 to 60,000 in 1963.

The principal American petroleum companies have been all over the world for many years. What chances would a newcomer have in this field where another strong segment of American business was already established? Take Phillips Petroleum Company as an example. The founder of the company—Frank Phillips—had laid down the dictum that the company would always be a domestic company. Not until 1959, did the company enter international markets. It tried licensing foreign companies to produce carbon black, but the market did not expand. In 1960 the company began to improve its position by buying into foreign companies, and in 1965 by buying out foreign companies. Its promotion has been vastly improved and the company is now in international business.[10]

Now let us look at two consumer products that sales promotion has established in the foreign market. One of these is Scotchbrite

---

[9] *Journal of Commerce,* July 3, 1964.
[10] *Forbes,* February 1, 1965.

Scouring Pads produced by MMM (Minnesota Mining and Manufacturing Company). The company first tried two different packages in which to sell its product and since both packages were successful, both were used. On both packages was depicted the pad in use, which proved a good sales promotion idea. MMM also designed a package that was difficult to stack and thus did not get mixed up with competitive products. The company also distributed sample cards telling the story of Scotchbrite and offered free samples to manufacturers of pots, pans, and stoves.

A classical example of a sales promotion campaign conducted by another well-known American company is that of the Procter and Gamble Company in Germany. As digested from *German-American Trade News* of May, 1965, this is the story:

In 1963, Procter and Gamble "jumped with both feet into a large, flourishing, and tradition-bound market" for soaps and detergents. *DASH* was introduced with "an assortment of techniques and gimmicks that are standard for detergent sales in the United States—sophisticated sales and distribution methods, trial samples, repetitive and motivation-oriented advertising spots replete with bright, hard-to-forget jingles." Henkel's *PERSIL,* which enjoyed 30 percent of the all-purpose detergent market until 1963, dropped to 20 percent by the end of 1964. Sunlicht's *OMO* dropped to 18 percent and *DASH* had risen to 15 percent in less than two years.

Each company offers discounts and rebates to the shopkeeper, making preferential stocking more attractive. Henkel gives special discounts upon the close of a sale that range from $16 for 400 cartons to over $60 for 1,200 cartons. Henkel also sends out a 4 percent rebate at the end of the year for sales over $7,500 as well as a "Christmas check" of 4 to 7 percent. Sunlicht has a discount of $2\frac{1}{2}$ percent for sales of $3,750 and a rebate by agreement for sales over $5,000. Procter and Gamble gives no cash rebate but offers one free package with every fifty ordered. Size of package is different for all competitors, and the housewife cannot make price comparisons. Package design, display, and familiarity of advertising jingle are paramount in promotion.

CONCLUSION

Competition in international trade is most severe because it involves both domestic and foreign competitors, while national markets are partially insulated from foreign competition. Therefore, a business firm that seeks entrance to international markets must have a distinctive product, an attractive price and/or terms, effective organization, and adequate promotion—in the latter deriving some assistance from its own government. The United States government, for example, is interested in aiding American exporters in competition with exporters of every other country. This is not a factor in domestic trade.

It is for the reasons considered in this chapter that a business firm entering international competition must be resolute in this endeavor. This was emphasized in Chapter 23 in the discussion of the need for executive backing. While there are business firms that initially engage in international competition on a hit-or-miss basis, this is no way to establish a permanent position in international business. International trade, therefore, is a serious undertaking and is best conducted along lines tried and proved in the fires of experience, reinforced by a daring to seize new opportunities in a rapidly changing world economy.

SUMMARY

1. International trade takes place in a widespread, ruthless, competitive environment.
2. The nature of international competition has undergone many changes since the close of World War II. The map of the world is drastically changed, with the Communist area separated from the Free World. Colonial empires have toppled and numerous politically independent nations have replaced them. Economic integration of nations is occurring, thus causing changes of a unique character in the international competitive scene. Technology has reached great levels in this scientific age and the end is not in sight. A new dynamism has ignited international competition causing this competition to be even more severe.
3. Since very few, if any, products possess an element of monopoly, the competitive position of a product is expressed essentially in terms of quality, style, and status.
4. Prices of staples that move in international trade are essentially world prices.
5. Producers set the prices of manufactured and semimanufactured products which are restrained by international competition. Generally speaking, export prices are the same as domestic, plus, of course, expenses incurred in reaching foreign markets. Occasionally, prices lower and sometimes higher than domestic prices are quoted.
6. Quoting prices in foreign currencies involves risks on the part of exporters. Very few currencies are actually used for international price quotations.
7. Terms may be of greater competitive advantage in international competition than price.

8. The organization of a company has a great bearing on its position in international competition. The highest development in organization is the global or multinational company where no distinction is made between domestic and international sales.
9. Governments of the developed nations actively promote their export trade by compiling trade information, lists of possible customers, reports on the standing of these customers, dispatching trade missions, and maintaining trade fairs and displays. All this is in addition to the normal government function of providing the proper environment for the conduct of international trade.
10. Export financing and credit guarantees are provided through government facilities of some countries.
11. Business firms with cogent and attractive promotion can meet international competition, despite severe obstacles.

QUESTIONS AND APPLICATIONS

1. Why is competition so severe in international trade?
2. Cite examples of products that have succeeded in meeting international competition.
3. Cite examples of services that have succeeded in meeting international competition.
4. How are the prices of staples that move in international trade determined?
5. Why would an exporter quote to a foreign customer a price lower than the domestic price of a given product?
6. Why would an exporter hesitate to quote a price in a foreign currency?
7. How may terms be more attractive than price to foreign customers?
8. Explain why the organization of a company is important as a factor influencing its position in international competition.
9. In what specific ways do the governments of developed countries promote export trade?
10. Cite examples of companies that have obtained prestige in international trade by sales promotion.

INDEX

A

Absolute quota, 256
"Adjustable peg" system of adjustment of balance of payments disequilibrium, 213; gold-exchange standard as an, 505
Adjustment assistance provision in Trade Expansion Act of 1962, 393, 394; to injured firm, 394; to workers, 394
Administrative protection, 268
Administrative restrictions, 387
Ad valorem duty, defined, 249; rates on U. S. imports, 389
Advertising, defined in agency and distributor contracts, 550
Africa, status in EEC, 412
Agencies, international trading, in foreign market, 545; in the home market, 542
Agency and distributor contracts, advertising obligations, 550; approval of order, 549; compensation, 550; direct and indirect sales, 549; duration of, 549; price change, 549; quotas, 549; service clause, 550; subagents and subdistributors, 548; terms of, 548; territory granted, 548; trademarks, 550
Agency for International Development, 447, 474
Agency, supporting, 517
Agent, 547; del credere, 547; exclusive, 548; general, 548; semiexclusive, 548
Agricultural Adjustment Act of 1933, 336, 384
Agricultural operations, 567
Agricultural Trade Development and Assistance Act, 448
Alliance for Progress, 447
Allied company, 540
Allocated quota, 256
Allocation, effects of a customs union, 412; of markets, by cartels, 319; of foreign exchange, 266
Alternative duty, 266; defined, 250
American Arbitration Association, 595
American Foreign Trade Definitions, Revised, 578
American selling price, as basis for customs valuation, 388
American Tariff League, 284
Amtorg Trading Corporation, 543
Antidumping Act, 418
Antidumping duty, 268
Antitrust provisions and policy in the EEC, 406; effectiveness of, 406
Approval of order, 549
Arbitrage, bilateral, 166; exchange, 166; interest, 172, 487; multilateral, 166; trilateral, 166
Arrival bill of exchange, 583
Association, as a form of cartel, 318
Association Convention of the EEC, 412
Atlantic Alliance, 419
Autarky, as an objective of international economic policy, 238
Automatic transferability agreements, defined, 291
Autonomous customs duty, 251
Autonomous items, defined, 177; in the U. S. balance of payments, 481, 484
Availability, as a determinant of trade, 115

B

Balance of payments, and quotas, 285, 347; as influenced by foreign exchange rates, 158, 213; commercial policy in the, 236; compilation of the, 136; concept of residence principle of the, 136; current and capital transactions principle of the, 138; deficit as a basis for Kennedy Round, 415; effect of changes in gross national income and product on, 197; effect of elasticities of supply and demand on, 221, 223; effect of exchange depreciation on, 218, 224, 228; effects of foreign investment on, 459, 470; equilibrium as an objective of international economic policy, 239; financial policy in the, 236; financial transfers, effect of, on, 456; foreign aid policy in the, 237; importance of the, 135; import duties, effect on equilibrium in, 282; international capital movements, 111, 139, 190; international transactions as debits and credits principle of the, 137; Marshall-Lerner condition effect on, 225; of the U. S., 141; projection of the developing nations, 435; transfer problems in the, 456, 489; why it balances, 148; *see also* Disequilibrium of the balance of payments *and* United States Balance of payments
Balance of Payments Yearbook, 533
Bank acceptance, 585
Bank bill, defined, 121
Bank for International Settlements, 364
Banks, government and international, 587; role in international trade, 586
Barcelona Statute on Freedom of Transit, 249
Bargaining and retaliation, as an argument for protection, 307
Basic deficit in U. S. balance of payments, 486
Basic transactions concept, 481; use of, by U. S. Department of Commerce, 482
Bilateral arbitrage, defined, 166
Bilateral offset agreements, defined, 291
Bilateral payments agreements, as an effect of exchange control, 290
Bilateral quota, 257
Bilateral swap agreements, 497; as a means of strengthening gold-exchange standard, 503
Bilateralism and inconvertibility, as effects of exchange control, 290
Bill of exchange, 582; accepted, 582; banker's, 124; clean, 122; date, 582; defined, 121; discounted, 582; documentary, 122; drawee of, 121; drawer of, 121; fluctuating rate of exchange, effect on, 214; parties to, 121; payee of, 121; sight, 582
Bill of lading, 596; ocean, 586
Bloomfield, Arthur J., 191
Board of Trade Journal, 531
Bonded warehouse, defined, 254
Bounties, 267
Branch office, 553
Bretton Woods Agreement, 505
British Exchange Equilization Account, as a stabilization agency, 162, 261
Built-in export department, 541
Bulletin of Agricultural Economics and Statistics, 533
Bureau of Mines, U. S. Department of the Interior, 592
Bureau of the Census, 530
Business associations, in the U. S. and abroad, 534
Business enterprise, in foreign manufacturing, 555; in home manufacturing, 556; for international competition, 617
Business Periodicals Index, 536
Businessman's Guide to Sources of Foreign Information, A, 532
"Buy-American" Act, 418; regulations, 386
Buyers, from abroad, 542

C

Capital, and profits, repatriation of, 565; **as a** factor supply of production, 100; basic transactions concept between short-term and long-term, 481; deficit in U. S. balance of payments as a consequence of long-term capital exports, 489; effect of technology on, 104, 106; export, 140, 456; flows, induced by interest arbitrage, 172; formation, in developing nations, 429, 430, 434; import, 140, 456; in foreign manufacturing,

625

555; in home manufacturing, 555; inflow, defined, 139; lack of social overhead capital in developing nations, 431, 476; liquidity concept in, 481; long-term capital flow to developing nations, 442, 447, 456, 476; measures to restrain U. S. private exports of, 494; mobility of, 60; net, 466; net outflow, and investment income, 466; outflow, defined, 139; risks, 599; short-term outflow of, as cause of U. S. balance of payments deficit, 485, 487; transactions, defined, 138; transfer of, 456
Capital flight, 170, 184, 214; and exchange speculation, 168; as a cause of exchange control, 263; effect on, IMF, 360; U. S. monetary authority measures to prevent, 498
Capital movements, 111, 486; international, 139; long-term (net), as entry of the U. S. balance of trade, 145; short-term, importance of, 190; short-term (net), as entry of the U. S. balance of trade, 145; U. S. monetary authority action to prevent, 497
Cartel, as a type of imperfect competition, 79; deferred, 317; *see also* International cartel
Cartel policy, in the EEC, 406; of other countries, 326; of the U. S., 325
Cash, in international trade, 581
Cassel, Gustav, 216
Center of interest, 136
Central American Common Market, 248, 368
Chamber of Commerce, of the U. S., 534
"Chicken war," 350
Clean bill, 122
Closed economy, 57, 195
Code law, as opposed to common law, 594
Code of Liberalization, 365
Combination export-management firm, 540
Combine, 318
Commercial agencies, 539
Commerical banks, role in transfer of international payments, 124
Commercial policy of the U. S., 373; an appraisal of, 394; basic economic policies of the, 374; comparison of objectives of Reciprocal Trade Agreements Act and Trade Expansion Act in the, 395; objectives under Trade Expansion Act of 1962, 395; Reciprocal Trade Agreements Act of 1934, effect on, 335, 378; Trade Expansion Act of 1962, 391
Commission houses, export and import, 544
Commission of the EEC, 400, 405, 409; administration of antitrust policy by the, 406; efforts by the, to achieve integration in social policy, 408
Commissions, government buying, 542
Commodity Credit Corporation, 159
Commodity, sources of information for analysis of, 535
Commodity terms of trade, 64; defined, 65; effects of exchange depreciation on, 228; effects of export duties on, 284; effects of import duties on, 281
Commodity Trade Statistics, 532
Common law, as opposed to code law, 594
Commonalities, as factor endowments, 97
Communications, as a function of the foreign exchange market, 123; as a supporting agency in international trade, 600
Company, allied, 540; organization of, for international trade, 540
Comparative cost advantage, 49
Comparative cost disadvantage, 49
Comparative costs theory, 47; absolute international differences in costs, 48; absolute international differences in prices, 47; dissimilar cost ratios, 49; dissimilar factor demand ratios, 55; dissimilar factor price ratios, 52; dissimilar factor supply ratios, 54; effect of capital movements on, 111; effect of decreasing costs on the, 77; effect of imperfect competition on, 78; effect of increasing costs on the, 75; effect of location on, 89; effect of many countries and many goods on the, 67; effect of service trades on, 111; effect of three countries and two commodities on the, 67; effect of Trade Expansion Act of 1962 on, 396; effect of transportation costs on the, 92, 111; effect of two countries and several commodities on the, 68; effect of unemployment on, 107; exchange control as a factor in, 293; factor endowments in, 95; identical cost ratios, 51; import duties, effect of, on, 281; international mobility of factors relation to, 58; measured by actual trade patterns, 115; recapitulation of, 112; technology, implications of, in, 102
Compendium of Social Statistics, 532
Compensation, in agency and distributor contracts, 550
Compensatory duty, defined, 250; use of drawback in lieu of, 253
Compensatory financing, 189; as an aid to correct a deficit disequilibrium, 180, 505; role of IMF in, 191, 354, 356; sources of, 190; to offset deteriorating terms of trade, 446
Compensatory items, defined, 177; in the U. S. balance of payments, 481, 487
Competition, as a factor in foreign market surveys, 526; as a reason for credit extension, 616, 619; effect of cartels on, 324; elimination of external, as an objective of cartels, 321; imperfect, 78; in EEC vs. U. S. firms, 407; monopolistic, defined, 79; nonprice, 79, 82; pure, defined, 48; *see also* International competition
Competitive depreciation, 217
Compound duty, defined, 250
Confirmed letter of credit, 584
Constructed value, as a basis for customs valuation, 388
Containers, used in international transportation, 598
Contractors, 543
Conventional customs duty, 252
Cost, opportunity, 49; real, 49
Cost ratios, comparative advantage, 49; comparative disadvantage, 49; dissimilar, 49; identical, 51
Costs, absolute international differences in, equalization of production, as an argument for protection, 312; increasing, 73; opportunity, 49; physical transfer, 84; real, 49; 48; constant, 74; decreasing, 77; effects of decreasing, on international trade, 77; effects of increasing on international trade, 75; theory of comparative, 47, 396; transportation and other transfer, 84
Costs and Competition: American Experience Abroad, 556
Council of Ministers of the EEC, 400, 402; Christmas eve and other marathons of the, 402; efforts by the, to achieve a common fiscal and monetary policy, 405; negotiations for common agricultural policy in the, 401; progress toward economic union by, 405
Countervailing duty, 267
Country, analysis of, as factor in foreign market survey, 524; commercial policy of, as factor in foreign market survey, 525; infrastructure of, as factor in foreign market survey, 524; marketing structure of, as factor in foreign market survey, 525
Court of Justice of the EEC, 401
Credit balance of trade, 142
Credit, in international trade, 576, 616, 619; sources of, 579; terms and prices, 515
Credit insurance, export, 492
Credit transactions, international, 137
Crisis of 1931, international financial, 260
Cross-rate, 168
Currency, inconvertibility, 13; used in international price quotations, 615
Current transactions, defined, 138
Customs Administration, 387
Customs area, 248
Customs duty, ad valorem, 249; alternative, 250; autonomous, 251; compound, 249; conventional, 252; export, 249; import, 249;

Index

kinds of, 249; scope of, 249; specific, 250; transit, 249
Customs house brokers used in international trade, 596
Customs Simplifications Acts, 387
Customs union, 248 allocation effects of, 412; as an objective of the EEC, 399, 401; effects of on trade, 411; growth effects of, 412
Customs valuation, basis of, 387

D

Date bill of exchange, 582
Debit transactions, international, 137
Debt service burden of the developing nations, 450
Decision making, 511; other decisions, 515
Defense essentiality amendment, to the Reciprocal Trade Agreements Act, 301, 380, 383
Defense Production Act of 1950, 385
Deficit and surplus concept in U. S. balance of payments, 481
De Gaulle, Charles, 368, 409
Del credere agent, 547
Demand, reciprocal, 63
Demographic Yearbook, 532
Developing nations, agricultural exports in, 439; and their potential trade gap, 423, 434, 435; and world trade, 423; balance of payments projection in, 435; capital formation in, 429; changes in external assistance advocated by, 450; common features of, 424; compensatory financing to offset deteriorating terms of trade in, 446; cultural blocks to economic growth in, 432; debt service burden of, 450; deterioration in terms of trade of, 441; Development Decade target in, 434; development process in, 429; *see also* Economic development; economic stagnation factors in, 431; export problems of, 436, 438; exports of compared to rest of world, 438; external assistance to, 446; foreign aid of international agencies to, 449; foreign aid of U. S. to, 447; *see also* Foreign aid; government aid programs for and private investment in, 446; growth rate of, 425; income gap in, 425, 434; indexes of value, quantum, and unit value of exports and imports in, 437, 442; investment treaties, role of, in, 472; lack of business managers and government administrators in, 431; lack of social overhead capital in, 431; long-term capital flow to, from industrial nations, 442, 447; obstacles to economic development in, 430; population explosion in, 433; population growth, effects of, on, 429, 430; potential trade gap of, 434; primary exports of, 439; primary production in industrial countries, effects on, 441; private investment and foreign aid in, 475; private investment in and government aid programs for, 446; reforms and trade policies advocated by, 444; repayment problems of, 458; stages of economic growth in, 426; *see also* Economic growth; trade policies and reforms advocated by, 444; U. S. investment guarantee program in, 474; which are the, 424
Development Assistance Committee of OECD, 366
Development Decade, 434, 436
Development Loan Fund, 447
Development loans, in foreign aid, 448
Dimensions of world trade, 17
Diminishing marginal productivity, principle of, 73
Direct investment, 459
Direct sales, 549
Direction of Trade, 533
Discounted bill of exchange, 582
Disequilibrium of the balance of payments, 176; *see also* Balance of payments, United States balance of payments; "adjustable-peg" system of adjustment, 213; adjustment via foreign trade multiplier, 201; capital flight as a source of 170, 184, 263; classical theory of adjustment, 192; compensatory and autonomous items of, 177; compensatory financing, 189, 202; correction in, after consultation with IMF, 355; cyclical, 183, 206; deficit in the, 179; destabilizing speculation as a source of, 184, 230; effect of competitive exchange depreciation and overvaluation, 217; effect of exchange depreciation, 218, 224; effect of savings leakage on adjustment, using foreign trade multiplier, 204; equilibrium rate of exchange, deciding on, 215, 217; exchange control as a source of, 185, 293; fluctuating-rate adjustment, 214; foreign repercussion effect of adjustment, 205; full-employment adjustment to, 202; gold standard, used to correct, 160, 191; income adjustment to payments deficit, 203, 205; income and price effects of exchange depreciation, 226; inflation as a source of, 183; influence of the domestic income multiplier, 200, 206; international reserves, measure of, 179; in the foreign exchange market, 126; long-run adjustment in a stable-rate system, 194; long-run adjustment using the foreign trade multiplier, 201; long-term investment capital outflow as a source of, 185; major sources of, 181; marginal propensities used in, 203; market and nonmarket adjustments, 186; national reserves, measure of, 179; operation of foreign trade multiplier in adjusting, 202, 226; price elasticities of supply and demand, effect on, 209; price-specie flow mechanism theory of adjustment, 192; remedial measures taken by U. S. to correct, 490; restrictions to eliminate, 186; role of price adjustment, 207, 209, 210; seasonal and random, 182; secular, 185; short-run adjustment in a stable-rate system, 189; short-run adjustment in a variable-rate system, 213, 214; short-run adjustment through occasional exchange depreciation, 215; sources of, 181; speculation as a source of, 184; stable-rate system of adjustment in, 189; stable vs. variable rate adjustment in solution of, 228; structural, 183; Suez crisis, beginning of United States, 358; suppressed, 164, 186, 211; suppression of, as an objective of exchange control, 263; surplus and deficit in, 179; tariff effects on, 277; trade restrictions used to control, 255; varieties of market adjustment, 186; *see also* Stable-rate system adjustment of disequilibrium *and* Variable-rate system adjustment of disequilibrium
Disequilibrium system, in the case for protection vs. free trade, 299
Dissimilar production functions, and technological innovations, 102; *see* Technology
Distributor, 547
Diversification for economic stability argument for protection, 305
Documentary bill, 122
Dollar, area, 261; importance of, to growth of international reserves, 501; maintaining gold value of, 497; shortage, 239, 470, 485; stabilization of, 497; U. S. as guardian of, 499
Domestic employment and quotas, 288
Domestic goods, 88
Domestic income multiplier, 200, 206
Domestic industry, defined, 382
Domestic investment, financing of, 430
Domestic price stability, as a measure to expand exports, 493
Double-column tariff schedule, 252
Drawback, defined, 253
Dumping, 308; defined, 267
Dutiable list, 251
Duty, ad valorem, 249; alternative, 250; antidumping, 268; autonomous customs, 251; compensatory, 250; compound, 250; conventional customs, 252; countervailing, 267; customs, 249; export, 249; export, the effects of, 284; import, *see* Import duty; specific, 249; transit, 249

E

East-West trade, 24; use of strategic export controls in, 385
Eastern Trading Area, 24
Economic development, as an objective of international economic policy, 240; cultural blocks to, 432; lack of business managers and government administrators as an impediment to, 431; lack of social overhead capital as an impediment to, 431; obstacles to, in developing nations, 430; population explosion as an obstacle in, 433; stagnation factors in, 431
Economic effects of tariffs, 278; of quotas, 285
Economic growth, capital formation, as a condition of, 429; cultural blocks to, 432; mass consumption, age of, in, 428; maturity, drive to, in, 428; obstacles to, 430; preconditions for takeoff in, 427; Rostow, W. W., stages of, 426; stages of, in developing nations, 426; stagnation factors in, 431; traditional society, the, 426; *see also* Economic development
Economic planning, as an argument against international trade, 10; objectives in free world countries, 264
Economic policies, as distinctive features of international trade, 14
Economic union, administration of and effectiveness of antitrust policy in accomplishing, 406; as an objective of the EEC, 399, 405; common policies for transportation and energy in accomplishing, 407; harmonization in the evolution of the, 405; harmonization of economic and social policies in order to achieve, 408; rules governing competition in accomplishing, 405; U. S. antitrust legislation compared with EEC antitrust legislation, 406
Economic warfare, as an objective of international economic policy, 240
Economic welfare, as an objective of international economic policy, 238
Economies of location, related to transportation costs, 91
Economies of scale, a new approach to trade theory, 114; a source of decreasing costs, 77; effects of customs union on, 412; external, 77; internal, 77
Education, as a supporting agency in international trade, 601
Elasticities, defined, 209; effect of tariffs on, 278; low income, 440
Ellsworth, P. T., 114
Embargoes, 385
Employment, as an argument for protection, 306; domestic, and quotas, 287; in U. S., 499
Energy, and transportation policies in the EEC, 407
Engel, Ernst, 440
Equalization of costs of production, as an argument for protection, 312
Equalization tax, on purchase of foreign securities, 463; interest, 495
Equations, adjustment and domestic expenditure, 201; domestic trade income multiplier, 200; foreign repercussion effect, 205; foreign trade income multiplier, 201; gross national income defined, 196; gross national income determined, 197; income, in a closed economy, 195, 201; income, in an open economy, 195; intended expenditures and savings, 198; marginal propensities, 199, 203, 205; national income in developing nations, 430
Equilibrium, effect of an import duty upon, 282; in the foreign exchange market, 126
Equilibrium rate of exchange, 63, 215
Erhard, Ludwig, 416
Escape clause, 314; provision of the extensions of the Reciprocal Trade Agreements Act, 380, 381; provision of the Trade Expansion Act of 1962, 392
European Atomic Energy Community (Euratom), 400, 407

European Coal and Steel Community, as a step toward economic integration, 367, 399, 407, 408
European Common Market, *see* European Economic Community
European Defense Community Treaty, 408
European Development Fund for Overseas, 413
European Economic Community, 78, 328, 337, 395, 396, 399, 493, 500, 533, 607; agricultural issue between U. S. and, 417; agricultural policy of the U. S. vs. that of the, 403; allocation and growth effects on, 412; and the Kennedy Round GATT Tariff Conference, 415; antitrust provisions and policy in the, 406; as a step toward European economic integration, 367, 399, 405; Association Convention in the, 412; cartel policy in, 406, 407; "chicken war" in the, 350; Commission of the, 400, 405; common external tariff in the, 411, 414; common trade policy, as a goal of, 408, 415; Council of Ministers of the, 400, 402; countries accorded preferential treatment in, 412; countries in, 399; Court of Justice of the, 401; customs union, as an objective of the, 248, 367, 399, 401, 402, 405; developing countries accorded preferential status by, 412, 418; development of, 400; economic union, as an objective of the, 399, 405; effectiveness of antitrust policy, 406; European Parliament of the, 401; exceptions lists between U. S. and, 417; free movement of persons, business enterprises, and services in the, 405; free trade in agricultural products, as a goal of, 405, 415; free trade in industrial products as a goal of, 401, 414; institutions of the, 400; issues between U. S. and, 416; negotiating authority of President under the Trade Expansion Act with, 393, 394; negotiations for a common agricultural policy in the, 402; nontariff trade barriers between U. S. and, 418; outlook for, 410; place of, in world trade, 410; political union, as an object of the, 399; Rome Treaty, establishing the, 367, 400, 405; significance of Kennedy Round in, 419; split in Western Europe, effect on, 413; structure of the common agricultural policy in the, 403; tariff disparities between U. S. and, 416; transportation and energy policies in the, 407; U. S. and the, 414; variable import levies in the, 411
European Free Trade Association, 533; as a step toward European economic integration, 367; effect of split in Western Europe on, 413; significance of Kennedy Round, 419; support to U. S., 414, 416
European Monetary Agreement, 365
European Parliament of the EEC, 401, 409
European Payments Union, 292; as a regional measure to liberalize trade and payments, 363, 365
Exchange arbitrage, defined, 166
Exchange control, 256, 260; abandonment of, after Suez crisis, 358; after World War I, 262; and the international financial crisis of 1931, 260; area, 261; arguments against, 293; bilateral payment agreements as an effect of, 290; creation of government revenue as an objective of, 265; defined, 14; effects of, 289; evasion of, as an effect of, 292; facilitation of national planning as an objective of, 264; inconvertibility and bilateralism as effects of, 290; licensing systems used with, 269; multiple rate systems of, 266; objectives of, 262; origins of, 260; proper use of, 293; protection of domestic industries as an objective of, 265; rate systems of, 266; redistribution as an effect of, 292; single rate systems, 266; suppression of balance of payments disequilibrium as an objective of, 263; under the IMF, 355
Exchange depreciation, competitive, and overvaluation of, 217; defined, 215; effect on terms of trade, 228; effects of, 218; elasticity of demand in, 209, 222, 223; elasticity

Index

of supply in, 209, 220, 223; income and price effects of, 226; Marshall-Lerner condition in, 225; operation of foreign trade multiplier in, 226; when successful?, 224; *see also* Stable-rate system *and* Variable-rate system
Exchange Equalization Fund, 162, 261
Exchange rate, adopting flexible, as an international monetary reform proposal, 505; concern of IMF, 354; defined, 13; effect of import duties on, 281; effect of transfer of capital on, 457; equilibrium, 63; occasional depreciation of, 215; *see also* Foreign exchange rates
Exchange risk, 127
Exchange settlement agreements, defined, 291
Exchange speculation, and capital flight, 168; proper, 169; stabilizing, 169
Exchange Stabilization Fund, 497
Exchange tax, defined, 266
Excise tax, 268
Export balance, fallacies of maintaining, 35; the U. S., 35
Export balance of trade, 142
Export, brokers, 543; department, 541; merchants, 543; organization of company, 540
Export controls, strategic, 385
Export Credit Insurance, 492
Export duty, defined, 249; the effects of, 284
Export Expansion Program, 492, 602
Export-Import Bank, 580; purpose of, 587
Export problems of developing nations, 436, 438; deterioration in terms of trade of developing nations, 441; displacement by synthetics, effects on, 440; expansion of industrial exports, 445; import restrictions by industrial countries, 441; improving commodity exports, 444; indexes of value, quantum, and unit value, 437, 442; low income elasticities, effects on, 440; new trade policies advocated by developing nations, 444; primary production in industrial countries, effects on, 441; reforms advocated by developing nations, 438; short-run price instability of commodity exports, 443; slow growth of commodity, 438
Export quota, 259
Export value, as a basis for customs valuation, 387
Exporters, defined, 546
Exports, agricultural, in developing nations, 439; commodity concentration of, in the United States, 38; direction of U. S., 39; domestic price stability as a measure to expand, 493; effects of price elasticities on, 209, 220; expansion of industrial, 445; expansion of, to combat U. S. balance of payments deficit, 491; improving commodity, 444; indexes of value, quantum, and unit value, 437, 442; Kennedy Round, as a measure to increase, 493; Korean War, effect on, 485; manufactured, of developing countries, 445; measures to restrain U. S. private capital, 494; of developing nations, 438; price-specie flow mechanism, effect of, on, 192; primary, in developing nations, 439, 445; short-run price instability of commodity, 443; Suez crisis, effect on, 485; Trade Expansion Act, as a measure to increase, 493; U. S. dependence on, 43
External assistance to developing nations, *see* Foreign aid; changes in, advocated by developing nations, 450

F

Factor, defined, 546
Factor endowments, change and heterogeneity in, 95; commonalities in, 97; effects on trade resulting from, 101; human, 98; land, 95; natural resources, 96; rareties in, 97; role of capital in, 100, 111; technological innovation as an agent in, 102; ubiquities in, 97; uniquities in, 97
Factor movements, international trade as a **substitute for,** 60

Factor prices, equalization of, 61, 209
Factor ratios, dissimilar demand, 55; dissimilar price, 52; dissimilar supply, 54
Factors of production, as an aspect of balance of payments disequilibrium, 184; capital, 100; effect of import duties on, 281; effect of mixing quotas on, 259; immobility of, as a distinctive feature of international trade, 12; in a closed economy, 57; labor and management, 59; land, 59; mobility of, 58; mobility of capital, 60; mobility of labor and management, 59; mobility of land, 59; price elasticities related to, 209; technological innovations as, 103
Favorable balance of trade, 142, 192
Federal Reserve Act of 1913, 595
Federal Reserve Board, 531
Federal Reserve Bulletin, 531
Federal Reserve System, 487, 496, 497, 498, 595
Financial supporting agencies in international business, 595
Financial transfer, defined, 456
Financing international trade, banking operations, 586; government and international banks, 587; illustrated, 585; meaning of, 575; nature of, 575; need for credit extension, 576; terms of payment, 580
Flexible exchange rate, adopting as an international monetary reform proposal, 505
Fluctuating-rate system of adjustment of balance of payments disequilibrium, 214
Food and Agricultural Organization, 533
Footloose production, 89
Fordney-McCumber Act, 377
Foreign Agriculture (Including Foreign Crops and Markets), 531
Foreign aid, Agency for International Development, 447; Alliance for Progress, 447; and private investment, 475; changes in, advocated by developing nations, 450; Development Loan Fund, 447; development loans in, 448; international agencies providing, 449; major categories of AID program for, 448; Marshall Plan, 447; of U. S. to developing nations, 447; supporting assistance, 448; technical assistance grants in, 448; U. S. deficit in balance of payments as a consequence of, 489, 494
Foreign assembly, 553
Foreign branch warehouse, 553
Foreign credit information, sources of, 579
Foreign credit insurance, 600
Foreign Credit Insurance Association, 493, 580
Foreign Credit Interchange Bureau, 579
Foreign economic policy, *see* International economic policy
Foreign exchange, activity of U. S. Exchange Stabilization Fund to stabilize, 497; compensatory financing to offset loss of, in developing countries, 446; dealers of, 122; defined, 120; demand for, 153; elasticity of, 220; need for, by developing nations, 430; net difference in, defined in U. S. balance of payments, 482; official settlements concept as an argument for stability in, 488; restrictions and inconvertibility, 559; shortage of, in developing nations, 435; supply of, 155
Foreign exchange market, as a method of making international payments, 120; communications function of, 123; dealers in, 122; functions of, 122; in disequilibrium, 126; in equilibrium, 126; provision of credit function of, 123; transfer of international payments function, 123
Foreign exchange rates, 151; active stabilization by monetary authorities, 162; "adjustable-peg" system of adjusting, 213; adjustment through occasional depreciation, 215; argument for flexible and variable, 228; arguments for stable, 158; at equilibrium, 215; base, 151; behavior of, 153; competitive depreciation and overvaluation of, 217; controlled, 164; deciding on equilibrium,

217; defined, 151; determination of, 156; effects of depreciation on, 218; "floating-rate" system of adjusting, 213; freely fluctuating, 153, 213, 228; gold-standard method of passive stabilization, 160, 191; influence on the balance of payments, 158; long-run adjustment with stable, 194; pattern of, 151; short-run adjustment through fluctuating, 214; short-run adjustment with stable, 189; speculation and capital flight in, 168; stable, 158; techniques of stabilization, 159, 213; variable-rate system of adjusting, 213
Foreign exchange restrictions and inconvertibility, 559
Foreign freight forwarders, 596
Foreign government intervention, 561
Foreign investment, by area, 464; contribution of U. S. investment to foreign economies, 468; direct, by major industries, 465; experience of the U. S., 461; guarantee program, 474; in the U. S., 463; nature of, 455; net capital outflow and investment income, 466; net creditor position of U. S., 463; policy of the U. S., 470; position of the U. S., 460; private, and foreign aid, 475; private, direct, 459, 462; private, portfolio, 459, 462; productive, 457; relationship to foreign assistance, 475; repayment problem, 457; sales, expenditures, and earnings of U. S. direct-investment enterprises abroad, 469; tax incentives and disincentives, 472; transfer problems, 456, 489; treaties, 471; unproductive, 457; U. S. abroad, 461; U. S. Department of Commerce survey of American company operations abroad, 468
Foreign laws and regulations, adverse, 562
Foreign manufacturing, 554; business enterprise, 555; capital, 555; labor, 554; land, 554, 565
Foreign market, international trading agencies in, 545
Foreign market research, characteristics of sources, 521; nature of, 521
Foreign market survey, 520; analysis of country, 524; commercial policy of country, 525; competition from producers, 526; economic activity of market, 524; infrastructure of country, 524; location of market, 524; marketing structure of country, 525; natural resources of country, 524; population, 524; prices of competitive products, 526; report, 527; sources of information, 529, 533; topics covered, 523
Foreign operations, adverse foreign laws and regulations, 562; branch office, 553; control over, 570; decision to invest abroad, 557; defined, 552; foreign assembly, 553; foreign branch warehouse, 553; foreign government intervention, 561; foreign manufacturing, 554; foreign primary production, 566; incentives to, 564; joint ventures, 571; licensing for, 568; obstacles, 557, 558
Foreign primary production, 566; agricultural operations, 567; mineral operations, 566
Foreign Trade, 531
Foreign trade multiplier, adjustment of balance of payments disequilibrium, 201; defined, 200; effect of savings leakage on, 204; foreign repercussion effect, 205; operation of, 202
Forward exchange, defined, 170
Forward rate of exchange, defined, 170
Free list, 251
Free port, defined, 254
Free trade, arguments against, 300; case for, 298; vs. protection, 299; *see* Protection
Free zone, defined, 254
Freight rates, a consideration in packing, 571; investigation of ocean, 87
Full employment, adjustment to balance of payments disequilibrium, 202; an exchange depreciation, 227; and gross national product, 202; as a national economic objective, 108; ignoring international consequences of, 108; sacrificing international trade to attain, 108; stability of, as an objective of international economic policy, 239

G

General Agreement on Tariffs and Trade, 304, 333, 342, 378, 384; activities, 345, 369; administration of, by OTC, 350; agricultural issue in, 417; and the Reciprocal Trade Agreements Act, 384; an international measure to liberalize trade and payments, 341; "chicken war" arbitrated by, 350; Committee on Trade and Development, 345; developing countries, treatment of, by GATT Tariff Conference, 418; EEC negotiations on tariffs at, 408; escape clause in, 343; exceptions list in, 417; import restrictions of, 344; major issues in Kennedy Round, 416; major provisions of, 343; necessity for compromises in, 244; necessity of U. S. support, 370; nontariff trade barriers, problem of GATT Tariff Conference, 418; other provisions, 345; OTC, offshoot of, 350; origin of, 342; principles agreed on in Kennedy Round Tariff Conference, 415; quantitative restrictions activity, 348; quantitative restrictions provision, 343; settlement of disputes activity, 349; significance of Kennedy Round to, 419; special provisions to promote trade of developing countries, 344; tariff bargaining, 346; tariff provision, 343; Tokyo session of, 348; Trade Negotiations Committee in, 416
General Arrangements to Borrow, of IMF, 358, 503
General Motors, 407
Geographical area, sources of information for analysis of, 535
Germany, difficulties experienced with cartels in, 323
Global corporation, 541
Global quota, 257
Gold bloc, 261
Gold-exchange standard, criticism of present, 502; strengthening the, 503
Gold export point, defined, 161
Gold import point, defined, 161
Gold, increasing price of, 503
Gold points, defined, 160
Gold standard, abandoned, 255, 260, 360; advantages of, 357; as a passive stabilization of foreign exchange, 160, 191; return to, 260
Gold tranche, 353, 482, 501, 503
Gold value of dollar, maintaining, 497
Goods, domestic, 88; international, 88
Government buying commissions, 542
Government regulation, as a distinctive feature of international trade, 14
Government revenue, the creation of, as an objective of exchange control, 265
Great Britain, state trading of, 331
Greece, status in EEC, 413
Gross domestic product and population of the free world, 424; per capita, 425
Gross National Income, *see* Gross National Product
Gross National Product, 195; and income equations, 195; compared with foreign aid, 448; defined, 195; determination of, 197; domestic and foreign trade income multipliers in, 226; effect of unemployment on, 226; gross national income and product of the U. S., 197, 499; in a closed economy, 195; in an open economy, 195; investment of, as a condition of development, 429; marginal propensities in, 199; *see also* National income and foreign trade
Growth effects of a customs union, 412
Growth of World Industry, The, 532

H

Haberler, G., 113
Hamilton, Alexander, 304, 375
Hawley-Smoot Act of 1930, 306, 377, 390, 458
Hedging, defined, 171
Home manufacturing, 555; business enterprise, 556; capital, 555; labor, 555; land, 555

Index

Home-market, as an argument for protection, 311; international trading agencies in, 542
Hume, David, 192

I

Imperfect competition, 78; types of, 79
Import, brokers, 543; declaration, 596; duties, low or reduced, 564; merchants, 543; organization, 541
Import duty, ad valorem rates of, 389; defined, 249; effect upon existing equilibrium, 282; nature of adjustment to, 281; no price change induced by, 278; price changes induced by, 278; price rise equal to the amount of duty induced by, 280; price rise greater than the amount of duty induced by, 281; price rise of less than the amount of duty induced by, 279
Import levy, variable, and the common external tariff, 411; defined, 404; inclusion of in Kennedy Round negotiations, 417
Import quota, absolute, 256, 384; allocated, 256; bilateral, 257; global, 257; mixing, 259; multilateral, 257; negotiated, 257; tariff, 258, 384; types of, 256, 384; unilateral, 256; uses, 384
Importers, defined, 546
Imports, commodity concentration of, in the U. S., 38; direction of U. S., 39; effect of depreciation on, 227; elasticity of demand, 222; elasticity of supply, 223; indexes of value, quantum, and unit value, 437, 442; Korean War, effect on, 485; price-specie flow mechanism, effect of on, 192; restriction by industrial countries, 441; Suez crisis, effect on, 485
Income injections, 198; leakage, 198
Income equations, adjustment and domestic expenditure, 201; domestic multipliers, 200; foreign multipliers, 201; foreign repercussion effect, 205; gross national income defined, 196; gross national income determined, 197; in a closed economy, 195, 201; in an open economy, 195; in developing nations, 430; intended expenditures and savings, 198; marginal propensities, 199, 203, 205
Inconvertibility and bilateralism, as effects of exchange control, 292; of currency, 13; of foreign investment capital, 559
Incoterms, 578
Indirect sales, 549
Industrial countries, import restriction by, 441; primary production in, 441
Industrial production and international trade, 18
Industrial Revolution, and export duties, 249; role of technology in, 104
Industry, domestic, defined, 382; domestic, the protection of, as an objective of exchange control, 265; infant, as an argument for protection, 303
Infant industry, argument of developing nations, 445; as an argument for protection, 303; protective tariffs used for developing, 323, 377
Instability, as an argument against international trade, 10; economic and political, 559
Inter-American Development Bank, 449, 587
Interbank debt, clearance of, 124
Interest arbitrage, 172
Interest Equalization Tax, 495
Intergovernmental Commodity Agreements, as a type of imperfect competition, 79; attitude of U. S. toward, 337; compared with cartels, 334; defined, 333; effects of, 334; favored by EEC, 418; policy of the U. S., 334; types of, 334; uses for, 334
International Bank for Reconstruction and Development, 341, 410, 449, 587
International business enterprise, definition of, 510
International business, relation of sovereignty to, 509; structure of, 516
International capital movements, 111, 139

International cartels, 317; allocation of markets as an objective of, 319; areas of activity of, 321; as a type of imperfect competition, 79; association form of, 318; benefits and drawbacks of, 322; classification of, 318; combine, as a type of cartel, 318; compared with intergovernmental commodity agreements, 334; control of prices as an objective of, 319; control of technological change as an objective of, 320; defined, 317; effects upon international trade, 323; elimination of external competition as an objective of, 321; examples of cases against, 319, 328; international regulation of, 327; nature of, 317; objectives of, 318; patents and processes form of, 318; policies of other countries regarding, 326; policy of EEC toward, 406, 407; policy of Germany, 324, 326; policy of United Kingdom, 326; policy of United States, 325; public policy toward, 324; restriction of supply as an objective of, 320
International Center for Settlement of Investment Disputes, 472
International Chamber of Commerce, 534, 578
International Commerce, 530
International commodity agreements, 333, 418; as a means of improving commodity exports, 444
International competition, 609; changing factors in, 605; organization of business enterprise, 617; price as a factor, 613; product as a factor, 609; promotion by government, 618; promotion by private business firms, 620; terms of sale, 616
International corporation, 511, 541
International Development Association, 449, 587
International economic policy, autarky as an objective of, 238; balance of payments equilibrium as an objective of, 239; commercial, 236; definition and scope of, 234; diversity and conflict of ends of, 241; economic development as an objective of, 240; economic warfare as an objective of, 240; economic welfare as an objective of, 238; ends of, 238; external conflict of ends, 243; financial, 236; foreign aid, 237; full employment as an objective of, 239; inadequacy of means of, 241; internal conflict of ends of, 242; lessening the conflict of ends in, 243; means of, 235; most-favored-nation treatment used in, 236; protectionism as an objective of, 239
International Finance Corporation, 449, 587
International financial centers, 130; decentralized and centralized, 130; London as one of the, 131; New York as one of the, 132
International Financial Statistics, 533
International goods, 88
International Monetary Fund, 162, 341, 351, 533, 588, 592; activities of, 356; "adjustable-peg" system sponsored by, 231; as an international central bank, 504; as an international measure to liberalize trade and payments, 359; compensatory financing of, 191, 354, 356; contribution of, to international trade, 359; deterioration of U. S. position in, 490; evaluation of, 357; exchange control by, 355; exchange rates, 354; gold quota of, 352; gold tranche, 353; necessity of U. S. support, 370; place of, in international monetary reform, 503; purposes of, 351; resources of, 352; revolving nature of resources of, 354; stand-by agreements used by countries in the, 353; stand-by credits used by, 503; Suez crisis effect on, 356; uses of resources, 352; **voting power of,** 352
International monetary reform, 500; flexible exchange rates, adopting to, 505; gold-exchange standard, criticism of present, 502; gold, increasing price of, to effect, 503; liquidity, question of, in, 500; multiple-currency system as a means of, 503; necessity for international monetary con-

ference to accomplish, 505; plans for, 503; strengthening gold-exchange standard as a means of, 503; the IMF as a central bank to effect, 504; Triffin Plan to accomplish, 504
International payments, as bank debits and credits, 127; contemporary systems of, 133; decentralized and centralized systems of, 130; disequilibrium and adjustment of, 175; monetary effect of the purchase of sterling exchange by an American bank, 128; monetary effect of the sale of sterling exchange by an American bank, 129; monetary effects of, 127; net monetary effects of a purchase and sale of sterling exchange by the American banking system on, 129; private compensation used to transfer, 119; systems, by group, 261; theory of adjustment of, 175; transfer of, 119, 123
International reserves, 179; of free world, composition of, 501
International trade, a broader interpretation of gains from, 65; abolition of restriction in, by the EEC, 399, 401, 406; absolute differences in productivity and wages, 66; and industrial production, 19; arguments against, 9; as a contribution to consumer welfare and national interest, 4; as a substitute for factor movements, 60; basis of, 56; basis of, explained by the theory of comparative costs, 47; cartels, effect of, on, 323; changing composition in, 437; changing factors in international competition, 605; contribution of IMF to, 359; credit extension, need for in, 576, 579, 616; credit in, 619; decisions to be made by the business enterprise, 511; developing nations in, 423; distinctive features of, 11; divisions of gains from, 65; East-West, 24, 385; economic planning as an argument against, 10; EEC, role of, in, 410; effect of decreasing costs on, 77; effect of increasing costs on, 75; effect of non-price competition on, 83; effect of transportation costs on, 85; exchange control used in, 260, 293; export problems of developing nations in, 438; factor movements as a substitute for, 60; financing, 575; foreign investment, necessity of, to, 455; foreign market agencies in, 545; gains from, 5, 62; government regulation of, as a distinctive feature of, 14; immobility of the factors of production as a distinctive feature of, 12; import duties, effects of, on, 281; in services, 111; inconvertibility of currency, effect on, 13; instability and economic planning argument against, 10; interest of consumers in, 3; interest of import-competing industries in, 3; interest of international business in, 2; inter-governmental commodity agreements, effects of, on, 333; international economic policy in, 233; languages and customs as a distinctive feature of, 15; multilateral structure of, 27; multilateral structure of contemporary, 29; national defense argument against, 10; national economic policies as a distinctive feature of, 14; national interest in, 2; national monetary systems as a distinctive feature of, 12; national sovereignty as a distinctive feature of, 11; net creditor position of U. S. in, 464; new approach to, theory of, 114; organization of company, for, 540; potential trade gap in, 434; price support program, used in, 337; protectionism as an argument against, 10; quotas, related to, 285; quotas, used as control in, 256; regional trade and payments arrangements, effect of, on, 359; restrictive measures against, 247, 267, 298; specialization in, 5; Sterling area, future of, in, 362; supporting agencies in, 590; tariffs, used in, 247, 274; technology, effect on, 105; trade restrictions on, 255; U. S. dependence on, 40; U. S. percentage of, 373; world, see World trade
International Trade Organization, 327, 337, 341

International trading agencies, in foreign market, 545; in the home market, 542
Interregional trade, 7
Intervention price, defined, 403
Intra-European Payments Scheme, 363
Investment, see Foreign investment
Invisible tariff, as an import restriction, 387; defined, 269
Irrevocable letter of credit, 584
Isard, Walter, 91, 92
Israel, status in EEC, 413

J

Jobbers, defined, 546
Joint Committee on the Economic Report, definition of U. S. foreign economic policy, 235
Joint Economic Committee, investigation of ocean freight rates, 87
Joint ventures, 571; going concern, 572; new, 572
Journal of Commerce, 534

K

Keep-money-at-home, as an argument for protection, 309
Kennedy Round, 269, 337, 346, 412, 414; agricultural issue in, 417; as a remedial measure to correct U. S. deficit, 493; exceptions list in, 417; GATT Tariff Conference principles agreed on, in, 416; major issues in, 416; nontariff trade barriers, a problem of, 218; significance of, 419; tariff disparities in, 416
Kravis, I. B., 115

L

Labor and management, as a factor supply of production, 59; mobility of, 59
Labor, in foreign manufacturing, 554; in home manufacturing, 555
Land, as a factor endowment, 95; as a factor supply of production, 59; in foreign manufacturing, 554; in home manufacturing, 555; mobility of, 59; offer of sites for foreign operations, 565
Latin America, economic integration in, 368
Latin American Free Trade Association, 369
Law against Restriction on Competitive Trade, 326
League of Nations, 251; study of, on multilateral trade, 31
Lebanon, status in EEC, 413
Legal supporting agencies in international trade, 593
Leontieff paradox, 113
Letters of credit, 583; confirmed, 584; irrevocable, 584; provision of, as a function of the foreign exchange market, 123; terms of credit, 583; revocable, 584
Licensing, abroad, 517; for foreign operations, 568; systems, 269
Licensing agreements, provisions of, 569; risk in, 569
Linder, Staffan B., 114
Linked-usage regulations, 259
Liquidity concept, 481; use of by U. S. Department of Commerce, 482
Liquidity deficit in U. S. balance of payments, 482; conclusions from review of, 486
Liquidity, IMF as a central bank to insure international, 504; question of, in international monetary reform, 500
List, Frederick, 304
Location, as a basis for filing international correspondence, 600; economics of, in production, 91; geographical, as a basic factor in foreign market surveys, 524; of production, as a factor in transportation costs, 89
London, as a financial center, 131
Low wages, as an argument for protection, 309

Index

M

MacDougall, G.D.A., 116
Magazines, as source of information in foreign market survey, 535
Managerial control, 459
Managua, Treaty of, 368
Manufacturing, foreign, 554; in the United States, 555
Marginal product-capital ratio, deferred, 429
Marginal productivity, of capital in developing nations, 429; principle of diminishing, 73
Marginal propensities, 199, 203, 205
Marine insurance, 599
Market adjustment, need for, 185; with variable exchange rates, 213; varieties of, 186; versus nonmarket, 186
Market, allocation of the, by cartels, 319; economic activity, as factor in foreign market survey, 524; home, as an argument for protection, 311; location of, as a factor in foreign market survey, 524
Market-oriented production, 89
Marshall-Lerner, condition of elasticity of export-import supply, 225
Marshall Plan, 356, 364, 399, 447, 448
Mass consumption, age of, in economic growth, 428
Maturity, drive to, in economic growth, 428
Measures, taken by U. S. monetary authorities, 497; to reduce U. S. government outlays abroad, 493; to restrain U. S. private capital exports, 494
Medium-term securities, sales of, 498
Merchandising, as a supporting agency of international trade, 592
Mezzogiorno program, 91
Mineral operations, 566
Minerals Yearbook, 531
Mint parity, defined, 160
Mixing quota, 259
Monetary authorities, bilateral swap agreements as a means of protecting gold reserves, 498; measures taken by U. S. to maintain gold value of dollar, 497; medium-term securities, sales of, to protect gold reserves, 498
Monetary reform, *see* International monetary reform
Monetary systems, as a distinctive feature of international trade, 12
Money incomes, the redistribution of, as an effect of exchange control, 292
Monnet, Jean, 408
Monopolist, defined, 164
Monopolistic competition, defined, 79
Monopoly, 48; and oligopoly prices, 80, 210; defined, 79; differences between oligopoly and, 81
Monopoly profits, 79; quotas as a source of, 285
Monopsonist, defined, 164
Monthly Bulletin of Statistics, of the United Nations, 532
Most-favored-nation treatment, definition and purpose of, 236; for developing countries, 445; of American investments, 471; quotas vs. tariffs under, 289; treaty, 252; under Reciprocal Trade Agreements Act, 379, 393
Multilateral arbitrage, defined, 166
Multilateral settlement, achievement of, 31; nature of, 30
Multilateral trade, basis of, 28; prewar system of, 31; structure of contemporary international, 29; structure of international, 27
Multinational corporation, 541
Multiple-currency system, as a proposal for international monetary reform, 503
Multiple rate system of exchange control, 266

N

National Association of Credit Management, 579
National Association of Manufacturers, 534
National Council of American Importers, 534
National defense, as an argument against international trade, 10
National Foreign Trade Council, 534
National income and foreign trade, 194; determination of, 197; domestic trade income multiplier, 200, 206; foreign repercussion, effect on, 205; foreign trade income multiplier, 200; gross national income and product of the U. S., 197; gross national income, defined, 196; gross national product, 195; in a closed economy, 195; in an open economy, 195; income equations, 195; income injections, 198; income leakages, 198, 201; intended expenditures and savings in, 198; marginal propensities, 199, 203, 205; operation of foreign trade multiplier, 202; payments adjustment via the foreign trade multiplier in, 201; relationship of expenditures, savings, and imports to, 198; role of price adjustment, 207, 209, 210
National Industrial Conference Board, 556
National planning, the facilitation of, as an objective of exchange control, 264
National security, as a restrictive power of the Trade Expansion Act, 392; as an argument for protection, 301
Nationalism, 563
Natural resources, as a factor endowment, 96; as a factor in foreign market survey, 524
Negotiated quota, 257
Negotiating authority of President under Trade Expansion Act, 391
Newspapers, as a source of information in foreign market survey, 534, 535
New York, as a financial center, 132
No-injury concept under the Reciprocal Trade Agreements Act and Trade Exapnsion Act, 393, 395
Nonintercourse Act of 1809, 376
Nonprice competition, 82; effect of, on international trade, 83
Nontariff restrictive policy, 384; administrative restrictions and other measures as, 387; Buy-American regulations as, 386; customs valuation, under the, 387; embargoes as, 385; import quotas as, 384; shipping restrictions and subsidies as, 386; strategic export controls as, 385

O

Obstacles to foreign operations, 557, 558
Ocean bill of lading, 586, 596
Ocean freight rates investigation, 87
Office of Defense and Civilian Mobilization, 383
Office of Emergency Planning, 383
Official settlement concept, 481; arguments for, 488
Official settlements deficit in the U. S. balance of payments, 487
Oligopoly, 48; defined, 79; difference between monopoly and, 81; prices, 80
Open account, 581
Open economy, 195
Opportunity cost, 49
Orderly marketing provision in the Trade Expansion Act, 393
Organization for Economic Cooperation and Development, 365, 533; developed economies target set by, 435; Development Assistance Committee of, 366; purposes of, 366
Organization for European Economic Cooperation, 399; as a regional arrangement to liberalize trade and payments, 362; creation of European Payments Union, 363; use of Code of Liberalization by, 365
Organization for Trade Cooperation, as an international measure to liberalize trade and payments, 350; object of, 350; role of U. S. in, 351
Overinvoicing, 293
Overseas Business Reports, 530

P

Packing, for international transportation, 598
Patents and processes, a form of cartel, 318
Payment, *see* Terms of payment
Payments policy, constraints imposed on U. S., 499
Payments restrictions, *see* Restrictions
Payments, *see* Balance of payments; *see also* International payments *and* United States balance of payments
Peril point, abandoned under Trade Expansion Act, 393; defined, 313; provision of the extensions of the Reciprocal Trade Act, 380, 381
Physical risks, 599
Political union, as an objective of the EEC, 408; opposition of France to, 409; outlook for, 410
Population, and gross domestic product of the free world, 424; as factor in foreign market survey, 524
Population explosion in developing countries, 433
Portfolio investment, 459
Positive balance of trade, 142
Posner, M. V., 115
Potential trade gap, definition, 435; policies and reforms advocated to close, 444
Prebisch, Raul, 442, 444
Preconditions for takeoff in economic growth, 427
Preferential tariff system, 253
Prevention-of-injury argument, for protection, 313
Price adjustment, obstacles to, 210; role of, 208; under a stable-rate system, 207
Price, as a factor in international competition, 613; change, 549; considerations of, before completing foreign market surveys, 526; determination in a closed economy, 56; intervention, defined, 403; structure of common grain policy in the EEC, 404; target, defined, 403; threshold, defined, 404
Price control, by cartels, 319
Price elasticities, defined, 209; effects of tariffs on, 278; price volatility of commodities, a result of, 443
Price quotations, 614; currency used, 615; international, 577
Price-specie flow mechanism, critique of, 193; explanation of the theory, 192
Price support, of U. S., 337
Prices, absolute international differences in, 47; monopoly and oligopoly, 80, 210
Prices and credit terms, 515
Principal trading countries, 20
Private compensation, a method of making international payments, 119
Proceedings of the National Foreign Convention, 534
Processing tax, 268
Product, and the foreign market, 514; as a factor in international competition, 609; nature of, 512; price of, as factor in foreign market survey, 526
Production, function, defined, 104; industrial, and international trade, 19; international differences in, 103; location of, as a factor in transportation costs, 89; restriction of, by cartels, 320; technical coefficients of, 53, 104
Production Yearbook, 533
Profits, monopoly, 79
Promotion, as a supporting agency in international trade, 590; treaty rights as a factor in, 590
Protection, administrative, 268; antidumping as an argument for, 308; arguments for, with qualified validity, 301; bargaining and retaliation as arguments for, 307; case for, 299; disequilibrium system in the case for, 300; diversification for economic stability argument for, 305; employment argument for, 306; equalization of costs of production argument for, 312; fallacious arguments for, 308; function of quotas in, 259, 288; function of tariffs in, 276, 288; Hawley-Smoot Act of 1930, as an instrument of, 377; home-market as an argument for, 311; infant-industry argument for, 303; keep-money-at-home argument for, 309; low wages as an argument for, 309; mixing quotas, a tool of, 259; national security argument for, 301; of domestic industries as an objective of exchange control, 265; persistence of, 314; prevention-of-injury argument for, 313; questionable arguments for, 305; Tariff Act of 1816, as a measure of, 376; terms-of-trade as an argument for, 307; vs. free trade, 298
Protectionism, after World War I, 376; as an argument against international trade, 10; as an argument against structural unemployment, 110; as an objective of international economic policy, 239; Hawley-Smoot Act of 1930, as an instrument of, 377; Tariff Act of 1816, as a measure of, 376
Public Information Service, 536
Purchasing-power parity doctrine, critique of, 216; defined, 216
Purchasing power, transfer of, 192
Pure competition, defined, 48

Q

Quantitative restrictions, 255; abolition of, under Code of Liberalization, 365; as a provision of GATT, 343; as an activity of GATT, 348; defined, 247; exchange control as, 256; import quotas as, 256, 350; nature of, 255; quotas as, 256; removal of, in Kennedy Round, 417; *see also* Restrictions
Quotas, 256; absolute, 256; agency and distributor contract, 549; allocated, 257; and domestic employment, 287; and the balance of payments, 287, 348; as a source of monopoly profits, 285; bilateral, 257; compared with tariffs, 288; controls, effects of, 384; economic effects of, 285; elimination of import quotas under GATT, 348; expansion of, to strengthen gold-exchange standard, 503; export, 259; global, 257; import, 256; IMF, 352; mixing, 259; negotiated, 257; tariff, 258; types of, 256, 384; unilateral, 256

R

Rareties, as a factor endowment, 97
Rate systems of exchange control, 266
Real cost, 49
Real transfer, defined, 456
Reciprocal demand, defined, 63
Reciprocal Trade Agreements (RTA), 335, 378; Act of 1934, 378; and the GATT, 384; authority granted to the President under, 379; authority to lower or raise duties under, 380; comparison of objectives of, with those of Trade Expansion Act, 395; defense-essentiality amendment to, 380, 383; deterioration of, 389; escape-clause provision of, 380, 381; extensions of 1945, 1955, 1958, 380, 382; function of Tariff Commission under, 381; impact of, 388; limitations placed upon the President under, 379; no-injury concept under, 393, 395; nontariff restrictive policy of, 384; objectives of, 378; peril-point provision of, 380, 381; postwar extensions of, 380; program, 375, 378
Redistribution of money incomes, as an effect of exchange control, 292
Regional trade and payments arrangements, 359; advantages and disadvantages of, 369; CACM, 368; economic integration in Latin America, 368; economic integration in Western Europe, 366; EEC, 367; effect of Code of Liberalization on, 365; effects of, on European economy, 359; EFTA, 367; EPU, 363; European Monetary Agreement,

365; free trade area, 367; LAFTA, 369; Managua, Treaty of, 368; OECD, 365; OEEC, 362; the Sterling Area, 360; United States support of, 360
Regulation of cartels, 327; of state trading, 332
Regulations, linked-usage, 259
Remedial measures taken by U. S. to correct deficit in balance of payments, 491; constraints imposed on U. S. payments policy, 499; to expand exports, 491; taken by U. S. monetary authorities, 497; to reduce U. S. government outlays abroad, 493; to restrain U. S. private capital exports, 494
Repatriation of capital and profits, 565
Repayment problem, in foreign investment, 457
Research, as a tool of business, 520; foreign market, 521
Reserves, composition of international, 501
Residence, concept of, 136
Resource-oriented production, 89
Restrictions, abolition of trade, as a goal of the EEC, 399, 401, 406; administrative protection, 268; antidumping duties, 268; countervailing duties, 267; exchange control, 260; excise and processing taxes, 268; foreign exchange, and inconvertibility, 559; import, by industrial countries, 441; payments, 247; quantitative, 247, 255; quotas as an instrument, 256; retaliation and discrimination under Trade Expansion Act as a tool of, 392; subsidies and bounties, 267; tariffs, as a tool of, 247
Restrictive authority of President under Trade Expansion Act of 1962, 391
Restrictive policy, nontariff, administrative restrictions and other measures, 387; Buy-American regulations, 386; embargoes, 385; quotas, 348; shipping restrictions and subsidies, 386; strategic export controls as, 385
Restrictive Practices Acts of 1948, 1953, and 1956, 326
Retailers, defined, 546
Retaliation and bargaining, as arguments for protection, 307
Retaliation and discrimination under Trade Expansion Act of 1962, 392
Revenue Act of 1962, 473, 495
Revenue function of tariffs, 275, 376
Revocable letter of credit, 584
Ricardo, David, 58
Risk bearing, as a supporting agency in international trade, 599
Rome Treaty, establishing the EEC, 405, 409; common tariff stipulations in, 411
Rostow, W. W., 426, 428, 429

S

Salesmen, from abroad, 542
Savings leakage, in adjusting the balance of payments disequilibrium, 204
Schuman, Maurice, 408
Self-sufficiency, as a method of solving the problem of national security, 301; economic, 6
Separate export department, 541
Service business, 511; and the foreign market, 514; in international competition, 613
Service clause, in agency and distributor contracts, 550
Services, use of international trade in, 111
Sherman Act of 1890, 325
Shipper's export declaration, 596
Shipping restrictions and subsidies, 386
Sight bill of exchange, 582, 586
Single-column tariff schedule, 252
Single rate system of exchange control, 266
Sovereignty, national, as a distinctive feature of international trade, 11; relation to international business, 509
Soviet Union, state trading in, 330
Specialization, in domestic and interregional trade, 7; in international trade, 5

Specific duty, defined, 250
Speculation, destabilizing, 169, 184; stabilizing, 169
Stability, economic, diversification for, as an argument for protection, 305; of exchange rates, 158
Stabilization, active, of foreign exchange rates by monetary authorities, 162; British Exchange Equalization Account, 162; passive stabilization by use of gold standard, 160
Stable-rate system adjustment to disequilibrium, 189; classical theory of adjustment, 192; compensatory financing in, 189; critique of price-specie flow mechanism, 193; domestic trade income multipliers in, 200, 206; foreign trade income multipliers in, 200; gold standard, used in, 191; gross national product in, 195; income equations using gross national income in, 196; income equations using gross national product in, 195; income injections and leakages in, 198, 201; intended expenditures and savings in, 198; long-run adjustment, 194; marginal propensities in, 199, 203, 205; national income determined in, 197; obstacles to price adjustment in, 210; operation of foreign trade multiplier in, 202; payments adjustment via foreign trade multiplier, 201; price elasticities in, 209; role of price adjustment in, 207; price-specie flow mechanism in, 192; short-run adjustment, 189; short-term capital movements, importance of, 190; sources of compensatory financing, 190; variable vs. stable rate, 228; *see also* National income and foreign trade
Stand-by agreements, 353
State trading, as a type of imperfect competition, 79; defined, 328; extent of, 330; in China, 331; in France, 332; in Great Britain, 331; in the Soviet Union, 330; in the United States, 332; nature and significance of, 328; objectives of, 330; regulation of, 332
Statistical Yearbook, of the United Nations, 532
Steamship conferences, 597
Steamship lines used in international trade, 597
Sterling Area, 133, 261; as a regional arrangement to liberalize trade and payments, 360; features of, 361; the future of, 362
Stern, Robert M., 116
Stockpiling, as a method of solving the problem of national security, 302
Strategic export controls, 385
Subagent, 548
Subdistributor, 548
Subsidization, as a method of solving the problem of national security, 302
Subsidy, 267
Suez crisis, effect of, on IMF, 356; beginning of balance of payments deficit of U. S., 358, 485
Supply, restriction of, by cartels, 322
Supporting agencies in international trade, 517, 590; communications, 600; education, 601; financial, 595; legal, 593; merchandising, 592; promotion, 590; risk-bearing, 599; transportation, 596
Supporting assistance, in foreign aid, 448
Surplus and deficit concept in U. S. balance of payments, 481
Survey of Current Business, The, 530
Survey of foreign markets, *see* Foreign market survey
Swing credit, 363; defined, 291
Synthetics, displacement of exports by, 440

T

Takeoff stage in economic growth, 427; cultural blocks as an impediment to, 432; lack of business managers and government administrators as an impediment to, 431; lack of social overhead capital as an impediment to, 431
Target price, defined, 403

Tariff Act of 1789, 374, 375; of 1816, 376; of 1922, 313; of 1930, 269, 313, 375
Tariff, agricultural issue between U. S. and EEC, 417; as a major provision of the GATT, 343; balance of payments function of, 277; bargaining as an activity of GATT, 346; classifications of, 250; common external and variable import levies in the EEC, 411, 414; common external, erection of, as a goal of the EEC, 399, 408, 411; compared with quotas, 288; defined, 247; disparities between U. S. and EEC, 416; economic effects of, 278; effect of price changes induced by an import duty, 278; EFTA support of Kennedy Round in tariff negotiations, 414; exceptions lists in Kennedy Round, 417; functions, 274; invisible, 269, 387; making, 274; measurement of, 284; mitigations of, 253; nature of, 248; negotiations in LAFTA, 369; nontariff trade barriers, 418; principles agreed on in Kennedy Round, 415; protective effect of common external tariff in EEC, 411, 414; protection function of, 276, 288, 376; revenue function, 275, 376; systems, 251; variable import levies and a common external tariff in the EEC, 411, 414
Tariff bargaining, an activity of GATT, 346
Tariff Commission, 280, 347, 381, 393, 394
Tariff policy of the U. S., adjustment assistance provision in Trade Expansion Act of 1962, as an innovation in, 393; authority granted to the President under the Reciprocal Trade Agreements Act of 1934, 379; effect of World War I upon, 376; evolution of, 374; Hawley-Smoot Act of 1930, 377, 390; limitations placed on the President by the Reciprocal Trade Agreements Act of 1934, 379; postwar extensions of the Reciprocal Trade Agreements Act, 380; Reciprocal Trade Agreements program, 375; Trade Expansion Act of 1962, 391
Tariff quota, 258, 384
Tariff schedule, double-column, 252; single-column, 252; triple-column, 253
Tariff systems, 251; preferential, 253
Taussig, Frank W., 194
Tax, excise, 268; import, 268; inducements, 564; processing, 268
Technical assistance grants, in foreign aid, 448
Technical coefficients of production, 53
Technological change, control over, by cartels, 320
Technology, agriculture, effect of, on, 104, 438, 441; as an agent in factor endowments, 102; capital movements related to, 111; definition of, 103; implications of in comparative costs, 103; Industrial Revolution, effect of, on 104; international differences in production as a result of, 103; international trade, effect of, on, 105, 438; or dissimilar production functions, 102, 104
Terms of payment, bill of exchange, 582; cash, 581; in international trade, 580; open account, 581
Terms of sale, 616, 619
Terms of trade, as an argument for protection, 307; commodity, 64, 65; compensatory financing to offset deteriorating, 446; deterioration of in developing countries, 437, 441; role of price adjustment in, 209
Territory, granted to agent or distributor, 548
Theory of trade, some new approaches to, 114
Threshold price, defined, 404
Tied loan, defined, 456
Trade, abolition of restrictions on, as a goal of the EEC, 399, 401; acceptance, 582; basis of multilateral, 28; "chicken war" dispute, 350; Code of Liberalization used to relax restrictions on, 365; compensatory financing to offset deteriorating terms of, 446; composition of United States, 36; composition of world, 26; creation of, 411; developing countries, concessions made to by GATT, 418; direction of United States, 39; diversion of, 411, 415; domestic specialization and interregional, 7; dominant countries in world, 20; East-West, 24, 385; effects of depreciation on, 223; gap of developing nations, 434; international, *see* International trade; new policies and reforms, demand for by developing nations, 444; of industrial and nonindustrial areas, 22; prewar system of multilateral, 31; promotion of, by GATT, for developing countries, 344; regional, *see* Regional trade and payments arrangements; retaliation and discrimination under Trade Expansion Act as a tool in restricting, 392; settlement of disputes by GATT, 349; terms of, 64, 65; theory of, 114; value and volume of U. S., 33; value and volume of world, 17; *see also* World trade
Trade Agreements Extension Act of 1958, 380
Trade bill, defined, 121
Trade Contact Service, 592
Trade Expansion Act of 1962, 314, 378, 391; adjustment assistance provision in, 393, 394; as a basis for Kennedy Round Tariff Conference, 415; as a remedial measure to correct U. S. deficit, 493; as a response to the EEC, 414; assistance to firms under, 394; comparison of objectives of, with those of the Reciprocal Trade Agreements Act, 395; escape clause in, 392, 393; implementation, methods of, 395; injured firms, forms of assistance to, 394; means for achieving objectives of, 391; national security requirements under, 392; negotiating authority of President under, 391; no-injury concept in, 393, 395; orderly marketing provision in, 393; purposes of, 391; restrictive authority of President under, 392; retaliation and discrimination under, 392; workers, assistance to, 394
Trade gap potential in developing nations, *see* Developing nations
Trade lists of countries, 530
Trade Negotiations Committee of Kennedy Round GATT Tariff Conference, 416
Trade Relations Council of the U. S., 284
Trade restrictions, abolition of, as a goal of the EEC, 399; administrative protection as, 269; antidumping duty as, 268; countervailing duty as, 267; exchange control as, 260; excise and processing taxes as, 268; licensing systems as, 270; quantitative, 255; quota systems as, 256; subsidies, duties, and taxes as, 267
Trade Yearbook, 533
Trademarks, 550
Trading houses, 544
Traditional society, as a characteristic in economic growth, 426
Transactions, international, as debits and credits, 137; current and capital, 138
Transfer costs, arising out of government regulation of foreign trade, 84; classification of, 84
Transfer of international payments, as a function of the foreign exchange market, 123; the role of commercial banks in the, 124; through private compensation, 119; through the banker's bill of exchange, 124; through the clearance of interbank debt, 124; through the foreign exchange market, 120
Transfer problem, U. S. deficit in balance of payments as, 489
Transit duties, defined, 249
Translation, as a supporting service, 601
Transportation and energy policies in the EEC, 407; as a supporting agency of international trade, 596; customs house brokers used in, 596; foreign freight forwarders used in, 596; packing for, 597; steamship conference in, 597; steamship lines, 597; travel agents used in, 599
Transportation costs, and other transfer costs, 84; discrimination against U. S. on, 87;

Index

economies of location and, 91; effects of, on international trade, 85, 111; effects of, on the location of industry and production, 89; footloose production and, 89; market-oriented production and, 89; resource-oriented production and, 89; weight-gaining products and, 90; weight-losing products and, 89
Travel agents, 599
Treasury and Post Office Department Appropriation Act of 1933, 386
Treaty establishing the EEC, 367
Treaty of Managua, 368
Triffin Plan, 504
Trilateral arbitrage, 166
Triple-column tariff schedule, 253
Turkey, status in EEC, 413

U

Ubiquities, as factor endowments, 97
Underinvoicing, 293
Unemployment, and comparative costs, 107; cyclical, 107; income and price effects of depreciation on, 226; protectionism against, 110; structural, 109; structural, as a factor of balance of payments disequilibrium, 184
Unilateral quota, 256
Uniquities, as factor endowments, 97
United Kingdom, international cartel policy, 326; rejection of, by France, as a member of EEC, 409
United Nations, and related agencies, 531; Conference on Trade and Development (UNCTAD), 418, 444, 450; Expanded Program of Technical Assistance, 450; General Assembly of, 434; publications of, 532; Special Fund, 450
United States and the EEC, *see* European Economic Community
United States balance of payments, 141; arguments for official settlements concept in, 488; autonomous items in, 177, 481; basic deficit in, 486; compensatory items in, 177, 481; compilation of, by U. S. Department of Commerce, 480, 482, 483; concepts of surplus and deficit, 481; constraints imposed on policy of, 499; deficit as a basis for Kennedy Round, 415, 493; deficit in, as a transfer problem, 489; effects of foreign investment on, 459, 470; errors and omissions, entry of the, 147; exports, expansion of, as a remedial measure to correct, 491; factors causing correction of deficit in, 499; failure of U. S. monetary authorities to reduce deficit in, 498; financial transfers, effect of, on, 456; government (net), entry of the, 144; income on investments, entry of the, 143; interest equalization tax, as a step to eliminate, 495; international monetary reforms to correct deficit in, 500; Kennedy Round, as a measure to alleviate deficit in, 493; liquidity, basic, and official settlements deficit in, 481, 484; liquidity, deficit in, 482, 484; long-term capital movements (net), entry of the, 145; Marshall-Lerner condition, effect on, 225; merchandise, excluding military, entry of the, 142; measures to reduce U. S. government outlays abroad to correct deficit in, 493; measures to restrain U. S. private capital export, 494; military expenditures, effect on, 494; military transactions, entry of the, 143; military transfers under grant (net), entry of the, 142; miscellaneous services, entry of the, 143; monetary authorities, measures taken by, 497; monetary gold (net), entry of the, 146; official settlements deficit in, 487; net balance on current account, entry of the, 144; net military transfers under grants, entry of the, 142; private remittances (net), entry of the, 144; remedial measures taken by U. S. to correct deficit in, 491; short-term capital movements (net), entry of the, 145; summary of the, 147; total unilateral transfers (net), entry of the, 144; Trade Expansion Act, as a measure to alleviate deficit in, 493; transfer problems in the, 456; transportation, entry of the, 142; travel, entry of the, 143; voluntary restraint program, as a measure to remedy deficit in, 495; *see also* Balance of payments
United States Business Defense and Services Administration, 592
United States cartel policy, 325
United States commercial policy, *see* Commercial policy
United States Department of Agriculture, 592; publications of, 531
United States Department of Commerce, 529; as a promotional agency in international trade, 591; Bureau of the Census of, 530; Export Expansion Program of, 492; guideline issued by, to restrain loans and investments abroad, 496; publications available through, 530, 592; sources of foreign credit information, 580; survey of operations of American companies abroad, 468; U. S. balance of payments measured by, 480, 482
United States Department of State, 591; sources of foreign credit information, 580
United States Department of the Interior, Bureau of Mines, 531, 592
United States policy on intergovernmental commodity agreements, 336
United States state trading, 332
United States Tariff Commission, 531
United States trade, commodity concentration of exports in, 38; commodity concentration of imports in, 38; composition of, 36; direction of, 39; direction of exports in, 39; direction of imports in, 39; role in world trade, 32; value and volume of, 33
United States value, as a basis for customs valuation, 387

V

Variable-import levy, and the common external tariff, 411; agricultural, 441; defined, 404; inclusion of, in Kennedy Round negotiations, 417
Variable-rate system adjustment to disequilibrium, 213; "adjustable-peg" system, 213; adjustment through occasional exchange depreciation, 215; arguments for, 228; competitive depreciation and overvaluation in a, 217; elasticity of foreign exchange demand in a, 222; elasticity of foreign exchange supply in a, 220; equilibrium rate, deciding on, 217; fluctuating-rate system, 214; kinds of, 213; opposition of governments and bankers to, 230; role of purchasing-power parity doctrine in, 216; stable vs. variable rate, 228; via foreign trade multiplier, 201
Vision, 535
Volume of world trade, 17
Voluntary Restraint Program, 495

W

Wages, differences in productivity and, 66; effect upon production costs of, 309
Warehouse, bonded, 254
Waybill, 597
Webb-Pomerene Act of 1918, 81, 325, 617
Weight-gaining products and transportation costs, 90
Weight-losing products and transportation costs, 89
Western Hemisphere Corporations, 472
Wholesalers, defined, 546
World Agricultural Production and Trade, 531
World Bank Group, 449
World Economic Conference of 1927, 251

World Economic Survey, 532
World trade, and the developing nations, 423, 428; composition of, 26, 437; countries in, afforded preferential status by EEC, 412; demand for restructure of, by developing nations, 444; dominant countries in, 20; East-West, role of, in, 24, 385; effect of common external tariff and variable import levies on, 411; effect of customs union on, 411; income gap in, between developing and developed countries, 425; indexes of value, quantum, and unit value of exports and imports in, 437, 442; liquidity, effect of international on, 501; of industrial and nonindustrial areas, 22, 436; place of EEC in, 410; *see also* European Economic Community; role of U. S. in, 32; significance of Kennedy Round to, 419; split in Western Europe, effect on, 413; U. S. dollar, as key reserve currency in, 490; value and volume of, 17; *see also* Trade *and* International trade
World Trade Directory, 530; reports, 580

Y

Yen area, 261
Yearbook of International Trade Statistics, 532

Z

Zimmermann, Erich W., 97
Zone, foreign-trade, 254; free, 254